THE FLOWER ADORNMENT SUTRA

An Annotated Translation of the Avataṃsaka Sutra

WITH A COMMENTARIAL SYNOPSIS OF THE FLOWER ADORNMENT SUTRA

VOLUME FOUR
CHAPTERS 33 – 38

Kalavinka Press
8603 39th Ave SW / Seattle, WA 98136 USA
(www.kalavinkapress.org)

Kalavinka Press is associated with the Kalavinka Dharma Association, a non-profit organized exclusively for religious educational purposes as allowed within the meaning of section 501(c)3 of the Internal RevenueCode. Kalavinka Dharma Association was founded in 1990 and gained formal approval in 2004 by the United States Internal Revenue Service as a 501(c)3 non-profit organization to which all donations are tax deductible.

> To refrain from doing any manner of evil,
> to respectfully perform all varieties of good,
> and to purify one's own mind—
> This is the teaching of all buddhas.
>
> The Ekottara Āgama Sūtra (T02 n.125 p.551a 13–14)

A Note on the Proper Care of Dharma Materials

Traditional Buddhist cultures treat books on Dharma as sacred. Hence it is considered disrespectful to place them in a low position, to read them when lying down, or to place them where they might be damaged by food or drink.

Kalavinka Press books are printed on acid-free paper.
Cover and interior designed by Bhikshu Dharmamitra.
Printed in the United States of America

The Flower Adornment Sutra

*The Great Expansive
Buddha's Flower Adornment Sutra*

An Annotated English Translation of the Avataṃsaka Sutra
By Bhikshu Dharmamitra

With a Commentarial Synopsis
Of the Flower Adornment Sutra

Volume Four

Kalavinka Press
Seattle, Washington
www.kalavinkapress.org

The Flower Adornment Sutra © 2025 Bhikshu Dharmamitra
Edition: HY-SA-1025-1.0 / Kalavinka Buddhist Classics Book 15a
The Six-Volume Set ISBN (paperback): 978-1-935413-47-9
This Volume Four ISBN: 978-1-935413-51-6
  Vol. 1 ISBN: 978-1-935413-48-6
  Vol. 2 ISBN: 978-1-935413-49-3
  Vol. 3 ISBN: 978-1-935413-50-9
  Vol. 5 ISBN: 978-1-935413-52-3
  Vol. 6 ISBN: 978-1-935413-53-0
The Six-Volume Set ISBN (Adobe PDF): 978-1-935413-54-7
Library of Congress Control Number: 2025947392

Publisher's Cataloging-in-Publication Data

Names: Dharmamitra, Bhikshu, 1948, translator. | Śikṣānanda, 652 CE, translator. | Prajñā, 734 CE, translator.

Title: The Flower Adornment Sutra. An Annotated Translation of the Avataṃsaka Sutra. With a Commentarial Synopsis of the Flower Adornment Sutra.

Other titles: *Mahāvaipulya Buddha Avataṃsaka Sūtra.* English

Description: HY-SA-1025-1.0-chinese/english. | Seattle, Washington : Kalavinka Press, 2025. | Series: Kalavinka Buddhist Classics, Book 15a | Includes bibliographical references. | English and Chinese. | Summary: "The Flower Adornment Sutra is Bhikshu Dharmamitra's extensively annotated original translation of the Mahāvaipulya Buddha Avataṃsaka Sūtra or "The Great Expansive Buddha's Flower Adornment Sutra" which he has rendered from Tripiṭaka Master Śikṣānanda's circa 699 ce Sanskrit-to-Chinese 80-fascicle translation as Da Fangguang Fo Huayan Jing (Taisho Vol. 10, no. 279). Appended here as the conclusion to Chapter 39 is Dharmamitra's English translation of Tripiṭaka Master Prajñā's translation into Chinese of "The Conduct and Vows of Samantabhadra" which is traditionally included as the conclusion of Chinese language editions of this sutra. Altogether, this sutra consists of 39 chapters that introduce an interpenetrating, infinitely expansive, and majestically grand multiverse of countless buddha worlds while explaining in great detail the cultivation of the bodhisattva path to buddhahood, most notably the ten highest levels of bodhisattva practice known as "the ten bodhisattva grounds." To date, this is the first and only complete English translation of the Avataṃsaka Sutra. This special bilingual edition (English / Chinese) includes the facing-page simplified and traditional Chinese scripts to facilitate close study by academic buddhologists, students in Buddhist universities, and Buddhists in Taiwan, Hong Kong, Mainland China, and the West."-- Provided by publisher.

Identifiers: LCCN 2025947392 | ISBN 9781935413479 (paperback) | ISBN 9781935413547 (adobe pdf)

Subjects: LCSH: Tripiṭaka. Sūtrapiṭaka. Avataṃsakasūtra. | Bodhisattva stages (Mahayana Buddhism)

LC record available at https://lccn.loc.gov/2025947392

Volume Four Table of Contents

Chapter 33 – The Inconceivable Dharmas of the Buddhas　2363
Chapter 34 – The Ocean of Major Marks of the Tathāgata's Ten Bodies　2445
Chapter 35 – Qualities of the Light of the Tathāgata's Secondary Signs　2481
Chapter 36 – The Practices of Samantabhadra　2499
Chapter 37 – The Manifestation of the Tathāgata　2543
Chapter 38 – Transcending the World　2703
Volume Four Endnotes　3113

The Flower Adornment Sutra

Volume Four

The Great Expansive
Buddha's Flower Adornment Sutra

The Mahāvaipulya Buddha Avataṃsaka Sūtra

(Taisho T10, no. 279)

Translated under Imperial Auspices by
Tripiṭaka Master Śikṣānanda from the State of Khotan

English Translation by Bhikshu Dharmamitra

正體字

```
242a02｜  大方廣佛華嚴經卷[*]第四十六
242a05｜    佛不思議法品第三十三之[1]一
242a06｜  爾時大會中。有諸菩薩。作是念。諸佛國土。云
242a07｜  何不思議。諸佛本願。云何不思議。諸佛種性。
242a08｜  云何不思議。諸佛出現。云何不思議。諸佛身。
242a09｜  云何不思議。諸佛音聲。云何不思議。諸佛智
242a10｜  慧。云何不思議。諸佛自在。云何不思議。諸佛
242a11｜  無礙。云何不思議。諸佛解脫。云何不思議。爾
242a12｜  時世尊。知諸菩薩心之所念。則以神力加持。
242a13｜  智慧攝受。光明照[2]曜。威勢充滿。令青蓮華
242a14｜  藏菩薩。住佛無畏。入佛法界。獲佛威德。神通
242a15｜  自在。得佛無礙廣大觀察。知一切佛種性次
242a16｜  第。住不可說佛法方便。爾時青蓮華藏菩薩。
242a17｜  則能通達無礙法界。則能安住離障深行。則
242a18｜  能成滿普賢大願。則能知見一切佛法。以大
242a19｜  悲心。觀察眾生。欲令清淨精勤修習。無有厭
242a20｜  怠。受行一切諸菩薩法。於一念中。出生佛智。
242a21｜  解了一切無盡智門。
```

简体字

大方广佛华严经卷第四十六
佛不思议法品第三十三之一

尔时,大会中有诸菩萨作是念:"诸佛国土云何不思议?诸佛本愿云何不思议?诸佛种性云何不思议?诸佛出现云何不思议?诸佛身云何不思议?诸佛音声云何不思议?诸佛智慧云何不思议?诸佛自在云何不思议?诸佛无碍云何不思议?诸佛解脱云何不思议?"

尔时,世尊知诸菩萨心之所念,则以神力加持,智慧摄受,光明照耀,威势充满,令青莲华藏菩萨住佛无畏,入佛法界,获佛威德,神通自在,得佛无碍广大观察,知一切佛种性次第,住不可说佛法方便。

尔时,青莲华藏菩萨则能通达无碍法界,则能安住离障深行,则能成满普贤大愿,则能知见一切佛法,以大悲心观察众生,欲令清净精勤修习无有厌怠,受行一切诸菩萨法,于一念中出生佛智,解了一切无尽智门,

Chapter 33
The Inconceivable Dharmas of the Buddhas

At that time, within that great congregation, there were bodhisattvas who had these thoughts:
> How are the lands of the buddhas inconceivable?
> How are the original vows of the buddhas inconceivable?
> How is the lineage of the buddhas inconceivable?
> How are the buddhas' appearances in the world inconceivable?
> How are the bodies of the buddhas inconceivable?
> How are the voices of the buddhas inconceivable?
> How is the wisdom of the buddhas inconceivable?
> How are the sovereign powers[1] of the buddhas inconceivable?
> How are the unimpeded qualities of the buddhas inconceivable?
> And how are the liberations of the buddhas inconceivable?

At that time, the Bhagavat, aware of the thoughts in the bodhisattvas' minds, then used his spiritual powers to aid them, used his wisdom to embrace them, used his radiance to illuminate them, and then filled them with his awesome strength. He then enabled Blue Lotus Treasury Bodhisattva to abide in the Buddha's fearlessness, to enter the Buddha's Dharma realm, to acquire the Buddha's awesome virtues and sovereign mastery of the spiritual superknowledges, to attain the Buddha's unimpeded vast contemplations, to know the order of succession in the lineages of all buddhas, and to dwell in the ineffably many skillful means in the Buddha's Dharma.

At that time, Blue Lotus Treasury Bodhisattva was then able to gain a penetrating comprehension of the unimpeded Dharma realm, was then able to securely abide in the profound practice free of obstacles, was then able to completely fulfill the great vows of Samantabhadra, and was then able to know and see the dharmas of all buddhas.

Contemplating beings with the mind of great compassion, he wished to enable them to attain purity and engage in intensely diligent cultivation free of weariness or indolence as they take on the practice of all bodhisattva dharmas. In but a single mind-moment, he then produced the wisdom of the Buddha, fully understood all the gateways to inexhaustible wisdom, and became fully possessed of

正體字

總持辯才。皆悉具足。承
佛神力。告蓮華藏菩薩言。佛子。諸佛世尊。有
無量住。所謂常住。大悲住。種種身作諸佛事
住。平等意轉淨法輪住。四辯才說無量法住。
不思議一切佛法住。清淨音遍無量土住。不
可說甚深法界住。現一切最勝神通住。能開
示無有障礙。究竟之法。佛子。諸佛世尊。有十
種法。普遍無量無邊法界。何等為十。所謂一
切諸佛有無邊際身。色相清淨。普入諸趣。而
無染著。一切諸佛有無邊際無障礙眼。於一
切法。悉能明見一切諸佛有無邊際無障礙
耳。悉能解了一切音聲。一切諸佛有無邊際
鼻。能到諸佛自在彼岸。一切諸佛有廣長舌。
出妙音聲。周遍法界。一切諸佛有無邊際身。
應眾生心。咸令得見。一切諸佛有無邊際意。
住於無礙平等法身。一切諸佛有無邊際無
礙解脫。示現無盡大神通力。一切諸佛有無
邊際清淨世界。隨眾生樂。現眾佛土。具足無
量。種種莊嚴。而於其中。不生染著。

简体字

总持、辩才皆悉具足；承佛神力，告莲华藏菩萨言："佛子，诸佛世尊有无量住，所谓：常住、大悲住、种种身作诸佛事住、平等意转净法轮住、四辩才说无量法住、不思议一切佛法住、清净音遍无量土住、不可说甚深法界住、现一切最胜神通住，能开示无有障碍究竟之法。

"佛子，诸佛世尊有十种法，普遍无量无边法界。何等为十？所谓：一切诸佛有无边际身，色相清净，普入诸趣而无染著；一切诸佛有无边际无障碍眼，于一切法悉能明见；一切诸佛有无边际无障碍耳，悉能解了一切音声；一切诸佛有无边际鼻，能到诸佛自在彼岸；一切诸佛有广长舌，出妙音声周遍法界；一切诸佛有无边际身，应众生心，咸令得见；一切诸佛有无边际意，住于无碍平等法身；一切诸佛有无边际无碍解脱，示现无尽大神通力；一切诸佛有无边际清净世界，随众生乐现众佛土，具足无量种种庄严，而于其中不生染著；

Chapter 33 — The Inconceivable Dharmas of the Buddhas

all the complete-retention *dhāraṇīs* and eloquence. Then, aided by the Buddha's spiritual powers, he told Lotus Treasury Bodhisattva:

> Sons of the Buddha, all buddhas, the *bhagavats*, have countless abodes, for example: the abode in which they forever dwell in great compassion; the abode in which, with many different types of bodies, they do the works of all buddhas; the abode in which, with an impartial mind, they turn the wheel of the pure Dharma; the abode in which, using the eloquence of the four unimpeded knowledges, they explain countless dharmas; the abode of the inconceivable dharmas of all buddhas; the abode in which their pure voices pervade countless lands; the abode of ineffably many extremely profound realms of Dharma; and the abode in which they manifest all of the most supreme spiritual superknowledges and are able to reveal and explain the unimpeded and ultimate Dharma.
>
> Sons of the Buddha, all buddhas, the *bhagavats*, have ten kinds of dharmas with which they go everywhere throughout the measureless and boundless Dharma realm. What are those ten? They are as follows:
>
>> All buddhas have the boundless body possessed of pure physical signs that everywhere enters all rebirth destinies and yet remains free of any defiling attachments;
>>
>> All buddhas have the boundlessly unimpeded eye faculty with which they are able to clearly see all dharmas;
>>
>> All buddhas have the boundlessly unimpeded ear faculty with which they are able to completely comprehend all sounds;
>>
>> All buddhas have the boundlessly sensitive olfactory faculty with which they are able to reach the far shore of perfection in all buddhas' sovereign powers;
>>
>> All buddhas have the vast and long tongue that produces their marvelous voice which reaches throughout the Dharma realm;
>>
>> All buddhas have the boundless body that, in response to the minds of beings, enables them all to see them;
>>
>> All buddhas have the boundless mind faculty that abides within the unimpeded and universally pervasive Dharma body;
>>
>> All buddhas have the boundlessly unimpeded liberations with which they manifest endless powers of the great spiritual superknowledges;
>>
>> All buddhas have boundless pure worlds with which, in accordance with beings' dispositions, they manifest a multitude of buddha lands replete with countless different kinds of adornments and yet do not cause them to engender any defiling attachment to them; and

正體字

一切諸佛。有無邊際菩薩行願。得圓滿智。遊戲自在。悉能通達一切佛法。佛子。是為如來應正等覺。普遍法界無邊際。十種佛法。佛子。諸佛世尊。有十種念念出生智。何等為十。所謂一切諸佛。於一念中。悉能示現無量世界從天來下。一切諸佛。於一念中。悉能示現無量世界菩薩受生。一切諸佛。於一念中。悉能示現無量世界出家學道。一切諸佛。於一念中。悉能示現無量世界菩提樹下。成等正覺。一切諸佛。於一念中。悉能示現無量世界轉妙法輪。一切諸佛。於一念中。悉能示現無量世界教化眾生。供養諸佛。一切諸佛。於一念中。悉能示現無量世界不可言說。種種佛身。一切諸佛。於一念中。悉能示現無量世界種種莊嚴。無數莊嚴。如來自在。一切智藏。一切諸佛。於一念中。悉能示現無量世界無量無數。清淨眾生。一切諸佛。於一念中。悉能示現無量世界三世諸佛。種種根性。種種精進。種種行解。於三世中。成等正覺。

简体字

一切诸佛有无边际菩萨行愿，得圆满智，游戏自在，悉能通达一切佛法。佛子，是为如来、应、正等觉普遍法界无边际十种佛法。

"佛子，诸佛世尊有十种念念出生智。何等为十？所谓：一切诸佛于一念中，悉能示现无量世界从天来下；一切诸佛于一念中，悉能示现无量世界菩萨受生；一切诸佛于一念中，悉能示现无量世界出家学道；一切诸佛于一念中，悉能示现无量世界菩提树下成等正觉；一切诸佛于一念中，悉能示现无量世界转妙法轮；一切诸佛于一念中，悉能示现无量世界教化众生供养诸佛；一切诸佛于一念中，悉能示现无量世界不可言说种种佛身；一切诸佛于一念中，悉能示现无量世界种种庄严、无数庄严、如来自在一切智藏；一切诸佛于一念中，悉能示现无量世界无量无数清净众生；一切诸佛于一念中，悉能示现无量世界三世诸佛种种根性、种种精进、种种行解，于三世中成等正觉。

All buddhas have the boundless conduct and vows of the bodhisattvas, acquire perfectly fulfilled wisdom, attain easeful mastery of the miraculous powers, and are entirely able to fully comprehend all dharmas of the Buddha.

Sons of the Buddha, these are the ten kinds of dharmas of the Tathāgata, the Arhat, the Right and Perfectly Enlightened One, everywhere throughout the boundless Dharma realm.

Sons of the Buddha, all buddhas, the *bhagavats*, have ten kinds of knowledge which they produce in each successive mind-moment. What are those ten? They are as follows:

In but a single mind-moment, all buddhas are able to manifest descent from the heavens in countless worlds;

In but a single mind-moment, all buddhas are able to manifest the bodhisattva's taking birth in countless worlds;

In but a single mind-moment, all buddhas are able to manifest leaving the home life and training in the path in countless worlds;

In but a single mind-moment, all buddhas are able to manifest realization of the universal and right enlightenment beneath the bodhi tree in countless worlds;

In but a single mind-moment, all buddhas are able to manifest the turning of the wheel of the sublime Dharma in countless worlds.

In but a single mind-moment, all buddhas are able to manifest the teaching of beings and the making of offerings to all buddhas in countless worlds;

In but a single mind-moment, all buddhas are able to manifest an ineffable number of many different kinds of buddha bodies in countless worlds;

In but a single mind-moment, all buddhas are able to manifest all the many different kinds of adornment and numberlessly many adornments in countless worlds along with the Tathāgata's sovereign masteries and treasury of all-knowledge;

In but a single mind-moment, all buddhas are able to manifest incalculably and innumerably many pure beings in countless worlds; and

In but a single mind-moment, all buddhas are able in countless worlds to manifest the many different kinds of faculties, many different kinds of vigor, and many different kinds of practice and understanding of all buddhas of the three periods of time and realize the universal and right enlightenment throughout the three periods of time.

是為十。佛子。諸佛世尊。有十種不失時。何等為十。所謂一切諸佛。成等正覺不失時。一切諸佛。成熟有緣不失時。一切諸佛。授菩薩記不失時。一切諸佛。隨眾生心。示現神力不失時。一切諸佛。隨眾生解。示現佛身不失時。一切諸佛。住於大捨不失時。一切諸佛。入諸聚落不失時。一切諸佛。攝諸淨信不失時。一切諸佛。調惡眾生不失時。一切諸佛。現不思議。諸佛神通不失時。是為十。佛子。諸佛世尊。有十種無比不思議境界。何等為十。所謂一切諸佛。一[3]跏趺坐。遍滿十方無量世界。一切諸佛。說一義句。悉能開示一切佛法。一切諸佛。放一光明。悉能遍照一切世界。一切諸佛。於一身中。悉能示現一切諸身。一切諸佛。於一處中。悉能示現一切世界。一切諸佛。於一智中。悉能決了一切諸法。無所罣礙。一切諸佛。於一念中。悉能遍往十方世界。一切諸佛。於一念中。悉現如來無量威德。一切諸佛。於一念中。普緣三世佛及眾生。心無雜亂。一切諸佛。於一念中。與去來今一切諸佛。體同無二。是為十。佛子。諸佛世尊。能出生十種智。何者為十。所謂一切諸佛。知一切法無所趣向。而能出生迴向願智。一切諸佛。知一切法皆無有身。

是为十。

"佛子，诸佛世尊有十种不失时。何等为十？所谓：一切诸佛成等正觉不失时；一切诸佛成熟有缘不失时；一切诸佛授菩萨记不失时；一切诸佛随众生心示现神力不失时；一切诸佛随众生解示现佛身不失时；一切诸佛住于大舍不失时；一切诸佛入诸聚落不失时；一切诸佛摄诸净信不失时；一切诸佛调恶众生不失时；一切诸佛现不思议诸佛神通不失时。是为十。

"佛子，诸佛世尊有十种无比不思议境界。何等为十？所谓：一切诸佛一跏趺坐，遍满十方无量世界；一切诸佛说一义句，悉能开示一切佛法；一切诸佛放一光明，悉能遍照一切世界；一切诸佛于一身中，悉能示现一切诸身；一切诸佛于一处中，悉能示现一切世界；一切诸佛于一智中，悉能决了一切诸法无所挂碍；一切诸佛于一念中，悉能遍往十方世界；一切诸佛于一念中，悉现如来无量威德；一切诸佛于一念中，普缘三世佛及众生，心无杂乱；一切诸佛于一念中，与去、来、今一切诸佛体同无二。是为十。

"佛子，诸佛世尊能出生十种智。何者为十？所谓：一切诸佛知一切法无所趣向，而能出生回向愿智；一切诸佛知一切法皆无有身，

These are the ten.

Sons of the Buddha, all buddhas, the *bhagavats*, have ten ways in which they do not miss the right time. What are those ten? They are as follows: All buddhas never miss the right time in realizing the universal and right enlightenment. All buddhas never miss the right time in ripening beings with whom they have affinities based on karmic conditions. All buddhas never miss the right time in bestowing predictions on bodhisattvas. All buddhas never miss the right time in manifesting spiritual powers adapted to the minds of beings. All buddhas never miss the right time in manifesting buddha bodies in accordance with beings' understandings. All buddhas never miss the right time in abiding in the great relinquishment. All buddhas never miss the right time in entering villages. All buddhas never miss the right time in attracting those with pure faith. All buddhas never miss the right time in training evil beings. And all buddhas never miss the right time in manifesting the inconceivable spiritual superknowledges of all buddhas. These are the ten.

Sons of the Buddha, all buddhas, the *bhagavats*, have ten kinds of incomparable and inconceivable spheres of action. What are those ten? They are as follows: When all buddhas sit in the lotus position, they fill up all worlds throughout the ten directions. When all buddhas utter a sentence with a single meaning, they are thereby able to explain all dharmas of the Buddha. When all buddhas emanate a single ray of light, they are able to illuminate all worlds. All buddhas are able with but a single body to manifest all bodies. All buddhas are able to reveal all worlds in but a single place. All buddhas are able with but a single type of knowledge to attain an unimpeded and decisive understanding of all dharmas. All buddhas are able in but a single mind-moment to go forth everywhere throughout the worlds of the ten directions. All buddhas are able in but a single mind-moment to manifest the Tathāgata's countless awesome virtues. All buddhas are able in but a single mind-moment to focus on all buddhas and beings of the three periods of time without experiencing any disorderliness in their own minds. And, in but a single mind-moment, all buddhas abide in substantially identical and non-dual identity with all buddhas of the past, future, and present. These are the ten.

Sons of the Buddha, all buddhas, the *bhagavats*, are able to produce ten kinds of wisdom. What are those ten? They are as follows: All buddhas know all dharmas have no tendencies, and yet they are able to produce the wisdom that makes dedications and vows. All buddhas know all dharmas have no body, and yet they are able to

正體字

而能出生
清淨身智。一切諸佛。知一切法本來無二。而
能出生能覺悟智。一切諸佛。知一切法無我
無眾生。而能出生調眾生智。一切諸佛。知一
切法本來無相。而能出生了諸相智。一切諸
佛。知一切世界。無有成壞。而能出生了成壞
智。一切諸佛。知一切法無有造作。而能出生
知業果智。一切諸佛。知一切法無有言說。而
能出生了言說智。一切諸佛。知一切法無有
染淨。而能出生知染淨智。一切諸佛。知一切
法無有生滅。而能出生了生滅智。是為十。佛
子。諸佛世尊。有十種普入法。何等為十。所謂
一切諸佛。有淨妙身。普入三世一切諸佛。皆
悉具足三種自在。普化眾生。一切諸佛。皆悉
具足諸陀羅尼。普能受持一切佛法。一切諸
佛。皆悉具足四種辯才。普轉一切清淨法輪。
一切諸佛。皆悉具足平等大悲。恒不捨離一
切眾生。一切諸佛。皆悉具足甚深禪定。恒普
觀察一切眾生。一切諸佛。皆悉具足利他善
根。調伏眾生。無有休息。一切諸佛。皆悉具足
無所礙心。普能安住一切法界。一切諸佛。皆
悉具足無礙神力。一念普現三世諸佛。一切
諸佛。皆悉具足無礙智慧。

简体字

而能出生清净身智；一切诸佛知一切法本来无二，而能出生能觉悟智；一切诸佛知一切法无我无众生，而能出生调众生智；一切诸佛知一切法本来无相，而能出生了诸相智；一切诸佛知一切世界无有成坏，而能出生了成坏智；一切诸佛知一切法无有造作，而能出生知业果智；一切诸佛知一切法无有言说，而能出生了言说智；一切诸佛知一切法无有染净，而能出生知染净智；一切诸佛知一切法无有生灭，而能出生了生灭智。是为十。

"佛子，诸佛世尊有十种普入法。何等为十？所谓：一切诸佛有净妙身，普入三世；一切诸佛皆悉具足三种自在，普化众生；一切诸佛皆悉具足诸陀罗尼，普能受持一切佛法；一切诸佛皆悉具足四种辩才，普转一切清净法轮；一切诸佛皆悉具足平等大悲，恒不舍离一切众生；一切诸佛皆悉具足甚深禅定，恒普观察一切众生；一切诸佛皆悉具足利他善根，调伏众生无有休息；一切诸佛皆悉具足无所碍心，普能安住一切法界；一切诸佛皆悉具足无碍神力，一念普现三世诸佛；一切诸佛皆悉具足无碍智慧，

Chapter 33 — *The Inconceivable Dharmas of the Buddhas*

produce the wisdom that manifests pure bodies. All buddhas know all dharmas are fundamentally non-dual, and yet they are able to produce the wisdom that enables awakening. All buddhas know all dharmas are devoid of any self and devoid of any being, and yet they are able to produce the wisdom with which they train beings. All buddhas know all dharmas are fundamentally signless, and yet they are able to produce the wisdom that understands all signs. All buddhas know all worlds have no creation or destruction and yet they are able to produce the wisdom that understands all creation and destruction. All buddhas know all dharmas have no endeavors in which they engage, and yet they are able to produce the wisdom that knows the retributions of karmic actions. All buddhas know all dharmas have no words or speech, and yet they are able to produce the wisdom that understands words and speech. All buddhas know all dharmas have no defilement or purity, and yet they are able to produce the wisdom that knows defilement and purity. And all buddhas know all dharmas have no arising or cessation, and yet they are able to produce the wisdom that understands arising and cessation. These are the ten.

Sons of the Buddha, all buddhas, the *bhagavats*, have ten kinds of dharmas of pervasive entry. What are those ten? They are as follows: All buddhas have a pure and marvelous body that everywhere enters the three periods of time. All buddhas have completely perfected all three kinds of sovereign mastery with which they everywhere teach beings.[2] All buddhas have completely perfected all of the *dhāraṇīs* by which they are everywhere able to take on and uphold all dharmas of the buddhas. All buddhas have completely perfected the eloquence of the four types of unimpeded knowledge by which they everywhere turn the wheel of the pure Dharma. All buddhas have completely perfected the impartial great compassion by which they never abandon any being. All buddhas have completely perfected the extremely deep *dhyāna* absorptions through which they constantly contemplate all beings everywhere. All buddhas have completely perfected the roots of goodness arising from benefiting others by which they ceaselessly engage in the training of beings. All buddhas have completely perfected the unimpeded mind by which they are everywhere able to securely abide throughout the entire Dharma realm. All buddhas have completely perfected the unimpeded spiritual powers by which, in but a single mind-moment, they everywhere manifest all buddhas of the three periods of time.[3] All buddhas have completely perfected the unimpeded wisdom by which, in but a single mind-moment,

正體字

一念普立三世劫
數。是為十。佛子。諸佛世尊。有十種難信受廣
大法。何等為十。所謂一切諸佛。悉能摧滅一
切諸魔。一切諸佛。悉能降伏一切外道。一切
諸佛。悉能調伏一切眾生。咸令歡悅。一切諸
佛。悉能往詣一切世界。化導群品。一切諸佛。
悉能智證甚深法界。一切諸佛。悉皆能以無
二之身。現種種身。充滿世界。一切諸佛。悉皆
能以清淨音聲。起四辯才。說法無斷。凡有信
受。功不唐捐。一切諸佛。皆悉能於一毛孔中。
出現諸佛。與一切世界微塵數等。無有斷絕。
一切諸佛。皆悉能於一微塵中。示現眾剎。與
一切世界微塵數等。具足種種上妙莊嚴。恒
於其中。轉妙法輪。教化眾生。而微塵不大。世
界不小。常以證智。安住法界。一切諸佛。皆悉
了達清淨法界。以智光明。破世癡闇。令於佛
法。悉得開曉。隨逐如來。住十力中。是為十。
佛子。諸佛世尊。有十種大功德。離過清淨。何
等為十。所謂一切諸佛。具大威德。離過清淨。
一切諸佛。悉於三世如來家生。種族調善。離
過清淨。一切諸佛。盡未來際。心無所住。離過
清淨。一切諸佛。於三世法。皆無所著。離過清
淨。

简体字

一念普立三世劫数。是为十。

"佛子,诸佛世尊有十种难信受广大法。何等为十?所谓:一切诸佛悉能摧灭一切诸魔;一切诸佛悉能降伏一切外道;一切诸佛悉能调伏一切众生咸令欢悦;一切诸佛悉能往诣一切世界化导群品;一切诸佛悉能智证甚深法界;一切诸佛悉皆能以无二之身现种种身充满世界;一切诸佛悉皆能以清净音声起四辩才说法无断,凡有信受功不唐捐;一切诸佛皆悉能于一毛孔中出现诸佛,与一切世界微尘数等,无有断绝;一切诸佛皆悉能于一微尘中示现众刹,与一切世界微尘数等,具足种种上妙庄严,恒于其中转妙法轮教化众生,而微尘不大、世界不小,常以证智安住法界;一切诸佛皆悉了达清净法界,以智光明破世痴暗,令于佛法悉得开晓,随逐如来住十力中。是为十。

"佛子,诸佛世尊有十种大功德,离过清净。何等为十?所谓:一切诸佛具大威德,离过清净;一切诸佛悉于三世如来家生,种族调善,离过清净;一切诸佛尽未来际心无所住,离过清净;一切诸佛于三世法皆无所著,离过清净;

Chapter 33 — The Inconceivable Dharmas of the Buddhas

they everywhere establish all the numerical categories of kalpas throughout the three periods of time. These are the ten.

Sons of the Buddha, all buddhas, the *bhagavats*, have ten kinds of vast dharmas that are difficult to believe in or accept. What are those ten? They are as follows: All buddhas are able to vanquish all *māras*. All buddhas are able to overcome the proponents of all non-Buddhist paths. All buddhas are able to train all beings and enable them all to be pleased. All buddhas are able to travel to visit all worlds, teaching and guiding the many kinds of beings. All buddhas are able with wisdom to attain realized knowledge of the extremely deep Dharma realm. All buddhas are able to use the non-dual body to manifest many different kinds of bodies that completely fill the world. All buddhas are able to use their pure voices to bring forth the eloquence of the four kinds of unimpeded knowledge to expound without interruption on the Dharma so that whoever accepts it with faith will not have done so in vain. All buddhas are able in but a single pore to ceaselessly manifest all buddhas as numerous as the atoms in all worlds. All buddhas are able to reveal multitudes of *kṣetras* within a single atom that are as numerous as the atoms in all worlds, all of which are replete with all different kinds of supremely marvelous adornments, this as they constantly turn the wheel of the sublime Dharma within them, thereby teaching beings, doing so even as those dust motes are not increased in size and those worlds are not made smaller, and as they always use realized wisdom to securely abide throughout the Dharma realm. All buddhas are able to completely penetrate the pure Dharma realm and use the light of wisdom to dispel the darkness of delusion among those abiding in the world, thereby enabling them to awaken to the Buddha's Dharma and follow the Tathāgata in coming to abide in the ten powers. These are the ten.

Sons of the Buddha, all buddhas, the *bhagavats*, possess ten kinds of great meritorious qualities embodying faultless purity. What are those ten? They are as follows:

All buddhas possess the faultless purity by which they possess great awesome virtue;

All buddhas possess the faultless purity of birth into the family of all *tathāgatas* of the three periods of time, the clan of those trained in goodness;

All buddhas possess the faultless purity by which, to the very end of future time, their mind has no place in which it dwells;

All buddhas possess the faultless purity by which they have no attachment to any dharmas throughout the three periods of time;

正體字

一切諸佛。知種種性。皆是一性。無所從來。離過清淨。一切諸佛。前際後際。福德無盡。等於法界。離過清淨。一切諸佛。無邊身相。遍十方刹。隨時調伏一切眾生。離過清淨。一切諸佛。獲四無畏。離諸恐怖。於眾會中。大師子吼。明了分別一切諸法。離過清淨。一切諸佛。於不可說不可說劫。入般涅槃。眾生聞名。獲無量福。如佛現在。功德無異。離過清淨。一切諸佛。遠在不可說不可說世界中。若有眾生。一心正念。則皆得見。離過清淨。是為十。佛子。諸佛世尊。有十種究竟清淨。何等為十。所謂一切諸佛。往昔大願。究竟清淨。一切諸佛。所持梵行。究竟清淨。一切諸佛。離世眾惑。究竟清淨。一切諸佛。莊嚴國土。究竟清淨。一切諸佛。所有眷屬。究竟清淨。一切諸佛。所有種族。究竟清淨。一切諸佛。色身相好。究竟清淨。一切諸佛。法身無染。究竟清淨。一切諸佛。一切智智。無有障礙。究竟清淨。一切諸佛。解脫自在。所作已[1]辦。到於彼岸。究竟清淨。是為十。佛子。諸佛世尊。於一切世界一切時。有十種佛事。何等為十。一者若有眾生。專心憶念。則現其前。二者若有眾生。心不調順。則為說法。

简体字

一切诸佛知种种性皆是一性，无所从来，离过清净；一切诸佛前际、后际福德无尽，等于法界，离过清净；一切诸佛无边身相遍十方刹，随时调伏一切众生，离过清净；一切诸佛获四无畏，离诸恐怖，于众会中大师子吼，明了分别一切诸法，离过清净；一切诸佛于不可说不可说劫入般涅槃，众生闻名获无量福，如佛现在功德无异，离过清净；一切诸佛远在不可说不可说世界中，若有众生一心正念则皆得见，离过清净。是为十。

"佛子，诸佛世尊有十种究竟清净。何等为十？所谓：一切诸佛往昔大愿究竟清净；一切诸佛所持梵行究竟清净；一切诸佛离世众惑究竟清净；一切诸佛庄严国土究竟清净；一切诸佛所有眷属究竟清净；一切诸佛所有种族究竟清净；一切诸佛色身相好究竟清净；一切诸佛法身无染究竟清净；一切诸佛一切智智无有障碍究竟清净；一切诸佛解脱自在，所作已办，到于彼岸，究竟清净。是为十。

"佛子，诸佛世尊于一切世界、一切时，有十种佛事。何等为十？一者、若有众生专心忆念，则现其前；二者、若有众生心不调顺，则为说法；

- All buddhas possess the faultless purity by which they realize that the many different kinds of nature are but a single nature which has no place from which it has come;
- All buddhas possess the faultless purity of endless past and future karmic merit commensurate in its vastness with the entire Dharma realm;
- All buddhas possess the faultless purity of the mark of the boundless body by which they pervade the *kṣetras* of the ten directions and adapt to the time in training all beings;
- All buddhas possess the faultless purity of having acquired the four fearlessnesses by which they have abandoned all fearfulness in roaring the great lion's roar in the midst of the assembled congregation and by which they clearly distinguish all dharmas;
- All buddhas possess the faultless purity by which, when they enter *parinirvāṇa* in an ineffable-ineffable number of kalpas, beings who hear their names acquire measureless merit indistinguishable from and just the same as if the buddhas were even now still residing in the world; and
- All buddhas possess the faultless purity by which, even if beings dwell at a great distance an ineffable-ineffable number of worlds away, so long as they engage in single-minded right mindfulness of those buddhas, they will then be able to see them.

These are the ten.

Sons of the Buddha, all buddhas, the *bhagavats*, possess ten kinds of ultimate purity. What are those ten? They are as follows: All buddhas' past vows are ultimately pure. All buddhas' *brahmacarya* is ultimately pure. All buddhas' separation from the many delusions of the world is ultimately pure. All buddhas' adornments of lands are ultimately pure. All buddhas' retinues are ultimately pure. All buddhas' lineages are ultimately pure. All buddhas' physical marks and secondary signs are ultimately pure. All buddhas' undefiled Dharma body is ultimately pure. All buddhas' unimpeded wisdom of all-knowledge is ultimately pure. All buddhas' liberations and sovereign masteries by which they have done what is to be done and reached the far shore—these are ultimately pure. These are the ten.

Sons of the Buddha, all buddhas, the *bhagavats*, in all worlds and at all times, have ten kinds of buddha works. What are those ten? They are as follows: First, if beings are single-mindedly mindful of them, they will manifest directly before them. Second, if beings have untrained minds, then they will speak Dharma for their sakes.

正體字

三者若有眾生。能生
淨信。必令獲得無量善根。四者若有眾生。能
入法位。悉皆現證。無不了知。五者教化眾生。
無有疲厭。六者遊諸佛剎。往來無礙。七者大
悲不捨一切眾生。八者現變化身。恒不斷絕。
九者神通自在。未嘗休息。十者安住法界。能
遍觀察。是為十。佛子。諸佛世尊。有十種無盡
智海法。何等為十。所謂一切諸佛。無邊法
身。無盡智海法。一切諸佛。無量佛事。無
盡智海法。一切諸佛。佛眼境界。無盡智
海法。一切諸佛。無量無數。難思善根。無
盡智海法。一切諸佛。普雨一切甘露妙法。
無盡智海法。一切諸佛。讚佛功德。無盡智
海法。一切諸佛。往昔所修。種種願行。無
盡智海法。一切諸佛。盡未來際。恒作佛
事。無盡智海法。一切諸佛。了知一切眾生心
行。無盡智海法。一切諸佛。福智莊嚴。無能過
者。無盡智海法。是為十。佛子。諸佛世尊。有
十種常法。何等為十。所謂一切諸佛。常行一
切諸波羅蜜。一切諸佛。於一切法。常離迷惑。
一切諸佛。常具大悲。一切諸佛。常有十力。一
切諸佛。常轉法輪。一切諸佛。常為眾生。示成
正覺。一切諸佛。常樂調伏一切眾生。一切諸
佛。心常正念不二之法。

简体字

三者、若有众生能生净信，必令获得无量善根；四者、若有众生能入法位，悉皆现证，无不了知；五者、教化众生无有疲厌；六者、游诸佛刹，往来无碍；七者、大悲不舍一切众生；八者、现变化身，恒不断绝；九者、神通自在，未尝休息；十者、安住法界，能遍观察。是为十。

"佛子，诸佛世尊有十种无尽智海法。何等为十？所谓：一切诸佛无边法身无尽智海法；一切诸佛无量佛事无尽智海法；一切诸佛佛眼境界无尽智海法；一切诸佛无量无数难思善根无尽智海法；一切诸佛普雨一切甘露妙法无尽智海法；一切诸佛赞佛功德无尽智海法；一切诸佛往昔所修种种愿行无尽智海法；一切诸佛尽未来际恒作佛事无尽智海法；一切诸佛了知一切众生心行无尽智海法；一切诸佛福智庄严无能过者无尽智海法。是为十。

"佛子，诸佛世尊有十种常法。何等为十？所谓：一切诸佛常行一切诸波罗蜜；一切诸佛于一切法常离迷惑；一切诸佛常具大悲；一切诸佛常有十力；一切诸佛常转法轮；一切诸佛常为众生示成正觉；一切诸佛常乐调伏一切众生；一切诸佛心常正念不二之法；

Third, if beings are able to develop pure faith, they will definitely enable them to acquire measureless great roots of goodness. Fourth, if beings are able to achieve entry into the Dharma position,[4] then they will all manifest direct realizations by which they have nothing they do not completely understand. Fifth, they never weary of teaching beings. Sixth, in traveling to all buddha *kṣetras*, they are unimpeded in coming and going. Seventh, their great compassion is such that they never abandon any being. Eighth, they manifest transformation bodies constantly and incessantly. Ninth, their sovereign mastery of the spiritual superknowledges is incessant. And tenth, they dwell in the Dharma realm and are able to carry out contemplations everywhere. These are the ten.

Sons of the Buddha, all buddhas, the *bhagavats*, have ten kinds of dharmas associated with their inexhaustible ocean of wisdom. What are those ten? They are as follows: The inexhaustible ocean-of-wisdom dharma of all buddhas' boundless Dharma body. The inexhaustible ocean-of-wisdom dharma of all buddhas' measureless buddha works. The inexhaustible ocean-of-wisdom dharma of all buddhas' sphere of cognition with the buddha eye. The inexhaustible ocean-of-wisdom dharma of all buddhas' measureless, innumerable, and inconceivable roots of goodness. The inexhaustible ocean-of-wisdom dharma of all buddhas' all-pervasive raining down of every kind of sublime elixir of immortality dharma. The inexhaustible ocean-of-wisdom dharma of all buddhas' praising of the Buddha's meritorious qualities. The inexhaustible ocean-of-wisdom dharma of all buddhas' many different kinds of vows and conduct cultivated in the past. The inexhaustible ocean-of-wisdom dharma of all buddhas' constant doing of buddha works to the end of future time. The inexhaustible ocean-of-wisdom dharma of all buddhas' complete knowing of all beings' mental actions. The inexhaustible ocean-of-wisdom dharma of all buddhas' adornment with merit and wisdom which no one can surpass. These are the ten.

Sons of the Buddha, all buddhas, the *bhagavats*, have ten kinds of dharmas which they always manifest. What are those ten? They are as follows: All buddhas always practice all of the *pāramitās*. All buddhas always abandon delusion regarding all dharmas. All buddhas always possess the great compassion. All buddhas always possess the ten powers. All buddhas always turn the wheel of Dharma. [All buddhas always liberate all beings.][5] All buddhas always demonstrate for beings the realization of the right enlightenment. All buddhas always delight in training all beings. All buddhas always maintain right mindfulness of the dharma of non-duality. All

正體字

一切諸佛。化眾生已。
常示入於無餘涅槃。諸佛境界。無邊際故。是
為十。佛子。諸佛世尊。有十種演說無量諸佛
法門。何等為十。所謂一切諸佛。演說無量眾
生界門。一切諸佛。演說無量眾生行門。一切
諸佛。演說無量眾生業果門。一切諸佛演說
無量化眾生門。一切諸佛。演說無量淨眾生
門。一切諸佛。演說無量菩薩行門。一切諸佛。
演說無量菩薩願門。一切諸佛。演說無量一
切世界。成壞劫門。一切諸佛。演說無量菩薩
深心。淨佛剎門。一切諸佛。演說無量[1]一切
世界。三世諸佛。於彼彼劫。次第出現門。一切
諸佛。演說一切諸佛智門。是為十。佛子。諸佛
世尊。有十種為眾生作佛事。何等為十。所謂
一切諸佛。示現色身。為眾生作佛事。一切諸
佛。出妙音聲。為眾生作佛事。一切諸佛。有所
受。為眾生作佛事。一切諸佛。無所受。為眾生
作佛事。一切諸佛。以地水火風。為眾生作佛
事。一切諸佛。神力自在。示現一切所緣境界。
為眾生作佛事。一切諸佛。種種名號。為眾生
作佛事。一切諸佛。以佛剎境界。為眾生作佛
事。一切諸佛。嚴淨佛剎。為眾生作佛事。一切
諸佛。寂[2]寞無言。為眾生作佛事。是為十。佛
子。諸佛世尊。有十種最勝法。何等為十。所謂
一切諸佛。大願堅固。不可沮壞。所言必作。言
無有二。

简体字

一切诸佛化众生已，常示入于无余涅槃，诸佛境界无边际故。是为十。

"佛子，诸佛世尊有十种演说无量诸佛法门。何等为十？所谓：一切诸佛演说无量众生界门；一切诸佛演说无量众生行门；一切诸佛演说无量众生业果门；一切诸佛演说无量化众生门；一切诸佛演说无量净众生门；一切诸佛演说无量菩萨行门；一切诸佛演说无量菩萨愿门；一切诸佛演说无量一切世界成坏劫门；一切诸佛演说无量菩萨深心净佛刹门；一切诸佛演说无量一切世界三世诸佛于彼彼劫次第出现门；一切诸佛演说一切诸佛智门。是为十。

"佛子，诸佛世尊有十种为众生作佛事。何等为十？所谓：一切诸佛示现色身为众生作佛事；一切诸佛出妙音声为众生作佛事；一切诸佛有所受为众生作佛事；一切诸佛无所受为众生作佛事；一切诸佛以地、水、火、风为众生作佛事；一切诸佛神力自在示现一切所缘境界为众生作佛事；一切诸佛种种名号为众生作佛事；一切诸佛以佛刹境界为众生作佛事；一切诸佛严净佛刹为众生作佛事；一切诸佛寂寞无言为众生作佛事。是为十。

"佛子，诸佛世尊有十种最胜法。何等为十？所谓：一切诸佛大愿坚固不可沮坏，所言必作，言无有二；

buddhas always demonstrate entry into the nirvāṇa without residue after they have finished teaching beings, doing so because the realm of all buddhas is boundless. These are the ten.

Sons of the Buddha, all buddhas, the *bhagavats*, have ten kinds of discourse on the countless Dharma gateways of all buddhas. What are those ten? They are as follows: All buddhas expound on the countless gateways related to the realms of beings. All buddhas expound on the countless gateways related to beings' actions. All buddhas expound on the countless gateways related to beings' karmic retributions. All buddhas expound on the countless gateways used in teaching beings. All buddhas expound on the countless gateways used in the purification of beings. All buddhas expound on the countless gateways related to the bodhisattva practices. All buddhas expound on the countless gateways related to the bodhisattva vows. All buddhas expound on the countless gateways related to the formation and destruction of the kalpas in all worlds. All buddhas expound on the countless gateways related to the bodhisattva's deep resolve to purify buddha *kṣetras*. All buddhas expound on the countless gateways related to the orderly appearance in all worlds and in each kalpa of all buddhas of the three periods of time. All buddhas expound on the wisdom gateways of all buddhas. These are the ten.

Sons of the Buddha, all buddhas, the *bhagavats*, have ten ways in which they do buddha works for beings. What are those ten? They are as follows: All buddhas manifest form bodies to accomplish buddha works for beings. All buddhas emanate sublime voices to accomplish buddha works for beings. All buddhas have that which they accept to accomplish buddha works for beings. All buddhas have that which they do not accept to accomplish buddha works for beings. All buddhas use earth, water, fire, and wind to accomplish buddha works for beings. All buddhas use sovereign mastery of spiritual powers to manifest all kinds of objective phenomena to accomplish buddha works for beings. All buddhas use all kinds of different names to accomplish buddha works for beings. All buddhas use buddha *kṣetra* realms to accomplish buddha works for beings. All buddhas purify buddha *kṣetras* to accomplish buddha works for beings. All buddhas may remain silent and refrain from speaking to accomplish buddha works for beings. These are the ten.

Sons of the Buddha, all buddhas, the *bhagavats*, have ten kinds of supreme dharmas. What are those ten? They are as follows:

> All buddhas' great and solid vows cannot be impeded. They definitely do whatever they say they will do. Hence their actions and their words do not differ.

正體字

一切諸佛。為欲圓滿一切功德。盡未
來劫。修菩薩行。不生懈倦。一切諸佛。為欲調
伏[3]一眾生故。往不可說不可說世界。如是而
為一切眾生。而無斷絕。一切諸佛。於信於毀
二種眾生。大悲普觀。平等無異。一切諸佛。從
初發心。乃至成佛。終不退失菩提之心。一切
諸佛。積集無量諸善功德。皆以迴向一切智
性。於諸世間。終無染著。一切諸佛。於諸佛
所。修學三業。唯行佛行。非二乘行。皆為迴向
一切智性。成於無上正等菩提。一切諸佛。放
大光明。其光平等。照一切處。及照一切諸佛
之法。令諸菩薩。心得清淨。滿一切智。一切諸
佛。捨離世樂。不貪不染。而普願世間離苦得
樂。無諸戲論。一切諸佛。愍諸眾生。受種種
苦。守護佛種。行佛境界。出離生死。逮十力
地。是為十。佛子。諸佛世尊。有十種無障礙
住。何等為十。所謂一切諸佛。皆能往一切世
界。無障礙住。一切諸佛。皆能住一切世界。無
障礙住。一切諸佛。皆能於一切世界。行住坐
臥。無障礙住。

简体字

一切诸佛为欲圆满一切功德，尽未来劫修菩萨行不生懈倦；一切诸佛为欲调伏一切众生故，往不可说不可说世界，如是而为一切众生而无断绝；一切诸佛于信、于毁二种众生，大悲普观，平等无异；一切诸佛从初发心乃至成佛，终不退失菩提之心；一切诸佛积集无量诸善功德，皆以回向一切智性，于诸世间终无染著；一切诸佛于诸佛所修学三业，唯行佛行，非二乘行，皆为回向一切智性，成于无上正等菩提；一切诸佛放大光明，其光平等照一切处，及照一切诸佛之法，令诸菩萨心得清净，满一切智；一切诸佛舍离世乐，不贪不染，而普愿世间离苦得乐，无诸戏论；一切诸佛愍诸众生受种种苦，守护佛种，行佛境界，出离生死，逮十力地。是为十。

"佛子，诸佛世尊有十种无障碍住。何等为十？所谓：一切诸佛皆能往一切世界无障碍住；一切诸佛皆能住一切世界无障碍住；一切诸佛皆能于一切世界行、住、坐、卧无障碍住；

All buddhas tirelessly cultivate the bodhisattva practices to the end of future kalpas because they wish to achieve complete fulfillment of all meritorious qualities.

All buddhas go forth to an ineffable-ineffable number of worlds because they wish to train all beings, ceaselessly engaging in their efforts on behalf of all beings.

All buddhas have great compassion by which they are impartial and no different in their universal regard for two kinds of beings, those who are faithful and those who disparage them.

All buddhas, from the time they make their initial resolve until they realize buddhahood, never retreat from their bodhi resolve.

All buddhas accumulate measureless excellent meritorious qualities and dedicate them all to the realization of all-knowledge while still never forming any defiling attachment to anything in the world.

All buddhas cultivate and train in the three kinds of karmic actions in the presence of all buddhas, only practice the practices associated with buddhahood, not the practices associated with the Two Vehicles, and then dedicate all of this to the realization of all-knowledge and the attainment of the utmost, right, and perfect bodhi.

All buddhas emanate great radiance, the light from which equally illuminates all places while also illuminating the Dharma of all buddhas, thereby enabling all bodhisattvas to attain purity of mind and fulfill all-knowledge.

All buddhas relinquish the pleasures of the world, do not crave them, are not defiled by them, and yet make the universal vow wishing to enable everyone in the world to leave suffering, attain bliss, and become free of all conceptual proliferation.

All buddhas, pitying all beings, undergo all different kinds of suffering as they guard and preserve the lineage of the buddhas, practice the Buddha's spheres of action, attain emancipation from *saṃsāra*, and arrive at the ground of the ten powers.

These are ten.

Sons of the Buddha, all buddhas, the *bhagavats*, have ten kinds of unimpeded abiding. What are those ten? They are as follows: All buddhas have the unimpeded abiding by which they are all able to go forth to all worlds. All buddhas have the unimpeded abiding by which they are all able to abide in all worlds. All buddhas have the unimpeded abiding by which they are all able to walk, stand, sit, and lie down in all worlds. All buddhas have the unimpeded

正體字	一切諸佛。[4]皆能於一切世界。演說正法。無障礙住。一切諸佛。[5]皆能於一切世界。住兜率天宮。無障礙住。一切諸佛。皆能入法界一切三世。無障礙住。一切諸佛。皆能坐法界一切道場。無障礙住。一切諸佛。皆能念念觀一切眾生心行。以三種自在。教化調伏。無障礙住。一切諸佛。皆能以一身。住無量不思議佛所及一切處。利益眾生。無障礙住。一切諸佛。皆能開示無量諸佛。所說正法。無障礙住。是為十。佛子。諸佛世尊。有十種最勝無上莊嚴。何等[6]為十。[7]一切諸佛。皆悉具足諸相隨好。是為諸佛第一最勝無上身莊嚴。一切諸佛。皆悉具足六十種音。一一音。有五百分。一一分。無量百千清淨之音。以為嚴好。能於法界一切眾中。無諸恐怖。大師子吼。演說如來甚深法義。眾生聞者。靡不歡喜。隨其根欲。悉得調伏。是為諸佛第二最勝無上語莊嚴。一切諸佛。皆具十力。諸大三昧。十八不共。莊嚴意業。所行境界。通達無礙一切佛法。咸得無餘法界莊嚴。而為莊嚴。法界眾生。心之所行。去來現在。各各差別。於一念中。悉能明見。
简体字	一切诸佛皆能于一切世界演说正法无障碍住；一切诸佛皆能于一切世界住兜率天宫无障碍住；一切诸佛皆能入法界一切三世无障碍住；一切诸佛皆能坐法界一切道场无障碍住；一切诸佛皆能念念观一切众生心行以三种自在教化调伏无障碍住；一切诸佛皆能以一身住无量不思议佛所及一切处利益众生无障碍住；一切诸佛皆能开示无量诸佛所说正法无障碍住。是为十。 "佛子，诸佛世尊有十种最胜无上庄严。何等为十？所谓：一切诸佛皆悉具足诸相随好，是为诸佛第一最胜无上身庄严。一切诸佛皆悉具足六十种音，一一音有五百分，一一分无量百千清净之音以为严好，能于法界一切众中无诸恐怖，大师子吼演说如来甚深法义，众生闻者靡不欢喜，随其根欲悉得调伏，是为诸佛第二最胜无上语庄严。一切诸佛皆具十力、诸大三昧、十八不共庄严意业，所行境界通达无碍，一切佛法咸得无余，法界庄严而为庄严，法界众生心之所行，去、来、现在各各差别，于一念中悉能明见，

abiding by which they are all able to expound on right Dharma in all worlds. All buddhas have the unimpeded abiding by which they are all able to dwell in the Tuṣita Heaven Palace in all worlds. All buddhas have the unimpeded abiding by which they are all able to enter the Dharma realm in all three periods of time. All buddhas have the unimpeded abiding by which they are all able to sit in all sites of enlightenment in the Dharma realm. All buddhas have the unimpeded abiding by which they are all able in each successive mind-moment to contemplate the mental actions of all beings and use their three kinds of sovereign mastery to teach and train them. All buddhas have the unimpeded abiding by which they are all able with but a single body to abide in all of the countless inconceivable abodes of all buddhas as well as all other places, bestowing benefit on beings. All buddhas have the unimpeded abiding by which they are all able to reveal and explain the right Dharma proclaimed by the incalculably many buddhas. These are the ten.

Sons of the Buddha, all buddhas, the *bhagavats*, have ten kinds of supreme and unsurpassable adornments. What are those ten? They are as follows:

All buddhas have completely perfected all of the major marks and secondary signs. This is the first of the buddhas' unsurpassably supreme adornments, those associated with the body.

All buddhas have completely perfected the sixty kinds of voices in every one of which there are five hundred subtypes in every one of which there are countless hundreds of thousands of pure voices which serve as fine adornments. They are able to fearlessly roar the great lion's roar in the midst of all assemblies throughout the Dharma realm, expounding on the Tathāgata's extremely profound meanings of the Dharma. When beings hear this, none of them are not delighted. In accordance with their faculties and inclinations, they are all able to receive the training. This is the second of the buddhas' unsurpassably supreme adornments, those associated with their speech.

All buddhas possess the ten powers, the great samādhis, and the eighteen dharmas exclusive to the buddhas which serve as adornments of their mental actions. In the sphere of cognition in which they act, they have an unimpededly penetrating comprehension of all dharmas of the Buddha. They all acquire as their adornments all of the Dharma realm's adornments without exception. In but a single mind-moment, they are able to clearly see every one of the different past, future, and present mental actions of all beings throughout the Dharma realm. This

正體字

是為諸佛第三最勝無上意莊
嚴。一切諸佛。皆悉能放無數光明。一一光明。
有不可說光明網。以為眷屬。普照一切諸佛
國土。滅除一切世間黑闇。示現無量諸佛出
興。其身平等。悉皆清淨。所作佛事。咸不唐
捐。能令眾生。至不退轉。是為諸佛第四最勝
無上光明莊嚴。一切諸佛。現微笑時。皆於口
中。放百千億那由他阿僧祇光明。一一光明。
各有無量不思議種種色。遍照十方一切世
界。於大眾中。發誠實語。授無量無數不思議
眾生。阿耨多羅三藐三菩提記。是為諸佛第
五離世癡惑最勝無上現微笑莊嚴。一切諸
佛。皆有法身清淨無礙。於一切法。究竟通達。
住於法界。無有邊際。雖在世間。不與世雜。了
世實性。行出世法。言語道斷。超蘊界處。是為
諸佛第六最勝無上法身莊嚴。一切諸佛。皆
有無量常妙光明。不可說不可說種種色相。
以為嚴好。為光明藏。出生無量圓滿光明。普
照十方。無有障礙。是為諸佛第七最勝無上
常妙光明莊嚴。一切諸佛。皆有無邊妙色。可
愛妙色。清淨妙色。隨心所現妙色。

简体字

是为诸佛第三最胜无上意庄严。一切诸佛皆悉能放无数光明，一一光明有不可说光明网以为眷属，普照一切诸佛国土，灭除一切世间黑暗，示现无量诸佛出兴，其身平等悉皆清净，所作佛事咸不唐捐，能令众生至不退转，是为诸佛第四最胜无上光明庄严。一切诸佛现微笑时，皆于口中放百千亿那由他阿僧祇光明，一一光明各有无量不思议种种色，遍照十方一切世界，于大众中发诚实语，授无量无数不思议众生阿耨多罗三藐三菩提记，是为诸佛第五离世痴惑最胜无上现微笑庄严。一切诸佛皆有法身清净无碍，于一切法究竟通达，住于法界无有边际，虽在世间不与世杂，了世实性，行出世法，言语道断，超蕴、界、处，是为诸佛第六最胜无上法身庄严。一切诸佛皆有无量常妙光明，不可说不可说种种色相以为严好为光明藏，出生无量圆满光明，普照十方无有障碍，是为诸佛第七最胜无上常妙光明庄严。一切诸佛皆有无边妙色、可爱妙色、清净妙色、随心所现妙色、

Chapter 33 — The Inconceivable Dharmas of the Buddhas

is the third of the buddhas' unsurpassably supreme adornments, those associated with their minds.

All buddhas are able to emanate countless light rays, every ray of which has a retinue of an ineffable number of light nets. They everywhere illuminate all buddha lands, extinguish the darkness in all worlds, and reveal the countless buddhas' coming forth and appearing in the world. Their bodies are all equal and they are all pure. Of all the buddha works that they accomplish, none of them are done in vain. They are thereby able to cause beings to reach irreversibility. This is the fourth of the buddhas' unsurpassably supreme adornments, those associated with their radiance.

When all buddhas manifest a subtle smile, they all emanate hundreds of thousands of *koṭīs* of *nayutas* of *asaṃkhyeyas* of light rays from their mouths, every ray of which possesses incalculably and inconceivably many different colors which everywhere illuminate all worlds of the ten directions and send forth in the midst of the great assembly the truthful speech that bestows the *anuttarā-samyak-saṃbodhi* prediction on incalculably, innumerably, and inconceivably many beings. This is the fifth of the buddhas' unsurpassably supreme adornments, those which transcend the world's delusions and are associated with their subtle smile.

All buddhas possess the pure and unimpeded Dharma body and have an ultimately penetrating comprehension of all dharmas. It abides in the Dharma realm and is boundless. Although they reside in the world, they do not mix with the world. They completely understand the true nature of the world and practice the world-transcending dharmas that cut short the path of words and speech and go beyond the aggregates, the sense realms and the sense bases. This is the sixth of the buddhas' unsurpassably supreme adornments, those associated with their Dharma body.

All buddhas have countless ever-marvelous lights which have an ineffable-ineffable number of various kinds of colors and appearances as their fine adornments. These form a treasury of light that sends forth countless spheres of light which everywhere and unimpededly illuminate the ten directions. This is the seventh of the buddhas' unsurpassably supreme adornments, those associated with their ever-marvelous lights.

All buddhas have boundlessly many marvelous forms, lovely marvelous forms, pure marvelous forms, marvelous forms appearing in response to whatever they wish, marvelous forms

正體字

映蔽一
244c24 ‖ 切三界妙色。到於彼岸無上妙色。是為諸
244c25 ‖ 佛第八最勝無上妙色莊嚴。一切諸佛。皆於
244c26 ‖ 三世佛種中生。積眾善寶。究竟清淨。無諸過
244c27 ‖ 失。離世譏謗。一切法中。最為殊勝清淨妙行
244c28 ‖ 之所莊嚴。具足成就一切智智。種族清淨。無
244c29 ‖ 能譏毀。是為諸佛第九最勝無上種族莊嚴。
245a01 ‖ 一切諸佛。以大慈力。莊嚴其身。究竟清淨。無
245a02 ‖ 諸渴愛。身行永息。心善解脫。見者無厭。大悲
245a03 ‖ 救護一切世間。第一福田。無上受者。哀愍利
245a04 ‖ 益一切眾生。悉令增長無量福德。智慧之聚。
245a05 ‖ 是為諸佛第十最勝無上大慈大悲功德莊
245a06 ‖ 嚴。是為十。佛子。諸佛世尊。有十種自在法。
245a07 ‖ 何等為十。所謂一切諸佛。於一切法。悉得自
245a08 ‖ 在。明達種種句身味身。演說諸法。辯才無礙。
245a09 ‖ 是為諸佛第一自在法。一切諸佛。教化眾生。
245a10 ‖ 未曾失時。隨其願樂。為說正法。咸令調伏。無
245a11 ‖ 有斷絕。是為諸佛第二自在法。一切諸佛。能
245a12 ‖ 令盡虛空界。無量無數種種莊嚴。一切世界。
245a13 ‖ 六種震動。

简体字

映蔽一切三界妙色、到于彼岸无上妙色，是为诸佛第八最胜无上妙色庄严。一切诸佛皆于三世佛种中生，积众善宝，究竟清净，无诸过失，离世讥谤，一切法中最为殊胜清净妙行之所庄严，具足成就一切智智，种族清净无能讥毁，是为诸佛第九最胜无上种族庄严。一切诸佛以大慈力庄严其身，究竟清净无诸渴爱，身行永息，心善解脱，见者无厌，大悲救护一切世间；第一福田、无上受者，哀愍利益一切众生，悉令增长无量福德、智慧之聚，是为诸佛第十最胜无上大慈大悲功德庄严。是为十。

　　"佛子，诸佛世尊有十种自在法。何等为十？所谓：一切诸佛于一切法悉得自在，明达种种句身、味身，演说诸法辩才无碍，是为诸佛第一自在法。一切诸佛教化众生未曾失时，随其愿乐为说正法，咸令调伏无有断绝，是为诸佛第二自在法。一切诸佛能令尽虚空界无量无数种种庄严，一切世界六种震动，

Chapter 33 — *The Inconceivable Dharmas of the Buddhas*

outshining everything throughout the three realms of existence, and unsurpassably marvelous forms which reach the far shore of perfection. This is the eighth of the buddhas' unsurpassably supreme adornments, those associated with their marvelous forms.

All buddhas are born into the lineage of all buddhas of the three periods of time in which they accumulate the many jewels of goodness, attain ultimate purity, become free of all faults, leave behind all of the world's censure and slander, adorn themselves with the most especially supreme purity in the practice of all dharmas, completely fulfill the wisdom of all-knowledge, and become possessed of the pure clan lineage which no one can criticize or disparage. This is the ninth of the buddhas' unsurpassably supreme adornments, those associated with their lineage.

All buddhas adorn themselves with the power of the great kindness, achieve the most ultimate purity, become free of all cravings, forever put to rest all physical actions, achieve thorough liberation of mind, become those whom no one ever wearies of seeing, use the great compassion to rescue and protect everyone in the world, serve as the foremost of all fields of merit unsurpassably supreme in their worthiness to accept offerings, deeply sympathize with and benefit all beings, and enable them all to increase their accumulations of measureless merit and wisdom. This is the tenth of the buddhas' unsurpassably supreme adornments, those associated with their meritorious qualities of great kindness and great compassion.

These are the ten.

Sons of the Buddha, all buddhas, the *bhagavats*, have ten kinds of dharmas of sovereign mastery. What are those ten? They are as follows:

All buddhas have achieved sovereign mastery in all dharmas by which they have a clear comprehension of the many different kinds of statements and syllables[6] and expound on all dharmas with unimpeded eloquence. This is the first of the buddhas' dharmas of sovereign mastery.

All buddhas never miss the right time in teaching beings. Adapting to their aspirations, they ceaselessly explain right Dharma for them, thereby enabling their training. This is the second of the buddhas' dharmas of sovereign mastery.

All buddhas are able to cause the six kinds of quaking in all of the incalculably and innumerably variously adorned worlds throughout all realms of space, thereby causing those worlds to

正體字

令彼世界。或舉或下。或大或小。或
合或散。未曾惱害。於一眾生。其中眾生。不覺
不知。無疑無怪。是為諸佛第三自在法。一切
諸佛。以神通力。悉能嚴淨一切世界。於一念
頃。普現一切世界莊嚴。此諸莊嚴。經無數劫。
說不能盡。悉皆離染。清淨無比。一切佛剎嚴
淨之事。皆令平等。入一剎中。是為諸佛第四
自在法。一切諸佛。見一眾生。應受化者。為其
住壽。經不可說不可說劫。乃至盡未來際。結
[＊]跏趺坐。身心無倦。專心憶念。未曾廢忘。方
便調伏。而不失時。如為一眾生。為一切眾生。
悉亦如是。是為諸佛第五自在法。一切諸佛。
悉能遍往一切世界。一切如來所行之處。而
不暫捨一切法界。十方各別。一一方有無
量世界海。一一世界海。有無量世界種。佛以
神力。一念咸到。轉於無礙清淨法輪。是為諸
佛第六自在法。一切諸佛。為欲調伏一切眾
生。念念中。成阿耨多羅三藐三菩提。而於一
切佛法。非已現覺。亦非當覺。亦不住於有學
之地。而悉知見。

简体字

令彼世界或举或下、或大或小、或合或散，未曾恼害于一众生，其中众生不觉不知、无疑无怪，是为诸佛第三自在法。一切诸佛以神通力悉能严净一切世界，于一念顷普现一切世界庄严，此诸庄严经无数劫说不能尽，悉皆离染，清净无比，一切佛刹严净之事，皆令平等入一刹中，是为诸佛第四自在法。一切诸佛见一众生应受化者，为其住寿，经不可说不可说劫，乃至尽未来际，结跏趺坐，身心无倦，专心忆念，未曾废忘，方便调伏而不失时；如为一众生，为一切众生悉亦如是，是为诸佛第五自在法。一切诸佛悉能遍往一切世界一切如来所行之处，而不暂舍一切法界；十方各别，一一方有无量世界海，一一世界海有无量世界种，佛以神力一念咸到，转于无碍清净法轮，是为诸佛第六自在法。一切诸佛为欲调伏一切众生，念念中成阿耨多罗三藐三菩提，而于一切佛法非已现觉，亦非当觉，亦不住于有学之地，而悉知见，

Chapter 33 — The Inconceivable Dharmas of the Buddhas 2389

rise or fall, to expand or contract, or to come together or scatter apart, doing so in a manner whereby not even a single being in them is ever subjected to distress or injury, and doing so in a manner whereby the beings in them are entirely unaware, unknowing, free of doubts, and unsurprised. This is the third of the buddhas' dharmas of sovereign mastery.

Using the power of spiritual superknowledges, all buddhas are able to engage in the purification of all worlds whereby, in but a single mind-moment, they may everywhere manifest adornments of all worlds. These adornments are such that one could never finish describing them even in countless kalpas. They are all free of defilements and are incomparably pure. They are able to cause all of the purifying phenomena throughout all buddha *kṣetras* to equally enter into but a single *kṣetra*. This is the fourth of the buddhas' dharmas of sovereign mastery.

When all buddhas observe any single being who should be taught, they may extend their own life spans for even up to an ineffable-ineffable number of kalpas which may extend to the end of future time during which time they may continue to sit in the lotus posture free of any weariness in either body or mind with their minds focused on and mindful of this being, never forgetting him as they use skillful means to train him, ensuring that they never miss the right time in doing so. Just as they may do this for a single being, so too may they also do this for all beings in the very same way. This is the fifth of the buddhas' dharmas of sovereign mastery.

All buddhas are able to go everywhere in all worlds to the places where all *tathāgatas* travel and yet never even briefly leave any other place throughout the entire Dharma realm. In every one of the different regions throughout the ten directions, there are oceans of countless worlds, and in every one of those oceans of worlds, there are countless world systems. Using their spiritual powers, in but a single mind-moment, the buddhas are able to go to all of them and turn the wheel of the unimpeded pure Dharma. This is the sixth of the buddhas' dharmas of sovereign mastery.

Wishing to train all beings, in each successive mind-moment, all buddhas manifest the realization of *anuttarā-samyak-saṃbodhi* even as, with respect to all dharmas of a buddha, they are not such as have already awakened or are now awakening, are not such as will be awakened in the future, and are not such as abide on the ground of those still in training. Still, they are possessed of the complete knowledge and vision by which they

正體字

通達無礙。無量智慧。無量自
在。教化調伏一切眾生。是為諸佛第七自在
法。一切諸佛。能以眼處。作耳處佛事。能以耳
處。作鼻處佛事。能以鼻處。作舌處佛事。能以
舌處。作身處佛事。能以身處。作意處佛事。能
以意處。於一切世界中。住世出世間種種
境界。一一境界中。能作無量廣大佛事。是為
諸佛第八自在法。一切諸佛。其身毛孔。一一
能容一切眾生。一一眾生。其身悉與不可說
諸佛剎等。而無[1]迫隘。一一眾生。步步能過
無數世界。如是展轉。盡無數劫。悉見諸佛出
現於世。教化眾生。轉淨法輪。開示過去未來
現在不可說法。盡虛空界。一切眾生。諸趣受
身。威儀往來。及其所受。種種樂具。皆悉具
足。而於其中。無所障礙。是為諸佛第九自在
法。一切諸佛。於一念頃。現一切世界微塵數
佛。一一佛。皆於一切法界。眾妙蓮華。廣大莊
嚴世界。蓮華藏師子座上。成等正覺。示現諸
佛自在神力。如於眾妙蓮華廣大莊嚴世界。
如是。於一切法界中。不可說不可說。

简体字

通达无碍，无量智慧，无量自在，教化调伏一切众生，是为诸佛第七自在法。一切诸佛能以眼处作耳处佛事，能以耳处作鼻处佛事，能以鼻处作舌处佛事，能以舌处作身处佛事，能以身处作意处佛事，能以意处于一切世界中住世、出世间种种境界，一一境界中能作无量广大佛事，是为诸佛第八自在法。一切诸佛，其身毛孔一一能容一切众生，一一众生其身悉与不可说诸佛刹等而无迫隘，一一众生步步能过无数世界，如是展转尽无数劫，悉见诸佛出现于世，教化众生，转净法轮，开示过去、未来、现在不可说法；尽虚空界一切众生诸趣受身，威仪、往来及其所受种种乐具皆悉具足，而于其中无所障碍，是为诸佛第九自在法。一切诸佛于一念顷现一切世界微尘数佛，一一佛皆于一切法界众妙莲华广大庄严世界莲华藏师子座上成等正觉，示现诸佛自在神力；如于众妙莲华广大庄严世界，如是于一切法界中不可说不可说

command unimpeded penetrating comprehension, measureless wisdom, and measureless sovereign mastery with which they teach and train all beings. This is the seventh of the buddhas' dharmas of sovereign mastery.

All buddhas are able with the eye sense base to do the buddha works of the ear sense base, are able with the ear sense base to do the buddha works of the nose sense base, are able with the nose sense base to do the buddha works of the tongue sense base, are able with the tongue sense base to do the buddha works of the body sense base, are able with the body sense base to do the buddha works of the mind sense base, are able with the mind sense base to abide in all worlds in the many different kinds of worldly and world-transcending realms, and are able in every one of those realms to do the incalculably many vast works of the Buddha. This is the eighth of the buddhas' dharmas of sovereign mastery.

Every one of the pores on the body of all buddhas is able to contain all beings even as every one of those beings' bodies, commensurate in size with an ineffable number of buddha *kṣetras*, remains entirely unconstricted within it. Every one of those beings is able with every step to pass by countless worlds. And so this may continue to the point that, continuing to the very end of countless kalpas, they see all buddhas coming forth into the worlds, teaching beings, turning the wheel of pure Dharma, and offering instruction in an ineffable number of dharmas of the past, future, and present, this even as all beings throughout the realm of space continue to take on bodies in all the rebirth destinies, continuing to go and come in their various ways of comporting themselves, and fully possessed of the various kinds of objects from which they derive their enjoyments. In all of this, no mutually obstructive interferences occur at all. This is the ninth of the buddhas' dharmas of sovereign mastery.

All buddhas are able in but a single mind-moment to reveal all buddhas as numerous as the atoms in all worlds with each of those buddhas throughout the entire Dharma realm in vastly adorned lotus flower worlds of many wonders seated on lotus dais lion thrones, realizing the perfect and right enlightenment, manifesting all buddhas' sovereign mastery of the spiritual powers.

And just as this occurs in this way in the vastly adorned lotus flower worlds of many wonders, so too does this also occur everywhere throughout the entire Dharma realm in an ineffable-ineffable number of pure worlds possessed of many

正體字

種種莊嚴。種種境界。種種形相。種種示現。種種劫數。清淨世界。如於一念。如是。於無量無邊阿僧祇劫。一切念中。一念一切現。一念無量住。而未曾用少方便力。是為諸佛第十自在法。佛子。諸佛世尊。有十種無量不思議圓滿佛法。何等為十。所謂一切諸佛。一一淨相。皆具百福。一切諸佛。皆悉成就一切佛法。一切諸佛。皆悉成就一切善根。一切諸佛。皆悉成就一切功德。一切諸佛。皆能教化一切眾生。一切諸佛。皆悉能為眾生作主。一切諸佛。皆悉成就清淨佛剎。一切諸佛。皆悉成就一切智智。一切諸佛。皆悉成就色身相好。見者獲益。功不唐捐。一切諸佛。皆具諸佛平等正法。一切諸佛。作佛事已。莫不示現入於涅槃。是為十。佛子。諸佛世尊。有十種善巧方便。何等為十。一切諸佛。了知諸法皆離戲論。而能開示諸佛善根。是為第一善巧方便。一切諸佛。知一切法。悉無所見。各不相知。無縛無解。無受無集。無成就自在究竟。到於彼岸。然於諸法真實。而知不異不別。而得自在。

简体字

种种庄严、种种境界、种种形相、种种示现、种种劫数清净世界；如于一念，如是于无量无边阿僧祇劫一切念中，一念一切现，一念无量住，而未曾用少方便力，是为诸佛第十自在法。

"佛子，诸佛世尊有十种无量不思议圆满佛法。何等为十？所谓：一切诸佛一一净相皆具百福；一切诸佛皆悉成就一切佛法；一切诸佛皆悉成就一切善根；一切诸佛皆悉成就一切功德；一切诸佛皆能教化一切众生；一切诸佛皆悉能为众生作主；一切诸佛皆悉成就清净佛刹；一切诸佛皆悉成就一切智智；一切诸佛皆悉成就色身相好，见者获益，功不唐捐；一切诸佛皆具诸佛平等正法；一切诸佛作佛事已，莫不示现入于涅槃。是为十。

"佛子，诸佛世尊有十种善巧方便。何等为十？一切诸佛了知诸法皆离戏论，而能开示诸佛善根，是为第一善巧方便。一切诸佛知一切法悉无所见、各不相知、无缚无解、无受无集、无成就，自在究竟到于彼岸，然于诸法真实而知不异不别，而得自在、

different kinds of adornments, many different kinds of realms, many different kinds of forms and appearances, many different kinds of manifestations, and many different kinds of numbers of kalpas.

And just as this is the case in a single mind-moment, so too is this also so in all the mind-moments in incalculably and boundlessly many *asaṃkhyeyas* of kalpas in which, in every single mind-moment, everything appears in this way, and in every single mind-moment, these incalculably many phenomena all abide therein, even as, in all of this, they are never required to use even the slightest sort of power of expedient means to cause this to occur in this way. This is the tenth of the buddhas' dharmas of sovereign mastery.

Sons of the Buddha, all buddhas, the *bhagavats*, have ten kinds of measureless and inconceivable perfectly fulfilled buddha dharmas. What are those ten? They are as follows: Every one of the pure marks of all buddhas embodies a hundredfold measure of merit. All buddhas perfect all the dharmas of a buddha. All buddhas perfect all roots of goodness. All buddhas perfect all meritorious qualities. All buddhas are able to teach all beings. All buddhas are able to serve as leaders for beings. All buddhas perfect pure buddha *kṣetras*. All buddhas perfect the wisdom of all-knowledge. All buddhas perfect the form body with its major marks and secondary signs that enables all who see it to acquire such benefit that their efforts will not have been in vain. All buddhas possess the equal and right Dharma of all buddhas. After all buddhas have completed their buddha works, none of them do not manifest the appearance of entering nirvāṇa. These are the ten.

Sons of the Buddha, all buddhas, the *bhagavats*, have ten kinds of skillful means. What are those ten? They are as follows:

All buddhas completely know all dharmas transcend all conceptual proliferation and thus they are able to reveal and provide instruction in all buddhas' roots of goodness. This is the first of their skillful means.

All buddhas realize that all dharmas have nothing they perceive, that each of them has no mutual awareness of any other, that they have no bondage and have no liberation, that they have no experiencing of anything and have no accumulation, and that they have no accomplishment, yet they independently ultimately reach the far shore of perfection. Thus they realize that the reality of all dharmas does not involve any differentiation or particularity and thus they attain sovereign mastery. They

正體字

無我無受。不
壞實際。已得至於大自在地。常能觀察一切
法界。是為第二善巧方便。一切諸佛。永離諸
相。心無所住。而能悉知不亂不錯。雖知一切
相皆無自性。而如其體性。悉能善入。而亦示
現無量色身。及以一切清淨佛土。種種莊嚴
無盡之相。集智慧燈。滅眾生惑。是為第三善
巧方便。一切諸佛。住於法界。不住過去未來
現在。如如性中。無去來今三世相故。而能演
說去來今世。無量諸佛。出現世間。令其聞者。
普見一切諸佛境界。是為第四善巧方便。一
切諸佛。身語意業。無所造作。無來無去。亦無
有住。離諸數法。到於一切諸法彼岸。而為眾
法藏。具無量智。了達種種世出世法。智慧無
礙。示現無量自在神力。調伏一切法界眾生。
是為第五善巧方便。一切諸佛。知一切法不
可見。非一非異。非量非無量。非來非去。皆無
自性。亦不違於世間諸法。一切智者。無自性
中。見一切法。於法自在。廣說諸法。

简体字

无我无受、不坏实际，已得至于大自在地，常能观察一切法界，是为第二善巧方便。一切诸佛永离诸相，心无所住，而能悉知不乱不错，虽知一切相皆无自性，而如其体性悉能善入，而亦示现无量色身，及以一切清净佛土种种庄严无尽之相，集智慧灯灭众生惑，是为第三善巧方便。一切诸佛住于法界，不住过去、未来、现在，如如性中无去、来、今三世相故，而能演说去、来、今世无量诸佛出现世间，令其闻者普见一切诸佛境界，是为第四善巧方便。一切诸佛身、语、意业，无所造作，无来无去，亦无有住，离诸数法，到于一切诸法彼岸，而为众法藏，具无量智，了达种种世、出世法，智慧无碍，示现无量自在神力，调伏一切法界众生，是为第五善巧方便。一切诸佛知一切法不可见，非一、非异、非量、非无量、非来、非去，皆无自性，亦不违于世间诸法；一切智者，无自性中见一切法，于法自在，广说诸法，

realize there is no self or anything that experiences and thus they do not contradict the apex of reality. They have already succeeded in reaching the ground of great sovereign mastery and are thereby always able to contemplate the entire Dharma realm. This is the second of their skillful means.

All buddhas have forever transcended all phenomenal characteristics. Their minds have no place in which they dwell and yet they are able to know them all in a way that is not disordered and that is not erroneous. Although they know all such characteristics have no inherent existence of their own, they are still able to skillfully penetrate them in a manner accordant with their essential nature and are still able to manifest countless form bodies and use the inexhaustible phenomenal characteristics associated with every sort of adornment in all pure buddha lands and accumulate lamps of wisdom to extinguish the delusions of beings. This is the third of their skillful means.

As all buddhas abide in the Dharma realm, they do not abide in the past, the future, or the present because, in the nature of suchness, there is no past, future, or present, the signs of the three periods of time. Even so, they are still able to expound on the coming forth into the world of the countless buddhas of the past, the future, and the present, thus enabling those who hear this to everywhere see the realms of all buddhas. This is the fourth of their skillful means.

In the physical, verbal, and mental actions of all buddhas, there is nothing that they do. They have no coming, no going, and no abiding. They transcend all dharmas of enumeration, reach the far shore of perfection in all dharmas, and yet become a treasury of the many dharmas possessed of measureless wisdom. They have a completely penetrating comprehension of the many different kinds of worldly and world-transcending dharmas and possess unimpeded wisdom. They manifest countless kinds of masterfully implemented spiritual powers and train all the beings of the Dharma realm. This is the fifth of their skillful means.

All buddhas know that all dharmas are imperceptible, neither singular nor different, neither measurable nor measureless, neither coming nor going, and in every case devoid of any inherently existent nature even as they still do not contradict [the conventional existence of] worldly dharmas. For those possessed of all-knowledge perceive all dharmas even in the midst of what is devoid of any inherent nature. With sovereign mastery in all dharmas, they extensively expound on all dharmas even as

正體字

而常安住
真如實性。是為第六善巧方便。一切諸佛。於
一時中。知一切時。具淨善根。入於正位。而無
所著。於其日月年劫成壞。如是等時。不住不
捨。而能示現。若晝若夜。初中後時。一日七
日。半月一月。一年百年。一劫多劫。不可思
劫。不可說劫。乃至盡於未來際劫。恒為眾
生。轉妙法輪。不斷不退。無有休息。是為第七
善巧方便。一切諸佛。恒住法界。成就諸佛無
量無畏。及不可數辯。不可量辯。無盡辯。無斷
辯。無邊辯。不共辯。無窮辯。真實辯。方便開
示一切句辯。一切法辯。隨其根性。及以欲解。
以種種法門。說不可說不可說百千億那由
他修多羅。初中後善。皆悉究竟。是為第八善
巧方便。一切諸佛。住淨法界。知一切法。本無
名字。無過去名。無現在名。無未來名。無眾生
名。無非眾生名。無國土名。無非國土名。無法
名。無非法名。無功德名。無非功德名。無菩
薩名。無佛名。無數名。無非數名。無生名。無
滅名。無有名。無無名。無一名。無種種名。

简体字

而常安住真如实性，是为第六善巧方便。一切诸佛于一时中知一切时，具净善根，入于正位而无所著，于其日月、年劫、成坏，如是等时不住不舍，而能示现若昼若夜、初中后时、一日、七日、半月、一月、一年、百年、一劫、多劫、不可思劫、不可说劫，乃至尽于未来际劫，恒为众生转妙法轮，不断不退，无有休息，是为第七善巧方便。一切诸佛恒住法界，成就诸佛无量无畏及不可数辩、不可量辩、无尽辩、无断辩、无边辩、不共辩、无穷辩、真实辩、方便开示一切句辩、一切法辩，随其根性及以欲解，以种种法门说不可说不可说百千亿那由他修多罗，初、中、后善，皆悉究竟，是为第八善巧方便。一切诸佛住净法界，知一切法本无名字，无过去名，无现在名，无未来名；无众生名，无非众生名；无国土名，无非国土名；无法名，无非法名；无功德名，无非功德名；无菩萨名，无佛名；无数名，无非数名；无生名，无灭名；无有名，无无名；无一名，无种种名。

Chapter 33 — The Inconceivable Dharmas of the Buddhas

they still always securely abide in the true nature of true suchness. This is the sixth of their skillful means.

All buddhas know all times in any single time. They possess pure roots of goodness and achieve entry into the right and fixed position,[7] and yet remain free of anything to which they are attached. They neither dwell within nor relinquish any of the creations and destructions occurring in days, months, years, kalpas, and other such periods of time, and yet they are able to manifest within them. Whether it be the beginning, middle, or ending periods of the day or the night, a single day, seven days, a half month, a month, a year, a century, one kalpa, many kalpas, inconceivably many kalpas, an ineffable number of kalpas, and so forth on through to the exhaustion of all kalpas of the future, they constantly and uninterruptedly turn the wheel of the sublime Dharma for the benefit of beings, never retreating from this and never resting in this. This is the seventh of their skillful means.

All buddhas constantly abide in the Dharma realm, perfect in the countlessly many fearlessnesses of all buddhas as well as their innumerable types of eloquence, their incalculable forms of eloquence, their interminable eloquence, their uninterrupted eloquence, their boundless eloquence, their exclusive forms of eloquence, their inexhaustible eloquence, their genuine eloquence, their eloquence that employs skillful means in the explanation of all statements, and their eloquence with respect to all dharmas. They adapt to beings' faculties and natures as well as to their aspirations and understandings, using then all kinds of different Dharma gateways to proclaim the ineffable-ineffable number of hundreds of thousands of *koṭīs* of *nayutas* of sutras that are good in the beginning, good in the middle, and good in the end, all of which are possessed of complete ultimacy. This is the eighth of their skillful means.

All buddhas abide in the pure Dharma realm knowing that all dharmas are fundamentally nameless, having no past names, no present names, no future names, no names of beings, no names of non-beings, no country names, no non-country names, no dharma names, no non-dharma names, no meritorious quality names, no non-meritorious quality names, no bodhisattva names, no buddha names, no numerical names, no non-numerical names, no names associated with production, no names associated with destruction, no names associated with existence, no names associated with nonexistence, no singular kinds of names, and no different kinds of names. And

正體字

	何
246a22	以故。諸法體性。不可說故。一切諸法。無方無
246a23	處。不可集說。不可散說。不可一說。不可多
246a24	說。音聲莫逮。言語悉斷。雖隨世俗種種言說。
246a25	無所攀緣。無所造作。遠離一切虛妄想著。如
246a26	是究竟。到於彼岸。是為第九善巧方便。一切
246a27	諸佛。知一切法本性寂靜。無生故非色。無戲
246a28	論故非受。無名數故非想。無造作故非行。無
246a29	執取故非識。無入處故非處。無所得故非界。
246b01	然亦不壞一切諸法。本性無起。如虛空故。一
246b02	切諸法。皆悉空寂。無業果。無修習。無成就。
246b03	無出生。非數非不數。非有非無。非生非滅。非
246b04	垢非淨。非入非出。非住非不住。非調伏非不
246b05	調伏。非眾生非無眾生。非壽命非無壽命。
246b06	非因緣非無因緣。而能了知

简体字

何以故？诸法体性不可说故。一切诸法无方无处，不可集说，不可散说，不可一说，不可多说，音声莫逮，言语悉断，虽随世俗种种言说，无所攀缘，无所造作，远离一切虚妄想著，如是究竟到于彼岸。是为第九善巧方便。一切诸佛知一切法本性寂静，无生故非色，无戏论故非受，无名数故非想，无造作故非行，无执取故非识，无入处故非处，无所得故非界，然亦不坏一切诸法，本性无起如虚空故。一切诸法皆悉空寂，无业果，无修习，无成就，无出生，非数、非不数，非有、非无，非生、非灭，非垢、非净，非入、非出，非住、非不住，非调伏、非不调伏，非众生、非无众生，非寿命、非无寿命，非因缘、非无因缘，而能了知

Chapter 33 — The Inconceivable Dharmas of the Buddhas

why is this? This is because the essential nature of all dharmas is indescribable. All dharmas are devoid of direction, devoid of place, indescribable in the aggregate, indescribable when scattered, indescribable with a single way of speaking, indescribable through multiple ways of speaking, entirely inaccessible to description by voice, and such as cut short any attempt to describe them with words and speech. Although [the buddhas] do conform to the many different kinds of worldly verbal discourse, in doing so, they have no objective conditions that they seize upon and have nothing that they create. They abandon all attachments to false conceptions. In all such matters they reach the most ultimately far shore of perfection. This is the ninth of their skillful means.

All buddhas know that the fundamental nature of all dharmas is quiescence. Because they are unproduced, they are not associated with the form aggregate. Because they are not accessible through conceptual proliferation, they are not associated with the feeling aggregate. Because they are devoid of any names or numerical categories, they are not associated with the perception aggregate. Because they are devoid of anything that is done, they are not associated with the karmic formative factor aggregate. Because they are devoid of any grasping at anything at all, they are not associated with the consciousness aggregate. Because they have no point of access, they are not associated with any of the sense bases. Because they are devoid of anything that is apprehensible, they are not associated with any of the sense realms. Even though this is the case, there is still no damage done to [the conventional existence of] any dharma. Their fundamental nature has no arising, for it is like empty space.

All dharmas are empty and quiescent, without any karmic retributions, without any cultivation, without any accomplishment, and without any production. They are neither enumerated nor non-enumerated, neither existent nor nonexistent, neither produced nor destroyed, neither defiled nor immaculate, neither entered nor exited, neither abiding nor non-abiding, neither associated with training nor unassociated with training, neither associated with beings nor unassociated with beings, neither consistent with a life span nor inconsistent with the existence of a life span, and they are neither within the sphere of causes and conditions nor devoid of causes and conditions. Even so, [the buddhas] are able to completely know [with regard to beings] whether they are in the group of those

正體字

正定邪定。及不
定聚。一切眾生。為說妙法。令到彼岸。成就十
力四無所畏。能師子吼。具一切智。住佛境界。
是為第十善巧方便。佛子。是為諸佛成就十
種。善巧方便。

[1]大方廣佛華嚴經卷第四十七

　　佛不思議法品第三十三之[2]二

佛子。諸佛世尊。有十種廣大佛事。無量無邊。
不可思議。一切世間。諸天及人。皆不能知。去
來現在。所有一切聲聞獨覺。亦不能知。唯除
如來威神之力。何等為十。所謂一切諸佛。於
盡虛空遍法界。一切世界。兜率陀天。皆現受
生。修菩薩行。作大佛事。無量色相。無量威
德。無量光明。無量音聲。無量言辭。無量三
昧。無量智慧。所行境界。攝取一切人天魔梵
沙門婆羅門。阿脩羅等。大慈無礙。大悲究竟。
平等饒益一切眾生。或令生天。或令生人。或
淨其根。或調其心。或時為說差別三乘。或時
為說圓滿一乘。普皆濟度。令出生死。是為第
一廣大佛事。佛子。一切諸佛。從兜率天。降神
母胎。以究竟三昧。觀受生法。如幻如化。如影
如空。如熱時焰。隨樂而受。無量無礙。入無諍
法。

简体字

正定、邪定及不定聚一切众生，为说妙法令到彼岸，成就十力、四无所畏，能师子吼，具一切智，住佛境界，是为第十善巧方便。佛子，是为诸佛成就十种善巧方便。

大方广佛华严经卷第四十七
佛不思议法品第三十三之二

　　"佛子，诸佛世尊有十种广大佛事，无量无边，不可思议，一切世间诸天及人皆不能知，去、来、现在所有一切声闻、独觉亦不能知，唯除如来威神之力。何等为十？所谓：

　　"一切诸佛于尽虚空遍法界一切世界兜率陀天，皆现受生，修菩萨行，作大佛事，无量色相，无量威德，无量光明，无量音声，无量言辞，无量三昧，无量智慧，所行境界摄取一切人、天、魔、梵、沙门、婆罗门、阿修罗等，大慈无碍，大悲究竟，平等饶益一切众生，或令生天，或令生人，或净其根，或调其心，或时为说差别三乘，或时为说圆满一乘，普皆济度，令出生死，是为第一广大佛事。

　　"佛子，一切诸佛从兜率天降神母胎，以究竟三昧观受生法如幻、如化、如影、如空、如热时焰，随乐而受，无量无碍，入无诤法，

Chapter 33 — The Inconceivable Dharmas of the Buddhas

fixed in the path of what is right, in the group of those fixed in the path of what is wrong, or in the group of those whose destiny is still unfixed. They expound on the sublime Dharma for all beings and thereby enable them to reach the far shore of liberation, to fully develop the ten powers and the four fearlessnesses, become able to roar the lion's roar, become possessed of all-knowledge, and dwell in the Buddha's sphere of cognition. This is the tenth of their skillful means.

Sons of the Buddha, these are what constitute all buddhas' perfection of the ten kinds of skillful means.

Sons of the Buddha, all buddhas, the *bhagavats*, have ten kinds of vast buddha works that are measureless, boundless, inconceivable, such as none of the world's devas or humans could ever know, such as no *śrāvaka* disciple or *pratyekabuddha* could ever know, and such as only can be known through the awesome spiritual powers of the Tathāgata. What are those ten? They are as follows:

Sons of the Buddha, when all buddhas are dwelling in the Tuṣita Heavens in all worlds to the very ends of empty space throughout the Dharma realm, they all manifest the taking on of births in which they cultivate bodhisattva practices and accomplish the great buddha works, appearing then with countless forms and appearances, countless kinds of awesome deportment, countless kinds of light, countless kinds of voices, countless kinds of language, countless samādhis, and countless spheres of cognition imbued with wisdom by all of which they draw forth all humans, devas, *māras*, Brahma Heaven devas, *śramaṇas*, brahmans, *asuras*, and others of these sorts, using their unimpeded great kindness and their ultimate great compassion to equally benefit all beings, perhaps enabling them to be born as devas, perhaps enabling them to be born as humans, perhaps purifying their faculties, perhaps training their minds, sometimes speaking for their benefit of three different vehicles, and sometimes speaking for their benefit of the perfectly complete One Vehicle, thereby rescuing and liberating them all through enabling them to escape from *saṃsāra*. This is the first of their vast buddha works.

Sons of the Buddha, when all buddhas spiritually descend from the Tuṣita Heaven into their mother's womb, they use the most ultimate samādhi to contemplate the dharmas involved in taking birth as like a magical conjuration, like a transformation, like a reflection, like space, or like a mirage in the hot season. It is in accordance with what pleases them that they take this on in a manner that is measurelessly unimpeded, enter into the dharma of noncontentiousness,

正體字

起無著智。離欲清淨。成就廣大妙莊嚴藏。受最後身。住大寶莊嚴樓閣。而作佛事。或以神力。而作佛事。或以正念。而作佛事。或現神通。而作佛事。或現智日。而作佛事。或現諸佛廣大境界。而作佛事。或現諸佛無量光明。而作佛事。或入無數廣大三昧。而作佛事。或現從彼諸三昧起。而作佛事。佛子。如來爾時。在母胎中。為欲利益一切世間。種種示現。而作佛事。所謂或現初生。或現童子。或現在宮。或現出家。或復示現成等正覺。或復示現轉妙法輪。或示現於入般涅槃。如是皆以種種方便。於一切方。一切網。一切[3]旋。一切種。一切世界中。而作佛事。是為第二廣大佛事。佛子。一切諸佛。一切善業。皆已清淨。一切生智。皆已明潔。而以生法。誘導群迷。令其開悟。具行眾善。為眾生故。示誕王宮。一切諸佛。於諸色欲宮殿妓樂。皆已捨離。無所貪染。常觀諸有。空無體性。一切樂具。悉不真實。持佛淨戒。究竟圓滿。觀諸內宮妻妾侍從。生大悲愍。

简体字

起无著智,离欲清净,成就广大妙庄严藏,受最后身,住大宝庄严楼阁而作佛事,或以神力而作佛事,或以正念而作佛事,或现神通而作佛事,或现智日而作佛事,或现诸佛广大境界而作佛事,或现诸佛无量光明而作佛事,或入无数广大三昧而作佛事,或现从彼诸三昧起而作佛事。佛子,如来尔时在母胎中,为欲利益一切世间种种示现而作佛事。所谓:或现初生,或现童子,或现在宫,或现出家,或复示现成等正觉,或复示现转妙法轮,或示现于入般涅槃,如是皆以种种方便,于一切方、一切网、一切旋、一切种、一切世界中而作佛事。是为第二广大佛事。

"佛子,一切诸佛一切善业皆已清净,一切生智皆已明洁,而以生法诱导群迷,令其开悟,具行众善。为众生故,示诞王宫,一切诸佛于诸色欲宫殿妓乐皆已舍离,无所贪染,常观诸有空无体性,一切乐具悉不真实,持佛净戒究竟圆满;观诸内宫妻妾、侍从生大悲愍,

bring forth unattached wisdom that is apart from desire and pure, perfect a treasury of vast and marvelous adornments, and then take on that very last body. They abide there in a great tower adorned with jewels, doing the Buddha's works, sometimes using their spiritual powers to do the Buddha's works, sometimes using right mindfulness to do the Buddha's works, sometimes manifesting the spiritual superknowledges to do the Buddha's works, sometime manifesting the wisdom sun to do the Buddha's works, sometimes manifesting the vast realms of the buddhas to do the Buddha's works, sometimes manifesting the measureless radiance of all buddhas to do the Buddha's works, sometimes entering into countless vast samādhis to do the Buddha's works, and sometimes manifesting their emergence from those samādhis to do the Buddha's works.

Sons of the Buddha, at that time, even as the Tathāgata resides in his mother's womb, because he wishes to benefit all beings, he may bring forth many different kinds of manifestations in doing the Buddha's works. For example, he may manifest his first taking birth, may manifest his existence as a youth, may manifest his residing within the palace, may manifest his leaving the home life, may once again manifest his realization of the perfect and right enlightenment, may once again manifest his turning of the wheel of the sublime Dharma, or may manifest his entry into *parinirvāṇa*. In this way, he always uses these many different kinds of skillful means in every region, in all the networks, in all the clans, in all the lineages, and in all the worlds as he accomplishes the Buddha's works. This is the second of their vast buddha works.

Sons of the Buddha, all buddhas have already achieved complete purity in all good karmic actions. All of their knowledge regarding the taking on of births having already become radiantly immaculate, they use the dharma of taking birth to gather in and guide the many confused beings, thus enabling them to awaken and completely practice the many kinds of goodness.

For the sake of beings, they manifest the appearance of being born into the palace of a king. All buddhas have already relinquished all sensual desires and pleasures of the palace life for they have nothing at all that they desire. They always contemplate all aspects of existence as empty and devoid of any essential nature and always contemplate all objects of pleasure as unreal. They have achieved the most ultimate and perfect fulfillment in observing a buddha's pure moral precepts.

In contemplating their wives, consorts, and retainers within the inner palace, they bring forth the pity of the great compassion for

正體字	觀諸眾生虛妄不實。起大慈心。觀諸世 246c24 ‖ 間無一可樂。而生大喜。於一切法。心得自在。 246c25 ‖ 而起大捨。具佛功德。現生法界。身相圓滿。眷 246c26 ‖ 屬清淨。而於一切。皆無所著。以隨類音。為眾 246c27 ‖ 演說。令於世法。深生厭離。如其所行。示所得 246c28 ‖ 果。復以方便。隨應教化。未成熟者。令其成 246c29 ‖ 熟。已成熟者。令得解脫。為作佛事。令不退 247a01 ‖ 轉。復以廣大慈悲之心。恒為眾生。說種種法。 247a02 ‖ 又為示現三種自在。令其開悟。心得清淨。雖 247a03 ‖ 處內宮。眾所咸覩。而於一切諸世界中。施作 247a04 ‖ 佛事。以大智慧。以大精進。示現種種諸佛神 247a05 ‖ 通。無礙無盡。恒住三種巧方便業。所謂身業 247a06 ‖ 究竟清淨。語業常隨智慧而行。意業甚深無 247a07 ‖ 有障礙。以是方便。利益眾生。是為第三廣大 247a08 ‖ 佛事。佛子。一切諸佛。示處種種莊嚴宮殿。觀 247a09 ‖ 察厭離。捨而出家。欲使眾生。了知世法皆是 247a10 ‖ 妄想。無常敗壞。深起厭離。不生染著。永斷世 247a11 ‖ 間貪愛煩惱。修清淨行。利益眾生。
简体字	观诸众生虚妄不实起大慈心,观诸世间无一可乐而生大喜,于一切法心得自在而起大舍;具佛功德,现生法界,身相圆满,眷属清净,而于一切皆无所著;以随类音为众演说,令于世法深生厌离,如其所行示所得果,复以方便随应教化;未成熟者令其成熟,已成熟者令得解脱,为作佛事令不退转;复以广大慈悲之心,恒为众生说种种法,又为示现三种自在,令其开悟,心得清净。虽处内宫,众所咸睹,而于一切诸世界中施作佛事;以大智慧,以大精进,示现种种诸佛神通,无碍无尽。恒住三种巧方便业,所谓:身业究竟清净、语业常随智慧而行、意业甚深无有障碍,以是方便利益众生。是为第三广大佛事。 　　"佛子,一切诸佛示处种种庄严宫殿,观察厌离,舍而出家,欲使众生了知世法皆是妄想、无常、败坏,深起厌离,不生染著,永断世间贪爱烦恼,修清净行,利益众生。

them. Contemplating all beings as false and unreal, they bring forth the mind of great kindness for them. Contemplating all worlds as devoid of anything in which one could delight, they bring forth the great sympathetic joy. And with their minds' acquisition of sovereign mastery in all dharmas, they bring forth the great equanimity.

Completely possessed of the meritorious qualities of a buddha, they manifest birth into the Dharma realm in bodies perfectly complete in their physical marks and are attended by retinues which are pure and thus they are free of any sort of attachment to any of them. With their voices adapted to the various types of beings, they expound on the Dharma for the sake of the many, thereby enabling those beings to bring forth a deep renunciation of worldly dharmas.

In accordance with the actions in which they engage, they instruct beings in the fruits that will thereby accrue to them. They also use skillful means adapted to those who should receive the benefit of their teachings. Those who have not yet become ripened, they enable to become ripened. Those who have already become ripened, they enable to attain liberation. So that they may do the works of the buddhas, they enable them to attain irreversibility.

Furthermore, they use their vast minds of kindness and compassion to constantly expound on the many different dharmas for the benefit of beings. They also manifest for them their three kinds of sovereign mastery, thus enabling them to awaken and achieve the purification of their own minds. Although they dwell within the inner palace where they are all seen by the multitudes, they still engage in the Buddha's works in all worlds. With great wisdom and with great vigor, they manifest many different kinds of unimpeded and endless acts of the Buddha's spiritual superknowledges. They constantly abide in the three kinds of expedient actions, namely the ultimate purity of their physical actions, the constant accordance of their verbal actions with wisdom, and their extremely profound and unimpeded mental actions. They use these skillful means to benefit beings. This is the third of their vast buddha works.

Sons of the Buddha, all buddhas manifest residence within palaces with all kinds of adornments and then contemplate them, renounce them, and abandon them to leave behind the home life. They wish to influence beings to fully realize that the dharmas of the world are all false conceptions which are impermanent and bound for destruction so that they will bring forth deep renunciation of them, so that they will not generate a defiling attachment to them, and so that they will forever cut off the world's desire-based afflictions and then cultivate the pure conduct and benefit beings.

正體字

當出家時。捨俗威儀。住無諍法。滿足本願無量功德。以大智光。滅世癡闇。為諸世間無上福田。常為眾生。讚佛功德。令於佛所。植諸善本。以智慧眼。見真實義。復為眾生。讚說出家。清淨無過。永得出離。長為世間智慧高幢。是為第四廣大佛事。佛子。一切諸佛。具一切智。於無量法。悉已知見。菩提樹下。成最正覺。降伏眾魔。威德特尊。其身充滿一切世界。神力所作。無邊無盡。於一切智所行之義。皆得自在。修諸功德。悉已圓滿。其菩提座。具足莊嚴。周遍十方一切世界。佛處其上。轉妙法輪。說諸菩薩所有行願。開示無量諸佛境界。令諸菩薩。皆得悟入。修行種種清淨妙行。復能示導一切眾生。令種善根。生於如來平等地中。住諸菩薩無邊妙行。成就一切功德勝法。一切世界。一切眾生。一切佛刹。一切諸法。一切菩薩。一切教化。一切三世。一切調伏。一切神變。一切眾生心之樂欲。悉善了知。而作佛事。是為第五廣大佛事。

简体字

当出家时，舍俗威仪，住无诤法，满足本愿无量功德，以大智光灭世痴暗，为诸世间无上福田，常为众生赞佛功德，令于佛所植诸善本，以智慧眼见真实义；复为众生赞说出家，清净无过，永得出离，长为世间智慧高幢。是为第四广大佛事。

"佛子，一切诸佛具一切智，于无量法悉已知见，菩提树下成最正觉，降伏众魔，威德特尊。其身充满一切世界，神力所作无边无尽，于一切智所行之义皆得自在，修诸功德悉已圆满。其菩提座具足庄严，周遍十方一切世界，佛处其上转妙法轮，说诸菩萨所有行愿，开示无量诸佛境界，令诸菩萨皆得悟入，修行种种清净妙行。复能示导一切众生令种善根，生于如来平等地中，住诸菩萨无边妙行，成就一切功德胜法，一切世界、一切众生、一切佛刹、一切诸法、一切菩萨、一切教化、一切三世、一切调伏、一切神变、一切众生心之乐欲，悉善了知而作佛事。是为第五广大佛事。

Chapter 33 — The Inconceivable Dharmas of the Buddhas

When they are about to leave the home life, they relinquish the behavior of the common person, abide within the dharma of non-contentiousness, fulfill the incalculable meritorious qualities of their original vows, use the great light of their wisdom to extinguish the darkness of the world's delusions, and serve as unexcelled fields of merit for the entire world. For the sake of beings, they always praise the meritorious qualities of the Buddha, thereby causing them to plant roots of goodness in relation to the buddhas. They use the wisdom eye to perceive the genuine meaning. For beings' sakes, they also praise the purity, absence of faults, and eternal emancipation associated with leaving the home life and then forever serving for the world as a highly placed banner of wisdom. This is the fourth of their vast buddha works.

Sons of the Buddha, all buddhas, being possessed of all-knowledge, have already come to completely know and see all of the countlessly many dharmas. They realize the utmost right enlightenment beneath the bodhi tree, vanquish the many *māras*, and become possessed of the most especially revered kinds of awesome virtue. Their bodies completely fill all worlds. What they accomplish through their spiritual powers is boundless and endless. They all attain sovereign mastery in the meaning of the practices related to all-knowledge. They have all already perfectly fulfilled the cultivation of every form of meritorious quality. Their bodhi thrones are perfectly complete in their adornments and everywhere pervade all the worlds of the ten directions. The buddhas abide on them, turning the wheel of the sublime Dharma, expounding on the practices and vows of all bodhisattvas, revealing and explaining the spheres of action of all the countlessly many buddhas, enabling all bodhisattvas to succeed in awakening to and entering them, enabling them also to cultivate the many different kinds of pure and marvelous practices, and, additionally, enabling them to instruct and guide all beings, enabling them to plant roots of goodness, to become born onto the level ground of the Tathāgata, to dwell in the boundless and marvelous practices of all bodhisattvas, and to perfect all the supreme dharmas of the meritorious qualities.

They skillfully and completely know all worlds, all beings, all buddha *kṣetras*, all dharmas, all bodhisattvas, all teachings, all three periods of time, all means of training, all the spiritual transformations, and all those matters that the minds of beings delight in and desire. So it is that they engage in doing the Buddha's works. This is the fifth of their vast buddha works.

正體字

佛子。一切諸佛。轉不退法輪。令諸菩薩。不退轉故。轉無量法輪。令一切世間。咸了知故。轉開悟一切法輪。能大無畏師子吼故。轉一切法智藏法輪。開法藏門。除闇障故。轉無礙法輪。等虛空故。轉無著法輪。觀一切法非有無故。轉照世法輪。令一切眾生。淨法眼故。轉開示一切智法輪。悉遍一切三世法故。轉一切佛同一法輪。一切佛法。不相違故。一切諸佛。以如是等無量無數百千億那由他法輪。隨諸眾生。心行差別。而作佛事。不可思議。是為第六廣大佛事。佛子。一切諸佛。入於一切王都城邑。為諸眾生。而作佛事。所謂人王都邑。天王都邑。龍王夜叉王。乾闥婆王。阿脩羅王。迦樓羅王。緊那羅王。摩睺羅伽王。羅剎王。毘舍闍王。如是等王。一切都邑。入城門時。大地震動。光明普照。盲者得眼。聾者得耳。狂者得心。裸者得衣。諸憂苦者。悉得安樂。一切樂器。不鼓自鳴。諸莊嚴具。若著不著。咸出妙音。眾生聞者。無不欣樂。一切諸佛。色身清淨。相好具足。見者無厭。能為眾生。作於佛事。所謂若顧視。若觀察。若動轉。若屈伸。若行若住。若坐若臥。若默若語。若現神通。

简体字

"佛子，一切诸佛转不退法轮，令诸菩萨不退转故；转无量法轮，令一切世间咸了知故；转开悟一切法轮，能大无畏师子吼故；转一切法智藏法轮，开法藏门，除暗障故；转无碍法轮，等虚空故；转无著法轮，观一切法非有无故；转照世法轮，令一切众生净法眼故；转开示一切智法轮，悉遍一切三世法故；转一切佛同一法轮，一切佛法不相违故。一切诸佛以如是等无量无数百千亿那由他法轮，随诸众生心行差别而作佛事不可思议。是为第六广大佛事。

"佛子，一切诸佛入于一切王都城邑，为诸众生而作佛事，所谓；人王都邑、天王都邑，龙王、夜叉王、乾闼婆王、阿修罗王、迦楼罗王、紧那罗王、摩睺罗伽王、罗刹王、毗舍阇王，如是等王一切都邑。入城门时，大地震动，光明普照，盲者得眼，聋者得耳，狂者得心，裸者得衣，诸忧苦者悉得安乐；一切乐器不鼓自鸣，诸庄严具若著、不著咸出妙音，众生闻者无不欣乐。一切诸佛色身清净，相好具足，见者无厌，能为众生作于佛事。所谓：若顾视，若观察，若动转，若屈伸，若行，若住，若坐，若卧，若默，若语，若现神通，

Chapter 33 — The Inconceivable Dharmas of the Buddhas

Sons of the Buddha, all buddhas turn the irreversible Dharma wheel to enable all bodhisattvas to attain irreversibility. They turn the measureless Dharma wheel to enable the entire world to reach complete understanding. They turn the Dharma wheel that awakens everyone to enable the attainment of the great fearlessnesses and the roaring of the lion's roar. They turn the Dharma wheel of the treasury of the knowledge of all dharmas to open the gates of the Dharma treasury and eliminate the obstacles associated with benightedness. They turn the unimpeded Dharma wheel to enable becoming the same as empty space. They turn the Dharma wheel of nonattachment to enable contemplation of all dharmas as neither existent nor nonexistent. They turn the world-illuminating Dharma wheel to enable all beings to purify the Dharma eye. They turn the Dharma wheel that explains the all-knowledge which completely extends to all dharmas of the three periods of time. They turn the Dharma wheel that is the same for all buddhas because the dharmas of all buddhas are not mutually contradictory. All buddhas use incalculable and innumerable hundreds of thousands of *koṭīs* of *nayutas* of kinds of Dharma wheels such as these to adapt to the differences in the mental actions of beings and thus accomplish their inconceivable buddha works. This is the sixth of their vast buddha works.

Sons of the Buddha, when all buddhas enter the capital cities of all kings, they accomplish buddha works for the sake of all beings. That is to say, when the buddhas enter the city gates of the cities of human kings, deva kings, dragon kings, *yakṣa* kings, *gandharva* kings, *asura* kings, *garuḍa* kings, *kiṃnara* kings, *mahoraga* kings, *rākṣasa* kings, *piśāca* kings, and other such kings, the great earth quakes, light illuminates everything, the blind gain sight, the deaf gain hearing, the insane come to their right minds, those who have no clothes obtain robes, all who are distressed and afflicted with suffering become happy, the musical instruments sound of their own accord without being played, all adornments, whether worn or not worn, emanate marvelous sounds, and, of all beings who hear this, there are none who are not pleased.

All buddhas have pure form bodies complete with all the major marks and secondary signs which, whoever beholds them, never wearies of seeing them. They are able to use them to perform the buddha works for the sake of beings. For example, whether they turn and look at a being, contemplate them, turn around, bend down or straighten up, walk along or stand, sit down or lie down, remain silent or speak, manifest spiritual superknowledges, speak

正體字

若為說法。若有教勅。如是一切。皆為眾生。而作佛事。一切諸佛。[1]昔於一切無數世界。種種眾生。心樂海中。勸令念佛。常勤觀察。種諸善根。修菩薩行。歎佛色相微妙第一。一切眾生。難可值遇。若有得見。而興信心。則生一切無量善法。集佛功德。普皆清淨。如是。稱讚佛功德已。分身普往十方世界。令諸眾生。悉得瞻奉。思惟觀察。承事供養。種諸善根。得佛歡喜。增長佛種。悉當成佛。以如是行。而作佛事。或為眾生。示現色身。或出妙音。或但微笑。令其信樂。頭頂禮敬。曲躬合掌。稱揚讚歎。問訊起居。而作佛事。一切諸佛。以如是等無量無數不可言說不可思議種種佛事。於一切世界中。隨諸眾生心之所樂。以本願力。大慈悲力。一切智力。方便教化。悉令調伏。是為第七廣大佛事。佛子。一切諸佛。或住阿蘭若處。而作佛事。或住寂靜處。而作佛事。或住空閑處。而作佛事。或住佛住處。而作佛事。或住三昧。而作佛事。或獨處園林。而作佛事。或隱身不現。而作佛事。

简体字

若为说法，若有教敕，如是一切皆为众生而作佛事。一切诸佛普于一切无数世界种种众生心乐海中，劝令念佛，常勤观察，种诸善根，修菩萨行；叹佛色相微妙第一，一切众生难可值遇，若有得见而兴信心，则生一切无量善法，集佛功德普皆清净。如是称赞佛功德已，分身普往十方世界，令诸众生，悉得瞻奉，思惟观察，承事供养，种诸善根，得佛欢喜，增长佛种，悉当成佛。以如是行而作佛事，或为众生示现色身，或出妙音，或但微笑，令其信乐，头顶礼敬，曲躬合掌，称扬赞叹，问讯起居而作佛事。一切诸佛以如是等无量无数不可言说不可思议种种佛事，于一切世界中，随诸众生心之所乐，以本愿力、大慈悲力、一切智力，方便教化，悉令调伏。是为第七广大佛事。

"佛子，一切诸佛或住阿兰若处而作佛事；或住寂静处而作佛事；或住空闲处而作佛事；或住佛住处而作佛事；或住三昧而作佛事；或独处园林而作佛事；或隐身不现而作佛事；

Dharma for them, or provide them with instructions, in all such cases as these, they are doing buddha works for the sake of beings.

Everywhere in all the countless worlds, in the midst of the ocean of mental dispositions of the many different kinds of beings, all buddhas encourage and enable them to practice mindfulness of the Buddha, to always diligently practice meditative contemplation, to plant roots of goodness, and to cultivate the bodhisattva practices. They praise the buddha's physical signs as the most sublime of all, as rarely encountered by any being, as being such that, if beings are able to see them and then bring forth minds of faith, then they will produce all of the countless good dharmas, will accumulate the buddhas' meritorious qualities, and will all become purified.

Having praised the Buddha's meritorious qualities in these ways, they send forth division bodies that go forth everywhere throughout the worlds of the ten directions, thus enabling all beings to look up with reverence, reflect upon, contemplate, serve, and make offerings to buddhas, thereby planting all kinds of roots of goodness, thereby eliciting the pleased approval of the buddhas, and thereby extending the lineage of the buddhas as they all become buddhas in the future.

It is through practices such as these that they accomplish buddha works. For beings' sakes, they sometimes manifest form bodies, sometimes speak with sublime voices, or sometimes simply smile a subtle smile that causes beings to bring forth resolute faith, to bow down in reverence, to bend low their bodies with pressed palms, to utter praises, to half-bow, or to stand up in respect. It is in ways such as these that they accomplish buddha works.

All buddhas use incalculably, innumerably, ineffably, and inconceivably many different kinds of buddha works such as these with which, in all worlds, they adapt to all beings' mental dispositions. Using the power of their original vows, the power of great kindness and great compassion, and the power of all-knowledge, they use skillful means to teach beings and enable them all to take on the training. This is the seventh of their vast buddha works.

Sons of the Buddha, all buddhas may abide in an *araṇya*, a forest dwelling, and thus accomplish buddha works, may abide in a quiet place and thus accomplish buddha works, may abide in a deserted place and thus accomplish buddha works, may abide where the Buddha dwells and thus accomplish buddha works, may abide in samādhi and thus accomplish buddha works, may dwell alone in a garden or grove and thus accomplish buddha works, may hide their bodies and not appear at all and thus accomplish buddha works,

正體字

或住甚深智。而作佛事。或住諸佛無比境界。而作佛事。或住不可見種種身行。隨諸眾生心樂欲解。方便教化。無有休息。而作佛事。或以天身求一切智。而作佛事。或以龍身。夜叉身。乾闥婆身。阿脩羅身。迦樓羅身。緊那羅身。摩睺羅伽。人非人等身。求一切智。而作佛事。或以聲聞身。獨覺身。菩薩身。求一切智。而作佛事。或時說法。或時寂默。而作佛事。或說一佛。或說多佛。而作佛事。或說諸菩薩。一切行。一切願。為一行願。而作佛事。或說諸菩薩。一行一願。為無量行願。而作佛事。或說佛境界即世間境界。而作佛事。或說世間境界即佛境界。而作佛事。或說佛境界即非境界。而作佛事。或住一日。或住一夜。或住半月。或住一月。或住一年。乃至住不可說劫。為諸眾生。而作佛事。是為第八廣大佛事。佛子。一切諸佛。是生清淨善根之藏。令諸眾生。於佛法中。生淨信解。諸根調伏。永離世間。令諸菩薩。於菩提道。具智慧明。不由他悟。或現涅槃。而作佛事。或現世間。皆悉無常。而作佛事。或說佛身。或說所作。皆悉已[1]辨。而作佛事。

简体字

或住甚深智而作佛事；或住诸佛无比境界而作佛事；或住不可见种种身行，随诸众生心乐欲解，方便教化无有休息，而作佛事；或以天身，求一切智而作佛事；或以龙身、夜叉身、乾闼婆身、阿修罗身、迦楼罗身、紧那罗身、摩睺罗伽、人非人等身，求一切智而作佛事；或以声闻身、独觉身、菩萨身，求一切智而作佛事；或时说法，或时寂默，而作佛事；或说一佛，或说多佛，而作佛事；或说诸菩萨一切行、一切愿，为一行愿而作佛事；或说诸菩萨一行、一愿，为无量行愿而作佛事；或说佛境界即世间境界而作佛事；或说世间境界即佛境界而作佛事；或说佛境界即非境界而作佛事；或住一日，或住一夜，或住半月，或住一月，或住一年，乃至住不可说劫，为诸众生而作佛事。是为第八广大佛事。

"佛子，一切诸佛是生清净善根之藏，令诸众生于佛法中生净信解，诸根调伏，永离世间；令诸菩萨于菩提道，具智慧明，不由他悟。或现涅槃而作佛事；或现世间皆悉无常而作佛事；或说佛身而作佛事；或说所作皆悉已办而作佛事；

may abide in extremely deep wisdom and thus accomplish buddha works, may abide in all buddhas' incomparable spheres of action and thus accomplish buddha works, or they may abide in all different kinds of invisible physical actions adapted to beings' mental dispositions, desires, and understandings, ceaselessly using skillful means in teaching and thus accomplish buddha works.

They may use the body of a deva seeking all-knowledge and thus accomplish buddha works, may use the body of a dragon, the body of *yakṣa*, the body of a *gandharva*, the body of an *asura*, the body of a *garuḍa*, the body of a *kiṃnara*, the body of a *mahoraga*, or the body of a human or nonhuman that, in each case, is seeking all-knowledge and thus accomplish buddha works, may use the body of a *śrāvaka* disciple, the body of a *pratyekabuddha*, or the body of a bodhisattva seeking all-knowledge and thus accomplish buddha works, may engage in speaking the Dharma or remain silent and thus accomplish buddha works, may speak of but a single buddha or speak of many buddhas and thus accomplish buddha works, may speak of all practices or all vows of bodhisattvas as but a single practice or vow and thus accomplish buddha works, or they may speak of a single practice or a single vow of bodhisattvas as constituting countless practices or vows and thus accomplish buddha works.

They may speak of the Buddha's realms as just the world's realms and thus accomplish buddha works, may speak of the world's realms as just the Buddha's realm and thus accomplish buddha works, or may speak of the Buddha's realms as not being realms at all and thus accomplish buddha works or, for the sake of all beings, they may remain for one day, one night, a half month, a whole month, a whole year, and so forth on up to their sometimes abiding even for an inexpressibly great number of kalpas and thus accomplish buddha works. This is the eighth of their vast buddha works.

Sons of the Buddha, all buddhas are a treasury which produces pure roots of goodness. They enable beings to develop pure resolute faith in the Buddha's Dharma, to acquire training of their faculties, and to forever transcend the world. They enable bodhisattvas to develop perfectly realized wisdom light on the path to bodhi and also cause them to acquire the awakening that does not depend on anyone else. For example, they may manifest entry into nirvāṇa and thus accomplish buddha works, may reveal all worlds as impermanent and thus accomplish buddha works, may speak of the body of the Buddha and thus accomplish buddha works, may speak of having already done what is to be done and thus accomplish buddha works, may speak of achieving perfectly fulfilled and flawless

正體字

或說功德圓滿無缺。而作佛事。或說永斷諸有根本。而作佛事。或令眾生。厭離世間。隨順佛心。而作佛事。或說壽命終歸於盡。而作佛事。或說世間無一可樂。而作佛事。或為宣說盡未來際。供養諸佛。而作佛事。或說諸佛轉淨法輪。令其得聞。生大歡喜。而作佛事。或為宣說諸佛境界。令其發心。而修諸行。而作佛事。或為宣說念佛三昧。令其發心。常樂見佛。而作佛事。或為宣說諸根清淨。勤求佛道。心無懈退。而作佛事。或詣一切諸佛國土。觀諸境界種種因緣。而作佛事。或攝一切諸眾生身。皆為佛身。令諸懈怠放逸眾生。悉住如來清淨禁戒。而作佛事。是為第九廣大佛事。佛子。一切諸佛。入涅槃時。無量眾生。悲號涕泣。生大憂惱。遞相瞻顧。而作是言。如來世尊。有大慈悲。哀愍饒益一切世間。與諸眾生。為救為歸。如來出現。難可值遇。無上福田。於今永滅。即以如是。令諸眾生。悲號戀慕。而作佛事。復為化度一切天人。龍神夜叉乾闥婆阿修羅迦樓羅緊那羅摩睺羅伽人非人等故。隨其樂欲。自碎其身。以為舍利。無量無數不可思議。令諸眾生。起淨信心。恭敬尊重。

简体字

或说功德圆满无缺而作佛事；或说永断诸有根本而作佛事；或令众生，厌离世间，随顺佛心，而作佛事；或说寿命终归于尽而作佛事；或说世间无一可乐而作佛事；或为宣说尽未来际供养诸佛而作佛事；或说诸佛转净法轮，令其得闻生大欢喜，而作佛事；或为宣说诸佛境界，令其发心而修诸行，而作佛事；或为宣说念佛三昧，令其发心常乐见佛，而作佛事；或为宣说诸根清净，勤求佛道，心无懈退，而作佛事；或诣一切诸佛国土，观诸境界种种因缘而作佛事；或摄一切诸众生身皆为佛身，令诸懈怠放逸众生悉住如来清净禁戒，而作佛事。是为第九广大佛事。

"佛子，一切诸佛入涅槃时，无量众生悲号涕泣，生大忧恼，递相瞻顾而作是言：'如来世尊有大慈悲，哀愍饶益一切世间，与诸众生为救为归。如来出现难可值遇，无上福田于今永灭。'即以如是，令诸众生悲号恋慕，而作佛事。复为化度一切天人、龙神、夜叉、乾闼婆、阿修罗、迦楼罗、紧那罗、摩睺罗伽、人非人等故，随其乐欲，自碎其身以为舍利，无量无数不可思议，令诸众生起净信心，恭敬尊重，

meritorious qualities and thus accomplish buddha works, may speak of forever severing the root of all realms of existence and thus accomplish buddha works, may enable beings to renounce the world and follow in accordance with the Buddha's resolve and thus accomplish buddha works, may speak of the life span as inevitably bound to end and thus accomplish buddha works, or they may speak of the world as devoid of even a single delightful thing and thus accomplish buddha works.

They may expound on the practice of making offerings to all buddhas to the end of the future and thus accomplish buddha works, may speak of all buddhas turning the wheel of the pure Dharma, thereby causing those who hear to be filled with great joy, and thus accomplish buddha works, may expound on all buddhas' spheres of action, thereby causing others to bring forth the resolve and cultivate all the practices and thus accomplish buddha works, may expound on the mindfulness of the Buddha samādhi, thereby causing others to bring forth the resolve by which they always delight in seeing the Buddha and thus accomplish buddha works, may expound on the purification of all one's faculties and the diligent pursuit of the path to buddhahood with a resolve that never rests or retreats and thus accomplish buddha works, may visit all buddha lands, contemplating the many different causes and conditions associated with all realms and thus accomplish buddha works, or they may unite the bodies of all beings into the body of a buddha, thereby causing all indolent and neglectful beings to abide in the pure moral precepts of the Tathāgata. This is the ninth of their vast Buddha works.

Sons of the Buddha, when all buddhas enter nirvāṇa, countless beings wail piteously, weep and cry, are beset with immense distress and affliction, and then look to each other and say, "The Tathāgata, the Bhagavat, possessed of the great kindness and compassion, deeply pities and benefits the entire world and serves beings as a rescuer and a refuge. The Tathāgata's appearance in the world is only rarely ever encountered. The most supreme of all fields of merit has now forever entered nirvāṇa." By causing beings to wail piteously and long for the Buddha in this way, they also accomplish buddha works.

Moreover, to teach and liberate all the devas, dragon spirits, *yakṣas, gandharvas, asuras, garuḍas, kiṃnaras, mahoragas,* humans, and nonhumans, they adapt to their aspirations, even grinding up their own bodies to serve as incalculably and innumerably many inconceivable *śarīra* relics which serve to cause beings to bring forth thoughts of pure faith, respect, reverence, and joyous delight

正體字	歡喜供養。修諸功德。具足圓滿。復起於 248a29　塔。種種嚴飾。於諸天宮。龍宮夜叉宮。乾闥 248b01　婆阿脩羅迦樓羅緊那羅摩睺羅伽人非人等 248b02　諸宮殿中。以為供養。牙齒爪髮。咸以起塔。令 248b03　其見者。皆悉念佛念法念僧。信樂不迴。誠敬 248b04　尊重。在在處處。布施供養。修諸功德。以是福 248b05　故。或生天上。或處人間。種族尊榮。財產備 248b06　足。所有眷屬。悉皆清淨。不入惡趣。常生善 248b07　道。恒得見佛。具眾白法。於三有中。速得出 248b08　離。各隨所願。獲自乘果。於如來所。知恩報 248b09　恩。永與世間。作所歸依。佛子。諸佛世尊。雖 248b10　般涅槃。仍與眾生。作不思議清淨福田。無盡 248b11　功德。最上福田。令諸眾生。善根具足。福德圓 248b12　滿。是為第十廣大佛事。佛子。此諸佛事。無量 248b13　廣大。不可思議。一切世間。諸天及人。及去來 248b14　今。聲聞獨覺。皆不能知。唯除如來威神所加。 248b15　佛子。諸佛世尊。有十種無二行自在法。何等 248b16　為十。所謂一切諸佛。悉能善說。授記言[2]辭。 248b17　決定無二。一切諸佛。悉能隨順眾生心念。令 248b18　其意滿。決定無二。一切諸佛。悉能現覺一切 248b19　諸法。
简体字	欢喜供养，修诸功德，具足圆满。复起于塔，种种严饰，于诸天宫、龙宫、夜叉宫，乾闼婆、阿修罗、迦楼罗、紧那罗、摩睺罗伽、人非人等诸宫殿中，以为供养。牙齿、爪发咸以起塔，令其见者皆悉念佛、念法、念僧，信乐不回，诚敬尊重，在在处处布施供养、修诸功德；以是福故，或生天上，或处人间，种族尊荣，财产备足，所有眷属悉皆清净，不入恶趣，常生善道，恒得见佛，具众白法，于三有中速得出离，各随所愿获自乘果，于如来所知恩报恩，永与世间作所归依。佛子，诸佛世尊虽般涅槃，仍与众生作不思议清净福田、无尽功德最上福田，令诸众生善根具足、福德圆满。是为第十广大佛事。 　　"佛子，此诸佛事无量广大、不可思议，一切世间诸天及人及去来今声闻、独觉皆不能知，唯除如来威神所加。 　　"佛子，诸佛世尊有十种无二行自在法。何等为十？所谓：一切诸佛悉能善说，授记言辞，决定无二；一切诸佛悉能随顺众生心念，令其意满，决定无二；一切诸佛悉能现觉一切诸法，

Chapter 33 — *The Inconceivable Dharmas of the Buddhas* 2417

in making offerings and cultivating all the meritorious qualities to complete fulfillment. They also erect stupas with all different kinds of adornments and make offerings in celestial palaces, dragon palaces, *yakṣa* palaces, and palaces of *gandharvas, asuras, garuḍas, kiṃnaras, mahoragas,* humans, nonhumans, and others.

They may also erect commemorative stupas to the buddhas' teeth, nails, or hair relics which inspire all those who see them to become mindful of the Buddha, mindful of the Dharma, and mindful of the Sangha while also causing them to develop unremitting resolute faith, to bring forth sincere respect and reverential esteem, to make gifts of offerings in place after place, and to cultivate all the meritorious qualities. Because of this merit, those beings may be reborn in the heavens or may come to dwell among humans in an honorable and illustrious clan where they are well endowed with wealth and possessions, are attended by a retinue of pure beings, and never enter the wretched destinies, but rather are always reborn in the good destinies where they are always able to see the Buddha, perfect the many dharmas of pristine purity, and swiftly succeed in gaining emancipation from the three realms of existence as they each reap the fruits of their own vehicles in accordance with whatever they have vowed to accomplish and then recognize and repay kindnesses bestowed on them by the *tathāgatas* and thus forever serve as those in whom those in the world can take refuge.

Sons of the Buddha, although all buddhas, the *bhagavats*, enter *parinirvāṇa*, they still continue to serve beings as inconceivable fields of pure merit and as the most supreme of all fields of merit for the generation of endless meritorious qualities, doing so in ways which enable all beings to fully develop roots of goodness and acquire the complete fulfillment of merit. This is the tenth of their vast buddha works.

Sons of the Buddha, these works of the buddhas are so immeasurably vast and so inconceivable that no deva or human in the entire world and no past, future, or present *śrāvaka* disciple or *pratyekabuddha* could ever know them unless they were aided by the awesome spiritual powers of the Tathāgata.

Sons of the Buddha, all buddhas, the *bhagavats*, have ten kinds of dharmas of masterful action in which it could not be otherwise. What are those ten? They are as follows: All buddhas are able to bestow predictions in which it definitely could not be otherwise.[8] All buddhas are able to adapt to the thoughts in beings' minds and enable their wishes to be fulfilled and it definitely could not be otherwise. All buddhas are able to manifest awakening to all dharmas

正體字

演說其義。決定無二。一切諸佛。悉能
具足去來今世。諸佛智慧。決定無二。一切諸
佛。悉知三世一切剎那。即一剎那決定無二。
一切諸佛。悉知三世一切佛剎。入一佛剎。決
定無[3]一。一切諸佛。悉知三世一切佛語。即
一佛語。決定無二。一切諸佛。悉知三世一切
諸佛。與其所化一切眾生。體性平等。決定無
二。一切諸佛悉知世法。及諸佛法。性無差別。
決定無二。一切諸佛。悉知三世一切諸佛。所
有善根。同一善根。決定無二。是為十。佛子。
諸佛世尊。有十種住。住一切法。何等為十。所
謂一切諸佛。住覺悟一切法界。一切諸佛。住
大悲語。一切諸佛。住本大願。一切諸佛。住不
捨調伏眾生。一切諸佛。住無自性法。一切諸
佛。住平等利益。一切諸佛。住無忘失法。一切
諸佛。住無障礙心。一切諸佛。住恒正定心。一
切諸佛。住等入一切法。不違實際相。是為十。
佛子。諸佛世尊。有十種知一切法盡無有餘。
何等為十。所謂知過去一切法。盡無有餘。知
未來一切法。盡無有餘。知現在一切法。盡無
有餘。知一切言語法。盡無有餘。知一切世間
道。盡無有餘。知一切眾生心。盡無有餘。知一
切菩薩善根。上中下。種種分位。盡無有餘。

简体字

演说其义，决定无二；一切诸佛悉能具足去、来、今世诸佛智慧，决定无二；一切诸佛悉知三世一切刹那即一刹那，决定无二；一切诸佛悉知三世一切佛刹入一佛刹，决定无二；一切诸佛悉知三世一切佛语即一佛语，决定无二；一切诸佛悉知三世一切诸佛，与其所化一切众生，体性平等，决定无二；一切诸佛悉知世法及诸佛法性无差别，决定无二；一切诸佛悉知三世一切诸佛所有善根同一善根，决定无二。是为十。

"佛子，诸佛世尊有十种住，住一切法。何等为十？所谓：一切诸佛住觉悟一切法界；一切诸佛住大悲语；一切诸佛住本大愿；一切诸佛住不舍调伏众生；一切诸佛住无自性法；一切诸佛住平等利益；一切诸佛住无忘失法；一切诸佛住无障碍心；一切诸佛住恒正定心；一切诸佛住等入一切法，不违实际相。是为十。

"佛子，诸佛世尊有十种知一切法尽无有余。何等为十？所谓：知过去一切法尽无有余；知未来一切法尽无有余；知现在一切法尽无有余；知一切言语法尽无有余；知一切世间道尽无有余；知一切众生心尽无有余；知一切菩萨善根上、中、下种种分位尽无有余；

and expound on their meaning and it definitely could not be otherwise. All buddhas are able to completely fulfill the wisdom of all buddhas of the past, future and present periods of time and it definitely could not be otherwise. All buddhas realize that all *kṣaṇa*-instants throughout the three periods of time are but a single *kṣaṇa*-instant and it definitely could not be otherwise. All buddhas realize that all buddha *kṣetras* of the three periods of time enter into a single buddha *kṣetra* and it definitely could not be otherwise. All buddhas realize that all speech of all buddhas of the three periods of time is identical to the speech of any single buddha and it definitely could not be otherwise. All buddhas realize that the essential nature of all buddhas of the three periods of time and the essential nature of all the beings they teach are identical and it definitely could not be otherwise. All buddhas realize that the nature of worldly dharmas and the nature of all buddhas' dharmas do not differ and it definitely could not be otherwise. All buddhas realize that all roots of goodness of all buddhas of the three periods of time are the same as any one of their roots of goodness and it definitely could not be otherwise. These are the ten.

Sons of the Buddha, all buddhas, the *bhagavats*, have ten kinds of abiding in which they abide in all dharmas. What are those ten? They are as follows: All buddhas abide in awakening to the entire Dharma realm. All buddhas abide in greatly compassionate speech. All buddhas abide in original great vows. All buddhas abide in the practice of not abandoning their training of beings. All buddhas abide in the dharma of the nonexistence of any inherent nature. All buddhas abide in impartially benefiting beings. All buddhas abide in never forgetting any dharma. All buddhas abide in the unimpeded mind. All buddhas abide in the mind of constant right meditative concentration. All buddhas abide in the equal penetration of all dharmas and never contradicting their having the characteristic [nature of] the apex of reality. These are the ten.

Sons of the Buddha, all buddhas, the *bhagavats*, have ten kinds of knowing of all dharmas without exception. What are those ten? They are as follows: They know all dharmas of the past without exception. They know all dharmas of the future without exception. They know all dharmas of the present without exception. They know all speech dharmas without exception. They know all worldly paths without exception. They know the thoughts of all beings without exception. They know without exception all of the superior, middling, and inferior roots of goodness of all bodhisattvas as well as all their many different stations on the path. They

正體字

知
248c13| 一切佛圓滿智。及諸善根。不增不減。盡無有
248c14| 餘。知一切法。皆從緣起。盡無有餘。知一切世
248c15| 界種。盡無有餘。知一切法界中。如因陀羅網。
248c16| 諸差別事。盡無有餘。是為十
248c17| 佛子。諸佛世尊。有十[4]種廣大力最上力。無
248c18| 量力。大威德力。難獲力不退力。堅固力不可
248c19| 壞力。一切世間不思議力。一切眾生無能動
248c20| [5]力。大那羅延幢勇健法。何者為十。所謂一
248c21| 切諸佛。身不可壞。命不可斷世間毒藥。所不
248c22| 能中。一切世界。水火風災。皆於佛身。不能為
248c23| 害。一切諸魔。天龍夜叉乾闥婆阿修羅迦樓
248c24| 羅緊那羅摩睺羅伽人非人毗舍闍羅剎等。盡
248c25| 其勢力。雨大金剛。如須彌山及鐵圍山。遍於
248c26| 三千大千世界。一時俱下。不能令佛心有驚
248c27| 怖。乃至一毛。亦不搖動。行住坐臥初無變易。
248c28| 佛所住處。四方遠近。不令其下。則不能雨。假
248c29| 使不制。而從雨之。終不為損。若有眾生。為佛
249a01| 所持。及佛所使。尚不可害。況如來身。是為諸
249a02| 佛第一大那羅延幢勇健法。佛子。一切諸佛。
249a03| 以一切法界。諸世界中。須彌山王。及鐵圍山。
249a04| 大鐵圍山。大海山林宮殿屋宅。置一毛孔。

简体字

知一切佛圆满智及诸善根不增不减尽无有余；知一切法皆从缘起尽无有余；知一切世界种尽无有余；知一切法界中如因陀罗网诸差别事尽无有余。是为十。

"佛子，诸佛世尊有十种力。何等为十？所谓：广大力、最上力、无量力、大威德力、难获力、不退力、坚固力、不可坏力、一切世间不思议力、一切众生无能动力。是为十。

"佛子，诸佛世尊有十种大那罗延幢勇健法。何者为十？所谓：

"一切诸佛，身不可坏，命不可断，世间毒药所不能中，一切世界水、火、风灾皆于佛身不能为害。一切诸魔、天、龙、夜叉、乾闼婆、阿修罗、迦楼罗、紧那罗、摩睺罗伽、人非人、毗舍阇、罗刹等，尽其势力，雨大金刚如须弥山及铁围山，遍于三千大千世界，一时俱下，不能令佛心有惊怖，乃至一毛亦不摇动，行、住、坐、卧初无变易。佛所住处四方远近，不令其下则不能雨；假使不制而从雨之，终不为损。若有众生为佛所持及佛所使，尚不可害，况如来身！是为诸佛第一大那罗延幢勇健法。

"佛子，一切诸佛以一切法界诸世界中须弥山王，及铁围山、大铁围山、大海、山林、宫殿、屋宅，置一毛孔，

Chapter 33 — The Inconceivable Dharmas of the Buddhas

know all without exception, neither more nor less, of all buddhas' perfectly fulfilled types of knowledge and roots of goodness. They know that all dharmas without exception arise from conditions. They know all the different world systems without exception. They know all the different phenomena without exception throughout the entire Dharma realm are like the net of Indra. These are the ten.

Sons of the Buddha, all buddhas, the *bhagavats*, have ten kinds of powers. What are those ten? They are as follows: vast powers, supreme powers, measureless powers, powers of great awesome virtue, powers that are difficult to acquire, irreversible powers, solidly enduring powers, indestructible powers, powers inconceivable to anyone in the world, and powers that cannot be shaken by any being. These are the ten.

Sons of the Buddha, all buddhas, the *bhagavats*, have ten kinds of great *nārāyaṇa* banner dharmas of bravery and strength. What are those ten? They are as follows:

All buddhas have indestructible bodies and lives which cannot be cut short. They cannot be poisoned by the world's poisons. Not even all the world's water, fire, and wind disasters can injure the Buddha's body. Even if all the demons, devas, dragons, *yakṣas*, *gandharvas*, *asuras*, *garuḍas*, *kiṃnaras*, *mahoragas*, humans, nonhumans, *piśācas*, *rākṣasas*, and other such beings all exhausted all of their strength in raining down great vajras as immense as Mount Sumeru or the Iron Ring Mountains all over all worlds of the entire great trichiliocosm, raining them down all at once, they would still remain unable to cause any fear in the mind of the Buddha, would still be unable to shake even a single hair on his body, and, even from the very beginning, would still be unable to cause any change at all in his walking, standing, sitting, or lying down. Wherever the Buddha dwells, whether near or far, if he does not allow them to descend, then they would be unable to rain down. And even if he did not restrain them and they then did in fact rain down, they would still remain unable to do him any harm. Not even any being supported by the Buddha or sent as an emissary of the Buddha could be the least bit harmed, how much the less could harm befall the body of the Tathāgata himself. This is the first of all buddhas' great *nārāyaṇa* banner dharmas of bravery and strength.

Sons of the Buddha, all buddhas may place into a single pore all of the contents of all the worlds throughout the entire Dharma realm, including Sumeru, the king of mountains, the Iron Ring Mountains, the Great Iron Ring Mountains, the great oceans, the mountains, the forests, the palaces, the buildings, and the dwellings, doing

正體字

盡未來劫。而諸眾生。不覺不知。唯除如來神力所被。佛子。爾時諸佛。於一毛孔。持於爾所一切世界。盡未來劫。或行或住。或坐或臥。不生一念勞倦之心。佛子。譬如虛空。普持一切遍法界中。所有世界。而無勞倦。一切諸佛。於一毛孔。持諸世界。亦復如是。是為諸佛第二大那羅延幢勇健法。佛子。一切諸佛。能於一念。起不可說不可說世界微塵數步。一一步。過不可說不可說佛剎微塵數國土。如是而行。經一切世界微塵數劫。佛子。假使有一大金剛山。與上所經一切佛剎。其量正等。如是量等。大金剛山。有不可說不可說佛剎微塵數諸佛。能以如是諸山。置一毛孔。佛身毛孔。與法界中一切眾生毛孔數等。一一毛孔。悉置爾許大金剛山。持爾許山。遊行十方。入盡虛空一切世界。從於前際。盡未來際。一切諸劫。無有休息。佛身無損。亦不勞倦。心常在定。無有散亂。是為諸佛第三大那羅延幢勇健法。

简体字

尽未来劫，而诸众生不觉不知，唯除如来神力所被。佛子，尔时，诸佛于一毛孔持于尔所一切世界，尽未来劫，或行、或住、或坐、或卧，不生一念劳倦之心。佛子，譬如虚空普持一切遍法界中所有世界而无劳倦，一切诸佛于一毛孔持诸世界亦复如是。是为诸佛第二大那罗延幢勇健法。

"佛子，一切诸佛能于一念起不可说不可说世界微尘数步，一一步过不可说不可说佛刹微尘数国土，如是而行，经一切世界微尘数劫。佛子，假使有一大金刚山，与上所经一切佛刹其量正等。如是量等大金刚山，有不可说不可说佛刹微尘数，诸佛能以如是诸山置一毛孔。佛身毛孔与法界中一切众生毛孔数等，一一毛孔悉置尔许大金刚山，持尔许山游行十方，入尽虚空一切世界，从于前际尽未来际，一切诸劫无有休息，佛身无损亦不劳倦，心常在定无有散乱。是为诸佛第三大那罗延幢勇健法。

Chapter 33 — The Inconceivable Dharmas of the Buddhas

so even to the very end of future kalpas even as all beings remain entirely unaware and incognizant of this unless they are assisted by the Tathāgata's spiritual powers.

Sons of the Buddha, at that time when the buddhas hold within a single pore all of those so very many worlds even to the very end of all kalpas of the future, whether they be walking, standing, sitting, or lying down, they never have even a single thought of weariness in this regard. Sons of the Buddha, just as empty space everywhere holds within it all the worlds throughout the entire Dharma realm without ever becoming wearied by this, so too it is with all buddhas as they hold all worlds within but a single pore. This is the second of all buddhas' great *nārāyaṇa* banner dharmas of bravery and strength.

Sons of the Buddha, all buddhas are able in but a single mind-moment to take a number of steps equal to the number of atoms in an ineffable-ineffable number of worlds and, in so doing, pass with every step beyond a number of worlds equal to the atoms contained within an ineffable-ineffable number of buddha *kṣetras* so that, as they walk along in this way, they may pass through a number of kalpas equal to the number of atoms contained in all worlds.

Sons of the Buddha, suppose that there was a great vajra mountain the size of which was precisely commensurate with all those buddha *kṣetras* that were passed by in the above description, and suppose too that there was a number of such great vajra mountains equal to the number of atoms in an ineffable-ineffable number of buddha *kṣetras*. The buddhas are able to take all such mountains and place them all inside of a single one of their pores. Even supposing that the number of pores on a buddha's body were equivalent to all the pores existing on the bodies of all beings throughout the entire Dharma realm, in every one of their pores, they can place just so very many great vajra mountains as this and, taking along just so very many mountains as this, they can then roam about throughout the ten directions, entering all the worlds throughout the entirety of empty space, doing so from the beginning of time on through to the end of all kalpas of the future, doing so without ever resting. and doing so without any injury to the Buddha's body, also doing so without any weariness occurring as a result of this, and doing so with the mind constantly residing in meditative concentration, entirely free of any scattering or disorder at all. This is the third of all buddhas' great *nārāyaṇa* banner dharmas of bravery and strength.

正體字

249a23　佛子。一切諸佛。一坐食已。結[1]跏趺坐。經前
249a24　後際不可說劫。入佛所受不思議樂。其身安
249a25　住。寂然不動。亦不廢捨化眾生事。佛子。假使
249a26　有人。於遍虛空一一世界。悉以毛端。次第度
249a27　量。諸佛能於一毛端處。結[＊]跏趺坐。盡未來
249a28　劫。如一毛端處。一切毛端處。悉亦如是。佛
249a29　子。假使十方一切世界。所有眾生。一一眾生。
249b01　其身大小。悉與不可說佛剎微塵數世界量
249b02　等。輕重亦爾。諸佛能以爾所眾生。置一指端。
249b03　盡於後際所有諸劫。一切指端。皆亦如是。盡
249b04　持爾許一切眾生。入遍虛空一一世界。盡於
249b05　法界。悉使無餘。而佛身心。曾無勞倦。是為諸
249b06　佛第四大那羅延幢勇健法。佛子。一切諸佛。
249b07　能於一身。化現不可說不可說佛剎微塵數
249b08　頭。一一頭。化現不可說不可說佛剎微塵數
249b09　舌。一一舌。化出不可說不可說佛剎微塵數
249b10　差別音聲。法界眾生。靡不皆聞。一一音聲。演
249b11　不可說不可說佛剎微塵數修多羅藏。

简体字

"佛子，一切诸佛一坐食已，结跏趺坐，经前后际不可说劫，入佛所受不思议乐，其身安住，寂然不动，亦不废舍化众生事。佛子，假使有人于遍虚空一一世界悉以毛端次第度量，诸佛能于一毛端处结跏趺坐，尽未来劫；如一毛端处，一切毛端处悉亦如是。佛子，假使十方一切世界所有众生，一一众生其身大小悉与不可说佛刹微尘数世界量等，轻重亦尔，诸佛能以尔所众生置一指端，尽于后际所有诸劫；一切指端皆亦如是，尽持尔许一切众生入遍虚空一一世界，尽于法界悉使无余，而佛身心曾无劳倦。是为诸佛第四大那罗延幢勇健法。

"佛子，一切诸佛能于一身化现不可说不可说佛刹微尘数头，一一头化现不可说不可说佛刹微尘数舌，一一舌化出不可说不可说佛刹微尘数差别音声，法界众生靡不皆闻，一一音声演不可说不可说佛刹微尘数修多罗藏，

Chapter 33 — The Inconceivable Dharmas of the Buddhas

Sons of the Buddha, after all buddhas have taken their meal in a single sitting, sitting in the lotus posture, they may pass through an ineffable number of kalpas of the past and future, immersed in the inconceivable bliss experienced by buddhas as, securely abiding there, their bodies remain quiescent and unmoving, this even as they still never desist from their work of teaching beings.

Sons of the Buddha, suppose there was a person who used the tip of a single hair to sequentially measure every one of the worlds throughout empty space. All buddhas are able to sit in the lotus position on the tip of but a single hair, doing so to the very end of all kalpas of the future. And just as this is so in the case of a single hair tip, so too may they do this on the tips of all hairs in the very same way.

Sons of the Buddha, suppose that every being among all the beings in all worlds throughout the ten directions was of a size equal to that of the aggregate of a number of worlds equivalent to the number of atoms in an ineffable number of buddha *kṣetras*. Suppose too that this was true of their weight as well. Even so, all buddhas would be able to place all those beings onto the tip of but a single one of their fingers, doing so on through to the end of all kalpas of the future while also doing so on each of their other fingertips in just this same way. They would be able to carry all of these very many beings into all places within every one of the worlds throughout all of empty space, doing so throughout all parts of the entire Dharma realm without exception, doing so without there ever being any weariness in either body or mind on the part of the buddhas. This is the fourth of all buddhas' great *nārāyaṇa* banner dharmas of bravery and strength.

Sons of the Buddha, all buddhas are able to transformationally manifest on but a single body a number of heads as numerous as the atoms within an ineffable-ineffable number of buddha *kṣetras* and are able to transformationally manifest on every one of those heads a number of tongues as numerous as the atoms in an ineffable-ineffable number of buddha *kṣetras*. In association with every one of those tongues, they are able to transformationally manifest a number of different voices as numerous as the atoms in an ineffable-ineffable number of buddha *kṣetras*, voices which no being anywhere in the Dharma realm could fail to hear.

With every one of those voices, they are able to expound upon a number of repositories of sutras as numerous as the atoms contained in an ineffable-ineffable number of buddha *kṣetras*. In association with every one of those repositories of sutras, they are able

正體字	一一 249b12 修多羅藏。演不可說不可說佛剎微塵數法。 249b13 一一法。有不可說不可說佛剎微塵數文字 249b14 句義。如是演說。盡不可說不可說佛剎微塵 249b15 數劫。盡是劫已。復更演說。盡不可說不可說 249b16 佛剎微塵數劫。如是次第。乃至盡於一切世 249b17 界微塵數。盡一切眾生心念數。未來際劫。猶 249b18 可窮盡。如來化身。所轉法輪。無有窮盡。所謂 249b19 智慧演說法輪。斷諸疑惑法輪。照一切法法 249b20 輪。開無礙藏法輪。令無量眾生。歡喜調伏法 249b21 輪。開示一切。諸菩薩行法輪。高[2]昇圓滿。大 249b22 智慧日法輪。普然照世。智慧明燈法輪。辯才 249b23 無畏。種種莊嚴法輪。如一佛身。以神通力。轉 249b24 如是等差別法輪。一切世法無能為[3]諭。如是 249b25 盡虛空界。一一毛端。分量之處。有不可說不 249b26 可說佛剎微塵數世界。一一世界中。念念現 249b27 不可說不可說佛剎微塵數化身。一一化身。 249b28 皆亦如是。所說音聲。文字句義。一一充滿一 249b29 切法界。其中眾生。皆得解了。
简体字	一一修多罗藏演不可说不可说佛刹微尘数法，一一法有不可说不可说佛刹微尘数文字句义；如是演说，尽不可说不可说佛刹微尘数劫；尽是劫已，复更演说，尽不可说不可说佛刹微尘数劫；如是次第，乃至尽于一切世界微尘数，尽一切众生心念数。未来际劫犹可穷尽，如来化身所转法轮无有穷尽。所谓：智慧演说法轮、断诸疑惑法轮、照一切法法轮、开无碍藏法轮、令无量众生欢喜调伏法轮、开示一切诸菩萨行法轮、高升圆满大智慧日法轮、普然照世智慧明灯法轮、辩才无畏种种庄严法轮。如一佛身以神通力转如是等差别法轮，一切世法无能为喻。如是，尽虚空界一一毛端分量之处，有不可说不可说佛刹微尘数世界，一一世界中念念现不可说不可说佛刹微尘数化身，一一化身皆亦如是，所说音声文字句义，一一充满一切法界，其中众生皆得解了，

Chapter 33 — The Inconceivable Dharmas of the Buddhas

to expound on a number of dharmas equal in number to all the atoms contained in an ineffable-ineffable number of buddha *kṣetras*. In association with every one of those dharmas, there are a number of passages, words, statements, and meanings as numerous as the atoms contained in an ineffable-ineffable number of buddha *kṣetras*.

They may expound in this way for a number of kalpas equal to all the atoms contained in an ineffable-ineffable number of *kṣetras*. Then, having exhausted so very many kalpas as these in doing so, they may yet again expound in this way throughout a number of kalpas as numerous as the atoms contained in an ineffable-ineffable number of buddha *kṣetras*. They may continue on sequentially in this way until they exhaust a number of kalpas equivalent to the atoms contained in all worlds and then exhaust a number of kalpas equivalent to the number of thoughts had by all beings.

Although one might conceivably exhaust all the kalpas of the future, the number of Dharma wheels turned by all transformation bodies of the Tathāgata are endless. This refers in particular to: the Dharma wheel of wise discourse, the Dharma wheel that severs all doubts, the Dharma wheel that illuminates all dharmas, the Dharma wheel that opens the treasury of the unimpeded, the Dharma wheel that enables the happiness and training of countless beings, the Dharma wheel that reveals and explains all bodhisattva practices, the Dharma wheel of the perfectly full sun of great wisdom that has risen high in the sky, the Dharma wheel of the brightly shining lamp of wisdom that everywhere illuminates the world, and the Dharma wheel adorned in many ways with fearless eloquence.

And just as a single buddha body, using the powers of spiritual superknowledges, turns so many different Dharma wheels as these that no analogy using worldly dharmas could describe them all, so too and in this very same way, throughout all realms of empty space, in every one of those places the size of the tip of a single hair, there are worlds as numerous as the atoms in an ineffable-ineffable number of buddha *kṣetras* and, within every one of those worlds, there are manifested in each successive mind-moment a number of transformation bodies as numerous as the atoms in an ineffable-ineffable number of buddha *kṣetras* in which the sounds of the teaching of passages, words, statements, and meanings uttered by every one of those transformation bodies also and in the very same way completely fill up the entire Dharma realm. All the beings within it are able to completely understand all of them. And as this occurs, the sound of those buddhas' words continues on,

正體字

而佛言音。無變無斷。無有窮盡。是為諸佛第五大那羅延幢勇健法。佛子。一切諸佛。皆以德相。莊嚴胸臆。猶若金剛不可損壞。菩提樹下。結跏趺坐。魔王軍眾。其數無邊。種種異形。甚可怖畏。眾生見者。靡不驚懾。悉發狂亂。或時致死。如是魔眾。遍滿虛空。如來見之。心無恐怖。容色不變。一毛不[4]豎。不動不亂。無所分別。離諸喜怒。寂然清淨。住佛所住。具慈悲力。諸根調伏。心無所畏。非諸魔眾。所能傾動。而能摧伏。一切魔軍。皆使迴心。稽首歸依。然後復以三輪教化。[今>令]其悉發阿耨多羅三藐三菩提意。永不退轉。是為諸佛第六大那羅延幢勇健法。佛子。一切諸佛。有無礙音。其音普遍十方世界。眾生聞者。自然調伏。彼諸如來。所出音聲。須彌盧等。一切諸山。不能為障。天宮龍宮。夜叉宮。乾闥婆阿脩羅迦樓羅緊那羅摩睺羅伽人非人等。一切諸宮。所不能障。一切世界。高大音聲。亦不能障。隨所應化。一切眾生。靡不皆聞文字句義悉得解了。是為諸佛第七大那羅延幢勇健法。

简体字

而佛言音无变、无断、无有穷尽。是为诸佛第五大那罗延幢勇健法。

"佛子,一切诸佛皆以德相庄严胸臆,犹若金刚不可损坏,菩提树下结跏趺坐。魔王军众其数无边,种种异形甚可怖畏,众生见者靡不惊慑,悉发狂乱或时致死。如是魔众遍满虚空,如来见之,心无恐怖,容色不变,一毛不竖,不动不乱,无所分别,离诸喜怒,寂然清净,住佛所住,具慈悲力,诸根调伏,心无所畏,非诸魔众所能倾动而能摧伏;一切魔军皆使回心,稽首归依,然后复以三轮教化,令其悉发阿耨多罗三藐三菩提意永不退转。是为诸佛第六大那罗延幢勇健法。

"佛子,一切诸佛有无碍音,其音普遍十方世界,众生闻者自然调伏。彼诸如来所出音声,须弥卢等一切诸山不能为障,天宫、龙宫、夜叉宫,乾闼婆、阿修罗、迦楼罗、紧那罗、摩睺罗伽、人非人等一切诸宫所不能障,一切世界高大音声亦不能障。随所应化,一切众生靡不皆闻,文字句义悉得解了。是为诸佛第七大那罗延幢勇健法。

unchanged, uninterrupted, and without end. This is the fifth of all buddhas' great *nārāyaṇa* banner dharmas of bravery and strength.

Sons of the Buddha, all buddhas have the sign of virtue adorning their chests and are all just as invulnerable to injury as vajra. Seated in the lotus posture beneath the bodhi tree, they are confronted by the boundless hordes of the king of the *māras* who appear in all kinds of different extremely fearsome forms such that, were beings to see them, none would not shrink in terror, be driven wildly insane, or perhaps even drop dead in fear.

In this circumstance, even though hordes of *māras* such as these completely fill all of empty space, when the Tathāgata sees them, his mind remains free of fear and his countenance remains unchanged. Not even a single hair is caused to rise on his body. Neither shaken nor flustered, he does not even indulge in any discriminations in this regard. He remains free of either joy or anger, remains in a state of serene purity, abides as a buddha abides, and embodies the power of kindness and compassion, with all of his faculties trained and restrained, and with his mind in a state of complete fearlessness. He is not one whom any of the armies of Māra could cause to quaver even slightly. Rather, he is able to vanquish all the armies of Māra and cause them all to change their minds, bow down their heads in reverence, and take refuge in him. He later uses the three spheres of action[9] to teach them and inspire them to bring forth the forever irreversible resolve to realize *anuttarā-samyak-saṃbodhi*. This is the sixth of all buddhas' great *nārāyaṇa* banner dharmas of bravery and strength.

Sons of the Buddha, all buddhas possess an unimpeded voice the sound of which reaches everywhere throughout the worlds of the ten directions. When beings hear it, they become spontaneously inclined to take on the training. The sound sent forth by all *tathāgatas* is such that it cannot be blocked by Mount Sumeru or any of the other mountains, cannot be blocked by any of the palaces of the devas, palaces of the dragons, palaces of the *yakṣas*, or palaces of any of the *gandharvas, asuras, garuḍas, kiṃnaras, mahoragas*, humans, nonhumans, or any other class of being, and is such that it cannot be blocked by any of the loudest sounds from anywhere in any world. In accordance with whichever beings should be taught, there are none of them who do not then fully hear and succeed in completely understanding its passages, words, statements, and meanings. This is the seventh of all buddhas' great *nārāyaṇa* banner dharmas of bravery and strength.

正體字

佛子。一切諸佛。心無障礙。於百千億那由他不可說不可說劫。恒善清淨。去來現在。一切諸佛。同一體性。無濁無翳。無我無我所。非內非外。了境空寂。不生妄想。無所依無所作。不住諸相。永斷分別。本性清淨。捨離一切攀緣憶念。於一切法。常無違諍。住於實際。離欲清淨。入真法界。演說無盡。離量非量。所有妄想。絕為無為。一切言說。於不可說無邊境界。悉已通達。無礙無盡。智慧方便。成就十力一切功德。莊嚴清淨。演說種種無量諸法。皆與實相。不相違背。於諸法界三世諸法。悉等無異。究竟自在。入一切法最勝之藏。一切法門。正念不惑。安住十方一切佛剎。而無動轉。得不斷智。知一切法究竟無餘。盡諸有漏。心善解脫。慧善解脫。住於實際。通達無礙。心常正定。於三世法。及以一切眾生心行。一念了達。皆無障礙。是為諸佛第八大那羅延幢勇健法。

简体字

"佛子，一切诸佛心无障碍，于百千亿那由他不可说不可说劫，恒善清净。去、来、现在一切诸佛同一体性，无浊、无翳，无我、无我所，非内、非外，了境空寂，不生妄想；无所依，无所作，不住诸相，永断分别；本性清净，舍离一切攀缘忆念，于一切法常无违诤；住于实际，离欲清净，入真法界，演说无尽；离量、非量所有妄想，绝为、无为一切言说，于不可说无边境界悉已通达；无碍无尽智慧方便，成就十力一切功德庄严清净，演说种种无量诸法，皆与实相不相违背；于诸法界三世诸法，悉等无异，究竟自在；入一切法最胜之藏，一切法门正念不惑，安住十方一切佛刹而无动转；得不断智，知一切法究竟无余，尽诸有漏，心善解脱，慧善解脱，住于实际，通达无碍，心常正定；于三世法及以一切众生心行，一念了达，皆无障碍。是为诸佛第八大那罗延幢勇健法。

Chapter 33 – The Inconceivable Dharmas of the Buddhas

Sons of the Buddha, all buddhas' minds are unimpeded. For hundreds of thousands of *koṭīs* of *nayutas* of ineffable-ineffable numbers of kalpas, they have constantly dwelt in goodness and purity. They are of the same single essential nature as that of all buddhas of the past, the future, and the present. They are free of all turbidity, are free of all obscurations, are devoid of any self or possessions of a self, and are neither inward nor outward. They realize the emptiness and quiescence of the objective realms, do not produce any erroneous perceptions, have nothing on which they depend and nothing they do, do not dwell on signs, and forever sever all discriminations. Their original nature is pure, they abandon all thought inclined to seize on objective conditions, they are ever free of any opposition or disputation regarding any dharmas, and they abide in the apex of reality. They have attained the purity apart from desires, and have entered the true Dharma realm where they expound on the Dharma endlessly. They have left behind all erroneous mental discursions associated with either perception or mistaken perception and have cut off all discussions of both the conditioned and the unconditioned.

They have already achieved a penetrating comprehension of an ineffable number of boundless realms. They possess unimpeded and endless wisdom and skillful means and have perfected the pure adornments of all of the meritorious qualities associated with the ten powers. They expound on the many different immeasurable dharmas in ways that never contradict the true character of dharmas. They have attained equal and indistinguishable ultimate sovereign mastery in all dharmas throughout the Dharma realm and the three periods of time. They have entered the supreme treasury of all dharmas and remain in a state of undeluded right mindfulness of all dharmas. They securely abide in all buddha *kṣetras* throughout the ten directions and yet remain motionless. They have acquired the uninterrupted wisdom that knows in the most ultimate way all dharmas without exception. They have put an end to all contaminants, have acquired the mind that is well liberated, have acquired the wisdom that is well liberated, and abide in an unimpeded penetrating comprehension of the apex of reality. Their minds are always in right meditative concentration and they are able in but a single mind-moment to attain an utterly penetrating and unimpeded comprehension of the mental activity of all beings throughout the three periods of time. This is the eighth of all buddhas' great *nārāyaṇa* banner dharmas of bravery and strength.

正體字

佛子。一切諸佛。同一法身。境界無量身。功德無邊身。世間無盡身。三界不染身。隨念示現身。非實非虛平等清淨身。無來無去無為不壞身。一相無相法自性身。無處無方遍一切身。神變自在。無邊色相身。種種示現普入一切身。妙法方便身。智藏普照身。示法平等身。普遍法界身。無動無分別非有非無常清淨身。非方便非不方便。非滅非不滅。隨所應化一切眾生。種種信解。而示現身。從一切功德寶所生身。具一切諸佛法真如身。本性寂靜。無障礙身。成就一切無礙法身。遍住一切清淨法界身。分形普遍一切世間身。無攀緣無退轉。永解脫。具一切智。普了達身。是為諸佛第九大那羅延幢勇健法。佛子。一切諸佛。等悟一切諸如來法。等修一切諸菩薩行。若願若智。清淨平等。猶如大海。悉得滿足。行力尊勝。未曾退怯。住諸三昧。無量境界。示一切道。勸善誡惡。智力第一。演法無畏。

简体字

"佛子，一切诸佛同一法身、境界无量身、功德无边身、世间无尽身、三界不染身、随念示现身、非实非虚平等清净身、无来无去无为不坏身、一相无相法自性身、无处无方遍一切身、神变自在无边色相身、种种示现普入一切身、妙法方便身、智藏普照身、示法平等身、普遍法界身、无动无分别非有非无常清净身、非方便非不方便非灭非不灭随所应化一切众生种种信解而示现身、从一切功德宝所生身、具一切诸佛法真如身、本性寂静无障碍身、成就一切无碍法身、遍住一切清净法界身、分形普遍一切世间身、无攀缘无退转永解脱具一切智普了达身，是为诸佛第九大那罗延幢勇健法。

"佛子，一切诸佛等悟一切诸如来法，等修一切诸菩萨行；若愿若智，清净平等，犹如大海，悉得满足；行力尊胜，未曾退怯，住诸三昧无量境界，示一切道，劝善诫恶；智力第一演法无畏，

Sons of the Buddha, all buddhas have: the same single Dharma body; the body possessed of countless objective realms; the body possessed of boundless meritorious qualities; the body that is endlessly present in the world; the body that remains undefiled by the three realms of existence; the body that manifests in accordance with thoughts; the body that, neither real nor false, is possessed of uniformly equal purity; the body that neither comes nor goes, that is unconditioned, and that is never destroyed; the body with the inherent nature of dharmas that has the single sign of signlessness; the body that, having no location and no region, pervades all places; the body possessed of masterful spiritual transformations with boundless forms and appearances; the body that possesses many different kinds of manifestations and everywhere enters all places; the body possessed of the sublime Dharma's skillful means; the body with the pervasive illumination of the treasury of wisdom; the body that reveals the uniform equality of dharmas; the body that everywhere pervades the Dharma realm; the body that is unmoving, free of all discriminations, neither existent nor nonexistent, and always pure; the body that is neither expedient nor nonexpedient, neither destroyed nor undestroyed, and that manifests in ways adapted to the many different kinds of resolute faith possessed by all beings who should be provided with teaching; the body that is born from the jewels of every sort of meritorious quality; the body possessed of the true suchness of the Dharma of all buddhas; the body with the original nature of unimpeded quiescence; the body that perfects all unimpeded dharmas; the body that abides everywhere throughout the pure Dharma realm; the body that divides its form and pervades all worlds; and the body free of grasping at objective conditions which is irreversibly and forever liberated, which is possessed of all-knowledge, and which has a complete comprehension of everything. This is the ninth of all buddhas' great *nārāyaṇa* banner dharmas of bravery and strength.

Sons of the Buddha, all buddhas have equally awakened to all dharmas of the *tathāgatas* and have equally cultivated all the bodhisattva practices. Whether it be their vows or their knowledge, they are pure, impartial, and as vast as the great ocean. Their practices and powers are venerable and supreme. They have never retreated in timidity from their cultivation. They abide in the measureless spheres of cognition of all samādhis. They provide instruction in all aspects of the paths, encouraging goodness and warning against evil. Their power of wisdom is foremost. They are fearless in expounding on the Dharma. They are able to offer skillful replies

正體字

隨有所問。悉能善
答。智慧說法。平等清淨。身語意行。悉皆無
雜。住佛所住。諸佛種性。以佛智慧。而作佛
事。住一切智。演無量法。無有根本。無有邊
際。神通智慧。不可思議。一切世間。無能解
了。智慧深入。見一切法。微妙廣大。無量無
邊。三世法門。咸善通達。一切世界。悉能開
曉。以出世智。於諸世間。作不可說種種佛
事。成不退智。入諸佛數。雖已證得不可言說
離文字法。而能開示種種言辭。以普賢智。集
諸善行。成就一念相應妙慧。於一切法。悉能
覺了。如先所念。一切眾生。皆依自乘。而施其
法。一切諸法。一切世界。一切眾生。一切三
世。於法界內。如是境界。其量無邊。以無礙
智。悉能知見。佛子。一切諸佛。於一念頃。隨
所應化。出興於世。住清淨土。成等正覺。現神
通力。開悟三世一切眾生。心意及識。不失於
時。佛子。眾生無邊。世界無邊。法界無邊。三
世無邊。諸佛最勝。亦無有邊。悉現於中。成等
正覺。以佛智慧。方便開悟。無有休息。

简体字

随有所问悉能善答,智慧说法平等清净,身、语、意行悉皆无杂,住佛所住诸佛种性,以佛智慧而作佛事;住一切智,演无量法,无有根本,无有边际,神通智慧不可思议,一切世间无能解了;智慧深入,见一切法微妙广大无量无边,三世法门咸善通达,一切世界悉能开晓;以出世智,于诸世间作不可说种种佛事,成不退智,入诸佛数;虽已证得不可言说离文字法,而能开示种种言辞;以普贤智集诸善行,成就一念相应妙慧,于一切法悉能觉了,如先所念一切众生,皆依自乘而施其法;一切诸法、一切世界、一切众生、一切三世,于法界内,如是境界其量无边,以无碍智悉能知见。佛子,一切诸佛于一念顷,随所应化出兴于世,住清净土,成等正觉,现神通力,开悟三世一切众生心、意及识不失于时。佛子,众生无边,世界无边,法界无边,三世无边,诸佛最胜亦无有边,悉现于中成等正觉,以佛智慧方便开悟无有休息。

Chapter 33 — The Inconceivable Dharmas of the Buddhas

to whatever is asked. Their wisdom in teaching the Dharma is uniformly pure and their physical, verbal, and mental actions are all free of any impurities. They dwell where the buddhas dwell, in the lineage of all buddhas. They use the Buddha's wisdom to do the buddha works and, dwelling in all-knowledge, they expound on the countless dharmas as devoid of any foundation or boundaries. Their spiritual superknowledges and wisdom are inconceivable and such that no one in the world is able to completely fathom them. Their wisdom with which they deeply penetrate and perceive all dharmas is sublime, vast, measureless, and boundless. With it, they have attained a thorough and penetrating comprehension of all Dharma gateways of the three periods of time. They are able to awaken those in all worlds. They use world-transcending wisdom to accomplish an ineffable number of buddha works of all different kinds everywhere in the world. Having realized irreversible wisdom, they have entered the ranks of all buddhas.

Although they have already realized the indescribable Dharma that transcends the written word, they are still able to explain all the many different kinds of expressions in language. Using the wisdom of Samantabhadra, they have accumulated all good practices and have perfected the sublime wisdom that responds in but a single mind-moment. They are able to command complete enlightenment with respect to all dharmas and, as befits all the beings they have just brought to mind, they rely on their individual vehicle and then proceed to give them their appropriate dharma. All dharmas, all worlds, all beings, and everything in the three periods of time—with their unimpeded wisdom, they are able to know and see all the boundless realms such as these throughout the Dharma realm.

Sons of the Buddha, in accordance with the needs of those who should be taught and in but a single mind-moment, all buddhas appear in the world. They dwell in pure lands, realize the perfect and right enlightenment, manifest the powers of their spiritual superknowledges, and awaken the minds, intentions, and consciousnesses of all beings of the three periods of time, never missing the appropriate time in doing so.

Sons of the Buddha, beings are boundless, worlds are boundless, the Dharma realm is boundless, the three periods of time are boundless, and all buddhas, the most supreme ones, are also boundless. [The buddhas] all manifest the realization of the perfect and right enlightenment in the midst of them all and are tireless in using a buddha's wisdom and skillful means to awaken them.

正體字

佛子。
一切諸佛。以神通力。現最妙身。住無邊處。大悲方便。心無障礙。於一切時。常為眾生。演說妙法。是為諸佛第十大那羅延幢勇健法。佛子。此一切諸佛大那羅延幢勇健法。無量無邊不可思議。去來現在一切眾生。及以二乘。不能解了。唯除如來神力所加。佛子。諸佛世尊。有十種決定法。何等為十。所謂一切諸佛。定從兜率壽盡下生。一切諸佛。定示受生。處胎十月。一切諸佛。定厭世俗。樂求出家。一切諸佛。決定坐於菩提樹下。成等正覺。悟諸佛法。一切諸佛。定於一念。悟一切法。一切世界。示現神力。一切諸佛。定能應時。轉妙法輪。一切諸佛。定能隨彼。所種善根。應時說法。而為授記。一切諸佛。定能應時。為作佛事。一切諸佛。定能為諸成就菩薩。而授記[1]別。一切諸佛。定能一念。普答一切眾生所問。是為十。佛子。諸佛世尊。有十種速疾法。何等為十。所謂一切諸佛。若有見者。速得遠離一切惡趣。一切諸佛。若有見者。速得圓滿殊勝功德。一切諸佛。若有見者。速能成就廣大善根。一切諸佛。若有見者。

简体字

佛子，一切诸佛以神通力，现最妙身，住无边处，大悲方便，心无障碍，于一切时常为众生演说妙法。是为诸佛第十大那罗延幢勇健法。

"佛子，此一切诸佛大那罗延幢勇健法无量无边、不可思议，去、来、现在一切众生及以二乘不能解了，唯除如来神力所加。

"佛子，诸佛世尊有十种决定法。何等为十？所谓：一切诸佛定从兜率寿尽下生；一切诸佛定示受生，处胎十月；一切诸佛定厌世俗，乐求出家；一切诸佛决定坐于菩提树下成等正觉，悟诸佛法；一切诸佛定于一念悟一切法，一切世界示现神力；一切诸佛定能应时转妙法轮；一切诸佛定能随彼所种善根，应时说法而为授记；一切诸佛定能应时为作佛事；一切诸佛定能为诸成就菩萨而授记莂；一切诸佛定能一念普答一切众生所问。是为十。

"佛子，诸佛世尊有十种速疾法。何等为十？所谓：一切诸佛若有见者，速得远离一切恶趣；一切诸佛若有见者，速得圆满殊胜功德；一切诸佛若有见者，速能成就广大善根；一切诸佛若有见者，

Chapter 33 — The Inconceivable Dharmas of the Buddhas

Sons of the Buddha, all buddhas use the power of their spiritual superknowledges to manifest their supremely marvelous bodies and dwell in boundlessly many places in which, with their great compassion, skillful means, and unimpeded minds, at all points in time, they forever expound on the sublime Dharma for the benefit of beings. This is the tenth of all buddhas' great *nārāyaṇa* banner dharmas of bravery and strength.

Sons of the Buddha, these great *nārāyaṇa* banner dharmas of bravery and strength of all buddhas are measureless, boundless, inconceivable, and such that they could never be completely understood by any of the beings or adherents of the Two Vehicles of the past, future or present with the sole exception of those who are aided by the spiritual powers of the Tathāgata.

Sons of the Buddha, all buddhas, the *bhagavats*, have ten kinds of definite dharmas. What are those ten? They are as follows: At the end of their lives in the Tuṣita Heaven, all buddhas then definitely descend to take birth. All buddhas definitely manifest the taking on of birth, dwelling in the womb for ten months. All buddhas definitely renounce the mundane ways of the world and delight in the quest to leave the home life. All buddhas definitely sit beneath the bodhi tree, realize the perfect and right enlightenment, and awaken to all the dharmas of buddhahood. All buddhas definitely awaken to all dharmas in but a single mind-moment and then manifest their spiritual powers in all worlds. All buddhas are definitely able to respond in accordance with the right time and turn the wheel of the sublime Dharma. All buddhas are definitely able to accord with the roots of goodness planted by others by speaking the Dharma for them at the appropriate time and then bestowing predictions for their benefit. All buddhas are definitely able to accord with the appropriate time in order to accomplish the buddha works. All buddhas are definitely able to bestow predictions for the sake of all fully accomplished bodhisattvas. And all buddhas are definitely able to reply in but a single mind-moment to all questions posed by any being. These are the ten.

Sons of the Buddha, all buddhas, the *bhagavats*, have ten kinds of swiftness dharmas. What are those ten? They are as follows: Whoever sees any buddha will swiftly leave all of the wretched rebirth destinies far behind. Whoever sees any buddha will swiftly succeed in the complete fulfillment of the especially supreme meritorious qualities. Whoever sees any buddha will swiftly become able to fully develop vast roots of goodness. Whoever sees any buddha will swiftly succeed in gaining rebirth into pure and

|正體字|速得往生淨妙
天上。一切諸佛。若有見者。速能除斷一切疑
惑。一切諸佛。若已發菩提心。而得見者。速得
成就廣大信解。永不退轉。能隨所應。教化眾
生。若未發心。即能速發阿耨多羅三藐三菩
提心。一切諸佛。若未入正位。而得見者。速入
正位。一切諸佛。若有見者。速能清淨世出世
間。一切諸根。一切諸佛。若有見者。速得除
滅一切障礙。一切諸佛。若有見者。速能獲得
無畏辯才。是為十。佛子。諸佛世尊。有十種應
[2]常憶念清淨法。何等為十。所謂一切諸佛。
過去因緣。一切菩薩。應常憶念。一切諸佛。清
淨勝行。一切菩薩。應常憶念。一切諸佛。滿足
諸度。一切菩薩。應常憶念。一切諸佛。成就大
願。一切菩薩。應常憶念。一切諸佛。積集善
根。一切菩薩。應常憶念。一切諸佛。已具梵
行。一切菩薩。應常憶念。一切諸佛。現成正
覺。一切菩薩。應常憶念。一切諸佛。色身無
量。一切菩薩。應常憶念。一切諸佛。神通無
量。一切菩薩。應常憶念。一切諸佛。十力無
畏。一切菩薩。應常憶念。是為十。佛子。諸佛
世尊。有十種一切智住。何等為十。所謂一切
諸佛。於一念中。悉知三世一切眾生。心心所
行。一切諸佛。於一念中。悉知三世一切眾生。
所集諸業。及業果報。一切諸佛。於一念中。悉
知一切眾生所宜。以三種輪。教化調伏。一切
諸佛。於一念中。盡知法界一切眾生。所有心
相。

简体字

速得往生净妙天上；一切诸佛若有见者，速能除断一切疑惑；一切诸佛若已发菩提心而得见者，速得成就广大信解永不退转，能随所应教化众生，若未发心即能速发阿耨多罗三藐三菩提心；一切诸佛若未入正位而得见者，速入正位；一切诸佛若有见者，速能清净世、出世间一切诸根；一切诸佛若有见者，速得除灭一切障碍；一切诸佛若有见者，速能获得无畏辩才。是为十。

"佛子，诸佛世尊有十种应常忆念清净法。何等为十？所谓：一切诸佛过去因缘，一切菩萨应常忆念；一切诸佛清净胜行，一切菩萨应常忆念；一切诸佛满足诸度，一切菩萨应常忆念；一切诸佛成就大愿，一切菩萨应常忆念；一切诸佛积集善根，一切菩萨应常忆念；一切诸佛已具梵行，一切菩萨应常忆念；一切诸佛现成正觉，一切菩萨应常忆念；一切诸佛色身无量，一切菩萨应常忆念；一切诸佛神通无量，一切菩萨应常忆念；一切诸佛十力无畏，一切菩萨应常忆念。是为十。

"佛子，诸佛世尊有十种一切智住。何等为十？所谓：一切诸佛于一念中，悉知三世一切众生心、心所行；一切诸佛于一念中，悉知三世一切众生所集诸业及业果报；一切诸佛于一念中，悉知一切众生所宜，以三种轮教化调伏；一切诸佛于一念中，尽知法界一切众生所有心相，

marvelous heavens. Whoever sees any buddha will swiftly become able to cut off all their doubts. Whoever, having already resolved to attain bodhi, sees any buddha—they will swiftly succeed in developing vast resolute faith, perpetual irreversibility, and the ability to teach beings in accordance with whatever is appropriate for them, whereas, in the case of those who have not yet resolved to attain bodhi, they will then swiftly be able to resolve to realize *anuttarā-samyak-saṃbodhi*. Whoever sees any buddha while not yet having entered the right and fixed position[10] will swiftly enter the right and fixed position. Whoever sees any buddha will swiftly be able to purify all worldly and world-transcending faculties. Whoever sees any buddha will swiftly succeed in eliminating all their obstacles. And whoever sees any buddha will swiftly be able to acquire fearless eloquence. These are the ten.

Sons of the Buddha, all buddhas, the *bhagavats*, have ten kinds of pure dharmas that one should always bear in mind. What are those ten? They are as follows: All bodhisattvas should always bear in mind all buddhas' past causes and conditions. All bodhisattvas should always bear in mind all buddhas' pure and supreme practices. All bodhisattvas should always bear in mind all buddhas' fulfillment of all the perfections. All bodhisattvas should always bear in mind all buddhas' perfection of great vows. All bodhisattvas should always bear in mind all buddhas' accumulation of roots of goodness. All bodhisattvas should always bear in mind all buddhas' past perfection of *brahmacarya*. All bodhisattvas should always bear in mind all buddhas' manifesting the realization of right enlightenment. All bodhisattvas should always bear in mind all buddhas' countless form bodies. All bodhisattvas should always bear in mind all buddhas' measureless spiritual superknowledges. And all bodhisattvas should always bear in mind all buddhas' ten powers and fearlessnesses. These are the ten.

Sons of the Buddha, all buddhas, the *bhagavats*, have ten kinds of omniscient abiding. What are those ten? They are as follows: In but a single mind-moment, all buddhas completely know all the actions of each successive thought of all beings throughout the three periods of time. In but a single mind-moment, all buddhas completely know all the karma and karmic retributions accumulated by all beings throughout the three periods of time. In but a single mind-moment, all buddhas completely know what is fitting for all beings in their use of the three spheres of action[11] to teach and train them. In but a single mind-moment, all buddhas exhaustively know with regard to all beings in the Dharma realm all their mental characteristics in

正體字

於一切處。普現佛興。令其得見。方便攝
受。一切諸佛。於一念中。普隨法界一切眾
生。心樂欲解。示現說法。[1]令其調伏。一切諸
佛。於一念中。悉知法界一切眾生心之所樂。
為現神力。一切諸佛。於一念中。遍一切處。隨
所應化一切眾生。示現出興。為說佛身。不可
取著。一切諸佛。於一念中。普至法界一切處。
一切眾生。彼彼諸道。一切諸佛。於一念中。
隨諸眾生。有憶念者。在在處處。無不往應。一
切諸佛。於一念中。悉知一切眾生解欲。為其
示現無量色相。是為十。佛子。諸佛世尊。有十
種無量不可思議佛三昧。何等為十。所謂一
切諸佛。恒在正定。於一念中。遍一切處。普為
眾生。廣說妙法。一切諸佛。恒在正定。於一念
中。遍一切處。普為眾生。說無我際。一切諸
佛。恒住正定。於一念中。遍一切處。普入三
世。一切諸佛。恒在正定。於一念中。遍一切
處。普入十方。廣大佛剎。一切諸佛。恒在正
定。於一念中。遍一切處。普現無量。種種佛
身。一切諸佛。恒在正定。於一念中。遍一切
處。隨諸眾生種種心解。現身語意。一切諸
佛。恒在正定。於一念中。遍一切處。說一切法
離欲真際。

简体字

于一切处普现佛兴，令其得见，方便摄受；一切诸佛于一念中，普随法界一切众生心乐欲解，示现说法，令其调伏；一切诸佛于一念中，悉知法界一切众生心之所乐，为现神力；一切诸佛于一念中，遍一切处，随所应化一切众生示现出兴，为说佛身不可取著；一切诸佛于一念中，普至法界一切处一切众生彼彼诸道；一切诸佛于一念中，随诸众生有忆念者，在在处处无不往应；一切诸佛于一念中，悉知一切众生解欲，为其示现无量色相。是为十。

"佛子，诸佛世尊有十种无量不可思议佛三昧。何等为十？所谓：一切诸佛恒在正定，于一念中遍一切处，普为众生广说妙法；一切诸佛恒在正定，于一念中遍一切处，普为众生说无我际；一切诸佛恒住正定，于一念中遍一切处，普入三世；一切诸佛恒在正定，于一念中遍一切处，普入十方广大佛剎；一切诸佛恒在正定，于一念中遍一切处，普现无量种种佛身；一切诸佛恒在正定，于一念中遍一切处，随诸众生种种心解现身、语、意；一切诸佛恒在正定，于一念中遍一切处，说一切法离欲真际；

Chapter 33 — *The Inconceivable Dharmas of the Buddhas* 2441

response to which they then everywhere manifest the appearance of buddhas and enable those beings to see them and be gathered in through the use of skillful means. In but a single mind-moment, all buddhas everywhere adapt to the inclinations, desires, and understandings of all beings throughout the Dharma realm and then manifest the speaking of Dharma for them to enable them to be trained. In but a single mind-moment, all buddhas completely know what delights the minds of all beings throughout the Dharma realm and then manifest spiritual powers for their sakes. In but a single mind-moment, all buddhas go forth to all places everywhere and, adapting to all those beings who should receive the teaching, they then manifest their appearance in the world and explain for beings that the body of the buddha is not graspable. In but a single mind-moment, all buddhas go everywhere throughout the Dharma realm into all the paths of all beings. In but a single mind-moment, all buddhas, in accordance with all beings who bring them to mind, go forth to every one of their locations, having none to whom they do not go in response. And, in but a single mind-moment, all buddhas completely know the understandings and desires of all beings and manifest countlessly many forms and appearances for their sakes. These are the ten.

Sons of the Buddha, all buddhas, the *bhagavats*, have ten kinds of measureless and inconceivable buddha samādhis. What are those ten? They are as follows: All buddhas constantly abide in right meditative concentration and, in but a single mind-moment, pervade all places, everywhere extensively expounding on the sublime Dharma for the benefit of beings. All buddhas constantly abide in right meditative concentration and, in but a single mind-moment, pervade all places, everywhere expounding for beings on the ultimate meaning of non-self. All buddhas constantly abide in right meditative concentration and, in but a single mind-moment, pervade all places, everywhere entering the three periods of time. All buddhas constantly abide in right meditative concentration and, in but a single mind-moment, pervade all places, everywhere entering the vast buddha *kṣetras* throughout the ten directions. All buddhas constantly abide in right meditative concentration and, in but a single mind-moment, pervade all places, everywhere manifesting incalculably many kinds of buddha bodies. All buddhas constantly abide in right meditative concentration and, in but a single mind-moment, pervade all places, manifesting physical, verbal, and mental deeds adapted to beings' many different types of inclinations. All buddhas constantly abide in right meditative concentration and,

正體字	一切諸佛。恒住正定。於一念中。遍 251a29 一切處。演說一切緣起自性。一切諸佛。恒住 251b01 正定。於一念中。遍一切處。示現無量世出世 251b02 間。廣大莊嚴。令諸眾生。常得見佛。一切諸 251b03 佛。恒住正定。於一念中。遍一切處。令諸眾 251b04 生。悉得通達一切佛法。無量解脫。究竟到於 251b05 無上彼岸。是為十。佛子。諸佛世尊。有十種無 251b06 礙解脫。何等為十。所謂一切諸佛。能於一塵。 251b07 現不可說不可說諸佛。出興於世。一切諸佛。 251b08 能於一塵。現不可說不可說諸佛。轉淨法輪。 251b09 一切諸佛。能於一塵。現不可說不可說眾生。 251b10 受化調伏。一切諸佛。能於一塵。現不可說不 251b11 可說諸佛國土。一切諸佛。能於一塵。現不可 251b12 說不可說菩薩[2]授記。一切諸佛。能於一塵。 251b13 現去來今一切諸佛。一切諸佛。能於一塵。現 251b14 去來今諸世界種。一切諸佛。能於一塵。現去 251b15 來今一切神通。一切諸佛。能於一塵。現去來 251b16 今。一切眾生。一切諸佛。能於一塵。現去來今 251b17 一切佛事。是為十。
简体字	一切诸佛恒住正定，于一念中遍一切处，演说一切缘起自性；一切诸佛恒住正定，于一念中遍一切处，示现无量世、出世间广大庄严，令诸众生常得见佛；一切诸佛恒住正定，于一念中遍一切处，令诸众生悉得通达一切佛法、无量解脱，究竟到于无上彼岸。是为十。 　　"佛子，诸佛世尊有十种无碍解脱。何等为十？所谓：一切诸佛能于一尘现不可说不可说诸佛出兴于世；一切诸佛能于一尘现不可说不可说诸佛转净法轮；一切诸佛能于一尘现不可说不可说众生受化调伏；一切诸佛能于一尘现不可说不可说诸佛国土；一切诸佛能于一尘现不可说不可说菩萨授记；一切诸佛能于一尘现去、来、今一切诸佛；一切诸佛能于一尘现去、来、今诸世界种；一切诸佛能于一尘现去、来、今一切神通；一切诸佛能于一尘现去、来、今一切众生；一切诸佛能于一尘现去、来、今一切佛事。是为十。"

in but a single mind-moment, pervade all places, expounding on all dharmas, transcendence of desire, and the apex of reality. All buddhas constantly abide in right meditative concentration and, in but a single mind-moment, pervade all places, expounding on the essential nature of everything arising through conditions. All buddhas constantly abide in right meditative concentration and, in but a single mind-moment, pervade all places, manifesting countless vast worldly and world-transcending adornments by which they enable all beings to always succeed in seeing the Buddha. And all buddhas constantly abide in right meditative concentration and, in but a single mind-moment, pervade all places, enabling beings to acquire a penetrating comprehension of all buddha dharmas, to achieve measureless liberation, and to ultimately reach the far shore of unsurpassed perfection. These are the ten.

Sons of the Buddha, all buddhas, the *bhagavats*, have ten kinds of unimpeded liberation. What are those ten? They are as follows: All buddhas are able to manifest within a single atom an ineffable-ineffable number of buddhas coming forth and appearing in the world. All buddhas are able to manifest within a single atom an ineffable-ineffable number of buddhas turning the wheel of the pure Dharma. All buddhas are able to manifest within a single atom an ineffable-ineffable number of beings receiving teaching and training. All buddhas are able to manifest within a single atom an ineffable-ineffable number of buddha lands. All buddhas are able to manifest within a single atom an ineffable-ineffable number of bodhisattvas receiving their predictions of buddhahood. All buddhas are able to manifest within a single atom all buddhas of the past, the future, and the present. All buddhas are able to manifest within a single atom all world systems of the past, the future, and the present. All buddhas are able to manifest within a single atom all spiritual superknowledges of the past, the future, and the present. All buddhas are able to manifest within a single atom all beings of the past, the future, and the present. And all buddhas are able to manifest within a single atom all buddha works throughout the past, the future, and the present. These are the ten.

The End of Chapter Thirty-Three

正體字

```
251b21  大方廣佛華嚴經卷[3]第四十八
251b24      如來十身相海品第三十四
251b25  爾時普賢菩薩摩訶薩。告諸菩薩言。佛子。今
251b26  當為汝。演說如來所有相海。佛子。如來頂上。
251b27  有三十二寶莊嚴大人相。其中。有大人相。名
251b28  光照一切方普放無量大光明網。一切妙寶。
251b29  以為莊嚴。寶髮周遍。柔軟密緻。一一咸放摩
251c01  尼寶光。充滿一切無邊世界。悉現佛身。色相
251c02  圓滿。是為一。次有大人相。名佛眼光明雲。以
251c03  摩尼王。種種莊嚴。出金色光。如眉間毫相。所
251c04  放光明。其光普照一切世界。是為二。次有大
251c05  人相。名充滿法界雲。上妙寶輪。以為莊嚴。放
251c06  於如來福智燈明。普照十方一切法界。諸世
251c07  界海。於中普現一切諸佛。及諸菩薩。是為三。
251c08  次有大人相。名示現普照雲。真金摩尼。種種
251c09  莊嚴。其諸妙寶。咸放光明。照不思議諸佛國
251c10  土。一切諸佛。於中出現。是為四。次有大人
251c11  相。名放寶光明雲。摩尼寶王。清淨莊嚴。毘瑠
251c12  璃寶。以為華蘂。
```

简体字

大方广佛华严经卷第四十八
如来十身相海品第三十四

尔时,普贤菩萨摩诃萨告诸菩萨言:"佛子,今当为汝演说如来所有相海。

"佛子,如来顶上有三十二宝庄严大人相。其中有大人相,名光照一切方普放无量大光明网,一切妙宝以为庄严,宝发周遍,柔软密致,一一咸放摩尼宝光,充满一切无边世界,悉现佛身色相圆满,是为一。

"次有大人相,名佛眼光明云,以摩尼王种种庄严出金色光,如眉间毫相所放光明,其光普照一切世界,是为二。

"次有大人相,名充满法界云,上妙宝轮以为庄严,放于如来福智灯明,普照十方一切法界诸世界海,于中普现一切诸佛及诸菩萨,是为三。

"次有大人相,名示现普照云,真金摩尼种种庄严,其诸妙宝咸放光明,照不思议诸佛国土,一切诸佛于中出现,是为四。

"次有大人相,名放宝光明云,摩尼宝王清净庄严,毗琉璃宝以为华蕊,

Chapter 34
The Ocean of Major Marks of the Tathāgata's Ten Bodies

At that time, Samantabhadra Bodhisattva-mahāsattva informed the bodhisattvas, saying:

Sons of the Buddha, I shall now explain for you the ocean of the Tathāgata's marks.[12] Sons of the Buddha, on the top of the Tathāgata's head, there is a mark of the great man adorned with thirty-two jewels. Among them is one of the marks of a great man that is known as "the light that illuminates all regions, everywhere emanating an immeasurably vast net of light rays." It is adorned with all kinds of marvelous jewels. All of his jewel-adorned hair is soft and dense. Every one of its strands emanates the light of *maṇi* jewels which completely fills all the boundlessly many worlds and completely reveals the perfect fulfillment of the buddha body's physical marks. This is the first.

Next, there is a mark of the great man known as "the cloud of light of the buddha eye." Adorned with all kinds of sovereign *maṇi* jewels, it emanates golden light like the light emanated by the hair mark between the Buddha's brows. Its light everywhere illuminates all worlds. This is the second.

Next, there is a mark of the great man known as "the cloud that fills the Dharma realm." Adorned with supremely marvelous jeweled spheres, it emanates the lamp light of the Tathāgata's merit and wisdom which pervasively illuminates the ocean of worlds throughout the ten directions of the entire Dharma realm and everywhere reveals all the buddhas and bodhisattvas within them. This is the third.

Next, there is a mark of the great man known as "the cloud that manifests pervasive illumination." Arrayed with many different kinds of adornments made of real gold and *maṇi* jewel adornments, its marvelous jewels all emanate light which illuminates inconceivably many buddha lands in which all buddhas appear. This is the fourth.

Next, there is a mark of the great man known as "the cloud that emanates the light of jewels." It is arrayed with pure adornments consisting of sovereign *maṇi* jewels. The stamens of the flowers are made of *vaiḍūrya* jewels. Its light illuminates the ten directions of the

正體字

光照十方一切法界。於中普
現種種神變。讚歎如來往昔所行。智慧功德。
是為五。次有大人相。名示現如來遍法界大
自在雲。菩薩神變。寶焰摩尼。以為其冠。具如
來力覺悟一切寶焰光輪。以為其鬘。其光普
照十方世界。於中示現一切如來。坐於道場。
一切智雲。充滿虛空無量法界。是為六。次有
大人相。名如來普燈雲。以能震動法界國土
大自在寶海。而為莊嚴。放淨光明。充滿法界。
於中普現十方諸菩薩功德海。過現未來。佛
智慧幢海。是為七。次有大人相。名普照諸佛
廣大雲。因陀羅寶如意王寶摩尼王寶。以為
莊嚴。常放菩薩焰燈光明。普照十方一切世
界。於中顯現一切諸佛。眾色相海。大音聲海。
清淨力海。是為八。次有大人相。名圓滿光明
雲。上妙瑠璃摩尼王種種寶華。以為莊嚴。一
切眾寶。舒大焰網。充滿十方一切世界。一切
眾生。悉見如來。現坐其前。讚歎諸佛。及諸菩
薩。法身功德。令入如來清淨境界。是為九。次
有大人相。名普照一切菩薩行藏光明雲。眾
寶妙華。以為莊嚴。寶光普照無量世界。

简体字

光照十方一切法界，于中普现种种神变，赞叹如来往昔所行智慧功德，是为五。

"次有大人相，名示现如来遍法界大自在云，菩萨神变宝焰摩尼以为其冠，具如来力觉悟一切宝焰光轮以为其鬘，其光普照十方世界，于中示现一切如来坐于道场，一切智云充满虚空无量法界，是为六。

"次有大人相，名如来普灯云，以能震动法界国土大自在宝海而为庄严，放净光明充满法界，于中普现十方诸菩萨功德海、过现未来佛智慧幢海，是为七。

"次有大人相，名普照诸佛广大云，因陀罗宝、如意王宝、摩尼王宝以为庄严，常放菩萨焰灯光明，普照十方一切世界，于中显现一切诸佛众色相海、大音声海、清净力海，是为八。

"次有大人相，名圆满光明云，上妙琉璃摩尼王种种宝华以为庄严，一切众宝舒大焰网充满十方，一切世界一切众生悉见如来现坐其前，赞叹诸佛及诸菩萨法身功德，令入如来清净境界，是为九。

"次有大人相，名普照一切菩萨行藏光明云，众宝妙华以为庄严，宝光普照无量世界，

entire Dharma realm, everywhere revealing many different kinds of spiritual transformations praising the Tathāgata's past practice of wisdom and meritorious qualities. This is the fifth.

Next, there is a mark of the great man known as "the cloud that reveals the great sovereign mastery of the Tathāgata throughout the Dharma realm." His crown is made of flaming jewel light *maṇi* jewels created by bodhisattvas' spiritual transformations and his floral chaplet is made of spheres of the flaming light of all jewels with the Tathāgata's power to awaken all beings. Their radiance illuminates all worlds throughout the ten directions and reveals all the *tathāgatas* in them sitting at their sites of enlightenment as clouds of all-knowledge everywhere fill empty space throughout the measureless Dharma realm. This is the sixth.

Next, there is a mark of the great man known as "the Tathāgata's cloud of universally pervasive lamplight" which is adorned with an ocean of great sovereign power jewels able to cause the quaking of all worlds throughout the Dharma realm. It emanates a pure radiance that completely fills the Dharma realm, revealing within it the ocean of meritorious qualities of all bodhisattvas throughout the ten directions as well as an ocean of wisdom banners of all buddhas of the past, the present, and the future. This is the seventh.

Next, there is a mark of the great man known as "the vast cloud that everywhere illuminates all buddhas." It is adorned with Indra jewels, sovereign wish-granting jewels, and sovereign *maṇi* jewels and always emanates the light of bodhisattvas' flaming lamps which everywhere illuminate all worlds of the ten directions and reveals the oceans of the many forms and appearances of all buddhas within them, their oceans of sounds, and their oceans of pure powers. This is the eighth.

Next, there is a mark of the great man known as "the cloud of light spheres." It is adorned with many different kinds of supremely marvelous bejeweled flowers made of *vaiḍūrya* and sovereign *maṇi* jewels. All those many jewels spread forth immense nets of flaming light which fill all the worlds of the ten directions. All the beings within them see the Tathāgata appearing, sitting directly before them, praising the meritorious qualities of the Dharma body of all buddhas and bodhisattvas, enabling them to enter the pure realms of the Tathāgata. This is the ninth.

Next, there is a mark of the great man known as "the light cloud that everywhere illuminates the treasury of all bodhisattvas' practices." Adorned with marvelous flowers made of the many kinds of jewels, its jewel light everywhere illuminates countless worlds. Its

寶焰

普覆一切國土。十方法界。通達無礙。震動佛
音。宣暢法海。是為十。次有大人相。名普光照
耀雲。毘瑠璃。因陀羅。金剛摩尼寶。以為莊
嚴。瑠璃寶光。色相明徹。普照一切諸世界
海出妙音聲。充滿法界。如是皆從諸佛智慧
大功德海之所化現。是為十一。次有大人相。
名正覺雲。以雜寶華。而為莊嚴。其諸寶華。悉
放光明。皆有如來坐於道場。充滿一切無邊
世界。令諸世界。普得清淨。永斷一切妄想分
別。是為十二。次有大人相。名光明照[1]曜雲。
以寶焰藏海。心王摩尼。而為莊嚴。放大光明。
光中顯現無量菩薩及諸菩薩。所行之行。一
切如來。智身法身。諸色相海。充滿法界。是為
十三。次有大人相。名莊嚴普照雲。以金剛華。
毘瑠璃寶。而為莊嚴。放大光明。光中有大寶
蓮華座。具足莊嚴。彌覆法界。自然演說四菩
薩行。其音普遍諸法界海。是為十四。次有大
人相。名現佛三昧海行雲。於一念中。示現如
來無量莊嚴。普遍莊嚴一切法界。不思議世
界海。是為十五。次有大人相。名變化海普照
雲。妙寶蓮華如須彌山。以為莊嚴。

宝焰普覆一切国土，十方法界通达无碍，震动佛音宣畅法海，是为十。

"次有大人相，名普光照耀云，毗琉璃、因陀罗、金刚摩尼宝以为庄严，琉璃宝光色相明彻，普照一切诸世界海，出妙音声充满法界，如是皆从诸佛智慧大功德海之所化现，是为十一。

"次有大人相，名正觉云，以杂宝华而为庄严，其诸宝华悉放光明，皆有如来坐于道场，充满一切无边世界，令诸世界普得清净，永断一切妄想分别，是为十二。

"次有大人相，名光明照耀云，以宝焰藏海心王摩尼而为庄严，放大光明，光中显现无量菩萨及诸菩萨所行之行，一切如来智身、法身、诸色相海充满法界，是为十三。

"次有大人相，名庄严普照云，以金刚华、毗琉璃宝而为庄严，放大光明，光中有大宝莲华座，具足庄严，弥覆法界，自然演说四菩萨行，其音普遍诸法界海，是为十四。

"次有大人相，名现佛三昧海行云，于一念中示现如来无量庄严，普遍庄严一切法界不思议世界海，是为十五。

"次有大人相，名变化海普照云，妙宝莲华如须弥山以为庄严，

flaming jewel light spreading everywhere over all lands throughout the ten directions of the Dharma realm is unimpeded in its pervasive penetration. It emanates the quake-inducing sound of the Buddha widely and freely expounding on the ocean of dharmas. This is the tenth.

Next, there is a mark of the great man known as "the universally illuminating cloud of dazzling light." It is adorned with *vaiḍūrya*, Indra jewels, vajra, and *maṇi* jewels. The colors of the light from the *vaiḍūrya* jewels brightly interpenetrate and everywhere illuminate the ocean of all worlds. It also sends forth marvelous sounds that fill the Dharma realm. All phenomena such as these are transformationally created manifestations produced from all buddhas' ocean of wisdom and great meritorious qualities. This is the eleventh.

Next, there is a mark of the great man known as "the cloud of the right enlightenment." It is adorned with flowers made of the various kinds of precious jewels. All those bejeweled flowers emanate rays of light in each of which there is a *tathāgata* seated in a site of enlightenment. They fill up all the boundless worlds, causing all those worlds to become purified and forever severing all erroneous thinking and discriminations. This is the twelfth.

Next, there is a mark of the great man known as "the cloud of dazzling light." It is adorned with an ocean of flaming jewel light treasuries and mind-king *maṇi* jewels which emanate a great light in which are revealed countless bodhisattvas and bodhisattva practices along with an ocean of forms and appearances of all *tathāgatas'* wisdom bodies and Dharma body which fills the Dharma realm. This is the thirteenth.

Next, there is a mark of the great man known as "the cloud of universally illuminating adornments." Adorned with vajra flowers and *vaiḍūrya* jewels, it emanates rays of light in which there are great fully adorned jeweled lotus thrones that spread all over the Dharma realm, spontaneously expounding on the four bodhisattva practices,[13] the sound from which everywhere pervades the ocean of the Dharma realm. This is the fourteenth.

Next, there is a mark of the great man known as "the cloud revealing the practice of the Buddha's ocean of samādhis." In but a single mind-moment, it reveals all the Tathāgata's measureless adornments that everywhere adorn the entire Dharma realm's inconceivable ocean of worlds. This is the fifteenth.

Next, there is a mark of the great man known as "the universally illuminating cloud of the ocean of transformations." It is adorned with a marvelous bejeweled lotus flower comparable to Mount

正體字

眾寶光明。
252a25 從佛願生。現諸變化。無有窮盡。是為十六。次
252a26 有大人相。名一切如來解脫雲。清淨妙寶。以
252a27 為莊嚴。放大光明。莊嚴一切佛師子座。示現
252a28 一切諸佛色像。及無量佛法。諸佛剎海。是為
252a29 十七。次有大人相。名自在方便普照雲。毘瑠
252b01 璃華。真金蓮華。摩尼王燈。妙法焰雲。以為莊
252b02 嚴。放一切諸佛。寶焰密雲。清淨光明。充滿法
252b03 界。於中普現一切妙好莊嚴之具。是為十八。
252b04 次有大人相。名覺佛種性雲。無量寶光。以為
252b05 莊嚴。具足千輪。內外清淨。從於往昔善根所
252b06 生。其光遍照十方世界。發明智日。宣布法海。
252b07 是為十九。次有大人相。名現一切如來相自
252b08 在雲。眾寶瓔珞。瑠璃寶華。以為莊嚴。舒大寶
252b09 焰。充滿法界。於中普現等一切佛剎微塵數
252b10 去來現在無量諸佛。如師子王。勇猛無畏。色
252b11 相智慧。皆悉具足。是為二十。次有大人相。名
252b12 遍照一切法界雲。如來寶相。清淨莊嚴。放大
252b13 光明。普照法界。顯現一切無量無邊諸佛菩
252b14 薩。智慧妙藏。是為二十一。次有大人相。名毘
252b15 盧遮那如來相雲。上妙寶華。及毘瑠璃。清淨
252b16 妙月。以為莊嚴。

简体字

众宝光明从佛愿生，现诸变化无有穷尽，是为十六。

"次有大人相，名一切如来解脱云，清净妙宝以为庄严，放大光明庄严一切佛师子座，示现一切诸佛色像及无量佛法诸佛刹海，是为十七。

"次有大人相，名自在方便普照云，毗琉璃华、真金莲华、摩尼王灯、妙法焰云以为庄严，放一切诸佛宝焰密云，清净光明充满法界，于中普现一切妙好庄严之具，是为十八。

"次有大人相，名觉佛种性云，无量宝光以为庄严，具足千轮，内外清净，从于往昔善根所生，其光遍照十方世界，发明智日，宣布法海，是为十九。

"次有大人相，名现一切如来相自在云，众宝璎珞、琉璃宝华以为庄严，舒大宝焰充满法界，于中普现等一切佛刹微尘数去、来、现在无量诸佛，如师子王勇猛无畏，色相、智慧皆悉具足，是为二十。

"次有大人相，名遍照一切法界云，如来宝相清净庄严，放大光明普照法界，显现一切无量无边诸佛菩萨智慧妙藏，是为二十一。

"次有大人相，名毗卢遮那如来相云，上妙宝华及毗琉璃清净妙月以为庄严，

Sumeru. The light of its many jewels arises from the Buddha's vows and reveals all of his endless transformations. This is the sixteenth.

Next, there is a mark of the great man known as "the cloud of all *tathāgatas'* liberations." Adorned with the pure and marvelous jewels, it emanates a great light that serves to adorn the lion thrones of all buddhas and reveal the physical appearances of all buddhas as well as the countless dharmas of the Buddha and the ocean of all buddha *kṣetras*. This is the seventeenth.

Next, there is a mark of the great man known as "the universally illuminating cloud of freely implemented expedient means." It is adorned with flowers made of *vaiḍūrya*, flowers made of real gold, sovereign *maṇi* jewel lamps, and clouds of the sublime Dharma's flaming radiance. It emanates a dense cloud of all buddhas' flaming jewel radiance, the pure light from which fills the Dharma realm and everywhere reveals within it all of its marvelously fine adornments. This is the eighteenth.

Next, there is a mark of the great man known as "the cloud instigating awakening to the lineage of the buddhas." Adorned with countless rays of jeweled light, it contains a thousand spheres and is possessed of inward and outward purity arising from past roots of goodness. Its radiance everywhere illuminates the worlds of the ten directions and ignites the light of the wisdom sun which proclaims the ocean of dharmas. This is the nineteenth.

Next, there is a mark of the great man known as "the cloud of sovereign powers revealing the marks of all *tathāgatas*." Adorned with necklaces of the many kinds of jewels and flowers made of *vaiḍūrya* jewels, it spreads forth the flaming radiance of immense jewels that fills up the Dharma realm and everywhere reveals within it countless past, future, and present buddhas as numerous as the atoms in all buddha *kṣetras* who are as courageous and fearless as the king of lions and who are replete in their physical marks and wisdom. This is the twentieth.

Next, there is a mark of the great man known as "the cloud that everywhere illuminates the entire Dharma realm." It possesses the pure adornments of the Tathāgata's precious signs and emanates a great radiance that everywhere illuminates the Dharma realm and reveals the marvelous treasury of wisdom possessed by all the countlessly and boundlessly many buddhas and bodhisattvas. This is the twenty-first.

Next, there is a mark of the great man known as "the cloud of Vairocana Tathāgata's marks." Adorned with supremely marvelous jewel flowers as well as with pure and marvelous moons made of

正體字

悉放無量百千萬億。摩尼寶光。充滿一切虛空法界。於中示現無量佛剎。皆有如來結[2]跏趺坐。是為二十二。次有大人相。名普照一切佛光明雲。眾寶妙燈。以為莊嚴。放淨光明。遍照十方一切世界。悉現諸佛轉於法輪。是為二十三。次有大人相。名普現一切莊嚴雲。種種寶焰。以為莊嚴。放淨光明。充滿法界。念念常現不可說不可說一切諸佛。與諸菩薩。坐於道場。是為二十四。次有大人相。名出一切法界音聲雲。摩尼寶海。上妙栴檀。以為莊嚴。舒大焰網。充滿法界。其中普演微妙音聲。示諸眾生一切業海。是為二十五。次有大人相。名普照諸佛變化輪雲。如來淨眼。以為莊嚴。光照十方一切世界。於中普現去來今佛。所有一切莊嚴之具。復出妙音。演不思議。廣大法海。是為二十六。次有大人相。名光照佛海雲。其光普照一切世界。盡于法界。無所障礙。悉有如來結[*]跏趺坐。是為二十七。次有大人相。名寶燈雲。放於如來廣大光明。普照十方一切法界。於中普現一切諸佛。及諸菩薩。不可思議。諸眾生海。是為二十八。

简体字

悉放无量百千万亿摩尼宝光，充满一切虚空法界，于中示现无量佛刹，皆有如来结跏趺坐，是为二十二。

"次有大人相，名普照一切佛光明云，众宝妙灯以为庄严，放净光明遍照十方一切世界，悉现诸佛转于法轮，是为二十三。

"次有大人相，名普现一切庄严云，种种宝焰以为庄严，放净光明充满法界，念念常现不可说不可说一切诸佛与诸菩萨坐于道场，是为二十四。

"次有大人相，名出一切法界音声云，摩尼宝海、上妙栴檀以为庄严，舒大焰网充满法界，其中普演微妙音声，示诸众生一切业海，是为二十五。

"次有大人相，名普照诸佛变化轮云，如来净眼以为庄严，光照十方一切世界，于中普现去、来、今佛所有一切庄严之具，复出妙音演不思议广大法海，是为二十六。

"次有大人相，名光照佛海云，其光普照一切世界，尽于法界无所障碍，悉有如来结跏趺坐，是为二十七。

"次有大人相，名宝灯云，放于如来广大光明，普照十方一切法界，于中普现一切诸佛及诸菩萨不可思议诸众生海，是为二十八。

Chapter 34 — The Ocean of Major Marks of the Tathāgata's Ten Bodies

vaiḍūrya, it emanates countless hundreds of thousands of myriads of *koṭīs* of *maṇi* jewel light rays that fill up all of empty space and the Dharma realm and reveal the countless buddha *kṣetras* therein, in each of which there sits a *tathāgata* seated in the lotus posture. This is the twenty-second.

Next, there is a mark of the great man known as "the light cloud that everywhere illuminates all buddhas." Adorned with marvelous lamps made of many kinds of jewels, it emanates pure light that pervasively illuminates all worlds of the ten directions, revealing in all of them the buddhas turning the wheel of the Dharma. This is the twenty-third.

Next, there is a mark of the great man known as "the cloud that everywhere reveals all adornments." Adorned with the many different kinds of flaming jewel light, it emanates pure radiance that fills the Dharma realm and, in each successive mind-moment, forever reveals an ineffable-ineffable number of all buddhas and bodhisattvas sitting in the sites of enlightenment. This is the twenty-fourth.

Next, there is a mark of the great man known as "the cloud that emanates all sounds of the Dharma realm." Adorned with oceans of *maṇi* jewels and supremely marvelous sandalwood, it spreads forth a great net of flaming radiance that fills the Dharma realm and everywhere emanates sublime voices instructing beings on the ocean of all karma. This is the twenty-fifth.

Next, there is a mark of the great man known as "the cloud that everywhere illuminates the sphere of all buddhas' spiritual transformations." Adorned by the pure eyes of the Tathāgata, its light illuminates all worlds of the ten directions and everywhere reveals within them all the adornments of all buddhas of the past, the future, and the present while also emanating sublime voices expounding on the inconceivably vast ocean of Dharma. This is the twenty-sixth.

Next, there is a mark of the great man known as "the cloud whose light illuminates the ocean of buddhas." Its light everywhere unimpededly illuminates all worlds throughout the entire Dharma realm, revealing them all as having *tathāgatas* in them who are seated in the lotus posture. This is the twenty-seventh.

Next, there is a mark of the great man known as "the cloud of bejeweled lamps." It emanates the vast radiance of the *tathāgatas* which everywhere illuminates the ten directions of the entire Dharma realm and reveals within it all buddhas as well as all bodhisattvas and the inconceivable ocean of all beings. This is the twenty-eighth.

正體字

次有大人相。名法界無差別雲。放於如
來大智光明。普照十方諸佛國土。一切菩薩。
道場眾會。無量法海。於中普現種種神通。復
出妙音。隨諸眾生心之所樂。演說普賢菩薩
行願。令其迴向。是為二十九。次有大人相。名
安住一切世界海普照雲。放寶光明。充滿一
切虛空法界。於中普現淨妙道場。及佛菩薩。
莊嚴身相。令其見者。得無所見。是為三十。次
有大人相。名一切寶清淨光焰雲。放於無量
諸佛菩薩。摩尼妙寶。清淨光明。普照十方一
切法界。於中普現諸菩薩海。莫不具足如來
神力。常遊十方盡虛空界。一切剎網。是為三
十一。次有大人相。名普照一切法界莊嚴雲。
最處於中。漸次隆起。閻浮檀金。因陀羅網。以
為莊嚴。放淨光雲。充滿法界。念念常現一切
世界諸佛菩薩。道場眾會。是為三十二。佛子。
如來頂上。有如是三十二種大人相。以為嚴
好。佛子。如來眉間。有大人相。名遍法界光明
雲。摩尼寶華。以為莊嚴。放大光明。

简体字

"次有大人相，名法界无差别云，放于如来大智光明，普照十方诸佛国土、一切菩萨道场众会无量法海，于中普现种种神通，复出妙音，随诸众生心之所乐演说普贤菩萨行愿，令其回向，是为二十九。

"次有大人相，名安住一切世界海普照云，放宝光明充满一切虚空法界，于中普现净妙道场及佛菩萨庄严身相，令其见者得无所见，是为三十。

"次有大人相，名一切宝清净光焰云，放于无量诸佛菩萨摩尼妙宝清净光明，普照十方一切法界，于中普现诸菩萨海，莫不具足如来神力，常游十方尽虚空界一切刹网，是为三十一。

"次有大人相，名普照一切法界庄严云，最处于中，渐次隆起，阎浮檀金、因陀罗网以为庄严，放净光云充满法界，念念常现一切世界诸佛菩萨道场众会，是为三十二。

"佛子，如来顶上有如是三十二种大人相以为严好。

"佛子，如来眉间有大人相，名遍法界光明云，摩尼宝华以为庄严，放大光明，

Next, there is a mark of the great man known as "the cloud of the undifferentiated Dharma realm." It emanates the light of the Tathāgata's great wisdom which everywhere illuminates the lands of all buddhas of the ten directions, all their congregations of bodhisattvas at their sites of enlightenment, and their measureless ocean of Dharma, everywhere revealing within them their many different kinds of spiritual superknowledges while also emanating marvelous voices which, adapting to beings' mental dispositions, expound on the conduct and vows of Samantabhadra Bodhisattva and inspire those beings to dedicate [their cultivation to emulating it]. This is the twenty-ninth.

Next, there is a mark of the great man known as "the pervasively illuminating cloud that abides in the ocean of all worlds." It emanates a jewel radiance that fills all of empty space and the Dharma realm and everywhere reveals the pure and marvelous sites of enlightenment within them as well as the signs adorning the bodies of the buddhas and bodhisattvas, thereby enabling all who behold this to gain the realization in which nothing whatsoever is perceived. This is the thirtieth.

Next, there is a mark of the great man known as "the cloud of all jewels' pure flaming radiance." It emanates the pure light of the countless buddhas, bodhisattvas, and marvelous *maṇi* jewels, everywhere illuminates the ten directions of the entire Dharma realm, and everywhere reveals the ocean of bodhisattvas within it, none of whom have not completely developed the Tathāgata's spiritual powers by which they forever roam about in the network of all *kṣetras* throughout the ten directions of space. This is the thirty-first.

Next, there is a mark of the great man known as "the cloud that everywhere illuminates the entire Dharma realm's adornments." It is located right in the very center where it gradually bulges upward [on the top of the Buddha's head]. It is adorned with an Indra's net of *jambūnada* gold and emanates a cloud of pure light that fills the Dharma realm. In each successive mind-moment, it forever reveals the congregations of all buddhas and bodhisattvas at the sites of enlightenment in all worlds. This is the thirty-second.

Sons of the Buddha, on the summit of the Tathāgata's head, there are thirty-two marks of the great man such as these which serve there as fine marks of adornment.

Sons of the Buddha, between the Tathāgata's eyebrows, there is a mark of the great man known as "the light cloud that pervades the Dharma realm." Adorned with flowers made of *maṇi* jewels, it emanates a great light that includes the colors of the many kinds of

具眾寶

色。猶如日月洞徹清淨。其光普照十方國土。於中顯現一切佛身。復出妙音。宣暢法海。是為三十三。如來眼。有大人相。名自在普見雲。以眾妙寶。而為莊嚴。摩尼寶光。清淨映徹。普見一切。皆無障礙。是為三十四。如來鼻。有大人相。名一切神通智慧雲。清淨妙寶。以為莊嚴。眾寶色光。彌覆其上。於中出現無量化佛。坐寶蓮華。往諸世界。為一切菩薩。一切眾生。演不思議。諸佛法海。是為三十五。如來舌。有大人相。名示現音聲影像雲。眾色妙寶。以為莊嚴。宿世善根之所成就。其舌廣長。遍覆一切諸世界海。如來若或熙怡微笑。必放一切摩尼寶光。其光普照十方法界。能令一切心得清涼。去來現在。所有諸佛。皆於光中。炳然顯現。悉演廣大微妙之音。遍一切剎。住無量劫。是為三十六。如來[1]舌。復有大人相。名法界雲。其掌安平。眾寶為嚴。放妙寶光。色相圓滿。猶如眉間。所放光明。其光普照一切佛剎。唯塵所成。無有自性。光中復現無量諸佛。咸發妙音。說一切法。是為三十七。

具众宝色,犹如日月洞彻清净,其光普照十方国土,于中显现一切佛身,复出妙音宣畅法海,是为三十三。

"如来眼有大人相,名自在普见云,以众妙宝而为庄严,摩尼宝光清净映彻,普见一切皆无障碍,是为三十四。

"如来鼻有大人相,名一切神通智慧云,清净妙宝以为庄严,众宝色光弥覆其上,于中出现无量化佛坐宝莲华,往诸世界为一切菩萨、一切众生演不思议诸佛法海,是为三十五。

"如来舌有大人相,名示现音声影像云,众色妙宝以为庄严,宿世善根之所成就,其舌广长遍覆一切诸世界海,如来若或熙怡微笑,必放一切摩尼宝光,其光普照十方法界,能令一切心得清凉,去、来、现在所有诸佛皆于光中炳然显现,悉演广大微妙之音,遍一切刹,住无量劫,是为三十六。

"如来舌复有大人相,名法界云,其掌安平,众宝为严,放妙宝光色相圆满,犹如眉间所放光明,其光普照一切佛刹,唯尘所成,无有自性,光中复现无量诸佛,咸发妙音说一切法,是为三十七。

jewels. Like the pure penetrating light of the sun and moon, its light everywhere illuminates the lands of the ten directions and reveals the bodies of all buddhas within them while also emanating a marvelous voice that sends forth proclamations of the ocean of dharmas. This is the thirty-third.

The Tathāgata's eyes have a mark of the great man known as "the cloud of independent pervasive vision." Adorned with many kinds of marvelous jewels, its *maṇi* jewel light's pure and penetrating brightness everywhere unimpededly sees all things. This is the thirty-fourth.

The Tathāgata's nose has a mark of the great man known as "the cloud of all spiritual superknowledges and wisdom." Adorned with pure and marvelous jewels, the colored light of the many kinds of precious gems spreads forth over all of it and reveals countless transformation buddhas in it who sit on bejeweled lotus flowers and go forth to all worlds, expounding on the inconceivable ocean of the Dharma of all buddhas for the benefit of all bodhisattvas and all beings. This is the thirty-fifth.

The Tathāgata's tongue has a mark of the great man known as "the cloud that manifests sounds and reflected images." It is adorned with marvelous multi-colored jewels and it is produced through roots of goodness created in former lifetimes. His tongue is vast and long and everywhere covers the oceans of all worlds. If perhaps the Tathāgata at times happily and subtly smiles, it certainly then emanates the radiance of all kinds of *maṇi* jewels, the light from which everywhere illuminates the ten directions of the Dharma realm in which it is able to bring about clarity and coolness in everyone's minds. All buddhas of the past, the future, and the present appear brilliantly shining within that radiance, all of them expounding with a vastly resonant and sublime voice that pervades all *kṣetras* and remains within them for countless kalpas. This is the thirty-sixth.

The Tathāgata's tongue also has a mark of the great man known as "the Dharma realm cloud." Its surface is perfectly flat and adorned with the many kinds of jewels. It emanates marvelous jewel light with perfect forms and appearances which is like the light emanated from between his brows. Those lights everywhere illuminate all buddha *kṣetras*, revealing them to be composed solely of atoms and hence entirely devoid of any inherently existent nature of their own. Those lights also reveal the countless buddhas all sending forth sublime voices expounding on all dharmas. This is the thirty-seventh.

正體字

如來舌端。有
大人相。名照法界光明雲。如意寶王。以為莊
嚴。自然恒出金色寶焰。於中影現一切佛海。
復震妙音。充滿一切無邊世界。一一音中。具
一切音。悉演妙法。聽者心悅。經無量劫。玩味
不忘。是為三十八。如來舌端。復有大人相。名
照[2]耀法界雲。摩尼寶王。以為嚴飾。演眾色
相。微妙光明。充滿十方無量國土。盡[3]于法
界。靡不清淨。於中悉有無量諸佛。及諸菩薩
各吐妙音。種種開示。一切菩薩。現前聽受。是
為三十九。如來口上齶。有大人相。名示現不
思議法界雲。因陀羅寶。毘瑠璃寶。以為莊嚴
放香燈焰。清淨光雲。充滿十方一切法界。示
現種種神通方便。普於一切諸世界海。開演甚
深不思議法。是為四十。如來口右輔下牙。有
大人相。名佛牙雲。眾寶摩尼。[4]卍字相輪。以
為莊嚴。放大光明。普照法界。於中普現一切
佛身。周流十方。開悟群生。是為四十一。如來
口右輔上牙。有大人相。名寶焰彌盧藏雲。摩
尼寶藏。以為莊嚴。放金剛香焰。清淨光明。一
一光明。充滿法界。示現一切諸佛神力。

简体字

"如来舌端有大人相，名照法界光明云，如意宝王以为庄严，自然恒出金色宝焰，于中影现一切佛海，复震妙音充满一切无边世界，一一音中具一切音，悉演妙法，听者心悦，经无量劫玩味不忘，是为三十八。

"如来舌端复有大人相，名照耀法界云，摩尼宝王以为严饰，演众色相微妙光明，充满十方无量国土，尽于法界靡不清净，于中悉有无量诸佛及诸菩萨各吐妙音种种开示，一切菩萨现前听受，是为三十九。

"如来口上腭有大人相，名示现不思议法界云，因陀罗宝、毗琉璃宝以为庄严，放香灯焰清净光云，充满十方一切法界，示现种种神通方便，普于一切诸世界海开演甚深不思议法，是为四十。

"如来口右辅下牙有大人相，名佛牙云，众宝摩尼卍字相轮以为庄严，放大光明普照法界，于中普现一切佛身，周流十方开悟群生，是为四十一。

"如来口右辅上牙有大人相，名宝焰弥卢藏云，摩尼宝藏以为庄严，放金刚香焰清净光明，一一光明充满法界，示现一切诸佛神力，

The tip of the Tathāgata's tongue has a mark of the great man known as "the light cloud that illuminates the Dharma realm." Adorned with sovereign wish-fulfilling gems, it spontaneously and constantly sends forth golden flaming jewel radiance in which the ocean of all buddhas is reflected. In addition, it emanates marvelous quake-inducing voices which fill all the boundlessly many worlds. In every one of those voices are contained all voices, all of which expound on the sublime Dharma, delighting the minds of all who hear them. This continues on for countless kalpas during which it continues to be appreciated and never forgotten. This is the thirty-eighth.

The tip of the Tathāgata's tongue has another mark of the great man known as "the cloud that illuminates the Dharma realm with dazzling radiance." Adorned with sovereign *maṇi* jewels, it emanates streams of sublime light of many colors which fill the countless lands of the ten directions throughout the Dharma realm, thereby purifying them all. Present within it are countless buddhas and bodhisattvas speaking in sublime voices with which they offer many different explanatory instructions to which all bodhisattvas directly listen. This is the thirty-ninth.

The upper palate of the Tathāgata's mouth has a mark of the great man known as "the cloud that reveals the inconceivable Dharma realm." Adorned with Indra jewels and *vaiḍūrya* gems, it emanates fragrant flaming lamplight in clouds of pure radiance which everywhere fill the ten directions of the Dharma realm and reveal the many different kinds of spiritual superknowledges and skillful means while also expounding on the extremely profound and inconceivable Dharma everywhere throughout the oceans of worlds. This is the fortieth.

The Tathāgata's lower right front teeth have a mark of the great man known as "the buddha tooth cloud." Adorned with the many kinds of precious gems and *maṇi* jewels forming *svastika*-emblem wheels, it emanates a great radiance that everywhere illuminates the Dharma realm and reveals everywhere within it the bodies of all buddhas flowing forth everywhere in the ten directions, awakening the many kinds of beings. This is the forty-first.

The Tathāgata's upper right front teeth have a mark of the great man known as "the cloud of flaming jewel light Sumeru treasuries." Adorned with treasuries of *maṇi* jewels, it emanates fragrant flaming vajra radiance, the pure light from each and every ray of which fills up the Dharma realm, revealing the spiritual powers of all buddhas while also revealing the pure and marvelous sites of

復現

正體字

```
253b09 | 一切十方世界。淨妙道場。是為四十二。如來
253b10 | 口左輔下牙。有大人相。名寶燈普照雲。一切
253b11 | 妙寶。舒華發香。以為莊嚴。放燈焰雲。清淨光
253b12 | 明。充滿一切諸世界海。於中顯現一切諸佛。
253b13 | 坐蓮華藏師子之座。諸菩薩眾。所共圍遶。是
253b14 | 為四十三。如來口左輔上牙。有大人相。名照
253b15 | 現如來雲。清淨光明。閻浮檀金。寶網寶華。以
253b16 | 為莊嚴。放大焰[5]輪。充滿法界。於中普現一
253b17 | 切諸佛。以神通力。於虛空中。流布法乳法燈
253b18 | 法寶。教化一切諸菩薩眾。是為四十四。如來
253b19 | 齒。有大人相。名普現光明雲。一一齒間。相海
253b20 | 莊嚴。若微笑時。悉放光明。具眾寶色。摩尼寶
253b21 | 焰。右旋宛轉。流布法界。靡不充滿。演佛言
253b22 | 音。說普賢行。是為四十五。如來脣。有大人
253b23 | 相。名影現一切寶光雲。放閻浮檀。真金色。蓮
253b24 | 華色。一切寶色。廣大光明。照[*]于法界。悉令
253b25 | 清淨。是為四十六。如來頸。有大人相。名普照
253b26 | 一切世界雲。摩尼寶王。以為莊嚴。紺蒲成就。
253b27 | 柔軟細滑。放毘盧遮那清淨光明。充滿十方
253b28 | 一切世界。於中普現一切諸佛。是為四十七。
253b29 | 如來右肩。有大人相。名佛廣大一切寶雲。放
253c01 | 一切寶色。真金色。蓮華色光明。
```

简体字

复现一切十方世界净妙道场，是为四十二。

"如来口左辅下牙有大人相，名宝灯普照云，一切妙宝舒华发香以为庄严，放灯焰云清净光明，充满一切诸世界海，于中显现一切诸佛坐莲华藏师子之座，诸菩萨众所共围绕，是为四十三。

"如来口左辅上牙有大人相，名照现如来云，清净光明、阎浮檀金、宝网、宝华以为庄严，放大焰轮充满法界，于中普现一切诸佛，以神通力于虚空中流布法乳、法灯、法宝，教化一切诸菩萨众，是为四十四。

"如来齿有大人相，名普现光明云，一一齿间相海庄严，若微笑时悉放光明，具众宝色摩尼宝焰右旋宛转，流布法界靡不充满，演佛言音说普贤行，是为四十五。

"如来唇有大人相，名影现一切宝光云，放阎浮檀真金色、莲华色、一切宝色广大光明，照于法界悉令清净，是为四十六。

"如来颈有大人相，名普照一切世界云，摩尼宝王以为庄严，绀蒲成就柔软细滑，放毗卢遮那清净光明，充满十方一切世界，于中普现一切诸佛，是为四十七。

"如来右肩有大人相，名佛广大一切宝云，放一切宝色、真金色、莲华色光明，

enlightenment throughout all worlds of the ten directions. This is the forty-second.

The Tathāgata's lower left front teeth have a mark of the great man known as "the universally illuminating cloud of jewel lamplight." Adorned with all kinds of marvelous jewels and emitting the fragrance of blooming flowers, it emanates a cloud of flaming lamplight, the pure radiance from which fills up all the oceans of worlds, revealing within it all their buddhas sitting on lotus dais lion thrones, surrounded by congregations of bodhisattvas. This is the forty-third.

The Tathāgata's upper left front teeth have a mark of the great man known as "the cloud that illuminates the Tathāgatas." Adorned with pure light, *jambūnada* gold, jeweled nets, and bejeweled flowers, it emanates a great orb of flaming radiance which fills the Dharma realm and everywhere reveals within it all buddhas using the powers of their spiritual superknowledges to distribute throughout space a flow of Dharma milk, Dharma lamplight, and Dharma jewels that teaches the congregations of all bodhisattvas. This is the forty-fourth.

The Tathāgata's teeth have a mark of the great man known as "the cloud that manifests light everywhere." Between each of his teeth, there are oceans of adorning signs. Whenever he smiles even slightly, they emanate jewel-colored light and the flaming light of *maṇi* jewels which circumambulate in a rightward direction, flowing throughout the Dharma realm, completely filling it, expounding with the voice of the Buddha on the practices of Samantabhadra. This is the forty-fifth.

The Tathāgata's lips have a mark of the great man known as "the cloud that reflects the light of all jewels." It emanates vast radiance the color of real *jambūnada* gold, the color of lotus flowers, and the color of every kind of jewel that illuminates the Dharma realm and causes everything to become purified. This is the forty-sixth.

The Tathāgata's neck has a mark of the great man known as "the cloud that everywhere illuminates all worlds." Adorned with sovereign *maṇi* jewels, possessed of the fully developed *kamboja*[14] feature, soft, and smooth, it emanates pure *vairocana* light that fills all worlds of the ten directions and everywhere reveals all the buddhas within them. This is the forty-seventh.

The Tathāgata's right shoulder has a mark of the great man known as "the Buddha's vast cloud of every kind of jewel." It emanates lights the colors of all kinds of jewels, the color of real gold, and the color of lotus flowers that form a web of flaming jewel light

正體字

成寶焰網。普照法界。於中普現一切菩薩。是為四十八。如來右肩。復有大人相。名最勝寶普照雲。其色清淨。如閻浮金。放摩尼光充滿法界。於中普現一切菩薩。是為四十九。如來左肩。有大人相。名最勝光照法界雲。猶如頂上。及以眉間。種種莊嚴。放閻浮檀金。及蓮華色。眾寶光明。成大焰網。充滿法界。於中示現一切神力。是為五十。如來左肩。復有大人相。名光明遍照雲。其相右旋。閻浮檀金色。摩尼寶王。以為莊嚴。放眾寶華。香焰光明。充遍法界。於中普現一切諸佛。及以一切嚴淨國土。是為五十一。如來左肩。復有大人相。名普照耀雲。其相右旋。微密莊嚴。放佛燈焰雲。清淨光明。充遍法界。於中顯現一切菩薩。種種莊嚴。悉皆妙好。是為五十二。如來胸臆。有大人相。形如[6]卍字。名吉祥海雲。摩尼寶華。以為莊嚴。放一切寶色。種種光焰輪。充滿法界。普令清淨。復出妙音。宣暢法海。是為五十三。吉祥相右邊。有大人相。名示現光照雲。因陀羅網。以為莊嚴。

简体字

成宝焰网普照法界，于中普现一切菩萨，是为四十八。

"如来右肩复有大人相，名最胜宝普照云，其色清净如阎浮金，放摩尼光充满法界，于中普现一切菩萨，是为四十九。

"如来左肩有大人相，名最胜光照法界云，犹如顶上及以眉间种种庄严，放阎浮檀金及莲华色众宝光明，成大焰网充满法界，于中示现一切神力，是为五十。

"如来左肩复有大人相，名光明遍照云，其相右旋，阎浮檀金摩尼宝王以为庄严，放众宝华，香焰光明充遍法界，于中普现一切诸佛及以一切严净国土，是为五十一。

"如来左肩复有大人相，名普照耀云，其相右旋，微密庄严，放佛灯焰云，清净光明充遍法界，于中显现一切菩萨种种庄严悉皆妙好，是为五十二。

"如来胸臆有大人相，形如卍字，名吉祥海云，摩尼宝华以为庄严，放一切宝色种种光焰轮，充满法界普令清净，复出妙音宣畅法海，是为五十三。

"吉祥相右边有大人相，名示现光照云，因陀罗网以为庄严，

everywhere illuminating the Dharma realm, revealing all the bodhisattvas within it. This is the forty-eighth.

The Tathāgata's right shoulder also has a mark of the great man known as "the cloud of supreme jewels' universal illumination." With colors as pure as *jambūnada* gold, it emanates *maṇi* jewel light that fills the Dharma realm and everywhere illuminates all the bodhisattvas within it. This is the forty-ninth.

The Tathāgata's left shoulder has a mark of the great man known as "the cloud of supreme light that illuminates the Dharma realm." Like that of the many different kinds of adornments on his summit and between his brows, it emanates light of the many kinds of jewels that is the color of *jambūnada* gold and lotus flowers and which forms a great net of flaming radiance that fills the Dharma realm and reveals all the spiritual powers being used within it. This is the fiftieth.

The Tathāgata's left shoulder also has a mark of the great man known as "the cloud of universally illuminating light." That mark swirls around in a rightward direction and is characterized by adornments the color of *jambūnada* gold and sovereign *maṇi* jewels. It emanates the light of flowers made of the many kinds of jewels and fragrant flaming light that pervasively fills the Dharma realm and everywhere reveals all the buddhas within it as well as all of their adorned pure lands. This is the fifty-first.

The Tathāgata's left shoulder also has a mark of the great man known as "the cloud of universally illuminating dazzling light." That mark swirls around in a rightward direction, is possessed of subtle and fine adornments, and emanates clouds of the Buddha's flaming lamplight. Its pure light everywhere fills the Dharma realm and reveals the many different kinds of adornments of all of the bodhisattvas within it, all of which are marvelously fine. This is the fifty-second.

The Tathāgata's chest has a mark of the great man shaped like a *svastika* emblem that is known as "the cloud of the ocean of auspiciousness." Adorned with flowers made of *maṇi* jewels, it emanates all kinds of flaming light spheres the color of every kind of jewel which fill the Dharma realm and cause everything to be purified while also sending forth marvelous sounds that freely propagate [the teachings in] the ocean of Dharma. This is the fifty-third.

To the right of this mark of auspiciousness, there is a mark of the great man known as "the cloud that manifests radiant illumination." Adorned by Indra's net, it emanates immense spheres of light

正體字

放大光輪。充滿法界。於中普現無量
諸佛。是為五十四。吉祥相右邊復有大人相。
名普現如來雲。以諸菩薩摩尼寶冠。而為莊
嚴。放大光明。普照十方一切世界。悉令清淨。
於中示現去來今佛。坐於道場。普現神力。廣
宣法海。是為五十五。吉祥相右邊。復有大人
相。名開敷華雲。摩尼寶華。以為莊嚴。放寶香
焰燈。清淨光明。狀如蓮華。充滿世界。是為五
十六。吉祥相右邊。復有大人相。名可悅樂金
色雲。以一切寶。心王藏摩尼王。而為莊嚴。放
淨光明。照于法界。於中普現。猶如佛眼。廣
大光明。摩尼寶藏。是為五十七。吉祥相右邊
復有大人相。名佛海雲。毘瑠璃寶。香燈華
鬘。以為莊嚴。放滿虛空。摩尼寶王。香燈大
焰。清淨光明。充遍十方一切國土。於中普現
道場眾會。是為五十八。吉祥相左邊。有大人
相。名示現光明雲。無數菩薩。坐寶蓮華。以為
莊嚴。放摩尼王。種種間錯。寶焰光明。普淨一
切諸法界海。於中示現無量諸佛。及佛妙音。
演說諸法。是為五十九。吉祥相左邊。復有大
人相。名示現遍法界光明雲。摩尼寶海。以為
莊嚴。放大光明。遍一切剎。於中普現諸菩薩
眾。是為六十。

简体字

放大光轮充满法界，于中普现无量诸佛，是为五十四。

"吉祥相右边复有大人相，名普现如来云，以诸菩萨摩尼宝冠而为庄严，放大光明普照十方一切世界悉令清净，于中示现去、来、今佛坐于道场，普现神力广宣法海，是为五十五。

"吉祥相右边复有大人相，名开敷华云，摩尼宝华以为庄严，放宝香焰灯清净光明，状如莲华，充满世界，是为五十六。

"吉祥相右边复有大人相，名可悦乐金色云，以一切宝心王藏摩尼王而为庄严，放净光明照于法界，于中普现犹如佛眼广大光明摩尼宝藏，是为五十七。

"吉祥相右边复有大人相，名佛海云，毗琉璃宝、香灯、华鬘以为庄严，放满虚空摩尼宝王香灯大焰清净光明，充遍十方一切国土，于中普现道场众会，是为五十八。

"吉祥相左边有大人相，名示现光明云，无数菩萨坐宝莲华以为庄严，放摩尼王种种间错宝焰光明，普净一切诸法界海，于中示现无量诸佛，及佛妙音演说诸法，是为五十九。

"吉祥相左边复有大人相，名示现遍法界光明云，摩尼宝海以为庄严，放大光明遍一切刹，于中普现诸菩萨众，是为六十。

which fill the Dharma realm and everywhere reveal the countless buddhas within it. This is the fifty-fourth.

To the right of the mark of auspiciousness, there is also a mark of the great man known as "the cloud that everywhere reveals the *tathāgatas.*" Adorned with bodhisattva *maṇi* jewel crowns, it emanates great radiance that everywhere illuminates all worlds of the ten directions, purifying them all and revealing the buddhas of the past, the future, and the present, seated in their sites of enlightenment, everywhere manifesting spiritual powers and extensively propagating [the teachings in] the ocean of Dharma. This is the fifty-fifth.

To the right of the mark of auspiciousness, there is also a mark of the great man known as "the cloud of blooming flowers." Adorned with flowers made of *maṇi* jewels, it emanates pure light from bejeweled fragrant flaming radiance lamps shaped like lotus flowers that fill the worlds. This is the fifty-sixth.

To the right of the mark of auspiciousness, there is also a mark of the great man known as "the delightful golden cloud." Adorned with sovereign *maṇi* jewels from the mind king treasury of all jewels, it emanates pure light that illuminates the Dharma realm, everywhere revealing within it vast radiant *maṇi* jewel treasuries resembling the eyes of the Buddha. This is the fifty-seventh.

To the right of the mark of auspiciousness, there is also a mark of the great man known as "the cloud of the ocean of buddhas." Adorned with *vaiḍūrya* gems, fragrant lamps, and floral garlands, it emanates the pure light filling empty space from sovereign *maṇi* jewels and fragrant lamps' great flaming radiance which pervades all lands of the ten directions and everywhere reveals within them the congregations at their sites of enlightenment. This is the fifty-eighth.

To the left of the mark of auspiciousness, there is a mark of the great man known as "the cloud that manifests light." Adorned with countless bodhisattvas sitting on bejeweled lotus flowers, it emanates the flaming light of many different kinds of jewels inlaid among sovereign *maṇi* jewels which everywhere purifies the entire ocean of the Dharma realm and reveals the countless buddhas within it while also making apparent the voices of those buddhas expounding on all dharmas. This is the fifty-ninth.

To the left of the mark of auspiciousness, there is also a mark of the great man known as "the cloud that manifests light throughout the Dharma realm." Adorned with an ocean of *maṇi* jewels, it emanates great light that pervades all *kṣetras* and everywhere reveals all the bodhisattvas within them. This is the sixtieth.

正體字

吉祥相左邊。復有大人相。名普
勝雲。日光明摩尼王寶輪鬘。而為莊嚴。放大
光焰。充滿法界。諸世界海。於中示現一切世
界。一切如來。一切眾生。是為六十一。吉祥相
左邊。復有大人相。名轉法輪妙音雲。一切法
燈。清淨香蘂。以為莊嚴。放大光明。充滿法
界。於中普現一切諸佛。所有相海。及以心海。
是為六十二。吉祥相左邊。復有大人相。名莊
嚴雲以去來今一切佛海。而為莊嚴。放淨光
明。嚴淨一切諸佛國土。於中普現十方一切
諸佛菩薩。及佛菩薩。所行之行。是為六十三。
如來右手。有大人相。名海照雲。眾寶莊嚴。恒
放月焰清淨光明。充滿虛空。一切世界。發大
音聲。歎美一切諸菩薩行。是為六十四。如來
右手。復有大人相。名影現照[*]耀雲。以毘瑠
璃。帝青摩尼寶華。而為莊嚴。放大光明。普照
十方菩薩所住。蓮華藏。摩尼藏等。一切世界。
於中悉現無量諸佛。以淨法身。坐菩提樹。
[1]震動一切十方國土。是為六十五。如來右
手。復有大人相。名燈焰鬘普嚴淨雲。毘盧遮
那寶。以為莊嚴。放大光明。成變化網。於中普
現諸菩薩眾。咸戴寶冠。演諸行海。是為六十
六。

简体字

"吉祥相左边复有大人相,名普胜云,日光明摩尼王宝轮鬘而为庄严,放大光焰充满法界诸世界海,于中示现一切世界、一切如来、一切众生,是为六十一。

"吉祥相左边复有大人相,名转法轮妙音云,一切法灯清净香蕊以为庄严,放大光明充满法界,于中普现一切诸佛所有相海及以心海,是为六十二。

"吉祥相左边复有大人相,名庄严云,以去、来、今一切佛海而为庄严,放净光明严净一切诸佛国土,于中普现十方一切诸佛菩萨及佛菩萨所行之行,是为六十三。

"如来右手有大人相,名海照云,众宝庄严,恒放月焰清净光明,充满虚空一切世界,发大音声叹美一切诸菩萨行,是为六十四。

"如来右手复有大人相,名影现照耀云,以毗琉璃、帝青、摩尼宝华而为庄严,放大光明普照十方菩萨所住莲华藏、摩尼藏等一切世界,于中悉现无量诸佛,以净法身坐菩提树,震动一切十方国土,是为六十五。

"如来右手复有大人相,名灯焰鬘普严净云,毗卢遮那宝以为庄严,放大光明成变化网,于中普现诸菩萨众,咸戴宝冠演诸行海,是为六十六。

To the left of the mark of auspiciousness, there is also a mark of the great man known as "the cloud of universal supremacy." Adorned with sunlight sovereign *maṇi* jewels, jeweled spheres, and garlands, it emanates a great flaming radiance that fills the oceans of worlds throughout the Dharma realm and reveals all the worlds, all the *tathāgatas*, and all the beings within them. This is the sixty-first.

To the left of the mark of auspiciousness, there is also a mark of the great man known as "the cloud of the marvelous sounds of turning the Dharma wheel." Adorned with all kinds of Dharma lamps and stamens exuding pure fragrance, it emanates a great radiance that fills the Dharma realm and everywhere reveals the ocean of all marks and the ocean of the mind of all buddhas. This is the sixty-second.

To the left of the mark of auspiciousness, there is also a mark of the great man known as "the cloud of adornments." Adorned with the ocean of all buddhas of the past, the future, and the present, it emanates a pure light that purifies all buddha lands and everywhere reveals within them all buddhas and bodhisattvas of the ten directions as well as all the practices they follow. This is the sixty-third.

The Tathāgata's right hand has a mark of the great man known as "the cloud of oceanic illumination." Adorned with the many kinds of jewels, it constantly emanates the pure radiance of shimmering moonlight that fills all the worlds throughout empty space and sends forth a great voice praising all the bodhisattva practices. This is the sixty-fourth.

The Tathāgata's right hand also has a mark of the great man known as "the cloud that reflects dazzling illumination." Adorned with flowers made of *vaiḍūrya*, sapphires, and *maṇi* jewels, it emanates a great radiance that everywhere illuminates all the lotus treasury worlds, *maṇi* jewel treasury worlds, and other worlds in which the bodhisattvas of the ten directions dwell while revealing the countless buddhas within them who, in reliance on the pure Dharma body, sit beneath the bodhi trees and cause all lands throughout the ten directions to quake. This is the sixty-fifth.

The Tathāgata's right hand also has a mark of the great man known as "the universally purifying cloud of flaming lamplight and garlands." Adorned with *vairocana* jewels, it emanates a great radiance that forms a net of transformations and everywhere reveals the congregations of bodhisattvas within it, all of whom wear jeweled crowns and expound upon the ocean of all practices. This is the sixty-sixth.

正體字

如來右手。復有大人相。名普現一切摩尼
雲。蓮華焰燈。而為莊嚴。放海藏光。充遍法
界。於中普現無量諸佛。坐蓮華座。是為六十
七。如來右手。復有大人相。名光明雲。摩尼焰
海。以為莊嚴。放眾寶焰。香焰華焰。清淨光
明。充滿一切諸世界網。於中普現諸佛道場。
是為六十八。如來左手。有大人相。名毘瑠璃
清淨燈雲。寶地妙色。以為莊嚴。放於如來。金
色光明。念念常現一切上妙莊嚴之具。是為
六十九。如來左手。復有大人相。名一切剎智
慧燈音聲雲。以因陀羅網。金剛華。而為莊嚴。
放閻浮檀金。清淨光明。普照十方一切世界。
是為七十。如來左手。復有大人相。名安住寶
蓮華光明雲。眾寶妙華。以為莊嚴。放大光明。
如須彌燈。普照十方一切世界。是為七十一。
如來左手。復有大人相。名遍照法界雲。以妙
寶鬘寶輪寶瓶。因陀羅網。及眾妙相。以為莊
嚴。放大光明。普照十方一切國土。於中示現
一切法界。一切世界海。一切如來。坐蓮華座。
是為七十二。如來右手指。有大人相。名現諸
劫剎海旋雲。水月焰藏摩尼王。一切寶華。以
為莊嚴。放大光明。充滿法界。

简体字

"如来右手复有大人相，名普现一切摩尼云，莲华焰灯而为庄严，放海藏光充遍法界，于中普现无量诸佛坐莲华座，是为六十七。

"如来右手复有大人相，名光明云，摩尼焰海以为庄严，放众宝焰、香焰、华焰清净光明，充满一切诸世界网，于中普现诸佛道场，是为六十八。

"如来左手有大人相，名毗琉璃清净灯云，宝地妙色以为庄严，放于如来金色光明，念念常现一切上妙庄严之具，是为六十九。

"如来左手复有大人相，名一切刹智慧灯音声云，以因陀罗网、金刚华而为庄严，放阎浮檀金清净光明，普照十方一切世界，是为七十。

"如来左手复有大人相，名安住宝莲华光明云，众宝妙华以为庄严，放大光明如须弥灯，普照十方一切世界，是为七十一。

"如来左手复有大人相，名遍照法界云，以妙宝鬘、宝轮、宝瓶、因陀罗网及众妙相以为庄严，放大光明普照十方一切国土，于中示现一切法界、一切世界海、一切如来坐莲华座，是为七十二。

"如来右手指有大人相，名现诸劫刹海旋云，水月焰藏摩尼王一切宝华以为庄严，放大光明充满法界，

The Tathāgata's right hand also has a mark of the great man known as "the cloud that everywhere reveals all *maṇi* jewels." Adorned with flaming lotus lamplight radiance, it emanates oceanic treasuries of light which fill the Dharma realm and everywhere reveal within them the countless buddhas sitting on lotus flower thrones. This is the sixty-seventh.

The Tathāgata's right hand also has a mark of the great man known as "the cloud of radiance." Adorned with an ocean of *maṇi* jewel flaming radiance, it emanates the pure light of the flaming radiance of the many kinds of jewels, the flaming radiance of incenses, and the flaming radiance of flowers which fills the net of all worlds and everywhere reveals within them the sites of enlightenment of all buddhas. This is the sixty-eighth.

The Tathāgata's left hand has a mark of the great man known as "the cloud of pure *vaiḍūrya* lamplight." Adorned with the marvelous colors of grounds made of jewels, it emanates the golden light of the Tathāgata and, in each successive mind-moment, forever reveals all the supremely marvelous adornments. This is the sixty-ninth.

The Tathāgata's left hand also has a mark of the great man known as "the cloud of voices of the lamps of wisdom throughout all *kṣetras*." Adorned with the net of Indra and vajra flowers, it emanates the pure light of *jambūnada* gold that everywhere illuminates all worlds of the ten directions. This is the seventieth.

The Tathāgata's left hand also has a mark of the great man known as "the cloud of light dwelling in a jeweled lotus." Adorned with marvelous flowers made of the many kinds of jewels, it emanates a great radiance as if from a lamp the size of Mount Sumeru which everywhere illuminates all worlds of the ten directions. This is the seventy-first.

The Tathāgata's left hand also has a mark of the great man known as "the cloud that everywhere illuminates the Dharma realm." Adorned with marvelous jeweled garlands, jeweled spheres, jeweled vases, Indra's nets, and the many marvelous of emblematic signs, it emanates a great radiance that everywhere illuminates all lands of the ten directions and reveals all the *tathāgatas* sitting on lotus flower thrones within the ocean of all worlds throughout the entire Dharma realm. This is the seventy-second.

The fingers of the Tathāgata's right hand have a mark of the great man known as "the swirling cloud revealing the ocean of all kalpas and *kṣetras*." Adorned with the sovereign *maṇi* jewels of the water moon's treasury of flaming radiance and flowers made of all kinds of jewels, it emanates a great light that fills the Dharma realm and

正體字

其中恒出微妙音聲。滿十方刹。是為七十三。如來左手指。有大人相。名安住一切寶雲。以帝青金剛寶。而為莊嚴。放摩尼王。眾寶光明。充滿法界。其中普現一切諸佛。及諸菩薩。是為七十四。如來右手掌。有大人相。名照[*]耀雲。以摩尼王。千輻寶輪。而為莊嚴。放寶光明。其光右旋。充滿法界。於中普現一切諸佛。一一佛身。光焰熾然。說法度人。淨諸世界。是為七十五。如來左手掌。有大人相。名焰輪普增長化現法界道場雲。以日光摩尼王。千輻輪。而為莊嚴。放大光明。充滿一切諸世界海。於中示現一切菩薩。演說普賢所有行海。普入一切諸佛國土。各各開悟無量眾生。是為七十六。如來陰藏。有大人相。名普流出佛音聲雲。一切妙寶。以為莊嚴。放摩尼燈。華焰光明。其光熾盛。具眾寶色。普照一切虛空法界。其中普現一切諸佛遊行往來。處處周遍。是為七十七。如來右臀。有大人相。名寶燈鬘普照雲。諸摩尼寶。以為莊嚴。放不思議寶焰光明。彌布十方一切法界。與虛空法界。同為一相。而能出生一切諸相。一一相中。悉現諸佛自在神變。是為七十八。

简体字

其中恒出微妙音声满十方刹,是为七十三。

"如来左手指有大人相,名安住一切宝云,以帝青、金刚宝而为庄严,放摩尼王众宝光明充满法界,其中普现一切诸佛及诸菩萨,是为七十四。

"如来右手掌有大人相,名照耀云,以摩尼王千辐宝轮而为庄严,放宝光明,其光右旋充满法界,于中普现一切诸佛,一一佛身光焰炽然,说法度人,净诸世界,是为七十五。

"如来左手掌有大人相,名焰轮普增长化现法界道场云,以日光摩尼王千辐轮而为庄严,放大光明充满一切诸世界海,于中示现一切菩萨,演说普贤所有行海,普入一切诸佛国土,各各开悟无量众生,是为七十六。

"如来阴藏有大人相,名普流出佛音声云,一切妙宝以为庄严,放摩尼灯华焰光明,其光炽盛,具众宝色,普照一切虚空法界,其中普现一切诸佛游行往来处处周遍,是为七十七。

"如来右臀有大人相,名宝灯鬘普照云,诸摩尼宝以为庄严,放不思议宝焰光明,弥布十方一切法界,与虚空法界同为一相,而能出生一切诸相,一一相中悉现诸佛自在神变,是为七十八。

constantly sends forth from within it sublime voices that fill the *kṣetras* of the ten directions. This is the seventy-third.

The fingers of the Tathāgata's left hand have a mark of the great man known as "the cloud that rests on all kinds of jewels." Adorned with sapphires and vajra gems, it emanates the light of sovereign *maṇi* jewels and the many kinds of precious gems which fill the Dharma realm, everywhere revealing all the buddhas and bodhisattvas within it. This is the seventy-fourth.

The Tathāgata's right palm has a mark of the great man known as "the cloud of dazzling illumination." Adorned with sovereign *maṇi* jewels and thousand-spoked jeweled wheels, it emanates the light of jewels that swirls around to the right and then fills the Dharma realm, everywhere revealing all the buddhas within it, the flaming light and blazing radiance of every one of their buddha bodies, as well as their speaking of Dharma to liberate people and their purification of all worlds. This is the seventy-fifth.

The Tathāgata's left palm has a mark of the great man known as "the cloud of flaming light spheres that everywhere increase the transformationally manifested sites of enlightenment throughout the Dharma realm." Adorned with thousand-spoked wheels of sovereign sunlight *maṇi* jewels, it emanates a great radiance that fills all the oceans of worlds and reveals all the bodhisattvas within them as they expound on Samantabhadra's ocean of practices and everywhere enter the lands of all buddhas where they each awaken countless beings. This is the seventy-sixth.

The Tathāgata's characteristic sign of genital ensheathment has a mark of the great man known as "the cloud that everywhere streams forth the voice of the Buddha." Adorned with every sort of marvelous jewel, it emanates the flaming floral light of *maṇi* jewel lamps, the light from which blazes fully with the colors of the many kinds of jewels, everywhere illuminates all of empty space and the Dharma realm, and everywhere reveals within them all the buddhas going forth and coming back as they everywhere roam about to place after place. This is the seventy-seventh.

The Tathāgata's right hip has a mark of the great man known as "the universally illuminating cloud of bejeweled lamps and garlands." Adorned with all kinds of *maṇi* jewels, it emanates an ineffable number of rays of flaming jewel radiance which spread forth across the entire Dharma realm. It is of the same single characteristic as the realm of empty space and the Dharma realm, and yet it is able to produce all the signs, each sign of which reveals the masterfully implemented spiritual transformations of all buddhas. This is the seventy-eighth.

正體字	如來左臀。有大人相。名示現一切法界 海光明彌覆虛空雲。猶如蓮華。清淨妙寶。以 為嚴飾。放光明網。遍照十方。一切法界。於中 普現種種相雲。是為七十九。如來右髀。有大 人相。名普現雲。以眾色摩尼。而為莊嚴。其髀 與[2]腨。上下相稱。放摩尼焰。妙法光明。於一 念中。能普示現一切寶王。遊步相海。是為八 十。如來左髀。有大人相。名現一切佛無量相 海雲。一切寶海。隨順安住。以為莊嚴。廣大遊 行。放淨光明。普照眾生。悉使希求無上佛法。 是為八十一。如來右邊。伊尼延鹿王腨。有大 人相。名一切虛空法界雲。光明妙寶。以為莊 嚴。其相圓直。善能遊步。放閻浮金色。清淨 光明。遍照一切諸佛世界。發大音聲。普皆震 動。復現一切諸佛國土。住於虛空。寶焰莊嚴。 無量菩薩。從中化現。是為八十二。如來左邊。 伊尼延鹿王腨。有大人相。名莊嚴海雲。色如 真金。能遍遊行一切佛剎。放一切寶清淨光 明。充滿法界。施作佛事。是為八十三。如來寶 腨上毛。有大人相。名普現法界影像雲。其毛 右旋。
简体字	"如来左臀有大人相,名示现一切法界海光明弥覆虚空云,犹如莲华,清净妙宝以为严饰,放光明网遍照十方一切法界,于中普现种种相云,是为七十九。 "如来右[月+坒]有大人相,名普现云,以众色摩尼而为庄严,其[月+坒]与腨上下相称,放摩尼焰妙法光明,于一念中能普示现一切宝王游步相海,是为八十。 "如来左[月+坒]有大人相,名现一切佛无量相海云,一切宝海随顺安住以为庄严,广大游行,放净光明普照众生,悉使希求无上佛法,是为八十一。 "如来右边伊尼延鹿王腨有大人相,名一切虚空法界云,光明妙宝以为庄严,其相圆直,善能游步,放阎浮金色清净光明,遍照一切诸佛世界,发大音声普皆震动,复现一切诸佛国土,住于虚空宝焰庄严,无量菩萨从中化现,是为八十二。 "如来左边伊尼延鹿王腨有大人相,名庄严海云,色如真金,能遍游行一切佛刹,放一切宝清净光明,充满法界施作佛事,是为八十三。 "如来宝腨上毛有大人相,名普现法界影像云,其毛右旋,

The Tathāgata's left hip has a mark of the great man known as "the cloud that reveals the light of the ocean of the entire Dharma realm and blankets empty space." Adorned with pure and marvelous jewels resembling lotus flowers, it emanates a net of light that everywhere illuminates the ten directions of the entire Dharma realm and everywhere reveals within it the many different kinds of clouds of signs. This is the seventy-ninth.

The Tathāgata's right thigh has a mark of the great man known as "the universally revealing cloud." Adorned with *maṇi* jewels of many different colors, above and below, his thighs and calves are proportionate in size and emanate flaming *maṇi* jewel radiance and the light of the sublime Dharma which, in but a single mind-moment, are able to everywhere reveal all the Jewel Kings'[15] freely roaming in the ocean of signs. This is the eightieth.

The Tathāgata's left thigh has a mark of the great man known as "the cloud that reveals the ocean of the countless signs of all buddhas." Adorned with an ocean of all kinds of jewels that follow along and remain with them in their vast roaming travels, they emanate a pure light that everywhere illuminates beings and causes them all to aspire to seek the unsurpassable Dharma of the Buddha. This is the eighty-first.

The Tathāgata's right calf, resembling that of the *aiṇeya* antelope, has a mark of the great man known as "the cloud of all of empty space and the Dharma realm." Adorned with marvelous radiant jewels and characterized by being round, straight, and well able to stride along in his wandering, it emanates the pure light of *jambūnada* gold that everywhere illuminates the worlds of all buddhas while also sending forth a great sound that everywhere causes a shaking movement. It also reveals the lands of all buddhas abiding in space, adorned with flaming jewel radiance, and it reveals as well the countless bodhisattvas transformationally manifested from within them. This is the eighty-second.

The Tathāgata's left calf, resembling that of the *aiṇeya* antelope, has a mark of the great man known as "the cloud of an ocean of adornments." Having a color like that of real gold, it is able to roam about, traveling everywhere to all the buddha *kṣetras*. It emanates the pure light of all the many kinds of jewels that fills the Dharma realm and performs buddha works. This is the eighty-third.

The hair on the Tathāgata's jewel-adorned calves has a mark of the great man known as "the cloud that everywhere reveals reflected images of the Dharma realm." Those hairs grow in a rightward spiraling direction and the tips of every one of those hairs

正體字	一一毛端。放寶光明。充滿十方一切法界。示現一切諸佛神力。其諸毛孔。悉放光明。一切佛剎。於中顯現。是為八十四。如來足下。有大人相。名一切菩薩海安住雲。色如金剛。閻浮檀金。清淨蓮華。放寶光明。普照十方諸世界海。寶香焰雲。處處周遍。舉足將步。香氣周流。具眾寶色。充滿法界。是為八十五。如來右足上。有大人相。名普照一切光明雲。一切眾寶。以為莊嚴。放大光明。充滿法界。示現一切諸佛菩薩。是為八十六。如來左足上。有大人相。名普現一切諸佛雲。寶藏摩尼。以為莊嚴。放寶光明。於念念中。現一切佛。神通變化。及其法海。所坐道場。盡未來際劫。無有間斷。是為八十七。如來右足指間。有大人相。名光照一切法界海雲。須彌燈摩尼王。千輻焰輪。種種莊嚴。放大光明。充滿十方一切法界。諸世界海。於中普現一切諸佛。所有種種寶莊嚴相。是為八十八。如來左足指間。有大人相。名現一切佛海雲。摩尼寶華。香焰燈鬘。一切寶輪。以為莊嚴。恒放寶海清淨光明。充滿虛空。普及十方一切世界。
简体字	一一毛端放宝光明，充满十方一切法界，示现一切诸佛神力，其诸毛孔悉放光明，一切佛刹于中显现，是为八十四。 　　"如来足下有大人相，名一切菩萨海安住云，色如金刚、阎浮檀金，清净莲华放宝光明，普照十方诸世界海，宝香焰云处处周遍，举足将步，香气周流，具众宝色充满法界，是为八十五。 　　"如来右足上有大人相，名普照一切光明云，一切众宝以为庄严，放大光明充满法界，示现一切诸佛菩萨，是为八十六。 　　"如来左足上有大人相，名普现一切诸佛云，宝藏摩尼以为庄严，放宝光明，于念念中现一切佛神通变化，及其法海所坐道场，尽未来际劫无有间断，是为八十七。 　　"如来右足指间有大人相，名光照一切法界海云，须弥灯摩尼王千辐焰轮种种庄严，放大光明充满十方一切法界诸世界海，于中普现一切诸佛所有种种宝庄严相，是为八十八。 　　"如来左足指间有大人相，名现一切佛海云，摩尼宝华、香焰、灯鬘、一切宝轮以为庄严，恒放宝海清净光明，充满虚空，普及十方一切世界，

emanates the light of jewels which fills the ten directions of the entire Dharma realm, revealing the spiritual powers of all buddhas. Those hair pores all emanate a radiance in which all buddha kṣetras are shown. This is the eighty-fourth.

The bottom of the Tathāgata's feet have a mark of the great man known as "the cloud in which the ocean of all bodhisattvas resides." It has a color like that of vajra, jambūnada gold, and pure lotus flowers and emanates a jewel radiance that everywhere illuminates the ocean of all worlds throughout the ten directions. A cloud of fragrant flaming jewel light spreads about everywhere into place after place. Whenever he raises a foot to begin a step, fragrant mists the colors of the many kinds of jewels flow about everywhere, filling the Dharma realm. This is the eighty-fifth.

The top of the Tathāgata's right foot has a mark of the great man known as "the light cloud that everywhere illuminates everything." Adorned with all of the many kinds of jewels, it emanates a great light that fills the Dharma realm and reveals all the buddhas and bodhisattvas. This is the eighty-sixth.

The top of the Tathāgata's left foot has a mark of the great man known as "the cloud that everywhere reveals all buddhas." Adorned with jewel treasury maṇi jewels, it emanates the light of jewels which in each successive mind-moment reveal all buddhas' spiritual superknowledges and transformations as well as their ocean of Dharma and the sites of enlightenment in which they sit uninterruptedly to the very end of all kalpas of the future. This is the eighty-seventh.

The spaces between the toes of the Tathāgata's right foot have a mark of the great man known as "the cloud that brightly illuminates the ocean of the entire Dharma realm." Adorned in all kinds of different ways with sumeru lamps, sovereign maṇi jewels, and thousand-spoked wheels of flaming radiance, they emanate a great light that fills all the oceans of worlds throughout the ten directions of the entire Dharma realm and everywhere reveal within them all the buddhas as well as all their many different kinds of signs adorned with jewels. This is the eighty-eighth.

The spaces between the toes of the Tathāgata's left foot have a mark of the great man known as "the cloud that reveals the ocean of all buddhas." Adorned with maṇi jewel flowers, fragrantly flaming lamps, garlands, and wheels made of every kind of jewel, they constantly emanate the pure light of an ocean of jewels that fills empty space and everywhere reaches all worlds throughout the ten directions, revealing all the buddhas and bodhisattvas within them as

正體字

於中示現一切
諸佛。及諸菩薩。圓滿音聲。[1]卍字等相。利益
無量一切眾生。是為八十九。如來右足跟。有
大人相。名自在照[*]耀雲。帝青寶末。以為莊
嚴。常放如來。妙寶光明。其光妙好。充滿法界。
皆同一相。無有差別。於中示現一切諸佛。坐
於道場。演說妙法。是為九十。如來左足跟。有
大人相。名示現妙音演說諸法海雲。以變化
海摩尼寶。香焰海須彌華摩尼寶。及毘瑠璃。
而為莊嚴。放大光明。充滿法界。於中普現諸
佛神力。是為九十一。如來右足跌。有大人相。
名示現一切莊嚴光明雲。眾寶所成。極妙莊
嚴。放閻浮檀金色。清淨光明。普照十方一切
法界。其光明相。猶如大雲。普覆一切諸佛道
場。是為九十二。如來左足跌。有大人相。名現
眾色相雲。以一切月焰藏。毘盧遮那寶。因陀
羅尼羅寶。而為莊嚴。念念遊行諸法界海。放
摩尼燈。香焰光明。其光遍滿一切法界。是為
九十三。如來右足四周。有大人相。名普藏雲。
因陀羅尼羅金剛寶。以為莊嚴。放寶光明。充
滿虛空。於中示現一切諸佛坐於道場。摩尼
寶王師子之座。是為九十四。如來左足四周。
有大人相。名光明遍照法界雲。摩尼寶華。以
為莊嚴。

简体字

于中示现一切诸佛及诸菩萨圆满音声、卍字等相,利益无量一切众生,是为八十九。

"如来右足跟有大人相,名自在照耀云,帝青、宝末以为庄严,常放如来妙宝光明,其光妙好充满法界,皆同一相无有差别,于中示现一切诸佛坐于道场演说妙法,是为九十。

"如来左足跟有大人相,名示现妙音演说诸法海云,以变化海摩尼宝、香焰海须弥华摩尼宝及毗琉璃而为庄严,放大光明充满法界,于中普现诸佛神力,是为九十一。

"如来右足跌有大人相,名示现一切庄严光明云,众宝所成,极妙庄严,放阎浮檀金色清净光明,普照十方一切法界,其光明相犹如大云,普覆一切诸佛道场,是为九十二。

"如来左足跌有大人相,名现众色相云,以一切月焰藏毗卢遮那宝、因陀罗尼罗宝而为庄严,念念游行诸法界海,放摩尼灯香焰光明,其光遍满一切法界,是为九十三。

"如来右足四周有大人相,名普藏云,因陀罗尼罗金刚宝以为庄严,放宝光明充满虚空,于中示现一切诸佛坐于道场摩尼宝王师子之座,是为九十四。

"如来左足四周有大人相,名光明遍照法界云,摩尼宝华以为庄严,

well as their perfectly full voices, their *svastika* emblems, and other such signs with which they benefit all the countlessly many beings. This is the eighty-ninth.

The Tathāgata's right heel has a mark of the great man known as "the cloud of freely shining dazzling illumination." Adorned with powdered sapphires, it always emanates the radiance of the Tathāgata's marvelous jewels, the marvelously fine light of which, all of it of the same appearance, free of any differences, fills the Dharma realm and reveals all the buddhas within it seated in their sites of enlightenment, expounding on the sublime Dharma. This is the ninetieth.

The Tathāgata's left heel has a mark of the great man known as "the cloud that reveals the marvelous voice expounding on the ocean of all dharmas." Adorned with ocean-of-transformations *maṇi* jewels, ocean-of-fragrant-flaming-light *sumeru* flower *maṇi* jewels, and *vaiḍūrya*, it emanates a great light that fills the Dharma realm and everywhere reveals within it the spiritual powers of all buddhas. This is the ninety-first.

The Tathāgata's right ankle has a mark of the great man known as "the light cloud that reveals all adornments." Possessed of the most ultimately marvelous adornments made of the many kinds of jewels, it emanates pure light the color of *jambūnada* gold that everywhere illuminates the ten directions of the Dharma realm. The appearance of its radiance is like that of a great cloud that everywhere covers the sites of enlightenment of all buddhas. This is the ninety-second.

The Tathāgata's left ankle has a mark of the great man known as "the cloud that reveals the many forms and appearances." Adorned with *vairocana* jewels and sapphires from the treasury of the shimmering light of all moons, in every mind-moment, it travels through all oceans of the Dharma realm emanating the fragrant flaming light of *maṇi* lamps. Its radiance everywhere fills the entire Dharma realm. This is the ninety-third.

The four-part circumference of the Tathāgata's right foot has a mark of the great man known as "the cloud of the universal treasury." Adorned with sapphire gems, and vajra jewels, it emanates the light of jewels that fills empty space and reveals within it all buddhas sitting in their sites of enlightenment on lion thrones made of sovereign *maṇi* jewels. This is the ninety-fourth.

The four sides of the Tathāgata's left foot have a mark of the great man known as "the cloud whose light everywhere illuminates the Dharma realm." Adorned with *maṇi* jewel flowers, it emanates a

正體字

放大光明。充滿法界。平等一相。於中示現一切諸佛。及諸菩薩。自在神力。以大妙音。演說法界。無盡法門。是為九十五。如來右足指端。有大人相。名示現莊嚴雲。甚可愛樂。閻浮檀清淨真金。以為莊嚴。放大光明。充滿十方一切法界。於中示現一切諸佛。及諸菩薩。無盡法海。種種功德。神通變化。是為九十六。如來左足指端。有大人相。名現一切佛神變雲。不思議佛光明。月焰普香。摩尼寶焰輪。以為莊嚴。放眾寶色。清淨光明。充滿一切。諸世界海。於中示現一切諸佛。及諸菩薩。演說一切諸佛法海。是為九十七。佛子。毘盧遮那如來。有如是等。十華藏世界海微塵數。大人相。一一身分。眾寶妙相。以為莊嚴

简体字

放大光明充满法界平等一相，于中示现一切诸佛及诸菩萨自在神力，以大妙音演说法界无尽法门，是为九十五。

"如来右足指端有大人相，名示现庄严云，甚可爱乐阎浮檀清净真金以为庄严，放大光明充满十方一切法界，于中示现一切诸佛及诸菩萨无尽法海种种功德、神通变化，是为九十六。

"如来左足指端有大人相，名现一切佛神变云，不思议佛光明、月焰普香、摩尼宝焰轮以为庄严，放众宝色清净光明，充满一切诸世界海，于中示现一切诸佛及诸菩萨演说一切诸佛法海，是为九十七。

"佛子，毗卢遮那如来有如是等十华藏世界海微尘数大人相；一一身分，众宝妙相以为庄严。"

great radiance of the same single character that fills the Dharma realm and reveals within it the sovereign spiritual powers of all buddhas and bodhisattvas as well as their use of a loud and sublime voice with which they expound on the endless Dharma gateways of the Dharma realm. This is the ninety-fifth.

The tips of the Tathāgata's right toes have a mark of the great man known as "the cloud that reveals adornments." Adorned with extremely lovely pure *jambūnada* gold, it emanates a great radiance that fills the ten directions of the Dharma realm, revealing within it all buddhas and bodhisattvas, their endless ocean of dharmas, their many different kinds of meritorious qualities, and the transformations produced by their spiritual superknowledges. This is the ninety-sixth.

The tips of the Tathāgata's left toes have a mark of the great man known as "the cloud that reveals the spiritual transformations of all buddhas." Adorned with the inconceivable light of the Buddha, the universally pervasive fragrance of shimmering moonlight, and wheels of flaming *maṇi* jewel radiance, it emanates a pure light the color of the many kinds of jewels that fills all the oceans of worlds, revealing within them all buddhas and bodhisattvas expounding on the ocean of the Dharma of all buddhas. This is the ninety-seventh.

Sons of the Buddha, Vairocana Tathāgata has marks of the great man such as these as numerous as the atoms in ten oceans of worlds such as the Flower Treasury World. Every one of the parts of his body is adorned with marvelous signs made of the many kinds of jewels.

The End of Chapter Thirty-Four

大方廣佛華嚴經如來隨好光明功德品
第三十五

爾時世尊。告寶手菩薩言。佛子。如來應正等覺。有隨好。名圓滿王。此隨好中。出大光明。名為熾盛。七百萬阿僧祇光明。而為眷屬。佛子。我為菩薩時。於兜率天宮。放大光明。名光幢王。照十佛剎微塵數世界。彼世界中。地獄眾生。遇斯光者。眾苦休息。得十種清淨眼。耳鼻舌身意。亦復如是。咸生歡喜。踊躍稱慶。從彼命終。生兜率天。天中有鼓。名甚可愛樂。彼天生已。此鼓發音。而告之言。諸天子。汝以心不放逸。於如來所。種諸[2]善根。往昔親近眾善知識。毘盧遮那。大威神力。於彼命終。來生此天。佛子。菩薩足下千輻輪。名光明普照王。此有隨好。名圓滿王。常放四十種光明。中有一光。名清淨功德。能照億那由他佛剎微塵數世界。隨諸眾生種種業行。種種欲樂。皆令成熟。阿鼻地獄。極苦眾生。遇斯光者。皆悉命終。生兜率天。既生天已。聞天鼓音。而告之言。

如来随好光明功德品第三十五

尔时，世尊告宝手菩萨言："佛子，如来、应、正等觉有随好，名圆满王。此随好中出大光明，名为炽盛，七百万阿僧祇光明而为眷属。佛子，我为菩萨时，于兜率天宫放大光明，名光幢王，照十佛刹微尘数世界。彼世界中地狱众生，遇斯光者，众苦休息，得十种清净眼，耳、鼻、舌、身、意亦复如是，咸生欢喜，踊跃称庆，从彼命终生兜率天。天中有鼓，名甚可爱乐。彼天生已，此鼓发音而告之言：'诸天子，汝以心不放逸，于如来所种诸善根，往昔亲近众善知识。毗卢遮那大威神力，于彼命终来生此天。'

"佛子，菩萨足下千辐轮，名光明普照王。此有随好，名圆满王，常放四十种光明。中有一光，名清净功德，能照亿那由他佛刹微尘数世界，随诸众生种种业行、种种欲乐皆令成熟。阿鼻地狱极苦众生，遇斯光者，皆悉命终生兜率天。既生天已，闻天鼓音而告之言：

Chapter 35
The Qualities of the Light of the Tathāgata's Secondary Signs

At that time, the Bhagavat told Jewel Hand Bodhisattva:

O Son of the Buddha, the Tathāgata, the Arhat, the One of Right and Perfect Enlightenment, has a subsidiary sign known as "the king of perfect fulfillment." From within this subsidiary sign there comes forth a great light known as "flourishing abundance" with a retinue consisting of seven hundred myriads of *asaṃkhyeyas* of light rays.

Son of the Buddha, when I was the bodhisattva abiding in the Tuṣita Heaven Palace, I emanated a great light known as "the king of light banners" that illuminated worlds as numerous as the atoms in ten buddha *kṣetras*. When the beings in the hells associated with those worlds encountered this light, their many sorts of sufferings ceased and they acquired ten kinds of pure eyes. So too did this occur with their ears, noses, tongues, bodies, and minds. They were all filled with joy and danced with celebratory delight. After their lives there came to an end, they were born in the Tuṣita Heaven. In that heaven, there was a drum called "delightful." After they were born in that heaven, this drum emanated a voice which announced to them: "Sons of the Devas, because your minds were not neglectful, because you planted roots of goodness with the Tathāgata, because you drew near to good spiritual guides in the past, and because of the great awesome spiritual powers of Vairocana, when your lives there came to an end, you came to be born in this heaven."

Sons of the Buddha, the thousand-spoked wheel emblem on the bottom of the bodhisattva's feet is known as "the king of universally illuminating light." This has a subsidiary sign known as "the king of perfect fulfillment" which always emanates forty kinds of light among which one of those lights is known as "pure meritorious qualities." It is able to illuminate worlds as numerous as the atoms in a *koṭī* of *nayutas* of buddha *kṣetras* and, adapting to all beings' many different kinds of karmic actions and many different sorts of aspirations, it enables them to become fully ripened. When beings undergoing the most extreme sufferings in the Avīci Hells encounter this light, once they all reach the end of their lives there, they are born in the Tuṣita Heaven. Having been reborn in this heaven, they then hear the sound of the celestial drum telling them: "Good

正體字

善哉善哉。諸天子。毘盧遮那菩薩。入離垢
三昧。汝當敬禮。爾時諸天子。聞天鼓音。如是
勸誨。咸生是念。奇哉希有。何因發此微妙之
音。是時天鼓。告諸天子言。我所發聲。諸善根
力之所成就。諸天子。如我說我。而不著我。不
著我所。一切諸佛。亦復如是。自說是佛。不著
於我。不著我所。諸天子。如我音聲。不從東方
來。不從南西北方四維上下來。業報成佛。亦
復如是。非十方來。諸天子。譬如汝等。昔在地
獄。地獄及身。非十方來。但由於汝顛倒惡業。
愚癡纏縛。生地獄身。此無根本。無有來處。諸
天子。毘盧遮那菩薩。威德力故。放大光明。而
此光明。非十方來。諸天子。我天鼓音。亦復如
是。非十方來。但以三昧善根力故。般若波羅
蜜威德力故。出生如是清淨音聲。示現如是
種種自在。諸天子。譬如須彌山王。有三十三
天。上妙宮殿。種種樂具。而此樂具。非十方
來。我天鼓音。亦復如是。非十方來。

简体字

'善哉！善哉！诸天子，毗卢遮那菩萨入离垢三昧，汝当敬礼。'

"尔时，诸天子闻天鼓音如是劝诲，咸生是念：'奇哉希有！何因发此微妙之音？'是时，天鼓告诸天子言：'我所发声，诸善根力之所成就。诸天子，如我说我，而不著我，不著我所；一切诸佛亦复如是，自说是佛，不著于我，不著我所。诸天子，如我音声不从东方来，不从南西北方、四维上下来；业报成佛亦复如是，非十方来。诸天子，譬如汝等昔在地狱，地狱及身非十方来，但由于汝颠倒恶业愚痴缠缚，生地狱身，此无根本、无有来处。诸天子，毗卢遮那菩萨威德力故放大光明，而此光明非十方来。诸天子，我天鼓音亦复如是，非十方来，但以三昧善根力故，般若波罗蜜威德力故，出生如是清净音声，示现如是种种自在。诸天子，譬如须弥山王有三十三天上妙宫殿种种乐具，而此乐具非十方来；我天鼓音亦复如是，非十方来。

Chapter 35 – The Qualities of the Light of the Tathāgata's Secondary Signs

indeed. Good indeed. Sons of the Devas, Vairocana Bodhisattva has entered the stainless samādhi. You should go and bow in reverence to him."

At that time, having heard this sound from the celestial drum encouraging and instructing them in this way, those devas' sons all have this thought: "How strange and rare! Why does it emanate this sublime sound?"

At this time, that celestial drum tells these devas' sons:

This sound that I have sent forth is produced by the power of all sorts of roots of goodness. Sons of the Devas, just as when I refer to "I," it is done without attaching to any self and without attaching to anything belonging to a self, so too it is with all buddhas, for when they refer to themselves as buddhas, this is done without any attachment to the existence of any self and without any attachment to anything belonging to a self.

Sons of the Devas, just as the sound that I emanate does not come from the east and does not come from the southerly, westerly, or northerly directions, the four midpoints, the zenith, or the nadir, so too it is with the karmic reward of realizing buddhahood, for it, too, does not come from any of the ten directions.

Sons of the Devas, this is just as when you previously dwelt in the hells, those hells as well as those bodies of yours did not come from any of the ten directions, but rather came from your own evil karmic deeds arising from inverted views and entangling bonds of delusion which caused rebirth into hell-realm bodies. These [hell-realm bodies] had no [other] originating basis and had no place from which they came.

Sons of the Devas, it is due to the power of Vairocana Bodhisattva's awesome virtue that he emanates great light even as this light does not come forth from any of the ten directions. Sons of the Devas, so too it is with the sound of my celestial drum. It does not come forth from any of the ten directions. It is only because of the power of roots of goodness associated with samādhi and because of the power of awesome virtue associated with the *prajñāpāramitā* that it emanates a pure sound such as this and manifests different sorts of sovereign powers such as these.

Sons of the Devas, this is just as in the case of the many different kinds of pleasing things within the supremely marvelous palace of the Trāyastriṃśa Heaven on Sumeru, king of the mountains. These pleasing things that are present there did not come there from any of the ten directions. So too it is with the sound of my celestial drum which is also not something that has come here from any of the ten directions.

諸天子。
譬如億那由他佛剎微塵數世界。盡末為塵。
我為如是塵數眾生。隨其所樂。而演說法。令
大歡喜。然我於彼。不生疲厭。不生退怯。不生
憍慢。不生放逸。諸天子。毘盧遮那菩薩。住離
垢三昧。亦復如是。於右手掌。一隨好中。放一
光明。出現無量。自在神力。一切聲聞。辟支
佛。尚不能知。況諸眾生。諸天子。汝當往詣彼
菩薩所。親近供養。勿復貪著五欲樂具。著五
欲樂。障諸善根。諸天子。譬如劫火。燒須彌
山。悉令除盡。無餘可得。貪欲纏心。亦復如
是。終不能生念佛之意。諸天子。汝等應當知
恩報恩。諸天子。其有眾生。不知報恩。多遭橫
死。生於地獄。諸天子。汝等昔在地獄之中。蒙
光照身。捨彼生此。汝等今者。宜疾迴向。增
長善根。諸天子。如我天鼓。非男非女。而能出
生無量無邊不思議事。汝天子天女。亦復如
是。非男非女。而能受用種種上妙。宮殿園林。
如我天鼓。不生不滅。色受想行識。亦復如是。
不生不滅。汝等若能於此悟解。應知則入無
依印三昧。

诸天子，譬如亿那由他佛刹微尘数世界尽末为尘，我为如是尘数众生，随其所乐而演说法，令大欢喜，然我于彼不生疲厌、不生退怯、不生憍慢、不生放逸。诸天子，毗卢遮那菩萨住离垢三昧亦复如是，于右手掌一随好中放一光明，出现无量自在神力，一切声闻、辟支佛尚不能知，况诸众生！诸天子，汝当往诣彼菩萨所亲近供养，勿复贪著五欲乐具，著五欲乐障诸善根。诸天子，譬如劫火烧须弥山，悉令除尽，无余可得；贪欲缠心亦复如是，终不能生念佛之意。诸天子，汝等应当知恩报恩。诸天子，其有众生不知报恩，多遭横死，生于地狱。诸天子，汝等昔在地狱之中，蒙光照身，舍彼生此；汝等今者宜疾回向，增长善根。诸天子，如我天鼓，非男非女，而能出生无量无边不思议事；汝天子、天女亦复如是，非男非女，而能受用种种上妙宫殿园林。如我天鼓不生不灭，色、受、想、行、识亦复如是不生不灭。汝等若能于此悟解，应知则入无依印三昧。'

Chapter 35 — The Qualities of the Light of the Tathāgata's Secondary Signs

Sons of the Devas, this is just as when, as I expound on the Dharma for beings as numerous as the atoms that would result from grinding to atoms a *koṭī* of *nayutas* of buddha *kṣetras*, speaking to them in accordance with what pleases them and thereby causing them to experience great joyous delight, doing so without growing weary, without shrinking from this, without becoming arrogant, and without becoming neglectful. So too it was, Sons of the Devas, with Vairocana Bodhisattva as he dwelt in the samādhi of stainless purity and, from a single subsidiary sign in his right palm, emanated a single ray of light that manifested countless sovereign spiritual powers which not even any *śrāvaka*-disciple or *pratyekabuddha* could ever know of, how much the less any other type of being.

Sons of the Devas, you should go to see that bodhisattva and draw near to him and make offerings to him. Do not indulge in any further desire-based attachment to any of the pleasurable objects of the five desires. Attachment to the pleasures of the five desires is an obstacle to the development of all roots of goodness. Sons of the Devas, just as the fires at the end of the kalpa burn up even Mount Sumeru, causing it to entirely disappear, leaving no residue that one can find, so too it is with the mind entangled in desire, for it prevents one from ever being able to bring forth any intention to abide in mindfulness of the Buddha.

Sons of the Devas, you should all know to recognize kindnesses and repay kindness. Sons of the Devas, wherever there are beings who do not know to repay kindnesses, they are more likely to meet an untimely death and be reborn in the hells. Sons of the Devas, you were all previously abiding in the hell realms, but then were able to encounter that light that illuminated your bodies, allowing you to relinquish that circumstance and take rebirth here. It would only be fitting if you were to now swiftly perform dedications to increase your roots of goodness.

Sons of the Devas, just as I, as a celestial drum, am neither male nor female, and yet I am able to bring forth countlessly and boundlessly many inconceivable phenomena, so too it is with you devas' sons and devas' daughters, for you are neither male nor female, and yet you are still able to enjoy the use of all sorts of different supremely marvelous palaces, parks, and groves. Just as my celestial drum is neither produced nor destroyed, so too it is with forms, feelings, perceptions, karmic formative factors, and consciousness, for they too are neither produced nor destroyed. If you are all able to awaken to and understand this, you should realize that you can then enter the samādhi with the seal of independence.

正體字

時諸天子。聞是音已。得未曾有。即皆化作一萬華雲。一萬香雲。一萬音樂雲。一萬幢雲。一萬蓋雲。一萬歌讚雲。作是化已。即共往詣毘盧遮那菩薩。所住宮殿。合掌恭敬。於一面立。欲申瞻覲。而不得見。時有天子。作如是言。毘盧遮那菩薩。已從此沒。生於人間。淨飯王家。乘栴檀樓閣。處摩耶夫人胎。時諸天子。以天眼。觀見菩薩身。處在人間淨飯王家。梵天欲天。承事供養。諸天子眾。咸作是念。我等若不往菩薩所問訊起居。乃至一念。於此天宮。而生愛著。則為不可。時一一天子。與十那由他眷屬。欲下閻浮提。時天鼓中。出聲告言。諸天子。菩薩摩訶薩。非此命終。而生彼間。但以神通。隨諸眾生心之所宜。令其得見。諸天子。如我今者。非眼所見。而能出聲。菩薩摩訶薩。入離垢三昧。亦復如是。非眼所見。而能處處。示現受生。離分別。除憍慢。無染著。諸天子。汝等應發阿耨多羅三藐三菩提心。淨治其意。住善威儀。悔除一切業障煩惱障。報障

简体字

"时,诸天子闻是音已,得未曾有,即皆化作一万华云、一万香云、一万音乐云、一万幢云、一万盖云、一万歌赞云;作是化已,即共往诣毗卢遮那菩萨所住宫殿,合掌恭敬,于一面立,欲申瞻觐而不得见。时,有天子作如是言:'毗卢遮那菩萨已从此没,生于人间净饭王家,乘栴檀楼阁,处摩耶夫人胎。'时,诸天子以天眼观见菩萨身,处在人间净饭王家,梵天、欲天承事供养。诸天子众咸作是念:'我等若不往菩萨所问讯起居,乃至一念于此天宫而生爱著,则为不可。'时,一一天子与十那由他眷属欲下阎浮提。时,天鼓中出声告言:'诸天子,菩萨摩诃萨非此命终而生彼间,但以神通,随诸众生心之所宜,令其得见。诸天子,如我今者,非眼所见,而能出声;菩萨摩诃萨入离垢三昧亦复如是,非眼所见,而能处处示现受生,离分别,除憍慢,无染著。诸天子,汝等应发阿耨多罗三藐三菩提心,净治其意,住善威仪,悔除一切业障、烦恼障、报障、

Having heard these sounds, those devas' sons attained what was unprecedented for them, whereupon they all transformationally created a myriad flower clouds, a myriad incense clouds, a myriad music clouds, a myriad banner clouds, a myriad canopy clouds, and a myriad clouds of singing praises, and, having transformationally created these, they all went together to the palace in which Vairocana Bodhisattva dwelt, and, having pressed their palms together respectfully, they stood off to one side wishing thus to be granted an audience with him. However they remained unable to see him. At that time, there was a devas' son who said, "Vairocana Bodhisattva has already disappeared from this place and descended to take rebirth among humans in the household of the Pure Rice King in which, residing within a sandalwood tower, he now abides in the womb of Lady Māyā."

At that time, those devas' sons used their heavenly eyes to see the body of that bodhisattva abiding in the human realm in the household of the Pure Rice King where he was being served and given offerings by the Brahma heaven devas and desire realm devas. That congregation of devas' sons then all had this thought, "So long as we have not gone to see the Bodhisattva and pay our respects, if we were to remain here and indulge so much as an instant of fond attachment for this heavenly palace, then that would be unacceptable."

At that time, every one of those devas' sons wished to descend to Jambudvīpa together with their retinues consisting of ten *nayutas* of retainers. The celestial drum then emanated a voice which told them:

> Sons of the Devas, it is not the case that this bodhisattva-mahāsattva reached the end of his life here and then took rebirth in that place. Rather, it is solely because of his spiritual superknowledges that, adapting to what is appropriate for the minds of beings, he has caused them to see this.
>
> Sons of the Devas, just as, even though I am now invisible, I am still able to emanate this voice, so too it is with the bodhisattva-mahāsattva who has entered the samādhi of stainless purity. Even though he is invisible, he is still able to manifest taking birth in place after place, having abandoned all discriminations, having done away with arrogance, and having become free of any defiled attachments.
>
> Sons of the Devas, you should all bring forth the resolve to attain *anuttara-samyak-saṃbodhi*, purify your minds, abide in the fine awesome deportment, repent of and rid yourselves of all karmic obstacles, all affliction obstacles, all retribution obstacles, and

正體字

見障。以盡法界。眾生數等身。以盡法界。眾生數等頭。以盡法界。眾生數等舌。以盡法界。眾生數等。善身業。善語業。善意業。悔除所有諸障過惡。時諸天子。聞是語已。得未曾有。心大歡喜。而問之言。菩薩摩訶薩。云何悔除一切過惡。爾時天鼓。以菩薩三昧善根力故。發聲告言。諸天子。菩薩。知諸業不從東方來。不從南西北方四維上下來。而共積集。止住於心。但從顛倒生。無有住處。菩薩如是。決定明見。無有疑惑。諸天子。如我天鼓。說業說報。說行說戒。說喜說安。說諸三昧。諸佛菩薩。亦復如是。說我說我所。說眾生說貪恚癡。種種諸業。而實無我。無有我所。諸所作業。六趣果報。十方推求。悉不可得。諸天子。譬如我聲。不生不滅。造惡諸天。不聞餘聲。唯聞以地獄覺悟之聲。一切諸業。亦復如是。非生非滅。隨有修集。則受其報。

简体字

见障；以尽法界众生数等身，以尽法界众生数等头，以尽法界众生数等舌，以尽法界众生数等善身业、善语业、善意业，悔除所有诸障过恶。'

"时，诸天子闻是语已，得未曾有，心大欢喜而问之言：'菩萨摩诃萨云何悔除一切过恶？'尔时，天鼓以菩萨三昧善根力故，发声告言：'诸天子，菩萨知诸业不从东方来，不从南西北方、四维上下来，而共积集，止住于心；但从颠倒生，无有住处。菩萨如是决定明见，无有疑惑。诸天子，如我天鼓，说业、说报、说行、说戒、说喜、说安、说诸三昧；诸佛菩萨亦复如是，说我、说我所、说众生、说贪恚痴种种诸业，而实无我、无有我所。诸所作业、六趣果报，十方推求悉不可得。诸天子，譬如我声，不生不灭，造恶诸天不闻余声，唯闻以地狱觉悟之声；一切诸业亦复如是，非生非灭，随有修集则受其报。

Chapter 35 — The Qualities of the Light of the Tathāgata's Secondary Signs

all obstacles arising from views. Using bodies as numerous as all beings throughout the Dharma realm, using heads as numerous as all beings throughout the Dharma realm, using tongues as numerous as all beings throughout the Dharma realm, and using good physical actions, good verbal actions, and good mental actions as numerous as all beings throughout the Dharma realm, you should repent of and rid yourselves of all obstacles and faults.

At that time, having heard these words, all those devas' sons experienced what was unprecedented for them. With minds filled with great joyous delight, they then asked [the celestial drum], "How then is it that the bodhisattva-mahāsattva repents of and rids himself of all faults?"

At that time, relying on the power of the bodhisattva's samādhi and roots of goodness, that celestial drum emanated a voice with which he told them:

Sons of the Devas, the bodhisattva realizes that karma does not come from the east and does not come from the south, the west, the north, the four midpoints, the zenith, or the nadir, and yet it all joins in accumulating and remaining in the mind. It arises solely from the inverted views and it has no place in which it dwells. It is in this way that the bodhisattva has a definite and clear perception of this which is free of any doubts.

Sons of the Devas, just as I, as a celestial drum, speak of karmic deeds, speak of karmic retributions, speak of actions, speak of the moral precepts, speak of joyousness, speak of peace, and speak of the samādhis, in this same way, the buddhas and bodhisattvas speak of a self, speak of possessions of a self, speak of beings, and speak of greed, hatred, delusion, and the many different kinds of karmic deeds, doing so even as, in truth, there is no self nor are there any possessions of a self and all karmic deeds that are done as well as the karmic rewards and retributions in the six destinies of rebirth are all such that, even if one were to search for them throughout the ten directions, none of them would be apprehensible.

Sons of the Devas, just as my voice is neither produced nor destroyed, and yet those devas who have done evil deeds will still hear no other sounds, but rather will only hear this sound that awakens them to the prospect of the hells, so too it is with all karmic deeds, for, even though they are neither produced nor destroyed, they still correspond to whatever one has cultivated and accumulated and hence they then result in experiencing their corresponding retributions.

正體字

諸天子。如我天鼓所出音聲。於無量劫。不可窮盡。無有間斷。若來若去。皆不可得。諸天子。若有去來。則有斷常。一切諸佛。終不演說有斷常法。除為方便。成熟眾生。諸天子。譬如我聲。於無量世界。隨眾生心。皆使得聞。一切諸佛。亦復如是。隨眾生心。悉令得見。諸天子。如有[1]玻瓈鏡。名為能照。清淨鑒徹。與十世界。其量正等。無量無邊諸國土中。一切山川。一切眾生。乃至地獄。畜生餓鬼。所有影像。皆於中現。諸天子。於汝意云何。彼諸影像。可得說言來入鏡中。從鏡去不。答言不也。諸天子。一切諸業。亦復如是。雖能出生諸[2]業果報。無來去處。諸天子。譬如幻師。幻惑人眼。當知諸業。亦復如是。若如是知。是真實懺悔。一切罪惡悉得清淨。說此法時。百千億那由他佛剎微塵數世界中。兜率陀諸天子。得無生法忍。無量不思議阿僧祇六欲諸天子。發阿耨多羅三藐三菩提心。六欲天中。一切天女。皆捨女身。發於無上菩提之意。爾時諸天子。聞說普賢廣大迴向。得十地故。獲諸力莊嚴三昧故。以眾生數等清淨三業。悔除一切諸重障故。

简体字

诸天子，如我天鼓所出音声，于无量劫不可穷尽、无有间断，若来若去皆不可得。诸天子，若有去来则有断常，一切诸佛终不演说有断常法，除为方便成熟众生。诸天子，譬如我声，于无量世界，随众生心皆使得闻；一切诸佛亦复如是，随众生心悉令得见。诸天子，如有颇梨镜，名为能照，清净鉴彻，与十世界其量正等；无量无边诸国土中，一切山川、一切众生，乃至地狱、畜生、饿鬼，所有影像皆于中现。诸天子，于汝意云何？彼诸影像可得说言来入镜中、从镜去不？'答言：'不也。''诸天子，一切诸业亦复如是，虽能出生诸业果报，无来去处。诸天子，譬如幻师幻惑人眼，当知诸业亦复如是。若如是知，是真实忏悔，一切罪恶悉得清净。'

"说此法时，百千亿那由他佛刹微尘数世界中兜率陀诸天子，得无生法忍；无量不思议阿僧祇六欲诸天子，发阿耨多罗三藐三菩提心；六欲天中一切天女，皆舍女身，发于无上菩提之意。尔时，诸天子闻说普贤广大回向，得十地故，获诸力庄严三昧故，以众生数等清净三业悔除一切诸重障故，

Chapter 35 — *The Qualities of the Light of the Tathāgata's Secondary Signs*

Sons of the Devas, sounds such as those emanating from my celestial drum, even in countless kalpas, can never come to an end and remain uninterrupted, even as, whether it be their coming or going, none of them are apprehensible at all. Sons of the Devas, if they were to have any coming or going, then that would involve either nihilism or eternalism. All buddhas never speak of the existence of any dharma of nihilism or eternalism except as an expedient to assist the ripening of beings.

Sons of the Devas, just as this sound of mine adapts to the minds of beings in countless worlds and enables them all, as fitting, to be able to hear it, so too it is with all buddhas who, adapting to the minds of beings, thereby enable them all to succeed in seeing them.

Sons of the Devas, it is as if there were a crystal mirror known as "able to illuminate" that, immaculately clean and possessed of penetrating clarity in its reflections, was precisely equal in size to ten worlds and was such that the reflections of all the countlessly and boundlessly many lands with all their mountains, rivers, and beings, and even their hells, animals, and hungry ghosts were all revealed there within it. Sons of the Devas, what do you think? Can one or can one not say of those reflected images that they come and enter the mirror and then depart from the mirror?

They replied, "No, one could not."

Sons of the Devas, so too it is with all karmic deeds. Although they are able to produce all kinds of karmic rewards and retributions, they have no place from whence they come and no place to which they go. Sons of the Devas, it is as if there were a master conjurer who used illusions to deceive people's vision. One should realize that all karmic deeds are just the same as this. If one knows them in this way, then this constitutes [the means of] genuine repentance by which all the evils of one's karmic offenses can be purified.

When he taught this Dharma, a number of Tuṣita Heaven devas' sons equal to the atoms in a hundred thousand *koṭīs* of *nayutas* of buddha kṣetras gained the unproduced-dharmas patience, incalculably and inconceivably many *asaṃkhyeyas* of Six Desire Heaven devas' sons resolved to attain *anuttara-samyak-saṃbodhi*, and all the female devas in the six desire heavens relinquished the female body and resolved to attain unsurpassed bodhi.

At that time, due to having reached the ten grounds by hearing the teaching of Samantabhadra's vast dedications, due to acquiring samādhis adorned with powers, and due to repenting and ridding themselves of all their heavy karmic obstacles by engaging in the three kinds of pure karmic actions as numerous as all beings, all those

正體字

```
257a08‖ 即見百千億那由他佛剎微塵數。七寶蓮華。
257a09‖ 一一華上。皆有菩薩。結[*]跏趺坐。放大光明。
257a10‖ 彼諸菩薩。一一隨好。放眾生數等光明。彼光
257a11‖ 明中。有眾生數等諸佛。結[*]跏趺坐。隨眾生
257a12‖ 心。而為說法。而猶未現離垢三昧少分之力
257a13‖ 爾時彼諸天子。以上眾華。復於身上。一一毛
257a14‖ 孔。化作眾生數等眾妙華雲。供養毘盧遮那
257a15‖ 如來。持以散佛。一切皆於佛身上住。其諸香
257a16‖ 雲。普雨無量佛剎。微塵數世界。若有眾生。身
257a17‖ 蒙香者。其身安樂。譬如比丘。入第四禪。一切
257a18‖ 業障。皆得[1]銷滅。若有聞者。彼諸眾生於色
257a19‖ 聲香味觸。其內具有五百煩惱。其外亦有五
257a20‖ 百煩惱。貪行多者。二萬一千。瞋行多者。二萬
257a21‖ 一千。癡行多者。二萬一千。等分行者。二萬一
257a22‖ 千。了知如是悉是虛妄。如是知已。成就香幢
257a23‖ 雲。自在光明。清淨善根。若有眾生。見其蓋者。
257a24‖ 種一清淨金網轉輪王一恒河沙善根。佛子。
257a25‖ 菩薩住此轉輪王位。於百千億那由他佛剎
257a26‖ 微塵數世界中。教化眾生。
```

简体字

即见百千亿那由他佛刹微尘数七宝莲华;一一华上皆有菩萨结跏趺坐,放大光明;彼诸菩萨一一随好,放众生数等光明;彼光明中,有众生数等诸佛结跏趺坐,随众生心而为说法,而犹未现离垢三昧少分之力。

"尔时,彼诸天子以上众华,复于身上一一毛孔化作众生数等众妙华云,供养毗卢遮那如来,持以散佛,一切皆于佛身上住。其诸香云,普雨无量佛刹微尘数世界。若有众生身蒙香者,其身安乐,譬如比丘入第四禅,一切业障皆得消灭。若有闻者,彼诸众生于色、声、香、味、触,其内具有五百烦恼,其外亦有五百烦恼,贪行多者二万一千,瞋行多者二万一千,痴行多者二万一千,等分行者二万一千,了知如是悉是虚妄。如是知已,成就香幢云自在光明清净善根。若有众生见其盖者,种一清净金网转轮王一恒河沙善根。

"佛子,菩萨住此转轮王位,于百千亿那由他佛刹微尘数世界中教化众生。

devas immediately saw seven-jeweled lotus flowers as numerous as the atoms in a hundred thousand *koṭīs* of *nayutas* of buddha *kṣetras*. Atop every one of those flowers, there was a bodhisattva seated in the lotus posture emanating a great light. Every one of the subsidiary signs of those bodhisattvas emanated light rays as numerous as all beings and, within those light rays, there were buddhas as numerous as all beings who were seated in the lotus posture, speaking the Dharma for beings in ways adapted to the minds of those beings, and yet they still had not yet manifested even a small amount of the powers of the samādhi of stainless purity.

At that time, issuing from every one of their hair pores, those devas' sons also transformationally created clouds of many different kinds of supremely fine flowers as numerous as beings which they then presented as offerings to Vairocana Tathāgata, doing so by taking them up and scattering them down over the Buddha, where all those flowers then remained suspended in the air above the Buddha's body. All their clouds of fragrance then everywhere rained down their fragrances across a number of worlds as numerous as the atoms in countless buddha *kṣetras*. Wherever any being's body received this fragrance, his body felt peace and happiness comparable to that of a bhikshu who, on entering the fourth *dhyāna*, then experiences the complete melting away of all of his karmic obstacles.

As for all those who heard this teaching, each of those beings possessed five hundred inwardly related afflictions and five hundred outwardly related afflictions related to their forms, sounds, smells, tastes and touchables. In the case of those more extensively coursing in desire, they had twenty-one thousand. In the case of those more extensively coursing in hatred, they had twenty-one thousand. In the case of those more extensively coursing in delusion, they had twenty-one thousand. In the case of those coursing equally in all of them, they also had twenty-one thousand. Whenever any of these beings smelled this fragrance, they completely realized the inherent unreality of all of these. Once they realized this in this way, they then created fragrance banner clouds and spontaneously radiant pure roots of goodness. Whenever any beings saw their canopy clouds, they thereby planted roots of goodness equal to those of pure gold net wheel-turning kings as numerous as the sands in the Ganges River.

> Sons of the Buddha, when a bodhisattva dwells in the position of this wheel-turning king, he teaches being in worlds as numerous as the atoms in a hundred thousand *koṭīs* of *nayutas* of buddha *kṣetras*.

正體字

佛子。譬如明鏡世界月智如來。常有無量諸世界中。比丘比丘尼。優婆塞優婆夷等。化現其身。而來聽法。廣為演說本生之事。未曾一念。而有間斷。若有眾生。聞其佛名。必得往生彼佛國土。菩薩安住清淨金網轉輪王位。亦復如是。若有暫得遇其光明。必獲菩薩第十地位。以先修行善根力故。佛子。如得初禪。雖未命終。見梵天處所有宮殿。而得受於梵世安樂。得諸禪者。悉亦如是。菩薩摩訶薩。住清淨金網轉輪王位。放摩尼髻。清淨光明。若有眾生。遇斯光者。皆得菩薩第十地位。成就無量智慧光明。得十種清淨眼。乃至十種清淨意。具足無量甚深三昧。成就如是清淨肉眼。佛子。假使有人。以億那由他佛剎。碎為微塵。一塵一剎。復以爾許微塵數佛剎。碎為微塵。如是微塵。悉置左手。持以東行。過爾[2]諸微塵數世界。乃下一塵。如是東行。盡此微塵。

简体字

佛子，譬如明镜世界月智如来，常有无量诸世界中比丘、比丘尼、优婆塞、优婆夷等化现其身而来听法，广为演说本生之事，未曾一念而有间断。若有众生闻其佛名，必得往生彼佛国土；菩萨安住清净金网转轮王位亦复如是，若有暂得遇其光明，必获菩萨第十地位，以先修行善根力故。佛子，如得初禅，虽未命终，见梵天处所有宫殿而得受于梵世安乐；得诸禅者悉亦如是。菩萨摩诃萨住清净金网转轮王位，放摩尼髻清净光明；若有众生遇斯光者，皆得菩萨第十地位，成就无量智慧光明，得十种清净眼，乃至十种清净意，具足无量甚深三昧，成就如是清净肉眼。

"佛子，假使有人以亿那由他佛刹碎为微尘，一尘一刹复以尔许微尘数佛刹碎为微尘，如是微尘悉置左手持以东行，过尔许微尘数世界乃下一尘，如是东行尽此微尘，

Chapter 35 — The Qualities of the Light of the Tathāgata's Secondary Signs

Sons of the Buddha, this circumstance is analogous to that of Lunar Wisdom Tathāgata in the Bright Mirror World who always has bhikshus, bhikshunis, *upāsakas, upāsikās*, and others from countless other worlds who transformationally manifest bodies in his presence, thereby coming to listen to his expounding on the Dharma, whereupon he then extensively discourses for their benefit on the events of his former lifetimes, never having so much as a single mind-moment in which his teaching is interrupted. In any instance where there is a being who so much as hears this buddha's name, he most certainly will then succeed in being reborn in that buddha's land.

So too it is in the case of a bodhisattva who comes to abide in the position of a pure gold net wheel-turning king. If one only briefly encounters a ray of his light, one thereby definitely becomes bound to attain the position of a bodhisattva on the tenth bodhisattva ground due to the power of having previously cultivated roots of goodness.

Sons of the Buddha, this is just as when one reaches the first *dhyāna*, even though one has not come to the end of this lifetime, he still sees all the palaces where the Brahma Heaven devas dwell and becomes able to enjoy the happiness of those who dwell in the Brahma World. When one reaches the other *dhyānas*, one's experiences are all of this same sort.

The bodhisattva-mahāsattva who abides in the position of a pure gold net wheel-turning king emanates pure light from his *maṇi* jewel topknot. If there are any beings who encounter this light, they all become bound to reach the station of the tenth bodhisattva ground, to completely develop the light of measureless wisdom, to acquire the ten kinds of pure eye faculty, and so forth, including their becoming bound to acquire the ten kinds of pure mind faculty, bound to completely fulfill countless extremely deep samādhis, and bound to perfect a pure fleshly eye of this same kind.

Sons of the Buddha, suppose that there was a person who ground into atoms a *koṭī* of *nayutas* of buddha *kṣetras* and then also ground to atoms yet another buddha *kṣetra* for each one of those resulting atoms and then took all of those atoms, placed them in his left hand, and then set out in an easterly direction, whereupon, only after passing beyond just such a number of worlds as all of those atoms would he then and only then set down a single one of those atoms, continuing to travel farther on to the east to the point where he finally used up all of these atoms, after which he then did this very same thing as he traveled off to the south, the west, the north,

正體字

南西北方四維上下。
亦復如是。如是十方所有世界。若著微塵。及不著者。悉以集成一佛國土。寶手。於汝意云何。如是佛土。廣大無量可思議不。答曰不也。如是佛土。廣大無量。希有奇特。不可思議。若有眾生。聞此譬[3]諭。能生信解。當知更為希有奇特。佛言寶手。如是如是。如汝所說。若有善男子善女人。聞此譬[*]諭。而生信者。我授彼記。決定當成阿耨多羅三藐三菩提。當獲如來無上智慧。寶手設復有人。以千億佛剎微塵數。如上所說。廣大佛土。末為微塵。以此微塵。依前譬[*]諭。一一下盡。乃至集成一佛國土。復末為塵。如是次第。展轉乃至經八十返。如是一切廣大佛土。所有微塵。菩薩業報。清淨肉眼。於一念中。悉能明見。亦見百億廣大佛剎微塵數佛。如[*]玻瓈鏡清淨光明。照十佛剎微塵數世界。寶手如是。皆是清淨金網轉輪王。甚深三昧福德善根之所成就

简体字

南西北方、四维上下亦复如是；如是十方所有世界若著微尘及不著者，悉以集成一佛国土。宝手，于汝意云何？如是佛土广大无量可思议不？"

答曰："不也！如是佛土广大无量，希有奇特，不可思议。若有众生闻此譬喻能生信解，当知更为希有奇特。"

佛言："宝手，如是，如是！如汝所说！若有善男子、善女人闻此譬喻而生信者，我授彼记，决定当成阿耨多罗三藐三菩提，当获如来无上智慧。宝手，设复有人以千亿佛刹微尘数如上所说广大佛土末为微尘，以此微尘依前譬喻一一下尽，乃至集成一佛国土，复末为尘，如是次第展转乃至经八十反；如是一切广大佛土所有微尘，菩萨业报清净肉眼于一念中悉能明见，亦见百亿广大佛刹微尘数佛，如颇梨镜清净光明，照十佛刹微尘数世界。宝手，如是皆是清净金网转轮王甚深三昧福德善根之所成就。"

the four midpoints, the zenith, and the nadir. Suppose then that one formed together into one single buddha land all those worlds of the ten directions that he had thereby passed, whether or not they were worlds in which he had set down one of those atoms. Jewel Hand, what do you think? Would the measureless vastness of a buddha land such as this be conceivable, or not?

He replied, "No, it would not be. A buddha land such as this would be so measurelessly vast, rare, and especially extraordinary as to be completely inconceivable. If there were to be any being at all who might hear this analogy and be able to develop resolute faith it, one should realize that they themselves would be even more rare and especially extraordinary than this."

The Buddha then said to Jewel Hand:

So it is. So it is. It is precisely as you say. If there were any son or daughter of good family who, hearing this analogy, was then able to believe in it, I would transmit to them their prediction prophesying that they would definitely be bound to realize *anuttara-samyaksaṃbodhi* and they would definitely be bound to realize the unsurpassable wisdom of the Tathāgata.

Jewel Hand, suppose that there was a person who ground to atoms a number of such vast buddha lands as this which were as numerous as the atoms in a thousand *koṭīs* of buddha *kṣetras* and, in accordance with this previously described analogy, he then took these atoms and set every one of them down until they were all gone, and so forth until we come once again to his putting so very many worlds together to form a single buddha world which he then yet again ground to atoms, continuing on sequentially in this way until he had passed through eighty such repeating cycles in this manner. The bodhisattva with the pure fleshly eye acquired as a karmic reward is able in but a single mind-moment to clearly see all the atoms resulting from grinding up all these vast buddha lands. He is also able to see a number of buddhas equal to the atoms contained in a hundred *koṭīs* of such vast buddha *kṣetras*, seeing them just as clearly as when that crystal mirror with its immaculate radiance illuminates a number of worlds equal to the atoms contained in ten buddha *kṣetras*.

Jewel Hand, all circumstances such as these are brought to perfect development through the extremely deep samādhi, merit, and roots of goodness of a pure gold net wheel-turning king.

The End of Chapter Thirty-Five

正體字

| 257c06 | [4]大方廣佛華嚴經卷第四十九
| 257c09 | 　　普賢行品第三十六
| 257c10 | 爾時普賢菩薩摩訶薩。復告諸菩薩大眾言。
| 257c11 | 佛子。如向所演。此但隨眾生根器所宜。略說
| 257c12 | 如來少分境界。何以故。諸佛世尊。為諸眾生。
| 257c13 | 無智作惡。計我我所。執著於身。顛倒疑惑。邪
| 257c14 | 見分別。與諸結縛。恒共相應。隨生死流。遠如
| 257c15 | 來道故。出興[6]于世。佛子。我不見一法為大過
| 257c16 | 失。如諸菩薩。於他菩薩。起瞋心者。何以故。
| 257c17 | 佛子。若諸菩薩。於餘菩薩。起瞋恚心。即成
| 257c18 | 就百萬障門故。何等為百萬障。所謂不見菩
| 257c19 | 提障。不聞正法障。生不淨世界障。生諸惡趣
| 257c20 | 障。生諸難處障。多諸疾病障。多被謗毀障。生
| 257c21 | 頑鈍諸趣障。

简体字

大方广佛华严经卷第四十九
普贤行品第三十六
　　尔时，普贤菩萨摩诃萨复告诸菩萨大众言："佛子，如向所演，此但随众生根器所宜，略说如来少分境界。何以故？诸佛世尊，为诸众生，无智作恶，计我、我所，执著于身，颠倒疑惑，邪见分别，与诸结缚恒共相应，随生死流远如来道故，出兴于世。佛子，我不见一法为大过失，如诸菩萨于他菩萨起瞋心者。何以故？佛子，若诸菩萨于余菩萨起瞋恚心，即成就百万障门故。何等为百万障？所谓：不见菩提障；不闻正法障；生不净世界障；生诸恶趣障；生诸难处障；多诸疾病障；多被谤毁障；生顽钝诸趣障；

Chapter 36
The Practices of Samantabhadra

At that time, Samantabhadra Bodhisattva-mahāsattva again addressed that immense congregation of bodhisattvas, saying:

Sons of the Buddha, as for the preceding proclamation, it represents only a general explanation of a small part of the Tathāgata's domain of objective experience that has been adapted as fitting to the faculties and capacities of beings. Why? All of the buddhas, the *bhagavats*, come forth into the world for the sake of beings, doing so because:

[Beings], having no wisdom, commit evil deeds;
They conceive the existence of a self and possessions of a self;
They are attached to the body;
They are affected by inverted views and skeptical doubt;
They engage in discriminations based on wrong views;
They constantly involve themselves with the fetters and the bonds;
They follow along with the flow of *saṃsāra*; and
They stray far away from the path of the Tathāgata.

Sons of the Buddha, I see no single dharma constituting a greater transgression than that of bodhisattvas who produce thoughts of hatred toward other bodhisattvas. And why is this? Sons of the Buddha, if bodhisattvas produce thoughts of hatred or anger toward other bodhisattvas, they immediately create a gateway to a million obstacles.

What sorts of circumstances constitute those million obstacles? They are as follows:

The obstacle of not perceiving bodhi;
The obstacle of not hearing right Dharma;
The obstacle of being reborn in an impure world;
The obstacle of being reborn in the wretched rebirth destinies;
The obstacle of being reborn into the [eight] difficult circumstances;[16]
The obstacle of being much beset by illnesses;
The obstacle of being extensively slandered by others;
The obstacle of being reborn in destinies where beings are unintelligent;[17]
The obstacle of diminished right mindfulness;

正體字	壞失正念障。闕少智慧障。眼障 耳障。鼻障舌障。身障意障。惡知識障。惡伴黨 障。樂習小乘障。樂近凡庸障。不信樂大威德 人障。樂與離正見人同住障。生外道家障。住 魔境界障。離佛正教障。不見善友障。善根留 難障。增不善法障。得下劣處障。生邊地障。生 惡人家障。生惡神中障。生惡龍惡夜叉。惡乾 闥婆。惡阿脩羅。惡迦樓羅。惡緊那羅。惡摩睺 羅伽。惡羅剎中障。不樂佛法障。習童蒙法障。 樂著小乘障。不樂大乘障。性多驚怖障。心常 憂惱障。愛著生死障。不專佛法障。不喜見聞 佛自在神通障。
简体字	坏失正念障；缺少智慧障；眼障；耳障；鼻障；舌障；身障；意障；恶知识障；恶伴党障；乐习小乘障；乐近凡庸障；不信乐大威德人障；乐与离正见人同住障；生外道家障；住魔境界障；离佛正教障；不见善友障；善根留难障；增不善法障；得下劣处障；生边地障；生恶人家障；生恶神中障；生恶龙、恶夜叉、恶乾闼婆、恶阿修罗、恶迦楼罗、恶紧那罗、恶摩睺罗伽、恶罗刹中障；不乐佛法障；习童蒙法障；乐著小乘障；不乐大乘障；性多惊怖障；心常忧恼障；爱著生死障；不专佛法障；不喜见闻佛自在神通障；

Chapter 36 — The Practices of Samantabhadra

The obstacle of deficient wisdom;
Obstacles associated with the eyes;
Obstacles associated with the ears;
Obstacles associated with the nose;
Obstacles associated with the tongue;
Obstacles associated with the body;
Obstacles associated with the mind;
The obstacle of association with bad spiritual guides;
The obstacle of association with bad companions;
The obstacle of merely delighting in Small Vehicle practice;
The obstacle of delighting in proximity to what is common and coarse;
The obstacle of not having resolute faith[18] in those possessed of great awesome virtue;
The obstacle of delighting in dwelling with those who have abandoned right views;
The obstacle of being reborn into households of those adhering to non-Buddhist paths;
The obstacle of abiding in realms of objective experience influenced by *māras*;
The obstacle of being separated from the Buddha's right teachings;
The obstacle of never encountering a good spiritual guide;[19]
The obstacle of encountering restraining difficulties[20] in developing roots of goodness;
The obstacle of increasing unwholesome dharmas;
The obstacle of coming upon inferior circumstances;[21]
The obstacle of birth into outlying lands;
The obstacle of birth into the household of evil people;
The obstacle of being born among evil spirits;
The obstacle of being born among evil dragons, evil *yakṣas*, evil *gandharvas*, evil *asuras*, evil *garuḍas*, evil *kiṃnaras*, evil *mahoragas*, or evil *rākṣasas*;
The obstacle of not delighting in the Buddha's Dharma;
The obstacle of habitually immature behavior;
The obstacle of delighting in attachment to the Small Vehicle;
The obstacle of not delighting in the Great Vehicle;
The obstacle of being naturally excessively fearful;
The obstacle of having a mind always afflicted by worry;
The obstacle of being fondly attached to [life in] *saṃsara*;
The obstacle of not remaining focused on the Buddha's Dharma;
The obstacle of not delighting in seeing or hearing of the Buddha's mastery of the spiritual superknowledges;

正體字	不得菩薩諸根障。不行菩薩 258a04 淨行障。退怯菩薩深心障。不生菩薩大願障。 258a05 不發一切智心障。於菩薩行懈怠障。不能淨 258a06 治諸業障。不能攝取大福障。智力不能明利 258a07 障。斷於廣大智慧障。不護持菩薩諸行障。樂 258a08 誹謗一切智語障。遠離諸佛菩提障。樂住眾 258a09 魔境界障。不專修佛境界障。不決定發菩薩 258a10 弘誓障。不樂與菩薩同住障。不求菩薩善根 258a11 障。性多見疑障。心常愚闇障。不能行菩薩平 258a12 等施故起不捨障。不能持如來戒故起破戒 258a13 障。不能入堪忍門故起愚癡惱害瞋恚障。不 258a14 能行菩薩大精進故起懈怠垢障。不能得諸 258a15 三昧故起散亂障。
简体字	不得菩萨诸根障；不行菩萨净行障；退怯菩萨深心障；不生菩萨大愿障；不发一切智心障；于菩萨行懈怠障；不能净治诸业障；不能摄取大福障；智力不能明利障，断于广大智慧障；不护持菩萨诸行障；乐诽谤一切智语障；远离诸佛菩提障；乐住众魔境界障；不专修佛境界障；不决定发菩萨弘誓障；不乐与菩萨同住障；不求菩萨善根障；性多见疑障；心常愚暗障；不能行菩萨平等施故，起不舍障；不能持如来戒故，起破戒障；不能入堪忍门故，起愚痴、恼害、瞋恚障；不能行菩萨大精进故，起懈怠垢障；不能得诸三昧故，起散乱障；

The obstacle of not acquiring the faculties of a bodhisattva;
The obstacle of not practicing the bodhisattva's pure practices;
The obstacle of timidly retreating from the bodhisattva's deep resolve;[22]
The obstacle of not making the bodhisattva's great vows;
The obstacle of not resolving to acquire all-knowledge;
The obstacle of indolence in carrying out the bodhisattva practices;
The obstacle of being unable to purify all of one's karma;
The obstacle of being unable to gather an immense accumulation of merit;
The obstacle of being unable to develop clarity and acuity in the power of one's knowledge;
The obstacle of interrupting one's development of vast wisdom;
The obstacle of not preserving and sustaining all the bodhisattva practices;
The obstacle of delighting in slandering the words of those who are omniscient;
The obstacle of distancing oneself from the bodhi of the buddhas;
The obstacle of delighting in abiding in the spheres of experience of the many *māras*;
The obstacle of not focusing on cultivating the Buddha's sphere of action;
The obstacle of not decisively making the bodhisattva's vast vows;
The obstacle of not delighting in dwelling together with bodhisattvas;
The obstacle of not seeking to develop the bodhisattva's roots of goodness;
The obstacle of being naturally inclined to hold numerous views and have many doubts;
The obstacle of having a mind that is always dull and dim;
The obstacle of not relinquishing things that arises due to an inability to practice the bodhisattva's impartial giving;
The obstacle of creating broken moral precepts that arises due to an inability to uphold the Tathāgata's moral prohibitions;
The obstacle of stupidity, maliciousness, and hatred that arises due to an inability to enter the gateway of patience;
The obstacle of indolence-related defilements that arises due to an inability to practice the bodhisattva's great vigor;
The obstacle of being scattered and disordered that arises due to an inability to acquire any of the samādhis;

|正體字|不修治般若波羅蜜故起惡慧障。於處非處中無善巧障。於度眾生中無方便障。於菩薩智慧中不能觀察障。於菩薩出離法中不能了知障。不成就菩薩十種廣大眼故。眼如生盲障。耳不聞無礙法故口如[1]啞羊障。不具相好故鼻根破壞障。不能辨了眾生語言故成就舌根障。輕賤眾生故成就身根障。心多狂亂故成就意根障。不持三種律儀故成就身業障。恒起四種過失故成就語業障。多生貪瞋邪見故成就意業障。賊心求法障。斷絕菩薩境界障。於菩薩勇猛法中心生退怯障。於菩薩出離道中心生嬾惰障。於菩薩智慧光明門中心生止息障。於菩薩念力中心生劣弱障。於如來教法中不能住持障。|

|简体字|不修治般若波罗蜜故，起恶慧障；于处、非处中无善巧障；于度众生中无方便障；于菩萨智慧中不能观察障；于菩萨出离法中不能了知障；不成就菩萨十种广大眼故，眼如生盲障；耳不闻无碍法故，口如哑羊障；不具相好故，鼻根破坏障；不能辨了众生语言故，成就舌根障；轻贱众生故，成就身根障；心多狂乱故，成就意根障；不持三种律仪故，成就身业障；恒起四种过失故，成就语业障；多生贪、瞋、邪见故，成就意业障；贼心求法障；断绝菩萨境界障；于菩萨勇猛法中心生退怯障；于菩萨出离道中心生懒惰障；于菩萨智慧光明门中心生止息障；于菩萨念力中心生劣弱障；于如来教法中不能住持障；|

Chapter 36 — The Practices of Samantabhadra 2505

The obstacle of developing an evil intelligence that arises due to failing to cultivate the *prajñāpāramitā*;

The obstacle of not having skillfulness sufficient to deal with various possible and impossible situations;[23]

The obstacle of having no skillful means with which to liberate beings;

The obstacle of being unable to apply analytic contemplations to the wisdom of the bodhisattva;

The obstacle of being unable to completely understand the dharmas by which a bodhisattva achieves emancipation;

The obstacle of having eyes like those born blind due to not perfecting the bodhisattva's ten kinds of great eyes;[24]

The obstacle of having verbal abilities like those who are mute because one's ears have never heard the unimpeded Dharma;

The obstacle of having diminished olfactory faculties because one does not possess the major marks and subsidiary characteristics;

The obstacle of impaired verbal skills due to being unable to distinguish and completely understand beings' speech;

The obstacle of impaired physical faculties due to having slighted other beings;

The obstacle of impaired mental faculties due to having a crazed and disordered mind;

Physical karmic obstacles due to not upholding three categories of moral precepts;[25]

Verbal karmic obstacles developed due to constantly committing four types of transgressions;[26]

Mental karmic obstacles developed due to much production of covetousness, ill will, and wrong views;[27]

The obstacle of seeking the Dharma with the mind of a thief;

The obstacle of having cut oneself off from the bodhisattva's domain of objective experience;

The obstacle of having a mind that timidly retreats from the bodhisattva's heroically courageous dharmas;

The obstacle of having a mind that is indolent in its pursuit of the bodhisattva's path of emancipation;

The obstacle of having a mind that stops and rests at the gateway to the bodhisattva's light of wisdom;

The obstacle of having a mind that becomes inferior and weak in developing the bodhisattva's power of mindfulness;

The obstacle of being unable to maintain and preserve the Tathāgata's teaching dharmas;

正體字

於菩薩離生道不能親近障。於菩薩
無失壞道不能修習障。隨順二乘正位障。遠
離三世諸佛菩薩種性障。佛子。若菩薩。於諸
菩薩。起一瞋心。則成就如是等百萬障門。何
以故。佛子。我不見有一法為大過惡。如諸菩
薩。於餘菩薩。起瞋心者。是故。諸菩薩摩訶
薩。欲疾滿足諸菩薩行。應勤修十種法。何等
為十。所謂心不棄捨一切眾生。於諸菩薩。生
如來想。永不誹謗一切佛法。知諸國土。無有
窮盡。於菩薩行。深生信樂。不捨平等虛空法
界。菩提之心。觀察菩提。入如來力。精勤修
習。無礙辯才。教化眾生。無有疲厭。住一切
世界。心無所著。是為十。佛子。菩薩摩訶薩。
安住此十法已。則能具足十種清淨。何等為
十。所謂通達甚深法清淨。親近善知識清淨。
護持諸佛法清淨。了達虛空界清淨。深入法
界清淨。觀察無邊心清淨。與一切菩薩同善
根清淨。

简体字

于菩萨离生道不能亲近障；于菩萨无失坏道不能修习障；随顺二乘正位障；远离三世诸佛菩萨种性障。

"佛子，若菩萨于诸菩萨起一瞋心，则成就如是等百万障门。何以故？佛子，我不见有一法为大过恶，如诸菩萨于余菩萨起瞋心者。是故，诸菩萨摩诃萨欲疾满足诸菩萨行，应勤修十种法。何等为十？所谓：心不弃舍一切众生，于诸菩萨生如来想，永不诽谤一切佛法，知诸国土无有穷尽，于菩萨行深生信乐，不舍平等虚空法界菩提之心，观察菩提入如来力，精勤修习无碍辩才，教化众生无有疲厌，住一切世界心无所著。是为十。

"佛子，菩萨摩诃萨安住此十法已，则能具足十种清净。何等为十？所谓：通达甚深法清净，亲近善知识清净，护持诸佛法清净，了达虚空界清净，深入法界清净，观察无边心清净，与一切菩萨同善根清净，

Chapter 36 — *The Practices of Samantabhadra*

> The obstacle of being unable to draw near to the bodhisattva's path of transcending births in cyclic existence;
>
> The obstacle of being unable to cultivate the uncorrupted path of the bodhisattva;
>
> The obstacle of pursuing realization of the Two Vehicles' right and fixed position;[28] and
>
> The obstacle of distancing oneself from the lineage of all buddhas and bodhisattvas of the three periods of time.

Sons of the Buddha, if a bodhisattva raises even a single thought of hatred for another bodhisattva, he then produces a million obstacles such as these. And why? Sons of the Buddha, I do not see any single dharma constituting such an immense transgression as that created by any bodhisattva who produces thoughts of hatred toward other bodhisattvas. Therefore, if a bodhisattva-mahāsattva wishes to swiftly fulfill all the bodhisattva practices, he should diligently cultivate ten kinds of dharmas. What then are those ten? They are as follows:

> His mind never abandons any being;
>
> He envisions all bodhisattvas as *tathāgatas*;
>
> He never slanders any dharma of the Buddha;
>
> He realizes that all lands are endless;
>
> He feels deep faith and delight in the bodhisattva practices;
>
> He never relinquishes a bodhi resolve that is commensurate with empty space and the Dharma realm;
>
> He contemplates bodhi and enters the powers of the Tathāgata;
>
> He is energetically diligent in cultivating unimpeded eloquence;
>
> He is tireless in teaching beings; and
>
> He abides in any world with a mind free of attachments.

These are the ten.

Sons of the Buddha, after the bodhisattva-mahāsattva comes to securely abide in these ten dharmas, he is then able to completely fulfill ten kinds of purity. What then are the ten? They are as follows:

> Purity in the penetrating comprehension of extremely profound dharmas;
>
> Purity in drawing close to good spiritual guides;
>
> Purity in guarding and preserving all dharmas of the Buddha;
>
> Purity in the complete penetration of the realm of empty space;
>
> Purity in deeply entering the Dharma realm;
>
> Purity in contemplation of the boundless mind;
>
> Purity in roots of goodness identical to those of all bodhisattvas;

正體字

不著諸劫清淨。觀察三世清淨。修行一切諸佛法清淨。是為十。佛子。菩薩摩訶薩。住此十法已。則具足十種廣大智。何等為十。所謂知一切眾生心行智。知一切眾生業報智。知一切佛法智。知一切佛法深密理趣智。知一切陀羅尼門智。知一切文字辯才智。知一切眾生語言音聲[2]辭辯善巧智。於一切世界中普現其身智。於一切眾會中普現影像智。於一切受生處中具一切智智。是為十。佛子。菩薩摩訶薩。住此十智已。則得入十種普入。何等為十。所謂一切世界入一毛道。一毛道入一切世界。一切眾生身入一身。一身入一切眾生身。不可說劫入一念。一念入不可說劫。一切佛法入一法。一法入一切佛法。不可說處入一處。一處入不可說處。不可說根入一根。一根入不可說根。

简体字

不著诸劫清净，观察三世清净，修行一切诸佛法清净。是为十。

"佛子，菩萨摩诃萨住此十法已，则具足十种广大智。何等为十？所谓：知一切众生心行智，知一切众生业报智，知一切佛法智，知一切佛法深密理趣智，知一切陀罗尼门智，知一切文字辩才智，知一切众生语言、音声、辞辩善巧智，于一切世界中普现其身智，于一切众会中普现影像智，于一切受生处中具一切智智。是为十。

"佛子，菩萨摩诃萨住此十智已，则得入十种普入。何等为十？所谓：一切世界入一毛道，一毛道入一切世界；一切众生身入一身，一身入一切众生身；不可说劫入一念，一念入不可说劫；一切佛法入一法，一法入一切佛法；不可说处入一处，一处入不可说处；不可说根入一根，一根入不可说根；

Chapter 36 — The Practices of Samantabhadra

Purity in refraining from attachment to any kalpa;
Purity in contemplation of the three periods of time; and
Purity in cultivation of all buddhas' dharmas.

These are the ten.

Sons of the Buddha, after the bodhisattva-mahāsattva abides in these ten dharmas, he then completely fulfills ten kinds of vast knowledge. What then are those ten? They are as follows:

The knowledge that knows the actions of all beings' minds;
The knowledge that knows the consequences of all beings' karma;
The knowledge that knows all dharmas of the Buddha;
The knowledge that knows the deeply secret principles and purport of all dharmas of the Buddha;
The knowledge that knows all *dhāraṇī* gateways;
The knowledge that knows and possesses eloquence in all written languages;
The knowledge by which one knows all beings' languages and speech and is skillful in the unimpeded knowledge of eloquent phrasing;[29]
The knowledge by which one everywhere manifests bodies in all worlds;
The knowledge by which one everywhere manifests reflected images within all congregations; and
The knowledge by which one possesses all-knowledge wherever one is born.

These are the ten.

Sons of the Buddha, after the bodhisattva-mahāsattva comes to abide in these ten types of knowledge, he then succeeds in entering into ten kinds of universal penetration. What then are those ten? They are as follows:

All worlds enter into a single hair pore and a single hair pore enters all worlds;
All beings' bodies enter a single body and a single body enters all beings' bodies;
An ineffable[30] number of kalpas enter a single mind-moment and a single mind-moment enters an ineffable number of kalpas;
All dharmas of the Buddha enter a single dharma and a single dharma enters all dharmas of the Buddha;
An ineffable number of places enter a single place and a single place enters an ineffable number of places;
An ineffable number of faculties enter a single faculty and a single faculty enters an ineffable number of faculties;

正體字

一切根入非根。非根入一切根。一切想入一想。一想入一切想。一切言音入一言音。一言音入一切言音。一切三世入一世。一世入一切三世。是為十。佛子。菩薩摩訶薩。如是觀察已。則住十種勝妙心。何等為十。所謂住一切世界語言非語言勝妙心。住一切眾生想念無所依止勝妙心。住究竟虛空界勝妙心。住無邊法界勝妙心。住一切深密佛法勝妙心。住甚深無差別法勝妙心。住除滅一切疑惑勝妙心。住一切世平等無差別勝妙心。住三世諸佛平等勝妙心。住一切諸佛力無量勝妙心。是為十。佛子。菩薩摩訶薩。住此十種勝妙心已。則得十種佛法善巧智。何等為十。所謂了達甚深佛法善巧智。出生廣大佛法善巧智。

简体字

一切根入非根，非根入一切根；一切想入一想，一想入一切想；一切言音入一言音，一言音入一切言音；一切三世入一世，一世入一切三世。是为十。

"佛子，菩萨摩诃萨如是观察已，则住十种胜妙心。何等为十？所谓：住一切世界语言、非语言胜妙心，住一切众生想念无所依止胜妙心，住究竟虚空界胜妙心，住无边法界胜妙心，住一切深密佛法胜妙心，住甚深无差别法胜妙心，住除灭一切疑惑胜妙心，住一切世平等无差别胜妙心，住三世诸佛平等胜妙心，住一切诸佛力无量胜妙心。是为十。

"佛子，菩萨摩诃萨住此十种胜妙心已，则得十种佛法善巧智。何等为十？所谓：了达甚深佛法善巧智，出生广大佛法善巧智，

Chapter 36 — The Practices of Samantabhadra

All faculties enter what is not a faculty at all and what is not a faculty at all enters all faculties;

All thoughts enter a single thought and a single thought enters all thoughts;

All sounds of speech enter a single sound of speech and a single sound of speech enters into all sounds of speech; and

All three periods of time enter a single period of time and a single period of time enters all three periods of time.

These are the ten.

Sons of the Buddha, after the bodhisattva-mahāsattva has contemplated in this way, he then abides in ten kinds of supremely sublime mind. What then are those ten? They are as follows:

He abides in the supremely sublime mind that comprehends all worlds' language and non-language;

He abides in the supremely sublime mind that comprehends that the thoughts of all beings have nothing whatsoever on which they rely;

He abides in the supremely sublime mind that comprehends the realm of ultimate emptiness;

He abides in the supremely sublime mind that comprehends the boundless Dharma realm;

He abides in the supremely sublime mind that comprehends all the deeply secret dharmas of the Buddha;

He abides in the supremely sublime mind that comprehends the extremely profound Dharma as free of any differentiations;

He abides in the supremely sublime mind that extinguishes all doubt;[31]

He abides in the supremely sublime mind that comprehends all periods of time[32] as the same and as free of any differentiation;

He abides in the supremely sublime mind that comprehends the equality of all buddhas of the three periods of time; and

He abides in the supremely sublime mind that comprehends the immeasurable powers of all buddhas.

These are the ten.

Sons of the Buddha, after the bodhisattva-mahāsattva has come to abide in these ten kinds of supremely sublime mind, he then acquires ten kinds of skillful knowledge with regard to the Dharma of the Buddha. What then are these ten? They are as follows:

The skillful knowledge that completely comprehends the extremely profound Dharma of the Buddha;

The skillful knowledge that brings forth the vast Dharma of the Buddha;

正體字

宣說種種佛
258c18 ‖ 法善巧智。證入平等佛法善巧智。明了差別
258c19 ‖ 佛法善巧智。悟解無差別佛法善巧智。深入
258c20 ‖ 莊嚴佛法善巧智。一方便入佛法善巧智。無
258c21 ‖ 量方便入佛法善巧智。知無邊佛法無差別
258c22 ‖ 善巧智。以自心自力於一切佛法不退轉善
258c23 ‖ 巧智。是為十。佛子。菩薩摩訶薩。聞此法已。
258c24 ‖ 咸應發心。恭敬受持。何以故。菩薩摩訶薩。持
258c25 ‖ 此法者。少作功力。疾得阿耨多羅三藐三菩
258c26 ‖ 提。皆得具足一切佛法。悉與三世諸佛法等
258c27 ‖ 爾時。佛神力故。法如是故。十方各有十不可
258c28 ‖ 說百千億那由他佛剎微塵數世界。六種震
258c29 ‖ 動。雨出過諸天一切華雲。香雲末香雲。衣蓋
259a01 ‖ 幢幡。摩尼寶等。及以一切莊嚴具雲。雨眾妓
259a02 ‖ 樂雲。雨諸菩薩雲。雨不可說如來色相雲。雨
259a03 ‖ 不可說讚歎如來善哉雲。雨如來音聲充滿一
259a04 ‖ 切法界雲。

简体字

宣说种种佛法善巧智，证入平等佛法善巧智，明了差别佛法善巧智，悟解无差别佛法善巧智，深入庄严佛法善巧智，一方便入佛法善巧智，无量方便入佛法善巧智，知无边佛法无差别善巧智，以自心自力于一切佛法不退转善巧智。是为十。

"佛子，菩萨摩诃萨闻此法已，咸应发心，恭敬受持。何以故？菩萨摩诃萨持此法者，少作功力，疾得阿耨多罗三藐三菩提，皆得具足一切佛法，悉与三世诸佛法等。"

尔时，佛神力故，法如是故，十方各有十不可说百千亿那由他佛刹微尘数世界六种震动，雨出过诸天一切华云、香云、末香云、衣盖、幢幡、摩尼宝等及以一切庄严具云，雨众妓乐云，雨诸菩萨云，雨不可说如来色相云，雨不可说赞叹如来善哉云，雨如来音声充满一切法界云，

The skillful knowledge that proclaims the many different kinds of dharmas of the Buddha;

The skillful knowledge that brings about realization of and entry into the equally accessible Dharma[33] of the Buddha;

The skillful knowledge that completely understands the different dharmas of the Buddha;

The skillful knowledge that awakens to and understands the absence of differences in the Dharma of the Buddha;

The skillful knowledge that deeply enters into the adornments of the Dharma of the Buddha;

The skillful knowledge that uses a single expedient means to penetrate the Dharma of the Buddha;

The skillful knowledge that uses countlessly many expedient means to penetrate the Dharma of the Buddha;

The skillful knowledge that knows the absence of differences in the boundlessly many dharmas of the Buddha;[34] and

The skillful knowledge by which, relying on one's own resolve and one's own powers, one does not retreat from any of the Buddha's dharmas.

These are the ten.[35]

Sons of the Buddha, once they have heard these dharmas, all bodhisattva-mahāsattvas should resolve to respectfully accept and uphold them. Why is this? By applying a small amount of effort, the bodhisattva-mahāsattvas who uphold these dharmas will be able to quickly reach *anuttara-samyak-saṃbodhi* and completely fulfill all dharmas of the Buddha which are equal to the dharmas of all buddhas of the three periods of time.

At that time, because of the Buddha's spiritual powers and because the Dharma is just this way, in worlds in each of the ten directions as numerous as the atoms in ten ineffable numbers of hundreds of thousands of *koṭīs* of *nayutas* of buddha *kṣetras*, there occurred the six kinds of shaking and moving along with the raining down of flower clouds superior even to those of the devas, incense clouds, powdered incense clouds, clouds of robes, canopies, banners, pennants, *maṇi* jewels, and other such things, as well as clouds of all manner of adornments.

There were clouds that rain the many kinds of music, clouds that rain bodhisattvas, clouds that rain an ineffable number of *tathāgatas'* physical signs, clouds that rain an ineffable number of praises of the Tathāgata, exclaiming "Good indeed!," clouds that rain *tathāgatas'* voices that fill the entire Dharma realm, clouds that rain an ineffable

正體字

雨不可說莊嚴世界雲。雨不可說
增長菩提雲。雨不可說光明照[1]耀雲。雨不可
說神力說法雲。如此世界四天下。菩提樹下。
菩提場。菩薩宮殿中。見於如來成等正覺。演
說此法。十方一切諸世界中。悉亦如是。爾時。
佛神力故。法如是故。十方各過十不可說佛
剎微塵數世界外。有十佛剎微塵數菩薩摩
訶薩。來詣此土。充滿十方。作如是言。善哉善
哉。佛子。乃能說此諸佛如來最大誓願。授記
深法。佛子。我等一切。同名普賢。各從普勝世
界。普幢自在如來所。來詣此土。悉以佛神力
故。於一切處。演說此法。如此眾會。如是所
說。一切平等無有增減。我等皆承佛威神力。
來此道場。為汝作證。如此道場。我等十佛剎。
微塵數菩薩。而來作證。十方一切諸世界中。
悉亦如是
爾時。普賢菩薩摩訶薩。以佛神力。自善根力。
觀察十方。泊[2]乎法界。欲開示菩薩行。欲宣
說如來菩提界。欲說大願界。欲說一切世界
劫數。

简体字

雨不可说庄严世界云，雨不可说增长菩提云，雨不可说光明照耀云，雨不可说神力说法云。如此世界四天下菩提树下菩提场菩萨宫殿中，见于如来成等正觉演说此法，十方一切诸世界中悉亦如是。

尔时，佛神力故，法如是故，十方各过十不可说佛刹微尘数世界外，有十佛刹微尘数菩萨摩诃萨来诣此土，充满十方，作如是言："善哉！善哉！佛子，乃能说此诸佛如来最大誓愿授记深法。佛子，我等一切同名普贤，各从普胜世界普幢自在如来所来诣此土，悉以佛神力故，于一切处演说此法；如此众会，如是所说，一切平等无有增减。我等皆承佛威神力，来此道场为汝作证。如此道场，我等十佛刹微尘数菩萨而来作证，十方一切诸世界中悉亦如是。"

尔时，普贤菩萨摩诃萨以佛神力、自善根力，观察十方洎于法界，欲开示菩萨行，欲宣说如来菩提界，欲说大愿界，欲说一切世界劫数，

Chapter 36 — The Practices of Samantabhadra

number of adorned worlds, clouds that rain an ineffable number of means to promote the realization of bodhi, clouds that rain an ineffable number of brightly shining lights, and clouds that rain an ineffable number of proclamations of Dharma through the use of spiritual powers.

And just as, in this world with its four continents, beneath the bodhi tree, in the *bodhimaṇḍa*, within the bodhisattva's palace, one could see the Tathāgata realize the universal and right enlightenment and then proclaim this Dharma, so too could one see this in all worlds throughout the ten directions.

At that time, because of the Buddha's spiritual powers and because the Dharma is just this way, from each of the ten directions, beyond a number of worlds as numerous as the atoms in ten ineffable numbers of large buddha *kṣetras*, bodhisattva-mahāsattvas as numerous as the atoms in ten buddha *kṣetras* came forth to this land to pay their respects and, filling up the ten directions, they spoke words such as these: "It is good indeed, good indeed, O Son of the Buddha, that you have now been able to speak of the profound dharmas of the greatest vows and the prediction of buddhahood of all buddhas, all *tathāgatas*.

"O Son of the Buddha, all of us have the same name, 'Samantabhadra.' We have each come to pay our respects in this land, coming here from the abode of Universal Banner of Mastery Tathāgata in the Universal Supremacy World. Through the Buddha's spiritual powers, all of us proclaim this Dharma everywhere just as it is set forth in the midst of this congregation, doing so in a way that everything is the same, free of any additions or omissions. Through having received the aid of the Buddha's awesome spiritual power, we have all come to this *bodhimaṇḍa* to serve as certifying witnesses for you. And just as we bodhisattvas as numerous as the atoms in ten buddha *kṣetras* have come to this *bodhimaṇḍa* to serve here as certifying witnesses, so too is this also so in all other worlds throughout the ten directions."

At that time, in reliance upon the Buddha's spiritual power and the power of his own roots of goodness, Samantabhadra Bodhisattva-mahāsattva surveyed the ten directions, including everywhere throughout the Dharma realm, and:

Wishing to provide instruction in the bodhisattva practices;
Wishing to proclaim his teaching on the Tathāgata's realm of bodhi;
Wishing to speak of the realm of great vows;
Wishing to explain all worlds' permutations of kalpas;

正體字

	欲明諸佛隨時出現。欲說如來隨根熟
259a24	眾生出現令其供養。欲明如來出世功不唐
259a25	捐。欲明所種善根。必獲果報。欲明大威德菩
259a26	薩為一切眾生現形說法令其開悟。而說頌
259a27	言
259a28	汝等應歡喜　捨離於諸蓋
259a29	一心恭敬聽　菩薩諸願行
259b01	往昔諸菩薩　最勝人師子
259b02	如彼所修行　我當次第說
259b03	亦說諸劫數　世界并諸業
259b04	及以無等尊　於彼而出興
259b05	如[3]是過去佛　大願出[4]于世
259b06	云何為眾生　滅除諸苦惱
259b07	一切論師子　所行相續滿
259b08	得佛平等法　一切智境界
259b09	見於過去世　一切人師子
259b10	放大光明網　普照十方界
259b11	思惟發是願　我當作世燈
259b12	具足佛功德　十力一切智

简体字

欲明诸佛随时出现，欲说如来随根熟众生出现令其供养，欲明如来出世功不唐捐，欲明所种善根必获果报，欲明大威德菩萨为一切众生现形说法令其开悟，而说颂言：

"汝等应欢喜，舍离于诸盖，
一心恭敬听，菩萨诸愿行。
往昔诸菩萨，最胜人师子，
如彼所修行，我当次第说。
亦说诸劫数，世界并诸业，
及以无等尊，于彼而出兴。
如是过去佛，大愿出于世，
云何为众生，灭除诸苦恼？
一切论师子，所行相续满，
得佛平等法，一切智境界。
见于过去世，一切人师子，
放大光明网，普照十方界。
思惟发是愿：我当作世灯，
具足佛功德，十力一切智。

Wishing to clarify the manner in which the buddhas appear in accordance with the time;

Wishing to explain how the Tathāgata appears for the sake of beings with ripened faculties to enable them to make offerings;

Wishing to clarify that the efforts of the Tathāgata in appearing in the world are never wasted;

Wishing to clarify that roots of goodness that have been planted will definitely result in harvesting karmic rewards; and

Wishing also to clarify the manner in which the bodhisattva possessed of great awesome virtue manifests his forms for the sake of all beings, speaking Dharma for them in a manner that causes them to awaken—

He then spoke verses, saying:

You should all be filled with joyous delight,
abandon all of the hindrances,
and single-mindedly and respectfully listen
to the vows and practices of the bodhisattva.

Just as it has been with all bodhisattvas of the distant past
as well as with the supreme lions among men,[36]
in accordance with what they have cultivated,
so shall I now explain it in accordance with its sequence.

I shall also describe the numbers of all kalpas,
the world systems, and all karma,
as well as the peerless Bhagavat's
coming forth and appearing within them,

how these buddhas of the past,
due to great vows, came forth into the world,
how it was that, for beings' sakes,
they extinguished sufferings and afflictions,

and how it has been that all the lions of reasoned discourse[37]
have so continuously fulfilled what they have practiced
and have acquired the Buddha's equal Dharma
and their omniscient sphere of cognition.

Seeing that all the Lions Among Men
throughout the past
have emanated a great net of light
that everywhere illuminates the worlds of the ten directions,

they reflected on this and then made this vow:
"I shall become a lamp for the world
and perfect the meritorious qualities of the Buddha,
the ten powers, and all-knowledge.

	259b13 ‖	一切諸眾生　　貪恚癡熾然
	259b14 ‖	我當悉救脫　　令滅惡道苦
	259b15 ‖	發如是誓願　　堅固不退轉
	259b16 ‖	具修菩薩行　　獲十無礙力
	259b17 ‖	如是誓願已　　修行無退怯
	259b18 ‖	所作皆不虛　　說名論師子
	259b19 ‖	於一賢劫中　　千佛出[*]于世
	259b20 ‖	彼所有普眼　　我當次第說
正體字	259b21 ‖	如一賢劫中　　無量劫亦然
	259b22 ‖	彼未來佛行　　我當分別說
	259b23 ‖	如一佛剎種　　無量剎亦然
	259b24 ‖	未來十力尊　　諸行我今說
	259b25 ‖	諸佛次興世　　隨願隨名號
	259b26 ‖	隨彼所得記　　隨其所壽命
	259b27 ‖	隨所修正法　　專求無礙道
	259b28 ‖	隨所化眾生　　正法住於世
	259b29 ‖	隨所淨佛剎　　眾生及法輪
	259c01 ‖	演說時非時　　次第淨群生
	259c02 ‖	隨諸眾生業　　所行及信解
	259c03 ‖	上中下不同　　化彼令修習
简体字		一切诸众生，贪恚痴炽然； 我当悉救脱，令灭恶道苦。 发如是誓愿，坚固不退转， 具修菩萨行，获十无碍力。 如是誓愿已，修行无退怯， 所作皆不虚，说名论师子。 于一贤劫中，千佛出于世， 彼所有普眼，我当次第说。 如一贤劫中，无量劫亦然， 彼未来佛行，我当分别说。 如一佛刹种，无量刹亦然， 未来十力尊，诸行我今说。 诸佛次兴世，随愿随名号， 随彼所得记，随其所寿命， 随所修正法，专求无碍道； 随所化众生，正法住于世； 随所净佛刹，众生及法轮， 演说时非时，次第净群生； 随诸众生业，所行及信解， 上中下不同，化彼令修习。

Chapter 36 — The Practices of Samantabhadra

The greed, hatred, and delusion
of all the many kinds of beings blazes intensely.
I shall rescue and liberate them all
and enable them to extinguish the wretched destinies' sufferings."

They have brought forth vows such as this
that are solid and irreversible
and, completely cultivating the bodhisattva practices,
they acquire the ten unimpeded powers.[38]

Having made vows such as this,
they then cultivate without ever retreating in fear
and whatever they do is never done in vain.
It is these who are known as "lions of reasoned discourse."

In this single age, "the worthy kalpa,"
a thousand buddhas come forth into the world.
All of those possessed of universally seeing eyes,
I shall proceed to describe here in an orderly fashion.

Just as this is the circumstance in this one "worthy kalpa,"
so too shall this be so in a measureless number of kalpas.
I shall now describe in a way that distinguishes them
the practices engaged in by those buddhas of the future.

Just as the circumstances exist in a single type of *kṣetra*,
so too do they also exist in a measureless number of *kṣetras*.
I shall now discuss all the practices
engaged in by those future *bhagavats* possessed of the ten powers.

Those buddhas sequentially appear in the world,
doing so in accordance with vows and their corresponding names,
in accordance with the predictions that they have received,
in accordance with the life spans they are destined to fulfill,

in accordance with the right Dharma they cultivate
and their focused quest to pursue the unimpeded path,
in accordance with those beings that they teach
and the right Dharma that abides in the world,

in accordance with the buddha *kṣetras* that they purify,
their beings, their turning of the wheel of Dharma,
and their expounding according to what is and is not the right time
as they pursue the orderly purification of the many types of beings,

and in accordance with all those beings' karmic deeds,
what they practice, what they resolutely believe in,
and how they differ due to superior, middling, and inferior capacities
as they teach them and influence them to pursue the cultivation.

正體字	259c04　入於如是智　修其最勝行 259c05　常作普賢業　廣度諸眾生 259c06　身業無障礙　語業悉清淨 259c07　意行亦如是　三世靡不然 259c08　菩薩如是行　究竟普賢道 259c09　出生淨智日　普照於法界 259c10　未來世諸劫　國土不可說 259c11　一念悉了知　於彼無分別 259c12　行者能趣入　如是最勝地 259c13　此諸菩薩法　我當說少分 259c14　智慧無邊際　通達佛境界 259c15　一切皆善入　所行不退轉 259c16　具足普賢慧　成滿普賢願 259c17　入於無等智　我當說彼行 259c18　於一微塵中　悉見諸世界 259c19　眾生若聞者　迷亂心發狂 259c20　如於一微塵　一切塵亦然 259c21　世界悉入中　如是不思議 259c22　一一塵中有　十方三世法 259c23　趣剎皆無量　悉能分別知	
简体字	入于如是智，修其最胜行， 常作普贤业，广度诸众生。 身业无障碍，语业悉清净， 意行亦如是，三世靡不然。 菩萨如是行，究竟普贤道， 出生净智日，普照于法界。 未来世诸劫，国土不可说， 一念悉了知，于彼无分别。 行者能趣入，如是最胜地， 此诸菩萨法，我当说少分。 智慧无边际，通达佛境界， 一切皆善入，所行不退转。 具足普贤慧，成满普贤愿， 入于无等智，我当说彼行。 于一微尘中，悉见诸世界， 众生若闻者，迷乱心发狂。 如于一微尘，一切尘亦然， 世界悉入中，如是不思议。 一一尘中有，十方三世法， 趣刹皆无量，悉能分别知。	

Chapter 36 — The Practices of Samantabhadra

[I shall describe as well] how they penetrate such types of knowledge,
cultivate their supreme types of practices,
and always perform the works of Samantabhadra,
and engage in the extensive liberation of beings,

doing so with physical actions that are never impeded,
with verbal actions that are entirely pure,
and with mental actions that are also of this same sort so that,
in all three periods of time, there are none that are not this way.

It is in this way that the bodhisattva practices
the ultimate path of Samantabhadra
and brings forth the rising of pure wisdom's sun
to everywhere illuminate the Dharma realm.

In all the kalpas of future time,
there are an ineffable number of lands.
In but a single mind-moment, they completely know them all
even as they make no discriminations regarding any of them.

The practitioner is able to progress into
such supreme grounds as these.
I shall now describe a minor portion
of these dharmas of the bodhisattva.

Their boundless wisdom penetratingly comprehends
the Buddha's spheres of cognition.
They skillfully enter them all
and never retreat from what they practice.

They become fully possessed of the wisdom of Samantabhadra,
completely fulfill the vows of Samantabhadra,
and enter into incomparable wisdom.
I shall describe their practices.

Within but a single atom,
they completely see all worlds.
If beings were to hear of this,
they would become so confused as to be driven insane.

Just as this is so with a single atom,
so too is this true of every atom.
The worlds all enter into them
in such an inconceivable manner as this.

In each and every atom there exist
the dharmas of the ten directions and three periods of time.
The rebirth destinies and *kṣetras* therein are countless,
yet they are able to distinguish and know them all.

	259c24	一一塵中有	無量種佛剎
	259c25	種種皆無量	於一靡不知
	259c26	法界中所有	種種諸異相
	259c27	趣類各差別	悉能分別知
	259c28	深入微細智	分別諸世界
	259c29	一切劫成壞	悉能明了說
	260a01	知諸劫修短	三世即一念
	260a02	眾行同不同	悉能分別知
正體字	260a03	深入諸世界	廣大非廣大
	260a04	一身無量剎	一剎無量身
	260a05	十方中所有	異類諸世界
	260a06	廣大無量相	一切悉能知
	260a07	一切三世中	無量諸國土
	260a08	具足甚深智	悉了彼成敗
	260a09	十方諸世界	有成或有壞
	260a10	如是不可說	賢德悉深了
	260a11	或有諸國土	種種地嚴飾
	260a12	諸趣亦復然	斯由業清淨
	260a13	或有諸世界	無量種雜染
	260a14	斯由眾生感	一切如其行

简体字

一一尘中有，无量种佛刹，
种种皆无量，于一靡不知。
法界中所有，种种诸异相，
趣类各差别，悉能分别知。
深入微细智，分别诸世界，
一切劫成坏，悉能明了说。
知诸劫修短，三世即一念，
众行同不同，悉能分别知。
深入诸世界，广大非广大，
一身无量刹，一刹无量身。
十方中所有，异类诸世界，
广大无量相，一切悉能知。
一切三世中，无量诸国土，
具足甚深智，悉了彼成败。
十方诸世界，有成或有坏，
如是不可说，贤德悉深了。
或有诸国土，种种地严饰；
诸趣亦复然，斯由业清净。
或有诸世界，无量种杂染；
斯由众生感，一切如其行。

Chapter 36 — The Practices of Samantabhadra

In each and every atom there exist
countless types of buddha *kṣetras*.
Every one of those types is measurelessly numerous,
yet there is not even a single one they do not know.

All of the Dharma realm's
many different types of varying aspects,
the rebirth destinies, and types of beings, each of which are different—
They are able to distinguish and know them all.

They deeply enter into the most subtly refined knowledge,
with which they distinguish all worlds
and they are able to thoroughly understand and explain
the development and destruction of all kalpas.

They know the length[39] of all kalpas
and know the three periods of time as but a single mind-moment.
They are able to distinguish and know
of the many types of practices, all their identities and differences.

They deeply enter into all worlds,
whether they be vast or not vast,
manifesting a single body in countless *kṣetras*,
or countless bodies within a single *kṣetra*.

With regard to the different types of worlds
throughout the ten directions
and their vastness as well as their countless other characteristics,
they are able to completely know them all.

With regard to all the countlessly many lands
throughout the three periods of time,
completely possessed of such extremely deep knowledge,
they entirely know both their creation and ruination.

In all the worlds throughout the ten directions,
some are just being formed and some are being destroyed.
Those possessed of the worthy's[40] virtue deeply comprehend
all the ineffable number of phenomena such as these.

Some have all kinds of lands
possessed of many different types of adornments of their grounds.
So too it is with their rebirth destinies.
This all arises from the purity of karmic deeds.

In some cases there are all kinds of worlds
possessed of countless types of defilement.
These arise as circumstances elicited by beings
that are all accordant with their own actions.

正體字	260a15	無量無邊剎	了知即一剎
	260a16	如是入諸剎	其數不可知
	260a17	一切諸世界	悉入一剎中
	260a18	世界不為一	亦復無雜亂
	260a19	世界有仰覆	或高或復下
	260a20	皆是眾生想	悉能分別知
	260a21	廣博諸世界	無量無有邊
	260a22	知種種是一	知一是種種
	260a23	普賢諸佛子	能以普賢智
	260a24	了知諸剎數	其數無邊際
	260a25	知諸世界化	剎化眾生化
	260a26	法化諸佛化	一切皆究竟
	260a27	一切諸世界	微細廣大剎
	260a28	種種異莊嚴	皆由業所起
	260a29	無量諸佛子	善學入法界
	260b01	神通力自在	普遍於十方
	260b02	眾生數等劫	說彼世界名
	260b03	亦不能令盡	唯除佛開示
	260b04	世界及如來	種種諸名號
	260b05	經於無量劫	說之不可盡
简体字	无量无边刹，了知即一刹， 如是入诸刹，其数不可知。 一切诸世界，悉入一刹中， 世界不为一，亦复无杂乱。 世界有仰覆，或高或复下， 皆是众生想，悉能分别知。 广博诸世界，无量无有边， 知种种是一，知一是种种。 普贤诸佛子，能以普贤智， 了知诸刹数，其数无边际。 知诸世界化，刹化众生化， 法化诸佛化，一切皆究竟。 一切诸世界，微细广大刹， 种种异庄严，皆由业所起。 无量诸佛子，善学入法界， 神通力自在，普遍于十方。 众生数等劫，说彼世界名， 亦不能令尽，唯除佛开示。 世界及如来，种种诸名号， 经于无量劫，说之不可尽。		

Chapter 36 — The Practices of Samantabhadra

They completely know the countless and boundless *kṣetras*
as identical with any single *kṣetra*.
In this way, they enter into all *kṣetras*
whose number is so great that it cannot be known.

All of those many worlds
entirely enter into but a single *kṣetra*
even as those worlds still do not become but one
and even as they still do not become mixed together or disordered.

Worlds may exist in either an upright or inverted position
and may be characterized by either lofty terrain or low-lying terrain.
In all cases, these circumstances reflect the thoughts of their beings.
They are able to distinguish and know all of these matters.

All of these vast worlds
are countlessly and boundlessly many.
They know the many different types to be but one
and know the one to be the many different types.

All of these Samantabhadras, these sons of the Buddha,
are able by using Samantabhadra's knowledge
to completely know the number of all these *kṣetras*
whose number is so boundlessly large.

They know the transformations of all worlds,
the transformations of the *kṣetras*, the transformations of beings,
the transformations of dharmas, and the transformations of buddhas,
and know them all to the most ultimate degree.

They know with regard to all worlds,
including the very small *kṣetras* as well as the vast *kṣetras*,
including, too, all of their many different kinds of adornments,
that all of these phenomena arise as a consequence of karmic actions.

Even if countless sons of the Buddha
who were well trained in entering the Dharma realm
and who were possessed of mastery in the spiritual powers
by which they could go everywhere throughout the ten directions

were to recite the names of all those worlds
for kalpas equal in number to that of all beings,
they would still be unable to come to the end of them all
unless this was disclosed to them by the Buddha.

Even if, in reciting all the many different names
of those worlds and their *tathāgatas*,
they continued to do so for a measureless number of kalpas,
they would still be unable to reach the end of their recitation.

正體字	260b06	何況最勝智	三世諸佛法
	260b07	從於法界生	充滿如來地
	260b08	清淨無礙念	無邊無礙慧
	260b09	分別說法界	得至於彼岸
	260b10	過去諸世界	廣大及微細
	260b11	修習所莊嚴	一念悉能知
	260b12	其中人師子	修佛種種行
	260b13	成於等正覺	示現諸自在
	260b14	如是未來世	次第無量劫
	260b15	所有人中尊	菩薩悉能知
	260b16	所有諸行願	所有諸境界
	260b17	如是勤修行	於中成正覺
	260b18	亦知彼眾會	壽命化眾生
	260b19	以此諸法門	為眾轉法輪
	260b20	菩薩如是知	住普賢行地
	260b21	智慧悉明了	出生一切佛
	260b22	現在世所攝	一切諸佛土
	260b23	深入此諸剎	通達於法界
	260b24	彼諸世界中	現在一切佛
	260b25	於法得自在	言論無所礙

简体字

何况最胜智，三世诸佛法，
从于法界生，充满如来地！
清净无碍念，无边无碍慧，
分别说法界，得至于彼岸。
过去诸世界，广大及微细，
修习所庄严，一念悉能知。
其中人师子，修佛种种行，
成于等正觉，示现诸自在。
如是未来世，次第无量劫，
所有人中尊，菩萨悉能知。
所有诸行愿，所有诸境界，
如是勤修行，于中成正觉。
亦知彼众会，寿命化众生，
以此诸法门，为众转法轮。
菩萨如是知，住普贤行地，
智慧悉明了，出生一切佛。
现在世所摄，一切诸佛土，
深入此诸剎，通达于法界。
彼诸世界中，现在一切佛，
于法得自在，言论无所碍。

Chapter 36 — The Practices of Samantabhadra

How much the less, with their supreme knowledge, could they do so
with the dharmas set forth by all buddhas of the three periods of time
which, having come forth from the Dharma realm,
completely pervade the ground of the Tathāgatas.

With pure and unimpeded mindfulness
and unimpeded wisdom,
they made distinctions as they explained the Dharma realm
and achieved complete perfection[41] in doing so.

As for all the worlds throughout the past,
whether vast or whether minute,
which were then adorned by cultivation—
they are able to know them all in but a single mind-moment,[42]

knowing as well how, within them, the lions among men
cultivated the many different types of practices of a buddha
and then reached the universal and right enlightenment
and manifested all the sovereign masteries.[43]

In this same way, during the course of the future,
how all of those most revered among men
will sequentially appear in countless ensuing kalpas—
these bodhisattvas are also able to know all of these matters,

including the content of all their practices and vows
and all of their domains of objective experience
as, in this way, they shall proceed with their diligent cultivation
and then will achieve right enlightenment during those times.

They also know their future congregations,
the life spans they will have, and the way they will teach beings
as, using all of these gateways into the Dharma,
they will turn the wheel of Dharma for the sake of the multitude.

Bodhisattvas who are possessed of these kinds of knowing
dwell on the ground of Samantabhadra's practices.
This wisdom that completely understands all these matters
is what gives birth to all buddhas.

All of the buddha lands
that exist during this present period of time—
they also deeply enter into all of those *kṣetras*
and command a penetrating comprehension of the Dharma realm

and all buddhas of the present
within all those worlds,
those who have gained sovereign mastery of the Dharma
and who are unimpeded in their discourse.

正體字	260b26	亦知彼眾會	淨土應化力
	260b27	盡無量億劫	常思惟是事
	260b28	調御世間尊	所有威神力
	260b29	無盡智慧藏	一切悉能知
	260c01	出生無礙眼	無礙耳鼻身
	260c02	無礙廣長舌	能令眾歡喜
	260c03	最勝無礙心	廣大普清淨
	260c04	智慧遍充滿	悉知三世法
	260c05	善學一切化	剎化眾生化
	260c06	世化調伏化	究竟化彼岸
	260c07	世間種種別	皆由於想住
	260c08	入佛方便智	於此悉明了
	260c09	眾會不可說	一一為現身
	260c10	悉使見如來	度脫無邊眾
	260c11	諸佛甚深智	如日出世間
	260c12	一切國土中	普現無休息
	260c13	了達諸世間	假名無有實
	260c14	眾生及世界	如夢如光影
	260c15	於諸世間法	不生分別見
	260c16	善離分別者	亦不見分別

简体字

亦知彼众会，净土应化力，
尽无量亿劫，常思惟是事。
调御世间尊，所有威神力，
无尽智慧藏，一切悉能知。
出生无碍眼，无碍耳鼻身，
无碍广长舌，能令众欢喜。
最胜无碍心，广大普清净，
智慧遍充满，悉知三世法。
善学一切化，剎化众生化，
世化调伏化，究竟化彼岸。
世间种种别，皆由于想住，
入佛方便智，于此悉明了。
众会不可说，一一为现身，
悉使见如来，度脱无边众。
诸佛甚深智，如日出世间，
一切国土中，普现无休息。
了达诸世间，假名无有实，
众生及世界，如梦如光影。
于诸世间法，不生分别见，
善离分别者，亦不见分别。

Chapter 36 — *The Practices of Samantabhadra*

They also know these buddhas' congregations,
their pure lands, and their powers to manifest in response to beings.
Throughout countless *koṭīs* of kalpas,
they always contemplate these matters.

All of the awesome spiritual powers
of these world-taming *bhagavats*
as well as their inexhaustible treasury of wisdom—
they are able to know them all.

They develop the unimpeded eye,
the unimpeded ear, nose, and body,
and the unimpeded vast and long tongue
with which they can inspire joyous delight in the many.

They develop supremely unimpeded minds
that are vast in their reach and thoroughly pure
and wisdom that is universally pervasive
with which they know all dharmas of the three periods of time.

They thoroughly train in all types of transformations,
including transformations of *kṣetras*, transformations among beings,
transformations of worlds, transformations in training beings,
and ultimately achieve perfection in the practice of transformations.[44]

That the world's many different kinds of distinctions
all arise and abide because of thought—
Through penetrating the Buddha's knowledge of skillful means,
they completely understand all of these matters.

They manifest bodies in each and every one
of an ineffable number of congregations,
enabling them all to see the Tathāgata,
and thereby liberating a boundless multitude of beings.

The extremely profound wisdom of all buddhas
is like the sun when it rises in the world.
Within all of the countries,
it keeps appearing everywhere incessantly.

They completely comprehend the entire world
as but artificial designations devoid of any reality,
while understanding both its beings and the world
as like dreams or like lights and shadows.

They do not produce any discriminations or views
regarding any of the world's dharmas.
They skillfully transcend "one who discriminates"
while also not even perceiving "that which is discriminated."

正體字	260c17 |	無量無數劫	解之即一念
	260c18 |	知念亦無念	如是見世間
	260c19 |	無量諸國土	一念悉超越
	260c20 |	經於無量劫	不動於本處
	260c21 |	不可說諸劫	即是須臾頃
	260c22 |	莫見修與短	究竟剎那法
	260c23 |	心住於世間	世間住於心
	260c24 |	於此不妄起	二非二分別
	260c25 |	眾生世界劫	諸佛及佛法
	260c26 |	一切如幻化	法界悉平等
	260c27 |	普於十方剎	示現無量身
	260c28 |	知身從緣起	究竟無所著
	260c29 |	依於無二智	出現人師子
	261a01 |	不著無二法	知無二非二
	261a02 |	了知諸世間	如焰如光影
	261a03 |	如響亦如夢	如幻如變化
	261a04 |	如是隨順入	諸佛所行處
	261a05 |	成就普賢智	普照深法界
	261a06 |	眾生剎染著	一切皆捨離
	261a07 |	而興大悲心	普淨諸世間
简体字	无量无数劫，解之即一念，知念亦无念，如是见世间。无量诸国土，一念悉超越，经于无量劫，不动于本处。不可说诸劫，即是须臾顷，莫见修与短，究竟刹那法。心住于世间，世间住于心，于此不妄起，二非二分别。众生世界劫，诸佛及佛法，一切如幻化，法界悉平等。普于十方刹，示现无量身，知身从缘起，究竟无所著。依于无二智，出现人师子，不著无二法，知无二非二。了知诸世间，如焰如光影，如响亦如梦，如幻如变化。如是随顺入，诸佛所行处，成就普贤智，普照深法界。众生刹染著，一切皆舍离，而兴大悲心，普净诸世间。		

They understand a period of measureless and countless kalpas
to be identical to a single mind moment even as
they realize mind-moments themselves are devoid of mind-moments.
It is in this way that they perceive the world.

They step beyond a measureless number of lands
in but a single mind-moment
and pass through a measureless number of kalpas
without ever moving from their original place.

An ineffable number of kalpas
are identical to a single instant.
To never even perceive "long" as opposed to "short"
is the ultimate *kṣaṇa* dharma.[45]

The mind abides in the world
and the world abides in the mind.
With regard to these, they do not erroneously generate
any discriminations construing them to be either dual or non-dual.

Beings, worlds, and kalpas,
the buddhas, and the dharmas of the buddhas—
They are all comparable to conjurations or transformations
even as the Dharma realm itself is everywhere the same.

They manifest incalculably many bodies
everywhere throughout the *kṣetras* of the ten directions
even as they realize that the body arises from conditions
and that there is ultimately nothing to which one can be attached.

Relying on their non-dual wisdom,
they come forth and appear as the lions among men
even as they do not become attached to non-dual dharmas
and realize that there is nothing that is either dual or non-dual.

They completely realize that the entire world
is like flames, like lights and shadows,
like echoes, like dreams,
like conjurations, or like transformations.

It is in this way that they accord with and enter into
the stations of all buddhas' action,
perfect the wisdom of Samantabhadra,
and everywhere illuminate the deep Dharma realm.

The defiling attachments associated with beings and *kṣetras*—
they completely relinquish all of them
and then raise up their minds of great compassion
to everywhere purify the entire world.

正體字	261a08	菩薩常正念	論師子妙法
	261a09	清淨如虛空	而興大方便
	261a10	見世常迷倒	發心咸救度
	261a11	所行皆清淨	普遍諸法界
	261a12	諸佛及菩薩	佛法世間法
	261a13	若見其真實	一切無差別
	261a14	如來法身藏	普入世間中
	261a15	雖在於世間	於世無所著
	261a16	譬如清淨水	影像無來去
	261a17	法身遍世間	當知亦如是
	261a18	如是離染著	身世皆清淨
	261a19	湛然如虛空	一切無有生
	261a20	知身無有盡	無生亦無滅
	261a21	非常非無常	示現諸世間
	261a22	除滅諸邪見	開示於正見
	261a23	法性無來去	不著我我所
	261a24	譬如工幻師	示現種種事
	261a25	其來無所從	去亦無所至
	261a26	幻性非有量	亦復非無量
	261a27	於彼大眾中	示現量無量

简体字

菩萨常正念，论师子妙法，
清净如虚空，而兴大方便。
见世常迷倒，发心咸救度，
所行皆清净，普遍诸法界。
诸佛及菩萨，佛法世间法，
若见其真实，一切无差别。
如来法身藏，普入世间中，
虽在于世间，于世无所著。
譬如清净水，影像无来去；
法身遍世间，当知亦如是。
如是离染著，身世皆清净，
湛然如虚空，一切无有生。
知身无有尽，无生亦无灭，
非常非无常，示现诸世间。
除灭诸邪见，开示于正见，
法性无来去，不著我我所。
譬如工幻师，示现种种事，
其来无所从，去亦无所至。
幻性非有量，亦复非无量，
于彼大众中，示现量无量。

The bodhisattvas always abide in right mindfulness
of the wondrous Dharma of the lions of reasoned discourse
and, with purity like that of empty space,
they then bring forth their great skillful means.

Seeing that the world always abides in confusion and inverted views,
they resolve to rescue and liberate everyone.
Whatever they practice is in all cases pure
as they go forth everywhere throughout the entire Dharma realm.

All buddhas as well as all bodhisattvas,
the Dharma of the Buddha, and the dharmas of the world—
If one perceives their reality,
one realizes they are all devoid of any differences.

The treasury of the Tathāgata's Dharma body
everywhere enters into the world.
Yet, although it abides within the world,
it has nothing in the world to which it is attached.

Just as it is true of a body of clear water
that the reflected images on it neither come into it nor leave it,
in the case of the Dharma body's pervasive presence in the world,
one should realize it is just the same as this.

In this same way, they transcend all defiling attachments,
both the body and the world are seen to be pure
and as quiescent as empty space,
and everything is realized as unproduced.

They realize that the body is endless,
that it is neither produced nor destroyed,
that it is neither permanent nor impermanent,
and that it manifests throughout the world.[46]

They extinguish all wrong views
and reveal right views.
They realize the nature of dharmas has no coming or going
and they are not attached to a self or anything belonging to a self.

It is just as in the case of a master conjurer
who manifests many different kinds of phenomena which,
when they appear, have no place from which they come,
and when they disappear, have no place to which they go.

The nature of those conjurations is not finite,
nor is it infinite.
Yet, in the midst of those large crowds,
he manifests both the finite and the infinite.

正體字	261a28	以此寂定心	修習諸善根
	261a29	出生一切佛	非量非無量
	261b01	有量及無量	皆悉是妄想
	261b02	了達一切趣	不著量無量
	261b03	諸佛甚深法	廣大深寂滅
	261b04	甚深無量智	知甚深諸趣
	261b05	菩薩離迷倒	心淨常相續
	261b06	巧以神通力	度無量眾生
	261b07	未安者令安	安者示道場
	261b08	如是遍法界	其心無所著
	261b09	不住於實際	不入於涅槃
	261b10	如是遍世間	開悟諸群生
	261b11	法數眾生數	了知而不著
	261b12	普雨於法雨	充洽諸世間
	261b13	普於諸世界	念念成正覺
	261b14	而修菩薩行	未曾有退轉
	261b15	世間種種身	一切悉了知
	261b16	如是知身法	則得諸佛身
	261b17	普知諸眾生	諸劫及諸剎
	261b18	十方無涯際	智海無不入

简体字

以此寂定心，修习诸善根，
出生一切佛，非量非无量。
有量及无量，皆悉是妄想，
了达一切趣，不著量无量。
诸佛甚深法，广大深寂灭，
甚深无量智，知甚深诸趣。
菩萨离迷倒，心净常相续，
巧以神通力，度无量众生。
未安者令安，安者示道场，
如是遍法界，其心无所著。
不住于实际，不入于涅槃，
如是遍世间，开悟诸群生。
法数众生数，了知而不著，
普雨于法雨，充洽诸世间。
普于诸世界，念念成正觉，
而修菩萨行，未曾有退转。
世间种种身，一切悉了知；
如是知身法，则得诸佛身。
普知诸众生，诸劫及诸刹，
十方无涯际，智海无不入。

Using this mind of quiescent meditative absorption,
they cultivate all roots of goodness
and bring about the birth of all buddhas.
This is not inherently either finite or infinite.

The finite and the infinite
are in every case merely erroneous perceptions.
They completely comprehend all destinies of rebirth
and do not become attached to either the finite or the infinite.

The extremely profound Dharma of all buddhas
is that of vast and deep quiescence.
Their extremely profound and measureless wisdom
knows the extremely profound aspects of all the rebirth destinies.

The bodhisattvas abandon confusion and inverted views.
The purity of their minds is continuous
as they skillfully use the powers of their spiritual superknowledges
to liberate countless beings.

Those who have not yet reached peace, they enable to find peace.
To those who have already found peace, they reveal the *bodhimaṇḍa*.
In this way, as they go everywhere throughout the Dharma realm,
their minds having nothing at all to which they are attached.

They do not dwell in ultimate reality
and do not opt for entry into nirvāṇa.
In this way, they go everywhere throughout the world,
awakening the many kinds of beings.

They completely understand and yet are not attached to
all the categories of dharmas and the categories of beings.
They everywhere rain down the Dharma rain,
causing it to completely drench the entire world.

Everywhere in all worlds and in each successive mind-moment,
they are achieving right enlightenment
and are cultivating the bodhisattva practices
without ever retreating from them.

They completely understand
all of the world's many different kinds of bodies,
and, by understanding the Dharma as it pertains to those bodies,
they are then able to acquire the body of all buddhas.

They everywhere know all beings,
all kalpas, and all *kṣetras*
throughout the boundless realms of the ten directions,
and they have no part of the ocean of wisdom they do not enter.

正體字	261b19 | 261b20 | 261b21 | 261b22 | 261b23 | 261b24 | 261b25 | 261b26 | 261b27 | 261b28 | 261b29 | 261c01 | 261c02 | 261c03 | 261c04 | 261c05 | 261c06 | 261c07 | 261c08 | 261c09 |	眾生身無量 佛身無有邊 一念之所知 經於無量劫 諸佛能現身 一念中無量 如是未來世 無量菩提心 如是三世中 一切悉能知 如是分別知 入於智慧處 微妙廣大智 入已不退轉 一切最勝尊 修行不退轉 無量無邊心 皆由想積集 染污非染污 不可說諸心	一一為現身 智者悉觀見 出現諸如來 稱揚不可盡 處處般涅槃 舍利各差別 有求於佛果 決定智悉知 所有諸如來 名住普賢行 無量諸行地 其輪不退轉 深入如來境 說名普賢慧 普入佛境界 得無上菩提 各各差別業 平等悉了知 學心無學心 念念中悉知
简体字	众生身无量，一一为现身； 佛身无有边，智者悉观见。 一念之所知，出现诸如来， 经于无量劫，称扬不可尽。 诸佛能现身，处处般涅槃， 一念中无量，舍利各差别。 如是未来世，有求于佛果， 无量菩提心，决定智悉知。 如是三世中，所有诸如来， 一切悉能知，名住普贤行。 如是分别知，无量诸行地， 入于智慧处，其轮不退转。 微妙广大智，深入如来境， 入已不退转，说名普贤慧。 一切最胜尊，普入佛境界， 修行不退转，得无上菩提。 无量无边心，各各差别业， 皆由想积集，平等悉了知。 染污非染污，学心无学心， 不可说诸心，念念中悉知。		

Chapter 36 — The Practices of Samantabhadra

The bodies of beings are incalculably many,
yet they manifest bodies for each of them.
Though the Buddha's bodies are boundlessly many,
the wise are able to contemplate and see them all.

What they know in a single mind-moment
about the manifestations of all *tathāgatas* is so much that,
were they to spend countless kalpas attempting to do so,
they still could never come to the end of their praises.

All buddhas are able to manifest bodies
that, in place after place, enter *parinirvāṇa*,
producing in but a single mind-moment countless
śarīra relics, each of them distinctly different from the others.

In this way, throughout the course of the future,
there will be those who seek the fruit of buddhahood
and there will be countless beings who resolve to attain bodhi.
With their definitive wisdom, they know all of these matters.

In this manner, they are all able to entirely know
all of the *tathāgatas*
throughout the three periods of time.
This is what is known as "dwelling in Samantabhadra's practices."

In this way, they distinguish and know
countless practices and grounds,
enter into the stations of wisdom,
and never retreat from their turning of the Dharma wheel.

Their sublime and vast wisdom
deeply penetrates the Tathāgata's domain of objective experience
and, once it has entered it, they attain irreversibility.
This is what is known as "Samantabhadra's wisdom."

All of these who become supremely revered ones
everywhere enter the Buddha's domain of objective experience,
cultivate the practices without ever retreating,
and attain unsurpassable bodhi.

The countlessly and boundlessly many minds—
each and every one of them has different karma
and it all accumulates due to thoughts.
They know all of them equally and completely.

Whether they be defiled or undefiled,
and whether they be minds still in training or minds beyond training,
in each successive mind-moment, they completely know
all of these ineffably numerous minds.

正體字	261c10　了知非一二　非染亦非淨
261c11　亦復無雜亂　皆從自想起
261c12　如是悉明見　一切諸眾生
261c13　心想各不同　起種種世間
261c14　以如是方便　修諸最勝行
261c15　從佛法化生　得名為普賢
261c16　眾生皆妄起　善惡諸趣想
261c17　由是或生天　或復墮地獄
261c18　菩薩觀世間　妄想業所起
261c19　妄想無邊故　世間亦無量
261c20　一切諸國土　想網之所現
261c21　幻網方便故　一念悉能入
261c22　眼耳鼻舌身　意根亦如是
261c23　世間想別異　平等皆能入
261c24　一一眼境界　無量眼皆入
261c25　種種性差別　無量不可說
261c26　所見無差別　亦復無雜亂
261c27　各隨於自業　受用其果報
261c28　普賢力無量　悉知彼一切
261c29　一切眼境界　大智悉能入
简体字	了知非一二，非染亦非净，
亦复无杂乱，皆从自想起。
如是悉明见，一切诸众生，
心想各不同，起种种世间。
以如是方便，修诸最胜行，
从佛法化生，得名为普贤。
众生皆妄起，善恶诸趣想，
由是或生天，或复堕地狱。
菩萨观世间，妄想业所起，
妄想无边故，世间亦无量。
一切诸国土，想网之所现，
幻网方便故，一念悉能入。
眼耳鼻舌身，意根亦如是，
世间想别异，平等皆能入。
一一眼境界，无量眼皆入，
种种性差别，无量不可说。
所见无差别，亦复无杂乱，
各随于自业，受用其果报。
普贤力无量，悉知彼一切，
一切眼境界，大智悉能入。

They completely realize that they are neither singular nor dual,
that they are neither defiled nor pure,
that they are also free of any mixing or disorder,
and that, in every case, they arise from one's own thoughts.

In this way, they completely and clearly see
with regard to all beings,
that their minds and thoughts are all different
and that this is what creates the many different kinds of worlds.

With skillful means such as these,
they cultivate all of the supreme practices,
become transformationally born from the Buddha's Dharma,
and come to be known as "Samantabhadra."[47]

Beings all erroneously generate
thoughts leading to the good and bad destinies.
Because of this, they may be reborn in the heavens
or else may fall into the hells.

The bodhisattvas contemplate the world
as produced by karmic actions based on erroneous thoughts.
Because erroneous thoughts are boundlessly numerous,
the worlds themselves are also measurelessly manifold.

All lands are manifestations
produced by networks of thoughts.
Due to skillful means addressing these networks of illusions,
they are able to enter them all in but a single mind-moment.

The eye, ear, nose, tongue, body,
and mind faculties are also like this,
for they each differ due to the thoughts of those in the world.
They are equally able to fathom all of them.

Each and every one of those realms of visual experience
as well as their countless eye faculties—they enter all of them.
So, too, in the case of the differences in all the various kinds of natures
which are measurelessly and ineffably numerous.

There are no differences in what each one sees,
nor is there any mixing up or disorder in this,
for each one, in accordance with his individual karma,
experiences his own resulting karmic consequences.

The powers of Samantabhadra are measureless.
They completely know all of those things.
Such great wisdom is able to completely penetrate
all of those realms of visual experience.

正體字

```
262a01 ‖    如是諸世間    悉能分別知
262a02 ‖    而修一切行    亦復無退轉
262a03 ‖    佛說眾生說    及以國土說
262a04 ‖    三世如是說    種種悉了知
262a05 ‖    過去中未來    未來中現在
262a06 ‖    三世互相見    一一皆明了
262a07 ‖    如是無量種    開悟諸世間
262a08 ‖    一切智方便    邊際不可得
```

简体字

如是诸世间，悉能分别知，
而修一切行，亦复无退转。
佛说众生说，及以国土说，
三世如是说，种种悉了知。
过去中未来，未来中现在，
三世互相见，一一皆明了。
如是无量种，开悟诸世间，
一切智方便，边际不可得。"

They are entirely able to distinguish and know
all such aspects of the world as these
even as they cultivate all of the practices
and still never retreat from practicing them.

The speech of the buddhas and the speech of beings
as well as the speech particular to various lands—
speech like this as it is spoken throughout the three periods of time—
they completely know it all in all its many different variations.

The future within the past,
the present within the future,
and all such mutual perceptions between the three periods of time—
they clearly know each and every one of them.

They use countlessly many different approaches such as these
to awaken everyone throughout the world.
Their all-knowledge and skillful means are so extensive
that their bounds could never be found.

The End of Chapter Thirty-Six

正體字

大方廣佛華嚴經卷[1]第五十
　　如來出現品第三十七之[3]一
爾時世尊。從眉間白毫相中。放大光明。名如
來出現。無量百千億那由他阿僧祇光明。以
為眷屬。其光普照十方盡虛空法界一切世
界右遶十匝。顯現如來無量自在。覺悟無數
諸菩薩眾。[4]震動一切十方世界。除滅一切諸
惡道苦。映蔽一切諸魔宮殿。顯示一切諸佛
如來。坐菩提座。成等正覺。及以一切道場眾
會。作是事已。而來右遶菩薩眾會。入如來性
起妙德菩薩頂。時此道場。一切大眾。身心踊
躍。生大歡喜。作如是念。甚奇希有。今者如
來。放大光明。必當演說甚深大法。爾時。如來
性起妙德菩薩。於蓮華座上。偏袒右肩。右跪
合掌。一心向佛。而說頌言

　　正覺功德大智出　　普達境界到彼岸
　　等於三世諸如來　　是故我今恭敬禮
　　已[5]昇無相境界岸　　而現妙相莊嚴身
　　放於離垢千光明　　破魔軍眾咸令盡

简体字

大方广佛华严经卷第五十
如来出现品第三十七之一

　　尔时，世尊从眉间白毫相中放大光明，名如来出现，无量百千亿那由他阿僧祇光明以为眷属。其光普照十方尽虚空法界一切世界，右绕十匝，显现如来无量自在，觉悟无数诸菩萨众，震动一切十方世界，除灭一切诸恶道苦，映蔽一切诸魔宫殿，显示一切诸佛如来坐菩提座成等正觉及以一切道场众会；作是事已，而来右绕菩萨众会，入如来性起妙德菩萨顶。

　　时，此道场一切大众身心踊跃，生大欢喜，作如是念："甚奇希有！今者如来放大光明，必当演说甚深大法。"

　　尔时，如来性起妙德菩萨于莲华座上，偏袒右肩，右跪合掌，一心向佛而说颂言：

　　　"正觉功德大智出，普达境界到彼岸，
　　　等于三世诸如来，是故我今恭敬礼。
　　　已升无相境界岸，而现妙相庄严身，
　　　放于离垢千光明，破魔军众咸令尽。

Chapter 37
The Manifestation of the Tathāgata

At that time, from the white hair mark between his brows, the Bhagavat emanated a great light known as "the manifestation of the Tathāgata" that had a retinue of countless hundreds of thousands of *koṭīs* of *nayutas* of *asaṃkhyeyas* of light rays. Its brilliance everywhere illuminated all worlds throughout the ten directions of space and the Dharma realm. It then circumambulated him ten times to his right, revealed the Tathāgata's measureless feats of sovereign spiritual powers, awakened a multitude of countless bodhisattvas, caused shaking and movement in all worlds of the ten directions, extinguished all the sufferings in the wretched destinies, obscured all the palaces of the *māras* with its brightness, revealed all the buddhas, the *tathāgatas*, seated on their bodhi seats, attaining the universal and right enlightenment, revealed too everyone within their *bodhimaṇḍas*' congregations, and then, having accomplished all of this, it came and circumambulated to their right the congregation of bodhisattvas and then entered the top of the head of Sublime Qualities of the Manifestations of the Tathāgata's Nature Bodhisattva.

At that time, everyone in the great assembly at this site of enlightenment was delighted in body and mind and filled with happiness, whereupon they had this thought, "How very extraordinary this is that the Tathāgata has now emanated this immensely brilliant light. Surely he is about to proclaim an extremely profound and great dharma."

Then, from his place where he was seated on a lotus, Sublime Qualities of the Manifestations of the Tathāgata's Nature Bodhisattva then bared his right shoulder, knelt on his right knee, joined his palms, single-mindedly faced the Buddha, and then spoke these verses:

> The Rightly Enlightened One's qualities arise from great wisdom
> whose universal penetration of the objective sphere has been perfected
> and equals that of all *tathāgatas* throughout the three periods of time.
> Therefore I now bow down in reverence.
>
> He has already ascended to the far shore of the realm of signlessness,
> and yet he manifests his body adorned with the marvelous marks.
> He emanates thousands of rays of immaculate radiance,
> vanquishes Māra's army's hordes, and causes them all to disappear.

正體字

262b04 ｜ 十方所有諸世界　悉能震動無有餘
262b05 ｜ 未曾恐怖一眾生　善逝威神力如是
262b06 ｜ 虛空法界性平等　已能如是而安住
262b07 ｜ 一切含生無數量　咸令滅惡除眾垢
262b08 ｜ 苦行勤勞無數劫　成就最上菩提道
262b09 ｜ 於諸境界智無[6]礙　與一切佛同其性
262b10 ｜ 導師放此大光明　震動十方諸世界
262b11 ｜ 已現無量神通力　而復還來入我身
262b12 ｜ 決定法中能善學　無量菩薩皆來集
262b13 ｜ 令我發起問法心　是故我今請法王
262b14 ｜ 今此眾會皆清淨　善能度脫諸世間
262b15 ｜ 智慧無邊無染著　如是賢勝咸來集
262b16 ｜ 利益世間尊導師　智慧精進皆無量
262b17 ｜ 今以光明照大眾　令我問於無上法
262b18 ｜ 誰於大仙深境界　而能真實具開演
262b19 ｜ 誰是如來法長子　世間尊導願顯示
262b20 ｜ 爾時如來。即於口中。放大光明。名無礙無畏。
262b21 ｜ 百千億阿僧祇光明。以為眷屬。普照十方盡
262b22 ｜ 虛空等法界。一切世界。右遶十匝。顯現如來
262b23 ｜ 種種自在。開悟無量諸菩薩眾。

简体字

十方所有诸世界，悉能震动无有余，
未曾恐怖一众生，善逝威神力如是。
虚空法界性平等，已能如是而安住，
一切含生无数量，咸令灭恶除众垢。
苦行勤劳无数劫，成就最上菩提道，
于诸境界智无碍，与一切佛同其性。
导师放此大光明，震动十方诸世界，
已现无量神通力，而复还来入我身。
决定法中能善学，无量菩萨皆来集，
令我发起问法心，是故我今请法王。
今此众会皆清净，善能度脱诸世间，
智慧无边无染著，如是贤胜咸来集。
利益世间尊导师，智慧精进皆无量，
今以光明照大众，令我问于无上法。
谁于大仙深境界，而能真实具开演？
谁是如来法长子？世间尊导愿显示！"
　　尔时，如来即于口中放大光明，名无碍无畏，百千亿阿僧祇光明以为眷属。普照十方尽虚空等法界一切世界，右绕十匝，显现如来种种自在，开悟无量诸菩萨众，

Chapter 37 — The Manifestation of the Tathāgata

He is able to cause shaking and movement
in all worlds of the ten directions without exception,
doing so without frightening even a single being.
The Well Gone One's awesome spiritual powers are of this very sort.

Equal to empty space and the nature of the Dharma realm—
he has already become able to abide in this way.
He is able to cause all of the countless and measurelessly many beings
to extinguish evil and eliminate their many defilements.

Exerting diligent effort in austere practices for countless kalpas,
he achieved success in the path to supreme bodhi,
acquired unimpeded wisdom in all realms,
and became identical in nature with all buddhas.

The Master Guide emanated this great light
and caused shaking and movement in all worlds of the ten directions.
Having shown the measureless powers of spiritual superknowledges,
they have returned and entered my body.

Having been well able to train well in the definitive Dharma,
these countless bodhisattvas have all come and gathered here,
thereby causing me to raise the thought to ask about the Dharma.
Therefore I shall now pose a question to the Dharma King.

Now this congregation is entirely pure
and well able to liberate everyone in the world.
Their wisdom is boundless and free of defiling attachments.
Such supreme worthies have all come and assembled here.

The revered Master Guide who benefits the world
is possessed of wisdom and vigor that are both beyond measure.
Now he has illuminated the great assembly with this great radiance
and thus caused me to inquire about the most supreme Dharma.

Who is it that is able to truly and completely expound
on the Great Rishi's deep spheres of action?
Who is the Tathāgata's most senior Dharma son?
We pray the revered Guide of the World will reveal this to us.

At that time, the Tathāgata immediately emanated a great light from his mouth known as "unimpeded fearlessness" that had a retinue of hundreds of thousands of *koṭīs* of *asaṃkhyeyas* of light rays. It everywhere illuminated all worlds throughout the ten directions of space commensurate with the entire Dharma realm. It then circumambulated him ten times to his right, revealed the Tathāgata's many different feats of sovereign spiritual powers, awakened a multitude of countless bodhisattvas, caused shaking and movement in all worlds

正體字

震動一切十
方世界。除滅一切諸惡道苦。映蔽一切諸魔
宮殿。顯示一切諸佛如來。坐菩提座。成等正
覺。及以一切道場眾會。作是事已。而來右遶。
菩薩眾會。入普賢菩薩摩訶薩口。其光入已。
普賢菩薩身。及師子座。過於本時。及諸菩薩。
身座百倍。唯除如來師子之座
爾時。如來性起妙德菩薩。問普賢菩薩摩訶
薩言。佛子。佛所示現。廣大神變。令諸菩薩。
皆生歡喜不可思議。世莫能知。是何瑞相。普
賢菩薩摩訶薩言。佛子。我於往昔。見諸如來
應正等覺。示現如是廣大神變。即說如來出
現法門。如我惟忖。今現此相。當說其法。說是
語時。一切大地。悉皆震動。出生無量問法光
明。時性起妙德菩薩。問普賢菩薩言。佛子。菩
薩摩訶薩。應云何知諸佛如來應正等覺。出
現之法。願為我說。佛子。此諸無量百千億那
由他。菩薩眾會。皆久修淨業。念慧成就。到於
究竟大莊嚴岸。具一切佛威儀之行。正念諸
佛。未曾忘失。大悲觀察一切眾生。

简体字

震动一切十方世界，除灭一切诸恶道苦，映蔽一切诸魔宫殿，显示一切诸佛如来坐菩提座成等正觉及以一切道场众会；作是事已，而来右绕菩萨众会，入普贤菩萨摩诃萨口。其光入已，普贤菩萨身及师子座，过于本时及诸菩萨身座百倍，唯除如来师子之座。

尔时，如来性起妙德菩萨问普贤菩萨摩诃萨言："佛子，佛所示现广大神变，令诸菩萨皆生欢喜，不可思议，世莫能知，是何瑞相？"

普贤菩萨摩诃萨言："佛子，我于往昔见诸如来、应、正等觉示现如是广大神变，即说如来出现法门。如我惟忖，今现此相，当说其法。"说是语时，一切大地悉皆震动，出生无量问法光明。

时，性起妙德菩萨问普贤菩萨言："佛子，菩萨摩诃萨应云何知诸佛如来、应、正等觉出现之法？愿为我说！佛子，此诸无量百千亿那由他菩萨众会，皆久修净业，念慧成就，到于究竟大庄严岸，具一切佛威仪之行，正念诸佛未曾忘失，大悲观察一切众生，

of the ten directions, extinguished all the sufferings in the wretched destinies, obscured all the palaces of the *māras* with its brightness, revealed all the buddhas, the *tathāgatas*, seated on their bodhi seats, attaining the universal and right enlightenment, revealed too everyone in their *bodhimaṇḍas'* congregations, and then, having accomplished all of this, it came and circumambulated to their right the congregation of bodhisattvas and entered the mouth of Samantabhadra Bodhisattva-mahāsattva. After that light had entered there, the splendor of Samantabhadra Bodhisattva's body and lion throne came to surpass their original state by a hundredfold, surpassing too that of the bodies and lion thrones of all the other bodhisattvas, with the sole exception of the Tathāgata's lion throne.

At that time, Sublime Qualities of the Manifestations of the Tathāgata's Nature Bodhisattva asked Samantabhadra Bodhisattva-mahāsattva, "O Son of the Buddha, the vast spiritual transformations manifested by the Buddha have caused all of these bodhisattvas to be filled with such inconceivable joyous delight that no one in the world could imagine it. What sort of auspicious sign is this?"

Samantabhadra Bodhisattva-mahāsattva then replied, "O Son of the Buddha, in the distant past, I have seen the Tathāgatas, the Right and Universally Enlightened Ones, manifest such vast spiritual transformations as this, whereupon they straightaway explained the Dharma gateway of 'the manifestation of the Tathāgata.' According to my assessment, that he has now displayed these signs indicates that he is about to teach that very dharma." When he spoke these words, the entire great earth shook and moved and sent forth measurelessly many rays of light associated with the requesting of Dharma.

Then Sublime Qualities of the Manifestations of the Tathāgata's Nature Bodhisattva asked Samantabhadra Bodhisattva, "O Son of the Buddha, how should the bodhisattva-mahāsattva know the dharma of the manifestation of the buddhas, the right and universally enlightened ones? Please speak about this matter for our sakes.

"Son of the Buddha, those in this congregation of countless hundreds of thousands of *koṭīs* of *nayutas* of bodhisattvas have all already long cultivated pure karmic works, have already completely developed their mindfulness and wisdom, have perfected the great adornments, have become possessed of the awesome deportment associated with the practices of all buddhas, and have established themselves in unfailing right mindfulness of all buddhas. They contemplate all beings with great compassion, definitely and completely know the

正體字

決定了知諸大菩薩神通境界。已得諸佛神力所加。能受一切如來妙法。具如是等無量功德。皆已來集。佛子。汝已曾於無量百千億那由他佛所。承事供養。成就菩薩最上妙行。於三昧門皆得自在。入一切佛祕密之處。知諸佛法。斷眾疑惑。為諸如來神力所加。知眾生根。隨其所樂。為說真實解脫之法。隨順佛智。演說佛法。到於彼岸。有如是等無量功德。善哉佛子。願說如來應正等覺。出現之法。身相言音。心意境界。所行之行。成道轉[7]法。乃至示現入般涅槃。見聞親近。所生善根。如是等事。願皆為說。時如來性起妙德菩薩。欲重明此義。向普賢菩薩。而說頌曰

　善哉無礙大智慧　　善覺無邊平等境
　願說無量佛所行　　佛子聞已皆欣慶
　菩薩云何隨順入　　諸佛如來出興世
　云何身語心境界　　及所行處願皆說
　云何諸佛成正覺　　云何如來轉法輪
　云何善逝般涅槃　　大眾聞已心歡喜

简体字

决定了知诸大菩萨神通境界，已得诸佛神力所加，能受一切如来妙法；具如是等无量功德，皆已来集。佛子，汝已曾于无量百千亿那由他佛所承事供养，成就菩萨最上妙行，于三昧门皆得自在，入一切佛秘密之处，知诸佛法，断众疑惑，为诸如来神力所加，知众生根，随其所乐为说真实解脱之法，随顺佛智演说佛法到于彼岸，有如是等无量功德。善哉！佛子，愿说如来、应、正等觉出现之法，身相、言音、心意境界，所行之行，成道转法轮，乃至示现入般涅槃，见闻亲近所生善根；如是等事，愿皆为说！

时，如来性起妙德菩萨欲重明此义，向普贤菩萨而说颂曰：

"善哉无碍大智慧，善觉无边平等境，
　愿说无量佛所行，佛子闻已皆欣庆！
　菩萨云何随顺入，诸佛如来出兴世？
　云何身语心境界？及所行处愿皆说！
　云何诸佛成正觉？云何如来转法轮？
　云何善逝般涅槃？大众闻已心欢喜。

spheres of action of the great bodhisattvas' spiritual superknowledges, have already acquired the assistance of all buddhas' spiritual powers, are able to take on the sublime Dharma of all *tathāgatas*, and, having become possessed of all such countlessly many meritorious qualities as these, have already come and assembled here.

"O Son of the Buddha, you have already served and made offerings to measurelessly many hundreds of thousands of *koṭīs* of *nayutas* of buddhas, have perfected the bodhisattva's most supremely marvelous practices, have achieved sovereign mastery in all gateways to samādhi, have entered the secret stations of all buddhas, have known all dharmas of the Buddha, have severed all of the many doubts, and have been assisted by the spiritual powers of all *tathāgatas*. You know the faculties of beings, adapt to whatever they find pleasing, and explain for them the dharmas of genuine liberation. You accord with the knowledge of the Buddha and thus achieve perfection in expounding the Dharma of the Buddha. You possess countlessly many meritorious qualities such as these.

"This is good indeed. O Son of the Buddha, we only wish that you will please speak about the dharma of the manifestation of the Tathāgata, the One of Universal and Right Enlightenment, about his physical signs, his voice, his mind's spheres of action, the practices in which he engages, his realization of the path, his turning of the Dharma wheel, and so forth, including his manifestation of entry into *parinirvāṇa*, the roots of goodness arising from seeing him, hearing him, and drawing near to him, as well as other such matters. We wish that you will please explain all of these matters for us."

At that time, wishing to clarify this meaning once again, Sublime Qualities of the Manifestations of the Tathāgata's Nature Bodhisattva addressed Samantabhadra Bodhisattva with verses, saying:

> It is good indeed, you who are possessed of unimpeded great wisdom
> and who has well awakened to the boundless realm of equality.
> Please speak about the countless practices of the buddha.
> Having listened, the sons of the Buddha will all feel joyous delight.
>
> How does the bodhisattva accord with and enter into
> the Buddha's, the Tathāgata's, emergence into the world?
> What are his physical, verbal, and mental spheres of action
> as well as the stations in which he practices? Please speak of all of this.
>
> How is it that all buddhas attain right enlightenment?
> How is it that the Tathāgata turns the wheel of the Dharma?
> And how is it that the Well Gone One enters *parinirvāṇa*?
> Hearing this, the minds of those in the Great Assembly will be happy.

正體字

```
263a04 |    若有見佛大法王    親近增長諸善根
263a05 |    願說彼諸功德藏    眾生見已何所獲
263a06 |    若有得聞如來名    若現在世若涅槃
263a07 |    於彼福藏生深信    有何等利願宣說
263a08 |    此諸菩薩皆合掌    瞻仰如來仁及我
263a09 |    大功德海之境界    淨眾生者願為說
263a10 |    願以因緣及譬[1]諭    演說妙法相應義
263a11 |    眾生聞已發大心    疑盡智淨如虛空
263a12 |    如遍一切國土中    諸佛所現莊嚴身
263a13 |    願以妙音及因[*]諭    示佛菩提亦如彼
263a14 |    十方千萬諸佛土    億那由他無量劫
263a15 |    如今所集菩薩眾    於彼一切悉難見
263a16 |    此諸菩薩咸恭敬    於微妙義生渴仰
263a17 |    願以淨心具開演    如來出現廣大法
263a18 | 爾時普賢菩薩摩訶薩。告如來性起妙德等
263a19 | 諸菩薩大眾言。佛子。此處不可思議。所[2]謂
263a20 | 如來應正等覺。以無量法。而得出現。何以故。
263a21 | 非以一緣。非以一事。如來出現。而得成就。以
263a22 | 十無量。百千阿僧祇事。而得成就。何等為十。
263a23 | 所謂過去無量攝受一切眾生。菩提心所成
263a24 | 故。
```

简体字

若有见佛大法王，亲近增长诸善根，
愿说彼诸功德藏，众生见已何所获？
若有得闻如来名，若现在世若涅槃，
于彼福藏生深信，有何等利愿宣说！
此诸菩萨皆合掌，瞻仰如来仁及我，
大功德海之境界，净众生者愿为说！
愿以因缘及譬喻，演说妙法相应义，
众生闻已发大心，疑尽智净如虚空。
如遍一切国土中，诸佛所现庄严身，
愿以妙音及因喻，示佛菩提亦如彼。
十方千万诸佛土，亿那由他无量劫，
如今所集菩萨众，于彼一切悉难见。
此诸菩萨咸恭敬，于微妙义生渴仰，
愿以净心具开演，如来出现广大法！"

尔时，普贤菩萨摩诃萨告如来性起妙德等诸菩萨大众言："佛子，此处不可思议，所谓如来、应、正等觉以无量法而得出现。何以故？非以一缘，非以一事，如来出现而得成就；以十无量百千阿僧祇事而得成就。何等为十？所谓：过去无量摄受一切众生菩提心所成故，

Chapter 37 — The Manifestation of the Tathāgata

> If there be anyone who sees the Buddha, the great king of the Dharma,
> or draws near to him, he will increase his roots of goodness.
> Please speak of the treasury of all his meritorious qualities
> and of what results shall be reaped after beings have seen him.
>
> If there be anyone who hears the Tathāgata's name,
> whether in the present era or after his nirvāṇa,
> and then develops deep faith in his treasury of merit,
> what benefit will then accrue to him? Please expound on this matter.
>
> All of these bodhisattvas have placed their palms together
> and gaze up in admiration at the Tathāgata, you, and me.
> The sphere of action of the Great Ocean of Meritorious Qualities
> and his purification of beings—please explain these matters for them.
>
> Please use causes and conditions as well as analogies
> to expound on the meanings of the sublime Dharma.
> Having heard this, beings will arouse the great resolve,
> their doubts will end, and their wisdom will become as pure as space.
>
> Just as it is set forth by the adorned bodies
> manifested by all buddhas everywhere in all lands,
> please use your sublime voice as well as causal factors and analogies
> to reveal the bodhi of the Buddha just as they do.
>
> Even in the hundreds of myriads of buddha lands in all ten directions
> throughout *koṭīs* of *nayutas* of incalculably long kalpas,
> an assembly of bodhisattvas such as has now assembled here,
> in all those circumstances, could only rarely be encountered.
>
> These bodhisattvas are all filled with reverential respect
> and have aroused a longing admiration for the sublime meaning.
> We all pray that, with your purified mind, you will fully expound
> on the vast dharma of the manifestation of the Tathāgata.

At that time, Samantabhadra Bodhisattva-mahāsattva informed the great assembly of Sublime Qualities of the Manifestations of the Tathāgata's Nature Bodhisattva and all the other bodhisattvas:

> Sons of the Buddha, this circumstance is inconceivable. That is to say, it is because of countless dharmas that the right and universal enlightenment of the Tathāgata, the Arhat, is able to manifest. How is this so? It is not because of but a single condition and not because of but a single matter that the manifestation of the Tathāgata is able to be accomplished. Rather it is because of ten measureless matters subsuming hundreds of thousands of *asaṃkhyeyas* of factors that it is able to be accomplished. What are those ten? They are as follows:
>
> > This is accomplished due to measureless past instances of the bodhi resolve in gathering in all beings;

|正體字|

過去無量清淨殊勝。志樂所成故。過去無
263a25　量救護一切眾生。大慈大悲。所成故。過去無
263a26　量。相續行願。所成故。過去無量。修諸福智。
263a27　心無厭足。所成故。過去無量。供養諸佛。教化
263a28　眾生。所成故。過去無量。智慧方便。清淨道所
263a29　成故。過去無量。清淨功德藏。所成故。過去無
263b01　量。莊嚴道智。所成故。過去無量。通達法義。
263b02　所成故。佛子。如是無量阿僧祇法門圓滿。成
263b03　於如來。佛子。譬如三千大千世界。非以一緣。
263b04　非以一事。而得成就。以無量緣無量事。方乃
263b05　得成。所謂興布大雲。降霪大雨。四種風輪。相
263b06　續為依。其四者何。一名能持。能持大水故。二
263b07　名能消。能消大水故。三名建立。建立一切
263b08　諸處所故。四名莊嚴。莊嚴分布。咸善巧故如是
263b09　皆由眾生共業。及諸菩薩。善根所起。令於其
263b10　中一切眾生。各隨所宜。而得受用。

|简体字|

过去无量清净殊胜志乐所成故，过去无量救护一切众生大慈大悲所成故，过去无量相续行愿所成故，过去无量修诸福智心无厌足所成故，过去无量供养诸佛教化众生所成故，过去无量智慧方便清净道所成故，过去无量清净功德藏所成故，过去无量庄严道智所成故，过去无量通达法义所成故。佛子，如是无量阿僧祇法门圆满，成于如来。佛子，譬如三千大千世界，非以一缘，非以一事，而得成就，以无量缘、无量事，方乃得成。所谓：兴布大云，降霪大雨，四种风轮相续为依。其四者何？一名能持，能持大水故；二名能消，能消大水故；三名建立，建立一切诸处所故；四名庄严，庄严分布咸善巧故。如是皆由众生共业及诸菩萨善根所起，令于其中一切众生各随所宜而得受用。

Chapter 37 — The Manifestation of the Tathāgata

This is accomplished due to measureless past instances of pure and especially supreme aspiration;

This is accomplished due to measureless past instances of great kindness and great compassion devoted to rescuing and protecting all beings;

This is accomplished due to measureless past instances of continuously implemented conduct and vows;

This is accomplished due to measureless past cultivation of merit and wisdom with insatiable resolve;

This is accomplished due to measureless past offerings to buddhas and teaching of beings;

This is accomplished due to measureless past uses of wisdom and skillful means on the path of purity;

This is accomplished due to measureless past accumulation of a treasury of pure meritorious qualities;

This is accomplished due to measureless past uses of path-adorning wisdom; and

This is accomplished due to measureless past penetrating comprehensions of Dharma's meanings.

Sons of the Buddha, it is through the complete fulfillment of measurelessly many *asaṃkhyeyas* of Dharma gateways such as these that one succeeds in becoming a *tathāgata*. Sons of the Buddha, this is just as the complete creation of the worlds of a great trichiliocosm is not accomplished solely due to a single condition or due to a single matter. Rather it is because of measurelessly many conditions and measurelessly many matters that it then and only then is created. For instance, there is the spreading forth of great clouds and the falling of the great drenching rains. There are the four kinds of spheres of wind upon which it continuously depends. What are those four? They are as follows:

The first is known as "able to retain" because of its ability to retain the waters;

The second is known as "able to dissipate" because of its ability to dissipate the great waters;

The third is known as "establishment" because it establishes all places; and

The fourth is known as "adornment" because the adornments and their distribution are all skillfully created.

All such phenomena as these arise due to beings' jointly created karma and also due to the bodhisattvas' roots of goodness which together allow all the beings therein to be able to obtain and use whatever is fitting for each of them.

正體字

佛子。如是等無量因緣。乃成三千大千世界。法性如是。無有生者。無有作者。無有知者。無有成者。然彼世界。而得成就。如來出現。亦復如是。非以一緣。非以一事。而得成就。以無量因緣。無量事相。乃得成就。所謂。曾於過去佛所。聽聞受持大法雲雨。因此能起如來四種大智風輪。何等為四。一者念持不忘陀羅尼大智風輪。能持一切如來大法雲雨故。二者出生止觀大智風輪。能消竭一切煩惱故。三者善巧迴向大智風輪。能成就一切善根故。四者出生離垢差別莊嚴大智風輪。令過去所化。一切眾生。善根清淨。成就如來無漏善根力故。如來如是成等正覺。法性如是無生無作。而得成就。佛子。是為如來應正等覺出現第一相。菩薩摩訶薩。應如是知。復次佛子。譬如三千大千世界。將欲成時。大雲降雨。名曰洪霔。

简体字

佛子，如是等无量因缘乃成三千大千世界，法性如是，无有生者，无有作者，无有知者，无有成者，然彼世界而得成就。如来出现亦复如是，非以一缘，非以一事，而得成就；以无量因缘，无量事相，乃得成就。所谓：曾于过去佛所听闻受持大法云雨，因此能起如来四种大智风轮。何等为四？一者、念持不忘陀罗尼大智风轮，能持一切如来大法云雨故；二者、出生止观大智风轮，能消竭一切烦恼故；三者、善巧回向大智风轮，能成就一切善根故；四者、出生离垢差别庄严大智风轮，令过去所化一切众生善根清净，成就如来无漏善根力故。如来如是成等正觉，法性如是，无生无作而得成就。佛子，是为如来、应、正等觉出现第一相，菩萨摩诃萨应如是知。

"复次，佛子，譬如三千大千世界将欲成时，大云降雨，名曰洪霔，

Chapter 37 — The Manifestation of the Tathāgata

Sons of the Buddha, it is because of countless causes and conditions such as these that there then occurs the creation of the worlds of a great trichiliocosm. The nature of dharmas is of this very sort. There is no one who produces them, no one who makes them, no one who knows them, and no one who creates them, and yet those worlds are still able to become completely established.

The manifestation of the Tathāgatas is also of this very sort. It is not due to but a single condition and not due to but a single matter that this circumstance is fully realized. Rather, it is due to countless causes and conditions and due to countless phenomenal characteristics that it is then able to become completely realized. In particular, in the presence of past buddhas, they have heard, absorbed, and retained the rains sent down by the great Dharma clouds. It is because of this that they were able to produce the four kinds of great wisdom wind spheres of a *tathāgata*. What are those four? They are as follows:

- The first is "the remembering and never forgetting *dhāraṇī* great wisdom wind sphere" by which they are able to retain the rains from the great Dharma clouds of all *tathāgatas*;
- The second is "the development of calming and contemplation great wisdom wind sphere" by which they are able to dissipate all afflictions;
- The third is "the skillful dedications great wisdom wind sphere" by which they are able to completely develop all roots of goodness; and
- The fourth is "the production of different immaculately pure adornments great wisdom wind sphere" by which they cause all beings they have taught in the past to acquire purified roots of goodness and then perfect the power of a *tathāgata*'s uncontaminated roots of goodness.

It is in this way that the Tathāgata brings about the realization of the universal and right enlightenment. It is in the very nature of Dharma that, in this way, even without any arising at all and without any creation at all, it is nonetheless brought to complete fulfillment.

Sons of the Buddha, this is the first of the marks of the manifestation of the Tathāgata, the Arhat, the One of Right and Universal Enlightenment. The bodhisattva-mahāsattva should know it in this way.

Moreover, Sons of the Buddha, this is just as when the great trichiliocosm is about to be created. Great clouds send down great rains known as "the vast torrential deluge" that no other place is

正體字

263b27	切方處。所不能受。所不能持。唯除大千界。將
263b28	欲成時。佛子。如來應正等覺。亦復如是。興大
263b29	法雲。雨大法雨。名成就如來出現。一切二乘。
263c01	心志狹劣。所不能受。所不能持。唯除諸大菩
263c02	薩。心相續力。佛子。是為如來應正等覺出現
263c03	第二相。菩薩摩訶薩。應如是知。復次佛子。譬
263c04	如眾生。以業力故。大雲降雨。來無所從。去無
263c05	所至。如來應正等覺。亦復如是。以諸菩薩。善
263c06	根力故。興大法雲。雨大法雨。亦無所從來。無
263c07	所至去。佛子。是為如來應正等覺出現第三
263c08	相。菩薩摩訶薩。應如是知。復次佛子。譬如大
263c09	雲。降霔大雨。大千世界。一切眾生。無能知數。
263c10	若欲算計。徒令發狂。唯大千世界主。摩醯首
263c11	羅。以過去所修善根力故。乃至一滴。無不明
263c12	了。佛子。如來應正等覺。亦復如是。興大法雲。
263c13	雨大法雨。一切眾生。聲聞獨覺。所不能知。若
263c14	欲思量。

简体字

一切方处所不能受、所不能持,唯除大千界将欲成时。佛子,如来、应、正等觉亦复如是,兴大法云,雨大法雨,名成就如来出现,一切二乘心志狭劣所不能受、所不能持,唯除诸大菩萨心相续力。佛子,是为如来、应、正等觉出现第二相,菩萨摩诃萨应如是知。

"复次,佛子,譬如众生以业力故,大云降雨,来无所从,去无所至。如来、应、正等觉亦复如是,以诸菩萨善根力故,兴大法云,雨大法雨,亦无所从来,无所至去。佛子,是为如来、应、正等觉出现第三相,菩萨摩诃萨应如是知。

"复次,佛子,譬如大云降霔大雨,大千世界一切众生,无能知数,若欲算计,徒令发狂;唯大千世界主——摩醯首罗,以过去所修善根力故,乃至一滴无不明了。佛子,如来、应、正等觉亦复如是,兴大法云,雨大法雨,一切众生、声闻、独觉所不能知,若欲思量,

able to absorb or able to retain aside from the great chiliocosms at such time as they are about to be created.

Sons of the Buddha, so too it is with the Tathāgata, the Arhat, the One of Right and Universal Enlightenment. He spreads forth the great Dharma clouds and rains down the great Dharma rain known as "establisher of the Tathāgata's manifestation," one that no practitioners of the two vehicles are able to absorb or retain. This is because of their narrow and inferior resolve. It is only the great bodhisattvas who are able to do so. This is because of the continuous power of their resolve.

Sons of the Buddha, this is the second of the marks of the manifestation of the Tathāgata, the Arhat, the One of Right and Universal Enlightenment. The bodhisattva-mahāsattva should know it in this way.

Moreover, Sons of the Buddha, this is just as when, due to the power of beings' karmic actions, the great clouds send down the rains, and yet, in coming, they have no place from which they come and, in going, they have no place to which they go.

So too it is with the Tathāgata, the Arhat, the One of Right and Universal Enlightenment. Due to the power of the bodhisattvas' roots of goodness, he spreads forth the great Dharma clouds and rains down the great Dharma rains even as they have no place from which they come and have no place to which they go.

Sons of the Buddha, this is the third of the marks of the manifestation of the Tathāgata, the Arhat, the One of Right and Universal Enlightenment. The bodhisattva-mahāsattva should know it in this way.

Moreover, Sons of the Buddha, this is just as when the great clouds send down the great drenching rains. There is no being anywhere in the great chiliocosm who would be able to know the number of those rain drops, and if they wished to count them, they would needlessly go insane. It is only Maheśvara, the lord of the great chiliocosm, who, because of the power of roots of goodness he cultivated in the past, is able to know this even to the extent that there would not be even a single drop about which he would not be completely clear.

Sons of the Buddha, so too it is with the Tathāgata, the Arhat, the One of Right and Universal Enlightenment. When he spreads forth the great Dharma clouds and rains down the great Dharma rain, there is no being, no *śrāvaka* disciple, and no *pratyekabuddha* who would be able to know the extent of this. Were they to even attempt to assess this through contemplation, their minds would

正體字

心必狂亂。唯除一切世間主。菩薩摩訶薩以過去所修。覺慧力故。乃至一文一[3]句。入眾生心。無不明了。佛子。是為如來應正等覺出現第四相。菩薩摩訶薩。應如是知。復次佛子。譬如大雲。降雨之時。有大雲雨。名為能滅。能滅火災。有大雲雨。名為能起。能起大水。有大雲雨。名為能止。能止大水。有大雲雨。名為能成。能成一切摩尼諸寶。有大雲雨。名為分別。分別三千大千世界。佛子。如來出現。亦復如是。興大法雲。雨大法雨。有大法雨。名為能滅。能滅一切眾生煩惱。有大法雨。名為能起。能起一切眾生善根。有大法雨。名為能止。能止一切眾生見惑。有大法雨。名為能成。能成一切智慧法寶。有大法雨。名為分別。分別一切眾生心樂。佛子。是為如來應正等覺出現第五相。菩薩摩訶薩。應如是知。

简体字

心必狂乱；唯除一切世间主——菩萨摩诃萨，以过去所修觉慧力故，乃至一文一句，入众生心，无不明了。佛子，是为如来、应、正等觉出现第四相，菩萨摩诃萨应如是知。

"复次，佛子，譬如大云降雨之时，有大云雨，名为能灭，能灭火灾；有大云雨，名为能起，能起大水；有大云雨，名为能止，能止大水；有大云雨，名为能成，能成一切摩尼诸宝；有大云雨，名为分别，分别三千大千世界。佛子，如来出现亦复如是，兴大法云，雨大法雨，有大法雨，名为能灭，能灭一切众生烦恼；有大法雨，名为能起，能起一切众生善根；有大法雨，名为能止，能止一切众生见惑；有大法雨，名为能成，能成一切智慧法宝；有大法雨，名为分别，分别一切众生心乐。佛子，是为如来、应、正等觉出现第五相，菩萨摩诃萨应如是知。

Chapter 37 — The Manifestation of the Tathāgata

certainly be bound to become crazed and confused. It is only the lords of all worlds, the bodhisattva-mahāsattvas, who, due to the power of their past cultivation of enlightened wisdom, could know this even to the extent that there would not be even a single passage or a single statement entering any being's mind about which they would not be completely clear.

Sons of the Buddha, this is the fourth of the marks of the manifestation of the Tathāgata, the Arhat, the One of Right and Universal Enlightenment. The bodhisattva-mahāsattva should know it in this way.

Moreover, Sons of the Buddha, this is just as when the great clouds send down their rains:

> There is a rain that falls from great clouds known as "able to extinguish" that is able to extinguish fire disasters;
> There is a rain that falls from great clouds known as "able to produce" that is able to produce great bodies of water;
> There is a rain that falls from great clouds known as "able to halt" that is able to halt great floods of water;
> There is a rain that falls from great clouds known as "able to create" that is able to create all kinds of *maṇi* jewels; and
> There is a rain that falls from great clouds known as "able to distinguish" that is able to distinguish all worlds of the great trichiliocosm.

Sons of the Buddha, so too it is with the manifestation of the Tathāgata in which he spreads forth the great Dharma clouds and rains down the great Dharma rains:

> There is a rain of great Dharma known as "able to extinguish" that is able to extinguish all beings' afflictions;
> There is a great Dharma rain known as "able to produce" that is able to produce roots of goodness in all beings;
> There is a rain of great Dharma known as "able to halt" that is able to halt all beings' view delusions;
> There is a rain of great Dharma known as "able to create" that is able to create the Dharma jewel of all-knowledge;
> And there is a rain of great Dharma known as "able to distinguish" that is able to distinguish whatever pleases the minds of all beings.

Sons of the Buddha, this is the fifth of the marks of the manifestation of the Tathāgata, the Arhat, the One of Right and Universal Enlightenment. The bodhisattva-mahāsattva should know it in this way.

正體字

復次佛子。譬如大雲。雨一味水。隨其所雨。無量差別。如來出現。亦復如是。雨於大悲一味法水。隨宜說法。無量差別。佛子。是為如來應正等覺出現第六相。菩薩摩訶薩。應如是知。復次佛子。譬如三千大千世界。初始成時。先成色界諸天宮殿。次成欲界諸天宮殿。次成於人及餘眾生。諸所住處。佛子。如來出現。亦復如是。先起菩薩諸行智慧。次起緣覺諸行智慧。次起聲聞善根諸行智慧。次起其餘眾生有為善根諸行智慧。佛子。譬如大雲。雨一味水。隨諸眾生。善根異故。所起宮殿。種種不同。如來大悲。一味法雨。隨眾生器。而有差別。佛子。是為如來應正等覺出現第七相。菩薩摩訶薩。應如是知。復次佛子。譬如世界。初欲成時。有大水生。遍滿三千大千世界。生大蓮華。名如來出現功德寶莊嚴。遍覆水上。光照十方一切世界。時摩醯首羅。淨居天等。見是華已。即決定知於此劫中。有爾所佛。出興[1]于世。

简体字

"复次，佛子，譬如大云雨一味水，随其所雨，无量差别。如来出现亦复如是，雨于大悲一味法水，随宜说法，无量差别。佛子，是为如来、应、正等觉出现第六相，菩萨摩诃萨应如是知。

"复次，佛子，譬如三千大千世界初始成时，先成色界诸天宫殿，次成欲界诸天宫殿，次成于人及余众生诸所住处。佛子，如来出现亦复如是，先起菩萨诸行智慧，次起缘觉诸行智慧，次起声闻善根诸行智慧，次起其余众生有为善根诸行智慧。佛子，譬如大云雨一味水，随诸众生善根异故，所起宫殿种种不同。如来大悲一味法雨，随众生器而有差别。佛子，是为如来、应、正等觉出现第七相，菩萨摩诃萨应如是知。

"复次，佛子，譬如世界初欲成时，有大水生，遍满三千大千世界；生大莲华，名如来出现功德宝庄严，遍覆水上，光照十方一切世界。时，摩醯首罗、净居天等见是华已，即决定知于此劫中有尔所佛出兴于世。

Chapter 37 — The Manifestation of the Tathāgata

Moreover, Sons of the Buddha, this is just as when a great cloud rains down rain of a single flavor and adapts to the countless differences in whatever it rains upon. So too it is with the manifestation of the Tathāgata when he rains down the waters of Dharma that have the singular flavor of great compassion with which he adapts to whatever is fitting in any given situation as he teaches the Dharma in accordance with countless differences.

Sons of the Buddha, this is the sixth of the marks of the manifestation of the Tathāgata, the Arhat, the One of Right and Universal Enlightenment. The bodhisattva-mahāsattva should know it in this way.

Moreover, Sons of the Buddha, this is just as when the great trichiliocosm is first being formed. First, the palaces of the form-realm devas are formed. Next, the palaces of the desire-realm devas are formed. And then all the dwelling places of humans and other beings are formed.

Sons of the Buddha, so too it is with the manifestation of the Tathāgata. First, he brings forth the wisdom associated with the bodhisattvas' practices. Next, he brings forth the wisdom associated with the *pratyekabuddhas*' practices. Next, he brings forth the wisdom associated with the *śrāvaka* disciples' roots of goodness and practices. And then he brings forth the wisdom associated with other beings' conditioned roots of goodness and practices.

Sons of the Buddha, this is just like when the great clouds rain down a single flavor of water and just like when, in accordance with differences in beings' roots of goodness, there are all kinds of differences in the palaces that are created. The single flavor of Dharma rain that comes forth from the Tathāgata's great compassion adapts to beings' capacities and thus possesses corresponding differences.

Sons of the Buddha, this is the seventh of the marks of the manifestation of the Tathāgata, the Arhat, the One of Right and Universal Enlightenment. The bodhisattva-mahāsattva should know it in this way.

Moreover, Sons of the Buddha, this is just as when the world is first about to be formed. A great flood arises everywhere filling the great trichiliocosm which then produces immense lotus blossoms known as "the jeweled adornments of the qualities of the Tathāgata's manifestation" which everywhere cover the surface of those waters and radiate light illuminating all worlds of the ten directions. Then, having seen these flowers, Maheśvara, the devas of the Pure Dwelling Heaven, and the others all immediately know with certitude that in this very kalpa there will be precisely just so very many buddhas that will come forth and appear in the world.[48]

正體字

佛子。爾時其中。有風輪起。名善淨光
明。能成色界諸天宮殿。有風輪起。名淨光莊
嚴。能成欲界諸天宮殿。有風輪起。名堅密無
能壞。能成大小諸輪圍山。及金剛山。有風輪
起。名勝高。能成須彌山王。有風輪起。名不
動。能成十大山王。何等為十。所謂。佉陀羅
山。仙人山。伏魔山。大伏魔山。持雙山。尼民
陀羅山。目真隣陀山。摩訶目真隣陀山。香山。
雪山。有風輪起。名為安住。能成大地。有風輪
起。名為莊嚴。能成地天宮殿。龍宮殿。乾闥婆
宮殿。有風輪起。名無盡藏。能成三千大千世
界。一切[2]大海。有風輪起。名普光明藏。能成
三千大千世界。諸摩尼寶。有風輪起。名堅固
根。能成一切諸如意樹。佛子。大雲所雨。一味
之水。無有分別。以眾生善根不同故。風輪不
同。風輪差別故。世界差別。佛子。如來出現。
亦復如是。具足一切善根功德。放於無上。大
智光明。名不斷如來種不思議智。普照十方
一切世界。與諸菩薩。一切如來。灌頂之記。

简体字

佛子，尔时，其中有风轮起，名善净光明，能成色界诸天宫殿。有风轮起，名净光庄严，能成欲界诸天宫殿。有风轮起，名坚密无能坏，能成大小诸轮围山及金刚山。有风轮起，名胜高，能成须弥山王。有风轮起，名不动，能成十大山王。何等为十？所谓：佉陀罗山、仙人山、伏魔山、大伏魔山、持双山、尼民陀罗山、目真邻陀山、摩诃目真邻陀山、香山、雪山。有风轮起，名为安住，能成大地。有风轮起，名为庄严，能成地天宫殿、龙宫殿、乾闼婆宫殿。有风轮起，名无尽藏，能成三千大千世界一切大海。有风轮起，名普光明藏，能成三千大千世界诸摩尼宝。有风轮起，名坚固根，能成一切诸如意树。佛子，大云所雨一味之水，无有分别；以众生善根不同故，风轮不同；风轮差别故，世界差别。佛子，如来出现亦复如是，具足一切善根功德，放于无上大智光明，名不断如来种不思议智，普照十方一切世界，与诸菩萨一切如来灌顶之记：

Chapter 37 — The Manifestation of the Tathāgata

Sons of the Buddha, at that time, in that very place:

There arises a sphere of wind known as "light of excellent purity" that is able to create the palaces of the form-realm devas;

There arises a sphere of wind known as "pure light adornment" that is able to create the palaces of the desire-realm devas;

There arises a sphere of wind known as "indestructibly solid and dense" that is able to create all of the greater and lesser mountain rings as well as the mountain of vajra;

There arises a sphere of wind known as "supremely lofty" that is able to create Sumeru, king of the mountains;

There arises a sphere of wind known as "immovable" that is able to create the ten great mountain kings. What are those ten? They are: Khadira Mountain, Rishi Mountain, Māra-Vanquishing Mountain, Great Māra-Vanquishing Mountain, Yugaṃdhara Mountain, Nemiṃdhara Mountain, Mucilinda Mountain, Mahāmucilinda Mountain, Incense Mountain, and Snow Mountain.

There arises a sphere of wind known as "stable abiding" that is able to create the great earth;

There arises a sphere of wind known as "adornment" that is able to create the palaces of the earthly devas, the palaces of the dragons, and the palaces of the *gandharvas*;

There arises a sphere of wind known as "endless treasury" that is able to create all the great oceans throughout the worlds of the great trichiliocosm;

There arises a sphere of wind known as "universal light treasury" that is able to create all the *maṇi* jewels throughout the worlds of the great trichiliocosm; and

There arises a sphere of wind known as "solid root" that is able to create all the wish-fulfilling trees.

Sons of the Buddha, the waters of a single flavor rained down from the great clouds has no distinctions. It is because of differences in beings' roots of goodness that the spheres of wind are different and it is because of differences in the spheres of wind that there are differences in the worlds.

Sons of the Buddha, so too it is with the manifestation of the Tathāgata. Perfectly replete in all meritorious qualities and roots of goodness, he emanates the light of unexcelled great wisdom known as "the inconceivable wisdom that prevents the severance of the lineage of the *tathāgatas*." It everywhere illuminates all worlds of the ten directions and bestows on all bodhisattvas the prediction that all *tathāgatas*' will give them their summit-anointing consecrations

正體字

當成正覺。出興於世。佛子。如來出現。復有無上。大智光明。名清淨離垢。能成如來。無漏無盡智。復有無上大智光明。名普照。能成如來普入法界不思議智。復有無上大智光明。名持佛種性。能成如來不傾動力。復有無上大智光明。名迥出無能壞。能成如來無畏無壞智。復有無上大智光明。名一切神通。能成如來諸不共法。一切智智。復有無上大智光明。名出生變化。能成如來。令見聞親近。所生善根。不失壞智。復有無上大智光明。名普隨順。能成如來無盡福德。智慧之身。為一切眾生。而作饒益。復有無上大智光明。名不可究竟。能成如來甚深妙智。隨所開悟。令三寶種。永不斷絕。復有無上大智光明。名種種莊嚴。能成如來相好嚴身。令一切眾生。皆生歡喜。復有無上大智光明。名不可壞。能成如來法界虛空界等。殊勝壽命。無有窮盡。

简体字

当成正觉出兴于世。佛子，如来出现复有无上大智光明，名清净离垢，能成如来无漏无尽智。复有无上大智光明，名普照，能成如来普入法界不思议智。复有无上大智光明，名持佛种性，能成如来不倾动力。复有无上大智光明，名迥出无能坏，能成如来无畏无坏智。复有无上大智光明，名一切神通，能成如来诸不共法、一切智智。复有无上大智光明，名出生变化，能成如来令见闻亲近所生善根不失坏智。复有无上大智光明，名普随顺，能成如来无尽福德智慧之身，为一切众生而作饶益。复有无上大智光明，名不可究竟，能成如来甚深妙智，随所开悟，令三宝种永不断绝。复有无上大智光明，名种种庄严，能成如来相好严身，令一切众生皆生欢喜。复有无上大智光明，名不可坏，能成如来法界、虚空界等殊胜寿命无有穷尽。

Chapter 37 — The Manifestation of the Tathāgata

after which they will attain right enlightenment and appear in the world [as buddhas].

Sons of the Buddha, in association with the manifestation of the Tathāgata:

There is also a light of unexcelled great wisdom known as "immaculately pure" that is able to produce the Tathāgata's uncontaminated and inexhaustible wisdom;

There is also a light of unexcelled great wisdom known as "universal illumination" that is able to produce the Tathāgata's inconceivable wisdom which everywhere enters the Dharma realm;

There is also a light of unexcelled great wisdom known as "sustainer of the Buddha's lineage" that is able to produce the Tathāgata's power to remain unshaken;

There is also a light of unexcelled great wisdom known as "utterly transcendent indestructibility" that is able to produce the Tathāgata's fearless and indestructible wisdom;

There is also a light of unexcelled great wisdom known as "all spiritual superknowledges" that is able to produce the Tathāgata's exclusive dharmas and the wisdom of all-knowledge;

There is also a light of unexcelled great wisdom known as "generating transformations" that is able to produce the Tathāgata's wisdom which prevents the loss or destruction of beings' roots of goodness acquired by seeing him, hearing him, or drawing near to him;

There is also a light of unexcelled great wisdom known as "universal adaptation" that is able to produce the Tathāgata's body endowed with inexhaustible merit and wisdom which does whatever is beneficial for all beings;

There is also a light of unexcelled great wisdom known as "interminable" that is able to produce the Tathāgata's extremely profound and sublime wisdom which, through those who are enlightened by it, prevents the lineage of the Three Jewels from ever being cut off;

There is also a light of unexcelled great wisdom known as "various adornments" that is able to produce the Tathāgata's body adorned with the major marks and subsidiary signs which causes all beings encountering it to be filled with joyous delight; and

There is also a light of unexcelled great wisdom known as "indestructible" that is able to produce the Tathāgata's extraordinary and supreme life span which is as endlessly enduring as the Dharma realm and the realms of empty space.

正體字	佛子。如來大悲。一味之水。無有分別。以諸眾生。欲樂不同。根性各別。而起種種大智風輪。令諸菩薩。成就如來。出現之法。佛子。一切如來。同一體性。大智輪中。出生種種智慧光明。佛子。汝等應知。如來於一解脫味。出生無量不可思議種種功德。眾生念言。此是如來。神力所造。佛子。此非如來。神力所造。佛子。乃至一菩薩。不於佛所。曾種善根。能得如來少分智慧。無有是處。但以諸佛威德力故。令諸眾生。具佛功德。而佛如來。無有分別。無成無壞。無有作者。亦無作法。佛子。是為如來應正等覺出現第八相。菩薩摩訶薩。應如是知。復次佛子。如依虛空。起四風輪。能持水輪。何等為四。一名安住。二名常住。三名究竟。四名堅固。此四風輪。能持水輪。水輪能持大地。令不散壞。是故說地輪依水輪。水輪依風輪。風輪依虛空。虛空無所依。雖無所依。能令三千大千世界。而得安住。佛子。如來出現。亦復如是。
简体字	佛子,如来大悲一味之水无有分别,以诸众生欲乐不同、根性各别,而起种种大智风轮,令诸菩萨成就如来出现之法。佛子,一切如来同一体性,大智轮中出生种种智慧光明。佛子,汝等应知,如来于一解脱味出生无量不可思议种种功德,众生念言:'此是如来神力所造。'佛子,此非如来神力所造。佛子,乃至一菩萨,不于佛所曾种善根,能得如来少分智慧,无有是处。但以诸佛威德力故,令诸众生具佛功德,而佛如来无有分别,无成无坏,无有作者,亦无作法。佛子,是为如来、应、正等觉出现第八相,菩萨摩诃萨应如是知。 　　"复次,佛子,如依虚空起四风轮,能持水轮。何等为四?一名安住,二名常住,三名究竟,四名坚固。此四风轮能持水轮,水轮能持大地令不散坏。是故说:地轮依水轮,水轮依风轮,风轮依虚空,虚空无所依。虽无所依,能令三千大千世界而得安住。佛子,如来出现亦复如是,

Chapter 37 — The Manifestation of the Tathāgata

Sons of the Buddha, the Tathāgata's waters with the single flavor of the great compassion are free of any discriminations. It is because beings' aspirations and predilections differ and because the nature of their faculties each differ that there then arise the various types of great wisdom wind spheres which cause the bodhisattvas to perfect the dharmas of the Tathāgata's manifestation.

Sons of the Buddha, the great wisdom sphere of all *tathāgatas'* identical essential nature produces all different kinds of wisdom light. Sons of the Buddha, you should all realize that, from the Tathāgata's single flavor of liberation, countlessly many different kinds of inconceivable meritorious qualities are produced. Beings think, "This is a something created by the Tathāgata's spiritual powers." However, Sons of the Buddha, this is not something created by the Tathāgata's spiritual powers.

Sons of the Buddha, it is utterly impossible that even a single bodhisattva might be able to acquire even a small amount of the Tathāgata's wisdom without having already planted roots of goodness in the presence of buddhas. It is only through the power of all buddhas' awesome virtue that any being is enabled to perfect any of the Buddha's meritorious qualities. And yet the Buddha, the Tathāgata, remains free of any discriminations. In this, there is no creation, no destruction, no agent of creative action, or any dharma of creation.

Sons of the Buddha, this is the eighth of the marks of the manifestation of the Tathāgata, the Arhat, the One of Right and Universal Enlightenment. The bodhisattva-mahāsattva should know it in this way.

Moreover, Sons of the Buddha, this is just as when, in reliance on empty space, there arise four wind spheres that are able to support the sphere of water. What are those four? The first is known as "stable abiding," the second is known as "forever abiding," the third is known as "ultimate," and the fourth is known as "solid."

These four spheres of wind are able to support the sphere of water and the sphere of water is able to support the great earth and prevent it from disintegrating. Therefore it is said that the sphere of earth depends on the sphere of water, the sphere of water depends on the spheres of wind, the spheres of wind depend on empty space, and empty space has nothing that it depends on. Although it has nothing upon which it depends, it enables the stable abiding of the entire great trichiliocosm.

Sons of the Buddha, so too it is with the manifestation of the Tathāgata, for it is in reliance on the light of unimpeded wisdom

正體字	依無礙慧 264c15 光明。起佛四種大智風輪。能持一切眾生善 264c16 根。何等為四。所謂普攝眾生皆令歡喜大智 264c17 風輪。建立正法令諸眾生皆生愛樂大智風 264c18 輪。守護一切眾生善根大智風輪。具一切方 264c19 便通達無漏界大智風輪。是為四。佛子。諸佛 264c20 世尊。大慈救護一切眾生。大悲度脫一切眾 264c21 生。大慈大悲。普遍饒益。然大慈大悲。依大方 264c22 便善巧。大方便善巧。依如來出現。如來出現。 264c23 依無礙慧光明。無礙慧光明。無有所依。佛子。 264c24 是為如來應正等覺出現第九相。菩薩摩訶 264c25 薩。應如是知復次佛子。譬如三千大千世界。 264c26 既成就已。饒益無量種種眾生。所謂水族眾 264c27 生。得水饒益。陸地眾生。得地饒益。宮殿眾 264c28 生。得宮殿饒益。虛空眾生。得虛空饒益。如 264c29 來出現。亦復如是。種種饒益無量眾生。所謂 265a01 見佛生歡喜者。得歡喜益。住淨戒者。得淨戒 265a02 益。住諸禪定。及無量者。得聖出世大神通益。
简体字	依无碍慧光明起佛四种大智风轮，能持一切众生善根。何等为四？所谓：普摄众生皆令欢喜大智风轮，建立正法令诸众生皆生爱乐大智风轮，守护一切众生善根大智风轮，具一切方便通达无漏界大智风轮。是为四。佛子，诸佛世尊，大慈救护一切众生，大悲度脱一切众生，大慈大悲普遍饶益。然大慈大悲依大方便善巧，大方便善巧依如来出现，如来出现依无碍慧光明，无碍慧光明无有所依。佛子，是为如来、应、正等觉出现第九相，菩萨摩诃萨应如是知。 　　"复次，佛子，譬如三千大千世界既成就已，饶益无量种种众生。所谓：水族众生得水饶益，陆地众生得地饶益，宫殿众生得宫殿饶益，虚空众生得虚空饶益。如来出现亦复如是，种种饶益无量众生。所谓：见佛生欢喜者，得欢喜益；住净戒者，得净戒益；住诸禅定及无量者，得圣出世大神通益；

Chapter 37 – The Manifestation of the Tathāgata

that the Buddha's four kinds of great wisdom wind spheres arise which are able to support all beings' roots of goodness. What are those four? They are:

The great wisdom wind sphere that everywhere attracts beings and causes them to be delighted;

The great wisdom wind sphere that establishes right Dharma and causes all beings to be pleased;

The great wisdom wind sphere that preserves and protects all beings' roots of goodness; and

The great wisdom wind sphere that possesses all skillful means and enables the penetrating comprehension of the realm that is free of the contaminants.

These are the four.

Sons of the Buddha, all of the buddhas, the *bhagavats*, use the great kindness in rescuing and protecting all beings and use the great compassion in liberating all beings. Their great kindness and great compassion bestow benefit on everyone everywhere. Even so, the great kindness and the great compassion rely on proficiency in the use of great skillful means. Proficiency in the use of great skillful means relies on the manifestation of the Tathāgata. The manifestation of the Tathāgata relies on the light of unimpeded wisdom. The light of unimpeded wisdom has nothing that it relies on.

Sons of the Buddha, this is the ninth of the marks of the manifestation of the Tathāgata, the Arhat, the One of Right and Universal Enlightenment. The bodhisattva-mahāsattva should know it in this way.

Moreover, Sons of the Buddha, this is just as when, after the great trichiliocosm has been completely formed, benefit is bestowed on the many different kinds of beings, for instance: water-coursing beings obtain the benefit of water; earth-coursing beings obtain the benefit of land; palace-dwelling beings obtain the benefit of palaces; and space-dwelling beings obtain the benefit of space.

So too it is with the manifestation of the Tathāgata which bestows many different kinds of benefit on countless beings, for instance:

Those who see the Buddha and experience joyous delight acquire that benefit of joyous delight;

Those who abide in the pure moral precepts acquire the benefit of the pure moral precepts;

Those who abide in the *dhyāna* absorptions or in the immeasurable minds acquire the benefit of the *āryas*' great world-transcending spiritual superknowledges;

正體字

住法門光明者。得因果不壞益。住無所有光
明者。得一切法不壞益。是故。說言如來出現
饒益一切無量眾生。佛子。是為如來應正等
覺出現第十相。菩薩摩訶薩。應如是知。佛子。
菩薩摩訶薩。知如來出現。則知無量。知成就
無量行故。則知廣大。知周遍十方故。則知無
來去。知離生住滅故。則知無行無所行。知離
心意識故。則知無身。知如虛空故。則知平等。
知一切眾生。皆無我故。則知無盡。知遍一切
剎。無有盡故。則知無退。知盡後際。無斷絕
故。則知無壞。知如來智。無有對故。則知無
二。知平等觀察。為無為故。則知一切眾生皆
得饒益。本願迴向自在滿足故。爾時普賢菩
薩摩訶薩。欲重明此義。而說頌言

　　十力大雄最無上　　譬如虛空無等等
　　境界廣大不可量　　功德第一超世間

简体字

住法门光明者，得因果不坏益；住无所有光明者，得一切法不坏益。是故说言：'如来出现，饶益一切无量众生。'佛子，是为如来、应、正等觉出现第十相，菩萨摩诃萨应如是知。

"佛子，菩萨摩诃萨知如来出现，则知无量；知成就无量行故，则知广大；知周遍十方故，则知无来去；知离生住灭故，则知无行、无所行；知离心、意、识故，则知无身；知如虚空故，则知平等；知一切众生皆无我故，则知无尽；知遍一切刹无有尽故，则知无退；知尽后际无断绝故，则知无坏；知如来智无有对故，则知无二；知平等观察为、无为故，则知一切众生皆得饶益，本愿回向自在满足故。"

尔时，普贤菩萨摩诃萨欲重明此义而说颂言：
"十力大雄最无上，譬如虚空无等等，
　境界广大不可量，功德第一超世间。

Chapter 37 — The Manifestation of the Tathāgata

Those who abide in the light of the Dharma gateways acquire the benefit of the indestructibility of cause and effect; and

Those who abide in the light of the nonexistence of anything at all acquire the benefit of the indestructibility of all dharmas.

Therefore it is said that the manifestation of the Tathāgata benefits all the countlessly many beings.

Sons of the Buddha, this is the tenth of the marks of the manifestation of the Tathāgata, the Arhat, the One of Right and Universal Enlightenment. The bodhisattva-mahāsattva should know it in this way.

Sons of the Buddha, as for the bodhisattva-mahāsattva:

If he knows the manifestation of the Tathāgatas, then he knows their measurelessness;

If he knows their perfection of the immeasurable practices, then he knows their vastness;

If he knows their universal presence throughout the ten directions, then he knows they have no coming or going;

If he knows their transcendence of birth, abiding, and destruction, then he knows the nonexistence of any practicing or anything that is practiced;

If he knows their transcendence of the mind, the intellect, and consciousness, then he knows they have no body;

If he knows their similarity to empty space, then he knows their uniform equality;

If he knows that all beings have no self, then he knows their endlessness;

If he knows their endless presence everywhere in all *kṣetras*, then he knows their irreversibility;

If he knows they are never cut off even to the end future time, then he knows their indestructibility;

If he knows the Tathāgatas' wisdom is free of any polar opposites, then he knows their non-duality; and

If he knows the uniformly equal contemplation of the conditioned and the unconditioned, then he knows that all beings acquire benefit because the Tathāgatas' dedication of their original vows to them is fulfilled with sovereign mastery.

At that time, wishing to restate the meaning of this, Samantabhadra Bodhisattva-mahāsattva then spoke these verses:

The great hero possessed of the ten powers is the most unsurpassable.
Comparable to space, he is the peer of even the peerless.
His sphere of action is measurelessly vast and
his meritorious qualities are foremost, surpassing any in the world.

正體字	265a19	十力功德無邊量	心意思量所不及
	265a20	人中師子一法門	眾生億劫莫能知
	265a21	十方國土碎為塵	或有算計知其數
	265a22	如來一毛功德量	千萬億劫無能說
	265a23	如人持尺量虛空	復有隨行計其數
	265a24	虛空邊際不可得	如來境界亦如是
	265a25	或有能於剎那頃	悉知三世眾生心
	265a26	設經眾生數等劫	不能知佛一念性
	265a27	譬如法界遍一切	不可見取為一切
	265a28	十力境界亦復然	遍於一切非一切
	265a29	真如離妄恒寂靜	無生無滅普周遍
	265b01	諸佛境界亦復然	體性平等不增減
	265b02	譬如實際而非際	普在三世亦非普
	265b03	導師境界亦如是	遍於三世皆無礙
	265b04	法性無作無變易	猶如虛空本清淨
	265b05	諸佛性淨亦如是	本性非性離有無
	265b06	法性不在於言論	無說離說恒寂滅
	265b07	十力境界性亦然	一切文辭莫能辯
	265b08	了知諸法性寂滅	如鳥飛空無有迹
	265b09	以本願力現色身	令見如來大神變

简体字

十力功德无边量，心意思量所不及，
人中师子一法门，众生亿劫莫能知。
十方国土碎为尘，或有算计知其数；
如来一毛功德量，千万亿劫无能说。
如人持尺量虚空，复有随行计其数，
虚空边际不可得，如来境界亦如是。
或有能于刹那顷，悉知三世众生心，
设经众生数等劫，不能知佛一念性。
譬如法界遍一切，不可见取为一切；
十力境界亦复然，遍于一切非一切。
真如离妄恒寂静，无生无灭普周遍；
诸佛境界亦复然，体性平等不增减。
譬如实际而非际，普在三世亦非普；
导师境界亦如是，遍于三世皆无碍。
法性无作无变易，犹如虚空本清净；
诸佛性净亦如是，本性非性离有无。
法性不在于言论，无说离说恒寂灭；
十力境界性亦然，一切文辞莫能辩。
了知诸法性寂灭，如鸟飞空无有迹，
以本愿力现色身，令见如来大神变。

Chapter 37 — The Manifestation of the Tathāgata

The Ten-Powered One's qualities are boundless and measureless
and such that the mind's reflections cannot reach.
Even a single Dharma gateway of the Lion Among Men
is such that no being could ever understand it even in a *koṭī* of kalpas.

If the lands throughout the ten directions were all ground to dust,
perhaps one might still be able to calculate the number of dust motes.
Still, even in ten million *koṭīs* of kalpas, no one could describe
the number of qualities creating but a single hair of the Tathāgata.

Just as if someone took up a ruler attempting to measure empty space
while someone else followed along and recorded his calculations,
they would still never be able to find the boundaries of space,
so too would it be in trying to fathom the Tathāgata's sphere of action.

Perhaps there might be someone able in but a single *kṣaṇa*'s instant
to know the minds of all beings throughout the three periods of time.
Still, even if he spent kalpas as numerous as all beings,
he could still never know the nature of but one thought of the Buddha.

Just as the Dharma realm pervades all things,
even as it cannot be seen and seized upon as being all things,
so too it is with the sphere of action of one possessing the ten powers,
for, although it pervades all things, it is not the case that it is all things.

True suchness transcends the false, is constantly quiescent,
is neither produced nor destroyed, and is universally pervasive.
So too it is with all buddhas' sphere of action:
Their essential nature, uniformly equal, is not increased or decreased.

Just as ultimate reality's limits are no limits at all and it is everywhere
in the three times yet is not identical with those universal phenomena,
so too it is with the Master Guide's sphere of action
which is unimpeded in its pervasion of the three periods of times.

The nature of dharmas is free of any actions, unchanging,
and, like empty space, it is fundamentally pure.
All buddhas' nature is pure in this very same way:
Its basic nature, not a nature, transcends existence and nonexistence.

The nature of dharmas does not reside in verbal discourse.
It has no speech, transcends speech, and is constantly quiescent.
So too it is with the sphere of action of he who has the ten powers,
for no literary phrasing could ever describe it.

He has completely fathomed the quiescence of all dharmas' nature
and he is like a bird flying through the sky without leaving any tracks.
It is by the power of original vows that he manifests his form bodies,
allowing all to witness the Tathāgata's great spiritual transformations.

正體字

265b10	若有欲知佛境界	當淨其意如虛空
265b11	遠離妄想及諸取	令心所向皆無礙
265b12	是故佛子應善聽	我以少譬明佛境
265b13	十力功德不可量	為悟眾生今略說
265b14	導師所現於身業	語業心業諸境界
265b15	轉妙法輪般涅槃	一切善根我今說
265b16	譬如世界初安立	非一因緣而可成
265b17	無量方便諸因緣	成此三千大千界
265b18	如來出現亦如是	無量功德乃得成
265b19	剎塵心念尚可知	十力生因莫能測
265b20	譬如劫初雲澍雨	而起四種大風輪
265b21	眾生善根菩薩力	成此三千各安住
265b22	十力法雲亦如是	起智風輪清淨意
265b23	昔所迴向諸眾生	普導令成無上果
265b24	如有大雨名洪澍	無有處所能容受
265b25	唯除世界將成時	清淨虛空大風力
265b26	如來出現亦如是	普雨法雨充法界
265b27	一切劣意無能持	唯除清淨廣大心
265b28	譬如空中澍大雨	無所從來無所去
265b29	作者受者悉亦無	自然如是普充洽

简体字

若有欲知佛境界，当净其意如虚空，
远离妄想及诸取，令心所向皆无碍。
是故佛子应善听，我以少譬明佛境，
十力功德不可量，为悟众生今略说。
导师所现于身业，语业心业诸境界，
转妙法轮般涅槃，一切善根我今说。
譬如世界初安立，非一因缘而可成，
无量方便诸因缘，成此三千大千界。
如来出现亦如是，无量功德乃得成，
刹尘心念尚可知，十力生因莫能测。
譬如劫初云澍雨，而起四种大风轮，
众生善根菩萨力，成此三千各安住。
十力法云亦如是，起智风轮清净意，
昔所回向诸众生，普导令成无上果。
如有大雨名洪澍，无有处所能容受，
唯除世界将成时，清净虚空大风力。
如来出现亦如是，普雨法雨充法界，
一切劣意无能持，唯除清净广大心。
譬如空中澍大雨，无所从来无所去，
作者受者悉亦无，自然如是普充洽。

Chapter 37 — The Manifestation of the Tathāgata

If one aspires to know the Buddha's sphere of action,
he should so purify his mind as to make it like empty space,
should abandon erroneous perceptions and all forms of grasping,
and thus allow the mind's pursuit of its aims to always be unimpeded.

Therefore, Sons of the Buddha, you should all listen well
as I use a few analogies to explain a buddha's sphere of action.
Although the qualities of the Ten-Powered One are measureless,
I shall now only briefly describe them in order to awaken beings.

I shall now describe all the roots of goodness associated with
all spheres of action manifested by the Master Guide
in physical actions, verbal actions, and mental actions,
from his turning the wheel of the sublime Dharma to his *parinirvāṇa*.

Just as it is with the initial establishment of the world
in which it is not by a single cause or condition that it can be formed,
but rather there are countless skillful means and causes and conditions
that bring about the establishment of this great trichiliocosm,

so too it is with the manifestation of the Tathāgata,
for it is only by countless meritorious qualities that it may then occur.
One may know the number of atoms in a *kṣetra* or of beings' thoughts,
but no one can fathom all the causes of the Ten-Powered One's birth.

Just as, at the beginning of a kalpa, clouds send down drenching rains
and then give rise to four kinds of great wind spheres which,
together with beings' roots of goodness and the bodhisattvas' powers,
all establish the secure abiding of the trichiliocosm,

so too it is with the Dharma clouds of the Ten-Powered One
that produce the wisdom wind spheres and the purified mind which,
together with past dedications made for the benefit of all beings,
all guide and cause the establishment of this unsurpassed fruition.

Just as when the great rains known as "the vast torrential deluge" fall,
there is no place able to take it in and contain it
with the sole exception of that time prior to the world's formation
when it purifies space together with the power of the great winds,

so too it is with the manifestation of the Tathāgata
who everywhere rains the Dharma rain that fills the Dharma realm.
Of all those of inferior mind, there are none who are able to retain it,
for it can only be retained by those with pure and vast minds.

Just as when great drenching rains fall from the sky,
they have no place from which they come, no place to which they go,
and those who create them and experience them are both nonexistent,
even as they naturally everywhere soak everything in this way,

正體字

```
265c01 | 十力法雨亦如是　無去無來無造作
265c02 | 本行為因菩薩力　一切大心咸聽受
265c03 | 譬如空雲澍大雨　一切無能數其滴
265c04 | 唯除三千自在王　具功德力悉明了
265c05 | 善逝法雨亦如是　一切眾生莫能測
265c06 | 唯除於世自在人　明見如觀掌中寶
265c07 | 譬如空雲澍大雨　能滅能起亦能斷
265c08 | 一切珍寶悉能成　三千所有皆分別
265c09 | 十力法雨亦如是　滅惑起善斷諸見
265c10 | 一切智寶皆使成　眾生心樂悉分別
265c11 | 譬如空中雨一味　隨其所雨各不同
265c12 | 豈彼雨性有分別　然隨物異法如是
265c13 | 如來法雨非一異　平等寂靜離分別
265c14 | 然隨所化種種殊　自然如是無邊[1]相
265c15 | 譬如世界初成時　先成色界天宮殿
265c16 | 次及欲天次人處　乾闥婆宮最後成
265c17 | 如來出現亦如是　先起無邊菩薩行
265c18 | 次化樂寂諸緣覺　次聲聞眾後眾生
265c19 | 諸天初見蓮華瑞　知佛當出生歡喜
265c20 | 水緣風力起世間　宮殿山川悉成立
```

简体字

十力法雨亦如是，无去无来无造作，
本行为因菩萨力，一切大心咸听受。
譬如空云澍大雨，一切无能数其滴，
唯除三千自在王，具功德力悉明了。
善逝法雨亦如是，一切众生莫能测，
唯除于世自在人，明见如观掌中宝。
譬如空云澍大雨，能灭能起亦能断，
一切珍宝悉能成，三千所有皆分别。
十力法雨亦如是，灭惑起善断诸见，
一切智宝皆使成，众生心乐悉分别。
譬如空中雨一味，随其所雨各不同，
岂彼雨性有分别，然随物异法如是。
如来法雨非一异，平等寂静离分别，
然随所化种种殊，自然如是无边相。
譬如世界初成时，先成色界天宫殿，
次及欲天次人处，乾闼婆宫最后成。
如来出现亦如是，先起无边菩萨行，
次化乐寂诸缘觉，次声闻众后众生。
诸天初见莲华瑞，知佛当出生欢喜；
水缘风力起世间，宫殿山川悉成立。

Chapter 37 — The Manifestation of the Tathāgata

so too it is with the Dharma rains of the Ten-Powered One
which have no going, no coming, and no one who creates them.
His original practices are the cause along with bodhisattvas' powers.
Hence all who have great minds then listen to and absorb them.

Just as, when the clouds in the sky pour down great rains,
there is no one able to count all its raindrops
with the sole exception of the trichiliocosm's sovereign king,[49] who,
by the power of his meritorious qualities, entirely knows all this,

so too it is with the Well Gone One's Dharma rain
which, even among all beings, there are none who can measure it
with the sole exception of those with sovereign mastery in the world
who clearly perceive all this as if looking at jewels in their own palms.

Just as clouds in the sky pouring down great rains can extinguish,
can generate, and can also put an end to things while also being able
to bring about the production of all kinds of precious jewels,
even as they are able to distinguish everything in the trichiliocosm,

so too it is with the Dharma rains of the Ten-Powered One
which extinguish delusions, produce goodness, put an end to views,
cause the creation of the jewels of all-knowledge,
and distinguish all the mental inclinations of beings.

Just as the rain falling from the sky is of but a single flavor
which then adapts to the differences in whatever it falls upon,
how could it be in the nature of that rain to have discriminations?
Still, in accordance with beings' differences, the Dharma is like this.

The Tathāgata's Dharma rain is neither the same nor different,
It is uniformly equal, quiescent, and free of discriminations.
Still, according with the many different distinctions in those taught,
it naturally manifests boundlessly many characteristics such as these.

Just as when the world is first being formed,
there is first the formation of the palaces of the form-realm devas,
then those of the desire-realm devas, then the human abodes,
and, finally, the *gandharvas*' palaces are the very last to be formed,

so too it is with the manifestation of the Tathāgata,
wherein first brought forth are the boundless bodhisattva practices,
then those used in teaching *pratyekabuddhas* delighting in stillness,
then those for the *śrāvaka* sangha, and, last, those for other beings.

On first seeing the auspicious sign of the lotus blossoms, the devas,
realizing the Buddha is about to appear, are filled with joyous delight.
The force of water interacting with wind gives rise to the world,[50]
whereupon its palaces, mountains, and rivers are all then established.

正體字

265c21	如來宿善大光明　　巧別菩薩與其記
265c22	所有智輪體皆淨　　各能開示諸佛法
265c23	譬如樹林依地有　　地依於水得不壞
265c24	水輪依風風依空　　而其虛空無所依
265c25	一切佛法依慈悲　　慈悲復依方便立
265c26	方便依智智依慧　　無礙慧身無所依
265c27	譬如世界既成立　　一切眾生獲其利
265c28	地水所住及空居　　二足四足皆[2]蒙益
265c29	法王出現亦如是　　一切眾生獲其利
266a01	若有見聞及親近　　悉使滅除諸惑惱
266a02	如來出現法無邊　　世間迷惑莫能知
266a03	為欲開悟諸含識　　無譬諭中說其譬
266a04	佛子。諸菩薩摩訶薩。應云何見如來應正等
266a05	覺身。佛子。諸菩薩摩訶薩。應於無量處。見如
266a06	來身。何以故。諸菩薩摩訶薩。不應於一法。一
266a07	事一身。一國土一眾生。見於如來。應遍一切
266a08	處。見於如來。佛子。譬如虛空遍至一切。色非
266a09	色處。非至非不至。何以故。虛空無身故。如來
266a10	身亦如是。遍一切處。遍一切眾生。遍一切法。
266a11	遍一切國土。非至非不至。何以故。如來身無
266a12	身故。為眾生故。示現其身。

简体字

如来宿善大光明，巧别菩萨与其记；
所有智轮体皆净，各能开示诸佛法。
譬如树林依地有，地依于水得不坏，
水轮依风风依空，而其虚空无所依。
一切佛法依慈悲，慈悲复依方便立，
方便依智智依慧，无碍慧身无所依。
譬如世界既成立，一切众生获其利，
地水所住及空居，二足四足皆蒙益。
法王出现亦如是，一切众生获其利，
若有见闻及亲近，悉使灭除诸惑恼。
如来出现法无边，世间迷惑莫能知，
为欲开悟诸含识，无譬喻中说其譬。
　　"佛子，诸菩萨摩诃萨应云何见如来、应、正等觉身？
　　"佛子，诸菩萨摩诃萨应于无量处见如来身。何以故？诸菩萨摩诃萨不应于一法、一事、一身、一国土、一众生见于如来，应遍一切处见于如来。佛子，譬如虚空遍至一切色、非色处，非至、非不至。何以故？虚空无身故。如来身亦如是，遍一切处，遍一切众生，遍一切法，遍一切国土，非至、非不至。何以故？如来身无身故，为众生故示现其身。

Chapter 37 — The Manifestation of the Tathāgata

The great illumination from the Tathāgata's goodness in previous lives
skillfully distinguishes the bodhisattvas and gives them predictions.
The essential nature of all the wisdom spheres is pure
and they are each able to reveal the Dharma of all buddhas.

Just as the forests exist in reliance on the earth,
the earth achieves its indestructibility in reliance on water,
the spheres of water rely on the wind, the wind relies on space,
and the space between them has nothing on which it depends,

so, too, all of the Buddha's dharmas rely on kindness and compassion,
kindness and compassion in turn rely on establishing skillful means,
skillful means rely on knowledge, knowledge relies on wisdom,
and the body of unimpeded wisdom has nothing on which it relies.

Just as, once the world has already become established,
all beings then acquire their respective benefits
so that those dwelling on land or in water and the space dwellers,
bipeds, and quadrupeds all then receive benefits,

so too it is with the manifestation of the Dharma King
when all beings then acquire their respective benefits.
Whether there are those who see, hear, or draw near to him,
they are all enabled to extinguish all their delusions and afflictions.

The dharmas of the Tathāgata's manifestation are boundless,
such that none of the world's deluded beings could know them.
In order to awaken all sentient beings,
amidst matters with no analogies, I have here set forth their analogies.

Sons of the Buddha, how is it that all bodhisattva-mahāsattvas should see the body of the Tathāgata, the Arhat, the One of Right and Universal Enlightenment? Sons of the Buddha, all bodhisattva-mahāsattvas should see the Tathāgata's body in countless places. How is this so? All bodhisattva-mahāsattvas should not see the Tathāgata in but a single dharma, in but a single phenomenon, in but a single body, in but a single land, or in but a single being, but rather they should see the Tathāgata everywhere and in all places.

Sons of the Buddha, he is like empty space which reaches everywhere to all places with and without form, but which still does not either reach or fail to reach them. How is this so? This is because empty space is nonphysical. So too it is with the body of the Tathāgata which pervades all places, pervades all beings, pervades all dharmas, and pervades all lands, but which still does not either reach them or fail to reach them. And how is this so? This is because the body of the Tathāgata is nonphysical. He only manifests his body for the sake of beings.

正體字

佛子。是為如來身
第一相。諸菩薩摩訶薩。應如是見。復次佛子。譬如虛空。寬廣非色。而能顯現一切諸色。而彼虛空。無有分別。亦無戲論。如來身亦復如是。以智光明。普照明故。令一切眾生世出世間諸善根業。皆得成就。而如來身。無有分別。亦無戲論。何以故。從本已來。一切執著。一切戲論。皆永斷故。佛子。是為如來身第二相。諸菩薩摩訶薩。應如是見。復次佛子。譬如日出於閻浮提。無量眾生。皆得饒益。所謂。破闇作明。變濕令燥。生長草木。成熟穀稼。廓徹虛空。開敷蓮華。行者見道。居者[1]辨業。何以故。日輪普放無量光故。佛子。如來智日。亦復如是。以無量事。普益眾生。所謂滅惡生善。破愚為智。大慈救護。大悲度脫。令其增長根力覺分。令生深信。捨離濁心。令得見聞。不壞因果。

简体字

佛子，是为如来身第一相，诸菩萨摩诃萨应如是见。

"复次，佛子，譬如虚空宽广非色，而能显现一切诸色，而彼虚空无有分别亦无戏论。如来身亦复如是，以智光明普照明故，令一切众生世、出世间诸善根业皆得成就，而如来身无有分别亦无戏论。何以故？从本已来，一切执著、一切戏论皆永断故。佛子，是为如来身第二相，诸菩萨摩诃萨应如是见。

"复次，佛子，譬如日出于阎浮提，无量众生皆得饶益。所谓：破暗作明，变湿令燥，生长草木，成熟谷稼，廓彻虚空，开敷莲华，行者见道，居者办业。何以故？日轮普放无量光故。佛子，如来智日亦复如是，以无量事普益众生。所谓：灭恶生善，破愚为智，大慈救护，大悲度脱；令其增长根、力、觉分；令生深信，舍离浊心；令得见闻，不坏因果；

Sons of the Buddha, this is the first of the marks of the Tathāgata's body. All bodhisattva-mahāsattvas should perceive it in this way.

Furthermore, Sons of the Buddha, just as empty space is vast and formless and yet is able to reveal all forms even as that empty space has no discriminations and also has no conceptual proliferation, so too it is with the Tathāgata's body. With the pervasively illuminating brightness of his wisdom light, he enables all beings to accomplish all the karmic works which establish their worldly and world-transcending roots of goodness, and yet the Tathāgata's body remains free of all discriminations and all conceptual proliferation. And how is this the case? This is because, from the very beginning to the present, he has forever severed all attachments and all forms of conceptual proliferation.

Sons of the Buddha, this is the second of the marks of the Tathāgata's body. All bodhisattva-mahāsattvas should perceive it in this way.

Furthermore, Sons of the Buddha, this is just as when the sun rises over the continent of Jambudvīpa, countless beings all acquire its benefits, namely:

It dispels darkness and creates brightness;

It transforms moisture and causes dryness;

It brings about the growth of the grasses and trees;

It ripens food grains;

Its illumination permeates empty space;

It causes the lotuses to bloom;

It allows travelers to see the road; and

It allows those who dwell there to do their work.

And why do these things occur? It is because the sun emanates measureless light which shines everywhere.

Sons of the Buddha, so too it is with the wisdom sun of the Tathāgata which, in countless matters, everywhere benefits beings, namely:

It extinguishes evil and produces goodness;

It demolishes stupidity and creates wisdom;

It rescues and protects beings with loving-kindness;

It liberates beings with great compassion;

It enables them to increase their development of the roots, powers, and limbs of enlightenment;[51]

It enables the development of deep faith and the abandonment of turbid thoughts;

It enables them to see and learn not to go against cause and effect;

正體字

令得天眼。見歿生處。令心無礙。不壞善根。令智修明。開敷覺華。令其發心。成就本行。何以故。如來廣大。智慧日身。放無量光。普照[2]耀故。佛子。是為如來身第三相。諸菩薩摩訶薩。應如是見。復次佛子。譬如日出於閻浮提。先照一切須彌山等諸大山王。次照黑山。次照高原。然後普照一切大地。日不作念。我先照此。後照於彼。但以山地有高下故。照有先後。如來應正等覺。亦復如是。成就無邊法界智輪。常放無礙智慧光明。先照菩薩摩訶薩等諸大山王。次照緣覺。次照聲聞。次照決定善根眾生。隨其心器。示廣大智。然後普照一切眾生。乃至邪定。亦皆普及。為作未來利益因緣。令成熟故。而彼如來大智日光。不作是念。我當先照菩薩大行。乃至後照邪定眾生。但放光明。平等普照。

简体字

令得天眼,见殁生处;令心无碍,不坏善根;令智修明,开敷觉华;令其发心,成就本行。何以故?如来广大智慧日身,放无量光普照耀故。佛子,是为如来身第三相,诸菩萨摩诃萨应如是见。

"复次,佛子,譬如日出于阎浮提,先照一切须弥山等诸大山王,次照黑山,次照高原,然后普照一切大地。日不作念:'我先照此,后照于彼。'但以山地有高下故,照有先后。如来、应、正等觉亦复如是,成就无边法界智轮,常放无碍智慧光明,先照菩萨摩诃萨等诸大山王,次照缘觉,次照声闻,次照决定善根众生,随其心器示广大智,然后普照一切众生,乃至邪定亦皆普及,为作未来利益因缘令成熟故。而彼如来大智日光不作是念:'我当先照菩萨大行,乃至后照邪定众生。'但放光明平等普照,

It enables them to acquire the heavenly eye and see the places where they have died and been reborn;

It enables their minds to become unimpeded and hence to refrain from ruining their roots of goodness;

It enables them to become wise and cultivate the illumination by which the flower of enlightenment may bloom; and

It enables them to arouse the resolve by which they can perfect their original practices.

And why do these things occur? It is because the body of the Tathāgata's vast wisdom sun emanates measureless light that shines brightly everywhere.

Sons of the Buddha, this is the third of the marks of the Tathāgata's body. All bodhisattva-mahāsattvas should perceive it in this way.

Furthermore, Sons of the Buddha, this is just as when the sun rises over Jambudvīpa, it first illuminates all the kings of mountains such as Mount Sumeru, then illuminates the black mountains, then illuminates the high plains, and then later everywhere illuminates the entire great earth. The sun does not think, "I shall first illuminate this and I shall later illuminate that." It is only because the mountains and the earth have higher and lower terrain that this illumination occurs either earlier or later.

So too it is with the Tathāgata, the Arhat, the One of Right and Universal Enlightenment, for, having fully developed the sphere of boundless Dharma realm wisdom, he always emanates the light of unimpeded wisdom which:

First illuminates the bodhisattva-mahāsattvas who are like the great kings of mountains;

Next illuminates the *pratyekabuddhas*;

Next illuminates *śrāvaka* disciples;

Next illuminates the beings possessed of definite roots of goodness, revealing vast wisdom to them in accordance with their mental capacities; and

Later on everywhere illuminates all beings, including even those fixated on wrong actions[52] so that it everywhere reaches even all of them in order that they may create causes and conditions for future benefit through which they will be caused to become fully ripened.

In doing so, that light of the Tathāgata's great wisdom sun does not think: "I should first illuminate the bodhisattvas who cultivate the great practices, and then should illuminate the others until, at the very last, I should illuminate the beings fixated on wrong actions." Rather it simply emanates its light that then equally and universally

正體字

無礙無障。無所
分別。佛子。譬如日月。隨時出現。大山幽谷。
普照無私。如來智慧。復亦如是。普照一切。無
有分別。隨諸眾生根欲不同。智慧光明。種種
有異。佛子。是為如來身第四相。諸菩薩摩訶
薩。應如是見。復次佛子。譬如日出。生盲眾
生。無眼根故。未曾得見。雖未曾見。然為日光
之所饒益。何以故。因此得知晝夜時節。受用
種種衣服飲食。令身調適。離眾患故。如來智
日。亦復如是。無信無解。毀戒毀見。邪命自
活。生盲之類。無信眼故。不見諸佛。智慧日
輪。雖不見佛智慧日輪。亦為智日之所饒益。
何以故。以佛威力。令彼眾生。所有身苦。及諸
煩惱。未來苦因。皆消滅故。佛子。如來有光
明。名積集一切功德。有光明名普照一切。有
光明。名清淨自在照。有光明。名出大妙音。有
光明。名普解一切語言法令他歡喜。有光明。
名示現永斷一切疑自在境界。

简体字

无碍无障，无所分别。佛子，譬如日月随时出现，大山、幽谷普照无私。如来智慧复亦如是，普照一切无有分别，随诸众生根欲不同，智慧光明种种有异。佛子，是为如来身第四相，诸菩萨摩诃萨应如是见。

"复次，佛子，譬如日出，生盲众生无眼根故，未曾得见。虽未曾见，然为日光之所饶益。何以故？因此得知昼夜时节，受用种种衣服、饮食，令身调适离众患故。如来智日亦复如是，无信、无解、毁戒、毁见、邪命自活生盲之类无信眼故，不见诸佛智慧日轮。虽不见佛智慧日轮，亦为智日之所饶益。何以故？以佛威力，令彼众生所有身苦及诸烦恼、未来苦因皆消灭故。佛子，如来有光明，名积集一切功德；有光明，名普照一切；有光明，名清净自在照；有光明，名出大妙音；有光明，名普解一切语言法令他欢喜；有光明，名示现永断一切疑自在境界；

Chapter 37 — The Manifestation of the Tathāgata

illuminates in a way that is unimpeded, free of all obstacles, and free of any sort of discriminations.

Sons of the Buddha, just as the sun and moon appear in accordance with the time and everywhere illuminate the great mountains and deep valleys without any selfishness in doing so, so too it is with the Tathāgata's wisdom. Rather, it everywhere illuminates everyone without making any discriminations. As it accords with differences in beings' faculties and aspirations, the light of wisdom manifests all kinds of differences.

Sons of the Buddha, this is the fourth of the marks of the Tathāgata's body. All bodhisattva-mahāsattvas should perceive it in this way.

Furthermore, Sons of the Buddha, this is just as when the sun rises, beings who are born blind have never been able to see it because they have no visual faculty. Although they have never been able to see it, they are still benefited by the sunlight. How is this so? This is because, on account of it, they are able to recognize the day, the night, and the seasons and put to use all different kinds of clothing, drink, and food which cause their bodies to remain well adapted and free from the many kinds of illnesses.

So too it is with the Tathāgata's wisdom sun. Those who have no faith, who have no understanding, who violate moral precepts, who denigrate [right] views, or who live by wrong livelihoods—because they do not have the eye of faith, they are of the same sort as those who are born blind. Hence they do not see the buddhas' wisdom sun. But, although they fail to see the buddhas' wisdom sun, they are still benefited by their sun of wisdom. And how is this so? This is because of the Buddha's awesome power to enable the complete melting away of all those beings' physical sufferings, afflictions, and causes of future suffering.

Sons of the Buddha, the Tathāgata [has the following kinds of lights]:

He has a light known as "accumulation of all meritorious qualities";
He has a light known as "universal illumination of everything";
He has a light known as "pure and freely produced illumination";
He has a light known as "emanation of the great sublime sound";
He has a light known as "universal comprehension of all language dharmas by which he delights others";
He has a light known as "manifestation of freely invoked spheres of experience by which he forever severs all doubts";

正體字

有光明。名無住智自在普照。有光明。名永斷一切戲論自在智。有光明。名隨所應出妙音聲。有光明。名出清淨自在音莊嚴國土成熟眾生。佛子如來一一毛孔。放如是等千種光明。五百光明。普照下方。五百光明。普照上方種種剎中。種種佛所。諸菩薩眾。其菩薩等。見此光明。一時皆得如來境界。十頭十眼。十耳十鼻。十舌十身。十手十足。十地十智。皆悉清淨。彼諸菩薩。先所成就。諸處諸地。見彼光明。轉更清淨。一切善根。皆悉成熟。趣一切智。住二乘者。滅一切垢。其餘一分。生盲眾生。身既快樂。心亦清淨。柔軟調伏。堪修念智。地獄餓鬼。畜生諸趣。所有眾生。皆得快樂。解脫眾苦。命終皆生天上人間。佛子。彼諸眾生不覺不知。以何因緣。以何神力。而來生此。彼生盲者。作如是念。我是梵天。我是梵化。是時如來。住普自在三昧。出六十種妙音。而告之言。汝等。非是梵天。亦非梵化。

简体字

有光明，名无住智自在普照；有光明，名永断一切戏论自在智；有光明，名随所应出妙音声；有光明，名出清净自在音庄严国土成熟众生。佛子，如来一一毛孔放如是等千种光明，五百光明普照下方，五百光明普照上方。种种刹中种种佛所诸菩萨众，其菩萨等见此光明，一时皆得如来境界，十头、十眼、十耳、十鼻、十舌、十身、十手、十足、十地、十智，皆悉清净。彼诸菩萨先所成就诸处诸地，见彼光明转更清净，一切善根皆悉成熟，趣一切智；住二乘者，灭一切垢；其余一分生盲众生，身既快乐，心亦清净，柔软调伏，堪修念智；地狱、饿鬼、畜生诸趣所有众生，皆得快乐，解脱众苦，命终皆生天上、人间。佛子，彼诸众生不觉不知，以何因缘、以何神力而来生此？彼生盲者作如是念：'我是梵天！我是梵化！'是时，如来住普自在三昧，出六十种妙音而告之言：'汝等非是梵天，亦非梵化，

Chapter 37 — The Manifestation of the Tathāgata

> He has a light known as "freely invoked universal illumination of the wisdom of non-abiding";
> He has a light known as "freely invoked wisdom that forever cuts off all conceptual proliferation";
> He has a light known as "sublime sounds emanated in accordance with whatever is fitting"; and
> He has a light known as "emanation of pure and freely produced sounds which adorn lands and ripen beings."

Sons of the Buddha, every one of the Tathāgata's pores emanates a thousand light rays such as these of which five hundred light rays everywhere illuminate the regions below and five hundred light rays everywhere illuminate the various congregations of bodhisattvas in the many different abodes of the buddhas in the many different kinds of kṣetras in the regions above. When those bodhisattvas see these light rays, they all at once acquire the Tathāgata's spheres of experience in which they are possessed of ten heads, ten pairs of eyes, ten pairs of ears, ten noses, ten tongues, ten bodies, ten pairs of hands, ten pairs of feet, the ten grounds, and the ten types of knowledge, all of which are completely purified. All of those bodhisattvas are ones who had previously perfected all the stations and all the grounds. On seeing those light rays, they achieve even greater levels of purity, accomplish the complete ripening of all their roots of goodness, and progress toward the realization of all-knowledge.

Those who abide in the two vehicles extinguish all their defilements. Another category of beings, those born blind, their bodies having experienced feelings of happiness, their minds then also become purified, pliant, well-trained, and capable of cultivating mindfulness and wisdom.[53] All the beings in the destinies of the hell realms, the hungry ghost realms, and the animal realms become happy and liberated from their many kinds of sufferings. Then, at the end of their lives, they are all reborn among the devas or within the human realm.

Sons of the Buddha, all those beings remain unaware and do not know due to which causes and conditions or because of what kinds of spiritual powers they came to be reborn here. Those born blind think, "I am a Brahma Heaven deva," or "I am an emanation of Brahmā."

At this time, the Tathāgata, abiding in the samādhi of universal sovereign mastery, sends forth sixty varieties of sublime voices[54] by which he tells them: "You are not Brahma Heaven devas, are not emanations of Brahmā, and are also not the creations of either Śakra

正體字

亦非帝釋護世所作。皆是如來。
威神之力。彼諸眾生。聞是語已。以佛神力。皆
知宿命。生大歡喜。心歡喜故。自然而出優曇
華雲。香雲音樂雲。衣雲蓋雲。幢雲幡雲。末香
雲寶雲。師子幢半月樓閣雲。歌詠讚歎雲。種
種莊嚴雲。皆以尊重心。供養如來。何以故。此
諸眾生。得淨眼故。如來與彼。授阿耨多羅三
藐三菩提記。佛子。如來智日。如是利益生盲
眾生。令得善根。具足成熟。佛子。是為如來身
第五相。諸菩薩摩訶薩。應如是見。復次佛子。
譬如月輪有四奇特。未曾有法。何等為四。一
者映蔽一切星宿光明。二者隨逐於時示現
虧盈。三者於閻浮提澄淨水中影無不現。四
者一切見者皆對目前。而此月輪。無有分別。
無有戲論。佛子。如來身月。亦復如是。有四奇
特未曾有法。何等為四。所謂映蔽一切聲聞
獨覺。學無學眾。隨其所宜。示現壽命修短不
同。而如來身。無有增減。一切世界。淨心眾
生。菩提器中。影無不現。

简体字

亦非帝释护世所作,皆是如来威神之力。'彼诸众生闻是语已,以佛神力皆知宿命,生大欢喜;心欢喜故,自然而出优昙华云、香云、音乐云、衣云、盖云、幢云、幡云、末香云、宝云、师子幢半月楼阁云、歌咏赞叹云、种种庄严云,皆以尊重心供养如来。何以故?此诸众生得净眼故,如来与彼授阿耨多罗三藐三菩提记。佛子,如来智日如是利益生盲众生,令得善根,具足成熟。佛子,是为如来身第五相,诸菩萨摩诃萨应如是见。

"复次,佛子,譬如月轮有四奇特未曾有法。何等为四?一者、映蔽一切星宿光明;二者、随逐于时示现亏盈;三者、于阎浮提澄净水中影无不现;四者、一切见者皆对目前,而此月轮无有分别、无有戏论。佛子,如来身月亦复如是,有四奇特未曾有法。何等为四?所谓:映蔽一切声闻、独觉、学、无学众;随其所宜,示现寿命修短不同,而如来身无有增减;一切世界净心众生菩提器中,影无不现;

or the World-protecting Heavenly Kings. All of this has occurred because of the awesome spiritual powers of the Tathāgata."

Once those beings hear these statements, due to the Buddha's spiritual powers, they all acquire the knowledge of their previous lifetimes and then feel great joyous delight. Because their minds feel joyous delight, they then spontaneously emanate clouds of *udumbara* flowers, clouds of perfumes, clouds of music, clouds of robes, clouds of canopies, clouds of banners, clouds of pennants, clouds of powdered incense, clouds of jewels, clouds of lion banners and half-moon towers, clouds of praise songs, and clouds of many different types of adornments, all of which they offer up to the Tathāgata with reverential minds. Why do they do so? This is because these beings have acquired purified eyes. The Tathāgata then bestows on them predictions of their future attainment of *anuttara-samyak-saṃbodhi*.

Sons of the Buddha, it is in ways such as these that the Tathāgata's wisdom sun benefits beings born blind, thereby enabling them to acquire roots of goodness that then become fully ripened.

Sons of the Buddha, this is the fifth of the marks of the Tathāgata's body. All bodhisattva-mahāsattvas should perceive it in this way.

Furthermore, Sons of the Buddha, this is comparable to the moon's four extraordinarily special and unprecedented dharmas. What are those four? They are:

First, it outshines the light of all the other stars and constellations;
Second, it displays its waning and waxing in accordance with the time;
Third, there is no still and clear body of water on the continent of Jambudvīpa in which its reflection does not appear; and
Fourth, to all who see it, it appears directly before their own eyes, and yet the orb of the moon is free of any discriminations or conceptual proliferation.

Sons of the Buddha, so too it is with the moon of the Tathāgata's body, for it has four extraordinarily special and unprecedented dharmas. What are those four? They are:

It outshines all *śrāvaka* disciples, *pratyekabuddhas*, and others in the congregations of those still in training or beyond training;
In accordance with what is fitting, it manifests with life spans of varying duration even as, in this circumstance, the Tathāgata's body itself does not undergo any increase or decrease;
Of all the pure-minded beings in all worlds who have the capacity to realize bodhi, there are none to whom his reflected image does not appear; and

正體字

一切眾生。有瞻對
者。皆謂如來。唯現我前。隨其心樂。而為說
法。隨其地位。令得解脫。隨所應化。令見佛
身。而如來身。無有分別。無有戲論。所作利
益。皆得究竟。佛子。是為如來身第六相。諸菩
薩摩訶薩。應如是見。復次佛子。譬如三千大
千世界。大梵天王。以少方便。於大千世界。普
現其身。一切眾生。皆見梵王現在[己>己]前。而此
梵王。亦不分身。無種種身。佛子。諸佛如來。亦
復如是。無有分別。無有戲論。亦不分身。無種
種身。而隨一切眾生心樂。示現其身。亦不作
念。現若干身。佛子。是為如來身第七相。諸菩
薩摩訶薩。應如是見。復次佛子。譬如醫王善
知眾藥及諸呪論。閻浮提中。諸所有藥。用無
不盡。復以宿世諸善根力。大明呪力。為方便
故。眾生見者。病無不愈。彼大醫王。知命將
終。作是念言。我命終後。一切眾生無所依怙。
我今宜應為現方便。是時醫王。合藥塗身。明
呪力持。

简体字

一切众生有瞻对者皆谓如来唯现我前，随其心乐而为说法，随其地位令得解脱，随所应化令见佛身，而如来身无有分别、无有戏论，所作利益皆得究竟。佛子，是为如来身第六相，诸菩萨摩诃萨应如是见。

"复次，佛子，譬如三千大千世界大梵天王，以少方便于大千世界普现其身，一切众生皆见梵王现在己前，而此梵王亦不分身、无种种身。佛子，诸佛如来亦复如是，无有分别，无有戏论，亦不分身，无种种身，而随一切众生心乐示现其身，亦不作念现若干身。佛子，是为如来身第七相，诸菩萨摩诃萨应如是见。

"复次，佛子，譬如医王善知众药及诸咒论，阎浮提中诸所有药用无不尽，复以宿世诸善根力、大明咒力，为方便故，众生见者病无不愈。彼大医王知命将终，作是念言：'我命终后，一切众生无所依怙，我今宜应为现方便。'是时，医王合药涂身，明咒力持，

Chapter 37 — The Manifestation of the Tathāgata

Of all beings who gaze with admiration upon it, they all feel that, "The Tathāgata is appearing only before me." Then, in accordance their mental dispositions, he speaks Dharma for them. In accordance with the particular ground on which they dwell, he enables them to achieve liberation. And, in accordance with those who should receive transformative teaching, he then causes them to see the body of a buddha. Yet the Tathāgata's body does not engage in any discriminations and does not engage in any conceptual proliferation as the benefits it bestows all achieve their ultimate ends.

Sons of the Buddha, this is the sixth of the marks of the Tathāgata's body. All bodhisattva-mahāsattvas should perceive it in this way.

Furthermore, Sons of the Buddha, this is just as when the great trichiliocosm's king of the Great Brahma Heaven uses a minor expedient to manifest his body everywhere throughout the worlds of a great chiliocosm. All of those beings then see the Brahma Heaven king manifesting directly before them, even as this Brahma Heaven king still does not divide his body and does not have many different bodies.

Sons of the Buddha, so too it is with the buddhas, the Tathāgatas. They do not engage in any discriminations, do not engage in any conceptual proliferation, do not divide their bodies, and do not have many different bodies. Even so, adapting to beings' mental dispositions, they manifest their bodies while still not thinking to create some particular number of bodies.

Sons of the Buddha, this is the seventh of the marks of the Tathāgata's body. All bodhisattva-mahāsattvas should perceive it in this way.

Furthermore, Sons of the Buddha, this is just as when some physician king who knows well the many kinds of medicines as well as the many kinds of mantras and treatises so that, of all the medicines on the continent of Jambudvīpa, there are none he does not extensively use.

Moreover, because of skillful means he has created through the power of roots of goodness from previous lives and the power of great bright mantras, among the beings who see him, there are none whose diseases are not cured.

When that great king of physicians realizes that his life is about to come to an end, he thinks, "After I die, all the beings will have no one on whom they can rely. It would be fitting if I were to manifest an expedient for them." Then that physician king mixes together a medicinal potion with which he smears his body and also uses the power of bright mantras to preserve it so that, after his death,

正體字

令其終後。身不分散。不萎不枯。威儀
267a28 ｜ 視聽。與本無別。凡所療治。悉得除差。佛子。
267a29 ｜ 如來應正等覺。無上醫王。亦復如是。於無量
267b01 ｜ 百千億那由他劫。[1]鍊治法藥。已得成就。修
267b02 ｜ 學一切方便善巧。大明呪力。皆到彼岸。善能
267b03 ｜ 除滅一切眾生。諸煩惱病。及住壽命。經無量
267b04 ｜ 劫。其身清淨。無有思慮。無有動用。一切佛
267b05 ｜ 事。未嘗休息。眾生見者。諸煩惱病。悉得消
267b06 ｜ 滅。佛子。是為如來身第八相。諸菩薩摩訶薩。
267b07 ｜ 應如是見。復次佛子。譬如大海有大摩尼寶。
267b08 ｜ 名集一切光明毘盧遮那藏。若有眾生。觸其
267b09 ｜ 光者。悉同其色。若有見者。眼得清淨。隨彼光
267b10 ｜ 明所照之處。雨摩尼寶。名為安樂。令諸眾生。
267b11 ｜ 離苦調適。佛子。諸如來身。亦復如是。為大寶
267b12 ｜ 聚一切功德大智慧藏。若有眾生。觸佛身寶
267b13 ｜ 智慧光者。同佛身色。若有見者。法眼清淨。隨
267b14 ｜ 彼光明所照之處。令諸眾生。離貧窮苦。乃至
267b15 ｜ 具足佛菩提樂。佛子。如來法身。無所分別。亦
267b16 ｜ 無戲論。而能普為一切眾生。作大佛事。佛子。
267b17 ｜ 是為如來身第九相。諸菩薩摩訶薩。應如是
267b18 ｜ 見。

简体字

令其终后身不分散、不萎不枯，威仪视听与本无别，凡所疗治悉得除差。佛子，如来、应、正等觉无上医王亦复如是，于无量百千亿那由他劫，炼治法药已得成就，修学一切方便善巧大明咒力皆到彼岸，善能除灭一切众生诸烦恼病及住寿命；经无量劫，其身清净无有思虑、无有动用，一切佛事未尝休息，众生见者诸烦恼病悉得消灭。佛子，是为如来身第八相，诸菩萨摩诃萨应如是见。

"复次，佛子，譬如大海有大摩尼宝，名集一切光明毗卢遮那藏；若有众生触其光者，悉同其色；若有见者，眼得清净。随彼光明所照之处，雨摩尼宝，名为安乐，令诸众生离苦调适。佛子，诸如来身亦复如是，为大宝聚一切功德大智慧藏；若有众生触佛身宝智慧光者，同佛身色；若有见者，法眼清净。随彼光明所照之处，令诸众生离贫穷苦，乃至具足佛菩提乐。佛子，如来法身无所分别亦无戏论，而能普为一切众生作大佛事。佛子，是为如来身第九相，诸菩萨摩诃萨应如是见。

Chapter 37 — The Manifestation of the Tathāgata

his body does not disintegrate, does not atrophy, does not wither. Consequently his appearance and the experience of seeing him are no different than before and, whichever diseases come for treatment, they are all able to be cured.

Sons of the Buddha, so too it is with the Tathāgata, the Arhat, the One of Right and Universal Enlightenment, the unsurpassed king of physicians who for countless hundreds of thousands of *koṭīs* of *nayutas* of kalpas has formulated the medicines of Dharma, has fulfilled the cultivation and study of all skillful uses of expedient means, and has perfected the powers of the great bright mantras. He is well able to eliminate the diseases of all beings' afflictions and, moreover, he dwells for a life span that continues for countless kalpas during which his body remains pristine and there is no reflective deliberation and no functional activity even as he never ceases to carry forth all the buddha works in such a way that the affliction-based diseases of all beings who see him can all be melted away.

Sons of the Buddha, this is the eighth of the marks of the Tathāgata's body. All bodhisattva-mahāsattvas should perceive it in this way.

Furthermore, Sons of the Buddha, this is just as it is in the case of an immense *maṇi* jewel found in the great ocean known as "the *vairocana* treasury that collects all light." If any beings contact its light, they all turn that same color, if any beings see it, their eyes become purified, and wherever its light shines, it rains *maṇi* jewels known as "happiness" jewels which cause all beings there to be relieved of suffering and experience well-being.

Sons of the Buddha, so too it is with the bodies of the Tathāgatas, for they constitute a great accumulation of jewels and a treasury of all meritorious qualities and great wisdom. If any beings contact the wisdom light emanating from the jewel of the Buddha's body, they become the same color as the Buddha's body and, if they so much as see it, their Dharma eyes then become purified. Wherever his light shines, it causes all beings to leave the suffering of poverty and ultimately enables them to fully possess the bliss of the Buddha's bodhi.

Sons of the Buddha, the Tathāgata's Dharma body is free of discriminations and also free of conceptual proliferation and yet it is still everywhere able to perform the Buddha's great works for the sake of all beings.

Sons of the Buddha, this is the ninth of the marks of the Tathāgata's body. All bodhisattva-mahāsattvas should perceive it in this way.

正體字

復次佛子。譬如大海有大如意摩尼寶王。
名一切世間莊嚴藏。具足成就百萬功德。隨
所住處。令諸眾生。災患消除。所願滿足。然此
如意摩尼寶王。非少福眾生所能得見。如來
身如意寶王。亦復如是。名為能令一切眾生
皆悉歡喜。若有見身聞名讚德。悉令永離生
死苦患。假使一切世界。一切眾生。一時專心。
欲見如來。悉令得見。所願皆滿。佛子。佛身非
是少福眾生所能得見。唯除如來自在神力。
所應調伏。若有眾生。因見佛身。便種善根。乃
至成熟。為成熟故。乃令得見如來身耳。佛子。
是為如來身第十相。諸菩薩摩訶薩。應如是
見。以其心無量遍十方故。所行無礙。如虛空
故。普入法界故。住真實際故。無生無滅故。等
住三世故。永離一切分別故。住盡後際誓願
故。嚴淨一切世界故。莊嚴一一佛身故。爾時。
普賢菩薩摩訶薩。欲重明此義。而說頌言

简体字

"复次，佛子，譬如大海有大如意摩尼宝王，名一切世间庄严藏，具足成就百万功德，随所住处，令诸众生灾患消除、所愿满足；然此如意摩尼宝王非少福众生所能得见。如来身如意宝王亦复如是，名为能令一切众生皆悉欢喜，若有见身、闻名、赞德，悉令永离生死苦患；假使一切世界一切众生，一时专心欲见如来，悉令得见，所愿皆满。佛子，佛身非是少福众生所能得见，唯除如来自在神力所应调伏；若有众生因见佛身便种善根乃至成熟，为成熟故，乃令得见如来身耳。佛子，是为如来身第十相，诸菩萨摩诃萨应如是见。以其心无量遍十方故，所行无碍如虚空故，普入法界故，住真实际故，无生无灭故，等住三世故，永离一切分别故，住尽后际誓愿故，严净一切世界故，庄严一一佛身故。"

尔时，普贤菩萨摩诃萨欲重明此义而说颂言：

Chapter 37 — The Manifestation of the Tathāgata

Furthermore, Sons of the Buddha, this is just as it is in the case of an immense sovereign wish-fulfilling *maṇi* jewel found in the great ocean known as "treasury of the entire world's adornments" which embodies the complete perfection of a million meritorious qualities and, wherever it is located, it enables the elimination of all beings' disastrous calamities and the fulfillment of whatever they wish for. However, this sovereign wish-fulfilling *maṇi* jewel is not something that beings possessed of but a small amount of merit would ever be able to see.

So too it is with the sovereign wish-fulfilling jewel of the Tathāgata's body known as "able to gladden all beings." If any beings see his body, hear his name, or praise his qualities, they are all thereby enabled to forever leave behind the sorrows and calamities of *saṃsāra*. If all beings in all worlds simultaneously and single-mindedly wished to see the Tathāgata, he would allow them all to see him and would ensure that all their wishes were fulfilled.

Sons of the Buddha, the Buddha's body is not something that beings possessed of a small amount of merit would be able to see, the sole exception to this being those whom the Tathāgata should use his freely invoked spiritual powers to train. If there are any beings who, because of seeing the Buddha's body, could then plant roots of goodness and even bring them to full maturity, he would then enable them to see the body of the Tathāgata.

Sons of the Buddha, this is the tenth of the marks of the Tathāgata's body. All bodhisattva-mahāsattvas should perceive them in these ways, doing so for these reasons:

> Because their minds are measureless and pervade the ten directions;
> Because their practice is as unimpeded as empty space itself;
> Because they everywhere enter the Dharma realm;
> Because they abide in the very apex of reality;
> Because they are beyond either production or destruction;
> Because they dwell equally in all three periods of time;
> Because they have forever abandoned all discriminations;
> Because they abide in vows that extend to the very end of future time;
> Because they purify all worlds; and
> Because they adorn the bodies of every buddha.

At that time, wishing to again clarify the meaning of this, Samantabhadra Bodhisattva-mahāsattva then spoke these verses:

	267c06 ‖	譬如虛空遍十方　　若色非色有非有
	267c07 ‖	三世眾生身國土　　如是普在無邊際
	267c08 ‖	諸佛真身亦如是　　一切法界無不遍
	267c09 ‖	不可得見不可取　　為化眾生而現形
	267c10 ‖	譬如虛空不可取　　普使眾生造眾業
	267c11 ‖	不念我今何所作　　云何我作為誰作
	267c12 ‖	諸佛身業亦如是　　普使群生修善法
	267c13 ‖	如來未曾有分別　　我今於彼種種作
正體字	267c14 ‖	譬如日出閻浮提　　光明破闇悉無餘
	267c15 ‖	山樹池蓮地眾物　　種種品類皆蒙益
	267c16 ‖	諸佛日出亦如是　　生長人天眾善行
	267c17 ‖	永除癡闇得智明　　恒受尊榮一切樂
	267c18 ‖	譬如日光出現時　　先照山王次餘山
	267c19 ‖	[從>後]照高原及大地　　而日未始有分別
	267c20 ‖	善逝光明亦如是　　先照菩薩次緣覺
	267c21 ‖	後照聲聞及眾生　　而佛本來無動念
	267c22 ‖	譬如生盲不見日　　日光亦為作饒益
	267c23 ‖	令知時節受飲食　　永離眾患身安隱
	267c24 ‖	無信眾生不見佛　　而佛亦為興義利
	267c25 ‖	聞名及以觸光明　　因此乃至得菩提

简体字	"譬如虚空遍十方，若色非色有非有，三世众生身国土，如是普在无边际。诸佛真身亦如是，一切法界无不遍，不可得见不可取，为化众生而现形。譬如虚空不可取，普使众生造众业，不念我今何所作？云何我作为谁作？诸佛身业亦如是，普使群生修善法，如来未曾有分别：我今于彼种种作。譬如日出阎浮提，光明破暗悉无余，山树池莲地众物，种种品类皆蒙益。诸佛日出亦如是，生长人天众善行，永除痴暗得智明，恒受尊荣一切乐。譬如日光出现时，先照山王次余山，后照高原及大地，而日未始有分别。善逝光明亦如是，先照菩萨次缘觉，后照声闻及众生，而佛本来无动念。譬如生盲不见日，日光亦为作饶益，令知时节受饮食，永离众患身安隐。无信众生不见佛，而佛亦为兴义利，闻名及以触光明，因此乃至得菩提。

Just as empty space pervades the ten directions,
reaching all that has form, is formless, exists, or does not exist
including the three times, beings' bodies, and lands,
thus being everywhere present and boundless in this way,

so too it is with the true body of the Buddha
which, in all the Dharma realm, has no place it does not pervade.
Although it cannot be seen and cannot be grasped,
it still manifests forms for the sake of teaching beings.

Just as empty space cannot be seized upon
even as it everywhere allows beings to do the many kinds of actions
and does not, in so doing, think, "This is what I am now doing,
this is how I am doing it, and these are those for whom I am doing it,"

so too it is with the physical actions of all buddhas by which
they everywhere cause the many beings to cultivate good dharmas,
for the Tathāgata never engages in any discrimination such as:
"I am now doing various kinds of things for them."

Just as when the sun rises over Jambudvīpa
and its light dispels all darkness without exception
and the mountains, trees, ponds, lotuses, and the many earthly beings
of many different categories and types all thereby receive its benefits,

so too it is with the rising of the Buddha sun
which begets and grows the many good actions of humans and devas
and forever dispels delusion's darkness so they attain wisdom's light
and always receive every happiness bestowed by the Glorious One.

Just as when the light of the sun first appears,
it first illuminates the mountain kings, then the other mountains,
and only afterward illuminates the high plains and the great earth
even as, in all of this, the sun has never had any discriminations,

so too it is with the radiant light of the Well Gone One
which first illuminates bodhisattvas, then the *pratyekabuddhas*,
and only afterward illuminates the *śrāvaka* disciples and other beings
even as, from the start, the Buddha has had no movement of thought.

Just as those born blind never see the sun
yet the sunlight still serves their benefit,
causes them to know time and season, to receive food and drink, and
to forever abandon the many calamities and gain physical security,

so too it is when beings without faith do not see the Buddha,
yet the Buddha still provides for their benefit,
so that those who hear his name or are touched by his light,
because of this, eventually achieve the realization of bodhi.

正體字	267c26 ∥	譬如淨月在虛空	能蔽眾星示盈缺
	267c27 ∥	一切水中皆現影	諸有觀瞻悉對前
	267c28 ∥	如來淨月亦復然	能蔽餘乘示修短
	267c29 ∥	普現天人淨心水	一切皆謂對其前
	268a01 ∥	譬如梵王住自宮	普現三千諸梵處
	268a02 ∥	一切人天咸得見	實不分身向於彼
	268a03 ∥	諸佛現身亦如是	一切十方無不遍
	268a04 ∥	其身無數不可稱	亦不分身不分別
	268a05 ∥	如有醫王善方術	若有見者病皆愈
	268a06 ∥	命雖已盡藥塗身	令其作務悉如初
	268a07 ∥	最勝醫王亦如是	具足方便一切智
	268a08 ∥	以昔妙行現佛身	眾生見者煩惱滅
	268a09 ∥	譬如海中有寶王	普出無量諸光明
	268a10 ∥	眾生觸者同其色	若有見者眼清淨
	268a11 ∥	最勝寶王亦如是	觸其光者悉同色
	268a12 ∥	若有得見五眼開	破諸塵闇住佛地
	268a13 ∥	譬如如意摩尼寶	隨有所求皆滿足
	268a14 ∥	少福眾生不能見	非是寶王有分別
	268a15 ∥	善逝寶王亦如是	悉滿所求諸欲樂
	268a16 ∥	無信眾生不見佛	非是善逝心棄捨
简体字		譬如净月在虚空，能蔽众星示盈缺，一切水中皆现影，诸有观瞻悉对前。如来净月亦复然，能蔽余乘示修短，普现天人净心水，一切皆谓对其前。譬如梵王住自宫，普现三千诸梵处，一切人天咸得见，实不分身向于彼。诸佛现身亦如是，一切十方无不遍，其身无数不可称，亦不分身不分别。如有医王善方术，若有见者病皆愈，命虽已尽药涂身，令其作务悉如初。最胜医王亦如是，具足方便一切智，以昔妙行现佛身，众生见者烦恼灭。譬如海中有宝王，普出无量诸光明，众生触者同其色，若有见者眼清净。最胜宝王亦如是，触其光者悉同色，若有得见五眼开，破诸尘暗住佛地。譬如如意摩尼宝，随有所求皆满足，少福众生不能见，非是宝王有分别。善逝宝王亦如是，悉满所求诸欲乐，无信众生不见佛，非是善逝心弃舍。	

Just as when the purely shining moon abiding up in space
is able to outshine the many stars and show its waxing and waning
as it appears reflected in all the many bodies of water
while all who gaze upon it see it as appearing directly before them,

So too, the brightly shining moon of the Tathāgata
is able to outshine other vehicles and appear for a long or short time
as he manifests in the waters of devas' and humans' pure minds
so that they all feel he is appearing directly before them.

Just as the Brahma Heaven King abiding in his palace
everywhere manifests in all the chiliocosm's abodes of Brahmā
so that all humans and devas are able to see him in all those places,
even as, in truth, he never divides his bodies or goes there,

so too it is with the Buddha's manifestation of his bodies
that have no place throughout the ten directions they do not pervade
as he displays so countlessly many bodies they cannot be described
even as he still does not divide his body or engage in discriminations.

Just as with the physician king skilled in the art of healing formulas
who, if anyone but saw him, their illnesses were all healed—
although his life had ended, having smeared his body with potions,
he was still able to continue performing all his works just as before—

so too it is with the supreme king of physicians
who is fully possessed of both skillful means and all-knowledge—
Because of his past marvelous practices, he manifests buddha bodies
which, if beings but see them, their afflictions are then extinguished.

Just as when there is a sovereign jewel in the ocean
which everywhere emanates countless rays of light
that, when beings are touched by them, they become the same color,
and, when they see them, their eyes are purified,

so too it is with the supreme king of all jewels who,
when beings are touched by his light, they all become the same color,
and when they see it, their five eyes all open so that it dispels
the darkness of sense objects and they dwell on the buddha ground.

Just as it is with a wish-fulfilling *maṇi* jewel
which completely fulfills all wishes for whatever is sought
even as beings of little merit are unable to even see it—
but it is not that the king of jewels discriminates against them.

So too it is with the Well Gone One, the King of Jewels,
who fulfills all wishes for whatever is sought
even as beings without faith are unable to even see the Buddha—
but it is not that the mind of the Well Gone One has forsaken them.

正體字

大方廣佛華嚴經[1]卷第五十一
　　如來出現品第三十七之二
佛子。菩薩摩訶薩。應云何知如來應正等覺
音聲。佛子。菩薩摩訶薩。應知如來音聲遍至
普遍無量諸音聲故。應知如來音聲。隨其心
樂。皆令歡喜。說法明了故。應知如來音聲。隨
其信解。皆令歡喜。心得清涼故。應知如來音
聲化不失時。所應聞者。無不聞故。應知如來
音聲無生滅。如呼響故。應知如來音聲無主。
修習一切。業所起故。應知如來音聲甚深。難
可度量故。應知如來音聲無邪曲。法界所生
故。應知如來音聲無斷絕。普入法界故。應知
如來音聲無變易。至於究竟故。佛子。菩薩摩
訶薩。應知如來音聲非量非無量。非主非無
主。非示非無示。何以故。佛子。譬如世界。將
欲壞時。無主無作。法爾而出四種音聲。其四
者何。一曰。汝等當知初禪安樂。離諸欲惡。
超過欲界。眾生聞已。自然而得成就初禪。捨
欲界身。生於梵天。

简体字

大方广佛华严经卷第五十一
如来出现品第三十七之二
　　"佛子，菩萨摩诃萨应云何知如来、应、正等觉音声？
　　"佛子，菩萨摩诃萨应知如来音声遍至，普遍无量诸音声故；应知如来音声随其心乐皆令欢喜，说法明了故；应知如来音声随其信解皆令欢喜，心得清凉故；应知如来音声化不失时，所应闻者无不闻故；应知如来音声无生灭，如呼响故；应知如来音声无主，修习一切业所起故；应知如来音声甚深，难可度量故；应知如来音声无邪曲，法界所生故；应知如来音声无断绝，普入法界故；应知如来音声无变易，至于究竟故。佛子，菩萨摩诃萨应知如来音声，非量、非无量，非主、非无主，非示、非无示。何以故？佛子，譬如世界将欲坏时，无主无作，法尔而出四种音声。其四者何？一曰：'汝等当知初禅安乐，离诸欲恶，超过欲界。'众生闻已，自然而得成就初禅，舍欲界身，生于梵天。

Sons of the Buddha, how is it that the bodhisattva-mahāsattva should know the voice of the Tathāgata, the Arhat, the One of Right and Universal Enlightenment? Sons of the Buddha, the bodhisattva-mahāsattva should know it in these ways:

> He should know the Tathāgata's voice as reaching everywhere because it everywhere pervades all the countless other sounds;
>
> He should know the Tathāgata's voice as enabling everyone to be delighted by conforming to their mental dispositions because his explanations of Dharma are clear and ultimate;
>
> He should know the Tathāgata's voice as enabling everyone to be delighted by adapting to their resolute beliefs because their minds are then able to experience clarity and coolness;
>
> He should know the Tathāgata's voice as teaching in a manner that never misses the right time because those who should listen to it are all able to hear it;
>
> He should know the Tathāgata's voice as neither produced nor destroyed because it is like a resounding echo;
>
> He should know the Tathāgata's voice as having no subjective agent of actions because it arises due to his having cultivated all the karmic works;
>
> He should know the Tathāgata's voice as extremely profound because it is difficult to fathom;
>
> He should know the Tathāgata's voice as free of any error or distortion because it arises from the Dharma realm itself;
>
> He should know the Tathāgata's voice as never ending because it everywhere penetrates the Dharma realm; and
>
> He should know the Tathāgata's voice as unchanging because it reaches the very ultimate.

Sons of the Buddha, the bodhisattva-mahāsattva should know the Tathāgata's voice as neither finite nor infinite, as neither possessed of nor devoid of any subjective agent, and as neither providing nor not providing instruction. And why is this? Sons of the Buddha, just as, when the world is about to be destroyed, even in the absence of any subjective agent and even in the absence of any deliberate action, there spontaneously arise four verbal declarations. What are those four?

The first of those voices says: "You should all come to know the happiness of the first *dhyāna* which leaves behind the bad aspects of the desires and surpasses the desire realm." Having heard this, beings are then naturally able to accomplish the attainment of the first *dhyāna* whereupon they relinquish their desire-realm bodies and take rebirth in the Brahma Heaven.

正體字

二曰。汝等當知二禪安樂。
無覺無觀。超於梵天。眾生聞已。自然而得成
就二禪。捨梵天身。生光音天。三曰。汝等當知
三禪安樂。無有過失。超光音天。眾生聞已。自
然而得成就三禪。捨光音身。生遍淨天。四曰。
汝等當知四禪寂靜。超遍淨天。眾生聞已。自
然而得成就四禪。捨遍淨身。生廣果天。是為
四。佛子。此諸音聲。無主無作。但從眾生諸善
業力之所出生。佛子。如來音聲。亦復如是。無
主無作。無有分別。非入非出。但從如來功德
法力。出於四種廣大音聲。其四者何。一曰。汝
等當知一切諸行。皆悉是苦。所謂地獄苦。畜
生苦。餓鬼苦。無福德苦。著我我所苦。作諸惡
行苦。欲生人天。當種善根。生人天中。離諸難
處。眾生聞已。捨離顛倒。修諸善行。離諸難
處。生人天中。

简体字

二曰：'汝等当知二禅安乐，无觉无观，超于梵天。'众生闻已，自然而得成就二禅，舍梵天身，生光音天。三曰：'汝等当知三禅安乐，无有过失，超光音天。'众生闻已，自然而得成就三禅，舍光音身，生遍净天。四曰：'汝等当知四禅寂静，超遍净天。'众生闻已，自然而得成就四禅，舍遍净身，生广果天。是为四。佛子，此诸音声无主无作，但从众生诸善业力之所出生。佛子，如来音声亦复如是，无主无作，无有分别，非入非出，但从如来功德法力，出于四种广大音声。其四者何？一曰：'汝等当知一切诸行皆悉是苦，所谓：地狱苦、畜生苦、饿鬼苦、无福德苦、著我我所苦、作诸恶行苦。欲生人、天当种善根；生人、天中，离诸难处。'众生闻已，舍离颠倒，修诸善行，离诸难处，生人、天中。

Chapter 37 — The Manifestation of the Tathāgata

The second of those voices says: "You should all come to know the happiness of the second *dhyāna* which is free of initial ideation and free of mental discursiveness and which surpasses the Brahma Heaven." Having heard this, beings are then naturally able to accomplish the attainment of the second *dhyāna* whereupon they relinquish their Brahma Heaven bodies and take rebirth in the Light-and-Sound Heaven.

The third of those voices says: "You should all come to know the happiness of the third *dhyāna* which is free of faults and which surpasses the Light-and-Sound Heaven." Having heard this, beings are then naturally able to accomplish the attainment of the third *dhyāna* whereupon they relinquish their Light-and-Sound Heaven bodies and take rebirth in the Universal Purity Heaven.

The fourth of those voices says: "You should all come to know the quiescence of the fourth *dhyāna* which surpasses the Universal Purity Heaven. Having heard this, beings are then naturally able to accomplish the attainment of the fourth *dhyāna* whereupon they relinquish their Universal Purity Heaven bodies and take rebirth in the Vast Fruition Heaven.

These are the four. Sons of the Buddha, all of these voices arise without any subjective agent of action and without any deliberate effort. They arise solely by the power of beings' good karmic deeds.

Sons of the Buddha, so too it is with the voice of the Tathāgata. It arises without any subjective agent of actions, without any deliberate effort, without any making of discriminations, and neither enters nor leaves. It is solely through the power of the dharma of the Tathāgata's meritorious qualities that there arise four kinds of vast voices. What are those four?

The first of those voices says: "You should all realize that all actions[55] are freighted with sufferings, in particular: the sufferings of the hell realms, the sufferings of the animal realms, the sufferings of the hungry ghost realms, the sufferings of an absence of karmic merit, the sufferings of seizing upon the existence of a self and possessions of a self, and the sufferings associated with all bad actions. If one wishes to attain rebirth in the human or heavenly realms, one must plant roots of goodness adequate to achieve rebirth in the human or heavenly realms apart from places beset by the difficulties."[56] Having heard this, beings then abandon their inverted views, cultivate the good actions, leave the places beset by the difficulties, and then achieve rebirth in the human or heavenly realms.

正體字

二曰。汝等當知一切諸行。眾
268b27　苦熾然。如熱鐵丸。諸行無常。是磨滅法。涅槃
268b28　寂靜。無為安樂。遠離熾然。消諸熱惱。眾生
268b29　聞已。勤修善法。於聲聞乘。得隨順音聲忍。三
268c01　曰。汝等當知聲聞乘者。隨他語解。智慧狹劣。
268c02　更有上乘。名獨覺乘。悟不由師。汝等應學。樂
268c03　勝道者。聞此音已。捨聲聞道。修獨覺乘。四
268c04　曰。汝等當知過二乘位。更有勝道。名為大乘。
268c05　菩薩所行。順六波羅蜜。不斷菩薩行。不捨菩
268c06　提心。處無量生死。而不疲厭。過於二乘。名為
268c07　大乘第一乘勝乘最勝乘上乘無上乘利益一
268c08　切眾生乘。若有眾生。信解廣大。諸根猛利。宿
268c09　種善根。為諸如來神力所加。有勝樂欲。希求
268c10　佛果。聞此音已。發菩提心。佛子。如來音聲。不
268c11　從身出。不從心出。而能利益無量眾生。佛子。
268c12　是為如來音聲第一相。諸菩薩摩訶薩。應如
268c13　是知。復次佛子。譬如呼響。因於山谷及音聲
268c14　起。無有形狀。不可覩見。亦無分別。而能隨逐
268c15　一切語言。如來音聲。亦復如是。無有形狀。不
268c16　可覩見。非有方所。

简体字

二曰：'汝等当知一切诸行众苦炽然，如热铁丸。诸行无常，是磨灭法；涅槃寂静，无为安乐，远离炽然，消诸热恼。'众生闻已，勤修善法，于声闻乘得随顺音声忍。三曰：'汝等当知声闻乘者，随他语解，智慧狭劣；更有上乘，名独觉乘，悟不由师，汝等应学。'乐胜道者闻此音已，舍声闻道，修独觉乘。四曰：'汝等当知过二乘位更有胜道，名为大乘。菩萨所行，顺六波罗蜜，不断菩萨行，不舍菩提心，处无量生死而不疲厌，过于二乘，名为大乘、第一乘、胜乘、最胜乘、上乘、无上乘、利益一切众生乘。'若有众生信解广大，诸根猛利，宿种善根，为诸如来神力所加，有胜乐欲，希求佛果；闻此音已，发菩提心。佛子，如来音声不从身出、不从心出，而能利益无量众生。佛子，是为如来音声第一相，诸菩萨摩诃萨应如是知。

"复次，佛子，譬如呼响，因于山谷及音声起，无有形状，不可睹见，亦无分别，而能随逐一切语言。如来音声亦复如是，无有形状，不可睹见，非有方所，

Chapter 37 — The Manifestation of the Tathāgata

The second of those voices says: "You should all realize that all actions are as ablaze with manifold sufferings as the burning hot iron pellets.[57] All actions are impermanent and are dharmas of destruction. The quiescence of nirvāṇa is the bliss of the unconditioned in which one leaves such burning heat far behind and eliminates all of the hot afflictions." Having heard this, beings then diligently cultivate good dharmas and acquire the "acquiescence in sounds" patience as it is found in the *śrāvaka*-disciple vehicle.[58]

The third of those voices says: "You should all realize that the *śrāvaka*-disciple vehicle's understanding developed by according with teachings from others produces narrow and inferior wisdom. There is also a superior vehicle known as the *pratyekabuddha* vehicle in which one becomes awakened without relying on a teacher. You should all train in it. Having heard this voice, those beings who delight in supreme paths relinquish the *śrāvaka*-disciple path and then cultivate the *pratyekabuddha* vehicle.

The fourth of those voices says: "You should all realize that, beyond the positions of the two vehicles, there is yet another superior path known as "the Great Vehicle" that is cultivated by the bodhisattvas who accord with the six *pāramitās*, never cease the bodhisattva practices, never relinquish the bodhi resolve, abide within it for countless births and deaths, and yet never weary of this. It surpasses the two vehicles and is known as "the Great Vehicle," "the foremost vehicle," "the supreme vehicle," "the most supreme vehicle," "the superior vehicle," "the unexcelled vehicle," and "the vehicle which benefits all beings." Wherever there are beings whose resolute faith is vast, whose faculties are especially sharp, who have planted roots of goodness in past lives, who are aided by the spiritual powers of the *tathāgatas*, who are possessed of supreme zeal, and who seek to acquire the fruit of buddhahood, once they have heard this voice, they then arouse the resolve to attain bodhi.

Sons of the Buddha, the Tathāgata's voice does not come forth from the body and does not come forth from the mind. Even so, it is able to benefit countless beings. Sons of the Buddha, this is the first of the marks of the Tathāgata's voice. All bodhisattva-mahāsattvas should perceive it in this way.

Furthermore, Sons of the Buddha, just as the echoes which occur due to the encounter between a mountain valley and voices have no form or appearance, cannot be seen, and have no discriminations even as they are still able to follow after everything that one says, so too it is with the Tathāgata's voice. It has no form or appearance, cannot be seen, and neither has a location nor does not have

正體字

非無方所。但隨眾生欲解
268c17| 緣出。其性究竟。無言無示。不可宣說。佛子。是
268c18| 為如來音聲第二相。諸菩薩摩訶薩。應如是
268c19| 知。復次佛子。譬如諸天有大法鼓。名為覺悟。
268c20| 若諸天子。行放逸時。於虛空中。出聲告言。汝
268c21| 等當知一切欲樂。皆悉無常。虛妄顛倒。須臾
268c22| 變壞。但誑愚夫。令其[3]戀著。汝莫放逸。若放
268c23| 逸者。墮諸惡趣。後悔無及。放逸諸天。聞此音
268c24| 已。生大[4]憂怖。捨自宮中所有欲樂。詣天王
268c25| 所。求法行道。佛子。彼天鼓音。無主無作。無起
268c26| 無滅。而能利益無量眾生。當知如來。亦復如
268c27| 是。為欲覺悟放逸眾生。出於無量妙法音聲。
268c28| 所謂無著聲。不放逸聲。無常聲。苦聲。無我聲。
268c29| 不淨聲。寂滅聲。涅槃聲。無有量自然智聲。不
269a01| 可壞菩薩行聲。至一切處如來無功用智地
269a02| 聲。以此音聲。遍法界中。而開悟之。無數眾
269a03| 生。聞是音已。皆生歡喜。勤修善法。各於自
269a04| 乘。而求出離。所謂或修聲聞乘。或修獨覺乘。
269a05| 或習菩薩無上大乘。而如來音。不住方所。無
269a06| 有言說。

简体字

非无方所；但随众生欲解缘出，其性究竟，无言无示，不可宣说。佛子，是为如来音声第二相，诸菩萨摩诃萨应如是知。

"复次，佛子，譬如诸天有大法鼓，名为觉悟。若诸天子行放逸时，于虚空中出声告言：'汝等当知一切欲乐皆悉无常，虚妄颠倒，须臾变坏，但诳愚夫令其恋著。汝莫放逸，若放逸者，堕诸恶趣，后悔无及。'放逸诸天闻此音已，生大忧怖，舍自宫中所有欲乐，诣天王所求法行道。佛子，彼天鼓音，无主无作，无起无灭，而能利益无量众生。当知如来亦复如是，为欲觉悟放逸众生，出于无量妙法音声，所谓：无著声、不放逸声、无常声、苦声、无我声、不净声、寂灭声、涅槃声、无有量自然智声、不可坏菩萨行声、至一切处如来无功用智地声，以此音声遍法界中而开悟之。无数众生闻是音已，皆生欢喜，勤修善法，各于自乘而求出离，所谓：或修声闻乘、或修独觉乘、或习菩萨无上大乘。而如来音，不住方所，无有言说。

a location. It arises solely in accordance with conditions associated with beings' aspirations and understandings. Its nature is ultimately devoid of either words or instruction and is inexpressible. Sons of the Buddha, this is the second of the marks of the Tathāgata's voice. All bodhisattva-mahāsattvas should perceive it in this way.

Furthermore, Sons of the Buddha, this is just as it is with the devas who have a great Dharma drum known as "the awakener." Whenever any of the devas' sons indulge in neglectful behavior, it emanates a voice from space that calls out, saying: "You should all realize that all desire-based pleasures are impermanent, false, born of inverted views, destined to fade away in an instant, and only serve to deceive foolish common people and cause them to become affectionately attached. You must not become neglectful. If you become neglectful, you will fall into the wretched destinies, at which point, it will be too late to regret this."

Having heard this voice, those neglectful devas then become filled with worry and fearfulness and relinquish all their desire-based pleasures in their palaces, and then go to pay their respects to the heavenly king and request the Dharma for practicing the path.

Sons of the Buddha, the voices emanating from that heavenly drum have no subjective agent, no deliberate actions, no arising, and no cessation, and yet they are able to benefit countless beings.

One should realize that the Tathāgata is also just like this. Wishing to awaken neglectful beings, he emanates countless voices speaking the sounds of the sublime Dharma, namely: the voice speaking of nonattachment, the voice speaking of avoiding neglectfulness, the voice speaking of impermanence, the voice speaking of the sufferings, the voice speaking of non-self, the voice speaking of impurity, the voice speaking of quiescence, the voice speaking of nirvāṇa, the voice speaking of measureless spontaneously arising wisdom, the voice speaking of the indestructible bodhisattva practices, and the universally pervading voice speaking of the Tathāgata's ground of effortless wisdom.

He uses these voices which reach everywhere throughout the Dharma realm to then bring about their awakening. Having heard these voices, countless beings become filled with joyous delight and diligently cultivate good dharmas, whereupon each of them seeks to achieve transcendence by resort to their own vehicle. For instance, some of them cultivate the *śrāvaka*-disciple vehicle, some of them cultivate the *pratyekabuddha* vehicle, and some of them cultivate the bodhisattva's unexcelled great vehicle, and yet the voices of the Tathāgata do not abide in any particular place and do not have anything they say.

正體字

佛子。是為如來音聲第三相。諸菩薩
摩訶薩。應如是知。復次佛子。譬如自在天王。
有天[1]采女。名曰善口。於其口中。出一音聲。
其聲則與百千種樂。而共相應。一一樂中。復
有百千差別音聲。佛子。彼善口女。從口一聲。
出於如是。無量音聲。當知如來。亦復如是。於
一音中。出無量聲。隨諸眾生心樂差別。皆悉
遍至。悉令得解。佛子。是為如來音聲第四相。
諸菩薩摩訶薩。應如是知。復次佛子。譬如大
梵天王。住於梵宮。出梵音聲。一切梵眾。靡不
皆聞。而彼音聲。不出眾外。諸梵天眾。咸生是
念。大梵天王。獨[2]與我語。如來妙音。亦復如
是。道場眾會。靡不皆聞。而其音聲。不出眾
外。何以故。根未熟者。不應聞故。其聞音者。
皆作是念。如來世尊。獨為我說。佛子。如來
音聲。無出無住。而能成就一切事業。是為如
來音聲第五相。諸菩薩摩訶薩。應如是知。復
次佛子。譬如眾水皆同一味。隨器異故。水有
差別。水無念慮。亦無分別。如來言音。亦復如
是。唯是一味。謂解脫味。隨諸眾生心器異故。
無量差別。而無念慮。亦無分別。佛子。是為
如來音聲第六相。諸菩薩摩訶薩。應如是知。

简体字

佛子，是为如来音声第三相，诸菩萨摩诃萨应如是知。

"复次，佛子，譬如自在天王有天媒女，名曰善口，于其口中出一音声，其声则与百千种乐而共相应，一一乐中复有百千差别音声。佛子，彼善口女从口一声，出于如是无量音声。当知如来亦复如是，于一音中出无量声，随诸众生心乐差别，皆悉遍至，悉令得解。佛子，是为如来音声第四相，诸菩萨摩诃萨应如是知。

"复次，佛子，譬如大梵天王住于梵宫出梵音声，一切梵众靡不皆闻，而彼音声不出众外。诸梵天众咸生是念：'大梵天王独与我语。'如来妙音亦复如是，道场众会靡不皆闻，而其音声不出众外。何以故？根未熟者不应闻故。其闻音者皆作是念：'如来世尊独为我说。'佛子，如来音声无出无住，而能成就一切事业。是为如来音声第五相，诸菩萨摩诃萨应如是知。

"复次，佛子，譬如众水皆同一味，随器异故水有差别，水无念虑亦无分别。如来言音亦复如是，唯是一味，谓解脱味，随诸众生心器异故无量差别，而无念虑亦无分别。佛子，是为如来音声第六相，诸菩萨摩诃萨应如是知。

Chapter 37 — The Manifestation of the Tathāgata

Sons of the Buddha, this is the third of the marks of the Tathāgata's voice. All bodhisattva-mahāsattvas should perceive it in this way.

Furthermore, Sons of the Buddha, this is just as it is with the Vaśavartin Heaven King's celestial palace maiden named Fine Mouth who is able to emanate a single voice from her mouth the sound of which resonates with a hundred thousand kinds of music of which each kind of music contains a hundred thousand different voices. Sons of the Buddha, as for that maiden Fine Mouth's emanation of so countlessly many voices from but a single voice—one should realize that the Tathāgata's voice is just like this, for from but a single sound, he emanates countless voices adapted to beings' different mental dispositions which then go everywhere and cause them all to understand.

Sons of the Buddha, this is the fourth of the marks of the Tathāgata's voice. All bodhisattva-mahāsattvas should perceive it in this way.

Furthermore, Sons of the Buddha, this is just as it is when the great Brahma Heaven King dwelling in the Brahma Heaven palace speaks with the voice of Brahmā and then no one in the assembly of Brahmā fails to hear this even as that voice does not go beyond that assembly and everyone in the assembly of Brahmā thinks, "The Brahma Heaven King is speaking solely to me."

So too it is with the sublime sound of the Tathāgata's voice. No one in the assembly at the site of enlightenment fails to hear it and yet it does not go beyond that congregation. Why is this so? This is because those whose faculties are not yet ripened should not hear it. Those who do hear his voice all think, "The Tathāgata, the Bhagavat, is speaking solely to me."

Sons of the Buddha, the Tathāgata's voice has no going forth or remaining and yet it is able to bring all kinds of karmic works to completion. This is the fifth of the marks of the Tathāgata's voice. All bodhisattva-mahāsattvas should perceive it in this way.

Furthermore, Sons of the Buddha, just as the many rivers' waters are all of the same flavor and yet, in accordance with different containers, those waters manifest differences without those waters thinking about this or making discriminations, so too it is with the voice of the Tathāgata which is of only a single flavor, namely the flavor of liberation. Because it adapts to differences in beings' mental capacities, it manifests countless differences and yet he does not think about this or make any discriminations in this regard.

Sons of the Buddha, this is the sixth of the marks of the Tathāgata's voice. All bodhisattva-mahāsattvas should perceive it in this way.

| 正體字 | 269a28
269a29
269b01
269b02
269b03
269b04
269b05
269b06
269b07
269b08
269b09
269b10
269b11
269b12
269b13
269b14
269b15
269b16
269b17 | 復次佛子。譬如阿那婆達多龍王。興大密雲。遍閻浮提。普霔甘雨。百穀苗稼。皆得生長。江河泉池。一切盈滿。此大雨水。不從龍王身心中出。而能種種。饒益眾生。佛子。如來應正等覺。亦復如是。興大悲雲。遍十方界。普雨無上甘露法雨。令一切眾生。皆生歡喜。增長善法。滿足諸乘。佛子。如來音聲。不從外來。不從內出。而能饒益一切眾生。是為如來音聲第七相。諸菩薩摩訶薩。應如是知。復次佛子。譬如摩那斯龍王。將欲降雨。未便即降。先起大雲。彌覆虛空。凝停七日。待諸眾生。作務究竟。何以故。彼大龍王。有慈悲心。不欲惱亂諸眾生故。過七日已。降微細雨。普潤大地。佛子。如來應正等覺。亦復如是。將降法雨。未便即降。先興法雲。成熟眾生。為欲令其心無驚怖。待其熟已。然後普降甘露法雨。演說甚深微妙善法。漸次令其滿足如來一切智智無上法味。佛子。是為如來音聲第八相。諸菩薩摩訶薩。應如是知。 |

简体字

"复次，佛子，譬如阿那婆达多龙王兴大密云，遍阎浮提普霔甘雨，百谷苗稼皆得生长，江河泉池一切盈满；此大雨水不从龙王身心中出，而能种种饶益众生。佛子，如来、应、正等觉亦复如是，兴大悲云遍十方界，普雨无上甘露法雨，令一切众生皆生欢喜，增长善法，满足诸乘。佛子，如来音声不从外来、不从内出，而能饶益一切众生。是为如来音声第七相，诸菩萨摩诃萨应如是知。

"复次，佛子，譬如摩那斯龙王将欲降雨，未便即降，先起大云弥覆虚空凝停七日，待诸众生作务究竟。何以故？彼大龙王有慈悲心，不欲恼乱诸众生故。过七日已，降微细雨普润大地。佛子，如来、应、正等觉亦复如是，将降法雨，未便即降，先兴法云成熟众生，为欲令其心无惊怖；待其熟已，然后普降甘露法雨，演说甚深微妙善法，渐次令其满足如来一切智智无上法味。佛子，是为如来音声第八相，诸菩萨摩诃萨应如是知。

Furthermore, Sons of the Buddha, this is just as it is when the dragon king, Anavatapta, spreads forth dense clouds that cover the entire continent of Jambudvīpa, everywhere sending down the sweet seasonal rains which allow the seedlings of the hundred kinds of grains to grow and which also allow all the rivers, springs, and ponds to become full. The waters of these great rains do not come forth from the body or mind of this dragon king and yet they are still able to bring beings many different kinds of benefits.

Sons of the Buddha, so too it is with the Tathāgata, the Arhat, the One of Right and Universal Enlightenment. He spreads forth the clouds of great compassion which cover all realms throughout the ten directions and which everywhere rain down the unexcelled sweet-dew Dharma rains that cause all beings to be filled with joyous delight, increase their development of good dharmas, and fulfill all the vehicles [of Dharma practice].

Sons of the Buddha, the Tathāgata's voice does not come from without and does emerge from within, and yet it is able to benefit all beings. This is the seventh of the marks of the Tathāgata's voice. All bodhisattva-mahāsattvas should perceive it in this way.

Furthermore, Sons of the Buddha, this is just as it is when the dragon king, Manasvin, is about to send down the rains. Since it would not be suitable to just let them suddenly descend, he first produces immense clouds that completely cover the entire sky and remain there for seven days, waiting for all beings to complete their work. And why does he do this? Because that great dragon king has thoughts of kindness and compassion and hence does not wish to distress or disrupt beings, he waits until seven days have passed before he sends down a fine drizzling rain that everywhere moistens the great earth.

Sons of the Buddha, so too it is with the Tathāgata, the Arhat, the One of Right and Universal Enlightenment. When he is about to send down the Dharma rains, since it would not be suitable to just let them suddenly descend, he first spreads forth Dharma clouds which ripen beings. Because he wishes to prevent their minds from becoming frightened, he waits until they have become ripened, after which he then everywhere sends down the sweet-dew Dharma rain with which he proclaims and explains the extremely profound and sublime good Dharma and gradually allows them to gain satisfaction with the flavor of the Tathāgata's unexcelled Dharma of the wisdom of all-knowledge.

Sons of the Buddha, this is the eighth of the marks of the Tathāgata's voice. All bodhisattva-mahāsattvas should perceive it in this way.

正體字

復次佛子。譬如海中。有大龍王。
名大莊嚴。於大海中。降雨之時。或降十種莊
嚴雨。或百或千。或百千種莊嚴雨。佛子。水無
分別。但以龍王不思議力。令其莊嚴。乃至百
千無量差別。如來應正等覺。亦復如是。為諸
眾生說法之時。或以十種。差別音說。或百或
千。或以百千。或以八萬四千音聲。說八萬四
千行。乃至或以無量百千億那由他音聲。各
別說法。令其聞者。皆生歡喜。如來音聲。無所
分別。但以諸佛於甚深法界。圓滿清淨。能隨
眾生根之所宜。出種種言音。皆令歡喜。佛子。
是為如來音聲第九相。諸菩薩摩訶薩。應如
是知。復次佛子。譬如娑竭羅龍王。欲現龍王
大自在力。饒益眾生。咸令歡喜。從四天下。乃
至他化自在天處。興大雲網。周匝彌覆。其雲
色相。無量差別。或閻浮檀金光明色。或毘瑠
璃光明色。或白銀光明色。或[3]玻瓈光明色。或
牟薩羅光明色。或碼碯光明色。或勝藏光明
色。或赤真珠光明色。

简体字

"复次，佛子，譬如海中有大龙王，名大庄严，于大海中降雨之时，或降十种庄严雨，或百、或千、或百千种庄严雨。佛子，水无分别，但以龙王不思议力令其庄严，乃至百千无量差别。如来、应、正等觉亦复如是，为诸众生说法之时，或以十种差别音说，或百、或千、或以百千，或以八万四千音声说八万四千行，乃至或以无量百千亿那由他音声各别说法，令其闻者皆生欢喜；如来音声无所分别，但以诸佛于甚深法界圆满清净，能随众生根之所宜，出种种言音皆令欢喜。佛子，是为如来音声第九相，诸菩萨摩诃萨应如是知。

"复次，佛子，譬如娑竭罗龙王，欲现龙王大自在力，饶益众生咸令欢喜，从四天下乃至他化自在天处，兴大云网周匝弥覆。其云色相无量差别，或阎浮檀金光明色，或毗琉璃光明色，或白银光明色，或玻璃光明色，或牟萨罗光明色，或玛瑙光明色，或胜藏光明色，或赤真珠光明色，

Furthermore, Sons of the Buddha, this is just as it is with the dragon king in the ocean known as Vāsuki or "Great Adornment." When he sends down the rains out in the great ocean, he may send down ten kinds of adorning rains, a hundred kinds, a thousand kinds, or a hundred thousand kinds of adorning rains. Sons of the Buddha, the rainwater itself has no discrimination by which it accomplishes this. Rather it is solely due to the inconceivable powers of that dragon king that he causes his adornments to manifest even up to countless hundreds of thousands of differences.

So too it is with the Tathāgata, the Arhat, the One of Right and Universal Enlightenment. When he explains the Dharma for beings, he may use ten different kinds of voices, may use a hundred, a thousand, a hundred thousand, or eighty-four thousand different kinds of voices in explaining eighty-four thousand different kinds of practices, or he may even use up to countless hundreds of thousands of *koṭīs* of *nayutas* of voices with each of which he teaches the Dharma in different ways, thereby causing all who hear them to be filled with joyous delight.

Still, the Tathāgata's voice remains entirely free of any kinds of discriminations. Rather, it is solely due to all buddhas' perfect fulfillment of purity throughout the extremely deep Dharma realm that he is able to accord with whatever is fitting for beings' faculties as he sends forth these many different kinds of voices and causes everyone to feel joyous delight.

Sons of the Buddha, this is the ninth of the marks of the Tathāgata's voice. All bodhisattva-mahāsattvas should perceive it in this way.

Furthermore, Sons of the Buddha, this is just as it is with the dragon king, Sāgara, when, wishing to display a dragon king's immense powers of sovereign mastery to benefit and delight beings, he then spreads forth a great net of clouds that extends all around, covering everything from the four continents on up to the Paranirmita-vaśavartin Heaven. Those clouds have countless different colors and characteristics:

Some glow with the color of *jambūnada* gold;
Some glow with the color of *vaiḍūrya*;
Some glow with the color of white silver;
Some glow with the color of crystal;
Some glow with the color of *musaragalva*;
Some glow with the color of emerald;
Some glow with the color of excellent-treasury jewels;
Some glow with the color of red pearls;

正體字

或無量香光明色。或無
269c07 | 垢衣光明色。或清淨水光明色。或種種莊嚴
269c08 | 具光明色。如是雲網。周匝彌布。既彌布已。出
269c09 | 種種色電光。所謂閻浮檀金色雲。出瑠璃色
269c10 | 電光。瑠璃色雲。出金色電光。銀色雲。出玻瓈
269c11 | 色電光。玻瓈色雲。出銀色電光。牟薩羅色雲。
269c12 | 出碼磂色電光。碼磂色雲。出牟薩羅電光。
269c13 | 勝藏寶色雲。出赤真珠色[4]電光。赤真珠色雲。
269c14 | 出勝藏寶色電光。無量香色雲。出無垢衣色
269c15 | 電光。無垢衣色雲。出無量香色電光。清淨水
269c16 | 色雲。出種種莊嚴具色電光。種種莊嚴具色
269c17 | 雲。出清淨水色電光。乃至種種色雲。出一色
269c18 | 電光。一色雲。出種種色電光。復於彼雲中。出
269c19 | 種種雷聲。隨眾生心。皆令歡喜。所謂或如天
269c20 | 女歌詠音。或如諸天[5]妓樂音。或如龍女歌詠
269c21 | 音。

简体字

或无量香光明色，或无垢衣光明色，或清净水光明色，或种种庄严具光明色，如是云网周匝弥布。既弥布已，出种种色电光。所谓：阎浮檀金色云出琉璃色电光，琉璃色云出金色电光，银色云出玻璃色电光，玻璃色云出银色电光，牟萨罗色云出玛瑙色电光，玛瑙色云出牟萨罗色电光，胜藏宝色云出赤真珠色电光，赤真珠色云出胜藏宝色电光，无量香色云出无垢衣色电光，无垢衣色云出无量香色电光，清净水色云出种种庄严具色电光，种种庄严具色云出清净水色电光；乃至种种色云出一色电光，一色云出种种色电光。复于彼云中出种种雷声，随众生心皆令欢喜，所谓：或如天女歌咏音，或如诸天妓乐音，或如龙女歌咏音，

Chapter 37 — The Manifestation of the Tathāgata

Some glow with the color of infinity incense;
Some glow with the color of stainless robes;
Some glow with the color of pure waters; and
Some glow with the color of all different kinds of adornments.

A net of clouds like this spreads everywhere over everything and then, after it has spread forth, it flashes with lightning bolts of many different colors, for instance:

Clouds the color of *jambūnada* gold send forth lightning flashes the color of *vaiḍūrya*;

Clouds the color of *vaiḍūrya* send forth lightning flashes the color of gold;

Clouds the color of silver send forth lightning flashes the color of crystal;

Clouds the color of crystal send forth lightning flashes the color of silver;

Clouds the color of *musaragalva* send forth lightning flashes the color of emeralds;

Clouds the color of emeralds send forth lightning flashes the color of *musaragalva*;

Clouds the color of excellent treasury jewels send forth lightning flashes the color of red pearls;

Clouds the color of red pearls send forth lightning flashes the color of excellent treasury jewels;

Clouds the color of infinity incense send forth lightning flashes the color of immaculate robes;

Clouds the color of immaculate robes send forth lightning flashes the color of infinity incense;

Clouds the color of pure waters send forth lightning flashes the color of various adornments; and

Clouds the color of various adornments send forth lightning flashes the color of pure waters.

And so these examples continue on through to the point where clouds of many different colors send forth lightning flashes of a single color and clouds of a single color send forth many-colored lightning flashes.

Furthermore, from within all of those clouds, there come forth many different types of thunder which, adapting to beings' minds, cause them all to feel joyous delight. For instance:

Some sound like the singing of celestial maidens;
Some sound like the music of celestial musicians;
Some sound like the singing of dragon maidens;

正體字

	或如乾闥婆女歌詠音。或如緊那羅女歌
269c22	詠音。或如大地震動聲。或如海水波潮聲。或
269c23	如獸王哮吼聲。或如好鳥鳴囀聲。及餘無量。
269c24	種種音聲。既震雷已。復起涼風。令諸眾生。心
269c25	生悅樂。然後乃降種種諸雨。利益安樂無量
269c26	眾生。從他化天。[6]至於地上。於一切處。所雨
269c27	不同。所謂於大海中。雨清冷水。名無斷絕。於
269c28	他化自在天。雨簫笛等種種樂音。名為美妙。
269c29	於化樂天。雨大摩尼寶。名放大光明。於兜率
270a01	天。雨大莊嚴具。名為垂髻。於夜摩天。雨大妙
270a02	華。名種種莊嚴具。於三十三天。雨眾妙香。名
270a03	為悅意。於四天王天。雨天寶衣。名為覆蓋。於
270a04	龍王宮。雨赤真珠。名涌出光明。於阿脩羅宮。
270a05	雨諸兵仗。名降伏怨敵。於此欝單越。雨種種
270a06	華。名曰開敷。餘三天下。悉亦如是。然各隨
270a07	其處。所雨不同。雖彼龍王。其心平等。無有
270a08	彼此。但以眾生善根異故。雨有差別。佛子如
270a09	來應正等覺

简体字

或如乾闼婆女歌咏音，或如紧那罗女歌咏音，或如大地震动声，或如海水波潮声，或如兽王哮吼声，或如好鸟鸣啭声，及余无量种种音声。既震雷已，复起凉风，令诸众生心生悦乐，然后乃降种种诸雨，利益安乐无量众生。从他化天至于地上，于一切处所雨不同，所谓：于大海中雨清冷水，名无断绝；于他化自在天雨箫笛等种种乐音，名为美妙；于化乐天雨大摩尼宝，名放大光明；于兜率天雨大庄严具，名为垂髻；于夜摩天雨大妙华，名种种庄严具；于三十三天雨众妙香，名为悦意；于四天王天雨天宝衣，名为覆盖；于龙王宫雨赤真珠，名涌出光明；于阿修罗宫雨诸兵仗，名降伏怨敌；于北郁单越雨种种华，名曰开敷；余三天下悉亦如是，然各随其处，所雨不同。虽彼龙王其心平等无有彼此，但以众生善根异故，雨有差别。佛子，如来、应、正等觉

Some sound like the singing of *gandharva* maidens;
Some sound like the singing of *kiṃnara* maidens;
Some sound like the great earth's quaking;
Some sound like the ocean waves' breaking surf;
Some sound like the king of beasts' roaring; and
Some sound like the pleasant singing of birds or like many other kinds of different sounds.

Following upon these manifestations of quaking thunder, there also arise cool breezes that cause beings' minds to be pleased, after which all different kinds of rain fall which bring benefit and happiness to countless beings from the Paranirmita-vaśavartin Heaven on down to the surface of the earth. In all these places, the rain that falls is different. For instance:

Out on the great ocean, there falls a rain of clear and cold waters known as "incessant."

In the Paranirmita-vaśavartin Heaven, there falls a rain sounding like the music of pipes and flutes known as "beautifully sublime."

In the Nirmāṇarati Heaven, there falls a rain of great *maṇi* jewels known as "great radiance emanation."

In the Tuṣita Heaven, there falls a rain of great adornments known as "hanging tresses."

In the Yama Heaven, there falls a rain of immense and marvelous flowers known as "all kinds of adornments."

In the Trāyastriṃśa Heaven, there falls a rain of many marvelous fragrances known as "pleasing the mind."

In the Heaven of the Four Heavenly Kings, there falls a rain of bejeweled celestial robes known as "covering."

In the palaces of the dragon kings, there falls a rain of red pearls known as "upwelling radiance."

In the palaces of the *asuras*, there falls a rain of weapons known as "conquering the enemy."

On this continent of Uttarakuru, there falls a rain of all kinds of different flowers known as "blooming" while, on the other three continents, all that transpires is also like this.

Thus, in accordance with each location, what falls as rain is different. Although the mind of that dragon king is impartial and free of any discriminations with regard to this one or that one, solely due to differences in beings' roots of goodness, the rain which falls has differences.

Sons of the Buddha, so too it is with the Tathāgata, the Arhat, the One of Right and Universal Enlightenment, the unsurpassed king

正體字

無上法王。亦復如是。欲以正法
教化眾生。先布身雲。彌覆法界。隨其樂欲。為
現不同。所謂或為眾生。現生身雲。或為眾生。
現化身雲。或為眾生。現力持身雲。或為眾生。
現色身雲。或為眾生。現相好身雲。或為眾生。
現福德身雲。或為眾生。現智慧身雲。或為眾
生。現諸力不可壞身雲。或為眾生。現無畏身
雲。或為眾生。現法界身雲。佛子如來。以如是
等。無量身雲。普覆十方一切世界。隨諸眾生
所樂各別。示現種種光明電光。所謂或為眾
生。現光明電光。名無所不至。或為眾生。現光
明電光。名無邊光明。或為眾生。現光明電光。
名入佛祕密法。或為眾生。現光明電光。名影
現光明。或為眾生。現光明電光。名光明照
[1]耀。或為眾生。現光明電光。名入無盡陀羅
尼門。或為眾生。現光明電光。名正念不亂。或
為眾生。現光明電光。名究竟不壞。或為眾生
現光明電光。名順入諸趣。或為眾生。現光明
電光。名滿一切願皆令歡喜。

简体字

无上法王亦复如是，欲以正法教化众生，先布身云弥覆法界，随其乐欲为现不同，所谓：或为众生现生身云，或为众生现化身云，或为众生现力持身云，或为众生现色身云，或为众生现相好身云，或为众生现福德身云，或为众生现智慧身云，或为众生现诸力不可坏身云，或为众生现无畏身云，或为众生现法界身云。佛子，如来以如是等无量身云，普覆十方一切世界，随诸众生所乐，各别示现种种光明电光，所谓：或为众生现光明电光，名无所不至；或为众生现光明电光，名无边光明；或为众生现光明电光，名入佛秘密法；或为众生现光明电光，名影现光明；或为众生现光明电光，名光明照曜；或为众生现光明电光，名入无尽陀罗尼门；或为众生现光明电光，名正念不乱；或为众生现光明电光，名究竟不坏；或为众生现光明电光，名顺入诸趣；或为众生现光明电光，名满一切愿皆令欢喜。

Chapter 37 — The Manifestation of the Tathāgata

of Dharma. When he is about to use right Dharma to teach beings, he first spreads forth clouds of bodies which cover the Dharma realm and appear for beings in different ways in accordance with their preferences. For instance:

> For some beings, he manifests clouds of mortal bodies;
> For some beings, he manifests clouds of emanation bodies;
> For some beings, he manifests clouds of bodies sustained by his powers;
> For some beings, he manifests clouds of form bodies;
> For some beings, he manifests clouds of bodies with the major marks and subsidiary signs;
> For some beings, he manifests clouds of merit bodies;
> For some beings, he manifests clouds of wisdom bodies;
> For some beings, he manifests clouds of bodies with indestructible powers;
> For some beings, he manifests clouds of fearless bodies; and
> For some beings, he manifests clouds of Dharma realm bodies.

Sons of the Buddha, the Tathāgata uses countless clouds of bodies such as these which spread everywhere across all worlds of the ten directions and adapt to the difference in beings' preferences by manifesting many different kinds of brilliant lightning. For instance:

> He may manifest brilliant lightning known as "reaching everywhere";
> He may manifest brilliant lightning known as "boundless radiance";
> He may manifest brilliant lightning known as "penetrating buddhas' secret dharmas";
> He may manifest brilliant lightning known as "reflected light";
> He may manifest brilliant lightning known as "dazzling illumination";
> He may manifest brilliant lightning known as "penetrating endless *dhāraṇī* gateways";
> He may manifest brilliant lightning known as "undisturbed right mindfulness";
> He may manifest brilliant lightning known as "ultimate indestructibility";
> He may manifest brilliant lightning known as "adaptive entry into all rebirth destinies"; or
> He may manifest brilliant lightning known as "causing joyous delight through fulfilling all wishes."

正體字

佛子。如來應正
270a28 等覺。現如是等無量光明電光已。復隨眾生
270a29 心之所樂。出生無量三昧雷聲。所謂善覺智
270b01 三昧雷聲。[2]明盛離垢海三昧雷聲。一切法自
270b02 在三昧雷聲。金剛輪三昧雷聲。須彌山幢三
270b03 昧雷聲。海印三昧雷聲。日燈三昧雷聲。無盡
270b04 藏三昧雷聲。不壞解脫力三昧雷聲。佛子。如
270b05 來身雲中。出如是等無量差別三昧雷聲已。
270b06 將降法雨。先現瑞相。開悟眾生。所謂從無障
270b07 礙。大慈悲心。現於如來大智風輪。名能令一
270b08 切眾生。生不思議。歡喜適悅。此相現已。一切
270b09 菩薩。及諸眾生。身之與心。皆得清涼。然後從
270b10 如來大法身雲。大慈悲雲。大不思議雲。雨不
270b11 思議廣大法雨。令一切眾生。身心清淨。所謂
270b12 為坐菩提場菩薩。雨大法雨。名法界無差別
270b13 為最後身菩薩。雨大法雨。名菩薩遊戲如來
270b14 祕密教。為一生所繫菩薩。雨大法雨。名清淨
270b15 普光明。為灌頂菩薩。雨大法雨。名如來莊嚴
270b16 具所莊嚴。為得忍菩薩。雨大法雨。

简体字

佛子,如来、应、正等觉现如是等无量光明电光已,复随众生心之所乐,出生无量三昧雷声,所谓:善觉智三昧雷声、炽然离垢海三昧雷声、一切法自在三昧雷声、金刚轮三昧雷声、须弥山幢三昧雷声、海印三昧雷声、日灯三昧雷声、无尽藏三昧雷声、不坏解脱力三昧雷声。佛子,如来身云中出如是等无量差别三昧雷声已,将降法雨,先现瑞相开悟众生,所谓:从无障碍大慈悲心,现于如来大智风轮,名能令一切众生生不思议欢喜适悦。此相现已,一切菩萨及诸众生,身之与心皆得清凉。然后从如来大法身云、大慈悲云、大不思议云,雨不思议广大法雨,令一切众生身心清净,所谓:为坐菩提场菩萨雨大法雨,名法界无差别;为最后身菩萨雨大法雨,名菩萨游戏如来秘密教;为一生所系菩萨雨大法雨,名清净普光明;为灌顶菩萨雨大法雨,名如来庄严具所庄严;为得忍菩萨雨大法雨,

Chapter 37 — The Manifestation of the Tathāgata

Sons of the Buddha, having displayed countless brilliant lightning flashes such as these, the Tathāgata, the Arhat, the One of Right and Universal Enlightenment then also adapts to what pleases beings' minds by manifesting countless kinds of samādhi-related thunder. For instance:

> The thunder of the "thoroughly awakened wisdom" samādhi.
> The thunder of the "brilliant immaculate ocean" samādhi.
> The thunder of the "sovereign mastery of all dharmas" samādhi.
> The thunder of the "vajra wheel" samādhi.
> The thunder of the "Mount Sumeru banner" samādhi.
> The thunder of the "oceanic imprint" samādhi.
> The thunder of the "solar lamp" samādhi.
> The thunder of the "endless treasury" samādhi.
> And the thunder of the "indestructible power of liberation" samādhi.

Sons of the Buddha, having emanated countless different kinds of samādhi-related thunder such as these from within the clouds of *tathāgata* bodies, in preparation for letting fall the Dharma rain, the Buddha first manifests an auspicious sign to awaken beings, for instance: From his unimpeded mind of great kindness and compassion, he manifests the Tathāgata's great wisdom wind sphere known as "able to cause all beings to experience inconceivable delight and enjoyment." Having manifested this sign, the bodies and minds of all bodhisattvas and other beings become clear and cool.

After this, from the Tathāgata's great Dharma body clouds, great kindness and compassion clouds, and great inconceivability clouds, there comes forth the raining down of inconceivably vast rains of Dharma that cause the bodies and minds of all beings to become purified. For instance:

> For bodhisattvas seated at the site enlightenment, he rains a great Dharma rain known as "the undifferentiated Dharma realm";
> For bodhisattvas in their very last body, he rains a great Dharma rain known as "the bodhisattva's easeful mastery of the Tathāgata's secret teachings";
> For bodhisattvas with but one more incarnation, he rains a great Dharma rain known as "pure universal light";
> For bodhisattvas at the stage of the crown-anointing consecration, he rains a great Dharma rain known as "adornment with the Tathāgata's adornments";
> For bodhisattvas who have achieved realization of the patience,[59] he rains a great Dharma rain known as "the bodhisattva's

名功德寶

270b17 　智慧華開敷不斷菩薩大悲行。為住向行菩
270b18 　薩。雨大法雨。名入現前變化甚深門而行菩
270b19 　薩行無休息無疲厭。為初發心菩薩。雨大法
270b20 　雨。名出生如來大慈悲行救護眾生。為求獨
270b21 　覺乘眾生。雨大法雨。名深知緣起法遠離二
270b22 　邊得不壞解脫果。為求聲聞乘眾生。雨大法
270b23 　雨。名以大智慧劍斷一切煩惱[3]怨。為積集善
270b24 　根決定不決定眾生。雨大法雨。名能令成就
270b25 　種種法門生大歡喜。佛子。諸佛如來。隨眾生
270b26 　心。雨如是等廣大法雨。充滿一切無邊世界。
270b27 　佛子。如來應正等覺。其心平等。於法無吝。但
270b28 　以眾生根欲不同。所雨法雨。示有差別。是為
270b29 　如來音聲第十相。諸菩薩摩訶薩。應如是知。
270c01 　復次佛子。應知如來音聲。有十種無量。何等
270c02 　為十。所謂如虛空界無量。至一切處故。如法
270c03 　界無量。無所不遍故。如眾生界無量。令一切
270c04 　心喜故。

正體字

名功德宝智慧华开敷不断菩萨大悲行；为住向行菩萨雨大法雨，名入现前变化甚深门而行菩萨行无休息无疲厌；为初发心菩萨雨大法雨，名出生如来大慈悲行救护众生；为求独觉乘众生雨大法雨，名深知缘起法远离二边得不坏解脱果；为求声闻乘众生雨大法雨，名以大智慧剑断一切烦恼冤；为积集善根决定、不决定众生雨大法雨，名能令成就种种法门生大欢喜。佛子，诸佛如来随众生心，雨如是等广大法雨，充满一切无边世界。佛子，如来、应、正等觉其心平等，于法无吝，但以众生根欲不同，所雨法雨示有差别。是为如来音声第十相，诸菩萨摩诃萨应如是知。

"复次，佛子，应知如来音声有十种无量。何等为十？所谓：如虚空界无量，至一切处故；如法界无量，无所不遍故；如众生界无量，令一切心喜故；

简体字

Chapter 37 — *The Manifestation of the Tathāgata*

unceasing practice of the great compassion arising from the jewels of meritorious qualities and the blooming of the flowers of wisdom";

For bodhisattvas at the stages of the dwellings, the dedications, or the practices,[60] he rains a great Dharma rain known as "entry into the extremely profound gateway of directly manifested transformations while incessantly and tirelessly practicing the bodhisattva practices";

For bodhisattvas who have made the initial resolve, he rains a great Dharma rain known as "rescuing and protecting beings through producing the Tathāgata's great kindness and compassion";

For beings seeking to cultivate the *pratyekabuddha* vehicle, he rains a great Dharma rain known as "deep realization of the dharma of conditioned arising, abandoning the two extremes, and acquiring the fruit of indestructible liberation";

For beings seeking to cultivate the *śrāvaka*-disciple vehicle, he rains a great Dharma rain known as "using great wisdom's sword to cut off all the affliction adversaries"; and

For beings who have accumulated either definite or indefinite roots of goodness, he rains a great Dharma rain known as "able to perfect many different Dharma gateways and produce immense joyous delight."

Sons of the Buddha, adapting to beings' minds, all buddhas, the *tathāgatas*, rain vast Dharma rains such as these which fill all the boundlessly many worlds. Sons of the Buddha, the mind of the Tathāgata, the Arhat, the One of Right and Universal Enlightenment, is impartial and free of any miserliness with respect to the Dharma. It is solely due to differences in beings' faculties and predilections that the Dharma rain they rain down manifests as having differences.

This is the tenth of the marks of the Tathāgata's voice. All bodhisattva-mahāsattvas should perceive it in this way.

Furthermore, Sons of the Buddha, one should realize that the Tathāgata's voice has ten kinds of measurelessness. What are those ten? They are as follows:

Because it reaches all places, it is as measureless as the realm of empty space;

Because it has no place it does not pervade, it is as measureless as Dharma realm;

Because it delights everyone's mind, it is as measureless as the realm of beings;

正體字

如諸業無量。說其果報故。如煩惱無
量。悉令除滅故。如眾生言音無量。隨解令聞
故。如眾生欲解無量。普觀救度故。如三世無
量。無有邊際故。如智慧無量。分別一切故。如
佛境界無量。入佛法界故。佛子。如來應正等
覺音聲。成就如是等阿僧祇無量。諸菩薩摩
訶薩。應如是知。爾時普賢菩薩摩訶薩。欲重
明此義。而說頌言

　　三千世界將壞時　　眾生福力聲告言
　　四禪寂靜無諸苦　　令其聞已悉離欲
　　十力世尊亦如是　　出妙音聲遍法界
　　為說諸行苦無常　　令其永度生死海
　　譬如深山大谷中　　隨有音聲皆響應
　　雖能隨逐他言語　　而響畢竟無分別
　　十力言音亦復然　　隨其根熟為示現
　　令其調伏生歡喜　　不念我今能演說
　　如天有鼓名能覺　　常於空中震法音
　　誡彼放逸諸天子　　令其聞已得離著

简体字

如诸业无量，说其果报故；如烦恼无量，悉令除灭故；如众生言音无量，随解令闻故；如众生欲解无量，普观救度故；如三世无量，无有边际故；如智慧无量，分别一切故；如佛境界无量，入佛法界故。佛子，如来、应、正等觉音声成就如是等阿僧祇无量，诸菩萨摩诃萨应如是知。"

尔时，普贤菩萨摩诃萨欲重明此义而说颂言：

"三千世界将坏时，众生福力声告言，
　四禅寂静无诸苦，令其闻已悉离欲。
　十力世尊亦如是，出妙音声遍法界，
　为说诸行苦无常，令其永度生死海。
　譬如深山大谷中，随有音声皆响应，
　虽能随逐他言语，而响毕竟无分别。
　十力言音亦复然，随其根熟为示现，
　令其调伏生欢喜，不念我今能演说。
　如天有鼓名能觉，常于空中震法音，
　诫彼放逸诸天子，令其闻已得离著。

Because it explains their resultant retributions, it is as measureless as all karmic actions;

Because it causes the complete extinguishing of all afflictions, it is as measureless as all afflictions;

Because it causes beings to hear in a manner adapted to their capacity to understand, it is as measureless as beings' speech;

Because it contemplates all beings and strives to rescue and liberate them, it is as measureless as all beings' individual aspirations and understandings;

Because it is boundless, it is as measureless as the three periods of time;

Because it distinguishes everything, it is as measureless as wisdom; and

Because it penetrates the realm of the Buddha's Dharma, it is as measureless as the Buddha's sphere of action.

Sons of the Buddha, the voice of the Tathāgata, the Arhat, the One of Right and Universal Enlightenment, has achieved *asaṃkhyeyas* of types of measurelessness such as these. All bodhisattva-mahāsattvas should know them in these ways.

At that time, wishing to once again clarify the meaning of this, Samantabhadra Bodhisattva-mahāsattva then spoke these verses:

When the trichiliocosm is about to be destroyed,
due to the power of beings' merit, a voice tells them:
"The quiescence of the four *dhyānas* is free of all forms of suffering,"
thus allowing all of them, having heard this, to abandon their desires.

So too it is with the Bhagavat possessed of the ten powers
who emanates a wondrous voice that pervades the Dharma realm and,
for beings' sakes, says, "All formations[61] are suffering and transient,"
thus allowing them to be forever liberated from the ocean of *saṃsāra*.

Just as when, in a great valley in the deep mountains,
whenever a voice calls out, there are always echoes which respond,
and, although they are able to follow upon the speech of others,
those echoes are still ultimately free of any discriminations—

so too it is in the case of the speech of the Ten-Powered One
which manifests for others in accordance with their faculties' ripeness,
thus enabling them to receive the training and feel joyous delight,
even as it never thinks, "I am now able to expound."

Just as, in the heavens, there is a drum called "able to awaken" that,
from the midst of space, always resounds with the sound of Dharma
and admonishes those sons of the devas who have become negligent,
thus enabling them, having heard this, to then abandon attachments—

正體字

270c22	十力法鼓亦如是	出於種種妙音聲
270c23	覺悟一切諸群生	令其悉證菩提果
270c24	自在天王有寶女	口中善奏諸音樂
270c25	一聲能出百千音	一一音中復百千
270c26	善逝音聲亦如是	一聲而出一切音
270c27	隨其性欲有差別	各令聞已斷煩惱
270c28	譬如梵王吐一音	能令梵眾皆歡喜
270c29	音唯及梵不出外	一一皆言己獨聞
271a01	十力梵王亦復然	演一言音充法界
271a02	唯霑眾會不遠出	以無信故未能受
271a03	譬如眾水同一性	八功德味無差別
271a04	因地在器各不同	是故令其種種異
271a05	一切智音亦如是	法性一味無分別
271a06	隨諸眾生行不同	故使聽聞種種異
271a07	譬如無熱大龍王	降雨普洽閻浮地
271a08	能令草樹皆生長	而不從身及心出
271a09	諸佛妙音亦如是	普雨法界悉充洽
271a10	能令生善滅諸惡	不從內外而得有
271a11	譬如摩那斯龍王	興雲七日未先雨
271a12	待諸眾生作務竟	然後始降成利益

简体字

十力法鼓亦如是，出于种种妙音声，
觉悟一切诸群生，令其悉证菩提果。
自在天王有宝女，口中善奏诸音乐，
一声能出百千音，一一音中复百千。
善逝音声亦如是，一声而出一切音，
随其性欲有差别，各令闻已断烦恼。
譬如梵王吐一音，能令梵众皆欢喜，
音唯及梵不出外，一一皆言己独闻。
十力梵王亦复然，演一言音充法界，
唯沾众会不远出，以无信故未能受。
譬如众水同一性，八功德味无差别，
因地在器各不同，是故令其种种异。
一切智音亦如是，法性一味无分别，
随诸众生行不同，故使听闻种种异。
譬如无热大龙王，降雨普洽阎浮地，
能令草树皆生长，而不从身及心出。
诸佛妙音亦如是，普雨法界悉充洽，
能令生善灭诸恶，不从内外而得有。
譬如摩那斯龙王，兴云七日未先雨，
待诸众生作务竟，然后始降成利益。

Chapter 37 — The Manifestation of the Tathāgata

so too it is with the Ten-Powered One's Dharma drum
that sends forth many different kinds of sublime voices
which awaken all the many kinds of beings,
thus enabling them all to attain the fruit of bodhi.

The king of the Paranirmita-vaśavartin Heaven has a precious maiden
from whose mouth comes the skillful singing of all kinds of music,
each sound of which is able to emanate a hundred thousand sounds,
every sound of which in turn makes a hundred thousand more.

So too it is with the voice of the Well Gone One
that, from a single sound, emanates all sounds
which adapt to the differences in others' natures and predilections,
thus allowing each being, having heard this, to cut off their afflictions.

Just as when the Brahma Heaven King utters but a single sound
able to cause delight in all his Brahma Heaven followers,
the sound reaches only Brahma devas and does not go beyond them
and every one of them claims he was the only one to hear it,

so too it is with the Brahma King of the Ten Powers,
who may utter a single sound that fills the Dharma realm
which only benefits those in the assembly and does not go farther, for,
because others have no faith, they would not yet be able to accept it.

Just as the many bodies of water have a single identical nature
in which the flavor of their eight qualities does not differ,
but, due to differences in lands of origin and vessels retaining them,
they are therefore caused to have many different kinds of distinctions,

so too it is with the voice of the Omniscient One—
The Dharma's nature is of a single flavor free of any discriminations,
but, because it adapts to the differences in beings' actions,
it is caused to acquire a variety of differences in what they hear.

Just as the dragon king Anavatapta
sends down rains everywhere moistening the lands of Jambudvīpa
which are able to cause all the grasses and trees to grow
even as those rains do not come forth from either his body or mind,

so too it is with the marvelous voices of all buddhas which let fall
rains throughout the Dharma realm, completely soaking everything.
They are able to cause growth of goodness and the cessation of evils
even as they do not come into existence either from within or without.

Just as the dragon king known as Manasvin
spreads forth rain clouds which stay for seven days before first raining
as he awaits beings' completion of their work
and only after that begins to let them fall and achieve their benefits,

正體字

```
271a13 |   十力演義亦如是    先化眾生使成熟
271a14 |   然後為說甚深法    令其聞者不驚怖
271a15 |   大莊嚴龍於海中    霔於十種莊嚴雨
271a16 |   或百或千百千種    水雖一味莊嚴別
271a17 |   究竟辯才亦如是    說十二十諸法門
271a18 |   或百或千至無量    不生心念有殊別
271a19 |   最勝龍王娑竭羅    興雲普覆四天下
271a20 |   於一切處雨各別    而彼龍心無二念
271a21 |   諸佛法王亦如是    大悲身雲遍十方
271a22 |   為諸修行雨各異    而於一切無分別
271a23 |   佛子。諸菩薩摩訶薩。應云何知如來應正等
271a24 |   覺心。佛子。如來心意識。俱不可得。但應以智
271a25 |   無量故。知如來心。譬如虛空為一切物所依。
271a26 |   而虛空無所依。如來智慧。亦復如是。為一切
271a27 |   世間出世間智所依。而如來智無所依。佛子。
271a28 |   是為如來心第一相。諸菩薩摩訶薩。應如是
271a29 |   知。復次佛子。譬如法界常出一切聲聞獨覺
271b01 |   菩薩解脫。而法界無增減。如來智慧。亦復如
271b02 |   是。恒出一切世間出世間。種種智慧。而如來
271b03 |   智無增減。佛子。是為如來心第二相。諸菩薩
271b04 |   摩訶薩。應如是知。
```

简体字

十力演义亦如是，先化众生使成熟，
然后为说甚深法，令其闻者不惊怖。
大庄严龙于海中，霔于十种庄严雨，
或百或千百千种，水虽一味庄严别。
究竟辩才亦如是，说十二十诸法门，
或百或千至无量，不生心念有殊别。
最胜龙王娑竭罗，兴云普覆四天下，
于一切处雨各别，而彼龙心无二念。
诸佛法王亦如是，大悲身云遍十方，
为诸修行雨各异，而于一切无分别。

"佛子，诸菩萨摩诃萨应云何知如来、应、正等觉心？佛子，如来心、意、识俱不可得，但应以智无量故，知如来心。

"譬如虚空为一切物所依，而虚空无所依；如来智慧亦复如是，为一切世间、出世间智所依，而如来智无所依。佛子，是为如来心第一相，诸菩萨摩诃萨应如是知。

"复次，佛子，譬如法界常出一切声闻、独觉、菩萨解脱，而法界无增减。如来智慧亦复如是，恒出一切世间、出世间种种智慧，而如来智无增减。佛子，是为如来心第二相，诸菩萨摩诃萨应如是知。

so too it is with the Ten-Powered One's expounding of meanings
in which he first teaches beings, thus causing their ripening,
and only later expounds the extremely deep Dharma for them,
thereby preventing those listening to him from being frightened.

Just as, out on the seas, the dragon known as Vāsuki
pours down ten kinds of adornment-filled rains,
perhaps of a hundred, or a thousand, or a hundred thousand types,
in which, though the water is of but one taste, the adornments differ,

so too it is with he who possesses the most ultimate eloquence
as he expounds on ten or twenty Dharma gateways,
or a hundred, or a thousand, on up to incalculably many,
yet still does not produce thoughts possessed of discriminations.

Just as Sāgara, the supreme king of the dragons,
spreads forth clouds which everywhere cover over the four continents
and sends down rains everywhere which differ in each place
and yet that dragon's mind remains free of twofold considerations,

so too it is with all the buddhas, the Dharma kings, whose clouds
of bodies motivated by the great compassion fill all ten directions
and send down rains for all who cultivate, each of whom are different,
and yet they stay free of any discriminations regarding any of them.

Sons of the Buddha, how should the bodhisattva-mahāsattva know the mind of the Tathāgata, the Arhat, the One of Right and Universal Enlightenment? Sons of the Buddha, the Tathāgata's mind, intellect, and consciousness are all inapprehensible. It is only by the measurelessness of his wisdom that one should know the mind of the Tathāgata. Just as empty space is relied upon by all things but has nothing on which it relies, so too it is with the wisdom of the Tathāgata, for it is relied upon by all worldly and world-transcending wisdom and yet the Tathāgata's wisdom has nothing on which it relies.

Sons of the Buddha, this is the first of the marks of the Tathāgata's mind. All bodhisattva-mahāsattvas should know it in this way.

Furthermore, Sons of the Buddha, just as the Dharma realm always produces the liberations of all *śrāvaka* disciples, *pratyekabuddhas*, and bodhisattvas and yet the Dharma realm itself is neither increased nor decreased, so to it is with the Tathāgata's wisdom which constantly produces all the different kinds of worldly and world-transcending wisdom and yet the Tathāgata's wisdom is neither increased nor decreased.

Sons of the Buddha, this is the second of the marks of the Tathāgata's mind. All bodhisattva-mahāsattvas should know it in this way.

正體字

復次佛子。譬如大海其水
潛流四天下地。及八十億。諸小洲中。有穿鑿
者。無不得水。而彼大海。不作分別。我出於
水。佛智海水。亦復如是。流入一切眾生心中。
若諸眾生。觀察境界。修習法門。則得智慧清
淨明了。而如來智。平等無二。無有分別。但隨
眾生心行異故。所得智慧。各各不同。佛子。是
為如來心第三相。諸菩薩摩訶薩。應如是知。
復次佛子。譬如大海有四寶珠。具無量德。能
生海內一切珍寶。若大海中。無此寶珠。乃至
一寶。亦不可得。何等為四。一名積集寶。二名
無盡藏。三名遠離熾然。四名具足莊嚴。佛子。
此四寶珠。一切凡夫。諸龍神等。悉不得見。何
以故。娑竭龍王。以此寶珠。端嚴方正。置於宮
中深密處故。佛子。如來應正等覺。大智慧海。
亦復如是。於中有四大智寶珠。具足無量福
智功德。由此能生一切眾生。聲聞獨覺。學無
學位。及諸菩薩智慧之寶。何等為四。所謂無
染著巧方便大智慧寶。善分別有為無為法
大智慧寶。分別說無量法而不壞法性大智
慧寶。

简体字

"复次，佛子，譬如大海，其水潜流四天下地及八十亿诸小洲中，有穿凿者无不得水，而彼大海不作分别：'我出于水。'佛智海水亦复如是，流入一切众生心中，若诸众生观察境界、修习法门，则得智慧清净明了，而如来智平等无二、无有分别，但随众生心行异故，所得智慧各各不同。佛子，是为如来心第三相，诸菩萨摩诃萨应如是知。

"复次，佛子，譬如大海有四宝珠，具无量德，能生海内一切珍宝；若大海中无此宝珠，乃至一宝亦不可得。何等为四？一名积集宝，二名无尽藏，三名远离炽然，四名具足庄严。佛子，此四宝珠，一切凡夫诸龙神等悉不得见。何以故？娑竭龙王以此宝珠端严方正置于宫中深密处故。佛子，如来、应、正等觉大智慧海亦复如是，于中有四大智宝珠，具足无量福智功德，由此能生一切众生声闻、独觉、学、无学位，及诸菩萨智慧之宝。何等为四？所谓：无染著巧方便大智慧宝、善分别有为无为法大智慧宝、分别说无量法而不坏法性大智慧宝、

Furthermore, Sons of the Buddha, just as the waters of the great ocean flow beneath the earth of the four continents as well as the eighty *koṭīs* of small islands so that, whenever someone drills down into them, no one fails to find water, and yet that great ocean does not make discriminations such as, "I shall send forth water," so too it is with the waters of the Buddha's wisdom ocean which flow into the minds of all beings. If any being contemplates the objective realms and cultivates the Dharma gateways, then he will acquire wisdom that is pure and utterly clear, and yet the Tathāgata's wisdom is impartial, non-dual, and free of discrimination, for it is solely in accordance with the differences in beings' mental actions that the wisdom they acquire differs for each of them.

Sons of the Buddha, this is the third of the marks of the Tathāgata's mind. All bodhisattva-mahāsattvas should know it in this way.

Furthermore, Sons of the Buddha, by way of analogy, consider the following: The great ocean contains four precious pearls possessed of countless qualities that can produce all the precious jewels in the ocean. If the great ocean did not contain these precious pearls, one would never be able to find even a single jewel. What are these four? The first is known as "accumulator of jewels," the second is known as "endless treasury," the third is known as "far from flaming fire," and the fourth is known as "replete with adornments."

Sons of the Buddha, these four precious pearls cannot be seen by any common person, dragon, spirit, or other such being. And why is this so? Because these precious pearls are so magnificent and perfectly formed that the dragon king, Sāgara, keeps them in a very secret place in his palace.

Sons of the Buddha, so too it is with the great ocean of wisdom of the Tathāgata, the Arhat, the One of Right and Universal Enlightenment. Within it, there are four precious pearls of great wisdom that are possessed of the qualities of measureless merit and wisdom. It is from these that there can be produced the jewels of wisdom possessed by all beings, by *śrāvaka* disciples, by *pratyekabuddhas*, by those at the stages of learning and beyond learning, and by all bodhisattvas. What are these four? They are:

> The great wisdom jewel of skillful means free of defiling attachments;
> The great wisdom jewel of skillful discernment of conditioned and unconditioned dharmas;
> The great wisdom jewel of differentiating discussion of countless dharmas without contradicting the nature of dharmas; and

正體字

知時非時未曾誤失大智慧寶。若諸如來。大智海中。無此四寶。有一眾生。得入大乘。終無是處。此四智寶。薄福眾生。所不能見。何以故。置於如來深密藏故。此四智寶。平均正直。端潔妙好。普能利益諸菩薩眾。令其悉得智慧光明。佛子。是為如來心第四相。諸菩薩摩訶薩。應如是知。復次佛子。譬如大海。有四熾然光明大寶。布在其底。性極猛熱。常能飲縮百川所注無量大水。是故大海。無有增減。何等為四。一名日藏。二名離潤。三名火焰光。四名盡無餘佛子。若大海中。無此四寶。從四天下乃至有頂。其中所有。悉被漂沒。佛子。此日藏大寶光明。照觸海水。悉變為乳。離潤大寶光明。照觸其乳。悉變為酪。火焰光大寶光明。照觸其酪。悉變為酥。盡無餘大寶光明。照觸其酥。變成醍醐。如火熾然。悉盡無餘。佛子。如來應正等覺。大智慧海。亦復如是。有四種大智慧寶。具足無量威德光明。

简体字

知时非时未曾误失大智慧宝。若诸如来大智海中无此四宝,有一众生得入大乘,终无是处。此四智宝,薄福众生所不能见。何以故？置于如来深密藏故。此四智宝,平均正直,端洁妙好,普能利益诸菩萨众,令其悉得智慧光明。佛子,是为如来心第四相,诸菩萨摩诃萨应如是知。

"复次,佛子,譬如大海,有四炽然光明大宝布在其底,性极猛热,常能饮缩百川所注无量大水,是故大海无有增减。何等为四？一名日藏,二名离润,三名火焰光,四名尽无余。佛子,若大海中无此四宝,从四天下乃至有顶,其中所有悉被漂没。佛子,此日藏大宝光明照触,海水悉变为乳；离润大宝光明照触,其乳悉变为酪；火焰光大宝光明照触,其酪悉变为酥；尽无余大宝光明照触,其酥变成醍醐；如火炽然,悉尽无余。佛子,如来、应、正等觉大智慧海亦复如是,有四种大智慧宝,具足无量威德光明；

Chapter 37 — *The Manifestation of the Tathāgata*

The great wisdom jewel of never erring in knowing what is and is not the right time.

If the *tathāgatas*' ocean of great wisdom did not contain these four jewels, it would be forever impossible for even a single being to enter the Great Vehicle. These four wisdom jewels cannot be seen by beings possessed of only meager merit. And why is this so? This is because they have been placed within the Tathāgata's extremely secret treasury.

These four wisdom jewels are equally symmetrical, rightly and evenly formed, exquisite, pristine, and marvelously fine. They are everywhere able to benefit the entire congregation of bodhisattvas and enable them to completely acquire the light of wisdom.

Sons of the Buddha, this is the fourth of the marks of the Tathāgata's mind. All bodhisattva-mahāsattvas should know it in this way.

Furthermore, Sons of the Buddha, by way of analogy, consider the following: The great ocean contains four immense jewels which radiate flaming light that are spread out on the ocean floor. By nature, they possess the most ultimately ferocious heat with which they are forever able to drink in and withdraw the measurelessly great volume of water that pours into the ocean from the hundred rivers. As a consequence, the great ocean neither increases nor decreases in volume. What are these four? The first is known as "solar treasury," the second is known as "moisture remover," the third is known as "blazing fire light," and the fourth is known as "complete consumption."

Sons of the Buddha, if the great ocean did not contain these four jewels, then everything from the four continents on up to the summit of existence would become inundated and submerged.

Sons of the Buddha, when the illumination created by the light of this immense "solar treasury" jewel contacts the ocean's waters, it transforms them all into milk. When the illumination created by the light of the immense "moisture remover" jewel contacts that milk, it is all transformed into curds. When the illumination created by the light of the immense "blazing fire light" jewel contacts those curds, they are all transformed into butter. And when the illumination created by the light of the immense "complete consumption" jewel contacts that butter, it is all transformed into ghee which, as if by blazing fire, is then completely consumed.

Sons of the Buddha, so too it is with the great ocean of wisdom of the Tathāgata, the Arhat, the One of Right and Universal Enlightenment. It contains four kinds of great wisdom jewels which are fully possessed of the light of measureless awesome virtue.

正體字

此智寶
光。觸諸菩薩乃至令得如來大智。何等為四。
所謂滅一切散善波浪大智慧寶。除一切法愛
大智慧寶。慧光普照大智慧寶。與如來平等
無邊無功用大智慧寶。佛子。諸菩薩。修[1]習
一切助道法時。起無量散善波浪。一切世間。
天人阿脩羅。所不能壞。如來以滅一切散善
波浪大智慧寶光明。觸彼菩薩。令捨一切散
善波浪。持心一境。住於三昧。又以除一切法
愛大智慧寶光明。觸彼菩薩。令捨離三昧味
著。起廣大神通。又以慧光普照大智慧寶光
明。觸彼菩薩。令捨所起廣大神通。住大明功
用行。又以與如來平等無邊無功用大智慧
寶光明。觸彼菩薩。令捨所起大明功用行。乃
至得如來平等地。息一切功用。令無有餘。佛
子。若無如來此四智寶。大光照觸。乃至有一
菩薩。得如來地。無有是處。佛子是為如來心
第五相。諸菩薩摩訶薩。應如是知。復次佛子。
如從水際。上至非想非非想天。其中所有。大
千國土。

简体字

此智宝光触诸菩萨,乃至令得如来大智。何等为四?所谓:灭一切散善波浪大智慧宝、除一切法爱大智慧宝、慧光普照大智慧宝、与如来平等无边无功用大智慧宝。佛子,诸菩萨修习一切助道法时,起无量散善波浪,一切世间天、人、阿修罗所不能坏;如来以灭一切散善波浪大智慧宝光明触彼菩萨,令舍一切散善波浪,持心一境,住于三昧;又以除一切法爱大智慧宝光明触彼菩萨,令舍离三昧味著,起广大神通;又以慧光普照大智慧宝光明触彼菩萨,令舍所起广大神通,住大明功用行;又以与如来平等无边无功用大智慧宝光明触彼菩萨,令舍所起大明功用行,乃至得如来平等地,息一切功用,令无有余。佛子,若无如来此四智宝大光照触,乃至有一菩萨得如来地,无有是处。佛子,是为如来心第五相,诸菩萨摩诃萨应如是知。

"复次,佛子,如从水际,上至非想非非想天,其中所有大千国土,

Chapter 37 — The Manifestation of the Tathāgata

When the light of these wisdom jewels touches the bodhisattvas, it causes them to ultimately attain the great wisdom of the Tathāgata. What are these four? They are:

The great wisdom jewel that stills all waves of scattered goodness;[62]
The great wisdom jewel that eliminates all affection for dharmas;
The great wisdom jewel that everywhere emanates wisdom light;
The jewel of boundless and effortless great wisdom equal to that of the Tathāgata;

Sons of the Buddha, when bodhisattvas cultivate all the path-assisting dharmas, they produce countless waves of scattered goodness which not even any of the world's devas, humans, or asuras can overcome. The Tathāgata sends forth light from "the great wisdom jewel that stills all waves of scattered goodness." When it touches those bodhisattvas, it causes them to leave behind all waves of scattered goodness, hold their minds on a single object, and dwell in samādhi.

He then also sends forth light from "the great wisdom jewel that eliminates all affection for dharmas." When it touches those bodhisattvas, it causes them to abandon any attachment to the delectable flavor of samādhi and produce vast spiritual superknowledges.

He then also sends forth light from "the great wisdom jewel that everywhere emanates wisdom light." When it touches those bodhisattvas, it causes them to relinquish the vast spiritual superknowledges they produced and abide in the practice of greatly radiant functional effort.

He then also sends forth light from "the jewel of boundless and effortless great wisdom equal to that of the Tathāgata." When it touches those bodhisattvas, it causes them to relinquish the practice of greatly radiant functional effort up until they reach the ground of equality with the Tathāgata where they put to rest all functional effort without exception.

Sons of the Buddha, if they had not been touched by the greatly radiant illumination cast by these four wisdom jewels of the Tathāgata, it would be utterly impossible for there to be even a single bodhisattva who could ever reach the ground of the Tathāgata.

Sons of the Buddha, this is the fifth of the marks of the Tathāgata's mind. All bodhisattva-mahāsattvas should know it in this way.

Furthermore, Sons of the Buddha, by way of analogy, consider the following: From the edge of [the sphere of] water[63] all the way up to the heaven of neither perception nor non-perception, of all the great chiliocosm's lands and of all the stations in which beings of the desire realm, form realm, and formless realms dwell, there are

正體字

欲色無色。眾生之處。莫不皆依虛空而起。虛空而住。何以故。虛空普遍故。雖彼虛空普容三界。而無分別。佛子。如來智慧。亦復如是若聲聞智。若獨覺智。若菩薩智。若有為行智。若無為行智。一切皆依如來智起。如來智住。何以故。如來智慧。遍一切故。雖復普容無量智慧。而無分別。佛子。是為如來心第六相。諸菩薩摩訶薩。應如是知。復次佛子。如雪山頂。有藥王樹。名無盡根。彼藥樹根。從十六萬八千由旬。下盡金剛地水輪際生。彼藥王樹。若生根時。令閻浮提一切樹根生。若生莖時。令閻浮提一切樹莖生。枝葉華果。悉皆如是。此藥王樹根能生莖。莖能生根。根無有盡。名無盡根。佛子。彼藥王樹。於一切處。皆令生長。唯於二處。不能為作生長利益。所謂地獄深坑。及水輪中。然亦於彼。初無厭捨。佛子。如來智慧。大藥王樹。亦復如是。

简体字

欲、色、无色众生之处，莫不皆依虚空而起、虚空而住。何以故？虚空普遍故；虽彼虚空，普容三界而无分别。佛子，如来智慧亦复如是，若声闻智，若独觉智，若菩萨智，若有为行智，若无为行智，一切皆依如来智起、如来智住。何以故？如来智慧遍一切故；虽复普容无量智慧而无分别。佛子，是为如来心第六相，诸菩萨摩诃萨应如是知。

"复次，佛子，如雪山顶有药王树，名无尽根。彼药树根从十六万八千由旬下尽金刚地水轮际生。彼药王树若生根时，令阎浮提一切树根生；若生茎时，令阎浮提一切树茎生；枝、叶、华、果悉皆如是。此药王树，根能生茎，茎能生根，根无有尽，名无尽根。佛子，彼药王树于一切处皆令生长，唯于二处不能为作生长利益，所谓：地狱深坑及水轮中；然亦于彼初无厌舍。佛子，如来智慧大药王树亦复如是，

none that do not entirely rely upon empty space for their origination while also relying upon empty space for their abiding. And why is this? It is because empty space is universally pervasive. Although that empty space completely includes within itself everything within the three realms of existence, it is still entirely free of any discrimination [with respect to any of them].

Sons of the Buddha, so too it is with the wisdom of the Tathāgata, for, whether it be the wisdom of *śrāvaka* disciples, the wisdom of *pratyekabuddhas*, the wisdom of bodhisattvas, the wisdom of conditioned practice, or the wisdom of unconditioned practice, they all rely upon the Tathāgata's wisdom for their origination while also relying upon the Tathāgata's wisdom for their abiding. And why is this? It is because the Tathāgata's wisdom is universally pervasive. Although it also completely includes all the countless other kinds of wisdom, it is still entirely free of any discrimination [with respect to any of them].

Sons of the Buddha, this is the sixth of the marks of the Tathāgata's mind. All bodhisattva-mahāsattvas should know it in this way.

Furthermore, Sons of the Buddha, by way of analogy, consider the following: There is a medicine king tree which grows on the summit of the Himalaya Mountains which is known as "endless roots." The roots of that medicine tree grow forth from one hundred and sixty-eight thousand *yojanas* below at the junction of the vajra ground and the sphere of water. When the roots of that medicine king tree began to grow, it caused the growth of all of Jambudvīpa's tree roots. When its trunk began to grow, it caused the growth of all of Jambudvīpa's tree trunks. So too it was with its branches, leaves, blossoms, and fruit.

It is due to the ability of the roots of this medicine king tree to cause the growth of trunks and due to its trunk's ability to cause the growth of roots that its roots are therefore endless. Hence it is known as "endless roots."

Sons of the Buddha, that medicine king tree is able to bring about growth in all places with the sole exception of two places in which it is unable to produce the benefits of growth. Specifically, those are in the deep abyss of the hell realms and within the wheel of water. Even so, even from the very beginning, it has still never had any sort of aversion for those places.

Sons of the Buddha, so too it is with the great medicine king tree of the Tathāgata's wisdom. It takes as its roots vast and greatly compassionate past vows to perfect all wise and good dharmas, vows which, extending everywhere and extending to all realms

正體字

以過去所發。成就一切智慧善法。普覆一切諸眾生界。除滅一切諸惡道苦。廣大悲願。而為其根。於一切如來真實智慧種性中生。堅固不動。善巧方便。以為其莖。遍法界智。諸波羅蜜。以為其枝。禪定解脫。諸大三昧。以為其葉。總持辯才。菩提分法。以為其華。究竟無變。諸佛解脫。以為其果。佛子。如來智慧。大藥王樹。何故得名為無盡根。以究竟無休息故。不斷菩薩行故。菩薩行即如來性。如來性即菩薩行。是故得名為無盡根。佛子。如來智慧。大藥王樹。其根生時。令一切菩薩。生不捨眾生大慈悲根。其莖生時。令一切菩薩。增長堅固精進深心莖。其枝生時。令一切菩薩。增長一切諸波羅蜜枝。其[1]葉生時。令一切菩薩。生長淨戒頭陀功德少欲知足葉。其華生時。令一切菩薩。具諸善根相好莊嚴華。其果生時。令一切菩薩。得無生忍。乃至一切佛灌頂忍果。佛子。如來智慧。大藥王樹。唯於二處。不能為作生長利益。所謂二乘墮於無為。廣大深阬。

简体字

以过去所发成就一切智慧善法、普覆一切诸众生界、除灭一切诸恶道苦广大悲愿而为其根,于一切如来真实智慧种性中生坚固不动善巧方便以为其茎,遍法界智、诸波罗蜜以为其枝,禅定、解脱、诸大三昧以为其叶,总持、辩才、菩提分法以为其华,究竟无变诸佛解脱以为其果。佛子,如来智慧大药王树,何故得名为无尽根?以究竟无休息故,不断菩萨行故;菩萨行即如来性,如来性即菩萨行,是故得名为无尽根。佛子,如来智慧大药王树,其根生时,令一切菩萨生不舍众生大慈悲根;其茎生时,令一切菩萨增长坚固精进深心茎;其枝生时,令一切菩萨增长一切诸波罗蜜枝;其叶生时,令一切菩萨生长净戒头陀功德少欲知足叶;其华生时,令一切菩萨具诸善根相好庄严华;其果生时,令一切菩萨得无生忍乃至一切佛灌顶忍果。佛子,如来智慧大药王树唯于二处不能为作生长利益,所谓:二乘堕于无为广大深坑

Chapter 37 — The Manifestation of the Tathāgata

of beings, are intent upon extinguishing all sufferings of the three wretched destinies. It grows forth from the lineage of all *tathāgatas'* genuine wisdom, takes solid and unshakable skillful means as its trunk, takes the wisdom which pervades the Dharma realm and the *pāramitās* as its branches, takes the *dhyāna* absorptions, the liberations, and the great samādhis as its leaves, takes the complete-retention *dhāraṇīs*, eloquence, and the dharmas of the factors of enlightenment as its blossoms, and takes all buddhas' ultimate and unchanging liberations as its fruits.

Sons of the Buddha, why is the great medicine king tree of the Tathāgata's wisdom known as "endless roots"? This is because it ultimately never rests and because it never allows the bodhisattva practices to be cut off. The bodhisattva practices are just the very nature of the Tathāgata. The nature of the Tathāgata is just the bodhisattva practices. It is for these reasons that it is known as "endless roots."

Sons of the Buddha, when the roots of the great medicine king tree of the Tathāgata's wisdom grow forth, they cause all bodhisattvas to produce the roots of the great kindness and compassion by which they never abandon beings.

When its trunk grows forth, it causes all bodhisattvas to increase the growth of the trunk of their solid vigor and deep resolve.

When its branches grow forth, they cause all bodhisattvas to increase the growth of the branches of all the *pāramitās*.

When its leaves grow forth, they cause all bodhisattvas to bring forth growth in the leaves of the pure precepts, the *dhūta* austerities, the meritorious qualities, and the ability to be easily satisfied with but few desires.

When its blossoms grow forth, they cause all bodhisattvas to acquire the blossoms consisting of the roots of goodness and the adornments of the major marks and subsidiary signs.

When its fruits grow forth, they cause all bodhisattvas to acquire the fruits of the unproduced-dharmas patience and so forth up to and including the patience associated with all buddhas' bestowal of the crown-anointing consecration.

Sons of the Buddha, the great medicine king tree of the Tathāgata's wisdom has only two places it is unable to provide the benefit of growth, namely the vast and deep abyss of the unconditioned into which the adherents of the two vehicles have fallen and also the immense river of wrong views and desires in which beings are drowning who have destroyed their roots of goodness and are

正體字

```
272b09 ‖  及壞善根。非器眾生。溺大邪見。貪愛之水。然
272b10 ‖  亦於彼。曾無厭捨。佛子。如來智慧。無有增減。
272b11 ‖  以根善安住。生無休息故。佛子。是為如來心
272b12 ‖  第七相。諸菩薩摩訶薩。應如是知。復次佛子。
272b13 ‖  譬如三千大千世界。劫火起時。焚燒一切。草
272b14 ‖  木叢林。乃至鐵圍大鐵圍山。皆悉熾然無有
272b15 ‖  遺餘。佛子。假使有人。手執乾草。投彼火中。
272b16 ‖  於意云何。得不燒不。答言不也。佛子。彼所投
272b17 ‖  草。容可不燒。如來智慧。分別三世一切眾生。
272b18 ‖  一切國土。一切劫數。一切諸法。無不知者。若
272b19 ‖  言不知。無有是處。何以故。智慧平等。悉明達
272b20 ‖  故。佛子。是為如來心第八相。諸菩薩摩訶薩。
272b21 ‖  應如是知。復次佛子。譬如風災。壞世界時。有
272b22 ‖  大風起。名曰散壞。能壞三千大千世界鐵圍
272b23 ‖  山等。皆成碎末。復有大風。名為能障。周匝三
272b24 ‖  千大千世界。障散壞風。不令得至餘方世界。
272b25 ‖  佛子。若令無此能障大風。十方世界。無不壞
272b26 ‖  盡。
```

简体字

及坏善根非器众生溺大邪见贪爱之水；然亦于彼曾无厌舍。佛子，如来智慧无有增减，以根善安住，生无休息故。佛子，是为如来心第七相，诸菩萨摩诃萨应如是知。

"复次，佛子，譬如三千大千世界劫火起时，焚烧一切草木丛林，乃至铁围、大铁围山皆悉炽然无有遗余。

"佛子，假使有人手执干草投彼火中，于意云何？得不烧不？"

答言："不也。"

"佛子，彼所投草容可不烧；如来智慧分别三世一切众生、一切国土、一切劫数、一切诸法，无不知者；若言不知，无有是处。何以故？智慧平等悉明达故。佛子，是为如来心第八相，诸菩萨摩诃萨应如是知。

"复次，佛子，譬如风灾坏世界时，有大风起，名曰散坏，能坏三千大千世界，铁围山等皆成碎末。复有大风，名为能障，周匝三千大千世界障散坏风，不令得至余方世界。佛子，若令无此能障大风，十方世界无不坏尽。

not fit vessels to receive it. Even so, he has never had any aversion for beings in those places.

Sons of the Buddha, the Tathāgata's wisdom neither increases nor decreases for, because its roots are well established, it grows incessantly.

Sons of the Buddha, this is the seventh of the marks of the Tathāgata's mind. All bodhisattva-mahāsattvas should know it in this way.

Furthermore, Sons of the Buddha, by way of analogy, consider the following: In the worlds of the great trichiliocosm, when the fires arise at the end of the kalpa, they incinerate everything from the grasses, trees, and dense forests to the iron ring mountains and the great iron ring mountains, burning them all so completely with their blazing flames that nothing is left.

Sons of the Buddha, if someone clutched up dry grasses in his hands and then threw them into those fires, what do you think? Is it possible that they would not be burned, or not?

They replied: "No, it would not be possible."

Sons of the Buddha, even supposing that somehow the grass they threw into the fires might not be burned, still, the Tathāgata's wisdom distinguishes all beings, all lands, all kalpa enumerations, and all dharmas of the three periods of time, having none among them it does not know. Were one to claim there is something it does not know, that would be an utter impossibility. And why is this so? It is because his wisdom has an equally and completely clear comprehension of everything.

Sons of the Buddha, this is the eighth of the marks of the Tathāgata's mind. All bodhisattva-mahāsattvas should know it in this way.

Furthermore, Sons of the Buddha, by way of analogy, consider the following: When the wind disaster that destroys the world occurs, a great wind arises known as "scattering destruction" that is able to so completely destroy even the great trichiliocosm's iron ring mountains and other features that they are all reduced to dust. Then another great wind known as "able to block" encircles the great trichiliocosm and blocks that "scattering destruction" wind and prevents it from being able to reach the worlds in any other regions.

Sons of the Buddha, if one somehow caused this "able to block" wind to no longer exist, none of the worlds of the ten directions would not be completely destroyed.

正體字

如來應正等覺。亦復如是。有大智風。名為
能滅。能滅一切諸大菩薩。煩惱習氣。有大智
風。名為巧持。巧持其根未熟菩薩。不令能滅。
大智風輪。斷其一切煩惱習氣。佛子。若無如
來巧持智風。無量菩薩。皆墮聲聞辟支佛地。
由此智故。令諸菩薩。超二乘地。安住如來究
竟之位。佛子。是為如來心第九相。諸菩薩摩
訶薩。應如是知。復次佛子。如來智慧。無處不
至。何以故。無一眾生。而不具有如來智慧。但
以妄想顛倒執著。而不證得。若離妄想。一切
智自然智無礙智。則得現前。佛子。譬如有大
經卷。量等三千大千世界。書寫三千大千世
界中事。一切皆盡。所謂書寫大鐵圍山中事。
量等大鐵圍山。書寫大地中事。量等大地。書
寫中千世界中事。量等中千世界。書寫小千
世界中事。量等小千世界。如是若四天下。若
大海。若須彌山。

简体字

如来、应、正等觉亦复如是，有大智风，名为能灭，能灭一切诸大菩萨烦恼习气；有大智风，名为巧持，巧持其根未熟菩萨不令能灭大智风轮断其一切烦恼习气。佛子，若无如来巧持智风，无量菩萨皆堕声闻、辟支佛地；由此智故，令诸菩萨超二乘地，安住如来究竟之位。佛子，是为如来心第九相，诸菩萨摩诃萨应如是知。

"复次，佛子，如来智慧无处不至。何以故？无一众生而不具有如来智慧，但以妄想颠倒执著而不证得；若离妄想，一切智、自然智、无碍智则得现前。佛子，譬如有大经卷，量等三千大千世界，书写三千大千世界中事，一切皆尽。所谓：书写大铁围山中事，量等大铁围山；书写大地中事，量等大地；书写中千世界中事，量等中千世界；书写小千世界中事，量等小千世界；如是，若四天下，若大海，若须弥山，

Chapter 37 — The Manifestation of the Tathāgata

So too it is with the Tathāgata, the Arhat, the One of Right and Universal Enlightenment, for he has a great wisdom wind known as "able to extinguish" which is able to extinguish the afflictions and habitual karmic propensities of all the great bodhisattvas. He also has a great wisdom wind known as "skillful sustenance" which skillfully sustains those bodhisattvas whose faculties have not yet become ripe by preventing the "able to extinguish" great wisdom whirlwind from cutting off all their afflictions and habitual karmic propensities.

Sons of the Buddha, if the Tathāgata's "skillful sustenance" wisdom wind did not exist, countless bodhisattvas would fall down to the grounds of *śrāvaka* disciples and *pratyekabuddhas*. It is due to this wisdom that all bodhisattvas are enabled to step beyond the grounds of the two vehicles practitioners and become securely established in the Tathāgata's ultimate position.

Sons of the Buddha, this is the ninth of the marks of the Tathāgata's mind. All bodhisattva-mahāsattvas should know it in this way.

Furthermore, Sons of the Buddha, the wisdom of the Tathāgata has no place it does not reach. And why is this so? This is because there is not a single being that does not possess the Tathāgata's wisdom. It is solely due to erroneous perceptions, inverted views, and attachments that they do not bring it to realization. If they were to abandon their erroneous thinking, then all-knowledge, spontaneous wisdom, and unimpeded wisdom would all manifest directly before them.

Sons of the Buddha, by way of analogy, consider the following: Suppose there was a great scriptural scroll equal in size to the great trichiliocosm in which there was exhaustively recorded everything in the great trichiliocosm, including for instance:

- A written record of everything within the area encircled by the iron ring mountains which was equal in size to the great iron ring mountains themselves;
- A written record of everything on the great earth which was equal in size to the great earth itself;
- A written record of everything throughout a medium-sized chiliocosm which was equal in size to that medium-sized chiliocosm itself;
- A written record of everything throughout a small chiliocosm which was equal in size to that small chiliocosm itself; and
- In this same way, written records of everything on the four continents, the great ocean, Mount Sumeru, the palaces of the earthly

正體字

若地天宮殿。若欲界空居天
272c14 ‖ 宮殿。若色界宮殿。若無色界宮殿。一一書寫。
272c15 ‖ 其量悉等此大經卷。雖復量等大千世界。而
272c16 ‖ 全住在一微塵中。如一微塵。一切微塵。皆亦
272c17 ‖ 如是。時有一人。智慧明達。具足成就清淨天
272c18 ‖ 眼。見此經卷。在微塵內。於諸眾生。無少利
272c19 ‖ 益。即作是念。我當以精進力。破彼微塵。出
272c20 ‖ 此經卷。令得饒益一切眾生。作是念已。即起
272c21 ‖ 方便。破彼微塵。出此[2]大經。令諸眾生。普得
272c22 ‖ 饒益。如於一塵。一切微塵。應知悉然。佛子。
272c23 ‖ 如來智慧。亦復如是。無量無礙。普能利益一
272c24 ‖ 切眾生。具足在於眾生身中。但諸凡愚。妄想
272c25 ‖ 執著。不知不覺。不得利益。爾時如來。以無障
272c26 ‖ 礙。清淨智眼。普觀法界一切眾生而作是言。
272c27 ‖ 奇哉奇哉。此諸眾生。云何具有如來智慧。愚
272c28 ‖ 癡迷惑。不知不見。我當教以聖道。令其永離
272c29 ‖ 妄想執著。自於身中。得見如來廣大智慧。與
273a01 ‖ 佛無異。即教彼眾生。修習聖道。令離妄想。離
273a02 ‖ 妄想已。證得如來無量智慧。利益安樂一切
273a03 ‖ 眾生。佛子。是為如來心第十相。諸菩薩摩訶
273a04 ‖ 薩。應如是知。

簡體字

若地天宫殿，若欲界空居天宫殿，若色界宫殿，若无色界宫殿，一一书写，其量悉等。此大经卷虽复量等大千世界，而全住在一微尘中；如一微尘，一切微尘皆亦如是。时，有一人智慧明达，具足成就清净天眼，见此经卷在微尘内，于诸众生无少利益，即作是念：'我当以精进力，破彼微尘，出此经卷，令得饶益一切众生。'作是念已，即起方便，破彼微尘，出此经卷，令诸众生普得饶益。如于一尘，一切微尘应知悉然。佛子，如来智慧亦复如是，无量无碍，普能利益一切众生，具足在于众生身中；但诸凡愚妄想执著，不知不觉，不得利益。尔时，如来以无障碍清净智眼，普观法界一切众生而作是言：'奇哉！奇哉！此诸众生云何具有如来智慧，愚痴迷惑，不知不见？我当教以圣道，令其永离妄想执著，自于身中得见如来广大智慧与佛无异。'即教彼众生修习圣道，令离妄想；离妄想已，证得如来无量智慧，利益安乐一切众生。佛子，是为如来心第十相，诸菩萨摩诃萨应如是知。

Chapter 37 — The Manifestation of the Tathāgata

devas, the palaces of the desire realm's space-dwelling devas, the palaces of the form realms, and the palaces of the formless realm devas, for every one of which these written records were equal in size to each of these phenomena.

Although these great scriptural scrolls might be equal in size to the great chiliocosm, they would all still be able to abide completely within a single atom. And just as this would be so with regard to a single atom, so too would this be so with regard to all atoms.

Suppose then that there was a single person possessed of clear and penetrating wisdom who, having completely purified the heavenly eye, saw this scriptural scroll within an atom and realized that it was not benefiting beings in the least, whereupon he thought, "I should use the power of vigor to break open this atom, draw forth this scriptural scroll, and then make it benefit all beings." Then, having thought in this way, suppose he immediately produced some skillful means to break open this atom, draw forth this immense scripture, and then use it to cause all beings to acquire its benefits. Then, just as he had done this with a single atom, one should realize he also did so with all atoms.

Sons of the Buddha, so too it is with the Tathāgata's wisdom. It is measureless, unimpeded, and universally able to benefit all beings. It is fully present in all beings.[64] It is solely because of all common people's erroneous perceptions and attachments that they do not know this, do not awaken to it, and thus fail to gain its benefits.

Then, the Tathāgata, using the unimpeded vision of his pure wisdom eye, everywhere contemplates all beings throughout the Dharma realm and speaks these words: "This is strange indeed, strange indeed! How could it be that all these beings completely possess the Tathāgata's wisdom, yet, because of foolishness and delusion, they do not realize this and do not perceive this? I should instruct them in the path of the *āryas* and enable them to forever abandon erroneous perceptions and attachments so that they can see in their own persons the vast wisdom of the Tathāgata which is no different than that of the Buddha himself."

He then instructs those beings in the cultivation of the path of the *āryas*, thereby enabling them to abandon their erroneous perceptions. Then, having abandoned their erroneous perceptions, they realize the measureless wisdom of the Tathāgata and bestow benefit and happiness on all beings.

Sons of the Buddha, this is the tenth of the marks of the Tathāgata's mind. All bodhisattva-mahāsattvas should know it in this way.

正體字

佛子。菩薩摩訶薩。應以如是等
無量無礙。不可思議廣大相。知如來應正等
覺心。爾時普賢菩薩摩訶薩。欲重明此義。而
說頌言
　欲知諸佛心　當觀佛智慧
　佛智無依處　如空無所依
　眾生種種樂　及諸方便智
　皆依佛智慧　佛智無依止
　聲聞與獨覺　及諸佛解脫
　皆依於法界　法界無增減
　佛智亦如是　出生一切智
　無增亦無減　無生亦無盡
　如水潛流地　求之無不得
　無念亦無盡　功力遍十方
　佛智亦如是　普在眾生心
　若有勤修行　疾得智光明
　如龍有四珠　出生一切寶
　置之深密處　凡人莫能見
　佛四智亦然　出生一切智
　餘人莫能見　唯除大菩薩
　如海有四寶　能飲一切水

简体字

"佛子，菩萨摩诃萨应以如是等无量无碍不可思议广大相，知如来、应、正等觉心。"
　　尔时，普贤菩萨摩诃萨欲重明此义而说颂言：
"欲知诸佛心，当观佛智慧，
　佛智无依处，如空无所依。
　众生种种乐，及诸方便智，
　皆依佛智慧，佛智无依止。
　声闻与独觉，及诸佛解脱，
　皆依于法界，法界无增减。
　佛智亦如是，出生一切智，
　无增亦无减，无生亦无尽。
　如水潜流地，求之无不得，
　无念亦无尽，功力遍十方。
　佛智亦如是，普在众生心，
　若有勤修行，疾得智光明。
　如龙有四珠，出生一切宝，
　置之深密处，凡人莫能见。
　佛四智亦然，出生一切智，
　余人莫能见，唯除大菩萨。
　如海有四宝，能饮一切水，

Chapter 37 — The Manifestation of the Tathāgata

Sons of the Buddha, the bodhisattva-mahāsattva should know the mind of the Tathāgata, the Arhat, the One of Right and Universal Enlightenment on the basis of countless unimpeded and inconceivably vast marks such as these.

At that time, wishing to once again clarify the meaning of this, Samantabhadra Bodhisattva-mahāsattva then spoke these verses:

> If one wishes to know the mind of all buddhas,
> one should contemplate the Buddha's wisdom.
> The Buddha's wisdom has no place on which it depends
> just as empty space has nothing on which it depends.

> Beings' many different ways of finding happiness
> as well as all their knowledge of skillful methods
> all rely on the wisdom of the Buddha,
> yet Buddha's wisdom has nothing on which it depends.

> The liberations gained by *śrāvaka* disciples,
> *pratyekabuddhas*, and buddhas
> all rely upon the Dharma realm,
> yet the Dharma realm is neither increased nor decreased.

> So too it is with the wisdom of the Buddha.
> It produces all forms of wisdom,
> yet it is neither increased nor decreased,
> and it is neither produced nor exhausted.

> Just as the water flowing beneath the earth
> is such that, if one searches for it, no one fails to find it, and just as,
> without thought and without ever being exhausted,
> its functions and powers reach throughout the ten directions,

> so too it is with the Buddha's wisdom
> which, being universally present in all beings' minds,
> is such that, if one diligently cultivates it,
> one will swiftly acquire the light of wisdom.

> Just as the dragon has four pearls
> which themselves create all other jewels
> and which he places in an extremely secret place
> so that no common person could ever even see them,

> So too it is with the Buddha's four types of wisdom
> which produce all other kinds of wisdom
> and which are such that no one could ever see them
> with the sole exception of the great bodhisattvas.

> Just as the ocean has four kinds of jewels
> that are able to drink in the waters of all the rivers

正體字	273a25	令海不流溢	亦復無增減
	273a26	如來智亦爾	息浪除法愛
	273a27	廣大無有邊	能生佛菩薩
	273a28	下方至有頂	欲色無色界
	273a29	一切依虛空	虛空不分別
	273b01	聲聞與獨覺	菩薩眾智慧
	273b02	皆依於佛智	佛智無分別
	273b03	雪山有藥王	名為無盡根
	273b04	能生一切樹	根莖葉華實
	273b05	佛智亦如是	如來種中生
	273b06	既得菩提已	復生菩薩行
	273b07	如人把乾草	置之於劫燒
	273b08	金剛猶洞然	此無不燒理
	273b09	三世劫與剎	及其中眾生
	273b10	彼草容不燒	此佛無不知
	273b11	有風名散壞	能壞於大千
	273b12	若無別風止	壞及無量界
	273b13	大智風亦爾	滅諸菩薩惑
	273b14	別有善巧風	令住如來地
	273b15	如有大經卷	量等三千界

简体字

令海不流溢，亦复无增减。
如来智亦尔，息浪除法爱，
广大无有边，能生佛菩萨。
下方至有顶，欲色无色界，
一切依虚空，虚空不分别。
声闻与独觉，菩萨众智慧，
皆依于佛智，佛智无分别。
雪山有药王，名为无尽根，
能生一切树，根茎叶华实。
佛智亦如是，如来种中生，
既得菩提已，复生菩萨行。
如人把干草，置之于劫烧，
金刚犹洞燃，此无不烧理。
三世劫与刹，及其中众生，
彼草容不烧，此佛无不知。
有风名散坏，能坏于大千；
若无别风止，坏及无量界。
大智风亦尔，灭诸菩萨惑；
别有善巧风，令住如来地。
如有大经卷，量等三千界，

Chapter 37 — The Manifestation of the Tathāgata

and thus prevent the oceans from overflowing,
while also ensuring that they neither increase nor decrease,

so too it is with the Tathāgata's wisdom
which stills the waves and eliminates all affection for dharmas,
which is so vast as to be boundless,
and which is able to give birth to buddhas and bodhisattvas.

Just as from the regions below on up to the peak of existence
throughout the desire realm, form realm, and formless realm,
everything whatsoever relies upon empty space,
even as empty space itself does not discriminate among them,

so too, the many types of wisdom of *śrāvaka* disciples,
pratyekabuddhas, and bodhisattvas
all rely upon the Buddha's wisdom
even as the Buddha's wisdom does not discriminate among them.

Just as the Himalaya Mountains have a medicine king tree
known as "endless roots"
which is able to bring about growth in all other trees,
including their roots, trunks, leaves, blossoms, and fruit,

so too it is with the wisdom of the Buddha
which comes forth from the lineage of the Tathāgatas,
and, having already attained the realization of bodhi,
still continues to bring forth the bodhisattva practices.

Supposing someone were to take up dry grasses
and place them into the kalpa-ending fires
in which even vajra would be completely incinerated,
there would be no basis for supposing they would not be burned,

but even supposing it was possible those grasses might not be burned,
of the three times' kalpas and *kṣetras*
as well as all the beings within them,
the Buddha would still have none of these matters he does not know.

Just as there is a wind known as "scattering destruction"
which is able to destroy the entire great chiliocosm,
one that, were it not for another wind's stopping it,
its destruction would extend to all the countlessly many other worlds,

so too it is with the wind of great wisdom
which extinguishes all the bodhisattvas' delusions
and which is attended by another wind possessed of an excellent skill
to enable them to dwell on the ground of the Tathāgata.

Just as, supposing there was an immense scriptural scroll
equal in size to the great trichiliocosm

正體字	273b16 273b17 273b18 273b19 273b20 273b21 273b22 273c02 273c05 273c06 273c07 273c08 273c09 273c10 273c11 273c12 273c13 273c14 273c15 273c16 273c17 273c18	在於一塵內　一切塵悉然 有一聰慧人　淨眼悉明見 破塵出經卷　普饒益眾生 佛智亦如是　遍在眾生心 妄想之所纏　不覺亦不知 諸佛大慈悲　令其除妄想 如是乃出現　饒益諸菩薩 大方廣佛華嚴經[＊]卷第五十二 　　如來出現品第三十七之三 佛子。菩薩摩訶薩。應云何知如來應正等覺 境界。佛子。菩薩摩訶薩。以無障無礙智慧。知 一切世間境界。是如來境界。知一切三世境 界。一切剎境界。一切法境界。一切眾生境界。真 如無差別境界。法界無障礙境界。實際無邊 際境界。虛空無分量境界。無境界境界。是如 來境界。佛子。如一切世間境界無量。如來境 界亦無量。如一切三世境界無量。如來境界 亦無量。乃至如無境界境界無量。如來境界 亦無量。如無境界境界一切處無有。如來境 界。亦如是。一切處無有。佛子。菩薩摩訶薩。應 知心境界是如來境界。如心境界。無量無邊。 無縛無脫。
简体字		在于一尘内，一切尘悉然。 有一聪慧人，净眼悉明见， 破尘出经卷，普饶益众生。 佛智亦如是，遍在众生心， 妄想之所缠，不觉亦不知。 诸佛大慈悲，令其除妄想， 如是乃出现，饶益诸菩萨。 大方广佛华严经卷第五十二 如来出现品第三十七之三 "佛子，菩萨摩诃萨应云何知如来、应、正等觉境界？佛子，菩萨摩诃萨以无障无碍智慧，知一切世间境界是如来境界，知一切三世境界、一切刹境界、一切法境界、一切众生境界、真如无差别境界、法界无障碍境界、实际无边际境界、虚空无分量境界、无境界境界是如来境界。佛子，如一切世间境界无量，如来境界亦无量；如一切三世境界无量，如来境界亦无量；乃至，如无境界境界无量，如来境界亦无量；如无境界境界一切处无有，如来境界亦如是一切处无有。佛子，菩萨摩诃萨应知心境界是如来境界。如心境界无量无边、无缚无脱，

Chapter 37 — The Manifestation of the Tathāgata

which resided within a single atom
and, in the same way, such scriptures resided in all other atoms—

and supposing, too, that there was a person of acute intelligence who,
with the purified eye, clearly saw them all
and then broke open those atoms, drew forth the scripture scrolls,
and used them to abundantly benefit beings everywhere—

So too it is with the wisdom of the Buddha
which is everywhere present within the minds of beings
in which it is bound up by their erroneous perceptions
so that they do not awaken to it or even know of it.

The buddhas then bring forth their great kindness and compassion
and enable them to rid themselves of such erroneous perceptions.
Thus, in this same way, they bring it forth and reveal it
so that it benefits all bodhisattvas.

Sons of the Buddha, how should the bodhisattva-mahāsattva know the objective realms of the Tathāgata, the Arhat, the One of Right and Universal Enlightenment? Sons of the Buddha, with unobstructed and unimpeded wisdom, the bodhisattva-mahāsattva knows the objective realms of all worlds as being the Tathāgata's objective realms, knows the objective realms of all three periods of time, the objective realms of all *kṣetras*, the objective realms of all dharmas, the objective realms of all beings, the undifferentiated objective realm of true suchness, the unimpeded objective realm of the Dharma realm, the limitless objective realm of the apex of reality, the undivided objective realm of empty space, and the objective realm of no objective realm at all—[he knows] these are the Tathāgata's objective realms.

Sons of the Buddha, just as the objective realms of all worlds are measureless, so too are the Tathāgata's objective realms also measureless. Just as the objective realms of all three periods of time are measureless, so too are the Tathāgata's objective realms also measureless, and so forth up to and including the fact that, just as the objective realm of no objective realm at all is measureless, so too is the Tathāgata's objective realm also measureless. And just as the objective realm of no objective realm at all does not exist anywhere, so too is this so of the Tathāgata's objective realm. It does not exist anywhere.

Sons of the Buddha, the bodhisattva-mahāsattva should know that the mind's objective realms are the Tathāgata's objective realms. Just as the mind's objective realms are measureless and boundless, neither bound up nor liberated, so too are the Tathāgata's objective

正體字

如來境界。亦無量無邊。無縛無脫。
何以故。以如是如是。思惟分別。如是如是。
無量顯現故。佛子。如大龍王。隨心降雨。其
雨不從內出。不從外出。如來境界。亦復如是。
隨於如是思惟分別。則有如是無量顯現。於
十方中。悉無來處。佛子。如大海水。皆從龍王
心力所起。諸佛如來。一切智海。亦復如是。皆
從如來往昔大願之所生起。佛子。一切智海。
無量無邊。不可思議。不可言說。然我今者。略
說譬諭。汝應諦聽。佛子。此閻浮提。有二千五
百河。流入大海。西拘耶尼。有五千河。流入大
海。東弗婆提。有七千五百河。流入大海。北
欝單越。有一萬河。流入大海。佛子。此四天
下。如是二萬五千河。相續不絕。流入大海。於
意云何。此水多不。答言甚多。佛子。復有十光
明龍王。雨大海中。水倍過前。百光明龍王。雨
大海中。水復倍前。大莊嚴龍王。摩那斯龍王。
雷震龍王。難陀跋難陀龍王。無量光明龍王。
連[1]霪不斷龍王。大勝龍王。

简体字

如来境界亦无量无边、无缚无脱。何以故？以如是如是思惟分别，如是如是无量显现故。佛子，如大龙王随心降雨，其雨不从内出、不从外出。如来境界亦复如是，随于如是思惟分别，则有如是无量显现，于十方中悉无来处。佛子，如大海水，皆从龙王心力所起。诸佛如来一切智海亦复如是，皆从如来往昔大愿之所生起。

　　"佛子，一切智海无量无边，不可思议，不可言说；然我今者略说譬喻，汝应谛听。佛子，此阎浮提有二千五百河流入大海，西拘耶尼有五千河流入大海，东弗婆提有七千五百河流入大海，北郁单越有一万河流入大海。

　　"佛子，此四天下，如是二万五千河相续不绝流入大海。于意云何？此水多不？"

　　答言："甚多。"

　　"佛子，复有十光明龙王，雨大海中水倍过前；百光明龙王，雨大海中水复倍前；大庄严龙王、摩那斯龙王、雷震龙王、难陀跋难陀龙王、无量光明龙王、连澍不断龙王、大胜龙王、

Chapter 37 — The Manifestation of the Tathāgata

realms also measureless and boundless and neither tied up nor liberated. And how is this so? This is because, it is due to just such kinds of thought and discrimination as these that there occur just such countless manifestations as these.

Sons of the Buddha, just as it is with the great dragon king for whom it is in accordance with his thoughts that he sends down the rain so that his rain then neither arises from within nor arises from without, so too it is with the Tathāgata's objective realms in which it is in accordance with just such thoughts and discriminations that there then occur just such countless manifestations throughout the ten directions, all of which have no place from which they come.

Sons of the Buddha, just as the waters of the great ocean all come forth from the power of the dragon king's mind, so too it is with the ocean of all-knowledge of all buddhas, the *tathāgatas*, which all arises from the Tathāgata's great vows made in the distant past.

Sons of the Buddha, the ocean of all-knowledge is measureless, boundless, inconceivable, and indescribable. Nonetheless, by way of analogy, I shall now present a general description. You should all listen closely.

Sons of the Buddha, this continent of Jambudvīpa has two thousand five hundred rivers that flow into the great ocean. The western continent of Aparagodānīya has five thousand rivers that flow into the great ocean. The eastern continent of Pūrvavideha has seven thousand five hundred rivers that flow into the great ocean. And the northern continent of Uttarakuru has ten thousand rivers that flow into the great ocean. Sons of the Buddha, in this way, these four continents have twenty-five thousand rivers that continuously and uninterruptedly flow into the great ocean. What do you think? Is this a great deal of water, or not?

They replied: "It is an extremely great amount."

Sons of the Buddha, in addition, there is the dragon king known as "Ten Light Rays" whose rains entering the great ocean amount to twice the volume of water described above. Moreover, the rains entering the great ocean sent down by the dragon king known as "Hundred Light Rays" amount to twice the previously mentioned volume of water.

In addition, the rains entering the great ocean sent down by Great Adornment Dragon King, Manasvin Dragon King, Rumbling Thunder Dragon King, Nanda Dragon King, Upananda Dragon King, Measureless Light Dragon King, Continuous Downpour Dragon King, Great Supremacy Dragon King, Great Bounding Speed

正體字

大奮迅龍王。如
是等八十億諸大龍王。各雨大海。皆悉展轉。
倍過於前。娑竭羅龍王太子。名閻浮幢。雨大
海中。水復倍前。佛子。十光明龍王。宮殿中
水。流入大海。復倍過前。百光明龍王。宮殿中
水。流入大海。復倍過前。大莊嚴龍王。摩那
斯龍王。雷[2]震龍王。難陀跋難陀龍王。無量光
明龍王。連[*]霔不斷龍王。大勝龍王。大奮迅
龍王。如是等八十億諸大龍王。宮殿各別。其
中有水。流入大海。皆悉展轉。倍過於前。娑竭
羅龍王太子。閻浮幢宮殿中水。流入大海。復
倍過前。佛子。娑竭羅龍王。連雨大海。水復倍
前。其娑竭羅龍王。宮殿中水。涌[3]出[4]入海。復
倍於前其所出水。紺瑠璃色。涌出有時。是故
大海。潮不失時。佛子。如是大海。其水無量。
眾寶無量。眾生無量。所依大地。亦復無量。佛
子。於汝意云何。彼大海。為無量不。答言。實為
無量。不可為[5]諭。佛子。此大海無量。於[6]如來
智海無量。百分不及一。千分不及一。乃至優
波尼沙陀分。不及其一。但隨眾生心。為作譬
諭。

简体字

大奋迅龙王，如是等八十亿诸大龙王，各雨大海，皆悉展转倍过于前；娑竭罗龙王太子，名阎浮幢，雨大海中水复倍前。佛子，十光明龙王宫殿中水流入大海，复倍过前；百光明龙王宫殿中水流入大海，复倍过前；大庄严龙王、摩那斯龙王、雷震龙王、难陀跋难陀龙王、无量光明龙王、连澍不断龙王、大胜龙王、大奋迅龙王，如是等八十亿诸大龙王，宫殿各别，其中有水流入大海，皆悉展转倍过于前；娑竭罗龙王太子阎浮幢宫殿中水流入大海，复倍过前。佛子，娑竭罗龙王连雨大海，水复倍前；其娑竭罗龙王宫殿中水涌出入海，复倍于前；其所出水绀琉璃色，涌出有时，是故大海潮不失时。佛子，如是大海，其水无量，众宝无量，众生无量，所依大地亦复无量。

"佛子，于汝意云何？彼大海为无量不？"

答言："实为无量，不可为喻。"

"佛子，此大海无量于如来智海无量，百分不及一，千分不及一，乃至优波尼沙陀分不及其一；但随众生心为作譬喻，

Chapter 37 — The Manifestation of the Tathāgata

Dragon King, and eighty *koṭīs* of other great dragon kings such as these in each case amount to twice that of the one before. And the rains entering the great ocean sent down by "Jambu Banner," the dragon prince son of the Dragon King, Sāgara, amount to twice that of the one before.

Sons of the Buddha, the waters flowing into the great ocean from the palace of Ten Light Rays Dragon King are twice the previous amount. So too, the waters flowing into the great ocean from the palace of Hundred Light Rays Dragon King are twice the previous amount. So too, the amount of water pouring into the great ocean from the palaces of Great Adornment Dragon King, Manasvin Dragon King, Rumbling Thunder Dragon King, Nanda Dragon King, Upananda Dragon King, Measureless Light Dragon King, Continuous Downpour Dragon King, Great Supremacy Dragon King, Great Bounding Speed Dragon King, and the eighty *koṭīs* of other great dragon kings is different in each case so that the amount of water flowing from each of these palaces is in turn twice that of the previous amount. And the water that flows into the great ocean from the palace of Jambu Banner, the dragon prince son of Sāgara, the Dragon King, is again twice that of the previous amount.

Sons of the Buddha, the waters pouring into the great ocean from the continuous rains of Sāgara, the dragon king, are again twice the previous amount. The waters gushing forth into the ocean from the palace of Sāgara, the dragon king, are again twice those previously described [that he sends down as rain]. The waters it gushes forth are purple colored and their gushing forth is timed so that the great ocean's tides never lose their normal timing.

Sons of the Buddha, just as, in this way, the waters of the great ocean are immeasurable, so too, its many jewels are measurelessly many, its beings are measurelessly many, and the ground of the great earth upon which they all rest is also measurelessly vast. Sons of the Buddha, What the do you think? Is that great ocean measureless, or not?

They replied: "It truly is measureless, so measureless as to be indescribable even by resort to analogy."

Sons of the Buddha, compared to the measurelessness of the Tathāgata's ocean of wisdom, the measurelessness of this great ocean does not amount to even a hundredth part, does not amount to even a thousandth part, and so forth until we come to its not amounting to even a single part in an *upaniṣad* of parts. It is solely to adapt to beings' minds that one makes such analogies, for the

正體字

而佛境界。非譬所及。佛子。菩薩摩訶薩。
應知如來智海無量。從初發心。修一切菩薩
行不斷故。應知寶聚無量。一切菩提分法。三
寶種不斷故。應知所住眾生無量。一切學無
學。聲聞獨覺。所受用故。應知住地無量。從初
歡喜地。乃至究竟無障礙地。諸菩薩所居故。
佛子。菩薩摩訶薩。為入無量智慧。利益一切
眾生故。於如來應正等覺境界。應如是知。爾
時。普賢菩薩摩訶薩。欲重明此義。而說頌言
　如心境界無有量　　諸佛境界亦復然
　如心境界從意生　　佛境如是應觀察
　如龍不離於本處　　以心威力[*]霑大雨
　雨水雖無來去處　　隨龍心故悉充洽
　十力牟尼亦如是　　無所從來無所去
　若有淨心則現身　　量等法界入毛孔
　如海珍奇無有量　　眾生大地亦復然
　水性一味等無別　　於中生者各蒙利

简体字

而佛境界非譬所及。佛子，菩萨摩诃萨应知如来智海无量，从初发心修一切菩萨行不断故；应知宝聚无量，一切菩提分法、三宝种不断故；应知所住众生无量，一切学、无学、声闻、独觉所受用故；应知住地无量，从初欢喜地乃至究竟无障碍地诸菩萨所居故。佛子，菩萨摩诃萨为入无量智慧利益一切众生故，于如来、应、正等觉境界应如是知。"

尔时，普贤菩萨摩诃萨欲重明此义而说颂言：
"如心境界无有量，诸佛境界亦复然；
　如心境界从意生，佛境如是应观察。
　如龙不离于本处，以心威力澍大雨，
　雨水虽无来去处，随龙心故悉充洽。
　十力牟尼亦如是，无所从来无所去，
　若有净心则现身，量等法界入毛孔。
　如海珍奇无有量，众生大地亦复然，
　水性一味等无别，于中生者各蒙利。

Chapter 37 — *The Manifestation of the Tathāgata*

objective realms of the Buddha cannot be described even by resort to analogies.

Sons of the Buddha, as for the bodhisattva-mahāsattva:

- He should realize that the Tathāgata's ocean of wisdom is measureless because, from the time of his initial resolve, he has incessantly cultivated the bodhisattva practices;
- He should realize that the aggregations of jewels within it are measureless because the dharmas constituting the limbs of bodhi and the lineage of the Three Jewels continue on incessantly;
- He should realize that the beings in which it abides are measureless because it is taken in and put to use by those still in training or beyond training, including by all *śrāvaka*-disciple and *pratyekabuddha* practitioners; and
- He should realize that the grounds on which they dwell are measureless because, from the first ground, the ground of joyfulness, on up to the most ultimate and unimpeded of all the grounds, those [grounds] are where all bodhisattvas reside.

Sons of the Buddha, in order to access measureless wisdom and benefit all beings, the bodhisattva-mahāsattva should know in these ways the objective realms of the Tathāgata, the Arhat, the One of Right and Universal Enlightenment.

At that time, wishing to once again clarify the meaning of this, Samantabhadra Bodhisattva-mahāsattva then spoke these verses:

> Just as the mind's objective realms are measureless,
> so too is this true of the Buddha's objective realms.
> Just as the mind's objective realms arise from the mind,
> so too should one contemplate the realms of the Buddha.

> Just as, even without leaving their original place, the dragons
> use their minds' awesome power to pour down the great rains
> and those rains have no place whence they come or to which they go,
> still, by according with the dragons' minds, they drench everything,

> so too it is that the Muni of Ten Powers
> who, though he has no place whence he comes or to which he goes,
> if there are any with pure minds, he manifests his body there so that,
> even being the size of the Dharma realm, he can enter a single pore.

> Just as the extraordinary jewels in the oceans are measureless
> just as are the number of beings and the size of the earth,
> and just as its waters by nature are of a single undifferentiated flavor,
> yet each being living within it receives its own benefit,

正體字

274b15	如來智海亦如是　　一切所有皆無量
274b16	有學無學住地人　　悉在其中得饒益
274b17	佛子。菩薩摩訶薩。應云何知如來應正等覺
274b18	行。佛子。菩薩摩訶薩。應知無礙行是如來行。
274b19	應知真如行是如來行。佛子如真如前際不
274b20	生後際不動現在不[7]起。如來行亦如是。不生
274b21	不動不起。佛子。如法界非量非無量無形故。
274b22	如來行亦如是。非量非無量無形故。佛子。譬
274b23	如鳥飛虛空。經於百年。已經過處。未經過處。
274b24	皆不可量。何以故。虛空界無邊際故。如來行
274b25	亦如是。假使有人。經百千億那由他劫分別
274b26	演說。已說未說。皆不可量。何以故。如來行無
274b27	邊際故。佛子。如來應正等覺。住無礙行。無有
274b28	住處。而能普為一切眾生。示現所行。令其見
274b29	已。出過一切諸障礙道。佛子。譬如金翅鳥王。
274c01	飛行虛空。迴翔不去。以清淨眼。觀察海內諸
274c02	龍宮殿。奮勇猛力。以左右翅。鼓揚海水。悉令
274c03	兩闢。知龍男女。命將盡者。而搏取之。

简体字

　　如来智海亦如是，一切所有皆无量，
　　有学无学住地人，悉在其中得饶益。
　"佛子，菩萨摩诃萨应云何知如来、应、正等觉行？佛子，菩萨摩诃萨应知无碍行是如来行，应知真如行是如来行。佛子，如真如，前际不生，后际不动，现在不起；如来行亦如是，不生、不动、不起。佛子，如法界，非量、非无量，无形故；如来行亦如是，非量、非无量，无形故。佛子，譬如鸟飞虚空，经于百年，已经过处、未经过处皆不可量。何以故？虚空界无边际故。如来行亦如是，假使有人经百千亿那由他劫分别演说，已说、未说皆不可量。何以故？如来行无边际故。佛子，如来、应、正等觉住无碍行，无有住处，而能普为一切众生示现所行，令其见已，出过一切诸障碍道。佛子，譬如金翅鸟王，飞行虚空，回翔不去，以清净眼观察海内诸龙宫殿，奋勇猛力，以左右翅鼓扬海水悉令两辟，知龙男女命将尽者而搏取之。

Chapter 37 — *The Manifestation of the Tathāgata*

so too it is with the Tathāgata's ocean of wisdom
in which everything it contains is measureless
and those in training, beyond training, or dwelling on its grounds
all acquire their own benefit there within it.

Sons of the Buddha, how should the bodhisattva-mahāsattva know the actions of the Tathāgata, the Arhat, the One of Right and Universal Enlightenment? Sons of the Buddha, the bodhisattva-mahāsattva should know that it is unimpeded action that constitutes the actions of the Tathāgata and he should know that it is actions of true suchness that constitute the actions of the Tathāgata.

Sons of the Buddha, just as true suchness was not created in the past, does not move into the future, and does not arise in the present, so too it is with the Tathāgata's actions which are not created, do not move, and do not arise.

Sons of the Buddha, just as the Dharma realm is not finite nor infinite because it has no form, so too it is with the Tathāgata's actions, for they are neither finite nor infinite because they have no form.

Sons of the Buddha, by way of analogy, it is just as if a bird flew through space for a hundred years, the regions already passed by and the regions not yet passed by would both be measureless. And why is this so? This is because the realm of space is boundless.

So too it is with the Tathāgata's actions for, even if someone spent a hundred thousand *koṭīs* of *nayutas* of kalpas in differentiating and expounding on them, what he had already described and what he had not yet described would both be measureless. And why is this so? This is because the Tathāgata's actions are boundless.

Sons of the Buddha, as he abides in unimpeded actions, the Tathāgata, the Arhat, the One of Right and Universal Enlightenment has no place in which he abides and yet he is able to manifest actions everywhere for the sake of all beings. Then, after they have been allowed to see them, they are able to step beyond all paths beset with obstacles.

Sons of the Buddha, by way of analogy, it is just as when the golden-winged king of birds, flying through the sky, begins to circle without flying on, and then uses his clear-eyed vision to look into the dragon palaces down in the waters of the ocean. Then, energetically exerting his courageous and fierce strength to sweep his left and then his right wings, he sweeps aside the ocean's waters and causes them to part, whereupon, knowing of those sons and daughters of the dragons which ones' lives are about to come to an end, he then pounces on them and snatches them up.

如來應正等覺金翅鳥王。亦復如是。住無礙行。以淨佛眼。觀察法界諸宮殿中一切眾生。若曾種善根。已成熟者。如來奮勇猛十力。以止觀兩翅。鼓揚生死大愛水海。使其兩闢而撮取之。置佛法中。令斷一切妄想戲論。安住如來無分別無礙行。佛子。譬如日月。獨無等侶。周行虛空。利益眾生。不作是念。我從何來。而至何所。諸佛如來。亦復如是。性本寂滅。無有分別。示現遊行一切法界。為欲饒益諸眾生故。作諸佛事。無有休息。不生如是戲論分別。我從彼來。而向彼去。佛子。菩薩摩訶薩應以如是等無量方便。無量性相。知見如來應正等覺。所行之行。爾時普賢菩薩。欲重明此義。而說頌言

譬如真如不生滅　　無有方所無能見
大饒益者行如是　　出過三世不可量
法界非界非非界　　非是有量非無量
大功德者行亦然　　非量無量無身故
如鳥飛行億千歲　　前後虛空等無別
眾劫演說如來行　　已說未說不可量

如来、应、正等觉金翅鸟王亦复如是，住无碍行，以净佛眼观察法界诸宫殿中一切众生，若曾种善根已成熟者，如来奋勇猛十力，以止观两翅鼓扬生死大爱水海，使其两辟而撮取之，置佛法中，令断一切妄想戏论，安住如来无分别无碍行。佛子，譬如日月，独无等侣，周行虚空，利益众生，不作是念：'我从何来，而至何所。'诸佛如来亦复如是，性本寂灭，无有分别，示现游行一切法界，为欲饶益诸众生故，作诸佛事无有休息，不生如是戏论分别：'我从彼来，而向彼去。'佛子，菩萨摩诃萨应以如是等无量方便、无量性相，知见如来、应、正等觉所行之行。"

尔时，普贤菩萨欲重明此义而说颂言：
"譬如真如不生灭，无有方所无能见；
大饶益者行如是，出过三世不可量。
法界非界非非界，非是有量非无量；
大功德者行亦然，非量无量无身故。
如鸟飞行亿千岁，前后虚空等无别；
众劫演说如来行，已说未说不可量。

Chapter 37 — The Manifestation of the Tathāgata

So too it is with the Tathāgata, the Arhat, the One of Right and Universal Enlightenment, the king of golden-winged birds. Abiding as he does in unimpeded actions, he uses his pure Buddha eye to contemplate all beings in all the palaces throughout the Dharma realm and, wherever there are those who have planted roots of goodness that have now become ripened, summoning the courageous strength of the ten powers, he uses his two wings of calming and contemplation to sweep aside the waters of *saṃsāra*'s great ocean of desires, thereby causing them to part. He then pulls forth those beings, places them within the Dharma, enables them to cut off all their erroneous perceptions and conceptual proliferations, and then establishes them in the nondiscriminating unimpeded actions of the Tathāgata.

Sons of the Buddha, just as the sun and moon, each alone and with no companions, circle through space, benefiting beings, never thinking as they do so, "I have come from such and such a place and am going on to such and such a place," so too it is with the buddhas, the *tathāgatas*, whose nature is originally quiescent and free of discriminations. They manifest as roaming throughout the entire Dharma realm, wishing to benefit all beings, and never resting. They do not produce conceptual proliferations and discriminations such as this: "I have come from that place and am going to that place."

Sons of the Buddha, it is by such measureless skillful means and measureless nature and marks that the bodhisattva-mahāsattva should know the actions engaged in by the Tathāgata, the Arhat, the One of Right and Universal Enlightenment.

At that time, wishing to once again clarify the meaning of this, Samantabhadra Bodhisattva-mahāsattva then spoke these verses:

> Just as true suchness is neither produced nor destroyed,
> has no place in which it resides, and cannot be seen by anyone,
> so too it is with the actions of the Greatly Beneficial One which,
> having transcended the three periods of time, are immeasurable.

> Just as the Dharma realm is neither a realm nor not a realm
> and is neither finite nor infinite,
> so too it is with the actions of the One of Great Meritorious Qualities
> who is neither finite nor infinite because he has no body at all.

> Just as when a bird has flown on for a thousand *koṭīs* of years,
> the regions of space behind and ahead are the same and no different,
> so too, if one expounded for many kalpas on the Tathāgata's actions,
> the already told of and not yet told of would both be measureless.

正體字	
274c24	金翅在空觀大海　　鬮水搏取龍男女
274c25	十力能拔善根人　　令出有海除眾惑
274c26	譬如日月遊虛空　　照臨一切不分別
274c27	世尊周行於法界　　教化眾生無動念
274c28	佛子。諸菩薩摩訶薩。應云何知如來應正等
274c29	覺成正覺。佛子。菩薩摩訶薩。應知如來成正
275a01	覺。於一切義。無所觀察。於法平等。無所疑
275a02	惑。無二無相。無行無止。無量無際。遠離二
275a03	邊。住於中道。出過一切文字言說。知一切眾
275a04	生。心念所行。根性欲樂。煩惱染習。舉要言
275a05	之。於一念中。悉知三世一切諸法。佛子。譬
275a06	如大海。普能印現四天下中。一切眾生。色身
275a07	形像。是故共說。以為大海。諸佛菩提。亦復如
275a08	是。普現一切眾生心念。根性樂欲。而無所現。
275a09	是故說名諸佛菩提。佛子。諸佛菩提。一切文
275a10	字所不能宣。一切音聲所不能及。一切言語
275a11	所不能說。但隨所應方便開示。

简体字

金翅在空观大海，辟水搏取龙男女；
十力能拔善根人，令出有海除众惑。
譬如日月游虚空，照临一切不分别；
世尊周行于法界，教化众生无动念。

"佛子，诸菩萨摩诃萨应云何知如来、应、正等觉成正觉？佛子，菩萨摩诃萨应知如来成正觉，于一切义无所观察，于法平等无所疑惑，无二无相，无行无止，无量无际，远离二边，住于中道，出过一切文字言说，知一切众生心念所行、根性欲乐、烦恼染习；举要言之，于一念中悉知三世一切诸法。佛子，譬如大海普能印现四天下中一切众生色身形像，是故共说以为大海；诸佛菩提亦复如是，普现一切众生心念、根性乐欲而无所现，是故说名诸佛菩提。佛子，诸佛菩提，一切文字所不能宣，一切音声所不能及，一切言语所不能说，但随所应方便开示。

As when the golden-winged bird in the sky looks at the great ocean,
parts the waters, pounces, and seizes the dragons' sons and daughters,
so too, the Ten-Powered One can pull forth those with good roots,
enable them to escape the ocean of existence, and be rid of their many
  delusions.

Just as the sun and moon roam through empty space
and their illumination reaches everyone without discrimination,
so too, the Bhagavat goes everywhere throughout the Dharma realm
and provides teaching to beings without ever moving a thought.

Sons of the Buddha, how should the bodhisattva-mahāsattva know the attainment of right enlightenment as achieved by the Tathāgata, the Arhat, the One of Right and Universal Enlightenment? Sons of the Buddha, the bodhisattva-mahāsattva should know the attainment of right enlightenment as achieved by the Tathāgata:

As not requiring any contemplation of any meaning;
As regarding all dharmas equally;
As free of doubt;
As non-dual and signless;
As neither going nor stopping;
As measureless and boundless;
As having abandoned the two extremes;
As abiding in the Middle Way;
As having gone beyond all language and speech; and
As knowing the actions of all beings' thoughts, the nature of their faculties, their aspirations, their afflictions, and their defiled habitual tendencies.

Or, to state it in terms of what is most essential, he should understand it as knowing in a single mind-moment all dharmas of the three periods of time.

Sons of the Buddha, just as the great ocean is known by all as "the great ocean" due to its ability to everywhere reflect the shapes and appearances of all beings on the four continents, so too it is with the bodhi of the Buddha which is known as "the Buddha's bodhi" due to its ability to everywhere manifesting all beings' thoughts, the nature of their faculties, and their aspirations, even without manifesting anything at all. Therefore it is known as "the bodhi of the Buddha."

Sons of the Buddha, the bodhi of all buddhas cannot be depicted by any literary passage, cannot be gotten at by any verbal description, and cannot be described in any language. It can only be explained by the use of skillful means adapted to what is most fitting.

正體字	佛子。如來應 275a12 ‖ 正等覺。成正覺時。得一切眾生量等身。得一 275a13 ‖ 切法量等身。得一切剎量等身。得一切三世 275a14 ‖ 量等身。得一切佛量等身。得一切語言量等 275a15 ‖ 身。得真如量等身。得法界量等身。得虛空界 275a16 ‖ 量等身。得無礙界量等身。得一切願量等身。 275a17 ‖ 得一切行量等身。得寂滅涅槃界量等身佛 275a18 ‖ 子。如所得身。言語及心。亦復如是。得如是 275a19 ‖ 等無量無數。清淨三輪。佛子。如來成正覺時。 275a20 ‖ 於其身中。普見一切眾生成正覺。乃至普見 275a21 ‖ 一切眾生入涅槃。皆同一性。所謂無性。無何 275a22 ‖ 等性。所謂無相性。無盡性。無生性。無滅性。 275a23 ‖ 無我性。無非我性。無眾生性。無非眾生性。無 275a24 ‖ 菩提性。無法界性。無虛空性。亦復無有成正 275a25 ‖ 覺性。知一切法。皆無性故。得一切智。大悲相 275a26 ‖ 續。救度眾生。
简体字	佛子，如来、应、正等觉成正觉时，得一切众生量等身，得一切法量等身，得一切刹量等身，得一切三世量等身，得一切佛量等身，得一切语言量等身，得真如量等身，得法界量等身，得虚空界量等身，得无碍界量等身，得一切愿量等身，得一切行量等身，得寂灭涅槃界量等身。佛子，如所得身，言语及心亦复如是，得如是等无量无数清净三轮。佛子，如来成正觉时，于其身中普见一切众生成正觉，乃至普见一切众生入涅槃，皆同一性，所谓：无性。无何等性？所谓：无相性、无尽性、无生性、无灭性、无我性、无非我性、无众生性、无非众生性、无菩提性、无法界性、无虚空性，亦复无有成正觉性。知一切法皆无性故，得一切智，大悲相续，救度众生。

Chapter 37 — The Manifestation of the Tathāgata

Sons of the Buddha, when the Tathāgata, the Arhat, the One of Right and Universal Enlightenment, attains right enlightenment:

He acquires bodies as measureless as all beings;
He acquires bodies as measureless as all dharmas;
He acquires bodies as measureless as all kṣetras;
He acquires bodies as measureless as the three periods of time;
He acquires bodies as measureless as all buddhas;
He acquires bodies as measureless as all languages;
He acquires bodies as measureless as true suchness;
He acquires bodies as measureless as the Dharma realm;
He acquires bodies as measureless as the realms of empty space;
He acquires bodies as measureless as the unimpeded realms;
He acquires bodies as measureless as all vows;
He acquires bodies as measureless as all practices; and
He acquires bodies as measureless as the realm of quiescent nirvāṇa.

Sons of the Buddha, just as it is with the bodies he acquires, so too it is with his speech and mind in which he also acquires just such measureless and innumerable endowments of all three of these pure spheres.[65]

Sons of the Buddha, when the Tathāgata attains right enlightenment, within his body, he sees all beings attaining right enlightenment, and so forth, including even seeing all beings entering nirvāṇa and including seeing them all as of a single identical nature, namely the absence of any nature at all. What kinds of nature do they not have? This refers to:

No nature of signs;
No nature of exhaustibility;
No nature of production;
No nature of destruction;
No nature of self;
No nature of non-self;
No nature of being any being;
No nature of not being any being;
No nature of bodhi;
No nature of the Dharma realm;
No nature of empty space; and
No nature of the attainment of right enlightenment.

Because they realize all dharmas have no nature, they therefore attain all-knowledge and the continuous great compassion with which they rescue and liberate beings.

正體字

	佛子。譬如虛空。一切世界。若
275a27	成若壞。常無增減。何以故。虛空無生故。諸佛
275a28	菩提。亦復如是。若成正覺。不成正覺。亦無增
275a29	減。何以故。菩提無相無非相。無一無種種故。
275b01	佛子。假使有人。能化作恒河沙等心。一一心
275b02	復化作恒河沙等佛。皆無色無形無相。如是
275b03	盡恒河沙等劫。無有休息。佛子。於汝意云何。
275b04	彼人化心。化作如來。凡有幾何。如來性起妙
275b05	德菩薩言。如我解於仁所說義。化與不化。等
275b06	無有別。云何問言凡有幾何。普賢菩薩言。善
275b07	哉善哉。佛子。如汝所說。設一切眾生。於一念
275b08	中。悉成正覺。與不成正覺。等無有異。何以
275b09	故。菩提無相故。若無有相。則無增無減。佛
275b10	子。菩薩摩訶薩。應如是知。成等正覺。同於菩
275b11	提。一相無相。如來成正覺時。以一相方便。入
275b12	善覺智三昧。入已於一成正覺廣大身。現一
275b13	切眾生數等身。住於身中。如一成正覺廣大
275b14	身。一切成正覺廣大身。悉亦如是。

简体字

佛子，譬如虛空，一切世界若成若坏，常无增减。何以故？虚空无生故。诸佛菩提亦复如是，若成正觉、不成正觉，亦无增减。何以故？菩提无相、无非相，无一、无种种故。佛子，假使有人能化作恒河沙等心，一一心复化作恒河沙等佛，皆无色、无形、无相，如是尽恒河沙等劫无有休息。佛子，于汝意云何？彼人化心，化作如来，凡有几何？"

如来性起妙德菩萨言："如我解于仁所说义，化与不化等无有别，云何问言凡有几何？"

普贤菩萨言："善哉！善哉！佛子，如汝所说，设一切众生，于一念中悉成正觉，与不成正觉等无有异。何以故？菩提无相故；若无有相，则无增无减。佛子，菩萨摩诃萨应如是知成等正觉同于菩提一相无相。如来成正觉时，以一相方便入善觉智三昧；入已，于一成正觉广大身，现一切众生数等身住于身中。如一成正觉广大身，一切成正觉广大身悉亦如是。

Chapter 37 — *The Manifestation of the Tathāgata*

Sons of the Buddha, this is just as it is with empty space which, whether all worlds are created or destroyed, is never either increased or decreased. Why is this so? This is because empty space is unproduced. So too it is with the bodhi of all buddhas which, whether beings do or do not attain right enlightenment, is still neither increased nor decreased. And how is this so? This is because bodhi is neither possessed of signs nor signless and neither singular nor multifarious.

Sons of the Buddha, suppose that there was someone who was able to transformationally create a Ganges' sands number of minds who was then also able to transformationally create from every one of those minds a Ganges' sands number of buddhas, all of whom were formless, shapeless, and signless, and suppose he ceaselessly continued on in this same way to the exhaustion of a Ganges' sands number of kalpas. Sons of the Buddha, what do you think? How many transformationally created *tathāgatas* would that man have created from those transformationally created minds?

Then Sublime Qualities of the Manifestations of the Tathāgata's Nature Bodhisattva replied: "As I understand the meaning of what the Humane One has described, there would be no difference between transformationally created and not being transformationally created. Why then would one even pose the question as to how many there would be all together in such a circumstance?"

Samantabhadra Bodhisattva replied:

Good indeed! Good indeed! Son of the Buddha, it is just as you have declared. Even supposing that all beings attained right enlightenment in but a single mind-moment, this would be the same and no different from when they had not yet attained right enlightenment. And why is this so? This is because bodhi is signless. If it is signless, then it would be neither increased nor decreased.

Sons of the Buddha, the bodhisattva-mahāsattva should understand this in this way. Attainment of the universal and right enlightenment is identical to bodhi in that its singular sign is signlessness. When the Tathāgata attains right enlightenment, he uses the skillful means of this singular sign to enter the "thoroughly enlightened wisdom" samādhi. Having entered it, within the singular vast body in which he realizes right enlightenment, he manifests a number of bodies as numerous as all beings, all of which dwell within that body. Then, just as it is with that single vast body in which he attains right enlightenment, so too is this so with all the vast bodies in which right enlightenment is attained.

佛子。如來有如是等無量成正覺門。是故應知。如來所現身無有量。以無量故。說如來身。為無量界。等眾生界。佛子。菩薩摩訶薩。應知。如來身一毛孔中。有一切眾生數等諸佛身。何以故。如來成正覺身。究竟無生滅故。如一毛孔。遍法界。一切毛孔。悉亦如是。當知無有少許處空無佛身。何以故。如來成正覺。無處不至故。隨其所能。隨其勢力。於道場菩提樹下師子座上。以種種身。成等正覺。佛子。菩薩摩訶薩。應知。自心念念。常有佛成正覺。何以故。諸佛如來。不離此心成正覺故。如自心。一切眾生心。亦復如是。悉有如來成等正覺。廣大周遍。無處不有。不離不斷。無有休息。入不思議方便法門。佛子。菩薩摩訶薩。應如是知。如來成正覺。爾時。普賢菩薩摩訶薩。欲重明此義。而說頌言

　　正覺了知一切法　　無二離二悉平等
　　自性清淨如虛空　　我與非我不分別
　　如海印現眾生身　　以此說其為大海

佛子，如来有如是等无量成正觉门，是故应知如来所现身无有量；以无量故，说如来身为无量界、等众生界。佛子，菩萨摩诃萨应知如来身一毛孔中，有一切众生数等诸佛身。何以故？如来成正觉身究竟无生灭故。如一毛孔遍法界，一切毛孔悉亦如是，当知无有少许处空无佛身。何以故？如来成正觉，无处不至故；随其所能，随其势力，于道场菩提树下师子座上，以种种身成等正觉。佛子，菩萨摩诃萨应知自心念念常有佛成正觉。何以故？诸佛如来不离此心成正觉故。如自心，一切众生心亦复如是，悉有如来成等正觉，广大周遍，无处不有，不离不断，无有休息，入不思议方便法门。佛子，菩萨摩诃萨应如是知如来成正觉。"

　　尔时，普贤菩萨摩诃萨欲重明此义而说颂言：
　　"正觉了知一切法，无二离二悉平等，
　　　自性清净如虚空，我与非我不分别。
　　　如海印现众生身，以此说其为大海；

Chapter 37 — The Manifestation of the Tathāgata

Sons of the Buddha, the Tathāgata has countless gateways such as these associated with the attainment of right enlightenment. One should therefore realize that the bodies manifested by the Tathāgata are measureless. Because they are measureless, it is said of the Tathāgata's bodies that they constitute a measureless realm equal in number to the realm of beings.

Sons of the Buddha, the bodhisattva-mahāsattva should realize that, in but a single pore of the Tathāgata's body, there are buddha bodies equal to the number of all beings' bodies. And how is this so? This is because, the body in which the Tathāgata attains right enlightenment is ultimately neither produced nor destroyed. Just as a single pore pervades the Dharma realm, so too is this true of all such pores. One should realize that there is not even the smallest empty place in which there is no buddha body. And how is this so? This is because, when the Tathāgata attains right enlightenment, there is no place he does not reach. In accordance with his abilities and in accordance with his powers, as he is seated on the lion throne at the site of enlightenment beneath the bodhi tree, he attains the universal and right enlightenment with many different types of bodies.

Sons of the Buddha, the bodhisattva-mahāsattva should realize that, within one's own mind, in each successive mind-moment, buddhas are always attaining right enlightenment. How is this so? This is because, it is not apart from this very mind that all buddhas, the *tathāgatas*, attain right enlightenment. And just as it is with one's own mind, so too it is with the minds of all beings. In all of them, there are *tathāgatas* attaining the universal and right enlightenment which, vast and universally pervasive, has no place in which it is not present. It is never abandoned, never cut off, and never ceases. So it is that one enters the gateway of inconceivable skillful means.

Sons of the Buddha, it is in these ways that the bodhisattva-mahāsattva should know the Tathāgata's attainment of right enlightenment.

At that time, wishing to once again clarify the meaning of this, Samantabhadra Bodhisattva-mahāsattva then spoke these verses:

> The Rightly Enlightened One completely knows all dharmas
> as non-dual, apart from duality, as all of a uniform equality,
> as possessed of an essential nature of purity comparable to space,
> and as not involving discriminations regarding "self" or "not-self."
>
> Just as the ocean reflects the bodies of beings
> and because of this is said to be "the great ocean,"

正體字

275c05	菩提普印諸心行　　是故說名為正覺
275c06	譬如世界有成敗　　而於虛空不增減
275c07	一切諸佛出世間　　菩提一相恒無相
275c08	如人化心化作佛　　化與不化[1]性無異
275c09	一切眾生成菩提　　成與不成無增減
275c10	佛有三昧名善覺　　菩提樹下入此定
275c11	放眾生等無量光　　開悟群品如蓮敷
275c12	如三世劫剎眾生　　所有心念及根欲
275c13	如是數等身皆現　　是故正覺名無量
275c14	佛子。菩薩摩訶薩。應云何知如來應正等覺
275c15	轉法輪。佛子。菩薩摩訶薩。應如是知。如來以
275c16	心自在力。無起無轉。而轉法輪。知一切法。恒
275c17	無起故。以三種轉。斷所應斷。而轉法輪。知一
275c18	切法。離邊[2]見故。離欲際非際。而轉法輪。入
275c19	一切法。虛空際故。無有言說。而轉法輪。知一
275c20	切法。不可說故。究竟寂滅。而轉法輪。知一切
275c21	法。涅槃性故。[3]一切文字。一切言語。而轉法
275c22	輪。如來音聲。無處不至故。知聲如響。而轉法
275c23	輪。了於諸法。真實性故。

简体字

菩提普印诸心行，是故说名为正觉。
譬如世界有成败，而于虚空不增减；
一切诸佛出世间，菩提一相恒无相。
如人化心化作佛，化与不化性无异；
一切众生成菩提，成与不成无增减。
佛有三昧名善觉，菩提树下入此定，
放众生等无量光，开悟群品如莲敷。
如三世劫刹众生，所有心念及根欲，
如是数等身皆现，是故正觉名无量。

"佛子，菩萨摩诃萨应云何知如来、应、正等觉转法轮？佛子，菩萨摩诃萨应如是知如来以心自在力无起无转而转法轮，知一切法恒无起故；以三种转断所应断而转法轮，知一切法离边见故；离欲际、非际而转法轮，入一切法虚空际故；无有言说而转法轮，知一切法不可说故；究竟寂灭而转法轮，知一切法涅槃性故；以一切文字、一切言语而转法轮，如来音声无处不至故；知声如响而转法轮，了于诸法真实性故；

so too, bodhi everywhere reflects all thoughts and actions
and is therefore described as "right enlightenment."

Just as when the worlds undergo creation and destruction,
empty space is still not thereby either increased or decreased,
so too, when all buddhas appear in the world,
bodhi still has but a single sign, that of being forever signless.

If someone conjured minds and transformed them into buddhas—
conjured and not-conjured, the nature of the matter would not differ.
So too, even if all beings were to realize bodhi, both after realization
and before realization, it would neither increase nor decrease.

The Buddha has a samādhi called "thoroughly enlightened wisdom."
It is beneath the bodhi tree that he enters this meditative absorption,
emanates countless light rays as numerous as beings,
and then awakens the many beings as if causing lotuses to bloom.

It is because of the manifestation of bodies as numerous
as the thoughts, faculties, and inclinations of all beings
throughout all the kalpas and *kṣetras* of the three periods of time
that right enlightenment is therefore described as "measureless."

Sons of the Buddha, how should the bodhisattva-mahāsattva know the turning of the Dharma wheel as accomplished by the Tathāgata, the Arhat, the One of Right and Universal Enlightenment? Sons of the Buddha, the bodhisattva-mahāsattva should know it in these ways:

> Through the sovereign power of the mind and without any arising and without any turning, the Tathāgata turns the wheel of Dharma, for he knows all dharmas as forever unarisen;
>
> Through three kinds of turning by which one cuts off what should be cut off he turns the wheel of Dharma, for he knows all dharmas transcend the extreme views;
>
> Through transcendence of both the extreme of desire and the extreme of its negation, he turns the wheel of Dharma, for he has penetrated to the utmost that all dharmas are like space;
>
> Without resort to speech, he turns the wheel of Dharma, for he knows all dharmas as ineffable;
>
> Through ultimate quiescence, he turns the wheel of Dharma, for he knows all dharmas as having the nature of nirvāṇa;
>
> Through all languages and through all forms of speech, he turns the wheel of Dharma, for there is no place the voice of the Tathāgata does not reach;
>
> Through knowing all sounds as like echoes, he turns the wheel of Dharma, for he completely understands the true nature of all dharmas;

正體字

於一音中。出一切
音。而轉法輪。畢竟無主故。無遺無盡。而轉
法輪。內外無著故。佛子。譬如一切文字語言。
盡未來劫。說不可盡。佛轉法輪。亦復如是。一
切文字。安立顯示。無有休息。無有窮盡。佛
子。如來法輪。悉入一切語言文字。而無所住。
譬如書字。普入一切事。一切語。一切算數。一
切世間出世間處。而無所住。如來音聲。亦復
如是。普入一切處。一切眾生。一切法。一切
業。一切報中。而無所住。一切眾生。種種語
言。皆悉不離如來法輪。何以故。言音實相。即
法輪故。佛子。菩薩摩訶薩。於如來轉法輪。應
如是知。復次佛子。菩薩摩訶薩。欲知如來。所
轉法輪。應知如來法輪。所出生處。何等為如
來法輪。所出生處。佛子。如來隨一切眾生。心
行欲樂。無量差別。出若干音聲。而轉法輪。佛
子。如來應正等覺。有三昧。名究竟無礙無畏。
入此三昧已。於成正覺。一一身一一口。各出
一切眾生數等言音。一一音中。眾音具足。各
各差別。而轉法輪。令一切眾生。皆生歡喜。

简体字

于一音中出一切音而转法轮，毕竟无主故；无遗无尽而转法轮，内外无著故。佛子，譬如一切文字语言，尽未来劫说不可尽；佛转法轮亦复如是，一切文字安立显示，无有休息，无有穷尽。佛子，如来法轮悉入一切语言文字而无所住。譬如书字，普入一切事、一切语、一切算数、一切世间出世间处而无所住；如来音声亦复如是，普入一切处、一切众生、一切法、一切业、一切报中而无所住。一切众生种种语言，皆悉不离如来法轮。何以故？言音实相即法轮故。佛子，菩萨摩诃萨于如来转法轮应如是知。

"复次，佛子，菩萨摩诃萨欲知如来所转法轮，应知如来法轮所出生处。何等为如来法轮所出生处？佛子，如来随一切众生心行欲乐无量差别，出若干音声而转法轮。佛子，如来、应、正等觉有三昧，名究竟无碍无畏，入此三昧已，于成正觉一一身、一一口，各出一切众生数等言音，一一音中众音具足，各各差别而转法轮，令一切众生皆生欢喜。

Through sending forth all voices from within a single voice, he turns the wheel of Dharma, for there is ultimately no subjective agent;[66] and

Through doing so endlessly and without omission, he turns the wheel of Dharma, for he is free of any inward or outward attachment.

Sons of the Buddha, just as one could never finish describing all that is expressed through language and speech even if one attempted to do so until the very end of all future kalpas, so too it is with the Buddha's turning of the wheel of Dharma for, even if one used every kind of language and ceaselessly described all that he has thereby established and revealed, one would never come to the end of it.

Sons of the Buddha, the Tathāgata's turning of the Dharma wheel enters all speech and language and yet does not abide there. Just as the alphabet everywhere enters all affairs, all speech, all numerical calculations, and all worldly and world-transcending circumstances and yet does not abide there, so too it is with [what has been described by] the Tathāgata's voice, for it everywhere enters all places, all beings, all dharmas, all karmic actions, and all karmic retributions, and yet it still has no place in which it abides.

None of the many different kinds of language of all beings exist apart from [what has been taught through] the Tathāgata's turning of the Dharma wheel. And how is this so? It is because the true character of words and speech is identical to the wheel of Dharma. Sons of the Buddha, the bodhisattva-mahāsattva should know the Tathāgata's turning of the Dharma wheel in this way.

Moreover, Sons of the Buddha, the bodhisattva-mahāsattva who wishes to know the Dharma wheel as it is turned by the Tathāgata should know the place of origination of the Tathāgata's wheel of Dharma. What then is the place of origination of the Tathāgata's wheel of Dharma? Sons of the Buddha, it is in accordance with the incalculably many differences in all beings' mental actions and inclinations that he sends forth just so very many voices in his turning of the wheel of Dharma.

Sons of the Buddha, the Tathāgata, the Arhat, the One of Right and Universal Enlightenment, has a samādhi known as "ultimate unimpeded fearlessness." Having entered this samādhi, in his state of realization of right enlightenment, from every mouth of every one of his bodies, he emanates voices as numerous as all beings. Every one of those voices is itself possessed of many voices, each of

正體字	能 276a14 ‖ 如是知轉法輪者。當知此人。則為隨順一切 276a15 ‖ 佛法。不如是知。則非隨順。佛子。諸菩薩摩訶 276a16 ‖ 薩。應如是知。佛轉法輪。普入無量眾生界故 276a17 ‖ 爾時普賢菩薩摩訶薩。欲重明此義。而說頌 276a18 ‖ 言 276a19 ‖ 　如來法輪無所轉　三世無起亦無得 276a20 ‖ 　譬如文字無盡時　十力法輪亦如是 276a21 ‖ 　如字普入而無至　正[1]覺法輪亦復然 276a22 ‖ 　入諸言音無所入　能令眾生悉歡喜 276a23 ‖ 　佛有三昧名究竟　入此定已乃說法 276a24 ‖ 　一切眾生無有邊　普出其音令悟解 276a25 ‖ 　一一音中復更演　無量言音各差別 276a26 ‖ 　於世自在無分別　隨其欲樂普使聞 276a27 ‖ 　文字不從內外出　亦不失壞無積聚 276a28 ‖ 　而為眾生轉法輪　如是自在甚奇特 276a29 ‖ 佛子。菩薩摩訶薩。應云何知如來應正等覺。 276b01 ‖ 般涅槃。佛子。菩薩摩訶薩。欲知如來大涅槃 276b02 ‖ 者。當須了知根本自性。如真如涅槃。如來涅 276b03 ‖ 槃亦如是。如實際涅槃。如來涅槃亦如是。
简体字	能如是知转法轮者，当知此人则为随顺一切佛法；不如是知，则非随顺。佛子，诸菩萨摩诃萨应如是知佛转法轮，普入无量众生界故。" 　　尔时，普贤菩萨摩诃萨欲重明此义而说颂言： 　　"如来法轮无所转，三世无起亦无得， 　　譬如文字无尽时，十力法轮亦如是。 　　如字普入而无至，正觉法轮亦复然， 　　入诸言音无所入，能令众生悉欢喜。 　　佛有三昧名究竟，入此定已乃说法， 　　一切众生无有边，普出其音令悟解。 　　一一音中复更演，无量言音各差别， 　　于世自在无分别，随其欲乐普使闻。 　　文字不从内外出，亦不失坏无积聚， 　　而为众生转法轮，如是自在甚奇特。 　　"佛子，菩萨摩诃萨应云何知如来、应、正等觉般涅槃？佛子，菩萨摩诃萨欲知如来大涅槃者，当须了知根本自性。如真如涅槃，如来涅槃亦如是；如实际涅槃，如来涅槃亦如是；

Chapter 37 — The Manifestation of the Tathāgata

which in turn is different in how it turns the wheel of Dharma and causes all beings to be filled with joyous delight.

One should realize that whoever is able to know the turning of the Dharma wheel in this way is one who accords with the Dharma of all buddhas. Whoever does not know it in this way is not one who accords with it.

Sons of the Buddha, all bodhisattva-mahāsattvas should know the Buddha's turning of the Dharma wheel in this way because it everywhere enters the countless realms of beings.

At that time, wishing to once again clarify the meaning of this, Samantabhadra Bodhisattva-mahāsattva then spoke these verses:

> When the Tathāgata turns the Dharma wheel, nothing at all is turned,
> In all three times, there is neither any arising nor any attainment.
> Just as there will be no time when all written words are exhausted,
> so too it is with the Dharma wheel as turned by the Ten-Powered One.
>
> Just as words can enter all places and yet still never reach them,
> so too it is with the Dharma wheel of the Rightly Enlightened One.
> It enters all verbal expressions and yet has nothing at all it enters
> even as it is still able to cause all beings to feel joyous delight.
>
> The Buddha has a samādhi called "ultimate unimpeded fearlessness."
> After he has entered this concentration, he then speaks the Dharma.
> For all the countless beings, he everywhere speaks in their languages,
> thereby causing them to awaken and thus then understand.
>
> Every one of those voices in turn additionally expounds
> in countlessly many languages, each of which are different,
> with which he freely holds forth in the world without discrimination,
> adapting to their individual dispositions, thus enabling all to hear.
>
> Those words do not arise from within or from without,
> are never lost, and are free of any accumulation,
> yet he thereby turns the wheel of Dharma for the sake of beings
> with just such sovereign mastery in his very extraordinary manner.

Sons of the Buddha, how should the bodhisattva-mahāsattva know the *parinirvāṇa* of the Tathāgata, the Arhat, the One of Right and Universal Enlightenment? Sons of the Buddha, the bodhisattva-mahāsattva who wishes to know the great nirvāṇa of the Tathāgata should and must completely know its fundamental and essential nature:

> Just as it is with the nirvāṇa of true suchness, so too it is with the Tathāgata's nirvāṇa;
> Just as it is with the nirvāṇa of the apex of reality, so too it is with the Tathāgata's nirvāṇa;

正體字

如法界涅槃。如來涅槃亦如是。如虛空涅槃。如來涅槃亦如是。如法性涅槃。如來涅槃亦如是。如離欲際涅槃。如來涅槃亦如是。如無相際涅槃。如來涅槃亦如是。如我性際涅槃。如來涅槃亦如是。如一切法性際涅槃。如來涅槃亦如是。如真如際涅槃。如來涅槃亦如是。何以故。涅槃無生無出故。若法無生無出。則無有滅。佛子。如來不為菩薩。說諸如來。究竟涅槃。亦不為彼。示現其事。何以故。為欲令見一切如來。常住其前。於一念中。見過去未來。一切諸佛。色相圓滿。皆如現在。亦不起二不二想。何以故。菩薩摩訶薩。永離一切諸想著故。佛子。諸佛如來。為令眾生。生欣樂故。出現於世。欲令眾生。生戀慕故。示現涅槃。而實如來。無有出世。亦無涅槃。何以故。如來常住清淨法界。隨眾生心。示現涅槃。佛子。譬如日出。普照世間。於一切淨水器中。影無不現。普遍眾處。而無來往。

简体字

如法界涅槃，如来涅槃亦如是；如虚空涅槃，如来涅槃亦如是；如法性涅槃，如来涅槃亦如是；如离欲际涅槃，如来涅槃亦如是；如无相际涅槃，如来涅槃亦如是；如我性际涅槃，如来涅槃亦如是；如一切法性际涅槃，如来涅槃亦如是；如真如际涅槃，如来涅槃亦如是。何以故？涅槃无生无出故；若法无生无出，则无有灭。佛子，如来不为菩萨说诸如来究竟涅槃，亦不为彼示现其事。何以故？为欲令见一切如来常住其前，于一念中见过去、未来一切诸佛色相圆满皆如现在，亦不起二、不二想。何以故？菩萨摩诃萨永离一切诸想著故。佛子，诸佛如来为令众生生欣乐故，出现于世；欲令众生生恋慕故，示现涅槃；而实如来无有出世，亦无涅槃。何以故？如来常住清净法界，随众生心示现涅槃。佛子，譬如日出，普照世间，于一切净水器中影无不现，普遍众处而无来往，

Just as it is with the nirvāṇa of the Dharma realm, so too it is with the Tathāgata's nirvāṇa;
Just as it is with the nirvāṇa of empty space, so too it is with the Tathāgata's nirvāṇa;
Just as it is with the nirvāṇa of the nature of dharmas, so too it is with the Tathāgata's nirvāṇa;
Just as it is with the nirvāṇa of the apex of dispassion, so too it is with the Tathāgata's nirvāṇa;
Just as it is with the nirvāṇa of the apex of signlessness, so too it is with the Tathāgata's nirvāṇa;
Just as it is with the nirvāṇa of the apex of the nature of a self, so too it is with the Tathāgata's nirvāṇa;
Just as it is with the nirvāṇa of the apex of the nature of all dharmas, so too it is with the Tathāgata's nirvāṇa; and
Just as it is with the nirvāṇa of the apex of true suchness, so too it is with the Tathāgata's nirvāṇa.

And how is this so? This is because nirvāṇa has no arising and no manifestation. If a dharma has no arising and no manifestation, then it has no cessation.

Sons of the Buddha, the Tathāgata does not speak about the *tathāgatas'* ultimate nirvāṇa for the bodhisattvas, nor does he show that matter to them. Why not? He prefers to enable them to see all *tathāgatas* always abiding directly before them so that, in but a single mind-moment, they also see all buddhas of the past and future with their perfectly fulfilled physical marks just as if they were here now, doing so without raising any dual or non-dual perceptions. And why? Because the bodhisattva-mahāsattvas have forever abandoned all attachments to perceptions.

Sons of the Buddha, it is in order to enable beings to find happiness that all buddhas, *tathāgatas,* appear in the world and it is out of a wish to cause beings to develop a fond admiration for it that they manifest the appearance of nirvāṇa. However, in truth, the Tathāgata has no emergence into the world nor does he have any nirvāṇa. How is this so? The Tathāgata forever dwells in the pure Dharma realm. It is as an adaptation to the minds of beings that he manifests the appearance of entering nirvāṇa.

Sons of the Buddha, by way of analogy, this is just as when the sun rises, it everywhere illuminates the world and, of all of its vessels containing pure water, there are none in which its reflection does not then appear. Its illumination reaches everywhere to all the many places even as it has neither any coming nor any going.

正體字

或一器破。便不現影。佛
子。於汝意云何。彼影不現。為日咎不。答言不
也。但由器壞。非日有咎。佛子。如來智日。亦
復如是。普現法界。無前無後。一切眾生。淨心
器中。佛無不現。心器常淨。常見佛身。若心濁
器破。則不得見。佛子。若有眾生。應以涅槃。
而得度者。如來則為示現涅槃。而實如來。無
生無歿。無有滅度。佛子。譬如火大。於一切世
間。能為火事。或時一處。其火息滅。於意云
何。豈一切世間。火皆滅耶。答言不也。佛子。
如來應正等覺。亦復如是。於一切世界。施作
佛事。或於一世界。能事已畢。示入涅槃。豈一
切世界。諸佛如來。悉皆滅度。佛子。菩薩摩訶
薩。應如是知。如來應正等覺。大般涅槃。復次
佛子。譬如幻師。善明幻術。以幻術力。於三千
大千世界。一切國土。城邑聚落。示現幻身。以
幻力持。經劫而住。然於餘處。幻事已訖。隱身
不現。

简体字

或一器破便不现影。佛子，于汝意云何？彼影不现为日咎不？"
　　答言："不也。但由器坏，非日有咎。"
　　"佛子，如来智日亦复如是，普现法界无前无后，一切众生净心器中佛无不现，心器常净常见佛身，若心浊器破则不得见。佛子，若有众生应以涅槃而得度者，如来则为示现涅槃，而实如来无生、无殁、无有灭度。佛子，譬如火大，于一切世间能为火事，或时一处其火息灭。于意云何？岂一切世间火皆灭耶？"
　　答言："不也。"
　　"佛子，如来、应、正等觉亦复如是，于一切世界施作佛事，或于一世界能事已毕示入涅槃，岂一切世界诸佛如来悉皆灭度？佛子，菩萨摩诃萨应如是知如来、应、正等觉大般涅槃。复次，佛子，譬如幻师善明幻术，以幻术力，于三千大千世界一切国土、城邑、聚落示现幻身，以幻力持经劫而住；然于余处，幻事已讫，隐身不现。

Sometimes one of these vessels breaks at which point it no longer shows the sun's reflection.

Sons of the Buddha, what do you think? When that reflection no longer appears, is that the fault of the sun, or not?

They replied: "No. It was only because the vessel was broken and not due to any fault on the part of the sun."

Sons of the Buddha, so too it is with the Tathāgata's wisdom sun. In its appearance everywhere throughout the Dharma realm, there is no before or after involved. Among all beings' vessels of the pure mind, there are none in which the Buddha does not appear. Wherever the vessel of the mind is forever pure, one always sees the body of the Buddha. If the mind becomes turbid and the vessel thereby breaks, then one is no longer able to see it.

Sons of the Buddha, wherever there is any being who should be able to achieve liberation through the appearance of nirvāṇa, the Tathāgata then manifests the appearance of nirvāṇa for him even though, in truth, the Tathāgata has no birth, has no death, and has no passage into nirvāṇa.

Sons of the Buddha, by way of analogy, fire as one of the great elements is able to create fires throughout the world, but sometimes in a particular time and place, its fire is extinguished. What do you think? Could it be that, as a result, all of the world's fires would be extinguished?

They replied: "No, that would not occur."

Sons of the Buddha, so too it is with the Tathāgata, the Arhat, the One of Right and Universal Enlightenment, who carries out the Buddha's works in all worlds. Sometimes, in a single world, when the works he has been able to accomplish have been concluded, he manifests the appearance of entry into nirvāṇa. How could it be then that, as a consequence, all buddhas, *tathāgatas*, in all worlds would then pass into nirvāṇa?

Sons of the Buddha, it is in this way that the bodhisattva-mahāsattva should know the great *parinirvāṇa* of the Tathāgata, the Arhat, the One of Right and Universal Enlightenment.

Moreover, Sons of the Buddha, it is as if there was a master magician who, understanding well the magical arts, used the powers of his magical conjuration to manifest the appearance of conjured bodies in all the cities and villages of all countries throughout the worlds of the great trichiliocosm and then used those magical powers to sustain their appearance throughout the entire kalpa. Then, in some other place where his magical performances had been finished, he allowed that conjured body to disappear.

正體字

佛子。於汝意云何。彼大幻師。豈於一處。隱身不現便一切處。皆隱滅耶。答言不也。佛子。如來應正等覺。亦復如是。善知無量智慧方便。種種幻術。於一切法界。普現其身。持令常住。盡未來際。或於一處。隨眾生心。所作事訖。示現涅槃。豈以一處。示入涅槃。便謂一切悉皆滅度。佛子。菩薩摩訶薩。應如是知如來應正等覺大般涅槃。復次佛子。如來應正等覺。示涅槃時。入不動三昧。入此三昧已。於一一身。各放無量百千億那由他大光明。一一光明各出阿僧祇蓮華。一一蓮華。各有不可說。妙寶華蘂。一一華蘂有師子座。一一座上。皆有如來。結[2]跏趺坐。其佛身數。正與一切眾生數等。皆具上妙功德莊嚴。從本願力之所生起。若有眾生。善根熟者。見佛身已。則皆受化。然彼佛身。盡未來際。究竟安住。隨宜化度一切眾生。未曾失時。佛子。如來身者。無有方處。非實非虛。但以諸佛本誓願力。

简体字

佛子，于汝意云何？彼大幻师岂于一处隐身不现，便一切处皆隐灭耶？"

答言："不也。"

"佛子，如来、应、正等觉亦复如是，善知无量智慧方便种种幻术，于一切法界普现其身，持令常住尽未来际；或于一处，随众生心，所作事讫，示现涅槃。岂以一处示入涅槃，便谓一切悉皆灭度？佛子，菩萨摩诃萨应如是知如来、应、正等觉大般涅槃。

"复次，佛子，如来、应、正等觉示涅槃时，入不动三昧；入此三昧已，于一一身各放无量百千亿那由他大光明，一一光明各出阿僧祇莲华，一一莲华各有不可说妙宝华蕊，一一华蕊有师子座，一一座上皆有如来结跏趺坐，其佛身数正与一切众生数等，皆具上妙功德庄严，从本愿力之所生起。若有众生善根熟者，见佛身已，则皆受化。然彼佛身，尽未来际究竟安住，随宜化度一切众生未曾失时。佛子，如来身者，无有方处，非实非虚，但以诸佛本誓愿力，

Sons of the Buddha, what do you think? Could it be that, having allowed a single body in a single place to disappear, all of them everywhere would therefore disappear?

They replied: "No, that would not occur."

Sons of the Buddha, so too it is with the Tathāgata, the Arhat, the One of Right and Universal Enlightenment. Being thoroughly cognizant of the many different kinds of supernatural arts used in implementing countless types of wise skillful means, he manifests his bodies everywhere throughout the entire Dharma realm and sustains their appearance so that they are allowed to abide forever to the very exhaustion of future time. It may happen that, in a particular single place, the works he has done in accordance with those beings' minds come to an end, whereupon he manifests entry into nirvāṇa there. How could one consequently claim that, just because he manifested entry into nirvāṇa in that one place, he would therefore pass into nirvāṇa everywhere?

Sons of the Buddha, it is in this way that the bodhisattva-mahāsattva should know the great *parinirvāṇa* of the Tathāgata, the Arhat, the One of Right and Universal Enlightenment.

Moreover, Sons of the Buddha, when the Tathāgata, the Arhat, the One of Right and Universal Enlightenment, manifests entry into nirvāṇa, he enters the "unshakable" samādhi and, having entered this samādhi, every one of his bodies then emanates incalculably many hundreds of thousands of *koṭīs* of *nayutas* of great light rays. Each of those light rays then sends forth an *asaṃkhyeya* of lotus flowers. Each of those lotus flowers has ineffably many marvelously bejeweled flower stamens.

Each of those flower stamens has a lion throne on it and, on each of those thrones, there is a *tathāgata* seated there in the lotus posture. The number of all of those buddha bodies is precisely equivalent to that of all beings. All of them possess supremely marvelous qualities of adornment which originate from the power of original vows.

Wherever there are any beings with ripened roots of goodness who see one of these buddha bodies, they all receive instruction. In this way, those buddha bodies continue to abide until the ultimate end of all future time during which, adapting to whatever is fitting, they teach and liberate all beings, never missing the right time in doing so.

Sons of the Buddha, the body of the Tathāgata has no location and is neither real nor false. It is only due to the power of the original vows of all buddhas that, if there are beings capable of being

正體字

眾
276c27‖ 生堪度。則便出現。菩薩摩訶薩。應如是知。如
276c28‖ 來應正等覺。大般涅槃。佛子。如來住於無量
276c29‖ 無礙。究竟法界。虛空界。真如法性。無生無滅。
277a01‖ 及以實際。為諸眾生。隨時示現。本願持故。無
277a02‖ 有休息。不捨一切眾生。一切剎。一切法。爾時
277a03‖ 普賢菩薩摩訶薩。欲重明此義。而說頌言
277a04‖ 　如日舒光[1]照法界　　器壞水漏影隨滅
277a05‖ 　最勝智日亦如是　　眾生無信見涅槃
277a06‖ 　如火世間作火事　　於一城邑或時息
277a07‖ 　人中最勝遍法界　　化事訖處示終盡
277a08‖ 　幻師現身一切剎　　能事畢處則便謝
277a09‖ 　如來化訖亦復然　　於餘國土常見佛
277a10‖ 　佛有三昧名不動　　化眾生訖入此定
277a11‖ 　一念身放無量光　　光出蓮華華有佛
277a12‖ 　佛身無數等法界　　有福眾生所能見
277a13‖ 　如是無數一一身　　壽命莊嚴皆具足
277a14‖ 　如無生性佛出興　　如無滅性佛涅槃
277a15‖ 　言辭譬[*]諭悉皆斷　　一切義成無與等
277a16‖ 佛子。菩薩摩訶薩。應云何知於如來應正等
277a17‖ 覺。見聞親近。所種善根。

简体字

众生堪度则便出现。菩萨摩诃萨应如是知如来、应、正等觉大般涅槃。佛子，如来住于无量无碍究竟法界、虚空界，真如法性无生无灭及以实际，为诸众生随时示现；本愿持故，无有休息，不舍一切众生、一切刹、一切法。"

尔时，普贤菩萨摩诃萨欲重明此义而说颂言：

"如日舒光照法界，器坏水漏影随灭；
最胜智日亦如是，众生无信见涅槃。
如火世间作火事，于一城邑或时息；
人中最胜遍法界，化事讫处示终尽。
幻师现身一切刹，能事毕处则便谢；
如来化讫亦复然，于余国土常见佛。
佛有三昧名不动，化众生讫入此定，
一念身放无量光，光出莲华华有佛。
佛身无数等法界，有福众生所能见，
如是无数一一身，寿命庄严皆具足。
如无生性佛出兴，如无灭性佛涅槃，
言辞喻悉皆断，一切义成无与等。

"佛子，菩萨摩诃萨应云何知于如来、应、正等觉见闻亲近所种善根？佛子，

liberated, they then appear. It is in this way that the bodhisattva-mahāsattva should know the great *parinirvāṇa* of the Tathāgata, the Arhat, the One of Right and Universal Enlightenment.

Sons of the Buddha, the Tathāgata abides in the measureless, unimpeded, and ultimate Dharma realm, the realm of empty space, the true suchness nature of dharmas, beyond production or destruction, in the apex of reality. Sustained by original vows, he then appears for beings in accordance with the appropriate time, doing so ceaselessly, never forsaking any being, any *kṣetra*, or any dharma.

Then, wishing to once again clarify the meaning of this, Samantabhadra Bodhisattva-mahāsattva then spoke these verses:

> Just as when the sun shines its light, illuminating the Dharma realm,
> when broken vessels' waters flow out, its reflections then disappear,
> so too it is with the wisdom sun of the Supreme One
> which beings without faith see as disappearing into nirvāṇa.
>
> This is just as when the fire element creates fires in the world,
> and then, in one town, perhaps the fires are temporarily extinguished,
> so too, the most supreme of men is everywhere in the Dharma realm,
> yet, when teaching works end somewhere, he manifests his final end.
>
> It is just as if a master conjurer manifested bodies in all *kṣetras*,
> then, when finishing his work in some place, he was able to disappear.
> When the Tathāgata's teachings end somewhere, he too does the same,
> but, even so, in other lands, one still always sees the Buddha.
>
> The Buddha has a samādhi known as "unshakable."
> On finishing teachings for particular beings, he enters this absorption.
> In but a single mind-moment, his body emanates countless light rays.
> Their light then manifests lotuses and those flowers all have buddhas.
>
> Those countless buddhas' bodies equal to the Dharma realm's beings
> are such that beings possessed of merit are able then to see them.
> Each of those countless bodies such as these
> are replete in both their life spans and their adornments.
>
> Though he has the nature of nonproduction, the Buddha still appears.
> Though he has the nature of nondestruction, Buddha enters nirvāṇa.
> Such phenomena cut short all verbal descriptions and analogies.
> Perfectly realizing every form of meaning, he is entirely without peer.

Sons of the Buddha, how should the bodhisattva-mahāsattva know the roots of goodness which are planted through seeing, hearing, or drawing near to the Tathāgata, the Arhat, the One of Right and Universal Enlightenment? Sons of the Buddha, the

正體字

佛子。菩薩摩訶薩。
應知於如來所。見聞親近。所種善根。皆悉不
虛。出生無盡覺慧故。離於一切障難故。決定
至究竟故。無有虛誑故。一切願滿故。不盡有
為行故。隨順無為智故。生諸佛智故。盡未來
際故。成一切種勝行故。到無功用智地故。佛
子。譬如丈夫。食少金剛。終竟不[2]消。要穿其
身。出在於外。何以故。金剛不與肉身雜穢。而
同止故。於如來所。種少善根。亦復如是。要穿
一切有為諸行。煩惱身過。到於無為究竟智
處。何以故。此少善根。不與有為諸行煩惱。而
共住故。佛子。假使乾草。積同須彌。投火於
中。如芥子許。必皆燒盡。何以故。火能燒故。
於如來所。種少善根。亦復如是。必能燒盡一
切煩惱。究竟得於無餘涅槃。何以故。此少善
根。性究竟故。

简体字

菩萨摩诃萨应知于如来所见闻亲近所种善根皆悉不虚，出生无尽觉慧故，离于一切障难故，决定至于究竟故，无有虚诳故，一切愿满故，不尽有为行故，随顺无为智故，生诸佛智故，尽未来际故，成一切种胜行故，到无功用智地故。佛子，譬如丈夫，食少金刚，终竟不消，要穿其身，出在于外。何以故？金刚不与肉身杂秽而同止故。于如来所种少善根亦复如是，要穿一切有为诸行烦恼身过，到于无为究竟智处。何以故？此少善根不与有为诸行烦恼而共住故。佛子，假使干草积同须弥，投火于中如芥子许，必皆烧尽。何以故？火能烧故。于如来所种少善根亦复如是，必能烧尽一切烦恼，究竟得于无余涅槃。何以故？此少善根性究竟故。

bodhisattva-mahāsattva should know that none of the roots of goodness planted in the presence of the Tathāgata through seeing him, hearing him, or drawing close to him are planted in vain. This is:

Because they produce the inexhaustible wisdom of enlightenment;

Because they allow one to leave behind the difficulties of all obstacles;

Because they ensure one will definitely reach the ultimate;

Because they are free of any false or deceptive aspects;

Because they enable one to fulfill all vows;

Because they lead one to never end one's practices in the realm of the conditioned;

Because they accord with unconditioned wisdom;

Because they produce the wisdom of all buddhas;

Because they continue on to the end of future time;

Because they lead to perfecting all the many kinds of supreme practices; and

Because they allow one to reach the ground of effortless wisdom.

Sons of the Buddha, by way of analogy, it is as if there were some great man who, having eaten a small piece of vajra, would then never finally be able to digest it, for it would pass through his body and be expelled to the outside. Why is this? This is because vajra cannot remain together with the various kinds of filth in the flesh body.

So too it is when one plants even a few roots of goodness in the presence of the Tathāgata. They will necessarily lead one to pass through and beyond all of the affliction-ridden body's practices in the realm of the conditioned and will finally lead one to reach the station of unconditioned ultimate wisdom. How is this so? It is because even these small roots of goodness will not remain together with the afflictions associated with conditioned practice.

Sons of the Buddha, even if one piled up a mass of dry grass the size of Mount Sumeru and then threw into it a flaming ember that was only the size of a mustard seed, it would still all definitely burn up. And why would this be so? This is because of fire's capacity to burn things. So too, even if one plants only small roots of goodness in the presence of the Tathāgata, one will still definitely be able to completely burn away all of one's afflictions and ultimately succeed in reaching the nirvāṇa without residue. And why is this? This is because of the ultimate nature of even these small roots of goodness.

正體字

佛子。譬如雪山。有藥王樹。名曰善見。若有見者。眼得清淨。若有聞者。耳得清淨。若有嗅者。鼻得清淨。若有嘗者。舌得清淨。若有觸者。身得清淨。若有眾生。取彼地土。亦能為作除病利益。佛子。如來應正等覺。無上藥王。亦復如是。能作一切饒益眾生。若有得見如來色身。眼得清淨。若有得聞如來名號。耳得清淨。若有得嗅如來戒香。鼻得清淨。若有得嘗如來法味。舌得清淨。具廣長舌。解語言法。若有得觸如來光者。身得清淨。究竟獲得無上法身。若於如來。生憶念者。則得念佛三昧清淨。若有眾生。供養如來。所經土地。及塔廟者。亦具善根。滅除一切諸煩惱患。得賢聖樂。佛子。我今告汝。設有眾生。見聞於佛。業障[3]纏覆。不生信樂。亦種善根。無空過者。乃至究竟。入於涅槃。佛子。菩薩摩訶薩。應如是知。於如來所。見聞親近。所種善根。悉離一切諸不善法。具足善法。佛子。如來以一切譬[*]諭。說種種事。無有譬[*]諭。能說此法。何以故。心智路絕。不思議故。

简体字

佛子，譬如雪山有药王树，名曰善见。若有见者，眼得清净；若有闻者，耳得清净；若有嗅者，鼻得清净；若有尝者，舌得清净；若有触者，身得清净；若有众生取彼地土，亦能为作除病利益。佛子，如来、应、正等觉无上药王亦复如是，能作一切饶益众生。若有得见如来色身，眼得清净；若有得闻如来名号，耳得清净；若有得嗅如来戒香，鼻得清净；若有得尝如来法味，舌得清净，具广长舌，解语言法；若有得触如来光者，身得清净，究竟获得无上法身；若于如来生忆念者，则得念佛三昧清净；若有众生供养如来所经土地及塔庙者，亦具善根，灭除一切诸烦恼患，得贤圣乐。佛子，我今告汝，设有众生见闻于佛，业障缠覆不生信乐，亦种善根无空过者，乃至究竟入于涅槃。佛子，菩萨摩诃萨应如是知于如来所见闻亲近所种善根，悉离一切诸不善法，具足善法。

"佛子，如来以一切譬喻说种种事，无有譬喻能说此法。何以故？心智路绝，不思议故。

Sons of the Buddha, by way of analogy, this is like the medicine king tree known as "Good to See" which grows in the Himalaya Mountains. When seen, the eyes become purified; when heard, the ears become purified; when smelled, the nose becomes purified; when tasted, the tongue becomes purified; and when touched, the body becomes purified. When any being so much as takes up some of its soil, that too can provide its healing benefits.

Sons of the Buddha, so too it is with the Tathāgata, the Arhat, the One of Right and Universal Enlightenment, the unexcelled physician king who is able to bestow every form of benefit on beings. If anyone is able to see the form body of the Tathāgata, his eyes will become purified; if anyone is able to hear the name of the Tathāgata, his ears will become purified; if anyone smells the fragrance of the Tathāgata's moral virtue, his nose will become purified; and if anyone is able to taste the flavor of the Tathāgata's Dharma, his tongue will become purified and he will possess the vast and long tongue and come to understand the dharma of languages. If anyone is able to be touched by the Tathāgata's light, his body will become purified and he will ultimately acquire the unexcelled Dharma body.

If anyone develops mindfulness of the Tathāgata, he will acquire the purification of the mindfulness-of-the-Buddha samādhi. If any being makes an offering to a spot of land the Tathāgata has passed through or makes an offering to one of his stupas or shrines, then he will acquire roots of goodness allowing him to extinguish all affliction-based troubles and he will also acquire the bliss of the worthies and the *āryas*.

Sons of the Buddha, I shall now tell you: Even if there is some being who sees or hears the Buddha, but then, due to being encumbered by karmic obstructions, fails to develop faith and feel happiness on this account, they still thereby plant roots of goodness which will not have been planted in vain, for even this will eventually culminate in his entering nirvāṇa.

Sons of the Buddha, it is in this way that the bodhisattva-mahāsattva should know the roots of goodness planted in the presence of the Tathāgata by seeing, hearing, or drawing near to him. This will in all cases lead to abandoning all bad dharmas and perfecting the good dharmas.

Sons of the Buddha, the Tathāgata uses all kinds of analogies to describe many different situations, yet he has no analogy adequate to describe this dharma. How is this so? This is because the road of intellectual knowledge ends here and because this matter is so inconceivable. All buddhas and bodhisattvas only use analogies

正體字

諸佛菩薩。但隨眾生心。令其歡喜。為說譬[*]諭。非是究竟。佛子。此法門。名為如來祕密之處。名一切世間所不能知。名入如來印。名開大智門。名示現如來種性。名成就一切菩薩。名一切世間所不能壞。名一向隨順如來境界。名能淨一切諸眾生界。名演說如來根本實性。不思議究竟法。佛子。此法門。如來不為[4]餘眾生說。唯為[5]趣向大乘菩薩說。唯為乘不思議乘菩薩說。此法門。不入一切餘眾生手。唯除諸菩薩摩訶薩。佛子。譬如轉輪聖王。所有七寶。因此寶故。顯示輪王。此寶不入餘眾生手。唯除第一夫人所生太子。具足成就聖王相者。若轉輪王。無此太子具眾德者。王命終後。此諸寶等。於七日中。悉皆散滅。佛子。此經珍寶。亦復如是。不入一切餘眾生手。唯除如來法王真子。生如來家。種如來相。諸善根者。佛子。若無此等佛之真子。如是法門。不久散滅。何以故。一切二乘。不聞此經。何況受持。讀誦書寫。

简体字

诸佛菩萨但随众生心，令其欢喜，为说譬喻，非是究竟。佛子，此法门名为如来秘密之处，名一切世间所不能知，名入如来印，名开大智门，名示现如来种性，名成就一切菩萨，名一切世间所不能坏，名一向随顺如来境界，名能净一切诸众生界，名演说如来根本实性不思议究竟法。佛子，此法门，如来不为余众生说，唯为趣向大乘菩萨说，唯为乘不思议乘菩萨说；此法门不入一切余众生手，唯除诸菩萨摩诃萨。佛子，譬如转轮圣王所有七宝，因此宝故显示轮王，此宝不入余众生手，唯除第一夫人所生太子，具足成就圣王相者。若转轮王无此太子具众德者，王命终后，此诸宝等于七日中悉皆散灭。佛子，此经珍宝亦复如是，不入一切余众生手，唯除如来法王真子，生如来家，种如来相诸善根者。佛子，若无此等佛之真子，如是法门不久散灭。何以故？一切二乘不闻此经，何况受持、读诵、书写、

when teaching in order to adapt to beings' minds and delight them. They are not ultimate.

Sons of the Buddha, this Dharma gateway:

Is known as the place which holds the Tathāgata's secrets;

Is known as that which no one in the world can know;

Is known as the entryway to the seal of the Tathāgata;

Is known as the gateway to developing great wisdom;

Is known as that which reveals the lineage of the Tathāgata;

Is known as that which perfects all bodhisattvas;

Is known as that which cannot be destroyed by anyone in the world;

Is known as that which continuously accords with the realm of the Tathāgata;

Is known as that which is able to purify all realms of beings; and

Is known as the inconceivable ultimate dharma which expounds the fundamental true nature of the Tathāgata.

Sons of the Buddha, this Dharma gateway is not spoken for the sake of any other beings: It is spoken only for bodhisattvas progressing in the Great Vehicle and is spoken only for bodhisattvas who have entered the inconceivable vehicle. This Dharma gateway is not to enter the hands of any other kinds of beings aside from those who are bodhisattva-mahāsattvas.

Sons of the Buddha, by way of analogy, this is like the seven treasures owned by a wheel-turning sage king on account of which he manifests as a wheel-turning king. These treasures of his do not pass into the hands of any other being aside from the prince born to his number one wife, the prince who is completely endowed with the marks of a sage king. If a wheel-turning king had no prince who was completely endowed with those many qualities, then, after the king's life came to an end, within seven days, all of those treasures and other such possessions would scatter and completely disappear.

Sons of the Buddha, the precious treasure of this sutra is also of this very sort. It is not to enter into the hands of any other beings with the exception of the true sons of the Tathāgata, the Dharma King, those sons born into the clan of the Tathāgata who have planted the roots of goodness which produce the marks of a *tathāgata*.

Sons of the Buddha, if there were no true sons of the Buddha such as these, Dharma gateways such as these would scatter and disappear before long. Why? All those who are adherents of the two vehicles do not even hear this sutra, how much the less could they accept it, preserve it, study it, recite it, write it out, and

正體字

分別
解說。唯諸菩薩。乃能如是。是故菩薩摩訶薩。
聞此法門。應大歡喜。以尊重心。恭敬頂受。何
以故。菩薩摩訶薩。信樂此經。疾得阿耨多羅
三藐三菩提故。佛子。設有菩薩。於無量百千
億那由他劫。行六波羅蜜。修習種種菩提分
法。若未聞此如來不思議。大威德法門。或時
聞已。不信不解。不順不入不得名為真實菩
薩。以不能生如來家故。若得聞此如來無量
不可思議。無障無礙。智慧法門。聞已信解。隨
順悟入。當知此人。生如來家。隨順一切如來
境界。具足一切諸菩薩法。安住一切種智境
界。遠離一切諸世間法。出生一切如來所行。
通達一切菩薩法性。於佛自在。心無疑惑。住
無師法。深入如來無礙境界。佛子。菩薩摩訶
薩。聞此法已。則能以平等智。知無量法。則能
以正直心。離諸分別。

简体字

分别解说！唯诸菩萨乃能如是。是故，菩萨摩诃萨闻此法门应大欢喜，以尊重心恭敬顶受。何以故？菩萨摩诃萨信乐此经，疾得阿耨多罗三藐三菩提故。佛子，设有菩萨于无量百千亿那由他劫行六波罗蜜，修习种种菩提分法。若未闻此如来不思议大威德法门，或时闻已不信、不解、不顺、不入，不得名为真实菩萨，以不能生如来家故。若得闻此如来无量不可思议无障无碍智慧法门，闻已信解，随顺悟入，当知此人生如来家，随顺一切如来境界，具足一切诸菩萨法，安住一切种智境界，远离一切诸世间法，出生一切如来所行，通达一切菩萨法性，于佛自在心无疑惑，住无师法，深入如来无碍境界。佛子，菩萨摩诃萨闻此法已，则能以平等智知无量法，则能以正直心离诸分别，

analytically explain it. It is only the bodhisattvas who are able to act in such ways. Therefore, the bodhisattva-mahāsattvas who hear this Dharma gateway should feel great happiness and then, with a reverential mind, they should accept it with the highest level of respect. And why? This is because, if a bodhisattva-mahāsattva has faith in and delights in this sutra, he will swiftly attain *anuttara-samyak-saṃbodhi*.

Sons of the Buddha, even if a bodhisattva practiced the six *pāramitās* and cultivated all the different aids to enlightenment, doing so for countless hundreds of thousands of *koṭīs* of *nayutas* of kalpas, still, if he had not yet heard this Dharma gateway of the Tathāgata's inconceivable and great awesome virtue, or if heard it at some point in time but failed to believe in it, failed to understand it, failed to accord with it, and failed to enter into it, then he does not qualify to be referred to as a genuine bodhisattva, for he has still been unable to achieve birth into the clan of the Tathāgata.

If one succeeds in hearing this Dharma gateway of the Tathāgata's incalculable, inconceivable, unobstructed, and unimpeded wisdom and then, having heard it, has faith in it, understands it, accords with it, awakens to it, and enters into it, one should know that this person:

Is one who has been born into the clan of the Tathāgata;
Is one who accords with the realm of all *tathāgatas*;
Is one who completely fulfills all the bodhisattva dharmas;
Is one who abides securely in the realm of the knowledge of all modes;
Is one who has left all worldly dharmas far behind;
Is one who has developed all of the Tathāgata's practices;
Is one who has a penetrating comprehension of the nature of all bodhisattva dharmas;
Is one whose mind is free of doubts about the Buddha's powers of transformation;
Is one who abides in the independently realized Dharma; and
Is one who has deeply entered the unimpeded realm of the Tathāgata.

Sons of the Buddha, after hearing this Dharma, the bodhisattva-mahāsattva:

Is able to use the knowledge of equality to know the immeasurable dharmas;
Is able to use the correct and straight mind to abandon all discriminations;

正體字	則能以勝欲樂。現見諸 277c28 ‖ 佛。則能以作意力。入平等虛空界。則能以自 277c29 ‖ 在念。行無邊法界。則能以智慧力。具一切功 278a01 ‖ 德。則能以自然智。離一切世間垢。則能以菩 278a02 ‖ 提心。入一切十方網。則能以大觀察。知三世 278a03 ‖ 諸佛。同一體性。則能以善根迴向智。普入如 278a04 ‖ 是法。不入而入。不於一法。而有攀緣。恒以一 278a05 ‖ 法。觀一切法。佛子。菩薩摩訶薩。成就如是功 278a06 ‖ 德。少作功力。得無師自然智。爾時普賢菩薩。 278a07 ‖ 欲重明此義。而說頌言 278a08 ‖ 　見聞供養諸如來　　所得功德不可量 278a09 ‖ 　於有為中終不盡　　要滅煩惱離眾苦 278a10 ‖ 　譬人吞服少金剛　　終竟不[*]消要當出 278a11 ‖ 　供養十力諸功德　　滅惑必至金剛智 278a12 ‖ 　如乾草積等須彌　　投芥子火悉燒盡 278a13 ‖ 　供養諸佛少功德　　必斷煩惱至涅槃 278a14 ‖ 　雪山有藥名善見　　見聞嗅觸[*]消眾疾 278a15 ‖ 　若有見聞於十力　　得勝功德到佛智
简体字	则能以胜欲乐现见诸佛，则能以作意力入平等虚空界，则能以自在念行无边法界，则能以智慧力具一切功德，则能以自然智离一切世间垢，则能以菩提心入一切十方网，则能以大观察知三世诸佛同一体性，则能以善根回向智普入如是法，不入而入；不于一法而有攀缘，恒以一法观一切法。佛子，菩萨摩诃萨成就如是功德，少作功力，得无师自然智。" 　　尔时，普贤菩萨欲重明此义而说颂言： 　　"见闻供养诸如来，所得功德不可量， 　　于有为中终不尽，要灭烦恼离众苦。 　　譬人吞服少金刚，终竟不消要当出； 　　供养十力诸功德，灭惑必至金刚智。 　　如干草[萉-且+只]等须弥，投芥子火悉烧尽； 　　供养诸佛少功德，必断烦恼至涅槃。 　　雪山有药名善见，见闻嗅触消众疾； 　　若有见闻于十力，得胜功德到佛智。"

Chapter 37 — The Manifestation of the Tathāgata

- Is able through supreme aspiration to see all buddhas directly before him;
- Is able through the power of mental engagement to enter a realm of uniform equality like empty space;[67]
- Is able through sovereign mastery of mindfulness to travel throughout the boundless Dharma realm;
- Is able to use the power of wisdom to possess all the meritorious qualities;
- Is able to use spontaneously arising wisdom to abandon all of the world's defilements;
- Is able to use the bodhi resolve to enter the web of all the ten directions;
- Is able to use great contemplation to know all buddhas of the three periods of time as of the same single essential nature; and
- Is able to use the wisdom that dedicates one's roots of goodness to everywhere enter dharmas such as these, not entering them and yet entering them, not seizing on even a single dharma even as he constantly contemplates all dharmas through but a single dharma.

Sons of the Buddha, the bodhisattva-mahāsattva perfects meritorious qualities such as these and, with the power of but a minor effort, acquires the spontaneously arising wisdom realized without the assistance of a teacher.

At that time, wishing to once again clarify the meaning of this, Samantabhadra Bodhisattva-mahāsattva then spoke these verses:

> If one sees, hears, or makes offerings to the Tathāgatas,
> the merit thus acquired is so measureless that
> it could never be exhausted even during all of conditioned existence.
> He will soon extinguish the afflictions and leave the many sufferings.

> Just as, if a man swallowed a small piece of vajra,
> it could never be digested and would necessarily be expelled,
> so too, merit acquired from offerings to the One of Ten Powers
> will extinguish the afflictions and definitely lead one to vajra wisdom.

> Just as, if one gathered dry grass equal in size to Mount Sumeru and
> threw only a mustard seed-sized ember into it, it would still all burn,
> so too, the small amount of merit gained from offerings to buddhas
> will definitely lead to cutting off the afflictions and arriving at nirvāṇa.

> The Himalaya Mountains have a medicine called "Good to See" that,
> when seen, heard, smelled, or touched, heals the many diseases.
> So too, if one but sees or hears the One of Ten Powers,
> one will gain supreme merit and then reach the Buddha's wisdom.

正體字	
278a16	爾時佛神力故。法如是故。十方各有十不可
278a17	說。百千億那由他世界。六種震動。所謂東
278a18	[1]涌西沒。西涌東沒。南涌北沒。北涌南沒。邊
278a19	涌中沒。中涌邊沒。十八相動。所謂動。遍動。等
278a20	遍動。起。遍起。等遍起。涌。遍涌。等遍涌。震。遍
278a21	震。等遍震。吼。遍吼。等遍吼。擊。遍擊。等遍擊。
278a22	雨出過諸天。一切華雲。一切蓋雲。幢雲幡雲。
278a23	香雲鬘雲。塗香雲。莊嚴具雲。大光明摩尼寶
278a24	雲。諸菩薩讚歎雲。不可說菩薩各差別身雲。
278a25	雨成正覺雲。嚴淨不思議世界雲。雨如來言
278a26	語音聲雲。充滿無邊法界。如此四天下。如來
278a27	神力。如是示現。令諸菩薩。皆大歡喜。周遍十
278a28	方一切世界。悉亦如是。是時十方。各過八十
278a29	不可說。百千億那由他佛剎微塵數世界外。
278b01	各有八十不可說百千億那由他佛剎微塵數
278b02	如來。同名普賢。皆現其前。而作是言。善哉佛
278b03	子。乃能承佛威力。

简体字

　　尔时，佛神力故，法如是故，十方各有十不可说百千亿那由他世界六种震动，所谓：东踊西没，西踊东没，南踊北没，北踊南没，边踊中没，中踊边没。十八相动，所谓：动、遍动、等遍动，起、遍起、等遍起，踊、遍踊、等遍踊，震、遍震、等遍震，吼、遍吼、等遍吼，击、遍击、等遍击。雨出过诸天一切华云、一切盖云、幢云、幡云、香云、鬘云、涂香云、庄严具云、大光明摩尼宝云、诸菩萨赞叹云、不可说菩萨各差别身云，雨成正觉云、严净不思议世界云，雨如来言语音声云，充满无边法界。如此四天下，如来神力如是示现，令诸菩萨皆大欢喜；周遍十方一切世界，悉亦如是。

　　是时，十方各过八十不可说百千亿那由他佛剎微尘数世界外，各有八十不可说百千亿那由他佛剎微尘数如来，同名普贤，皆现其前而作是言："善哉！佛子，乃能承佛威力，

Chapter 37 — The Manifestation of the Tathāgata

At that time, due to the Buddha's spiritual powers and also because Dharma is of this very sort, ten ineffable numbers of hundreds of thousands of *koṭīs* of *nayutas* of worlds in each of the ten directions all moved and shook in six ways, namely upward thrusting in the east together with sinking in the west, upward thrusting in the west together with sinking in the east, upward thrusting in the south together with sinking in the north, upward thrusting in the north together with sinking in the south, upward thrusting at the periphery together with sinking in the middle, and upward thrusting in the middle together with sinking at the periphery. Eighteen types of movement then occurred, namely movement, pervasive movement, universally pervasive movement, rising, pervasive rising, universally pervasive rising, upward thrusting, universal upward thrusting, universally pervasive upward thrusting, shaking, universal shaking, universally pervasive shaking, roaring, universal roaring, universally pervasive roaring, striking, universal striking, and universally pervasive striking.

Rains of adornments then fell which were superior even to those in all the heavens. They consisted of all kinds of flower blossom clouds, all kinds of canopy clouds, banner clouds, pennant clouds, fragrance clouds, garland clouds, perfume clouds, adornment clouds, clouds of immensely radiant *maṇi* jewels, clouds of all kinds of bodhisattva praises, clouds of an ineffable number of many different types of bodhisattva bodies, clouds raining displays of realizations of right enlightenment, clouds causing the purification of inconceivably many worlds, and clouds raining down sounds of the Tathāgata's sayings. They completely filled the boundless Dharma realm. Just as, within these four continents, due to the Tathāgata's spiritual powers, there were manifestations such as these which caused the bodhisattvas to all be filled with great joyous delight, so too did this occur everywhere throughout all worlds of the ten directions.

At that time, from beyond a number of worlds off in each of the ten directions as numerous as the atoms in eighty ineffable numbers of hundreds of thousands of *koṭīs* of *nayutas* of buddha kṣetras, there came *tathāgatas* as numerous as the atoms in eighty ineffable numbers of hundreds of thousands of *koṭīs* of *nayutas* of buddha kṣetras. They were all identically named "Samantabhadra." They all appeared directly before them and said:

> It is good indeed, good indeed, Son of the Buddha, that you have been able to receive the assistance of the Buddha's awesome powers

正體字

隨順法性。演說如來出現
不思議法。佛子。我等十方八十不可說百千
億那由他佛剎微塵數。同名諸佛。皆說此法。
如我所說。十方世界。一切諸佛。亦如是說。佛
子。今此會中。十萬佛剎微塵數。菩薩摩訶
薩。得一切菩薩。神通三昧。我等皆與授記。一
生當得阿耨多羅三藐三菩提。佛剎微塵數
眾生。發阿耨多羅三藐三菩提心。我等亦與
授記。於當來世。經不可說佛剎微塵數劫。皆
得成佛。同號佛殊勝境界。我等為令未來諸
菩薩。聞此法故。皆共護持。如此四天下。所度
眾生。十方百千億那由他。無數無量。乃至不
可說不可說。法界虛空等。一切世界中。所度
眾生。皆亦如是。爾時十方諸佛[2]威神力故。
毘盧遮那本願力故。法如是故。善根力故。如
來起智不[3]越念故。如來應緣不失時故。隨時
覺悟諸菩薩故。往昔所作無失壞故。

简体字

随顺法性,演说如来出现不思议法。佛子,我等十方八十不可说百千亿那由他佛刹微尘数同名诸佛皆说此法;如我所说,十方世界一切诸佛亦如是说。佛子,今此会中,十万佛刹微尘数菩萨摩诃萨,得一切菩萨神通三昧;我等皆与授记,一生当得阿耨多罗三藐三菩提。佛刹微尘数众生,发阿耨多罗三藐三菩提心;我等亦与授记,于当来世经不可说佛刹微尘数劫,皆得成佛,同号佛殊胜境界。我等为令未来诸菩萨闻此法故,皆共护持。如此四天下所度众生,十方百千亿那由他无数无量,乃至不可说不可说法界虚空等一切世界中所度众生,皆亦如是。"

尔时,十方诸佛威神力故,毗卢遮那本愿力故,法如是故,善根力故,如来起智不越念故,如来应缘不失时故,随时觉悟诸菩萨故,往昔所作无失坏故,

and, according with the nature of dharmas, expound upon the inconceivable Dharma of the manifestation of the Tathāgata. Son of the Buddha, all of us identically named buddhas from each of the ten directions, in each case as numerous as the atoms in eighty ineffable numbers of hundreds of thousands of *koṭīs* of *nayutas* of buddha *kṣetras*—we all speak this very Dharma. And just as it is what is spoken by us, so too is it also what is spoken by all buddhas of the ten directions.

O Son of the Buddha, now, within this congregation, there are bodhisattva-mahāsattvas as numerous as the atoms in ten myriads of buddha *kṣetras* who have acquired the spiritual superknowledges and samādhis of all bodhisattvas. We now bestow upon them their predictions of being bound to realize *anuttara-samyak-saṃbodhi* in but one more lifetime.

There are also beings here as numerous as the atoms in a buddha *kṣetra* who have resolved to attain *anuttara-samyak-saṃbodhi*. We also bestow predictions on them that, in a future age, after passing through kalpas as numerous as the atoms in an ineffable number of buddha *kṣetras*, they will all succeed in attaining buddhahood at which time they will all be identically named "Especially Supreme Realm of the Buddha." In order to enable future bodhisattvas to hear this Dharma, we shall all join in protecting and preserving it.

Just as it is so for the beings brought across to liberation here in these four continents, so too is this so for the beings brought across to liberation in the ten directions' countlessly and immeasurably many hundreds of thousands of *koṭīs* of *nayutas* of worlds even up to all the ineffable-ineffable number of worlds throughout the Dharma realm and the realm of empty space.

At that time:

Because of the awesome spiritual powers of all buddhas of the ten directions;

Because of the power of the original vows of Vairocana;

Because Dharma is of this very sort;

Because of the power of roots of goodness;

Because the arising of the Tathāgata's wisdom never skips even a single mind-moment;

Because the Tathāgata's responses to conditions never fail to occur at the right time;

Because they awaken all bodhisattvas in accordance with the right time;

Because whatever they have done in the distant past is never lost;

正體字

令得普
賢廣大行故。顯現一切智自在故。十方各過
十不可說百千億那由他佛剎微塵數世界
外。各有十不可說百千億那由他佛剎微塵
數菩薩。來詣於此。充滿十方一切法界。示現
菩薩廣大莊嚴。放大光明網。震動一切十方
世界。壞散一切諸魔宮殿。[＊]消滅一切諸惡道
苦。顯現一切如來威德。歌詠讚歎。如來無量
差別功德法。普雨一切種種雨。示現無量差
別身。領受無量諸佛法。以佛神力。各作是言。
善哉佛子。乃能說此如來不可壞法。佛子。我
等一切皆名普賢。各從普光明世界。普幢自
在如來所。而來於此。彼一切處。亦說是法。如
是文句。如是義理。如是宣說。如是決定。皆同
於此。不增不[4]減。我等皆以佛神力故。得如
來法故。來詣此處。為汝作證。如我來此。十方
等虛空遍法界。一切世界。諸四天下。亦復如
是
爾時普賢菩薩。承佛神力。觀察一切菩薩大
眾。欲重明如來出現。廣大威德。如來正法。不
可沮壞。

简体字

令得普贤广大行故，显现一切智自在故，十方各过十不可说百千亿那由他佛刹微尘数世界外，各有十不可说百千亿那由他佛刹微尘数菩萨来诣于此，充满十方一切法界，示现菩萨广大庄严，放大光明网，震动一切十方世界，坏散一切诸魔宫殿，消灭一切诸恶道苦，显现一切如来威德，歌咏赞叹如来无量差别功德法，普雨一切种种雨，示现无量差别身，领受无量诸佛法，以佛神力各作是言："善哉！佛子，乃能说此如来不可坏法。佛子，我等一切皆名普贤，各从普光明世界普幢自在如来所而来于此，彼一切处亦说是法，如是文句，如是义理，如是宣说，如是决定，皆同于此，不增不减。我等皆以佛神力故，得如来法故，来诣此处为汝作证。如我来此，十方等虚空遍法界一切世界诸四天下亦复如是。"

尔时，普贤菩萨承佛神力，观察一切菩萨大众，欲重明如来出现广大威德，如来正法不可沮坏，

> Because they enable the attainment of Samantabhadra's vast practices; and
>
> Because they manifest the sovereign mastery of all-knowledge—

From beyond a number of worlds in each of the ten directions equal to the atoms in ten ineffable numbers of hundreds of thousands of *koṭīs* of *nayutas* of buddha *kṣetras*, there then came, intent on paying their respects, bodhisattvas from each of those directions as numerous as the atoms in ten ineffable numbers of hundreds of thousands of *koṭīs* of *nayutas* of buddha *kṣetras* who, completely filling up the entire Dharma realm's ten directions, then manifested the bodhisattva's vast adornments, emanated an immense net of light rays, caused quaking in all worlds of the ten directions, caused the destruction and scattering of all the palaces of the *māras*, melted away all the sufferings in all the wretched destinies, displayed the awesome virtue of all *tathāgatas*, sang the praises of the Tathāgata's incalculably many different meritorious dharmas, everywhere rained down all the many different kinds of rain, manifested countlessly many different kinds of bodies, and received the Dharma of incalculably many buddhas.

Then, aided by the Buddha's spiritual powers, they each proclaimed:

> It is good indeed, Son of the Buddha, that you have been able to speak about this indestructible Dharma of the Tathāgata. Son of the Buddha, we are all identically named "Samantabhadra" and we have all come here from the presence of the *tathāgata* named "Universal Banner of Sovereign Mastery" in worlds known as "Universal Light." In all those places, they also teach this very Dharma with just such phrasings as these, just such principles as these, just such explanations as these, and just such certitude as this. They are all the same as found here, neither more nor less.
>
> It is due to the aid of the Buddha's spiritual powers and due to having acquired the Dharma of the Tathāgata that we have come here to pay our respects and bear witness for you. And just as we have come here for this purpose, so too is this also occurring in just this same way in all of the four-continent worlds throughout the ten directions of empty space everywhere throughout the Dharma realm.

At that time, aided by the Buddha's spiritual powers, Samantabhadra Bodhisattva surveyed that entire great congregation of bodhisattvas, and, wishing to once again clarify:

> The vast awesome virtue of the manifestation of the Tathāgata;
>
> The indestructibility of the Tathāgata's right Dharma;

無量善根。皆悉不空。諸佛出世。必具一切最勝之法。善能觀察諸眾生心。隨應說法。未曾失時。生諸菩薩。無量法光。一切諸佛。自在莊嚴。一切如來。一身無異。從本大行之所生起。而說頌言

一切如來諸所作　世間譬[5]諭無能及
為令眾生得悟解　非諭為[*]諭而顯示
如是微密甚深法　百千萬劫難可聞
精進智慧調伏者　乃得聞此祕奧義
若聞此法生欣慶　彼曾供養無量佛
為佛加持所攝受　人天讚歎常供養
此為超世第一財　此能救度諸群品
此能出生清淨道　汝等當持莫放逸

无量善根皆悉不空,诸佛出世必具一切最胜之法,善能观察诸众生心,随应说法未曾失时,生诸菩萨无量法光,一切诸佛自在庄严,一切如来一身无异,从本大行之所生起,而说颂言:

"一切如来诸所作,世间譬喻无能及,
为令众生得悟解,非喻为喻而显示。
如是微密甚深法,百千万劫难可闻;
精进智慧调伏者,乃得闻此秘奥义。
若闻此法生欣庆,彼曾供养无量佛,
为佛加持所摄受,人天赞叹常供养。
此为超世第一财,此能救度诸群品,
此能出生清净道,汝等当持莫放逸。"

Chapter 37 — The Manifestation of the Tathāgata

> The non-futility of planting measureless roots of goodness;
> The inevitability that, when all buddhas appear in the world, they will be completely possessed of all the most superior dharmas;
> Their excellent ability to contemplate the minds of all beings;
> Their adaptation to whatever is appropriate in speaking the Dharma without ever missing the right time;
> Their production of all bodhisattvas' measureless light of Dharma;
> The miraculous adornment of all buddhas;
> All *tathāgatas'* sharing of a single body free of individual differences; and
> Their arising from their great original practices—

He then spoke these verses:

> All that is done by all the *tathāgatas* is so indescribable
> that none of the worlds' analogies could even come close.
> Still, to enable beings to awaken and understand,
> in what is inaccessible to analogies, I make analogies to instruct.

> Such subtle, secret, and extremely deep Dharma
> could only rarely be heard in a hundred thousand myriads of kalpas.
> It is only those who are vigorous, wise, and well trained
> who are then able to hear these mysterious and abstruse meanings.

> Whoever, on hearing this Dharma, is filled with rejoicing
> is one who has already made offerings to incalculably many buddhas,
> is one who is supported and drawn forth by the Buddha, and
> is one to whom men and devas give praise and always make offerings.

> This constitutes the foremost world-transcending wealth,
> this is able to rescue and liberate all the many kinds of beings,
> and this is able to bring forth the path of purity.
> You should all uphold it and must never be neglectful in doing so.

The End of Chapter Thirty-Seven

正體字

[1]大方廣佛華嚴經卷第五十三

離世間品第三十八之一

爾時世尊。在摩竭提國阿蘭若法菩提場中普光明殿。坐蓮華藏師子之座。妙悟皆滿。二行永絕。達無相法。住於佛住。得佛平等。到無障處。不可轉法。所行無礙。立不思議。普見三世。身恒充遍一切國土。智恒明達一切諸法。了一切行。盡一切疑。無能測身。一切菩薩。等所求智。到佛無二究竟彼岸。具足如來平等解脫。證無中邊。佛平等地。盡於法界。等虛空界。與不可說。百千億那由他佛剎微塵數。菩薩摩訶薩俱。皆一生當得阿耨多羅三藐三菩提。各從他方。種種國土而共來集。悉具菩薩。方便智慧。所謂

简体字

大方广佛华严经卷第五十三
离世间品第三十八之一

尔时，世尊在摩竭提国阿兰若法菩提场中普光明殿，坐莲华藏师子之座，妙悟皆满，二行永绝，达无相法；住于佛住，得佛平等，到无障处不可转法；所行无碍，立不思议，普见三世；身恒充遍一切国土，智恒明达一切诸法；了一切行，尽一切疑，无能测身；一切菩萨等所求智，到佛无二究竟彼岸，具足如来平等解脱，证无中边佛平等地，尽于法界等虚空界。与不可说百千亿那由他佛剎微尘数菩萨摩诃萨俱，皆一生当得阿耨多罗三藐三菩提，各从他方种种国土而共来集，悉具菩萨方便智慧。所谓：

Chapter 38
Transcending the World

At that time, the Bhagavat, dwelling in the state of Magadha, was residing at the site of enlightenment in accordance with the *araṇya* dharma of forest dwelling, seated on a lotus flower dais lion throne in the Hall of Universal Light where:

His marvelous awakening was in all respects completely fulfilled;
He had forever cut off the two kinds of action;[68]
He had acquired the penetrating comprehension of the dharma of signlessness;
He had come to dwell where buddhas dwell;[69]
He had attained the equality of the buddhas;[70]
He had reached the station free of obstacles;
He had attained the Dharma that cannot be overturned;[71]
He had become unimpeded in his actions;[72]
He had established what is inconceivable;[73] and
He had attained the universal vision of the three periods of time.

His body constantly and completely pervaded all lands, his wisdom constantly and clearly penetrated all dharmas, and he had completed all the practices.[74] He had put an end to all doubts, had acquired the body that no one is able to fathom, and had acquired the wisdom that all bodhisattvas equally seek to acquire. He had achieved the ultimate perfection in the non-duality of the Buddha, had completely fulfilled the liberations which are the same for all *tathāgatas*, and had realized the ground equally shared by all buddhas in which neither the middle nor the extremes exist and he is present throughout the entire Dharma realm and commensurate with the realm of empty space.

He dwelt together there with bodhisattva-mahāsattvas as numerous as the atoms in an ineffable number of hundreds of thousands of *koṭīs* of *nayutas* of buddha *kṣetras*, all of whom had reached the stage of having but one more lifetime before they would realize *anuttarasamyaksaṃbodhi*. They had all come and gathered there from many different countries in other regions and all of them possessed the bodhisattva's skillful means and wisdom. That is to say:

正體字

善能觀察一切眾生。以方便
力。令其調伏。住菩薩法。善能觀察一切世界。
以方便力。普皆往詣。善能觀察涅槃境界。思
惟籌量。永離一切戲論分別。而修妙行。無有
間斷。善能攝受一切眾生。善入無量諸方便
法。知諸眾生。空無所有。而不壞業果。善知眾
生心。使諸根境界方便。種種差別。悉能受持
三世佛法。自得解了。復為他說。於世出世無
量諸法。皆善安住。知其真實。於有為無為。一
切諸法。悉善觀察。知無有二。於一念中。悉能
獲得三世諸佛。所有智慧。於念念中。悉能示
現成等正覺。令一切眾生。發心成道。於一眾
生心之所緣。悉知一切眾生境界。雖入如來
一切智地。而不捨菩薩行。諸所作業。智慧方
便。而無所作。為一一眾生。住無量劫。而於
阿僧祇劫。難可值遇。轉正法輪。調伏眾生。皆
不唐捐。三世諸佛。清淨行願。悉已具足。

简体字

善能观察一切众生，以方便力，令其调伏，住菩萨法；善能观察一切世界，以方便力，普皆往诣；善能观察涅槃境界，思惟筹量永离一切戏论分别，而修妙行无有间断；善能摄受一切众生，善入无量诸方便法，知诸众生空无所有而不坏业果；善知众生心使、诸根境界方便，种种差别悉能受持；三世佛法，自得解了，复为他说；于世、出世无量诸法，皆善安住，知其真实；于有为、无为一切诸法，悉善观察，知无有二；于一念中，悉能获得三世诸佛所有智慧；于念念中，悉能示现成等正觉，令一切众生发心成道；于一众生心之所缘，悉知一切众生境界；虽入如来一切智地，而不舍菩萨行诸所作业，智慧方便而无所作；为一一众生住无量劫，而于阿僧祇劫难可值遇，转正法轮调伏众生皆不唐捐，三世诸佛清净行愿悉已具足；

Chapter 38 — *Transcending the World*

They were well able to contemplate all beings and use the power of skillful means to enable them to undergo the training and dwell in the bodhisattva dharmas;

They were well able to contemplate all worlds and use the power of skillful means to go forth everywhere to visit them all;

They were well able to contemplate the realm of nirvāṇa, reflect upon it, and assess it;

They forever abandoned all conceptual proliferation and discriminations and incessantly cultivated the marvelous practices;

They were well able to attract all beings and skillfully penetrated all the countless dharmas of skillful means;

They realized all beings are empty and nonexistent and yet they still did not deny the fruits of karmic actions;

They thoroughly knew all of the many kinds of differences in beings' minds, latent tendencies, faculties, spheres of cognition, and skillful means;

They were able to take on and uphold the dharmas of all buddhas of the three periods of time, to completely understand them by themselves, and to then also explain them for others;

They skillfully and securely dwelt in the countless worldly and world-transcending dharmas while also knowing them in accordance with reality;

They skillfully contemplated all conditioned and unconditioned dharmas and realized their non-dual character;

In but a single mind-moment, they were able to acquire all the wisdom of all buddhas of the three periods of time;

They were able in each successive mind-moment to manifest the realization of the right and perfect enlightenment and enable all beings to resolve to attain enlightenment;

In the objective conditions focused on by a single being, they thoroughly knew all beings' spheres of cognition;

Although they entered the Tathāgata's ground of all-knowledge, they still did not relinquish the bodhisattva practices;

They use wisdom and skillful means in all the works they do, and yet they have nothing at all that they do;

They dwelt for countless kalpas for the sake of every being, and yet they were difficult to encounter even in *asaṃkhyeyas* of kalpas;

They turned the wheel of right Dharma and trained beings, never doing so in vain;

They had already completely fulfilled the pure conduct and vows of all buddhas of the three periods of time; and

成就

正體字

如是無量功德。一切如來。於無邊劫。說不可盡。其名曰普賢菩薩。普眼菩薩。普化菩薩。普慧菩薩。普見菩薩。普光菩薩。普觀菩薩。普照菩薩。普幢菩薩。普覺菩薩。如是等十不可說百千億那由他佛剎微塵數。皆悉成就普賢行願。深心大願。皆已圓滿。一切諸佛。出興世處。悉能往詣。請轉法輪。善能受持諸佛法眼。不斷一切諸佛種性。善知一切諸佛興世。授記次第。名號國土。成等正覺。轉於法輪。無佛世界。現身成佛。能令一切雜染眾生。皆悉清淨。能滅一切菩薩業障。入於無礙清淨法界爾時普賢菩薩摩訶薩入廣大三昧。名佛華莊嚴。入此三昧時。十方所有。一切世界。六種十八相動。出大音聲。靡不皆聞。然後從其三昧而起。爾時普慧菩薩。知眾已集。問普賢菩薩言。佛子。願為演說。何等為菩薩摩訶薩依。何等為奇特想。何等為行。何等為善知識。

简体字

成就如是无量功德，一切如来于无边劫说不可尽。其名曰：普贤菩萨、普眼菩萨、普化菩萨、普慧菩萨、普见菩萨、普光菩萨、普观菩萨、普照菩萨、普幢菩萨、普觉菩萨。如是等十不可说百千亿那由他佛刹微尘数，皆悉成就普贤行愿，深心大愿皆已圆满；一切诸佛出兴世处，悉能往诣请转法轮；善能受持诸佛法眼，不断一切诸佛种性；善知一切诸佛兴世授记次第、名号、国土、成等正觉、转于法轮；无佛世界现身成佛，能令一切杂染众生皆悉清净；能灭一切菩萨业障，入于无碍清净法界。

尔时，普贤菩萨摩诃萨入广大三昧，名佛华庄严；入此三昧时，十方所有一切世界六种、十八相动，出大音声靡不皆闻；然后从其三昧而起。

尔时，普慧菩萨知众已集，问普贤菩萨言："佛子，愿为演说：何等为菩萨摩诃萨依？何等为奇特想？何等为行？何等为善知识？

Chapter 38 — *Transcending the World*

They had all perfected countless meritorious qualities such as these which were so extensive that, even if all *tathāgatas* tried to do so for boundlessly many kalpas, they could still never finish describing them.

Their names were: Universal Worthy [Samantabhadra][75] Bodhisattva, Universal Eye Bodhisattva, Universal Transformation Bodhisattva, Universal Wisdom Bodhisattva, Universal Vision Bodhisattva, Universal Radiance Bodhisattva, Universal Contemplation Bodhisattva, Universal Illumination Bodhisattva, Universal Banner Bodhisattva, and Universal Enlightenment Bodhisattva.

Bodhisattvas such as these were as numerous as the atoms in ten ineffables of hundreds of thousands of *koṭīs* of *nayutas* of buddha *kṣetras*. They had all already perfected the conduct and vows of Samantabhadra. They had already completely fulfilled all their deep-minded great vows. Wherever any buddha appeared in the world, they were all able to go forth there, pay their respects, and request the turning of the Dharma wheel. They were well able to take on and sustain the Dharma eye of all buddhas. They ensured that the lineage of all buddhas would never be cut off. They knew well the sequence of all buddhas' appearances in the world and their bestowing of predictions, their names, their lands, their realization of the right and perfect enlightenment, and their turning of the Dharma wheel. In worlds without buddhas, they manifested bodies realizing buddhahood. They were able to cause all beings possessed of defilements to become purified. They were able to extinguish the karmic obstacles of all bodhisattvas. And they entered the unimpeded pure Dharma realm.

At that time, Samantabhadra Bodhisattva-Mahāsattva entered a vast samādhi known as "the flower adornment of the Buddha." When he entered this samādhi, all worlds of the ten directions shook in six ways, moved in eighteen ways, and produced a loud sound that no one did not hear. After this, he arose from his samādhi.

Then Universal Wisdom Bodhisattva, knowing that the assembly had already gathered together there, proceeded to pose questions to Samantabhadra Bodhisattva, saying:

O Son of the Buddha, please expound on the following matters:
    What does the bodhisattva-mahāsattva rely on?
    What constitutes his extraordinary kinds of thought?
    What constitutes his practices?
    What serves as his good spiritual guide?

正體字

何等為勤精進。何等為心得安隱。何等為成就眾生。何等為戒。何等為自知受記。何等為入菩薩。何等為入如來。何等為入眾生心行。何等為入世界。何等為入劫。何等為說三世。何等為入三世。何等為發無疲厭心。何等為差別智。何等為陀羅尼。何等為演說佛。何等為發普賢心。何等為普賢行法。以何等故。而起大悲。何等為發菩提心因緣。何等為於善知識。起尊重心。何等為清淨。何等為諸波羅蜜。何等為智隨覺。何等為證知。何等為力。何等為平等。何等為佛法實義句。何等為說法。何等為持。何等為辯才。何等為自在。何等為無著性。

简体字

何等为勤精进？何等为心得安隐？何等为成就众生？何等为戒？何等为自知受记？何等为入菩萨？何等为入如来？何等为入众生心行？何等为入世界？何等为入劫？何等为说三世？何等为知三世？何等为发无疲厌心？何等为差别智？何等为陀罗尼？何等为演说佛？何等为发普贤心？何等为普贤行法？以何等故而起大悲？何等为发菩提心因缘？何等为于善知识起尊重心？何等为清净？何等为诸波罗蜜？何等为智随觉？何等为证知？何等为力？何等为平等？何等为佛法实义句？何等为说法？何等为持？何等为辩才？何等为自在？何等为无著性？

Chapter 38 — Transcending the World

What constitutes his diligent vigor?
What constitutes his bases for attaining peace of mind?
What constitutes his ways to develop beings?
What constitutes his moral precepts?
What constitutes his bases for realizing he is bound to receive his prediction?
What constitutes his entry among the bodhisattvas?
What constitutes his entry among the *tathāgatas*?
What constitutes his penetration of beings' mental actions?
What constitutes his entry into worlds?
What constitutes his entry into kalpas?
What constitutes his ways of speaking of the three periods of time?
What constitutes his penetrating knowledge of the three periods of time?
What constitutes his bringing forth of the tireless mind?
What constitutes his knowledge of differences?
What constitutes his *dhāraṇīs*?
What constitutes his proclamations regarding buddhas?[76]
What constitutes his bringing forth of the universally worthy mind [of Samantabhadra]?[77]
What constitutes his dharmas of universally worthy practice [of Samantabhadra]?
What constitutes his reasons for generating the great compassion?
What constitutes the causes and conditions for his arousing the bodhi resolve?
What are the types of mind he uses in revering the good spiritual guide?
What constitutes his purity?
What constitutes his *pāramitās*?
What constitutes his knowledge pursuant to awakening?
What constitutes his knowing based on realizations?
What constitutes his powers?
What constitutes his equal regard?
What constitutes his statements on the true meaning of the dharmas of the Buddha?
What constitutes his speaking about dharmas?
What constitutes what he preserves?
What constitutes his eloquence?
What constitutes his sovereign masteries?
What is the nature of his nonattachment?

正體字

何等為平等心。何等為出生智慧。何等為變化。何等為力持。何等為得大欣慰。何等為深入佛法。何等為依止。何等為發無畏心。何等為發無疑惑心。何等為不思議。何等為巧密語。何等為巧分別智。何等為入三昧。何等為遍入。何等為解脫門。何等為神通。何等為明。何等為解脫。何等為園林。何等為宮殿。何等為所樂。何等為莊嚴。何等為發不動心。何等為不捨深大心。何等為觀察。何等為說法。何等為清淨。何等為印。何等為智光照。何等為無等住。何等為無下劣心。何等為如山增上心。何等為入無上菩提如海智。何等為如寶住。何等為發如金剛大乘誓願心。何等為大發起。何等為究竟大事。

简体字

何等为平等心？何等为出生智慧？何等为变化？何等为力持？何等为得大欣慰？何等为深入佛法？何等为依止？何等为发无畏心？何等为发无疑惑心？何等为不思议？何等为巧密语？何等为巧分别智？何等为入三昧？何等为遍入？何等为解脱门？何等为神通？何等为明？何等为解脱？何等为园林？何等为宫殿？何等为所乐？何等为庄严？何等为发不动心？何等为不舍深大心？何等为观察？何等为说法？何等为清净？何等为印？何等为智光照？何等为无等住？何等为无下劣心？何等为如山增上心？何等为入无上菩提如海智？何等为如宝住？何等为发如金刚大乘誓愿心？何等为大发起？何等为究竟大事？

Chapter 38 — *Transcending the World*

What constitutes his types of impartial mind?
What constitutes his ways of developing wisdom?
What constitutes his transformations?
What constitutes his means of empowerment?
What constitutes the bases for great happiness and satisfaction?
What constitutes his deep penetration of the Buddha's Dharma?
What constitutes those things on which he is based?
What constitutes his ways of arousing fearless resolve?
What constitutes his ways of arousing doubt-free resolve?
What constitutes his inconceivability?
What constitutes his skillful and esoteric speech?
What constitutes his skillfully distinguishing wisdom?
What constitutes his kinds of entry into samādhi?
What constitutes his kinds of pervasive penetration?
What constitutes his gateways to liberation?
What constitutes his spiritual superknowledges?
What constitutes his clarities?
What constitutes his liberations?
What constitutes his gardens and groves?
What constitutes his palaces?
What constitutes his bases of delight?
What constitutes his kinds of adornments?
What constitutes his manifestations of the unshakable mind?
What constitutes his kinds of never-relinquished profound and great resolve?
What constitutes his kinds of [wise] contemplations?[78]
What constitutes his explanations of dharmas?
What constitutes his [other] kinds of purity?[79]
What constitutes his seals?
What constitutes his illumination with the light of wisdom?
What constitutes his peerless dwelling?
What constitutes his types of flawless resolve?
What constitutes his types of especially superior mountain-like mind?
What constitutes his oceanic wisdom by which he enters unexcelled bodhi?
What constitutes his jewel-like abiding?
What constitutes his generation of the vajra-like Great Vehicle resolve?
What constitutes his great undertakings?
What constitutes his ultimate and great endeavors?

正體字

何等為不壞信。
何等為授記。何等為善根迴向。何等為得智
慧。何等為發無邊廣大心。何等為伏藏。何等
為律儀。何等為自在。何等為無礙用。何等為
眾生無礙用。何等為剎無礙用。何等為法無
礙用。何等為身無礙用。何等為願無礙用。何
等為境界無礙用。何等為智無礙用。何等為
神通無礙用。何等為神力無礙用。何等為力
無礙用。何等為遊戲。何等為境界。何等為力。
何等為無畏。何等為不共法。何等為業。何等
為身。何等為身業。何等為身。何等為語。何等
為淨修語[3]業。何等為得守護。何等為成[4]辨
大事。何等為心。何等為發心。何等為周遍心。

简体字

何等为不坏信？何等为授记？何等为善根回向？何等为得智慧？何等为发无边广大心？何等为伏藏？何等为律仪？何等为自在？何等为无碍用？何等为众生无碍用？何等为刹无碍用？何等为法无碍用？何等为身无碍用？何等为愿无碍用？何等为境界无碍用？何等为智无碍用？何等为神通无碍用？何等为神力无碍用？何等为力无碍用？何等为游戏？何等为境界？何等为力？何等为无畏？何等为不共法？何等为业？何等为身？何等为身业？何等为身？何等为语？何等为净修语业？何等为得守护？何等为成办大事？何等为心？何等为发心？何等为周遍心？

Chapter 38 — *Transcending the World*

What constitutes his indestructible faith?
What constitutes his ways of receiving the prediction [of future buddhahood]?
What constitutes his ways of dedicating roots of goodness?
What constitutes his ways of attaining wisdom?
What constitutes his ways of arousing boundlessly vast resolve?
What constitutes his hidden treasures?
What constitutes his types of moral standards?
What constitutes his sovereign masteries?
What constitutes his unimpeded functions?
What constitutes his unimpeded functions in relation to beings?
What constitutes his unimpeded functions in relation to *kṣetras*?
What constitutes his unimpeded functions in relation to dharmas?
What constitutes his unimpeded functions in relation to bodies?
What constitutes his unimpeded functions in relation to vows?
What constitutes his unimpeded functions in relation to realms?
What constitutes his unimpeded functions in relation to knowledge?
What constitutes his unimpeded functions in relation to the spiritual superknowledges?
What constitutes his unimpeded functions in relation to the spiritual powers?
What constitutes his unimpeded functions in relation to the powers?
What constitutes his easeful mastery?[80]
What constitutes his spheres of action?[81]
What constitutes his [other kinds of] powers?[82]
What constitutes his kinds of fearlessness?
What constitutes his exclusive dharmas?
What constitutes his works?
What constitutes his bodies?
What constitutes his physical actions?
What constitutes his [other] bodies?[83]
What constitutes his speech?
What constitutes his ways of purifying speech?
What constitutes his sources of protection?
What constitutes his accomplishment of great endeavors?
What constitutes his types of mind?
What constitutes his resolutions?
What constitutes his types of all-pervasive mind?

正體字	280a02 何等為諸根。何等為深心。何等為增上深心。 280a03 何等為勤修。何等為決定解。何等為決定解 280a04 入世界。何等為決定解入眾生界。何等為習 280a05 氣。何等為取。何等為修。何等為成就佛法。何 280a06 等為退失佛法道。何等為離生道。何等為決 280a07 定法。何等為出生佛法道。何等為大丈夫名 280a08 號。何等為道。何等為無量道。何等為助道。何 280a09 等為修道。何等為莊嚴道。何等為足。何等為 280a10 手。何等為腹。何等為藏。何等為心。何等為 280a11 被甲。何等為器仗。何等為首。何等為眼。何等 280a12 為耳。何等為鼻。何等為舌。何等為身。何等為 280a13 意。何等為行。何等為住。何等為坐。
简体字	何等为诸根？何等为深心？何等为增上深心？何等为勤修？何等为决定解？何等为决定解入世界？何等为决定解入众生界？何等为习气？何等为取？何等为修？何等为成就佛法？何等为退失佛法道？何等为离生道？何等为决定法？何等为出生佛法道？何等为大丈夫名号？何等为道？何等为无量道？何等为助道？何等为修道？何等为庄严道？何等为足？何等为手？何等为腹？何等为藏？何等为心？何等为被甲？何等为器仗？何等为首？何等为眼？何等为耳？何等为鼻？何等为舌？何等为身？何等为意？何等为行？何等为住？何等为坐？

Chapter 38 — *Transcending the World*

What constitutes his faculties?
What constitutes his deep mind?
What constitutes his kinds of especially superior deep mind?
What constitutes his diligent cultivation?
What constitutes his definite understanding?
What constitutes his definite understanding in entering worlds?[84]
What constitutes his definite understanding in entering the realms of beings?[85]
What constitutes his habitual karmic propensities?
What constitutes his grasping?
What constitutes his cultivation?
What constitutes his fulfillment of the dharmas of the Buddha?
What constitutes the ways of retreating from the path of the Buddha's Dharma?[86]
What constitutes his paths for transcendence of rebirths?
What constitutes his definite dharmas?
What constitutes the paths by which he develops the dharmas of the Buddha?
What constitutes his names that are used for great men?
What constitutes his paths?
What constitutes his measureless paths?
What constitutes his provisions for enlightenment?[87]
What constitutes his cultivation of the path?[88]
What constitutes his adornments of the path?
What constitutes his feet?
What constitutes his hands?
What constitutes his stomach?
What constitutes his inner organs?
What constitutes his heart?
What constitutes his armor?
What constitutes his weapons?
What constitutes his head?
What constitutes his eyes?
What constitutes his ears?
What constitutes his nose?
What constitutes his tongue?
What constitutes his body?
What constitutes his mind?
What constitutes his practices?
What constitutes his abiding?
What constitutes his sitting?

正體字	何等為臥。何等為所住處。何等為所行處。何等為觀察。何等為普觀察。何等為奮迅。何等為師子吼。何等為清淨施。何等為清淨戒。何等為清淨忍。何等為清淨精進。何等為清淨定。何等為清淨慧。何等為清淨慈。何等為清淨悲。何等為清淨喜。何等為清淨捨。何等為義。何等為法。何等為福德助道具。何等為智慧助道具。何等為明足。何等為求法。何等為明了法。何等為修行法。何等為魔。何等為魔業。何等為捨離魔業。何等為見佛。何等為佛業。何等為慢業。何等為智業。何等為魔所攝持。何等為佛所攝持。何等為法所攝持。何等為住兜率天所作業。何故於兜率天宮歿。
简体字	何等为卧？何等为所住处？何等为所行处？何等为观察？何等为普观察？何等为奋迅？何等为师子吼？何等为清净施？何等为清净戒？何等为清净忍？何等为清净精进？何等为清净定？何等为清净慧？何等为清净慈？何等为清净悲？何等为清净喜？何等为清净舍？何等为义？何等为法？何等为福德助道具？何等为智慧助道具？何等为明足？何等为求法？何等为明了法？何等为修行法？何等为魔？何等为魔业？何等为舍离魔业？何等为见佛？何等为佛业？何等为慢业？何等为智业？何等为魔所摄持？何等为佛所摄持？何等为法所摄持？何等为住兜率天所作业？何故于兜率天宫殁？

(280a14–280a26)

Chapter 38 – Transcending the World

What constitutes his recumbence?
What constitutes his abodes?
What constitutes his places of practice?
What constitutes his [other] contemplations?[89]
What constitutes his universal contemplations?
What constitutes his swiftness?
What constitutes his lion's roar?
What constitutes his pure giving?
What constitutes his pure moral precepts?
What constitutes his pure patience?
What constitutes his pure vigor?
What constitutes his pure meditative concentration?
What constitutes his pure wisdom?
What constitutes his pure kindness?
What constitutes his pure compassion?
What constitutes his pure sympathetic joy?
What constitutes his pure equanimity?
What constitutes his meanings?
What constitutes his dharmas?
What constitutes his merit-based provisions for the enlightenment?
What constitutes his wisdom-based provisions for enlightenment?
What constitutes his completely developed clarities?
What constitutes his ways of seeking the Dharma?
What constitutes his dharmas for attaining complete understanding?
What constitutes his cultivation dharmas?
What constitutes the *māras*?
What constitutes the works of the *māras*?
What constitutes the ways of abandoning the works of the *māras*?
What constitutes the ways of seeing the Buddha?
What constitutes the buddha works?
What constitutes the arrogant actions?
What constitutes the wise actions?
What constitutes the ways of being possessed by Māra?
What constitutes the ways of being possessed by the Buddha?
What constitutes the ways of being possessed by the Dharma?
What constitutes the works accomplished while dwelling in the Tuṣita Heaven?
Why does he pass away from his dwelling in the Tuṣita Heaven?

正體字

280a27 何故現處胎。何等為現微細趣。何故現初生。
280a28 何故現微笑。何故示行七步。何故現童子地。
280a29 何故現處內宮。何故現出家。何故示苦行。云
280b01 何往詣道場。云何坐道場。何等為坐道場時
280b02 奇特相。何故示降魔。何等為成如來力。云何
280b03 轉法輪。何故因轉法輪。得白淨法。何故如來
280b04 應正等覺。示般涅槃。善哉佛子。如是等法。願
280b05 為演說
280b06 爾時普賢菩薩。告普慧等。諸菩薩言。佛子。菩
280b07 薩摩訶薩。有十種依。何等為十。所謂以菩提
280b08 心為依。恒不忘失故。以善知識為依。和合如
280b09 一故。以善根為依。修[1]集增長故。以波羅蜜
280b10 為依。具足修行故。以一切法為依。究竟出離
280b11 故。以大願為依。增長菩提故。以諸行為依。普
280b12 皆成就故。

简体字

何故现处胎？何等为现微细趣？何故现初生？何故现微笑？何故示行七步？何故现童子地？何故现处内宫？何故现出家？何故示苦行？云何往诣道场？云何坐道场？何等为坐道场时奇特相？何故示降魔？何等为成如来力？云何转法轮？何故因转法轮得白净法？何故如来、应、正等觉示般涅槃？善哉！佛子，如是等法，愿为演说！"

尔时，普贤菩萨告普慧等诸菩萨言："佛子，菩萨摩诃萨有十种依。何等为十？所谓：以菩提心为依，恒不忘失故；以善知识为依，和合如一故；以善根为依，修习增长故；以波罗蜜为依，具足修行故；以一切法为依，究竟出离故；以大愿为依，增长菩提故；以诸行为依，普皆成就故；

Chapter 38 — *Transcending the World*

> Why does he manifest as dwelling within the womb?
> What then constitutes his manifestation of subtle endeavors?
> Why does he manifest as having just taken birth?
> Why does he manifest a subtle smile?
> Why does he manifest the walking seven steps?
> Why does he manifest on the ground of the pure youth?
> Why does he manifest abiding within the inner palace?
> Why does he manifest as leaving the household life?
> Why does he manifest as practicing the austerities?
> Why does he then go to the site of enlightenment?
> Why does he then sit at the site of enlightenment?
> What constitutes the extraordinary signs that occur when he sits at the site of enlightenment?
> Why does he manifest as conquering the *māras*?
> What constitutes his realization of the Tathāgata's powers?
> Why does he turn the wheel of the Dharma?
> How is it that, because of turning the wheel of the Dharma, he acquires the dharmas of purity?
> Why does the Tathāgata, the Arhat, the One of Right and Perfect Enlightenment manifest *parinirvāṇa*?

It would be good indeed, O Son of the Buddha, if you would please expound on dharmas such as these for our benefit.

Samantabhadra Bodhisattva then told Universal Wisdom and the other bodhisattvas:

> Sons of the Buddha, the bodhisattva-mahāsattva has ten kinds of things upon which he relies. What are those ten? They are as follows:
>
>> He relies on the resolve to attain bodhi, doing so through never forgetting or losing it;
>>
>> He relies on the good spiritual guide, doing so by remaining as harmoniously united with him as if they were one;
>>
>> He relies on roots of goodness, doing so through cultivating, accumulating, and increasing them;
>>
>> He relies on the *pāramitās*, doing so through cultivating them to complete fulfillment;
>>
>> He relies on all dharmas, doing so because they ultimately result in emancipation;
>>
>> He relies on great vows, doing so because they cause the growth of bodhi;
>>
>> He relies on all the practices, doing so by completely developing them all;

正體字

以一切菩薩為依。同一智慧故。以供養諸佛為依。信心清淨故。以一切如來為依。如慈父教誨不斷故。是為十。若諸菩薩。安住此法。則得為如來無上大智。所依處。佛子。菩薩摩訶薩。有十種奇特想。何等為十。所謂於一切善根。生自善根想。於一切善根。生菩提種子想。於一切眾生。生菩提器想。於一切願。生自願想。於一切法。生出離想。於一切行。生自行想。於一切法。生佛法想。於一切語言法。生語言道想。於一切佛。生慈父想。於一切如來。生無二想。是為十。若諸菩薩。安住此法。則得無上善巧想。佛子。菩薩摩訶薩。有十種行。何等為十。所謂一切眾生行。普令成熟故。一切求法行。咸悉修學故。一切善根行。悉使增長故。一切三昧行。一心不亂故。一切智慧行。無不了知[2]故。一切修習行。無不能修故。一切佛剎行。皆悉莊嚴故。

简体字

以一切菩萨为依，同一智慧故；以供养诸佛为依，信心清净故；以一切如来为依，如慈父教诲不断故。是为十。若诸菩萨安住此法，则得为如来无上大智所依处。

"佛子，菩萨摩诃萨有十种奇特想。何等为十？所谓：于一切善根生自善根想；于一切善根生菩提种子想；于一切众生生菩提器想；于一切愿生自愿想；于一切法生出离想；于一切行生自行想；于一切法生佛法想；于一切语言法生语言道想；于一切佛生慈父想；于一切如来生无二想。是为十。若诸菩萨安住此法，则得无上善巧想。

"佛子，菩萨摩诃萨有十种行。何等为十？所谓：一切众生行，普令成熟故；一切求法行，咸悉修学故；一切善根行，悉使增长故；一切三昧行，一心不乱故；一切智慧行，无不了知故；一切修习行，无不能修故；一切佛刹行，皆悉庄严故；

Chapter 38 — *Transcending the World*

He relies on all the bodhisattvas, doing so because they share the same single [body of] wisdom;

He relies on offerings to all buddhas, doing so through maintaining purity in the mind of faith; and

He relies on all *tathāgatas* because, like a kindly father, they incessantly provide him with instruction.

These are the ten. If bodhisattvas abide in these dharmas, then they themselves will succeed in becoming abodes of the Tathāgata's unexcelled wisdom.

Sons of the Buddha, the bodhisattva-mahāsattva has ten kinds of extraordinary thought. What are those ten? They are as follows:

He thinks of all roots of goodness as his own roots of goodness;

He thinks of all roots of goodness as seeds of bodhi;

He thinks of all beings as vessels of bodhi;

He thinks of all vows as his own vows;

He thinks of all dharmas as [means of attaining] emancipation;

He thinks of all practices as his own practices;

He thinks of all dharmas as dharmas of the Buddha;

He thinks of all dharmas of speech as constituting the path of speech;

He thinks of all buddhas as kindly fathers; and

He thinks of all *tathāgatas* as non-dual.

These are the ten. If bodhisattvas abide in these dharmas, then they acquire thought which is unexcelled in its skillful means.

Sons of the Buddha, the bodhisattva-mahāsattva has ten kinds of practices. What are those ten? They are as follows:

Practices related to all beings, to enable them all to become ripened;

Practices related to all means of seeking Dharma, to cultivate and train in them all;

Practices related to all roots of goodness, to cause them all to grow;

Practices related to all samādhis, to bring about undistracted single-mindedness;

Practices related to all [aspects of] wisdom, to have none of them he does not completely understand;

[Practices related to all the spiritual superknowledges, to facilitate sovereign mastery in spiritual transformations];[90]

Practices related to all means of cultivation, to have none he is unable to cultivate;

Practices related to all buddha *kṣetras, to* adorn them all;

正體字	一切善友行。恭敬供養故。一切如來行。尊重承事故。是為十。若諸菩薩。安住此法。則得如來無上大智慧行。佛子。菩薩摩訶薩。有十種善知識。何等為十。所謂令住菩提心善知識。令生善根善知識。令行諸波羅蜜善知識。令解說一切法善知識。令成熟一切眾生善知識。令得決定辯才善知識。令不著一切世間善知識。令於一切劫。修行無厭倦善知識。令安住普賢行善知識。令入一切佛智所入善知識。是為十。佛子。菩薩摩訶薩。有十種勤精進。何等為十。所謂教化一切眾生勤精進。深入一切法勤精進。嚴淨一切世界勤精進。修行一切菩薩所學勤精進。滅除一切眾生惡勤精進。止息一切三惡道苦勤精進。摧破一切眾魔勤精進。願為一切眾生。作清淨眼勤精進。供養一切諸佛勤精進。

(280b29–280c15)

简体字：

一切善友行，恭敬供养故；一切如来行，尊重承事故；一切神通行，变化自在故。是为十。若诸菩萨安住此法，则得如来无上大智慧行。

"佛子，菩萨摩诃萨有十种善知识。何等为十？所谓：令住菩提心善知识；令生善根善知识；令行诸波罗蜜善知识；令解说一切法善知识；令成熟一切众生善知识；令得决定辩才善知识；令不著一切世间善知识；令于一切劫修行无厌倦善知识；令安住普贤行善知识；令入一切佛智所入善知识。是为十。

"佛子，菩萨摩诃萨有十种勤精进。何等为十？所谓：教化一切众生勤精进；深入一切法勤精进；严净一切世界勤精进；修行一切菩萨所学勤精进；灭除一切众生恶勤精进；止息一切三恶道苦勤精进；摧破一切众魔勤精进；愿为一切众生作清净眼勤精进；供养一切诸佛勤精进；

Chapter 38 — *Transcending the World*

Practices related to all good spiritual guides, to respect and make offerings to them; and

Practices related to all *tathāgatas*, to revere and serve them.

These are the ten. If bodhisattvas abide in these dharmas, then they acquire practices related to the unexcelled great wisdom of the Tathāgata.

Sons of the Buddha, the bodhisattva-mahāsattva has ten kinds of good spiritual guides. What are those ten? They are as follows:

The good spiritual guide who enables one to abide in the bodhi resolve;

The good spiritual guide who enables one to produce roots of goodness;

The good spiritual guide who enables one to practice the *pāramitās*;

The good spiritual guide who enables one to explain all dharmas;

The good spiritual guide who enables one to ripen all beings;

The good spiritual guide who enables one to acquire decisive eloquence;

The good spiritual guide who enables one to not become attached to anything in the world;

The good spiritual guide who enables one to cultivate tirelessly throughout all kalpas;

The good spiritual guide who enables one to securely abide in the practices of Samantabhadra; and

The good spiritual guide who enables one to penetrate everything penetrated by the wisdom of all buddhas.

These are the ten.

Sons of the Buddha, the bodhisattva-mahāsattva has ten kinds of diligent vigor. What are those ten? They are as follows:

The diligent vigor with which he teaches all beings;

The diligent vigor with which he deeply penetrates all dharmas;

The diligent vigor with which he purifies all worlds;

The diligent vigor with which he cultivates everything in which all bodhisattvas train;

The diligent vigor with which he extinguishes the evil of all beings;

The diligent vigor with which he stops all the sufferings in the three wretched destinies;

The diligent vigor with which he vanquishes all the many *māras*;

The diligent vigor with which he wishes to serve all beings as their purified vision;

正體字

令一切如來。皆悉歡喜勤精進。是為
十。若諸菩薩安住此法。則得具足如來無上
精進波羅蜜。佛子。菩薩摩訶薩。有十種心得
安隱。何等為十。所謂自住菩提心。亦當令他
住菩提心。心得安隱。自究竟離忿諍。亦當令
他離忿諍。心得安隱。自離凡愚法。亦令他離
凡愚法。心得安隱。自勤修善根。亦令他勤修
善根。心得安隱。自住波羅蜜道。亦令他住波
羅蜜道。心得安隱。自生在佛家。亦當令他生
於佛家。心得安隱。自深入無自性真實法。亦
令他入無自性真實法。心得安隱。自不誹謗
一切佛法。亦令他不誹謗一切佛法。心得安
隱。自滿一切智菩提願。亦令他滿一切智菩
提願。心得安隱。自深入一切如來。無盡智藏。
亦令他入一切如來。無盡智藏。心得安隱。是
為十。若諸菩薩。安住此法。則得如來無上大
智安隱。

简体字

令一切如来皆悉欢喜勤精进。是为十。若诸菩萨安住此法，则得具足如来无上精进波罗蜜。

"佛子，菩萨摩诃萨有十种心得安隐。何等为十？所谓：自住菩提心，亦当令他住菩提心，心得安隐；自究竟离忿诤，亦当令他离忿诤，心得安隐；自离凡愚法，亦令他离凡愚法，心得安隐；自勤修善根，亦令他勤修善根，心得安隐；自住波罗蜜道，亦令他住波罗蜜道，心得安隐；自生在佛家，亦当令他生于佛家，心得安隐；自深入无自性真实法，亦令他入无自性真实法，心得安隐；自不诽谤一切佛法，亦令他不诽谤一切佛法，心得安隐；自满一切智菩提愿，亦令他满一切智菩提愿，心得安隐；自深入一切如来无尽智藏，亦令他入一切如来无尽智藏，心得安隐。是为十。若诸菩萨安住此法，则得如来无上大智安隐。

Chapter 38 — *Transcending the World*

> The diligent vigor with which he makes offerings to all buddhas; and
>
> The diligent vigor with which he pleases all *tathāgatas*.

These are the ten. If bodhisattvas abide in these dharmas, then they are able to completely fulfill the Tathāgata's *pāramitā* of unexcelled vigor.

Sons of the Buddha, the bodhisattva-mahāsattva has ten bases for attaining peace of mind. What are those ten? They are as follows:

> He attains peace of mind through personally dwelling in the resolve to attain bodhi while also feeling he should enable others to dwell in the resolve to attain bodhi;
>
> He attains peace of mind through personally ultimately abandoning anger and disputation while also feeling he should enable others to abandon anger and disputation;
>
> He attains peace of mind through personally abandoning the dharmas of the foolish common person while also enabling others to abandon the dharmas of the foolish common person;
>
> He attains peace of mind through personally diligently cultivating roots of goodness while also enabling others to diligently cultivate roots of goodness;
>
> He attains peace of mind through personally dwelling in the path of the *pāramitās* while also enabling others to dwell in the path of the *pāramitās*;
>
> He attains peace of mind through personally being born into the family of the buddhas while also feeling he should enable others to be born into the family of the buddhas;
>
> He attains peace of mind through personally deeply penetrating the genuine dharma of the nonexistence of any inherently existent nature while also enabling others to penetrate the genuine dharma of the nonexistence of any inherently existent nature;
>
> He attains peace of mind through personally refraining from ever slandering the Dharma of all buddhas while also enabling others to refrain from ever slandering the Dharma of all buddhas;
>
> He attains peace of mind through personally fulfilling the bodhi vow to attain all-knowledge while also enabling others to fulfill the bodhi vow to attain all-knowledge; and
>
> He attains peace of mind through personally deeply entering all *tathāgatas'* treasury of inexhaustible wisdom while also enabling others to enter all *tathāgatas'* treasury of inexhaustible wisdom.

These are the ten. If bodhisattvas abide in these dharmas, then they attain the peace of mind of the Tathāgata's unexcelled great wisdom.

正體字

佛子。菩薩摩訶薩。有十種成就眾生。
何等為十。所謂以布施成就眾生。以色身成
就眾生。以說法成就眾生。以同行成就眾生。
以無染著成就眾生。以開示菩薩行。成就眾
生。以熾然示現一切世界。成就眾生。以示現
佛法大威德。成就眾生。以種種神通變現。成
就眾生。以種種微密。善巧方便。成就眾生。是
為十。菩薩以此。成就眾生界。佛子。菩薩摩訶
薩。有十種戒。何等為十。所謂不捨菩提心戒。
遠離二乘地戒。觀察利益一切眾生戒。令一
切眾生住佛法戒。修一切菩薩所學戒。於一
切法。無所得戒。以一切善根。迴向菩提戒。不
著一切如來身戒。思惟一切法。離取著戒。

简体字

"佛子，菩萨摩诃萨有十种成就众生。何等为十？所谓：以布施成就众生；以色身成就众生；以说法成就众生；以同行成就众生；以无染著成就众生；以开示菩萨行成就众生；以炽然示现一切世界成就众生；以示现佛法大威德成就众生；以种种神通变现成就众生；以种种微密善巧方便成就众生。是为十。菩萨以此成就众生界。

"佛子，菩萨摩诃萨有十种戒。何等为十？所谓：不舍菩提心戒；远离二乘地戒；观察利益一切众生戒；令一切众生住佛法戒；修一切菩萨所学戒；于一切法无所得戒；以一切善根回向菩提戒；不著一切如来身戒；思惟一切法离取著戒；

Chapter 38 — *Transcending the World*

Sons of the Buddha, the bodhisattva-mahāsattva has ten ways of developing beings. What are these ten? They are as follows:

He develops beings through giving;

He develops beings through use of the form body;

He develops beings through speaking Dharma;

He develops beings through engaging in joint endeavors with them;

He develops beings through remaining free of defiling attachments;

He develops beings through providing instruction in the bodhisattva practices;

He develops beings through brightly revealing all worlds to them;

He develops beings through revealing the great awesome virtue of the Buddha's Dharma;

He develops beings through using the appearance of many different kinds of transformations produced by his spiritual super-knowledges; and

He develops beings through using many different kinds of subtle and esoteric skillful means.

These are the ten. The bodhisattva uses these to develop those in the realms of beings.

Sons of the Buddha, the bodhisattva-mahāsattva has ten kinds of moral precepts. What are those ten? They are as follows:

The moral precept requiring that one never relinquish the bodhi resolve;

The moral precept requiring that one abandon the grounds of the two vehicles;

The moral precept requiring one to contemplate and benefit all beings;

The moral precept requiring one to enable all beings to abide in the Buddha's Dharma;

The moral precept requiring one to cultivate everything in which all bodhisattvas train;

The moral precept requiring one to realize that all dharmas are inapprehensible;[91]

The moral precept requiring one to dedicate all roots of goodness to the realization of bodhi;

The moral precept requiring one to remain unattached to any of the bodies of all *tathāgatas*;

The moral precept that requires one to reflect on all dharmas and abandon any attachment to them; and

正體字

諸根律儀戒。是為十。若諸菩薩。安住此法。則得如來無上廣大。戒波羅蜜。佛子。菩薩摩訶薩。有十種受記法。菩薩以此。自知受記。何等為十。所謂以殊勝意。發菩提心。自知受記。永不厭捨諸菩薩行。自知受記。住一切劫。行菩薩行。自知受記。修一切佛法。自知受記。於一切佛教。一向深信。自知受記。修一切善根。皆令成就。自知受記。置一切眾生。於佛菩提。自知受記。於一切善知識。和合無二。自知受記。於一切善知識。起如來想。自知受記。恒勤守護菩提本願。自知受記。是為十。佛子。菩薩摩訶薩。有十種入。入諸菩薩。何等為十。所謂入本願。入行入聚。入諸波羅蜜。

简体字

诸根律仪戒。是为十。若诸菩萨安住此法，则得如来无上广大戒波罗蜜。

"佛子，菩萨摩诃萨有十种受记法，菩萨以此自知受记。何等为十？所谓：以殊胜意发菩提心，自知受记；永不厌舍诸菩萨行，自知受记；住一切劫行菩萨行，自知受记；修一切佛法，自知受记；于一切佛教一向深信，自知受记；修一切善根皆令成就，自知受记；置一切众生于佛菩提，自知受记；于一切善知识和合无二，自知受记；于一切善知识起如来想，自知受记；恒勤守护菩提本愿，自知受记。是为十。

"佛子，菩萨摩诃萨有十种入，入诸菩萨。何等为十？所谓：入本愿；入行；入聚；入诸波罗蜜；

Chapter 38 — Transcending the World

The moral precept requiring that one observe the right regulation of all one's faculties.

These are the ten. If bodhisattvas abide in these dharmas, then then they acquire the Tathāgata's unexcelled and vast *pāramitā* of moral virtue.

Sons of the Buddha, the bodhisattva-mahāsattva has ten dharmas associated with receiving the prediction [of future buddhahood]. It is due to these that the bodhisattva knows he is bound to receive the prediction. What are those ten? They are as follows:

It is through especially superior will in generating the bodhi resolve that he knows he is bound to receive the prediction;

It is through never wearying of or abandoning any of the bodhisattva practices that he knows he is bound to receive the prediction;

It is through abiding throughout all kalpas in practicing the bodhisattva practices that he knows he is bound to receive the prediction;

It is through cultivating all dharmas of the Buddha that he knows he is bound to receive the prediction;

It is through always having deep faith in all teachings of the Buddha that he knows he is bound to receive the prediction;

It is through cultivating all roots of goodness and causing them all to become completely developed that he knows he is bound to receive the prediction;

It is through establishing all beings in the Buddha's bodhi that he knows he is bound to receive the prediction;

It is through joining together harmoniously with all good spiritual guides in a state of non-dual unity that he knows he is bound to receive the prediction;

It is through envisioning all good spiritual guides as *tathāgatas* that he knows he is bound to receive the prediction; and

It is through constantly diligent preservation of his original vow to realize bodhi that he knows he is bound to receive the prediction.

These are the ten.

Sons of the Buddha, the bodhisattva-mahāsattva has ten kinds of entry among the bodhisattvas. What are those ten? They are as follows:

Entry into their original vows;
Entry into their practices;
Entry into their accumulations;[92]
Entry into their *pāramitās*;

正體字

入成就。入差別
願。入種種解。入莊嚴佛土。入神力自在。入示
現受生。是為十。菩薩以此。普入三世一切菩
薩。佛子。菩薩摩訶薩。有十種入。入諸如來。
何等為十。所謂入無邊成正覺。入無邊轉法
輪。入無邊方便法。入無邊差別音聲。入無邊
調伏眾生。入無邊神力自在。入無邊種種差
別身。入無邊三昧。入無邊力無所畏。入無邊
示現涅槃。是為十。菩薩以此。普入三世一切
如來。佛子。菩薩摩訶薩。有十種入眾生行。何
等為十。所謂入一切眾生過去行。入一切眾
生未來行。入一切眾生現在行。入一切眾生
善行。入一切眾生不善行。入一切眾生心行。
入一切眾生根行。入一切眾生解行。入一切
眾生。煩惱習氣行。入一切眾生。教化調伏。時
非時行。

简体字

入成就；入差别愿；入种种解；入庄严佛土；入神力自在；入示现受生。是为十。菩萨以此普入三世一切菩萨。

"佛子，菩萨摩诃萨有十种入，入诸如来。何等为十？所谓：入无边成正觉；入无边转法轮；入无边方便法；入无边差别音声；入无边调伏众生；入无边神力自在；入无边种种差别身；入无边三昧；入无边力、无所畏；入无边示现涅槃。是为十。菩萨以此普入三世一切如来。

"佛子，菩萨摩诃萨有十种入众生行。何等为十？所谓：入一切众生过去行；入一切众生未来行；入一切众生现在行；入一切众生善行；入一切众生不善行；入一切众生心行；入一切众生根行；入一切众生解行；入一切众生烦恼习气行；入一切众生教化调伏时、非时行。

Chapter 38 — *Transcending the World*

Entry into their successful achievements;
Entry into their various different vows;
Entry into their many different kinds of understandings;
Entry into their adornment of buddha lands;
Entry into their sovereign mastery of the spiritual powers; and
Entry into their manifesting the taking on of births.

These are the ten. The bodhisattva uses these to everywhere enter among all bodhisattvas of the three periods of time.

Sons of the Buddha, the bodhisattva-mahāsattva has ten kinds of entry among the Tathāgatas. What are those ten? They are as follows:

Entry into their boundless realization of right enlightenment;
Entry into their boundless turning of the Dharma wheel;
Entry into their boundless dharmas of skillful means;
Entry into their boundlessly many different voices;
Entry into their boundless training of beings;
Entry into their boundless sovereign mastery of the spiritual powers;
Entry into their boundlessly many different kinds of bodies;
Entry into their boundless samādhis;
Entry into their boundless powers and fearlessnesses; and
Entry into their boundless manifestations of nirvāṇa.

These are the ten. The bodhisattva uses these to everywhere enter among all *tathāgatas* of the three periods of time.

Sons of the Buddha, the bodhisattva-mahāsattva has ten kinds of penetration of beings' actions. What are those ten? They are as follows:

Penetration of all beings' past actions;
Penetration of all beings' future actions;
Penetration of all beings' present actions;
Penetration of all beings' good actions;
Penetration of all beings' bad actions;
Penetration of all beings' mental actions;
Penetration of all beings' actions arising from their faculties;
Penetration of all beings' actions arising from their understandings;
Penetration of all beings' actions arising from their affliction-based habitual karmic propensities; and
Penetration of all beings' actions in relation to their teaching and training and whether it was provided at the right time or the wrong time.

正體字

是為十。菩薩以此。普入一切諸眾生
行。佛子。菩薩摩訶薩。有十種入世界。何等為
十。所謂入染世界。入淨世界。入小世界。入大
世界。入微塵中世界。入微細世界。入覆世界。
入仰世界。入有佛世界。入無佛世界。是為十。
菩薩以此。普入十方一切世界。佛子。菩薩摩
訶薩。有十種入劫。何等為十。所謂入過去劫。
入未來劫。入現在劫。入可數劫。入不可數劫。
入可數劫即不可數劫。入不可數劫即可數
劫。入一切劫即非劫。入非劫即一切劫。入一
切劫即一念。是為十。菩薩以此。普入一切劫。
佛子。菩薩摩訶薩。有十種說三世。何等為十。
所謂過去世說過去世。過去世說未來世。過
去世說現在世。未來世說過去世。未來世說
現在世。未來世說無盡。

简体字

是为十。菩萨以此普入一切诸众生行。

"佛子,菩萨摩诃萨有十种入世界。何等为十?所谓:入染世界;入净世界;入小世界;入大世界;入微尘中世界;入微细世界;入覆世界;入仰世界;入有佛世界;入无佛世界。是为十。菩萨以此普入十方一切世界。

"佛子,菩萨摩诃萨有十种入劫。何等为十?所谓:入过去劫;入未来劫;入现在劫;入可数劫;入不可数劫;入可数劫即不可数劫;入不可数劫即可数劫;入一切劫即非劫;入非劫即一切劫;入一切劫即一念。是为十。菩萨以此普入一切劫。

"佛子,菩萨摩诃萨有十种说三世。何等为十?所谓:过去世说过去世;过去世说未来世;过去世说现在世;未来世说过去世;未来世说现在世;未来世说无尽;

Chapter 38 — *Transcending the World*

These are the ten. The bodhisattva uses these to everywhere penetrate the practices of all beings.

Sons of the Buddha, the bodhisattva-mahāsattva has ten kinds of entry into worlds. What are those ten? They are as follows:

Entry into defiled worlds;
Entry into pure worlds;
Entry into small worlds;
Entry into large worlds;
Entry into worlds within atoms;
Entry into minute worlds;
Entry into inverted worlds;
Entry into upward-facing worlds;
Entry into worlds in which buddhas are present; and
Entry into worlds without buddhas.

These are the ten. The bodhisattva uses these to everywhere enter all worlds of the ten directions.

Sons of the Buddha, the bodhisattva-mahāsattva has ten kinds of entry into kalpas. What are those ten? They are as follows:

Entry into past kalpas;
Entry into future kalpas;
Entry into present kalpas;
Entry into calculably many kalpas;
Entry into incalculably many kalpas;
Entry into calculably many kalpas that are just incalculably many kalpas;
Entry into incalculably many kalpas that are just calculably many kalpas;
Entry into all kalpas that are just non-kalpas;
Entry into non-kalpas that are just all kalpas; and
Entry into all kalpas that are just a single mind-moment.

These are the ten. The bodhisattva uses these to enter all kalpas.

Sons of the Buddha, the bodhisattva-mahāsattva has ten ways of speaking of the three periods of time. What are those ten? They are as follows:

Speaking of past periods of time in the past;
Speaking of future periods of time in the past;
Speaking of present periods of time in the past;
Speaking of past periods of time in the future;
Speaking of present periods of time in the future;
Speaking of the future as endless;

正體字

現在世說過去世。現
在世說未來世。現在世說平等。現在世說三
世即一念。是為十。菩薩以此。普說三世。佛
子。菩薩摩訶薩。有十種知三世。何等為十。所
謂知諸安立。知諸語言。知諸談議。知諸軌則。
知諸稱[1]謂。知諸制令。知其假名。知其無盡。
知其寂滅。知一切空。是為十。菩薩以此。普知
一切三世諸法。佛子。菩薩摩訶薩。發十種無
疲厭心。何等為十。所謂供養一切諸佛無疲
厭心。親近一切善知識無疲厭心。求一切法
無疲厭心。聽聞正法無疲厭心。宣說正法無
疲厭心。教化調伏一切眾生無疲厭心。置一
切眾生。於佛菩提無疲厭心。於一一世界。經
不可說不可說劫。行菩薩行無疲厭心。遊行
一切世界無疲厭心。觀察思惟一切佛法無疲
厭心。

简体字

现在世说过去世；现在世说未来世；现在世说平等；现在世说三世即一念。是为十。菩萨以此普说三世。

"佛子，菩萨摩诃萨有十种知三世。何等为十？所谓：知诸安立；知诸语言；知诸谈议；知诸轨则；知诸称谓；知诸制令；知其假名；知其无尽；知其寂灭；知一切空。是为十。菩萨以此普知一切三世诸法。

"佛子，菩萨摩诃萨发十种无疲厌心。何等为十？所谓：供养一切诸佛无疲厌心；亲近一切善知识无疲厌心；求一切法无疲厌心；听闻正法无疲厌心；宣说正法无疲厌心；教化调伏一切众生无疲厌心；置一切众生于佛菩提无疲厌心；于一一世界经不可说不可说劫行菩萨行无疲厌心；游行一切世界无疲厌心；观察思惟一切佛法无疲厌心。

Chapter 38 — *Transcending the World*

Speaking of the past in the present;
Speaking of the future in the present;
Speaking of their uniform equality in the present; and
Speaking in the present of the three periods of time being equal to but a single mind-moment.

These are the ten. The bodhisattva uses these to speak of all three periods of time.

Sons of the Buddha, the bodhisattva-mahāsattva has ten kinds of knowing of the three periods of time. What are those ten? They are as follows:

He knows all of their arrangements;
He knows all of their languages;
He knows all of their discussions;
He knows all of their rules and regulations;
He knows all of their declarations;
He knows all of their edicts;
He knows all of their false designations;
He knows their endlessness;
He knows their quiescence; and
He knows them all as entirely empty [of inherent existence].

These are the ten. The bodhisattva uses these to know all dharmas of the three periods of time.

Sons of the Buddha, the bodhisattva-mahāsattva brings forth ten kinds of tireless mind. What are those ten? They are as follows:

The mind that is tireless in making offerings to all buddhas;
The mind that is tireless in drawing near to all good spiritual guides;
The mind that is tireless in seeking all dharmas;
The mind that is tireless in listening to right Dharma;
The mind that is tireless in proclaiming and explaining right Dharma;
The mind that is tireless in teaching and training all beings;
The mind that is tireless in establishing all beings in the bodhi of the Buddha;
The mind that is tireless in passing through an ineffable-ineffable number of kalpas in each and every world as he practices the bodhisattva practices;
The mind that is tireless in traveling to all worlds; and
The mind that is tireless in contemplating and reflecting on all dharmas of the Buddha.

正體字

是為十。若諸菩薩。安住此法。則得如來
無疲厭無上大智。佛子。菩薩摩訶薩。有十種
差別智。何等為十。所謂知眾生差別智。知諸
根差別智。知業報差別智。知受生差別智。知
世界差別智。知法界差別智。知諸佛差別智。
知諸法差別智。知三世差別智。知一切語言
道差別智。是為十。若諸菩薩。安住此法。則得
如來無上廣大差別智。佛子。菩薩摩訶薩。有
十種陀羅尼。何等為十。所謂聞持陀羅尼持
一切法。不忘失故。修行陀羅尼。如實巧觀一
切法故。思惟陀羅尼。了知一切諸法性故。法
光明陀羅尼。照不思議諸佛法故。三昧陀羅
尼。普於現在一切佛所。聽聞正法。心不亂故。
圓音陀羅尼。解了不思議。音聲語言故。三世
陀羅尼。演說三世不可思議。諸佛法故。種種
[2]辯才陀羅尼。演說無邊諸佛法故。

简体字

是为十。若诸菩萨安住此法，则得如来无疲厌无上大智。

"佛子，菩萨摩诃萨有十种差别智。何等为十？所谓：知众生差别智；知诸根差别智；知业报差别智；知受生差别智；知世界差别智；知法界差别智；知诸佛差别智；知诸法差别智；知三世差别智；知一切语言道差别智。是为十。若诸菩萨安住此法，则得如来无上广大差别智。

"佛子，菩萨摩诃萨有十种陀罗尼。何等为十？所谓：闻持陀罗尼，持一切法不忘失故；修行陀罗尼，如实巧观一切法故；思惟陀罗尼，了知一切诸法性故；法光明陀罗尼，照不思议诸佛法故；三昧陀罗尼，普于现在一切佛所听闻正法心不乱故；圆音陀罗尼，解了不思议音声语言故；三世陀罗尼，演说三世不可思议诸佛法故；种种辩才陀罗尼，演说无边诸佛法故；

Chapter 38 — *Transcending the World*

These are the ten. If bodhisattvas abide in these dharmas, then they acquire the Tathāgata's tireless and unexcelled great wisdom.

Sons of the Buddha, the bodhisattva-mahāsattva has ten kinds of knowledge of differences. What are those ten? They are as follows:

The knowledge that knows the differences in beings;
The knowledge that knows the differences in their faculties;
The knowledge that knows the differences in their karmic consequences;
The knowledge that knows the differences in their taking on of rebirths;
The knowledge that knows the differences in the worlds;
The knowledge that knows the differences in the Dharma realm;
The knowledge that knows the differences among all buddhas;
The knowledge that knows the differences in all dharmas;
The knowledge that knows the differences throughout the three periods of time; and
The knowledge that knows the differences in the paths of speech.

These are the ten. If bodhisattvas abide in these dharmas, then they acquire the Tathāgata's unexcelled and vast knowledge of differences.

Sons of the Buddha, the bodhisattva-mahāsattva has ten kinds of *dhāraṇīs*. What are those ten? They are as follows:

The "listening-and-retaining" *dhāraṇī*, so called because, through it, one retains all dharmas and never forgets them;
The "cultivation" *dhāraṇī*, so called because it facilitates the skillful contemplation of all dharmas in accordance with reality;
The "reflective contemplation" *dhāraṇī*, so called because it facilitates the complete knowing of the nature of all dharmas;
The "Dharma light" *dhāraṇī*, so called because it facilitates illumination of the inconceivable Dharma of all buddhas;
The "samādhi" *dhāraṇī*, so called because it facilitates remaining unconfused with regard to right Dharma as heard in the abodes of all buddhas of the present;
The "perfect sound" *dhāraṇī*, so called because it facilitates the complete understanding of inconceivably many voices and languages;
The "three periods of time" *dhāraṇī*, so called because it facilitates expounding on inconceivably many dharmas of all buddhas of the three periods of time;
The "various forms of eloquence" *dhāraṇī*, so called because it facilitates expounding the boundless Dharma of all buddhas;

正體字

出生無礙耳陀羅尼。不可說佛所說之法。悉能聞故。一切佛法陀羅尼。安住如來力無畏故。是為十。若諸菩薩。欲得此法當勤修學。佛子。菩薩摩訶薩。說十種佛。何等為十。所謂成正覺佛。願佛。業報佛。住持佛。涅槃佛。法界佛。心佛。三昧佛。本性佛。隨樂佛。是為十。

佛子。菩薩摩訶薩。發十種普賢心。何等為十。所謂發大慈心。救護一切眾生故。發大悲心。代一切眾生受苦故。發一切施心。悉捨所有故。發念一切智為首心。樂求一切佛法故。發功德莊嚴心。學一切菩薩行故。發如金剛心。一切處受生。不忘失故。發如海心。一切白淨法。悉流入故。發如大山王心。一切惡言。皆忍受故。發安隱心。施一切眾生。無怖畏故。

简体字

出生无碍耳陀罗尼，不可说佛所说之法悉能闻故；一切佛法陀罗尼，安住如来力、无畏故。是为十。若诸菩萨欲得此法，当勤修学。

"佛子，菩萨摩诃萨说十种佛。何等为十？所谓：成正觉佛；愿佛；业报佛；住持佛；涅槃佛；法界佛；心佛；三昧佛；本性佛；随乐佛。是为十。

"佛子，菩萨摩诃萨发十种普贤心。何等为十？所谓：发大慈心，救护一切众生故；发大悲心，代一切众生受苦故；发一切施心，悉舍所有故；发念一切智为首心，乐求一切佛法故；发功德庄严心，学一切菩萨行故；发如金刚心，一切处受生不忘失故；发如海心，一切白净法悉流入故；发如大山王心，一切恶言皆忍受故；发安隐心，施一切众生无怖畏故；

Chapter 38 — *Transcending the World*

The "producer of the unimpeded ear" *dhāraṇī*, so called because it facilitates the ability to hear all Dharma spoken by an ineffable number of buddhas; and

The "Dharma of all buddhas" *dhāraṇī*, so called because it facilitates abiding in the Tathāgata's powers and fearlessnesses.

These are the ten. If bodhisattvas wish to acquire these dharmas, then they should engage in diligent cultivation and training [in them].

Sons of the Buddha, the bodhisattva-mahāsattva speaks of ten kinds of buddhas. What are those ten? They are as follows:

The rightly enlightened buddha;
The buddha of vows;
The buddha of karmic rewards;
The abiding and sustaining buddha;
The nirvāṇa buddha;
The Dharma realm buddha;
The mind buddha;
The samādhi buddha;
The buddha of the fundamental nature; and
The buddha who adapts to the dispositions [of beings].

These are the ten.

Sons of the Buddha, the bodhisattva-mahāsattva brings forth ten kinds of universally worthy mind [of Samantabhadra]. What are those ten? They are as follows:

He brings forth the mind of great kindness to rescue and protect all beings;

He brings forth the mind of great compassion to substitute for all beings in undergoing sufferings;

He brings forth the mind that gives away everything to relinquish all that he owns;

He brings forth the mind that takes mindfulness of all-knowledge as what is foremost to happily seek all dharmas of the Buddha;

He brings forth the mind adorned with meritorious qualities to train in all the bodhisattva practices;

He brings forth the vajra-like mind to never forget any of the places he has taken rebirth;

He brings forth the ocean-like mind so that all the dharmas of purity will flow into it;

He brings forth the mind like the great king of mountains to patiently endure all harsh speech;

He brings forth the peaceful and secure mind to remain fearless in giving away everything to beings;

正體字

發般若波羅蜜究竟心。巧觀一切法。無所有故。是為十。若諸菩薩。安住此心。疾得成就普賢善巧智。佛子。菩薩摩訶薩。有十種普賢行法。何等為十。所謂願住未來一切劫普賢行法。願供養恭敬[1]本來一切佛普賢行法。願安置一切眾生。於普賢菩薩行普賢行法。願積集一切善根普賢行法。願入一切波羅蜜普賢行法。願滿足一切菩薩行普賢行法。願莊嚴一切世界普賢行法。願生一切佛刹普賢行法。願善觀察一切法普賢行法。願於一切佛國土。成無上菩提普賢行法。是為十。若諸菩薩。勤修此法。疾得滿足普賢行願。佛子。菩薩摩訶薩。以十種觀眾生。而起大悲。何等為十。所謂觀察眾生。無依無怙。而起大悲。觀察眾生。性不調順。而起大悲。觀察眾生。貧無善根。而起大悲。

简体字

发般若波罗蜜究竟心,巧观一切法无所有故。是为十。若诸菩萨安住此心,疾得成就普贤善巧智。

"佛子,菩萨摩诃萨有十种普贤行法。何等为十?所谓:愿住未来一切劫普贤行法;愿供养恭敬未来一切佛普贤行法;愿安置一切众生于普贤菩萨行普贤行法;愿积集一切善根普贤行法;愿入一切波罗蜜普贤行法;愿满足一切菩萨行普贤行法;愿庄严一切世界普贤行法;愿生一切佛刹普贤行法;愿善观察一切法普贤行法;愿于一切佛国土成无上菩提普贤行法。是为十。若诸菩萨勤修此法,疾得满足普贤行愿。

"佛子,菩萨摩诃萨以十种观众生而起大悲。何等为十?所谓:观察众生无依无怙而起大悲;观察众生性不调顺而起大悲;观察众生贫无善根而起大悲;

Chapter 38 — Transcending the World

> He brings forth the ultimate mind of the *prajñāpāramitā* to skillfully contemplate all dharmas as devoid of anything at all that exists.

These are the ten. If bodhisattvas abide in these types of minds, then they swiftly succeed in perfecting the universally worthy skillful wisdom [of Samantabhadra].

Sons of the Buddha, the bodhisattva-mahāsattva has ten kinds of universally worthy practice [of Samantabhadra]. What are those ten? They are as follows:

> The universally worthy practice dharma of vowing to remain [in the world] for all kalpas of the future;
>
> The universally worthy practice dharma of vowing to make offerings to and revere all buddhas of the future;
>
> The universally worthy practice dharma of vowing to establish all beings in the practices of Samantabhadra;
>
> The universally worthy practice dharma of vowing to accumulate all kinds of roots of goodness;
>
> The universally worthy practice dharma of vowing to enter all the *pāramitās*;
>
> The universally worthy practice dharma of vowing to completely fulfill all the bodhisattva practices;
>
> The universally worthy practice dharma of vowing to adorn all worlds;
>
> The universally worthy practice dharma of vowing to take on rebirths in all buddha *kṣetras*;
>
> The universally worthy practice dharma of vowing to skillfully contemplate all dharmas; and
>
> The universally worthy practice dharma of vowing to realize the unsurpassed bodhi in all buddha lands.

These are the ten. If bodhisattvas diligently cultivate these dharmas, then they swiftly succeed in completely fulfilling the universally worthy conduct and vows [of Samantabhadra].

Sons of the Buddha, the bodhisattva-mahāsattva arouses the great compassion by using ten kinds of contemplations of beings. What are those ten? They are as follows:

> Arousing the great compassion by contemplating beings as having no one to depend upon or rely on;
>
> Arousing the great compassion by contemplating beings as being, by their very nature, untrained and non-compliant;
>
> Arousing the great compassion by contemplating beings as poverty-stricken through having no roots of goodness;

正體字

觀察眾生。長夜睡眠。而起大悲。觀察
眾生。行不善法。而起大悲。觀察眾生。欲縛所
縛。而起大悲。觀察眾生。沒生死海。而起大
悲。觀察眾生。長嬰疾苦。而起大悲。觀察眾
生。無善法欲。而起大悲。觀察眾生。失諸佛法。
而起大悲。是為十。菩薩恒以此心。觀察眾生。
佛子。菩薩摩訶薩。有十種發菩提心因緣。何
等為十。所謂為教化調伏一切眾生故。發菩
提心。為除滅一切眾生苦聚故。發菩提心。為
與一切眾生。具足安樂故。發菩提心。為斷一
切眾生愚癡故。發菩提心。為與一切眾生佛
智故。發菩提心。為恭敬供養一切諸佛故。發
菩提心。為隨如來教。[2]令佛[歎>歡]喜故。發菩提
心。為見一切佛。色身相好故。發菩提心。為入
一切佛。廣大智慧故。發菩提心。為顯現諸佛
力無所畏故。發菩提心。是為十。佛子。若菩薩
發無上菩提心。為悟入一切智智故。

简体字

观察众生长夜睡眠而起大悲；观察众生行不善法而起大悲；观察众生欲缚所缚而起大悲；观察众生没生死海而起大悲；观察众生长婴疾苦而起大悲；观察众生无善法欲而起大悲；观察众生失诸佛法而起大悲。是为十。菩萨恒以此心观察众生。

"佛子，菩萨摩诃萨有十种发菩提心因缘。何等为十？所谓：为教化调伏一切众生故，发菩提心；为除灭一切众生苦聚故，发菩提心；为与一切众生具足安乐故，发菩提心；为断一切众生愚痴故，发菩提心；为与一切众生佛智故，发菩提心；为恭敬供养一切诸佛故，发菩提心；为随如来教，令佛欢喜故，发菩提心；为见一切佛色身相好故，发菩提心；为入一切佛广大智慧故，发菩提心；为显现诸佛力、无所畏故，发菩提心。是为十。

"佛子，若菩萨发无上菩提心，为悟入一切智智故，

Chapter 38 — *Transcending the World*

Arousing the great compassion by contemplating beings as sleeping throughout the long night [of ignorance];

Arousing the great compassion by contemplating beings as practicing unwholesome dharmas;

Arousing the great compassion by contemplating beings as tied up by the bonds of desire;

Arousing the great compassion by contemplating beings as sunken into the ocean of *saṃsāra*;

Arousing the great compassion by contemplating beings as forever entangled in the suffering of sickness;

Arousing the great compassion by contemplating beings as having no wish to practice wholesome dharmas; and

Arousing the great compassion by contemplating beings as having lost the Dharma of the buddhas.

These are the ten. The bodhisattva constantly uses these types of thoughts in contemplating beings.

Sons of the Buddha, the bodhisattva-mahāsattva has ten kinds of causes and conditions for arousing the bodhi resolve. What are those ten? They are as follows:

He arouses the bodhi resolve to teach and train all beings;

He arouses the bodhi resolve to do away with all beings' accumulations of sufferings;

He arouses the bodhi resolve to bestow complete happiness on all beings;

He arouses the bodhi resolve to cut off all beings' delusions;

He arouses the bodhi resolve to bestow the wisdom of the Buddha on all beings;

He arouses the bodhi resolve to revere and make offerings to all buddhas;

He arouses the bodhi resolve to accord with the Tathāgata's teachings and please the Buddha;

He arouses the bodhi resolve to see the major marks and secondary signs of all buddhas' form bodies;

He arouses the bodhi resolve to enter the vast wisdom of all buddhas; and

He arouses the bodhi resolve to reveal the powers and fearlessnesses of all buddhas.

These are the ten.

Sons of the Buddha, if the bodhisattva brings forth the unexcelled bodhi resolve in order to awaken to and enter the wisdom of all-knowledge, when drawing near to and making offerings to the

親近供

正體字

養善知識時。應起十種心。何等為十。所謂起給侍心。歡喜心。無違心。隨順心。無異求心。一向心。同善根心。同願心。如來心。同圓滿行心。是為十。佛子。若菩薩摩訶薩。起如是心。則得十種清淨。何等為十。所謂深心清淨。到於究竟無失壞故。色身清淨。隨其所宜。為示現故。音聲清淨。了達一切諸語言故。辯才清淨。善說無邊諸佛法故。智慧清淨。捨離一切愚癡暗故。受生清淨。具足菩薩。自在力故。眷屬清淨。成就過去同行眾生。諸善根故。果報清淨。除滅一切諸業障故。大願清淨。與諸菩薩。性無二故。諸行清淨。以普賢乘。而出離故。是為十。佛子。菩薩摩訶薩。有十種波羅蜜。何等為十。所謂施波羅蜜。悉捨一切諸所有故。戒波羅蜜。淨佛戒故。

简体字

亲近供养善知识时，应起十种心。何等为十？所谓：起给侍心、欢喜心、无违心、随顺心、无异求心、一向心、同善根心、同愿心、如来心、同圆满行心。是为十。

"佛子，若菩萨摩诃萨起如是心，则得十种清净。何等为十？所谓：深心清净，到于究竟无失坏故；色身清净，随其所宜为示现故；音声清净，了达一切诸语言故；辩才清净，善说无边诸佛法故；智慧清净，舍离一切愚痴暗故；受生清净，具足菩萨自在力故；眷属清净，成就过去同行众生诸善根故；果报清净，除灭一切诸业障故；大愿清净，与诸菩萨性无二故；诸行清净，以普贤乘而出离故。是为十。

"佛子，菩萨摩诃萨有十种波罗蜜。何等为十？所谓：施波罗蜜，悉舍一切诸所有故；戒波罗蜜，净佛戒故；

Chapter 38 — *Transcending the World*

good spiritual guide, he should arouse ten kinds of mind. What are those ten? They are as follows:

The mind intent on serving him;
The mind of joyous delight;
The mind that is free of any opposition;
The mind that is compliant;
The mind that has no differing motivations;
The mind that is single-mindedly focused;
The mind that shares the same roots of goodness;
The mind that shares the same vows;
The mind of the Tathāgata; and
The mind intent on fulfilling the same practices.

These are the ten.

Sons of the Buddha, if the bodhisattva-mahāsattva arouses types of mind such as these, then he acquires ten kinds of purity. What are those ten? They are as follows:

Purity of deep resolve which reaches all the way to its ultimate destination without ever deteriorating;
Purity of the physical body which manifests for others in accordance with what is appropriate;
Purity of voice to ensure comprehension of all speech;
Purity of eloquence to skillfully expound on the boundlessly many dharmas of all buddhas;
Purity of wisdom to leave behind all the darkness of delusion;
Purity in the taking on of births through complete fulfillment of the bodhisattva's sovereign powers;
Purity of retinue through developing all roots of goodness with other beings who have joined in the same practices in the past;
Purity of karmic rewards and consequences through extinguishing all karmic obstacles;
Purity of great vows through having a nature no different from that of all other bodhisattvas; and
Purity of practice through achieving emancipation in reliance on the universally worthy vehicle [of Samantabhadra].

These are the ten.

Sons of the Buddha, the bodhisattva-mahāsattva has ten kinds of *pāramitās*. What are those ten? They are as follows:

The *pāramitā* of giving based on the complete relinquishing of everything one possesses;
The *pāramitā* of moral virtue based on purity in the Buddha's moral precepts;

正體字

忍波羅蜜。住佛忍故。精進波羅蜜。一切所作。不退轉故。禪波羅蜜。念一境故。般若波羅蜜。如實觀察一切法故。智波羅蜜。入佛力故。願波羅蜜。滿足普賢諸大願故。神通波羅蜜。示現一切自在用故。法波羅蜜。普入一切諸佛法故。是為十。若諸菩薩。安住此法。則得具足如來無上大智波羅蜜。佛子。菩薩摩訶薩。有十種智隨覺。何等為十。所謂一切世界。無量差別智隨覺。一切眾生界。不可思議智隨覺。一切諸法。一入種種。種種入一智隨覺。一切法界。廣大智隨覺。一切虛空界。究竟智隨覺。一切世界。入過去世智隨覺。一切世界入未來世智隨覺一切世界。入現在世智隨覺。一切如來。無量行願。皆於一智。而得圓滿智隨覺。

简体字

忍波罗蜜,住佛忍故;精进波罗蜜,一切所作不退转故;禅波罗蜜,念一境故;般若波罗蜜,如实观察一切法故;智波罗蜜,入佛力故;愿波罗蜜,满足普贤诸大愿故;神通波罗蜜,示现一切自在用故;法波罗蜜,普入一切诸佛法故。是为十。若诸菩萨安住此法,则得具足如来无上大智波罗蜜。

"佛子,菩萨摩诃萨有十种智随觉。何等为十?所谓:一切世界无量差别智随觉;一切众生界不可思议智随觉;一切诸法一入种种,种种入一智随觉;一切法界广大智随觉;一切虚空界究竟智随觉;一切世界入过去世智随觉;一切世界入未来世智随觉;一切世界入现在世智随觉;一切如来无量行愿皆于一智而得圆满智随觉;

Chapter 38 — *Transcending the World*

The *pāramitā* of patience based on abiding in the Buddha's patience;
The *pāramitā* of vigor based on irreversibility in all that one does;
The *pāramitā* of *dhyāna* based on mindfulness focused on a single object;
The *pāramitā* of *prajñā* based on contemplation of all dharmas in accordance with reality;
The *pāramitā* of knowledge based on entering the Buddha's powers;[93]
The *pāramitā* of vows based on complete fulfillment of all the great vows of Samantabhadra;
The *pāramitā* of spiritual superknowledges based on manifesting all the functions of sovereign spiritual powers; and
The *pāramitā* of Dharma based on penetrating all the dharmas of all buddhas.[94]

These are the ten. If bodhisattvas abide in these dharmas, then they achieve the complete fulfillment of the Tathāgata's unexcelled *pāramitā* of great wisdom.

Sons of the Buddha, the bodhisattva-mahāsattva has ten kinds of knowledge pursuant to awakening. What are those ten? They are as follows:

The knowledge pursuant to awakening that knows the countlessly many differences in all worlds;
The knowledge pursuant to awakening that knows the inconceivability of all realms of beings;
The knowledge pursuant to awakening that knows with regard to all dharmas how any single phenomenon enters into all the many different phenomena and how all the many different phenomena enter into any single phenomenon;
The knowledge pursuant to awakening that knows the vastness of the entire Dharma realm;
The knowledge pursuant to awakening that knows the ultimate nature of all realms of empty space;
The knowledge pursuant to awakening that knows all worlds as they entered the past;
The knowledge pursuant to awakening that knows all worlds as they enter the future;
The knowledge pursuant to awakening that knows all worlds as they enter the present; and
The knowledge pursuant to awakening that knows the countless practices and vows of all *tathāgatas* can all be fulfilled with a single [act of] cognition;

正體字

三世諸佛。皆同一行。
而得出離智隨覺是為十。若諸菩薩。安住此
法。則得一切法。自在光明。所願皆滿。於一念
頃。悉能解了一切佛法。成等正覺。佛子。菩薩
摩訶薩。有十種證知。何等為十。所謂知一切
法一相。知一切法無量相。知一切法在一念。
知一切眾生心行無礙。知一切眾生諸根平
等。知一切眾生煩[3]惱習氣行。知一切眾生心
使行。知一切眾生善不善行。知一切菩薩願
行自在。住持變化。知一切如來具足十力。成
等正覺。是為十。若諸菩薩。安住此法。則得一
切法善巧方便。佛子。菩薩摩訶薩。有十種力。
何等為十。所謂入一切法自性力。入一切法
如化力。入一切法如幻力。入一切法皆是佛
法力。於一切法無染著力。於一切法甚明解
力。於一切善知識。恒不捨離。尊重心力。

简体字

三世诸佛皆同一行而得出离智随觉。是为十。若诸菩萨安住此法，则得一切法自在光明，所愿皆满，于一念顷悉能解了一切佛法成等正觉。

"佛子，菩萨摩诃萨有十种证知。何等为十？所谓：知一切法一相；知一切法无量相；知一切法在一念；知一切众生心行无碍；知一切众生诸根平等；知一切众生烦恼习气行；知一切众生心使行；知一切众生善、不善行；知一切菩萨愿行自在住持变化；知一切如来具足十力成等正觉。是为十。若诸菩萨安住此法，则得一切法善巧方便。

"佛子，菩萨摩诃萨有十种力。何等为十？所谓：入一切法自性力；入一切法如化力；入一切法如幻力；入一切法皆是佛法力；于一切法无染著力；于一切法甚明解力；于一切善知识恒不舍离尊重心力；

> The knowledge pursuant to awakening that knows all buddhas of the three periods of time as all sharing a single practice to attain emancipation.

These are the ten. If bodhisattvas abide in these dharmas, then they acquire the radiance of sovereign mastery in all dharmas, all their vows become fulfilled, and, in but the instant of a single mind-moment, they all become able to completely comprehend all dharmas of the Buddha and realize the right and perfect enlightenment.

Sons of the Buddha, the bodhisattva-mahāsattva has ten kinds of knowing based on realizations. What are those ten? They are as follows:

> He knows all dharmas have but a single sign;
>
> He knows all dharmas have measurelessly many signs;
>
> He knows all dharmas reside in but a single mind-moment;
>
> He knows the unimpeded nature of all beings' mental actions;
>
> He knows the faculties of all beings are the same;
>
> He knows the actions arising from all beings' afflictions and habitual karmic propensities;
>
> He knows the actions associated with the latent tendencies in the minds of all beings;[95]
>
> He knows all beings' good and bad actions;
>
> He knows all bodhisattvas' sovereign mastery of conduct and vows, their preservation [of the Dharma], and their spiritual transformations; and
>
> He knows the *tathāgatas'* complete fulfillment of the ten powers as well as their realization of the right and perfect enlightenment.

These are the ten. If bodhisattvas abide in these dharmas, then they acquire skillful means in all dharmas.

Sons of the Buddha, the bodhisattva-mahāsattva has ten kinds of powers. What are those ten? They are as follows:

> The power to comprehend the inherent nature of all dharmas;
>
> The power to comprehend all dharmas as comparable to transformationally created phenomena;
>
> The power to comprehend all dharmas as comparable to mere illusory conjurations;
>
> The power to comprehend all dharmas as dharmas of the Buddha;
>
> The power to remain free of any defiling attachment to any dharma;
>
> The power to possess a very clear understanding of all dharmas;
>
> The power to never abandon the reverential mind toward all good spiritual guides;

正體字

令一切善根。順至無上智王力。於一切佛法。深信不謗力。令一切智心。不退善巧力。是為十。若諸菩薩。安住此法。則具如來無上諸力。佛子。菩薩摩訶薩。有十種平等。何等為十。所謂。於一切眾生平等。一切法平等。一切剎平等。一切深心平等。一切善根平等。一切菩薩平等。一切願平等。一切波羅蜜平等。一切行平等。一切佛平等。是為十。若諸菩薩。安住此法。則得一切諸佛無上平等法。佛子。菩薩摩訶薩。有十種佛法實義句。何等為十。所謂。一切法但有名。一切法猶如幻。一切法猶如影。一切法但緣起。一切法業清淨。一切法但文字所作。一切法實際。一切法無相。一切法第一義。一切法法界。是為十。若諸菩薩。安住此法。則善入一切智智無上真實義。

简体字

令一切善根顺至无上智王力；于一切佛法深信不谤力；令一切智心不退善巧力。是为十。若诸菩萨安住此法，则具如来无上诸力。

"佛子，菩萨摩诃萨有十种平等。何等为十？所谓：于一切众生平等、一切法平等、一切刹平等、一切深心平等、一切善根平等、一切菩萨平等、一切愿平等、一切波罗蜜平等、一切行平等、一切佛平等。是为十。若诸菩萨安住此法，则得一切诸佛无上平等法。

"佛子，菩萨摩诃萨有十种佛法实义句。何等为十？所谓：一切法但有名；一切法犹如幻；一切法犹如影；一切法但缘起；一切法业清净；一切法但文字所作；一切法实际；一切法无相；一切法第一义；一切法法界。是为十。若诸菩萨安住此法，则善入一切智智无上真实义。

Chapter 38 — *Transcending the World*

> The power to enable all roots of goodness to lead to the unexcelled king of all types of wisdom;
>
> The power to maintain deep faith in the Dharma of all buddhas and never slander it; and
>
> The power to skillfully ensure that one will never retreat from one's resolve to attain all-knowledge.

These are the ten. If bodhisattvas abide in these dharmas, then they come to possess all of the unexcelled powers of the Tathāgata.

Sons of the Buddha, the bodhisattva-mahāsattva has ten kinds of equal regard. What are those ten? They are as follows:

> Equal regard for all beings;
>
> Equal regard for all dharmas;
>
> Equal regard for all *kṣetras*;
>
> Equal regard for all kinds of resolute intentions;
>
> Equal regard for all roots of goodness;
>
> Equal regard for all bodhisattvas;
>
> Equal regard for all vows;
>
> Equal regard for all *pāramitās*;
>
> Equal regard for all the practices; and
>
> Equal regard for all buddhas.

These are the ten. If bodhisattvas abide in these dharmas, then they acquire all buddhas' unexcelled dharma of equal regard for all.

Sons of the Buddha, the bodhisattva-mahāsattva has ten kinds of statements on true meaning according to the dharmas of the Buddha. What are those ten? They are as follows:

> All of these dharmas only have names;
>
> All of these dharmas are like mere conjurations;
>
> All of these dharmas are like reflections;
>
> All of these dharmas arise solely from conditions;
>
> All actions based on these dharmas are pure;
>
> All of these dharmas are merely creations of language;
>
> All of these dharmas are synonymous with the apex of reality;
>
> All of these dharmas are signless;
>
> All of these dharmas are synonymous with the ultimate truth; and
>
> All of these dharmas are synonymous with the Dharma realm.

These are the ten. If bodhisattvas abide in these dharmas, then they skillfully penetrate the unexcelled and genuine meaning of the wisdom of all-knowledge.

正體字

佛子。菩薩摩訶
薩。說十種法。何等為十。所謂說甚深法。說廣
大法。說種種法。說一切智法。說隨順波羅蜜
法。說出生如來力法。說三世相應法。說令菩
薩不退法。說讚歎佛功德法。說一切菩薩學
一切佛平等。一切如來境界相應法。是為十。
若諸菩薩。安住此法。則得如來無上巧說法。
佛子。菩薩摩訶薩。有十種持。何等為十。所謂
持所集一切福德善根。持一切如來所說法。
持一切譬[1]諭。持一切法理趣門。持一切出生
陀羅尼門。持一切除疑惑法。持成就一切菩
薩法。持一切如來所說平等三昧門。持一切
法照明門。持一切諸佛神通遊戲力。是為十。
若諸菩薩。安住此法。則得如來無上大智住
持力。佛子。菩薩摩訶薩。有十種辯才。何等為
十。所謂

简体字

"佛子，菩萨摩诃萨说十种法。何等为十？所谓：说甚深法；说广大法；说种种法；说一切智法；说随顺波罗蜜法；说出生如来力法；说三世相应法；说令菩萨不退法；说赞叹佛功德法；说一切菩萨学一切佛平等、一切如来境界相应法。是为十。若诸菩萨安住此法，则得如来无上巧说法。

"佛子，菩萨摩诃萨有十种持。何等为十？所谓：持所集一切福德善根；持一切如来所说法；持一切譬喻；持一切法理趣门；持一切出生陀罗尼门；持一切除疑惑法；持成就一切菩萨法；持一切如来所说平等三昧门；持一切法照明门；持一切诸佛神通游戏力。是为十。若诸菩萨安住此法，则得如来无上大智住持力。

"佛子，菩萨摩诃萨有十种辩才。何等为十？所谓：

Sons of the Buddha, the bodhisattva-mahāsattva speaks of ten kinds of dharmas. What are those ten? They are as follows:

They speak of very profound dharmas;
They speak of vast dharmas;
They speak of all kinds of different dharmas;
They speak of the dharma of all-knowledge;
They speak of dharmas which accord with the *pāramitās*;
They speak of dharmas which produce the Tathāgata's powers;
They speak of dharmas related to the three periods of time;
They speak of dharmas which enable the bodhisattva's irreversibility;
They speak of dharmas of praise for the Buddha's meritorious qualities; and
They speak of dharmas corresponding to all bodhisattvas' training, the equality of all buddhas, and all *tathāgatas'* spheres of cognition and action.

These are the ten. If bodhisattvas abide in these dharmas, then they acquire the Tathāgata's unexcelled skill in speaking about the Dharma.

Sons of the Buddha, the bodhisattva-mahāsattva has ten kinds of things he preserves. What are those ten? They are as follows:

He preserves all the merit and roots of goodness he has accumulated;
He preserves all dharmas spoken by the Tathāgata;
He preserves all analogies;
He preserves all the gateways to the principles and purport of the Dharma;
He preserves all gateways to the production of *dhāraṇīs*;
He preserves all the dharmas for doing away with doubts;
He preserves all the dharmas used to bring about the complete development of all bodhisattvas;
He preserves all the gateways to the samādhis of equality taught by the Tathāgata;
He preserves all the gateways to the bright illumination of dharmas; and
He preserves all the powers of all buddhas' easeful mastery in the spiritual superknowledges.

These are the ten. If bodhisattvas abide in these dharmas, then they acquire the powers of preservation of the Tathāgata's unexcelled and great wisdom.

Sons of the Buddha, the bodhisattva-mahāsattva has ten kinds of eloquence. What are those ten? They are as follows:

正體字

於一切法。無分別辯才。於一切法。無
所作辯才。於一切法。無所著辯才。於一切法。
了達空辯才。於一切法。無疑暗辯才。於一切
法。佛加被辯才。於一切法。自覺悟辯才。於一
切法。文句差別。善巧辯才。於一切法。真實說
辯才。隨一切眾生。心令歡喜辯才。是為十。若
諸菩薩。安住此法。則得如來無上巧妙辯才。
佛子。菩薩摩訶薩。有十種自在。何等為十。所
謂教化調伏一切眾生自在。普照一切法自
在。修一切善根行自在。廣大智自在。無所依
戒自在。一切善根迴向菩提自在。精進不退
轉自在。智慧摧破一切眾魔自在。隨所樂欲
令發菩提心自在。隨所應化現成正覺自在。
是為十。若諸菩薩。安住此法。則得如來無上
大智自在。

简体字

于一切法无分别辩才；于一切法无所作辩才；于一切法无所著辩才；于一切法了达空辩才；于一切法无疑暗辩才；于一切法佛加被辩才；于一切法自觉悟辩才；于一切法文句差别善巧辩才；于一切法真实说辩才；随一切众生心令欢喜辩才。是为十。若诸菩萨安住此法，则得如来无上巧妙辩才。

"佛子，菩萨摩诃萨有十种自在。何等为十？所谓：教化调伏一切众生自在；普照一切法自在；修一切善根行自在；广大智自在；无所依戒自在；一切善根回向菩提自在；精进不退转自在；智慧摧破一切众魔自在；随所乐欲令发菩提心自在；随所应化现成正觉自在。是为十。若诸菩萨安住此法，则得如来无上大智自在。

Chapter 38 — *Transcending the World*

The eloquence that remains free of discriminations in speaking of all dharmas;

The eloquence that remains effortless in speaking of all dharmas;

The eloquence that remains free of attachment in speaking of all dharmas;

The eloquence that completely comprehends emptiness in speaking of all dharmas;

The eloquence that remains free of doubts or dullness in speaking of all dharmas;

The eloquence that receives the assistance of the Buddha in speaking of all dharmas;

The eloquence that brings about self-awakening in speaking of all dharmas;

The eloquence that is skillful in explaining differences in textual passages in speaking of all dharmas;

The eloquence that accords with reality in speaking of all dharmas; and

The eloquence that gladdens all beings by adapting to their minds.

These are the ten. If all bodhisattvas abide in these dharmas, then they acquire the Tathāgata's unexcelled skillful and sublime eloquence.

Sons of the Buddha, the bodhisattva-mahāsattva has ten kinds of sovereign mastery. What are those ten? They are as follows:

Sovereign mastery in the teaching and training of all beings;

Sovereign mastery in the universal illumination of all dharmas;

Sovereign mastery in cultivating the practices producing all roots of goodness;

Sovereign mastery in vast wisdom;

Sovereign mastery in the moral virtue that has nothing at all that it relies on;

Sovereign mastery in dedicating all roots of goodness to the realization of bodhi;

Sovereign mastery in irreversible vigor;

Sovereign mastery in the wisdom that utterly vanquishes all the many kinds of *māras*;

Sovereign mastery in enabling beings to resolve to attain bodhi by adapting to their individual inclinations;

Sovereign mastery in manifesting the realization of right enlightenment in accordance with those who should be taught.

These are the ten. If bodhisattvas abide in these dharmas, then they acquire the sovereign mastery of the Tathāgata's unexcelled great wisdom.

正體字	佛子。菩薩摩訶薩。有十種無著。何 283b18 等為十。所謂於一切世界無著。於一切眾生無 283b19 著。於一切法無著。於一切所作無著。於一切 283b20 善根無著。於一切受生處無著。於一切願無 283b21 著。於一切行無著。於一切菩薩無著。於一切 283b22 佛無著。是為十。若諸菩薩。安住此法。則能速 283b23 轉一切眾想。得無上清淨智慧。佛子。菩薩摩 283b24 訶薩。有十種平等心。何等為十。所謂積集一 283b25 切功德平等心。發一切差別願平等心。於一 283b26 切眾生身平等心。於一切眾生業報平等心。 283b27 於一切法平等心。於一切淨穢國土平等心。 283b28 於一切眾生解平等心。於一切行無所分別 283b29 平等心。於一切佛力無[異>畏]平等心。於一切如 283c01 來智慧平等心。是為十。若諸菩薩。安住其中。 283c02 則得如來無上大平等心。佛子。菩薩摩訶薩。 283c03 有十種出生智慧。何等為十。所謂知一切眾 283c04 生解。出生智慧。知一切佛剎。種種差別。出生 283c05 智慧。

"佛子，菩薩摩訶薩有十種無著。何等為十？所謂：于一切世界無著；于一切眾生無著；于一切法無著；于一切所作無著；于一切善根無著；于一切受生處無著；于一切願無著；于一切行無著；于一切菩薩無著；于一切佛無著。是為十。若諸菩薩安住此法，則能速轉一切眾想，得無上清淨智慧。

"佛子，菩薩摩訶薩有十種平等心。何等為十？所謂：積集一切功德平等心；發一切差別願平等心；于一切眾生身平等心；于一切眾生業報平等心；于一切法平等心；于一切淨穢國土平等心；于一切眾生解平等心；于一切行無所分別平等心；于一切佛力無畏平等心；于一切如來智慧平等心。是為十。若諸菩薩安住其中，則得如來無上大平等心。

"佛子，菩薩摩訶薩有十種出生智慧。何等為十？所謂：知一切眾生解出生智慧；知一切佛剎種種差別出生智慧；

Chapter 38 — *Transcending the World*

Sons of the Buddha, the bodhisattva-mahāsattva has ten kinds of nonattachment. What are those ten? They are as follows:

Nonattachment to any world;
Nonattachment to any being;
Nonattachment to any dharma;
Nonattachment to anything he does;
Nonattachment to any roots of goodness;
Nonattachment to any place in which he takes on rebirth;
Nonattachment to any vows;
Nonattachment to any practices;
Nonattachment to any bodhisattva; and
Nonattachment to any buddha.

These are the ten. If bodhisattvas abide in these dharmas, then they are able to swiftly transform all the many kinds of thought into the attainment of unexcelled and pure wisdom.

Sons of the Buddha, the bodhisattva-mahāsattva has ten kinds of impartial mind. What are those ten? They are as follows:

The mind that impartially accumulates all meritorious qualities;
The mind that impartially makes all the different kinds of vows;
The mind that is impartial toward the bodies of all beings;
The mind that is impartial toward the karmic consequences of all beings;
The mind that is impartial toward all dharmas;
The mind that is impartial toward all lands no matter whether they are pure or defiled;
The mind that is impartial toward all beings no matter what their levels of understanding might be;
The mind that is impartial and nondiscriminating toward all practices;
The mind that is impartial toward all the powers and fearlessnesses of the buddhas; and
The mind that is impartial toward all the types of wisdom of the *tathāgatas*.

These are the ten. If bodhisattvas abide in these, then they acquire the Tathāgata's unexcelled great mind of impartial regard for all.

Sons of the Buddha, the bodhisattva-mahāsattva has ten ways of developing wisdom. What are those ten? They are as follows:

Developing wisdom through knowing all beings' levels of understanding;
Developing wisdom through knowing the many kinds of differences in all buddha *kṣetras*;

正體字

知十方網分齊。出生智慧。知覆仰等一切世界。出生智慧。知一切法。一性種種性。廣大住。出生智慧。知一切種種身。出生智慧。知一切世間顛倒妄想。悉無所著。出生智慧。知一切法究竟。皆以一道出離。出生智慧。知如來神力。能入一切法界。出生智慧。知三世一切眾生。佛種不斷。出生智慧。是為十。若諸菩薩。安住此法。則於諸法。無不了達。佛子。菩薩摩訶薩。有十種變化。何等為十。所謂一切眾生變化。一切身變化。一切剎變化。一切供養變化。一切音聲變化。一切行願變化。一切教化調伏眾生變化。一切成正覺變化。一切說法變化。一切加持變化。是為十。若諸菩薩。安住此法。則得具足一切無上變化法。佛子。菩薩摩訶薩。有十種力持。何等為十。所謂佛力持。法力持。眾生力持。

简体字

知十方网分齐出生智慧；知覆仰等一切世界出生智慧；知一切法一性、种种性广大住出生智慧；知一切种种身出生智慧；知一切世间颠倒妄想悉无所著出生智慧；知一切法究竟皆以一道出离出生智慧；知如来神力能入一切法界出生智慧；知三世一切众生佛种不断出生智慧。是为十。若诸菩萨安住此法，则于诸法无不了达。

"佛子，菩萨摩诃萨有十种变化。何等为十？所谓：一切众生变化；一切身变化；一切刹变化；一切供养变化；一切音声变化；一切行愿变化；一切教化调伏众生变化；一切成正觉变化；一切说法变化；一切加持变化。是为十。若诸菩萨安住此法，则得具足一切无上变化法。

"佛子，菩萨摩诃萨有十种力持。何等为十？所谓：佛力持；法力持；众生力持；

Chapter 38 — *Transcending the World*

Developing wisdom through knowing the distinct details throughout the network of the ten directions;

Developing wisdom through knowing all the inverted worlds, upward-facing worlds, and other kinds of worlds;

Developing wisdom through knowing with respect to all dharmas their single nature, their many different types of natures, and their vast scale of abiding;

Developing wisdom through knowing all the different kinds of bodies;

Developing wisdom through knowing all the worlds' inverted views and false conceptions while having no attachment to any of them;

Developing wisdom through knowing all dharmas ultimately bring about emancipation through but a single path;

Developing wisdom through knowing the Tathāgata's spiritual powers are able to enter the entire Dharma realm; and

Developing wisdom through knowing that the seed of buddhahood in all beings of the three periods of time is never cut off.

These are the ten. If bodhisattvas abide in these dharmas, then they have no dharma that they do not completely comprehend.

Sons of the Buddha, the bodhisattva-mahāsattva has ten kinds of transformations that he performs. What are those ten? They are as follows:

Transformations of all kinds of beings;
Transformations of all kinds of bodies;
Transformations of all kinds of *kṣetras*;
Transformations of all kinds of offerings;
Transformations of all kinds of voices;
Transformations of all kinds of conduct and vows;
Transformations of all ways to teach and train beings;
Transformations of all ways of realizing right enlightenment;
Transformations in all ways of speaking the Dharma; and
Transformations of all means of empowerment.

These are the ten. If bodhisattvas abide in these dharmas, then they achieve complete fulfillment of all the unexcelled dharmas of transformation.

Sons of the Buddha, the bodhisattva-mahāsattva has ten kinds of empowerment. What are those ten? They are as follows:

Empowerment by the Buddha;
Empowerment by the Dharma;
Empowerment by beings;

正體字

業力持。行力持。
願力持。境界力持。時力持。善力持。智力持。
是為十。若諸菩薩。安住此法。則於一切法得
無上自在力持

大方廣佛華嚴經卷[＊]第五十四

離世間品第三十八之二

佛子。菩薩摩訶薩。有十種大欣慰。何等為十。
所謂諸菩薩。發如是心。盡未來世。所有諸佛。
出興[1]于世。我當皆得隨逐承事。令生歡喜。
如是思惟。心大欣慰。復作是念。彼諸如來。出
興於世。我當悉以無上供具。恭敬供養。如是
思惟。心大欣慰。復作是念。我於諸佛所。興供
養時。彼諸如來。必示誨我法。我悉以深心。恭
敬聽受。如說修行。於菩薩地。必得已生。現生
當生。如是思惟。心大欣慰。復作是念。我當於
不可說不可說劫。行菩薩行。常與一切諸佛
菩薩。而得共俱。如是思惟。心大欣慰。復作是
念。我於往昔。未發無上大菩提心。有諸怖畏。
所謂不活畏。惡名畏。死畏。墮惡道畏。大眾威
德畏。自一發心。悉皆遠離。不驚不恐。

简体字

业力持；行力持；愿力持；境界力持；时力持；善力持；智力持。是为十。若诸菩萨安住此法，则于一切法得无上自在力持。

大方广佛华严经卷第五十四

离世间品第三十八之二

　　"佛子，菩萨摩诃萨有十种大欣慰。何等为十？所谓：诸菩萨发如是心：'尽未来世所有诸佛出兴于世，我当皆得随逐承事令生欢喜。'如是思惟，心大欣慰。复作是念：'彼诸如来出兴于世，我当悉以无上供具恭敬供养。'如是思惟，心大欣慰。复作是念：'我于诸佛所兴供养时，彼诸如来必示诲我法，我悉以深心恭敬听受、如说修行，于菩萨地必得已生、现生、当生。'如是思惟，心大欣慰。复作是念：'我当于不可说不可说劫行菩萨行，常与一切诸佛菩萨而得共俱。'如是思惟，心大欣慰。复作是念：'我于往昔未发无上大菩提心，有诸怖畏，所谓：不活畏、恶名畏、死畏、堕恶道畏、大众威德畏。自一发心，悉皆远离，不惊不恐，

Chapter 38 — *Transcending the World*

    Empowerment by karmic actions;
    Empowerment by the practices;
    Empowerment by vows;
    Empowerment by spheres of cognition;
    Empowerment by time;
    Empowerment by goodness; and
    Empowerment by knowledge.

These are the ten. If bodhisattvas abide in these dharmas, then, in all dharmas, they will attain unsurpassed mastery of empowerments.

Sons of the Buddha, the bodhisattva-mahāsattva has ten kinds of bases for feeling great happiness and satisfaction. What are those ten? They are as follows:

    All bodhisattvas make a resolution such as this: "To the very end of future time, when buddhas appear in the world, I shall follow, serve, and please them all." When they think in this way, they experience great happiness and satisfaction;

    They also think: "When those *tathāgatas* appear in the world, I shall reverently make offerings of unexcelled gifts to all of them." When they think in this way, they experience great happiness and satisfaction;

    They also think: "When, in the presence of all those buddhas, I present offerings to them, those *tathāgatas* will certainly provide me with instruction in the Dharma. In all such instances, with deep resolve, I shall respectfully listen and cultivate in accordance with what they teach so that it must certainly be the case that I have attained birth on the bodhisattva grounds in the past, that I have been reborn there in the present, and that will continue to be reborn there in the future." When they think in this way, they experience great happiness and satisfaction;

    They also think: "I shall practice the bodhisattva practices for an ineffable-ineffable number of future kalpas and shall always succeed in dwelling together with all buddhas and bodhisattvas." When they think in this way, they experience great happiness and satisfaction;

    They also think: "In the past, before I resolved to attain the unexcelled great bodhi, I had all kinds of fears, namely: the fear of not surviving, the fear of a bad reputation, the fear of death, the fear of falling into the wretched destinies, and the fear of the awesome virtue of great assemblies.[96] However, once I made that resolve, I abandoned all those fears so that I am no longer alarmed, no longer full of trepidation, no longer fearful, no

正體字	不畏不懼。不怯不怖。一切眾魔。及諸外道。所不能壞。如是思惟。心大欣慰。復作是念。我當令一切眾生。成無上菩提。成菩提已。我當於彼佛所。修菩薩行。盡其形壽。以大信心。興所應供佛。諸供養具。而為供養。及涅槃後。各起無量塔。供養舍利。及受持守護。所有遺法。如是思惟。心大欣慰。又作是念。十方所有一切世界。我當悉以無上莊嚴。而莊嚴之。皆令具足。種種奇妙。平等清淨。復以種種。大神通力住持[2]震動。光明照[3]曜。普使周遍。如是思惟。心大欣慰。復作是念。我當斷一切眾生疑惑。淨一切眾生欲樂。啟一切眾生心意。滅一切眾生煩惱。閉一切眾生惡道門。開一切眾生善趣門。破一切眾生黑闇。與一切眾生光明。令一切眾生。離眾魔業。使一切眾生。至安隱處。如是思惟。心大欣慰。菩薩摩訶薩。復作是念。諸佛如來。如優曇華。難可值遇。於無量劫。莫能一見。我當於未來世。欲見如來。則便得見。諸佛如來。常不捨我。恒住我所。令我得見。為我說法。無有斷絕。既聞法已。
简体字	不畏不惧，不怯不怖，一切众魔及诸外道所不能坏。'如是思惟，心大欣慰。复作是念：'我当令一切众生成无上菩提；成菩提已，我当于彼佛所修菩萨行尽其形寿，以大信心兴所应供佛诸供养具而为供养；及涅槃后，各起无量塔供养舍利，及受持守护所有遗法。'如是思惟，心大欣慰。又作是念：'十方所有一切世界，我当悉以无上庄严而庄严之，皆令具足种种奇妙平等清净，复以种种大神通力住持震动，光明照耀普使周遍。'如是思惟，心大欣慰。复作是念：'我当断一切众生疑惑，净一切众生欲乐，启一切众生心意，灭一切众生烦恼，闭一切众生恶道门，开一切众生善趣门，破一切众生黑暗，与一切众生光明，令一切众生离众魔业，使一切众生至安隐处。'如是思惟，心大欣慰。菩萨摩诃萨复作是念：'诸佛如来如优昙华，难可值遇，于无量劫莫能一见。我当于未来世欲见如来则便得见，诸佛如来常不舍我，恒住我所，令我得见，为我说法无有断绝；既闻法已，

longer beset with terror, no longer timid, and no longer scared. I have become invulnerable to being destroyed by any of the many kinds of *māras* or any of the adherents of non-Buddhist paths." When they think in this way, they experience great happiness and satisfaction;

They also think: "I shall enable all beings to attain unexcelled bodhi and, once they have attained bodhi, I shall cultivate the bodhisattva practices in the presence of those buddhas where, to the very end of their lives, with a mind of great faith, I shall engage in extensively bestowing offerings of all kinds of gifts appropriate for presenting to buddhas, doing so all the way up to the time when they enter nirvāṇa, after which I shall raise up countless stupas commemorating each of them. I shall then make offerings to their *śarīra* and see to the preservation and protection of the Dharma they leave behind." When they think in this way, they experience great happiness and satisfaction;

They also think: "I shall use the most unexcelled adornments to adorn all worlds of the ten directions, thereby ensuring that they all are fully adorned with the many different kinds of extraordinarily marvelous adornments and are all then equally purified. Moreover, I shall then use many different kinds of great spiritual powers through which I cause them all to quake, move, and become everywhere illuminated with brilliant radiance." When they think in this way, they experience great happiness and satisfaction;

They also think: "I shall sever all beings' doubts, purify all beings' inclinations, open up of all beings' minds, extinguish all beings' afflictions, close all beings' gates to the wretched destinies, open all beings' gates to the good destinies, dispel all beings' darkness, shine light on all beings, enable all beings to depart from the works of the many kinds of *māras*, and influence all beings to reach the place of peace and security." When they think in this way, they experience great happiness and satisfaction;

The bodhisattva-mahāsattva also thinks: "The buddhas, the *tathāgatas*, are as rarely met as the blooming of the *udumbara* flower and are so rare that one may never see them even once in a measureless number of kalpas. May it be that, in the future, when I wish to see the Tathāgata, I will then succeed in seeing all the buddhas, the *tathāgatas*. May it then be that they will never abandon me, but rather will constantly dwell wherever I am, allowing me to see them, speaking Dharma for my sake, doing so ceaselessly so that, having heard that Dharma, my mind will

正體字

心意清淨。遠離
諂曲。質直無偽。於念念中。常見諸佛。如是思
惟。心大欣慰。復作是念。我於未來。當得成
佛。以佛神力。於一切世界。為一切眾生。各別
示現成等正覺。清淨無畏。大師子吼。以本大
願周遍法界。擊大法鼓。雨大法雨。作大法施。
於無量劫。常演正法。大悲所持。身語意業。無
有疲厭。如是思惟。心大欣慰。佛子。是為菩薩
摩訶薩。十種大欣慰。若諸菩薩。安住此法。則
得無上成正覺智慧。大欣慰。佛子。菩薩摩訶
薩。有十種深入佛法。何等為十。所謂入過去
世一切世界。入未來世一切世界。入現在世
世界數。世界行。世界說。世界清淨。入一切世
界種種性。入一切眾生。種種業報。入一切菩
薩種種行。知過去一切佛次第。知未來一
切佛次第。知現在十方虛空法界等。一切
諸佛。國土眾會。說法調伏。

简体字

心意清净,远离谄曲,质直无伪,于念念中常见诸佛。'如是思惟,心大欣慰。复作是念:'我于未来当得成佛,以佛神力,于一切世界,为一切众生各别示现成等正觉清净无畏大师子吼,以本大愿周遍法界,击大法鼓,雨大法雨,作大法施,于无量劫常演正法,大悲所持身、语、意业无有疲厌。'如是思惟,心大欣慰。佛子,是为菩萨摩诃萨十种大欣慰。若诸菩萨安住此法,则得无上成正觉智慧大欣慰。

"佛子,菩萨摩诃萨有十种深入佛法。何等为十?所谓:入过去世一切世界;入未来世一切世界;入现在世世界数、世界行、世界说、世界清净;入一切世界种种性;入一切众生种种业报;入一切菩萨种种行;知过去一切佛次第;知未来一切佛次第;知现在十方虚空法界等一切诸佛、国土众会、说法调伏;

Chapter 38 — *Transcending the World*

become purified and I will abandon flattery and deviousness and become straightforward in character and entirely free of falseness, whereupon I may then always be able to see all buddhas in each successive mind-moment." When they think in this way, they experience great happiness and satisfaction; and

They also think: "May it be that, in the future, I will realize buddhahood and become able then to use a buddha's spiritual powers to individually manifest the realization of the right and perfect enlightenment for each one of all the beings, manifesting purity, fearlessness, and the great lion's roar, using great original vows to go everywhere throughout the entire Dharma realm, beating the great Dharma drum, raining down the great Dharma rain, and engaging in the great Dharma giving whereby, throughout countless kalpas, I constantly expound right Dharma, sustained in this by the great compassion so that I remain tireless in all associated physical, verbal, and mental karmic deeds." When they think in this way, they experience great happiness and satisfaction.

Sons of the Buddha, these are the bodhisattva-mahāsattva's ten kinds of bases for great happiness and satisfaction. If bodhisattvas abide in these dharmas, then they acquire the great happiness and satisfaction of the wisdom arising from the realization of the unexcelled right enlightenment.

Sons of the Buddha, the bodhisattva-mahāsattva has ten kinds of deep penetration of the Buddha's Dharma. What are those ten? They are as follows:

They enter all worlds of the past;

They enter all worlds of the future;

They enter the worlds of the present, including the numbers of those worlds, the practices of those worlds, the speech of those worlds, and the purity of those worlds;

They penetrate the many different kinds of natures of all worlds;

They penetrate the many different kinds of karmic consequences of all beings;

They penetrate the many different kinds of practices of all bodhisattvas;

They know the sequence of all buddhas of the past;

They know the sequence of all buddhas of the future;

They know with regard to all present-era buddhas throughout the Dharma realm and the ten directions of empty space their lands, their congregations, their speaking of Dharma, and their training of beings;

正體字

知世間法。聲聞
法獨覺法。菩薩法如來法。雖知諸法。皆無
分別。而說種種法。悉入法界。無所入故。如其
法說。無所取著。是為十。若諸菩薩。安住此
法。則得入於阿耨多羅三藐三菩提。大智慧
甚深性。佛子。菩薩摩訶薩。有十種依止。菩薩
依此。行菩薩行。何等為十。所謂依止供養一
切諸佛。行菩薩行。依止調伏一切眾生。行菩
薩行。依止親近一切善友。行菩薩行。依止
積集一切善根。行菩薩行。依止嚴淨一切佛
土。行菩薩行。依止不捨一切眾生。行菩薩行。
依止深入一切波羅蜜。行菩薩行。依止滿足
一切菩薩願。行菩薩行。依止無量菩提心。
行菩薩行。依止一切佛菩提。行菩薩行。是
為十。菩薩依此行菩薩行。佛子。菩薩摩訶
薩。有十種發無畏心。何等為十。所謂滅一
切障礙業。發無畏心。

简体字

知世间法、声闻法、独觉法、菩萨法、如来法,虽知诸法皆无分别而说种种法,悉入法界无所入故,如其法说无所取著。是为十。若诸菩萨安住此法,则得入于阿耨多罗三藐三菩提大智慧甚深性。

"佛子,菩萨摩诃萨有十种依止,菩萨依此行菩萨行。何等为十?所谓:依止供养一切诸佛,行菩萨行;依止调伏一切众生,行菩萨行;依止亲近一切善友,行菩萨行;依止积集一切善根,行菩萨行;依止严净一切佛土,行菩萨行;依止不舍一切众生,行菩萨行;依止深入一切波罗蜜,行菩萨行;依止满足一切菩萨愿,行菩萨行;依止无量菩提心,行菩萨行;依止一切佛菩提,行菩萨行。是为十。菩萨依此行菩萨行。

"佛子,菩萨摩诃萨有十种发无畏心。何等为十?所谓:灭一切障碍业,发无畏心;

Chapter 38 — *Transcending the World*

They know the dharmas of the world, the dharmas of *śrāvaka* disciples, the dharmas of *pratyekabuddhas*, the dharmas of bodhisattvas, and the dharmas of the Tathāgata and, although they know all these dharmas have no bases for discriminations, they still speak about the many different kinds of dharmas. They completely penetrate the Dharma realm, and because, in so doing, they have nothing whatsoever that they penetrate, in accordance with their Dharma discourse, they have nothing at all to which they become attached.

These are the ten. If bodhisattvas abide in these dharmas, then they succeed in entering the extremely profound nature of the great wisdom of *anuttarasamyaksaṃbodhi*.

Sons of the Buddha, the bodhisattva-mahāsattva has ten kinds of bases. The bodhisattva bases himself on these as he practices the bodhisattva practices. What are these ten? They are as follows:

He bases himself on making offerings to all buddhas as he practices the bodhisattva practices;

He bases himself on training all beings as he practices the bodhisattva practices;

He bases himself on drawing near to all good spiritual friends as he practices the bodhisattva practices;

He bases himself on accumulating all kinds of roots of goodness as he practices the bodhisattva practices;

He bases himself on purifying all buddha lands as he practices the bodhisattva practices;

He bases himself on never abandoning any being as he practices the bodhisattva practices;

He bases himself on deeply entering all the *pāramitās* as he practices the bodhisattva practices;

He bases himself on completely fulfilling all the bodhisattva vows as he practices the bodhisattva practices;

He bases himself on the measureless bodhi resolve as he practices the bodhisattva practices; and

He bases himself on the bodhi of all buddhas as he practices the bodhisattva practices.

These are the ten. The bodhisattva bases himself on these as he practices the bodhisattva practices.

Sons of the Buddha, the bodhisattva-mahāsattva has ten kinds of arousal of fearless resolve. What are those ten? They are as follows:

The arousal of fearless resolve by which he extinguishes all obstructive karma;

正體字

於佛滅後。護持正法。
發無畏心。降伏一切魔。發無畏心。不惜身
命。發無畏心。摧破一切外道邪論。發無畏心。
令一切眾生歡喜。發無畏心。令一切眾會。皆
悉歡喜。發無畏心。調伏一切天龍夜叉。乾闥
婆阿脩羅迦樓羅緊那羅摩睺羅伽。發無畏
心。離二乘地。入甚深法。發無畏心。於不可說
不可說劫。行菩薩行。心無疲厭。發無畏心。是
為十。若諸菩薩。安住此法。則得如來無上大
智。無所畏心。佛子。菩薩摩訶薩。發十種無疑
心。於一切佛法。心無疑[4]惑。何等為十。所謂
菩薩摩訶薩。發如是心。我當以布施。攝一切
眾生。以戒忍精進禪定智慧。慈悲喜捨。攝一
切眾生。發此心時。決定無疑。若生疑心。無有
是處。是為第一發無疑心。菩薩摩訶薩。又作
是念。未來諸佛。出興[*]于世。我當一切承事
供養。發此心時。決定無疑。若生疑心。無有是
處。是為第二發無疑心。

简体字

于佛灭后护持正法，发无畏心；降伏一切魔，发无畏心；不惜身命，发无畏心；摧破一切外道邪论，发无畏心；令一切众生欢喜，发无畏心；令一切众会皆悉欢喜，发无畏心；调伏一切天、龙、夜叉、乾闼婆、阿修罗、迦楼罗、紧那罗、摩睺罗伽，发无畏心；离二乘地，入甚深法，发无畏心；于不可说不可说劫行菩萨行，心无疲厌，发无畏心。是为十。若诸菩萨安住此法，则得如来无上大智无所畏心。

"佛子，菩萨摩诃萨发十种无疑心，于一切佛法心无疑惑。何等为十？所谓：菩萨摩诃萨发如是心：'我当以布施，摄一切众生；以戒、忍、精进、禅定、智慧、慈、悲、喜、舍，摄一切众生。'发此心时，决定无疑；若生疑心，无有是处。是为第一发无疑心。菩萨摩诃萨又作是念：'未来诸佛出兴于世，我当一切承事供养。'发此心时，决定无疑；若生疑心，无有是处。是为第二发无疑心。

Chapter 38 — *Transcending the World*

> The arousal of fearless resolve by which he protects and preserves right Dharma after the Buddha enters nirvāṇa;
>
> The arousal of fearless resolve by which he conquers all *māras*;
>
> The arousal of fearless resolve by which he does not even spare his own body or life;
>
> The arousal of fearless resolve by which he utterly vanquishes the deviant doctrines of all adherents of the non-Buddhist paths;
>
> The arousal of fearless resolve by which he causes all beings to rejoice;
>
> The arousal of fearless resolve by which he causes all congregations to rejoice;
>
> The arousal of fearless resolve by which he trains all the devas, dragons, *yakṣas, gandharvas, asuras, garuḍas, kiṃnaras,* and *mahoragas*;
>
> The arousal of fearless resolve by which he abandons the grounds of the two vehicles and enters the extremely profound Dharma; and
>
> The arousal of fearless resolve by which he tirelessly practices the bodhisattva practices for an ineffable-ineffable number of kalpas.

These are the ten. If bodhisattvas abide in these dharmas, then they acquire the fearless resolve accompanying the Tathāgata's unexcelled great wisdom.

Sons of the Buddha, the bodhisattva-mahāsattva has ten ways of arousing doubt-free resolve by which his mind remains free of doubt regarding any of the Buddha's dharmas. What are those ten? They are as follows:

> The bodhisattva-mahāsattva arouses resolve such as this: "I should use giving to gather in all beings and shall use moral virtue, patience, vigor, *dhyāna* concentration, wisdom, kindness, compassion, sympathetic joy, and equanimity to gather in all beings." When he arouses this resolve, he is resolutely decisive and free of all doubt. Hence there is no possibility that he might produce any thoughts of doubt. This is the first of his ways of arousing doubt-free resolve;
>
> The bodhisattva-mahāsattva also arouses this resolve: "When all buddhas of the future come forth and appear in the world, I shall serve and make offerings to them all." When he arouses this resolve, he is resolutely decisive and free of all doubt. Hence there is no possibility that he might produce any thoughts of doubt. This is the second of his ways of arousing doubt-free resolve;

正體字

菩薩摩訶薩。又作是
念。我當以種種奇妙光明網。周遍莊嚴一切
世界。發此心時。決定無疑。若生疑心。無有是
處。是為第三發無疑心。菩薩摩訶薩。又作是
念。我當盡未來劫。修菩薩行。無數無量無邊
無等。不可數不可稱不可思不可量不可說不
可說不可說。過諸算數。究竟法界虛空界。一
切眾生。我當悉以無上教化調伏法。而成熟
之。發此心時。決定無疑。若生疑心。無有是
處。是為第四發無疑心。菩薩摩訶薩。又作是
念。我當修菩薩行。滿大誓願。具一切智。安住
其中。發此心時。決定無疑。若生疑心。無有是
處。是為第五發無疑心。菩薩摩訶薩。又作是
念。我當普為一切世間。行菩薩行。為一切法
清淨光明。照明一切所有佛法。發此心時。決
定無疑。若生疑心。無有是處。是為第六發無
疑心。菩薩摩訶薩。又作是念。我當知一切法
皆是佛法。隨眾生心。為其演說。悉令開悟。發
此心時。決定無疑。若生疑心。無有是處。是為
第七發無疑心。

简体字

菩萨摩诃萨又作是念：'我当以种种奇妙光明网，周遍庄严一切世界。'发此心时，决定无疑；若生疑心，无有是处。是为第三发无疑心。菩萨摩诃萨又作是念：'我当尽未来劫修菩萨行。无数、无量、无边、无等、不可数、不可称、不可思、不可量、不可说、不可说不可说，过诸算数，究竟法界、虚空界一切众生，我当悉以无上教化调伏法而成熟之。'发此心时，决定无疑；若生疑心，无有是处。是为第四发无疑心。菩萨摩诃萨又作是念：'我当修菩萨行，满大誓愿，具一切智，安住其中。'发此心时，决定无疑；若生疑心，无有是处。是为第五发无疑心。菩萨摩诃萨又作是念：'我当普为一切世间行菩萨行，为一切法清净光明，照明一切所有佛法。'发此心时，决定无疑；若生疑心，无有是处。是为第六发无疑心。菩萨摩诃萨又作是念：'我当知一切法皆是佛法，随众生心，为其演说，悉令开悟。'发此心时，决定无疑；若生疑心，无有是处。是为第七发无疑心。

Chapter 38 — *Transcending the World*

The bodhisattva-mahāsattva also arouses this resolve: "I shall use many different kinds of extraordinarily marvelous nets of light to everywhere adorn all worlds." When he arouses this resolve, he is resolutely decisive and free of all doubt. Hence there is no possibility that he might produce any thoughts of doubt. This is the third of his ways of arousing doubt-free resolve;

The bodhisattva-mahāsattva also arouses this resolve: "I shall cultivate the bodhisattva practices until the very end of all kalpas of the future during which time I shall use all the unexcelled teaching and training dharmas to ripen all beings to the very ends of the Dharma realm and the realm of empty space in which those beings are so countlessly many, measurelessly many, boundlessly many, incomparably many, innumerably many, inexpressibly many, inconceivably many, immeasurably many, ineffably many, and ineffably-ineffably many as to entirely surpass all means of numerical calculation." When he arouses this resolve, he is resolutely decisive and free of all doubt. Hence there is no possibility that he might produce any thoughts of doubt. This is the fourth of his ways of arousing doubt-free resolve;

The bodhisattva-mahāsattva also arouses this resolve: "I shall cultivate the bodhisattva practices, fulfill the great vows, become possessed of all-knowledge, and abide within it." When he arouses this resolve, he is resolutely decisive and free of all doubt. Hence there is no possibility that he might produce any thoughts of doubt. This is the fifth of his ways of arousing doubt-free resolve;

The bodhisattva-mahāsattva also arouses this resolve: "For the sake of everyone in all worlds, I shall everywhere practice the bodhisattva practices and become a pure light of all dharmas which clearly illuminates all dharmas of the Buddha." When he arouses this resolve, he is resolutely decisive and free of all doubt. Hence there is no possibility that he might produce any thoughts of doubt. This is the sixth of his ways of arousing doubt-free resolve;

The bodhisattva-mahāsattva also arouses this resolve: "I shall realize that all dharmas are dharmas of the Buddha and shall adapt to beings' minds as I expound on the Dharma for them to enable them all to awaken." When he arouses this resolve, he is resolutely decisive and free of all doubt. Hence there is no possibility that he might produce any thoughts of doubt. This is the seventh of his ways of arousing doubt-free resolve;

正體字

菩薩摩訶薩。又作是念。我當於一切法。得無障礙門。知一切障礙。不可得故。其心如是。無有疑惑。住真實性。乃至成於阿耨多羅三藐三菩提。發此心時。決定無疑。若生疑心。無有是處。是為第八發無疑心。菩薩摩訶薩。又作是念。我當知一切法。莫不皆是出世間法。遠離一切。妄想顛倒。以一莊嚴。而自莊嚴。而無所莊嚴。於此自了。不由他悟。發此心時。決定無疑。若生疑心。無有是處。是為第九發無疑心。菩薩摩訶薩。又作是念。我當於一切法。成最正覺。離一切妄想顛倒故。得一念相應智故。若一若異。不可得故。離一切數故。究竟無為故。離一切言說故。住不可說境界際故。發此心時。決定無疑。若生疑心。無有是處。是為第十發無疑心。若諸菩薩。安住此法。則於一切佛法。心無所疑。佛子。菩薩摩訶薩。有十種不可思議。何等為十。所謂一切善根。不可思議。一切誓願。不可思議。知一切法如幻不可思議。

简体字

菩萨摩诃萨又作是念：'我当于一切法得无障碍门，知一切障碍不可得故；其心如是，无有疑惑，住真实性，乃至成于阿耨多罗三藐三菩提。'发此心时，决定无疑；若生疑心，无有是处。是为第八发无疑心。菩萨摩诃萨又作是念：'我当知一切法莫不皆是出世间法，远离一切妄想颠倒，以一庄严而自庄严而无所庄严；于此自了，不由他悟。'发此心时，决定无疑；若生疑心，无有是处。是为第九发无疑心。菩萨摩诃萨又作是念：'我当于一切法成最正觉，离一切妄想颠倒故，得一念相应智故，若一若异不可得故，离一切数故，究竟无为故，离一切言说故，住不可说境界际故。'发此心时，决定无疑；若生疑心，无有是处。是为第十发无疑心。若诸菩萨安住此法，则于一切佛法心无所疑。

"佛子，菩萨摩诃萨有十种不可思议。何等为十？所谓：一切善根，不可思议。一切誓愿，不可思议。知一切法如幻，不可思议。

Chapter 38 — *Transcending the World*

- The bodhisattva-mahāsattva also arouses this resolve: "I shall acquire the unobstructed gateway to all dharmas through realizing all obstructions are inapprehensible." In this way his mind becomes free of doubts and he abides in the nature of reality all the way until he realizes *anuttarasamyaksaṃbodhi*. When he arouses this resolve, he is resolutely decisive and free of all doubt. Hence there is no possibility that he might produce any thoughts of doubt. This is the eighth of his ways of arousing doubt-free resolve;
- The bodhisattva-mahāsattva also arouses this resolve: "I shall realize that there are no dharmas that are not world-transcending dharmas, shall abandon all false conceptions and inverted views, and shall use a single kind of adornment to accomplish the self-adornment in which there is no one at all who is adorned so that, in this way, I reach complete understanding myself and become awakened without relying on anyone else." When he arouses this resolve, he is resolutely decisive and free of all doubt. Hence there is no possibility that he might produce any thoughts of doubt. This is the ninth of his ways of arousing doubt-free resolve; and
- The bodhisattva-mahāsattva also arouses this resolve: "I shall achieve the most supreme and right enlightenment with regard to all dharmas, accomplishing this through abandoning all false conceptions and inverted views, through acquiring the wisdom that responds in but a single mind-moment, through realizing that whether it be unity or difference, such things are all inapprehensible, through transcending all enumerations, through realizing the ultimate state of the unconditioned, through transcending all words and speech, and through abiding at the very apex of the ineffable sphere of cognition." When he arouses this resolve, he is resolutely decisive and free of all doubt. Hence there is no possibility that he might produce any thoughts of doubt. This is the tenth of his ways of arousing doubt-free resolve.

If bodhisattvas abide in these dharmas, then their minds remain free of any doubts regarding any of the Buddha's dharmas.

Sons of the Buddha, the bodhisattva-mahāsattva has ten kinds of inconceivability. What are those ten? They are as follows:

- The inconceivability of all his roots of goodness;
- The inconceivability of all his vows;
- The inconceivability of his knowing that all dharmas are like mere conjurations;

正體字

發菩提心。修菩薩行。善
根不失。無所分別。不可思議。雖深入一切法。
亦不取滅度。以一切願。未成滿故。不可思議。
修菩薩道。而示現降神。入胎誕生。出家苦行。
[1]往詣道場。降伏眾魔。成最正覺。轉正法輪。
入般涅槃。神變自在無有休息。不捨悲願。救
護眾生。不可思議。雖能示現如來十力神變
自在。而亦不捨等法界心。教化眾生。不可思
議。知一切法無相是相。相是無相。無分別是
分別。分別是無分別。非有是有。有是非有。無
作是作。作是無作。非說是說。說是非說。不可
思議。知心與菩提等。知菩提與心等。心及菩
提。與眾生等。亦不生心顛倒。想顛倒。見顛
倒。不可思議。於念念中。入滅盡定。盡一切
漏。而不證實際。亦不盡有漏善根。雖知一切
法無漏。而知漏盡。亦知漏滅。雖知佛法即世
間法。世間法即佛法。而不於佛法中。分別世
間法。

简体字

发菩提心修菩萨行，善根不失，无所分别，不可思议。虽深入一切法，亦不取灭度，以一切愿未成满故，不可思议。修菩萨道而示现降神、入胎、诞生、出家、苦行、往诣道场、降伏众魔、成最正觉、转正法轮、入般涅槃，神变自在无有休息，不舍悲愿救护众生，不可思议。虽能示现如来十力神变自在，而亦不舍等法界心教化众生，不可思议。知一切法无相是相，相是无相，无分别是分别，分别是无分别，非有是有，有是非有，无作是作，作是无作，非说是说，说是非说，不可思议。知心与菩提等，知菩提与心等，心及菩提与众生等，亦不生心颠倒、想颠倒、见颠倒，不可思议。于念念中入灭尽定，尽一切漏而不证实际，亦不尽有漏善根；虽知一切法无漏，而知漏尽，亦知漏灭；虽知佛法即世间法，世间法即佛法，而不于佛法中分别世间法，

Chapter 38 — Transcending the World

The inconceivability of his arousal of the resolve to attain bodhi, his cultivation of the bodhisattva practices, his never losing his roots of goodness, and his remaining free of discriminations;

The inconceivability of the fact that, although he has already deeply penetrated all dharmas, he still does not choose to enter nirvāṇa because his vows have not yet all been fulfilled;

The inconceivability of his cultivating the bodhisattva path, manifesting the appearance of his spirit's descent [from the Tuṣita Heavens], entering the womb, being reborn, leaving the home life, engaging in the austerities, going to the site of enlightenment, conquering the many *māras*, realizing the supreme and right enlightenment, turning the wheel of right Dharma, entering *parinirvāṇa*, incessantly manifesting mastery of the spiritual transformations, never relinquishing his compassionate vows, and rescuing and protecting beings;

The inconceivability of the fact that, although he is able to manifest the Tathāgata's ten powers and mastery of the spiritual transformations, he still never relinquishes his resolve as vast as the Dharma realm to continue teaching beings;

The inconceivability of his knowing with regard to all dharmas that whatever is signless is possessed of signs, that whatever is possessed of signs is signless, that whatever is free of discriminations involves discriminations, that whatever involves discriminations is free of discriminations, that nonexistence is existence, that existence is nonexistence, that effortlessness is effortful, that what is effortful is effortless, that what is unspoken is spoken, and that what is spoken is unspoken;

The inconceivability of his knowing that the mind is the same as bodhi, bodhi is the same as the mind, and the mind, bodhi, and beings are the same, this even as he still avoids producing inverted thoughts, inverted conceptions, or inverted views; and

The inconceivability of his entering the complete cessation absorption in each successive mind-moment while putting an end to all the contaminants, this even as he still refrains from entering the realization of the apex of reality and still refrains from putting an end to his roots of goodness associated with the contaminants. Although he does know all dharmas are free of the contaminants, he does know the ending of the contaminants and also does know the extinguishing of the contaminants. Although he knows that the dharmas of the Buddha are just the dharmas of the world and does know that the dharmas of the world are just the dharmas of the Buddha, he still does not distinguish worldly dharmas within the dharmas

正體字

不於世間法中。分別佛法。一切諸法。悉
入法界。無所入故。知一切法。皆無二。無變易
故。是為第十不可思議。佛子。是為菩薩摩訶
薩。十種不可思議。若諸菩薩。安住其中。則得
一切諸佛無上不可思議法。佛子。菩薩摩訶
薩。有十種巧密語。何等為十。所謂於一切佛
經中巧密語。於一切受生處巧密語。於一切
菩薩。神通變現。成等正覺巧密語。於一切眾
生。業報巧密語。於一切眾生。所起染淨巧密
語。於一切法。究竟無障礙門巧密語。於一切
虛空界。一一方處。悉有世界。或成或壞。間無
空處巧密語。於一切法界。一切十方。乃至微
細處。悉有如來。示現初生。乃至成佛。入般涅
槃。充滿法界。悉分別見巧密語。見一切眾生。
平等涅槃。無變易故。而不捨大願。以一切智
願。未得圓滿。令滿足故巧密語。雖知一切法
不由他悟。

简体字

不于世间法中分别佛法；一切诸法悉入法界，无所入故；知一切法皆无二，无变易故；是为第十不可思议。佛子，是为菩萨摩诃萨十种不可思议。若诸菩萨安住其中，则得一切诸佛无上不可思议法。

"佛子，菩萨摩诃萨有十种巧密语。何等为十？所谓：于一切佛经中，巧密语；于一切受生处，巧密语；于一切菩萨神通变现、成等正觉，巧密语；于一切众生业报，巧密语；于一切众生所起染净，巧密语；于一切法究竟无障碍门，巧密语；于一切虚空界，一一方处悉有世界或成或坏，间无空处，巧密语；于一切法界、一切十方，乃至微细处，悉有如来示现初生，乃至成佛、入般涅槃，充满法界悉分别见，巧密语；见一切众生平等涅槃无变易故，而不舍大愿，以一切智愿未得圆满令满足故，巧密语；虽知一切法不由他悟，

Chapter 38 — *Transcending the World*

of the Buddha and still does not distinguish the dharmas of the Buddha within the dharmas of the world, this because all dharmas enter the Dharma realm even as there is no entry that occurs at all, and also because he knows all dharmas are in all cases non-dual due to their being free of any transformation at all. This is the tenth of these kinds of inconceivability.

Sons of the Buddha, these are the bodhisattva-mahāsattva's ten kinds of inconceivability. If bodhisattvas abide in them, then they acquire all buddhas' unexcelled dharmas of inconceivability.

Sons of the Buddha, the bodhisattva-mahāsattva has ten kinds of skillful and esoteric speech. What are those ten? They are as follows:

Skillful and esoteric speech in all the Buddha's sutras;

Skillful and esoteric speech regarding all the stations of rebirth;

Skillful and esoteric speech regarding all bodhisattvas, their spiritual superknowledges, their transformations, and their realization of the right and perfect enlightenment;

Skillful and esoteric speech regarding all beings' karmic consequences;

Skillful and esoteric speech regarding the defilement and purity created by all beings;

Skillful and esoteric speech regarding the gateway by which there are ultimately no obstacles with regard to any dharmas;

Skillful and esoteric speech regarding the presence of worlds in each and every place throughout all realms of space that, whether they are being created or destroyed, have no empty places between them;

Skillful and esoteric speech regarding the existence of the *tathāgatas* in even the most minute locations in all places throughout the ten directions of the entire Dharma realm, including their manifestation of the appearance of first taking birth, and so forth up to and including their realization of buddhahood, their entry into *parinirvāṇa*, and their completely filling the entire Dharma realm in which they all may be distinctly seen;

Skillful and esoteric speech regarding perceiving all beings as equally abiding in nirvāṇa because they are completely unchanging, and yet he, [the bodhisattva-mahāsattva], still never relinquishes his great vow because he has not yet completely fulfilled his vow to attain all-knowledge and hence he persists in fulfilling it; and

Skillful and esoteric speech regarding his knowing that all dharmas do not depend on awakening induced by others even as

正體字

而不捨離諸善知識。於如來所。轉
加尊敬。與善知識。和合無二。於諸善根。修
[2]集種植。迴向安住。同一所作。同一體性。同
一出離。同一成就巧密語。是為十。若諸菩薩。
安住其中。則得如來無上善巧微密語。佛子。
菩薩摩訶薩。有十種巧分別智。何等為十。所
謂入一切剎。巧分別智。入一切眾生處。巧分
別智。入一切眾生心行。巧分別智。入一切眾
生根。巧分別智。入一切眾生業報。巧分別智。
入一切聲聞行。巧分別智。入一切獨覺行。巧
分別智。入一切菩薩行。巧分別智。入一切世
間法。巧分別智。入一切佛法。巧分別智。是為
十。若諸菩薩。安住其中。則得一切諸佛無上
善巧。分別諸法智。佛子。菩薩摩訶薩。有十種
入三昧。何等為十。所謂於一切世界入三昧。
於一切眾生身入三昧。於一切法入三昧。見
一切佛入三昧。住一切劫入三昧。

简体字

而不舍离诸善知识，于如来所转加尊敬，与善知识和合无二，于诸善根修习种植，回向安住，同一所作，同一体性，同一出离，同一成就，巧密语。是为十。若诸菩萨安住其中，则得如来无上善巧微密语。

"佛子，菩萨摩诃萨有十种巧分别智。何等为十？所谓：入一切刹巧分别智；入一切众生处巧分别智；入一切众生心行巧分别智；入一切众生根巧分别智；入一切众生业报巧分别智；入一切声闻行巧分别智；入一切独觉行巧分别智；入一切菩萨行巧分别智；入一切世间法巧分别智；入一切佛法巧分别智。是为十。若诸菩萨安住其中，则得一切诸佛无上善巧分别诸法智。

"佛子，菩萨摩诃萨有十种入三昧。何等为十？所谓：于一切世界入三昧；于一切众生身入三昧；于一切法入三昧；见一切佛入三昧；住一切劫入三昧；

he still never abandons his good spiritual guides, but rather ever increases his venerating esteem toward the Tathāgata and becomes so closely united with his good spiritual guides as to be as if no different in his cultivation, accumulation, and planting of all forms of roots of goodness, in his dedications, in his abiding, in his same endeavors, in his same essential nature, in his same emancipation, and in his same fulfillment.

These are the ten. If bodhisattvas abide in these, then they acquire the Tathāgata's unexcelled skillful and esoteric discourse.

Sons of the Buddha, the bodhisattva-mahāsattva has ten kinds of skillfully distinguishing wisdom. What are those ten? They are as follows:

Skillfully distinguishing wisdom that penetrates all *kṣetras*;

Skillfully distinguishing wisdom that penetrates every place that there are beings;

Skillfully distinguishing wisdom that penetrates all beings' mental actions;

Skillfully distinguishing wisdom that penetrates all beings' faculties;

Skillfully distinguishing wisdom that penetrates all beings' karmic consequences;

Skillfully distinguishing wisdom that penetrates all the *śrāvaka*-disciple practices;

Skillfully distinguishing wisdom that penetrates all the *pratyekabuddha* practices;

Skillfully distinguishing wisdom that penetrates all the bodhisattva practices;

Skillfully distinguishing wisdom that penetrates all worldly dharmas; and

Skillfully distinguishing wisdom that penetrates all dharmas of the Buddha.

These are the ten. If bodhisattvas abide in these, then they acquire all buddhas' unexcelled skillfully distinguishing wisdom with respect to all dharmas.

Sons of the Buddha, the bodhisattva-mahāsattva has ten kinds of entry into samādhi. What are those ten? They are as follows:

He may enter samādhis in all worlds;

He may enter samādhis in the bodies of all beings;

He may enter samādhis on all dharmas;

He may enter samādhis in which he sees all buddhas;

He may enter samādhis in which he abides in all kalpas;

正體字

從三昧起。
現不思議身入三昧。於一切佛身入三昧。覺悟一切眾生平等入三昧。一念中入一切菩薩三昧智入三昧。一念中以無礙智。成就一切諸菩薩行願。無有休息入三昧。是為十。若諸菩薩。安住其中。則得一切諸佛無上善巧三昧法。佛子。菩薩摩訶薩。有十種遍入。何等為十。所謂眾生遍入。國土遍入。世間種種相遍入。火災遍入。水災遍入。佛遍入。莊嚴遍入。如來無邊功德身遍入。一切種種說法遍入。一切如來種種供養遍入。是為十。若諸菩薩。安住其中。則得如來無上大智遍入法。佛子。菩薩摩訶薩。有十種解脫門。何等為十。所謂一身周遍一切世界解脫門。於一切世界。示現無量種種色相解脫門。以一切世界。入一佛剎解脫門。普加持一切眾生界解脫門。以一切佛莊嚴身。充滿一切世界解脫門。

简体字

从三昧起现不思议身入三昧；于一切佛身入三昧；觉悟一切众生平等入三昧；一念中入一切菩萨三昧智入三昧；一念中以无碍智成就一切诸菩萨行愿无有休息入三昧。是为十。若诸菩萨安住其中，则得一切诸佛无上善巧三昧法。

"佛子，菩萨摩诃萨有十种遍入。何等为十？所谓：众生遍入；国土遍入；世间种种相遍入；火灾遍入；水灾遍入；佛遍入；庄严遍入；如来无边功德身遍入；一切种种说法遍入；一切如来种种供养遍入。是为十。若诸菩萨安住其中，则得如来无上大智遍入法。

"佛子，菩萨摩诃萨有十种解脱门。何等为十？所谓：一身周遍一切世界解脱门；于一切世界示现无量种种色相解脱门；以一切世界入一佛刹解脱门；普加持一切众生界解脱门；以一切佛庄严身充满一切世界解脱门；

Chapter 38 — Transcending the World

He may enter samādhis in which, when he arises from samādhi, he manifests inconceivably many bodies;
He may enter samādhis focused on the bodies of all buddhas;
He may enter samādhis in which he awakens to the equality of all beings;
He may enter samādhis in which, in but a single mind-moment, he enters the samādhis and wisdom of all bodhisattvas; and
He may enter samādhis in which, in but a single mind-moment, he uses unimpeded wisdom to ceaselessly fulfill the practices and vows of all bodhisattvas.

These are the ten. If bodhisattvas abide in these, then they acquire all buddhas' unexcelled dharmas of skillful samādhi practice.

Sons of the Buddha, the bodhisattva-mahāsattva has ten kinds of pervasive penetration. What are those ten? They are as follows:

Pervasive penetration of beings;
Pervasive penetration of lands;
Pervasive penetration of the world's many different kinds of signs;
Pervasive penetration of fire disasters;
Pervasive penetration of flood disasters;
Pervasive penetration among buddhas;
Pervasive penetration of adornments;
Pervasive penetration of the Tathāgata's body possessed of boundless meritorious qualities;
Pervasive penetration of all of the many different ways of explaining the Dharma; and
Pervasive penetration of the many different kinds of offerings made to all buddhas.

These are the ten. If bodhisattvas abide in these dharmas, then they acquire the Tathāgata's unexcelled dharmas of pervasive penetration with great wisdom.

Sons of the Buddha, the bodhisattva-mahāsattva has ten kinds of gateways to liberation. What are those ten? They are as follows:

The gateway of liberation in which a single body everywhere pervades all worlds;
The gateway of liberation in which one manifests incalculably many different kinds of forms and appearances in all worlds;
The gateway of liberation in which one enables all worlds to enter but a single buddha *kṣetra*;
The gateway of liberation in which one provides supportive empowerment to all realms of beings;
The gateway of liberation in which the adorned bodies of all buddhas completely fill all worlds;

正體字

286a16 於自身中。見一切世界解脫門。一念中往一
286a17 切世界解脫門。於一世界。示現一切如來出
286a18 世解脫門。一身充滿一切法界解脫門。一念
286a19 中示現一切佛遊戲神通解脫門。是為十。若
286a20 諸菩薩。安住其中。則得如來無上解脫門。佛
286a21 子。菩薩摩訶薩。有十種神通。何等為十。所謂
286a22 憶念宿命。方便智通。天耳無礙。方便智通。知
286a23 他眾生不思議心行。方便智通。天眼觀察。無
286a24 有障礙。方便智通。隨眾生心。現不思議大神
286a25 通力。方便智通。一身普現無量世界。方便智
286a26 通。一念遍入不可說不可說世界。方便智通。
286a27 出生無量莊嚴具。莊嚴不思議世界。方便智
286a28 通。示現不可說變化身。方便智通。隨不思議
286a29 眾生心。於不可說世界。現成阿耨多羅三藐
286b01 三菩提方便智通。是為十。若諸菩薩。安住其
286b02 中。則得如來無上大善巧神通。

简体字

于自身中见一切世界解脱门；一念中往一切世界解脱门；于一世界示现一切如来出世解脱门；一身充满一切法界解脱门；一念中示现一切佛游戏神通解脱门。是为十。若诸菩萨安住其中，则得如来无上解脱门。

"佛子，菩萨摩诃萨有十种神通。何等为十？所谓：忆念宿命方便智通；天耳无碍方便智通；知他众生不思议心行方便智通；天眼观察无有障碍方便智通；随众生心现不思议大神通力方便智通；一身普现无量世界方便智通；一念遍入不可说不可说世界方便智通；出生无量庄严具，庄严不思议世界方便智通；示现不可说变化身方便智通；随不思议众生心，于不可说世界现成阿耨多罗三藐三菩提方便智通。是为十。若诸菩萨安住其中，则得如来无上大善巧神通，

Chapter 38 — *Transcending the World*

The gateway of liberation in which one sees all worlds within one's own body;

The gateway of liberation in which, in but a single mind-moment, one goes to all worlds;

The gateway of liberation in which one manifests all *tathāgatas* coming forth into the world within but a single world;

The gateway of liberation in which a single body completely fills the entire Dharma realm; and

The gateway of liberation in which, in but a single mind-moment, one manifests all buddhas' easeful mastery of the spiritual superknowledges.

These are the ten. If bodhisattvas abide in these, then they acquire the Tathāgata's unexcelled gateways to liberation.

Sons of the Buddha, the bodhisattva-mahāsattva has ten kinds of spiritual superknowledges. What are those ten? They are as follows:

The expedient superknowledge with which he remembers past lives;

The expedient superknowledge with which he possesses the unimpeded heavenly ear;

The expedient superknowledge with which he knows the inconceivable mental actions of other beings;

The expedient superknowledge with which his heavenly eye is unimpeded in what it observes;

The expedient superknowledge with which he adapts to the minds of beings in manifesting the inconceivably great power of the spiritual superknowledges;

The expedient superknowledge in which a single body appears everywhere in countless worlds;

The expedient superknowledge with which, in but a single mind-moment, he everywhere enters an ineffable-ineffable number of worlds;

The expedient superknowledge with which he produces countless adornments with which he adorns an inconceivable number of worlds;

The expedient superknowledge with which he manifests an ineffable number of transformation bodies; and

The expedient superknowledge with which he adapts to the minds of inconceivably many beings in an ineffable number of worlds for whom he manifests the realization of *anuttarasamyaksaṃbodhi*.

These are the ten. If bodhisattvas abide in these, then they acquire the Tathāgata's unexcelled great expedient superknowledges with

正體字

為一切眾生。種種示現。令其修學。佛子。菩薩摩訶薩。有十種明。何等為十。所謂知一切眾生。業報善巧智明。知一切眾生境界。寂滅清淨。無諸戲論。善巧智明。知一切眾生種種所緣。唯是一相。悉不可得。一切諸法。皆如金剛。善巧智明。能以無量微妙音聲。普聞十方一切世界。善巧智明。普壞一切心所染著。善巧智明。能以方便。示現受生。或不受生。善巧智明。捨離一切想受境界。善巧智明。知一切法非相非無相。一性無性。無所分別。而能了知種種諸法。於無量劫。分別演說。住於法界。成阿耨多羅三藐三菩提。善巧智明。菩薩摩訶薩。知一切眾生。生本無有生。了達受生。不可得故。而知因知緣。知事。知境界。知行。知生知滅。知言說。知迷惑知離迷惑。知顛倒知離顛倒。知雜染知清淨。知生死知涅槃。知可得知不可得。知執著知無執著。知住

简体字

为一切众生种种示现，令其修学。

"佛子，菩萨摩诃萨有十种明。何等为十？所谓：知一切众生业报，善巧智明。知一切众生境界，寂灭清净，无诸戏论，善巧智明。知一切众生种种所缘唯是一相悉不可得，一切诸法皆如金刚，善巧智明。能以无量微妙音声，普闻十方一切世界，善巧智明。普坏一切心所染著，善巧智明。能以方便示现受生或不受生，善巧智明。舍离一切想、受境界，善巧智明。知一切法非相、非无相，一性无性，无所分别，而能了知种种诸法，于无量劫分别演说，住于法界，成阿耨多罗三藐三菩提，善巧智明。菩萨摩诃萨知一切众生生本无有生，了达受生不可得故，而知因、知缘、知事、知境界、知行、知生、知灭、知言说、知迷惑、知离迷惑、知颠倒、知离颠倒、知杂染、知清净、知生死、知涅槃、知可得、知不可得、知执著、知无执著、知住、

Chapter 38 — *Transcending the World*

which they bring forth many different kinds of manifestations for all beings in order to enable them to cultivate and pursue the training.

Sons of the Buddha, the bodhisattva-mahāsattva has ten kinds of clarities. What are those ten? They are as follows:

The skillful cognitive clarity with which he knows all beings' karmic consequences;

The skillful cognitive clarity with which he knows all beings' spheres of cognition as quiescent, pure, and free of all conceptual proliferation;

The skillful cognitive clarity with which he knows all beings' many different objective conditions have but a single sign, that of inapprehensibility, and with which he knows all dharmas are [as indestructible] as vajra;

The skillful cognitive clarity with which he is able to use countless extremely subtle sounds to be heard in all worlds throughout the ten directions;

The skillful cognitive clarity with which he destroys all of the mind's defiling attachments;

The skillful cognitive clarity with which he is able to use skillful means to manifest as either being reborn or as not being reborn;

The skillful cognitive clarity with which he abandons all objects of perception and feeling;

The skillful cognitive clarity with which he knows all dharmas as neither possessed of signs nor signless, with which he knows them to be of but a single nature, that of having no nature, with which he remains free of discriminations yet is still able to completely know all the many different kinds of dharmas throughout measureless kalpas, distinguishing them and expounding on them, and with which he abides in the Dharma realm, realizing *anuttarasamyaksaṃbodhi*;

The skillful cognitive clarity with which he knows all beings as born and yet as originally unborn because he completely understands that taking birth is inapprehensible, and with which he knows causes, knows conditions, knows phenomena, knows spheres of cognition, knows actions, knows production, knows cessation, knows words and speech, knows delusion, knows the transcendence of delusion, knows inverted views, knows the transcendence of inverted views, knows defilement, knows purity, knows *saṃsāra*, knows *nirvāṇa*, knows apprehensibility, knows inapprehensibility, knows attachment, knows the absence of attachment, knows abiding, knows

正體字	知動。知去知還。知起 知不起。知失壞。知出離。知成熟。知諸根。知 調伏。隨其所應。種種教化。未曾忘失菩薩所 行。何以故。菩薩但為利益眾生故。發阿耨多 羅三藐三菩提心。無餘所為。是故菩薩。常化 眾生。身無疲倦。不違一切世間所作。是名緣 起善巧智明。菩薩摩訶薩。於佛無著。不起著 心。於法無著。不起著心。於剎無著。不起著 心。於眾生無著。不起著心。不見有眾生。而行 教化。調伏說法。然亦不捨菩薩諸行。大悲大 願。見佛聞法。隨順修行。依於如來。種諸善 根。恭敬供養。無有休息。能以神力。[＊]震動十 方無量世界。其心廣大。等法界故。知種種說 法。知眾生數。知眾生差別。知苦生。知苦滅。 知一切行皆如影像。行菩薩行。永斷一切受 生根本。但為救護一切眾生。行菩薩行。而無 所行。隨順一切諸佛種性。發如大山王心。知 一切虛妄顛倒。入一切種智門。智慧廣大。不 可傾動。
简体字	知动、知去、知还、知起、知不起、知失坏、知出离、知成熟、知诸根、知调伏，随其所应种种教化，未曾忘失菩萨所行。何以故？菩萨但为利益众生故，发阿耨多罗三藐三菩提心，无余所为。是故，菩萨常化众生，身无疲倦，不违一切世间所作。是名缘起善巧智明。菩萨摩诃萨于佛无著，不起著心；于法无著，不起著心；于刹无著，不起著心；于众生无著，不起著心；不见有众生而行教化调伏说法，然亦不舍菩萨诸行，大悲大愿，见佛闻法，随顺修行，依于如来种诸善根，恭敬供养无有休息，能以神力震动十方无量世界，其心广大等法界故，知种种说法，知众生数，知众生差别，知苦生，知苦灭，知一切行皆如影像，行菩萨行，永断一切受生根本，但为救护一切众生，行菩萨行而无所行，随顺一切诸佛种性，发如大山王心，知一切虚妄颠倒，入一切种智门，智慧广大不可倾动，

movement, knows going, knows returning, knows arising, knows non-arising, knows destruction, knows emancipation, knows ripening, knows faculties, and knows training—and thus, by adapting to what is appropriate, he provides all different kinds of teaching and never forgets what the bodhisattva practices. And how is this the case? It is solely in order to benefit beings that the bodhisattva brings forth the resolve to attain *anuttarasamyaksaṃbodhi*. He has no other motivation aside from this. The bodhisattva therefore always pursues the teaching of beings without ever becoming weary and without opposing what those in the worlds do. This is known as the skillful cognitive clarity with respect to conditioned arising; and

The skillful cognitive clarity by which the bodhisattva-mahāsattva has no attachment to the buddha and does not produce any thoughts of attachment thereto, has no attachment to the Dharma and does not generate any thoughts of attachment thereto, has no attachment to *kṣetras* and does not generate any thoughts of attachment thereto, has no attachment to beings and does not generate any thoughts of attachment thereto, and does not perceive the existence of beings and yet still engages in teaching, training, and teaching Dharma for their benefit. Thus he still never abandons any of the bodhisattva practices including the great compassion, the great vows, the seeing of buddhas, the hearing of the Dharma, the cultivation in accordance with it, the reliance upon the Tathāgata, the planting of all kinds of roots of goodness, and the respectful making of offerings, all of which he incessantly continues to pursue. In this, he is able to use his spiritual powers to cause quaking and movement in the countless worlds of the ten directions, this because his mind is as vast as the Dharma realm. In this, he knows the many different ways of explaining the Dharma, knows how many beings there are, knows the differences among beings, knows the arising of suffering, knows the cessation of suffering, knows all actions as like reflected images, practices the bodhisattva practices, and forever severs the very root of all rebirths. It is only for the sake of rescuing and protecting all beings that he practices the bodhisattva practices, and yet he has nothing whatsoever that he practices. He accords with the lineage of all buddhas and brings forth a resolve [as unshakable as] the great king of mountains. He recognizes that even all falseness and inverted views are subsumed within the gateway of the knowledge of all modes. His wisdom is so vast that it cannot be the least bit shaken. He is one who is bound for

正體字

當成正覺。於生死海。平等濟[1]渡一切眾生。善巧智明。是為十。若諸菩薩。安住其中。則得如來無上大善巧智明。佛子。菩薩摩訶薩。有十種解脫。何等為十。所謂煩惱解脫。邪見解脫。諸取解脫。蘊界處解脫。超二乘解脫。無生法忍解脫。於一切世間。一切剎。一切眾生。一切法。離著解脫。無邊住解脫。發起一切菩薩行。入如來無分別地解脫。於一念中。悉能了知一切三世解脫。是為十。若諸菩薩。安住此法。則能施作無上佛事。教化成熟一切眾生。佛子。菩薩摩訶薩。有十種園林。何等為十。所謂生死是菩薩園林。無厭捨故。教化眾生。是菩薩園林。不疲倦故。住一切劫。是菩薩園林。攝諸大行故。清淨世界。是菩薩園林。自所止住故。一切魔宮殿。是菩薩園林。降伏彼眾故。思惟所聞法。是菩薩園林。如理觀察故。六波羅蜜。四攝事。三十七菩提分法。是菩薩園林。紹繼慈父境界故。

简体字

当成正觉,于生死海平等济渡一切众生,善巧智明。是为十。若诸菩萨安住其中,则得如来无上大善巧智明。

"佛子,菩萨摩诃萨有十种解脱。何等为十?所谓:烦恼解脱;邪见解脱;诸取解脱;蕴、处、界解脱;超二乘解脱;无生法忍解脱;于一切世间、一切剎、一切众生、一切法离著解脱;无边住解脱;发起一切菩萨行入如来无分别地解脱;于一念中悉能了知一切三世解脱。是为十。若诸菩萨安住此法,则能施作无上佛事,教化成熟一切众生。

"佛子,菩萨摩诃萨有十种园林。何等为十?所谓:生死是菩萨园林,无厌舍故;教化众生是菩萨园林,不疲倦故;住一切劫是菩萨园林,摄诸大行故;清净世界是菩萨园林,自所止住故;一切魔宫殿是菩萨园林,降伏彼众故;思惟所闻法是菩萨园林,如理观察故;六波罗蜜、四摄事、三十七菩提分法是菩萨园林,绍继慈父境界故;

Chapter 38 — *Transcending the World*

realization of the right enlightenment who equally rescues all beings from the ocean of births and deaths.

These are the ten. If bodhisattvas abide in these, then they acquire the Tathāgata's unexcelled great skillful cognitive clarity.

Sons of the Buddha, the bodhisattva-mahāsattva has ten kinds of liberations. What are those ten? They are as follows:

The liberation from afflictions;

The liberation from wrong views;

The liberation from all grasping;

The liberation from the aggregates, sense realms, and sense bases;

The liberation that steps beyond the two vehicles;

The liberation of the unproduced-dharmas patience;

The liberation that abandons attachment to all worlds, all *kṣetras*, all beings, and all dharmas;

The liberation of boundless dwelling;

The liberation by which he begins all the bodhisattva practices and enters the Tathāgata's ground of nondiscrimination; and

The liberation by which, in but a single mind-moment, he is able to completely know all three periods of time.

These are the ten. If bodhisattvas abide in these dharmas, then they are able to carry out the unexcelled buddha works, teaching and ripening all beings.

Sons of the Buddha, the bodhisattva-mahāsattva has ten kinds of gardens and groves. What are those ten? They are as follows:

Saṃsāra is the bodhisattva's garden and grove because he does not loathe and abandon it;

Teaching beings is the bodhisattva's garden and grove because he never wearies of it;

Dwelling in all kalpas is the bodhisattva's garden and grove because he thereby accumulates all the great practices;

Pure worlds are the bodhisattva's garden and grove because this is where he dwells;

All the palaces of the *māras* are the bodhisattva's garden and grove because he conquers their hordes;

Meditative contemplation on the Dharma that he hears is the bodhisattva's garden and grove because he contemplates it in accordance with principle;

The six *pāramitās*, the four means of attraction,[97] and the thirty-seven aids to enlightenment are the bodhisattva's garden and grove because he thereby sustains the realm passed on by the kindly father;[98]

正體字

十力四無所畏。十
八不共。乃至一切佛法。是菩薩園林。不念餘
法故。示現一切菩薩。威力自在神通。是菩薩
園林。以大神力。轉正法輪。調伏眾生。無休息
故。一念於一切處。為一切眾生。示成正覺。是
菩薩園林。法身周遍。盡虛空一切世界故。是
為十。若諸菩薩。安住此法。則得如來無上離
憂惱。大安樂行。佛子。菩薩摩訶薩。有十種宮
殿。何等為十。所謂菩提心是菩薩宮殿。恒不
忘失故。十善業道。福德智慧。是菩薩宮殿。教
化欲界眾生故。四梵住禪定。是菩薩宮殿。教
化色界眾生故。生淨居天。是菩薩宮殿。一切
煩惱不染故。生無色界。是菩薩宮殿。令諸眾
生。離難處故。生雜染世界。是菩薩宮殿。令一
切眾生。斷煩惱故。現處内宮妻子眷屬。是菩
薩宮殿。成就往昔同行眾生故。現居輪王護
世釋梵。是菩薩宮殿。為調伏自在心眾生故。

简体字

十力、四无所畏、十八不共乃至一切佛法是菩萨园林，不念余法故；示现一切菩萨威力自在神通是菩萨园林，以大神力转正法轮调伏众生无休息故；一念于一切处为一切众生示成正觉是菩萨园林，法身周遍尽虚空一切世界故。是为十。若诸菩萨安住此法，则得如来无上离忧恼、大安乐行。

"佛子，菩萨摩诃萨有十种宫殿。何等为十？所谓：菩提心是菩萨宫殿，恒不忘失故；十善业道福德智慧是菩萨宫殿，教化欲界众生故；四梵住禅定是菩萨宫殿，教化色界众生故；生净居天是菩萨宫殿，一切烦恼不染故；生无色界是菩萨宫殿，令诸众生离难处故；生杂染世界是菩萨宫殿，令一切众生断烦恼故；现处内宫妻子、眷属是菩萨宫殿，成就往昔同行众生故；现居轮王、护世、释、梵是菩萨宫殿，为调伏自在心众生故；

The ten powers, four fearlessnesses, eighteen dharmas exclusive to the buddhas, and so forth until we come to all dharmas of the buddhas are the bodhisattva's garden and grove because he does not devote mindfulness to any other kinds of dharmas;

The manifestation of all bodhisattvas' awesome powers and sovereign spiritual superknowledges are the bodhisattva's garden and grove because he uses those great spiritual powers to ceaselessly turn the wheel of right Dharma, thereby training beings; and

The manifestation of the realization of right enlightenment for all beings in every place in but a single mind-moment is the bodhisattva's garden and grove because the Dharma body everywhere pervades all worlds throughout empty space.

These are the ten. If bodhisattvas abide in these dharmas, then they acquire the Tathāgata's unexcelled, worry-free, and immensely blissful conduct.

Sons of the Buddha, the bodhisattva-mahāsattva has ten kinds of palaces. What are those ten? They are as follows:

The resolve to attain bodhi is the bodhisattva's palace because he never forgets it;

The ten courses of good karmic action, merit, and wisdom are the bodhisattva's palace because he uses them to teach the beings of the desire realm;

The *dhyāna* absorptions corresponding to the four abodes of Brahma[99] are the bodhisattva's palace because he uses them to teach the beings of the form realm;

Birth into the Pure Dwelling Heavens is the bodhisattva's palace because there he remains undefiled by any of the afflictions;

Birth into the formless realm is the bodhisattva's palace because he thereby enables beings to leave behind the stations beset by the difficulties;[100]

Birth into defiled worlds is the bodhisattva's palace because there he enables all beings to sever the afflictions;

Manifesting as dwelling in the inner palace with wife, children, and retinue is the bodhisattva's palace because there he thereby assists the development of those beings he has practiced with in the past;

Manifesting as dwelling in the position of a wheel-turning king, a world-protecting deva king, Śakra, or Brahma is the bodhisattva's palace because it is done in order to train beings with the mind of a sovereign;

正體字

住一切菩薩行。遊戲神通。皆得自在。是菩薩宮殿。善遊戲諸禪解脫三昧智慧故。一切佛所受。無上自在。一切智王灌頂記。是菩薩宮殿。住十力莊嚴。作一切法王自在事故。是為十。若諸菩薩。安住其中。則得法灌頂。於一切世間。神力自在。佛子。菩薩摩訶薩。有十種所樂。何等為十。所謂樂正念。心不散亂故。樂智慧。分別諸法故。樂往詣一切佛所。聽法無厭故。樂諸佛充滿十方無邊際故。樂菩薩。自在為諸眾生。以無量門。而現身故。樂諸三昧門。於一三昧門。入一切三昧門故。樂陀羅尼。持法不忘。轉[1]受眾生故。樂無礙辯才。於一文一句。經不可說劫。分別演說。無窮盡故。樂成正覺。為一切眾生。以無量門。示現於身。成正覺故。樂轉法輪。摧滅一切異道法故。

简体字

住一切菩萨行游戏神通皆得自在是菩萨宫殿,善游戏诸禅解脱三昧智慧故;一切佛所受无上自在、一切智王灌顶记是菩萨宫殿,住十力庄严作一切法王自在事故。是为十。若诸菩萨安住其中,则得法灌顶,于一切世间神力自在。

"佛子,菩萨摩诃萨有十种所乐。何等为十?所谓:乐正念,心不散乱故;乐智慧,分别诸法故;乐往诣一切佛所,听法无厌故;乐诸佛,充满十方无边际故;乐菩萨,自在为诸众生以无量门而现身故;乐诸三昧门,于一三昧门入一切三昧门故;乐陀罗尼,持法不忘转受众生故;乐无碍辩才,于一文一句经不可说劫分别演说无穷尽故;乐成正觉,为一切众生以无量门示现于身成正觉故;乐转法轮,摧灭一切异道法故。

Chapter 38 — *Transcending the World*

Abiding in all the bodhisattva practices with easeful mastery of the spiritual superknowledges, in all cases attaining sovereign mastery of them—this is the bodhisattva's palace because he thereby skillfully acquires easeful mastery in all the *dhyānas*, liberations, samādhis, and wisdom; and

As received from all buddhas, the summit-anointing consecration and prediction of attaining unsurpassed sovereign mastery as a king of all-knowledge—this is the bodhisattva's palace because he thereby comes to abide in the adornment of the ten powers and thereby accomplishes the masterful works of all the Dharma kings.

These are the ten. If bodhisattvas abide in these, then they acquire the crown-anointing consecration of the Dharma and will attain sovereign mastery in the use of spiritual powers throughout all worlds.

Sons of the Buddha, the bodhisattva-mahāsattva has ten bases for delight. What are those ten? They are as follows:

He delights in right mindfulness because his mind is thereby neither scattered nor confused;

He delights in wisdom because he thereby distinguishes all dharmas;

He delights in visiting all buddhas because he is tireless in listening to the Dharma;

He delights in all buddhas because they fill the boundless realms of the ten directions;

He delights in bodhisattvas because of their sovereign mastery in using countless approaches to manifest bodies for the benefit of beings;

He delights in all the samādhi gateways because, through entering but a single samādhi gateway, he enters all samādhi gateways;

He delights in the *dhāraṇīs* because he thereby retains the Dharma, never forgets it, and then transmits it on to beings;

He delights in unimpeded eloquence because, by resort to it, he may endlessly distinguish and expound upon but a single passage or a single sentence for an ineffable number of kalpas;

He delights in the realization of right enlightenment because it entails using countless means to manifest bodies and realize right enlightenment for the benefit of beings; and

He delights in turning the wheel of the Dharma because he thereby utterly vanquishes the dharmas promoted by all non-Buddhist paths.

正體字

是為十。
287a28 若諸菩薩。安住此法。則得一切諸佛如來無
287a29 上法樂。佛子。菩薩摩訶薩。有十種莊嚴。何等
287b01 為十。所謂力莊嚴不可壞故。無畏莊嚴。無能
287b02 伏故。義莊嚴。說不可說義無窮盡故。法莊嚴。
287b03 八萬四千法聚。觀察演說。無忘失故。願莊嚴。
287b04 一切菩薩。所發弘誓。無退轉故。行莊嚴。修普
287b05 賢行。而出離故。刹莊嚴。以一切刹。作一刹
287b06 故。普音莊嚴。周遍一切諸佛世界。雨法雨故。
287b07 力持莊嚴。於一切劫。行無數行。不斷絕故。
287b08 變化莊嚴。於一眾生身。示現一切眾生數等
287b09 身。令一切眾生。悉得知見。求一切智。無退轉
287b10 故。是為十。若諸菩薩。安住此法。則得如來一
287b11 切無上法莊嚴。佛子。菩薩摩訶薩。發十種不
287b12 動心。何等為十。所謂於一切所有。悉皆能捨
287b13 不動心。思惟觀察一切佛法不動心。憶念供
287b14 養一切諸佛不動心。於一切眾生。誓無惱害
287b15 不動心。普攝眾生。不[2]揀怨親不動心。求一
287b16 切佛法。無有休息不動心。

简体字

是为十。若诸菩萨安住此法，则得一切诸佛如来无上法乐。

"佛子，菩萨摩诃萨有十种庄严。何等为十？所谓：力庄严，不可坏故；无畏庄严，无能伏故；义庄严，说不可说义无穷尽故；法庄严，八万四千法聚观察演说无忘失故；愿庄严，一切菩萨所发弘誓无退转故；行庄严，修普贤行而出离故；刹庄严，以一切刹作一刹故；普音庄严，周遍一切诸佛世界雨法雨故；力持庄严，于一切劫行无数行不断绝故；变化庄严，于一众生身示现一切众生数等身，令一切众生悉得知见，求一切智无退转故。是为十。若诸菩萨安住此法，则得如来一切无上法庄严。

"佛子，菩萨摩诃萨发十种不动心。何等为十？所谓：于一切所有悉皆能舍不动心；思惟观察一切佛法不动心；忆念供养一切诸佛不动心；于一切众生誓无恼害不动心；普摄众生不拣怨亲不动心；求一切佛法无有休息不动心；

These are the ten. If bodhisattvas abide in these dharmas, then they acquire the unexcelled Dharma bliss of all buddhas, the *tathāgatas*.

Sons of the Buddha, the bodhisattva-mahāsattva has ten kinds of adornment. What are those ten? They are as follows:

Adornment with the powers, because they are indestructible;

Adornment with the fearlessnesses, because they are insurmountable;

Adornment with meanings, because he endlessly expounds on ineffably many meanings;

Adornment with Dharma, because he contemplates and expounds on the collection of eighty-four thousand dharmas, never forgetting any of them;

Adornment with vows, because of the irreversibility of the vast vows made by all bodhisattvas;

Adornment with practices, because he attains emancipation by cultivating Samantabhadra's practices;

Adornment with *kṣetras*, because he makes a single *kṣetra* of all *kṣetras*;

Adornment with the universally pervasive voice, because it everywhere pervades all buddha worlds, raining the Dharma rain;

Adornment with empowerments, because he thereby incessantly practices innumerable practices throughout all kalpas; and

Adornment with transformations, because he manifests bodies as numerous as all beings in the body of a single being, thus enabling all beings to acquire knowledge and vision and seek all-knowledge without ever retreating.

These are the ten. If bodhisattvas abide in these dharmas, then they acquire all of the Tathāgata's unexcelled Dharma adornments.

Sons of the Buddha, the bodhisattva-mahāsattva manifests ten kinds of unshakable mind. What are those ten? They are as follows:

The unshakable mind that is able to relinquish all his possessions;

The unshakable mind that reflects upon and contemplates all dharmas of the Buddha;

The unshakable mind that recollects and makes offerings to all buddhas;

The unshakable mind that vows to refrain from tormenting or injuring any being;

The unshakable mind that gathers in all beings without distinguishing between adversaries and close relations;

The unshakable mind that ceaselessly seeks all dharmas of the Buddha;

正體字

一切眾生數等不
可說不可說劫。行菩薩行。不生疲厭。亦無退
轉不動心。成就有根信。無濁信。清淨信。極清
淨信。離垢信。明徹信。恭敬供養一切佛信。不
退轉信。不可盡信。無能壞信。大歡喜踊躍信
不動心。成就出生一切智方便道不動心。聞
一切菩薩行法。信受不謗不動心。是為十。若
諸菩薩。安住此法。則得無上一切智不動心。
佛子。菩薩摩訶薩。有十種不捨深大心。何等
為十。所謂不捨成滿一切佛菩提深大心。不
捨教化調伏一切眾生深大心。不捨不斷一
切諸佛種性深大心。不捨親近一切善知識深
大心。不捨供養一切諸佛深大心。不捨專求
一切大乘功德法深大心。不捨於一切佛所。
修行梵行。護持淨戒深大心。不捨親近一切
菩薩深大心。不捨求一切佛法方便護持深
大心。

简体字

一切众生数等不可说不可说劫，行菩萨行不生疲厌亦无退转不动心；成就有根信、无浊信、清净信、极清净信、离垢信、明彻信、恭敬供养一切佛信、不退转信、不可尽信、无能坏信、大欢喜踊跃信不动心；成就出生一切智方便道不动心；闻一切菩萨行法信受不谤不动心。是为十。若诸菩萨安住此法，则得无上一切智不动心。

"佛子，菩萨摩诃萨有十种不舍深大心。何等为十？所谓：不舍成满一切佛菩提深大心；不舍教化调伏一切众生深大心；不舍不断一切诸佛种性深大心；不舍亲近一切善知识深大心；不舍供养一切诸佛深大心；不舍专求一切大乘功德法深大心；不舍于一切佛所修行梵行、护持净戒深大心；不舍亲近一切菩萨深大心；不舍求一切佛法方便护持深大心；

Chapter 38 — *Transcending the World*

> The unshakable mind that tirelessly and irreversibly practices the bodhisattva practices for an ineffable-ineffable number of kalpas as numerous as all beings;
>
> The unshakable mind that develops deeply-rooted faith, faith free of turbidity, pure faith, ultimately pure faith, immaculate faith, faith with radiant clarity, faith associated with revering and making offerings to all buddhas, irreversible faith, endless faith, indestructible faith, and faith suffused with exultant joyfulness;
>
> The unshakable mind that perfects the path of skillful means leading to the development of all-knowledge; and
>
> The unshakable mind that, on hearing the Dharma of all the bodhisattva practices, believes in, accepts, and never disparages them.

These are the ten. If bodhisattvas abide in these dharmas, then they acquire the unexcelled unshakable mind of all-knowledge.

Sons of the Buddha, the bodhisattva-mahāsattva has ten kinds of never-relinquished profound and great resolve. What are those ten? They are as follows:

> He never relinquishes the profound and great resolve to completely fulfill the bodhi of all buddhas;
>
> He never relinquishes the profound and great resolve to teach and train all beings;
>
> He never relinquishes the profound and great resolve to ensure that the lineage of all buddhas will never be cut off;
>
> He never relinquishes the profound and great resolve to draw near to all good spiritual guides;
>
> He never relinquishes the profound and great resolve to make offerings to all buddhas;
>
> He never relinquishes the profound and great resolve to especially focus on seeking to acquire all dharmas possessed of the Great Vehicle's meritorious qualities;
>
> He never relinquishes the profound and great resolve to practice *brahmacarya* and preserve the pure precepts in the presence of all buddhas;
>
> He never relinquishes the profound and great resolve to draw near to all bodhisattvas;
>
> He never relinquishes the profound and great resolve to seek the skillful means by which to protect and preserve all dharmas of the Buddha; and

正體字

不捨滿一切菩薩行願集一切諸佛法
深大心。是為十。若諸菩薩。安住其中。則能
不捨一切佛法。佛子。菩薩摩訶薩。有十種智
慧觀察。何等為十。所謂善巧分別。說一切法
智慧觀察。了知三世一切善根智慧觀察。了
知一切諸菩薩行。自在變化智慧觀察。了知
一切諸法義門智慧觀察。了知一切諸佛威
力智慧觀察。了知一切陀羅尼門智慧觀察。
於一切世界普說正法智慧觀察。入一切法
界智慧觀察。知一切十方不可思議智慧觀
察。知一切佛法智慧光明。無有障礙智慧觀
察。是為十。若諸菩薩。安住其中。則得如來無
上大智慧觀察。佛子。菩薩摩訶薩。有十種說
法。何等為十。所謂說一切法。皆從緣起。說一
切法。皆悉如幻。說一切法。無有乖諍。說一切
法。無有邊際。說一切法。無所依止。說一切
法。猶如金剛。說一切法。皆悉如如。說一切
法。皆悉寂靜。

简体字

不舍满一切菩萨行愿、集一切诸佛法深大心。是为十。若诸菩萨安住其中，则能不舍一切佛法。

"佛子，菩萨摩诃萨有十种智慧观察。何等为十？所谓：善巧分别说一切法智慧观察；了知三世一切善根智慧观察；了知一切诸菩萨行自在变化智慧观察；了知一切诸法义门智慧观察；了知一切诸佛威力智慧观察；了知一切陀罗尼门智慧观察；于一切世界普说正法智慧观察；入一切法界智慧观察；知一切十方不可思议智慧观察；知一切佛法智慧光明无有障碍智慧观察。是为十。若诸菩萨安住其中，则得如来无上大智慧观察。

"佛子，菩萨摩诃萨有十种说法。何等为十？所谓：说一切法皆从缘起；说一切法皆悉如幻；说一切法无有乖诤；说一切法无有边际；说一切法无所依止；说一切法犹如金刚；说一切法皆悉如如；说一切法皆悉寂静；

Chapter 38 — *Transcending the World*

He never relinquishes the profound and great resolve to fulfill the conduct and vows of all bodhisattvas and accumulate the dharmas of all buddhas.

These are the ten. If bodhisattvas abide in these, then they are able to never relinquish any of the dharmas of the Buddha.

Sons of the Buddha, the bodhisattva-mahāsattva has ten kinds of wise contemplations. What are those ten? They are as follows:

The wise contemplation by which he skillfully distinguishes and expounds on all dharmas;

The wise contemplation by which he completely knows all roots of goodness of the three periods of time;

The wise contemplation by which he completely knows all the practices of all bodhisattvas as well as their sovereign mastery of spiritual transformations;

The wise contemplation by which he completely knows all the gateways to the meaning of all dharmas;

The wise contemplation by which he completely knows the awesome powers of all buddhas;

The wise contemplation by which he completely knows all of the *dhāraṇī* gateways;

The wise contemplation by which he expounds on right Dharma everywhere in all worlds;

The wise contemplation by which he enters the entire Dharma realm;

The wise contemplation by which he knows the inconceivability everywhere throughout the ten directions; and

The wise contemplation by which he knows the unimpeded wisdom light of all dharmas of the Buddha.

These are the ten. If bodhisattvas abide in these, then they acquire the Tathāgata's unexcelled and greatly wise contemplations.

Sons of the Buddha, the bodhisattva-mahāsattva has ten kinds of explanations about dharmas. What are those ten? They are as follows:

He explains all dharmas as arising from conditions;

He explains all dharmas as like conjurations;

He explains all dharmas as free of any mutual contradiction;

He explains all dharmas as boundless;

He explains all dharmas as independent;

He explains all dharmas as like vajra;

He explains all dharmas as characterized by true suchness;

He explains all dharmas as quiescent;

正體字	說一切法。皆悉出離。說一切 287c21 法。皆住一義。本性成就。是為十。若諸菩薩。 287c22 安住其中。則能善巧。說一切法。佛子。菩薩摩 287c23 訶薩。有十種清淨。何等為十。所謂深心清淨。 287c24 斷疑清淨。離見清淨。境界清淨。求一切智清 287c25 淨。辯才清淨。無畏清淨。住一切菩薩智清淨。 287c26 受一切菩薩律儀清淨。具足成就無上菩提。 287c27 三十二種百福相白淨法一切善根清淨。是 287c28 為十。若諸菩薩。安住其中。則得一切如來無 287c29 上清淨法。佛子。菩薩摩訶薩。有十種印。何等 288a01 為十。所謂菩薩摩訶薩。知苦苦壞苦行苦。專 288a02 求佛法。不生懈怠。行菩薩行。無有疲懈。不驚 288a03 不畏。不恐不怖。不捨大願。求一切智。堅固不 288a04 退。究竟阿耨多羅三藐三菩提。是為第一印。 288a05 菩薩摩訶薩。見有眾生愚癡狂亂。或以麁弊 288a06 惡語。而相毀辱。或以刀杖瓦石。而加損害。終 288a07 不以此境界。捨菩薩心。但忍辱柔和。專修佛 288a08 法。
简体字	说一切法皆悉出离；说一切法皆住一义，本性成就。是为十。若诸菩萨安住其中，则能善巧说一切法。 　　"佛子，菩萨摩诃萨有十种清净。何等为十？所谓：深心清净；断疑清净；离见清净；境界清净；求一切智清净；辩才清净；无畏清净；住一切菩萨智清净；受一切菩萨律仪清净；具足成就无上菩提、三十二种百福相、白净法、一切善根清净。是为十。若诸菩萨安住其中，则得一切如来无上清净法。 　　"佛子，菩萨摩诃萨有十种印。何等为十？所谓：菩萨摩诃萨知苦苦、坏苦、行苦，专求佛法，不生懈怠，行菩萨行无有疲懈，不惊不畏，不恐不怖，不舍大愿，求一切智坚固不退，究竟阿耨多罗三藐三菩提，是为第一印。菩萨摩诃萨见有众生愚痴狂乱，或以粗弊恶语而相毁辱，或以刀杖瓦石而加损害，终不以此境界舍菩萨心，但忍辱柔和，专修佛法，

Chapter 38 — *Transcending the World* 2801

He explains all dharmas as leading to emancipation; and

He explains all dharmas as in every case abiding in ultimate truth[101] and as perfect by virtue of their original nature.

These are the ten. If bodhisattvas abide in these, then they are able to skillfully explain all dharmas.

Sons of the Buddha, the bodhisattva-mahāsattva has ten [other] kinds of purity. What are those ten? They are as follows:

Purity of deep resolve;

Purity in severing doubts;

Purity in abandoning views;

Purity of spheres of cognition and action;

Purity in the quest for all-knowledge;

Purity in eloquence;

Purity in fearlessness;

Purity in abiding in the wisdom of all bodhisattvas;

Purity in taking on the moral code of all bodhisattvas; and

Purity in the complete perfection of unexcelled bodhi, the thirty-two marks of hundredfold merit, the dharmas of purity, and all roots of goodness.

These are the ten. If bodhisattvas abide in these, then they acquire all *tathāgatas'* dharmas of unexcelled purity.

Sons of the Buddha, the bodhisattva-mahāsattva has ten kinds of seals. What are those ten? They are as follows:

The bodhisattva-mahāsattva knows the suffering of suffering, the suffering of deterioration, and the suffering of the *saṃskāras'* karmic formative factors.[102] He especially focuses on the quest for the Buddha's Dharma. He never indulges the arising of any indolence in his tireless practice of the bodhisattva practices, is never alarmed, never fearful, never beset by trepidation, and is never struck with terror. He never relinquishes the great vows, he is solid and unretreating in his quest for all-knowledge, and thus he ultimately reaches *anuttarasamyaksaṃbodhi*. This is the first of his seals;

When the bodhisattva-mahāsattva observes that there are beings who are crazed and confused by stupidity who may use coarse and vile words in defaming and vilifying him, or who may use knives, staves, tiles, or stones to injure him, he still never allows these kinds of objective circumstances to cause him to relinquish the bodhisattva resolve. Rather, he simply endures such abuse and persists in the gentle, harmonious, and especially focused cultivation of the Buddha's Dharma, abides in the

正體字

住最勝道。入離生位。是為第二印。菩薩摩
訶薩。聞說與一切智相應。甚深佛法。能以自
智。深信忍可。解了趣入。是為第三印。菩薩摩訶
薩。又作是念。我發深心。求一切智。我當
成佛。得阿耨多羅三藐三菩提。一切眾生。流
轉五趣。受無量苦。亦當令其發菩提心。深信
歡喜。勤修精進。堅固不退。是為第四印。菩薩
摩訶薩。知如來智無有邊際。不以齊限測如
來智。菩薩曾於無量佛所。聞如來智無有邊
際故。能不以齊限測度一切世間。文字所說
皆有齊限。悉不能知如來智慧。是為第五印。
菩薩摩訶薩。於阿耨多羅三藐三菩提。得最
勝欲。甚深欲。廣欲大欲。種種欲。無能勝欲。
無上欲。堅固欲。眾魔外道并其眷屬無能壞
欲。求一切智不退轉欲。菩薩住如是等欲。於
無上菩提。畢竟不退。是為第六印。菩薩摩訶
薩。行菩薩行。不顧身命。無能沮壞。發心趣向
一切智故。一切智性。常現前故。得一切佛智
光明故。終不捨離佛菩提。終不捨離善知識。
是為第七印。

简体字

住最胜道,入离生位,是为第二印。菩萨摩诃萨闻说与一切智相应甚深佛法,能以自智,深信忍可,解了趣入,是为第三印。菩萨摩诃萨又作是念:'我发深心求一切智,我当成佛得阿耨多罗三藐三菩提。一切众生流转五趣受无量苦,亦当令其发菩提心,深信欢喜,勤修精进,坚固不退。'是为第四印。菩萨摩诃萨知如来智无有边际,不以齐限测如来智;菩萨曾于无量佛所闻如来智无有边际故,能不以齐限测度;一切世间文字所说皆有齐限,悉不能知如来智慧;是为第五印。菩萨摩诃萨于阿耨多罗三藐三菩提得最胜欲、甚深欲、广欲、大欲、种种欲、无能胜欲、无上欲、坚固欲、众魔外道并其眷属无能坏欲、求一切智不退转欲,菩萨住如是等欲,于无上菩提毕竟不退,是为第六印。菩萨摩诃萨行菩萨行,不顾身命,无能沮坏,发心趣向一切智故,一切智性常现前故,得一切佛智光明故,终不舍离佛菩提,终不舍离善知识,是为第七印。

Chapter 38 — *Transcending the World*

supreme path, and enters the positions [on the path] in which births are transcended. This is the second of his seals;

When the bodhisattva hears teachings related to all-knowledge from the extremely profound Dharma of the Buddha, relying on his own wisdom, he is able to recognize their validity with deep faith, completely comprehends them, and enters them. This is the third of his seals;

The bodhisattva-mahāsattva also thinks thus: "Just as I who have brought forth the deep resolve to seek all-knowledge am thereby bound to become a buddha and realize *anuttarasamyaksaṃbodhi*, so too, given that all beings, flowing along and turning about in the five destinies, are thus bound to undergo measureless suffering, I should also enable them to bring forth the bodhi resolve, to develop deep faith and joyous delight, to become diligent and vigorous in cultivation, and to become solidly irreversible in this." This is the fourth of his seals;

The bodhisattva-mahāsattva realizes that the Tathāgata's wisdom is so boundless that one could never fathom the Tathāgata's wisdom through the use of limited means. Because the bodhisattva has already heard the Tathāgata's boundless wisdom under countless buddhas, he is able to refrain from using such limited means to fathom it. He realizes that discussions using any of the world's languages are so limited that they would all be incapable of knowing the Tathāgata's wisdom. This is the fifth of his seals;

The bodhisattva-mahāsattva acquires for his quest to realize *anuttarasamyaksaṃbodhi* the most supreme zeal,[103] extremely profound zeal, vast zeal, great zeal, all different forms of zeal, indomitable zeal, unexcelled zeal, solid zeal, zeal indestructible by any of the many *māras*, non-Buddhists, or their retinues, and zeal that is irreversible in its quest for all-knowledge. Abiding in types of zeal such as these, the bodhisattva achieves ultimate irreversibility with respect to the attainment of unexcelled bodhi. This is the sixth of his seals;

In his practice of the bodhisattva practices, the bodhisattva-mahāsattva, being unconcerned with preserving his own body or life, cannot be hindered by anyone. Because he has generated the resolve to proceed toward all-knowledge, because the nature of all-knowledge always manifests directly before him, and because he has acquired the wisdom light of all buddhas, he never abandons the bodhi of the buddhas and never abandons his good spiritual guides. This is the seventh of his seals;

正體字

菩薩摩訶薩。若見善男子善女人趣大乘者。令其增長求佛法心。令其安住一切善根。令其攝取一切智心。令其不退無上菩提。是為第八印。菩薩摩訶薩。令一切眾生。得平等心。勸令勤修一切智道。以大悲心。而為說法。令於阿耨多羅三藐三菩提。永不退轉。是為第九印。菩薩摩訶薩。與三世諸佛。同一善根。不斷一切諸佛種性。究竟得至一切智智。是為第十印。佛子。是為菩薩摩訶薩十種印。菩薩以此。速成阿耨多羅三藐三菩提。具足如來一切法無上智印。佛子。菩薩摩訶薩。有十種智光照。何等為十。所謂知定當成阿耨多羅三藐三菩提智光照。見一切佛智光照。見一切眾生。死此生彼智光照。解一切修多羅法門智光照。依善知識。發菩提心。集諸善根智光照。示現一切諸佛智光照。教化一切眾生。悉令安住如來地智光照。

简体字

菩萨摩诃萨若见善男子、善女人趣大乘者，令其增长求佛法心，令其安住一切善根，令其摄取一切智心，令其不退无上菩提，是为第八印。菩萨摩诃萨令一切众生得平等心，劝令勤修一切智道，以大悲心而为说法，令于阿耨多罗三藐三菩提永不退转，是为第九印。菩萨摩诃萨与三世诸佛同一善根，不断一切诸佛种性，究竟得至一切智智，是为第十印。佛子，是为菩萨摩诃萨十种印。菩萨以此速成阿耨多罗三藐三菩提，具足如来一切法无上智印。

"佛子，菩萨摩诃萨有十种智光照。何等为十？所谓：知定当成阿耨多罗三藐三菩提智光照；见一切佛智光照；见一切众生死此生彼智光照；解一切修多罗法门智光照；依善知识发菩提心集诸善根智光照；示现一切诸佛智光照；教化一切众生悉令安住如来地智光照；

Chapter 38 — *Transcending the World*

> When the bodhisattva-mahāsattva observes a son or daughter of good family who is progressing in the Great Vehicle, he enables them to increase their resolve to seek the Buddha's Dharma, enables them to abide in all kinds of roots of goodness, enables them to consolidate their resolve for all-knowledge, and enables them to become irreversible in their quest for unexcelled bodhi. This is the eighth of his seals;
>
> The bodhisattva-mahāsattva enables all beings to acquire the mind of equal regard for all and encourages them to diligently cultivate the path to all-knowledge. With the mind of great compassion, he explains the Dharma for them and enables them to become forever irreversible in their progress toward *anuttarasamyaksaṃbodhi*. This is the ninth of his seals; and
>
> The bodhisattva-mahāsattva possesses roots of goodness that are one and the same with those of all buddhas of the three periods of time. He never allows the severance of the lineage of all buddhas and ultimately succeeds in acquiring the wisdom of all-knowledge. This is the tenth of his seals.

Sons of the Buddha, these are the ten kinds of seals of the bodhisattva-mahāsattva. Relying on these, the bodhisattva swiftly succeeds in realizing *anuttarasamyaksaṃbodhi* and in completely perfecting the seal of the Tathāgata's unexcelled wisdom in all dharmas.

Sons of the Buddha, the bodhisattva-mahāsattva has ten kinds of illumination with the light of wisdom. What are those ten? They are as follows:

> The illumination with the light of wisdom by which he knows he will definitely attain *anuttarasamyaksaṃbodhi*;
>
> The illumination with the light of wisdom by which he sees all buddhas;
>
> The illumination with the light of wisdom by which he sees all beings dying in this place and being reborn in that place;
>
> The illumination with the light of wisdom by which he understands all the Dharma gateways contained in the sutras;
>
> The illumination with the light of wisdom by which he relies on the good spiritual guide, makes the bodhi resolve, and accumulates all roots of goodness;
>
> The illumination with the light of wisdom by which all buddhas are revealed;
>
> The illumination with the light of wisdom by which he teaches all beings and enables them all to abide on the ground of the Tathāgata;

演

說不可思議。廣大法門智光照。善巧了知一切諸佛。神通威力智光照。滿足一切諸波羅蜜智光照。是為十。若諸菩薩。安住此法。則得一切諸佛無上智光照。佛子。菩薩摩訶薩。有十種無等住。一切眾生。聲聞獨覺。悉無與等。何等為十。所謂菩薩摩訶薩。雖觀實際。而不取證。以一切願。未成滿故。是為第一無等住。菩薩摩訶薩。種等法界一切善根。而不於中有少執著。是為第二無等住。菩薩摩訶薩。修菩薩行。知其如化。以一切法。悉寂滅故。而於佛法。不生疑惑。是為第三無等住。菩薩摩訶薩。雖離世間所有妄想。然能作意。於不可說劫。行菩薩行。滿足大願。終不中起疲厭之心。是為第四無等住。菩薩摩訶薩。於一切法。無所取著。以一切法性寂滅故。而不證涅槃。何以故。一切智道。未成滿故。是為第五無等住。菩薩摩訶薩。知一切劫皆即非劫。而真實說一切劫數。是為第六無等住。

演说不可思议广大法门智光照；善巧了知一切诸佛神通威力智光照；满足一切诸波罗蜜智光照。是为十。若诸菩萨安住此法，则得一切诸佛无上智光照。

"佛子，菩萨摩诃萨有十种无等住，一切众生、声闻、独觉悉无与等。何等为十？所谓：菩萨摩诃萨虽观实际而不取证，以一切愿未成满故，是为第一无等住。菩萨摩诃萨种等法界一切善根，而不于中有少执著，是为第二无等住。菩萨摩诃萨修菩萨行，知其如化，以一切法悉寂灭故，而于佛法不生疑惑，是为第三无等住。菩萨摩诃萨虽离世间所有妄想，然能作意，于不可说劫行菩萨行，满足大愿，终不中起疲厌之心，是为第四无等住。菩萨摩诃萨于一切法无所取著，以一切法性寂灭故，而不证涅槃。何以故？一切智道未成满故，是为第五无等住。菩萨摩诃萨知一切劫皆即非劫，而真实说一切劫数，是为第六无等住。

Chapter 38 — *Transcending the World*

> The illumination with the light of wisdom by which he expounds on the inconceivable and vast gateways to the Dharma;
>
> The illumination with the light of wisdom by which he skillfully and completely knows the spiritual superknowledges and awesome powers of all buddhas; and
>
> The illumination with the light of wisdom by which he completely fulfills all the *pāramitās*.

These are the ten. If bodhisattvas abide in these dharmas, then they acquire all buddhas' unexcelled illumination with the light of wisdom.

Sons of the Buddha, the bodhisattva-mahāsattva has ten kinds of peerless dwelling which are unequaled by any being, any *śrāvaka* disciple, or any *pratyekabuddha*. What are those ten? They are as follows:

> Although the bodhisattva-mahāsattva contemplates the apex of reality, he still does not choose to bring it to full realization because all his vows have not yet been completely fulfilled. This is the first of his peerless dwellings;
>
> The bodhisattva-mahāsattva plants all roots of goodness equal in their expansiveness to the Dharma realm and yet he does not retain even the slightest attachment to any of them. This is the second of his peerless dwellings;
>
> In his cultivation of the bodhisattva practices, the bodhisattva-mahāsattva realizes that they are like transformationally created phenomena because all dharmas are quiescent. Even so, he never develops any doubts regarding the Buddha's Dharma. This is the third of his peerless dwellings;
>
> Although the bodhisattva-mahāsattva has abandoned all the world's false conceptions, he is still able to engage in mental actions devoted to practicing the bodhisattva practices for an ineffable number of kalpas, completely fulfilling the great vows and never having any thought of weariness in this. This is the fourth of his peerless dwellings;
>
> The bodhisattva-mahāsattva has no attachment to any dharma, this because all dharmas are by nature quiescent. Still, he refrains from opting for the realization of nirvāṇa. Why? Because he has not yet completely fulfilled the path to the acquisition of all-knowledge. This is the fifth of his peerless dwellings;
>
> The bodhisattva-mahāsattva knows all kalpas are just non-kalpas and yet he still truthfully speaks of all the types of kalpas.[104] This is the sixth of his peerless dwellings;

菩薩摩訶薩。知一切法悉無所作。而不捨作道。求諸佛法。是為第七無等住。菩薩摩訶薩。知三界唯心。三世唯心。而了知其心無量無邊。是為第八無等住。菩薩摩訶薩。為一眾生。於不可說劫行菩薩行。欲令安住一切智地。如為一眾生。為一切眾生。悉亦如是而不生疲厭。是為第九無等住。菩薩摩訶薩。雖修行圓滿。而不證菩提。何以故。菩薩作如是念。我之所作。本為眾生。是故我應久處生死。方便利益。皆令安住無上佛道。是為第十無等住。佛子。是為菩薩摩訶薩。十種無等住。若諸菩薩。安住其中。則得無上大智。一切佛法。無等住。

大方廣佛華嚴經[*]卷第五十五

　　離世間品第三十八之三

佛子。菩薩摩訶薩。發十種無下劣心。何等為十。佛子。菩薩摩訶薩。作如是念。我當降伏一切天魔。及其眷屬。是為第一無下劣心。又作是念。我當悉破一切外道。及其邪法。是為第二無下劣心。又作是念。我當於一切眾生。善言開[1]諭。皆令歡喜。是為第三無下劣心。又作是念。我當成滿遍法界一切波羅蜜行。是為第四無下劣心。

菩萨摩诃萨知一切法悉无所作，而不舍作道，求诸佛法，是为第七无等住。菩萨摩诃萨知三界唯心、三世唯心，而了知其心无量无边，是为第八无等住。菩萨摩诃萨为一众生，于不可说劫行菩萨行，欲令安住一切智地；如为一众生，为一切众生悉亦如是，而不生疲厌，是为第九无等住。菩萨摩诃萨虽修行圆满，而不证菩提。何以故？菩萨作如是念：'我之所作本为众生，是故我应久处生死，方便利益，皆令安住无上佛道。'是为第十无等住。佛子，是为菩萨摩诃萨十种无等住。若诸菩萨安住其中，则得无上大智、一切佛法无等住。

大方广佛华严经卷第五十五

离世间品第三十八之三

　　"佛子，菩萨摩诃萨发十种无下劣心。何等为十？佛子，菩萨摩诃萨作如是念：'我当降伏一切天魔及其眷属。'是为第一无下劣心。又作是念：'我当悉破一切外道及其邪法。'是为第二无下劣心。又作是念：'我当于一切众生善言开喻皆令欢喜。'是为第三无下劣心。又作是念：'我当成满遍法界一切波罗蜜行。'是为第四无下劣心。

Chapter 38 — *Transcending the World*

The bodhisattva-mahāsattva realizes that all dharmas have no actions at all that they perform and yet he still never relinquishes the actions in which he engages on the path in seeking the Dharma of all buddhas. This is the seventh of his peerless dwellings;

The bodhisattva-mahāsattva realizes that the three realms are only mind and that the three periods of time are only mind even as he completely realizes his mind is measureless and boundless. This is the eighth of his peerless dwellings;

For the sake of but a single being, the bodhisattva-mahāsattva may practice the bodhisattva practices for an ineffable number of kalpas, wishing thereby to enable that being to dwell on the ground of all-knowledge. And just as he may do so for but a single being, so too may he also do so for all beings in this very same way, and yet he still never grows weary of this. This is the ninth of his peerless dwellings; and

Although the bodhisattva-mahāsattva achieves the complete fulfillment of his cultivation, he still refrains from the complete realization of bodhi. And why is this? This is because the bodhisattva thinks: "Whatever I do is originally done for the sake of beings. Therefore I should remain for a long time in *saṃsāra*, using skillful means to benefit them and enable them all to dwell securely in the unexcelled path to buddhahood." This is the tenth of his peerless dwellings.

These are the ten peerless dwellings of the bodhisattva-mahāsattva. If bodhisattvas abide in them, then they acquire the peerless dwelling in the unexcelled great wisdom with regard to all dharmas of the Buddha.

Sons of the Buddha, the bodhisattva-mahāsattva makes ten kinds of flawless resolve.[105] What are those ten? Sons of the Buddha:

The bodhisattva-mahāsattva thinks thus: "I should subdue all the deva-*māras* along with all their retinues." This is the first of his kinds of flawless resolve;

He also thinks thus: "I should demolish all the non-Buddhist paths and their deviant dharmas." This is the second of his kinds of flawless resolve;

He also thinks thus: "I should present such skillfully worded explanations to all beings that they are all delighted." This is the third of his kinds of flawless resolve;

He also thinks thus: "I should fulfill the *pāramitā* practices everywhere throughout the Dharma realm." This is the fourth of his kinds of flawless resolve;

正體字

又作是念。我當積集一切
福德藏。是為第五無下劣心。又作是念。無上
菩提廣大難成。我當修行。悉令圓滿。是為第
六無下劣心。又作是念。我當以無上教化。無
上調伏。教化調伏一切眾生。是為第七無下
劣心。又作是念。一切世界。種種不同。我當以
無量身。[1]成等正覺。是為第八無下劣心。又
作是念。我修菩薩行時。若有眾生。來從我乞
手足耳鼻。血肉骨髓。妻子象馬。乃至王位。如
是一切悉皆能捨。不生一念憂悔之心。但為
利益一切眾生。不求果報。以大悲為首。大慈
究竟。是為第九無下劣心。又作是念。三世所
有。一切諸佛。一切佛法。一切眾生。一切國
土。一切世間。一切三世。一切虛空界。一切法
界。一切語言施設界。一切寂滅涅槃界。如是
一切種種諸法。我當以一念相應慧。悉知悉
覺。悉見悉證。悉修悉斷。然於其中。無分別離
分別。無種種差別。無功德無境界。非有非無。
非一非二。以不二智。知一切二。以無相智。知
一切相。以無分別智。知一切分別。

简体字

又作是念：'我当积集一切福德藏。'是为第五无下劣心。又作是念：'无上菩提广大难成，我当修行悉令圆满。'是为第六无下劣心。又作是念：'我当以无上教化、无上调伏，教化调伏一切众生。'是为第七无下劣心。又作是念：'一切世界种种不同，我当以无量身成等正觉。'是为第八无下劣心。又作是念：'我修菩萨行时，若有众生来从我乞手足、耳鼻、血肉、骨髓、妻子、象马乃至王位，如是一切悉皆能舍，不生一念忧悔之心，但为利益一切众生，不求果报，以大悲为首，大慈究竟。'是为第九无下劣心。又作是念：'三世所有一切诸佛，一切佛法、一切众生、一切国土、一切世间、一切三世、一切虚空界、一切法界、一切语言施设界、一切寂灭涅槃界，如是一切种种诸法，我当以一念相应慧，悉知悉觉，悉见悉证，悉修悉断，然于其中无分别、离分别、无种种差别、无功德、无境界、非有非无、非一非二。以不二智知一切二，以无相智知一切相，以无分别智知一切分别，

Chapter 38 — *Transcending the World*

He also thinks thus: "I should accumulate a treasury of all kinds of merit." This is the fifth of his kinds of flawless resolve;

He also thinks thus: "Although the unexcelled bodhi is vast and difficult to fully realize, I should cultivate it and bring it to complete fulfillment." This is the sixth of his kinds of flawless resolve;

He also thinks thus: "I should use unexcelled teaching and unexcelled training to teach and train all beings." This is the seventh of his kinds of flawless resolve;

He also thinks thus: "All worlds have various kinds of differences. I should use countless bodies in accomplishing the realization of the right and perfect enlightenment." This is the eighth of his kinds of flawless resolve;

He also thinks thus: "If, when I am cultivating the bodhisattva practices, beings come and beg from me my hands, feet, ears, nose, blood, flesh, bones, marrow, wives, sons, elephants, horses, and so forth until we come to the position of kingship, I shall be able to relinquish all such things, doing so without even an instant of worried or regretful thought, doing so solely to benefit all beings, and doing so without seeking karmic rewards, taking the great compassion as what is foremost and the great kindness as what is ultimate." This is the ninth of his kinds of flawless resolve; and

He also thinks thus: "As for all that exists in the three periods of time, all buddhas, all dharmas of the Buddha, all beings, all lands, all worlds, all three periods of time, all realms of space, the entire Dharma realm, all realms established through words and speech, all realms of quiescent nirvāṇa—with wisdom that responds in but a single mind-moment, I should completely know, completely awaken to, completely perceive, completely realize, completely cultivate, and completely sever all the many different kinds of dharmas such as these. However, with regard to everything among them, I should remain free of discriminations and abandon discriminations, should remain free of [any conception of] the many kinds of differences, free of [any conception of] meritorious qualities or objective realms, and free of [any conception of] "neither existent nor nonexistent" or "neither singular nor dual," and:

I should use non-dual wisdom to know all dual phenomena;
I should use signless wisdom to know all signs;
I should use nondiscriminating wisdom to know all discriminations;

正體字

以無異智。知一[2]切異。以無差別智。知一切差別。以無世間智。知一切世間。以無世智。知一切世。以無眾生智。知一切眾生。以無執著智。知一切執著。以無住處智。知一切住處。以無雜染智。知一切雜染。以無盡智。知一切盡。以究竟法界智。於一切世界。示現身。以離言音智。示不可說言音。以一自性智。入於無自性。以一境界智。現種種境界。知一切法不可說。而現大自在言說。證一切智地。為教化調伏一切眾生故。於一切世間。示現大神通變化。是為第十無下劣心。佛子。是為菩薩摩訶薩。發十種無下劣心。若諸菩薩。安住此心。則得一切最上無下劣佛法。佛子。菩薩摩訶薩。於阿耨多羅三藐三菩提。有十種如山增上心。何等為十。佛子。菩薩摩訶薩。常作意勤修一切智法。是為第一如山增上心。

简体字

以无异智知一切异，以无差别智知一切差别，以无世间智知一切世间，以无世智知一切世，以无众生智知一切众生，以无执著智知一切执著，以无住处智知一切住处，以无杂染智知一切杂染，以无尽智知一切尽，以究竟法界智于一切世界示现身，以离言音智示不可说言音，以一自性智入于无自性，以一境界智现种种境界；知一切法不可说，而现大自在言说，证一切智地；为教化调伏一切众生故，于一切世间示现大神通变化。'是为第十无下劣心。佛子，是为菩萨摩诃萨发十种无下劣心。若诸菩萨安住此心，则得一切最上无下劣佛法。

"佛子，菩萨摩诃萨于阿耨多罗三藐三菩提，有十种如山增上心。何等为十？佛子，菩萨摩诃萨常作意勤修一切智法，是为第一如山增上心。

Chapter 38 — *Transcending the World*

> I should use nondifferentiating wisdom to know all differences;
> I should use the wisdom that does not conceive of differences to know all distinctions;
> I should use the wisdom that realizes the nonexistence of the world to know the entire world;
> I should use the wisdom that realizes the nonexistence of the periods of time to know all periods of time;
> I should use the wisdom that realizes the nonexistence of beings to know all beings;
> I should use the wisdom free of attachments to know all attachments;
> I should use non-abiding wisdom to know all abodes;
> I should use undefiled wisdom to know all defilements;
> I should use endless wisdom to know all endings;
> I should use the wisdom that reaches throughout the Dharma realm to manifest bodies in all worlds;
> I should use the wisdom that transcends words and voice to manifest ineffably many words and voices;
> I should use the wisdom cognizing but a single inherent nature to penetrate the nonexistence of any inherent nature at all;
> I should use the wisdom of the singular objective realm to manifest all kinds of different objective realms;
> I should know all dharmas are ineffable and yet manifest great sovereign mastery in the use of words and speech;
> I should realize entry into the ground of all-knowledge; and
> For the sake of teaching and training all beings, I should manifest transformations in all worlds with the great spiritual superknowledges."
> This is the tenth of his kinds of flawless resolve.

Sons of the Buddha, these are the ten kinds of flawless resolve made by the bodhisattva-mahāsattva. If bodhisattvas abide in these types of resolve, then they acquire all of the most supreme and flawless dharmas of the Buddha.

Sons of the Buddha, regarding *anuttarasamyaksaṃbodhi*, the bodhisattva-mahāsattva has ten kinds of especially superior mountain-like mind.[106] What are those ten? Sons of the Buddha:

> The bodhisattva-mahāsattva is always determined to diligently cultivate the dharma of all-knowledge. This is the first of his types of especially superior mountain-like mind;

正體字	恒觀一切法本性空
	289b08 ‖ 無所得。是為第二如山增上心。願於無量劫。
	289b09 ‖ 行菩薩行。修一切白淨法。以住一切白淨法
	289b10 ‖ 故。知見如來無量智慧。是為第三如山增上
	289b11 ‖ 心。為求一切佛法故。等心敬奉諸善知識。無
	289b12 ‖ 異希求。無盜法心。唯生尊重。未曾有懈。一切
	289b13 ‖ 所有。悉皆能捨。是為第四如山增上心。若有
	289b14 ‖ 眾生。罵辱毀謗。打棒屠割。苦其形體。乃至斷
	289b15 ‖ 命。如是等事。悉皆能受。終不因此生動亂心。
	289b16 ‖ 生瞋害心。亦不退捨大悲弘誓。更令增長。無
	289b17 ‖ 有休息。何以故。菩薩於一切法。如實出離。捨
	289b18 ‖ 成就故。證得一切諸如來法。忍辱柔和。已自
	289b19 ‖ 在故。是為第五如山增上心。菩薩摩訶薩。成
	289b20 ‖ 就增上大功德。所謂天增上功德。人增上功
	289b21 ‖ 德。色增上功德。力增上功德。眷屬增上功德。
	289b22 ‖ 欲增上功德。王位增上功德。

简体字

恒观一切法本性空无所得，是为第二如山增上心。愿于无量劫行菩萨行，修一切白净法，以住一切白净法故，知见如来无量智慧，是为第三如山增上心。为求一切佛法故，等心敬奉诸善知识，无异希求，无盗法心，唯生尊重，未曾有懈，一切所有悉皆能舍，是为第四如山增上心。若有众生骂辱、毁谤、打棒、屠割，苦其形体，乃至断命，如是等事悉皆能受，终不因此生动乱心、生瞋害心，亦不退舍大悲弘誓，更令增长无有休息。何以故？菩萨于一切法如实出离，舍成就故；证得一切诸如来法，忍辱柔和已自在故。是为第五如山增上心。菩萨摩诃萨成就增上大功德，所谓：天增上功德、人增上功德、色增上功德、力增上功德、眷属增上功德、欲增上功德、王位增上功德、

Chapter 38 — *Transcending the World*

He constantly contemplates all dharmas as having the original nature characterized by emptiness [of inherent existence] and the absence of anything that is apprehensible. This is the second of his types of especially superior mountain-like mind;

He vows to practice the bodhisattva practices for incalculably many kalpas during which he cultivates all the dharmas of purity. Due to abiding in all those dharmas of purity, he comes to know and perceive the Tathāgata's measureless wisdom. This is the third of his types of especially superior mountain-like mind;

In order to seek out all dharmas of the Buddha, with a mind of equal regard for them all, he reverently serves all good spiritual guides, doing so without any other kinds of aspirations, and doing so without any intention to steal their Dharma. He only brings forth reverential esteem for them and never indulges any [other kinds of] intentions. In this, he is able to relinquish everything that he possesses. This is the fourth of his types of especially superior mountain-like mind;

If beings curse him, vilify him, disparage him, slander him, strike him with cudgels, butcher him, or otherwise inflict suffering on his physical body even to the point that they cut short his life, he is able to endure all such circumstances as these and never allows his mind to become either shaken or confused by this, nor does he raise even a single thought motivated by hatred or the intent to harm others. Nor does he then retreat from or abandon his greatly compassionate and vast vows. Rather, it causes them to incessantly grow ever stronger. And why is this? This is because, due to the complete development of his equanimity, the bodhisattva, according with reality, has become emancipated from [any attachment to] any dharma. It is also because he has realized the dharmas of all *tathāgatas* and because he has already developed sovereign mastery of gentle and harmonious patience. This is the fifth of his types of especially superior mountain-like mind;

The bodhisattva-mahāsattva perfects supreme great meritorious qualities, namely:

The supreme meritorious qualities of the devas;
The supreme meritorious qualities of humans;
The supreme meritorious qualities of his physical form;
The supreme meritorious qualities of his powers;
The supreme meritorious qualities of his retinue;
The supreme meritorious qualities of his aspirations;
The supreme meritorious qualities of a king;

正體字

自在增上功德。
289b23 ｜ 福德增上功德。智慧增上功德。雖復成就如
289b24 ｜ 是功德。終不於此。而生染著。所謂不著味。不
289b25 ｜ 著欲。不著財富。不著眷屬。但深樂法。隨法
289b26 ｜ 去。隨法住。隨法趣向。隨法究竟。以法為依。
289b27 ｜ 以法為救。以法為歸。以法為舍。守護法。愛樂
289b28 ｜ 法。希求法。思惟法。佛子。菩薩摩訶薩。雖復
289b29 ｜ 具受種種法樂。而常遠離眾魔境界。何以故。
289c01 ｜ 菩薩摩訶薩。於過去世。發如是心。我當令一
289c02 ｜ 切眾生。皆悉永離眾魔境界。住佛境[3]界故。
289c03 ｜ 是為第六如山增上心。菩薩摩訶薩。為求阿
289c04 ｜ 耨多羅三藐三菩提。已於無量阿僧祇劫。行
289c05 ｜ 菩薩道。精勤匪懈。猶謂我今始發阿耨多羅
289c06 ｜ 三藐三菩提心。行菩薩行。亦不驚亦不怖。亦
289c07 ｜ 不畏。雖能一念即成阿耨多羅三藐三菩提。
289c08 ｜ 然為眾生故。於無量劫。行菩薩行。無有休息。
289c09 ｜ 是為第七如山增上心。菩薩摩訶薩。知一切
289c10 ｜ 眾生。性不和善。難調難度。不能知恩。不能報
289c11 ｜ 恩。是故為其。發大誓願。

简体字

自在增上功德、福德增上功德、智慧增上功德。虽复成就如是功德，终不于此而生染著，所谓：不著味、不著欲、不著财富、不著眷属；但深乐法，随法去、随法住、随法趣向、随法究竟，以法为依、以法为救、以法为归、以法为舍，守护法、爱乐法、希求法、思惟法。佛子，菩萨摩诃萨虽复具受种种法乐，而常远离众魔境界。何以故？菩萨摩诃萨于过去世发如是心：'我当令一切众生皆悉永离众魔境界，住佛境故。'是为第六如山增上心。菩萨摩诃萨为求阿耨多罗三藐三菩提，已于无量阿僧祇劫行菩萨道精勤匪懈，犹谓：'我今始发阿耨多罗三藐三菩提心。'行菩萨行，亦不惊、亦不怖、亦不畏。虽能一念即成阿耨多罗三藐三菩提，然为众生故，于无量劫行菩萨行无有休息，是为第七如山增上心。菩萨摩诃萨知一切众生性不和善，难调难度，不能知恩，不能报恩，是故为其发大誓愿，

Chapter 38 — Transcending the World

The supreme meritorious qualities of his sovereign masteries;

The supreme meritorious qualities of his merit; and

The supreme meritorious qualities of his wisdom.

Although he develops meritorious qualities such as these, he never develops any kind of defiling attachment for any of these things. In particular, he is not attached to whatever is delectable, he is not attached to the desires, he is not attached to wealth, and he is not attached to any retinue. He only deeply delights in the Dharma and thus goes forth in accordance with the Dharma, abides in accordance with the Dharma, progresses along in accordance with the Dharma, reaches the most ultimate point in accordance with the Dharma, takes the Dharma as what he relies upon, take the Dharma as the source of his rescue, takes the Dharma as his refuge, takes the Dharma as his shelter, preserves and guards the Dharma, cherishes and delights in the Dharma, seeks the Dharma, and reflects on the Dharma.

Sons of the Buddha, although the bodhisattva-mahāsattva completely experiences all the many different kinds of Dharma bliss, he still always abandons the realms of the many kinds of *māras*. And why is this? This is because, in the past, the bodhisattva-mahāsattva brought forth this kind of resolve: "I shall enable all beings to forever abandon the many realms of the *māras* and shall instead enable them to abide in the realms of the Buddha." This is the sixth of his types of especially superior mountain-like mind;

For the sake of his quest to reach *anuttarasamyaksaṃbodhi*, the bodhisattva-mahāsattva has already cultivated the bodhisattva path for incalculably many *asaṃkhyeyas* of kalpas during which he has been intensely diligent and never indolent. Even so, he still thinks, "I have only now just brought forth my initial resolve to gain *anuttarasamyaksaṃbodhi*." In his practice of the bodhisattva practices, he is neither terrified nor frightened nor beset with fearfulness. Although he is able in but a single mind-moment to immediately realize *anuttarasamyaksaṃbodhi*, for the sake of beings, he still incessantly practices the bodhisattva practices for incalculably many kalpas. This is the seventh of his types of especially superior mountain-like mind;

The bodhisattva-mahāsattva realizes that all beings by nature are not harmonious and good, that they are difficult to train and difficult to liberate, that they are unable to feel gratitude for kindnesses bestowed on them, and they are unable to repay kindnesses bestowed on them. As a consequence, he makes a great vow for their sakes in which he wishes to enable them all

正體字

欲令皆得心意自在。
所行無礙。捨離惡念。不於他所。生諸煩惱。是
為第八如山增上心。菩薩摩訶薩。復作是念。
非他令我發菩提心。亦不待人助我修行。我
自發心。集諸佛法。誓期自勉。盡未來劫。行菩
薩道。成阿耨多羅三藐三菩提。是故我今修
菩薩行。當淨自心。亦淨他心。當知自境界。亦
知他境界。我當悉與三世諸佛。境界平等。是
為第九如山增上心。菩薩摩訶薩。作如是觀。
無有一法修菩薩行。無有一法滿菩薩行。無
有一法教化調伏一切眾生。無有一法供養
恭敬一切諸佛。無有一法於阿耨多羅三藐
三菩提。已成今成當成。無有一法已說今說
當說。說者及法。俱不可得。而亦不捨阿耨多
羅三藐三菩提願。何以故。菩薩求一切法。皆
無所得。如是出生阿耨多羅三藐三菩提。是
故於法。雖無所得。而勤修習增上善業。清淨
對治。智慧圓滿。念念增長。一切具足。其心
於此。不驚不怖。不作是念。若一切法。皆悉寂
滅。我有何義。求於無上菩提之道。

简体字

欲令皆得心意自在，所行无碍，舍离恶念，不于他所生诸烦恼，是为第八如山增上心。菩萨摩诃萨复作是念：'非他令我发菩提心，亦不待人助我修行。我自发心，集诸佛法，誓期自勉，尽未来劫行菩萨道，成阿耨多罗三藐三菩提。是故我今修菩萨行，当净自心亦净他心，当知自境界亦知他境界，我当悉与三世诸佛境界平等。'是为第九如山增上心。菩萨摩诃萨作如是观：'无有一法修菩萨行，无有一法满菩萨行，无有一法教化调伏一切众生，无有一法供养恭敬一切诸佛，无有一法于阿耨多罗三藐三菩提已成、今成、当成，无有一法已说、今说、当说，说者及法俱不可得，而亦不舍阿耨多罗三藐三菩提愿。'何以故？菩萨求一切法皆无所得，如是出生阿耨多罗三藐三菩提。是故，于法虽无所得，而勤修习增上善业，清净对治，智慧圆满，念念增长，一切具足。其心于此不惊不怖，不作是念：'若一切法皆悉寂灭，我有何义求于无上菩提之道？'

to attain sovereign mastery of the mind, to remain unimpeded in their actions, to abandon evil thoughts, and to refrain from generating afflicted emotions toward others. This is the eighth of his types of especially superior mountain-like mind;

The bodhisattva-mahāsattva also has this thought: "It is not the case that anyone else has caused me to bring forth the bodhi resolve, nor is it the case that I wait on others to assist me in cultivation. Rather it is I alone who make this resolve to accumulate all the Buddha dharmas and exhort myself to practice the bodhisattva path to the end of all future kalpas in order to realize *anuttarasamyaksaṃbodhi*. It is for this reason that I now cultivate the bodhisattva practices. I shall purify my own mind and shall also assist others in purifying their own minds. I should know my own sphere of cognition and should know the spheres of cognition of others as well. I should develop a sphere of cognition which is the same as that of all buddhas of the three periods of time." This is the ninth of his types of especially superior mountain-like mind; and

The bodhisattva-mahāsattva takes up a contemplation of this sort: "There is not so much as a single dharma by which one cultivates the bodhisattva practices, not so much as a single dharma by which one fulfills the bodhisattva practices, not so much as a single dharma by which one teaches and trains all beings, not so much as a single dharma by which one makes offerings to and reveres all buddhas, not so much as a single dharma by which *anuttarasamyaksaṃbodhi* has ever been realized, is now realized, or ever will be realized in the future, and there is not so much as a single dharma that has ever been spoken, is now spoken, or ever will be spoken in the future. The one who speaks as well as the dharmas that are spoken are both inapprehensible."

Even so, he still does not abandon his vow to attain *anuttarasamyaksaṃbodhi*. And why is this? Whenever the bodhisattva seeks to find any dharma at all, they are all inapprehensible. And so it is that he succeeds in bringing forth [the realization of] *anuttarasamyaksaṃbodhi*. Therefore, although nothing is apprehensible in any dharma, he still diligently cultivates the especially superior good works, the pure means of counteraction, and the complete fulfillment of wisdom, increasing these in each successive mind-moment to the point that he completely perfects them all. In this, his mind is never frightened or fearful, nor does he have this thought: "If it is the case that all dharmas are quiescent, what meaning could there be for me in continuing to seek the path to unexcelled bodhi?"

正體字

是為第十
如山增上心。佛子。是為菩薩摩訶薩。於阿耨
多羅三藐三菩提。十種如山增上心。若諸菩
薩。安住其中。則得如來無上大智山王增上
心。佛子。菩薩摩訶薩。有十種入阿耨多羅三
藐三菩提如海智。何等為十。所謂入一切無
量眾生界。是為第一如海智。入一切世界。而
不起分別。是為第二如海智。知一切虛空界
無量無礙。普入十方一切差別世界網。是為
第三如海智。菩薩摩訶薩。善入法界。所謂無
礙入。不斷入。不常入。無量入。不生入。不滅
入。一切入。悉了知故。是為第四如海智。菩薩
摩訶薩。於過去未來現在諸佛。菩薩法師。聲
聞獨覺。及一切凡夫。所集善根。已集現集當
集。三世諸佛。於阿耨多羅三藐三菩提。已成
今成當成。所有善根。三世諸佛。說法調伏一
切眾生。已說今說當說。所有善根。於彼一切
皆悉了知。深信隨喜。願樂修習。無有厭足。是
為第五如海智。菩薩摩訶薩。於念念中。入過
去世不可說劫。於一劫中。

简体字

是为第十如山增上心。佛子，是为菩萨摩诃萨于阿耨多罗三藐三菩提十种如山增上心。若诸菩萨安住其中，则得如来无上大智山王增上心。

"佛子，菩萨摩诃萨有十种入阿耨多罗三藐三菩提如海智。何等为十？所谓：入一切无量众生界，是为第一如海智。入一切世界而不起分别，是为第二如海智。知一切虚空界无量无碍，普入十方一切差别世界网，是为第三如海智。菩萨摩诃萨善入法界，所谓：无碍入、不断入、不常入、无量入、不生入、不灭入、一切入，悉了知故，是为第四如海智。菩萨摩诃萨于过去、未来、现在诸佛、菩萨、法师、声闻、独觉及一切凡夫所集善根已集、现集、当集，三世诸佛于阿耨多罗三藐三菩提已成、今成、当成所有善根，三世诸佛说法调伏一切众生已说、今说、当说所有善根，于彼一切皆悉了知，深信随喜，愿乐修习，无有厌足，是为第五如海智。菩萨摩诃萨于念念中入过去世不可说劫，于一劫中，

Chapter 38 — *Transcending the World*

This is the tenth of his types of especially superior mountain-like mind.

Sons of the Buddha, these are the bodhisattva-mahāsattva's ten kinds of especially superior mountain-like mind in relation to *anuttarasamyaksaṃbodhi*. If bodhisattvas abide in these, then they acquire the especially superior mind associated with the Tathāgata's mountain king of unexcelled great wisdom.

Sons of the Buddha, the bodhisattva-mahāsattva has ten kinds of oceanic wisdom with which he enters *anuttarasamyaksaṃbodhi*. What are those ten? They are as follows:

That by which he enters all the realms of the incalculably many beings. This is the first of his types of oceanic wisdom;

That by which he enters all worlds and yet never generates any discriminations. This is the second of his types of oceanic wisdom;

That by which he knows all the measureless and unimpeded realms of empty space and everywhere enters the network of all the different worlds of the ten directions. This is the third of his types of oceanic wisdom;

The bodhisattva-mahāsattva skillfully enters the Dharma realm, namely through endless entry, noneternal entry, measureless entry, unproduced entry, undestroyed entry, and comprehensive entry, accomplishing this because he completely knows them all. This is the fourth of his types of oceanic wisdom;

With regard to all the roots of goodness collected in the past, collected in the present, and collected in the future by all past, future, and present buddhas, bodhisattvas, masters of the Dharma, *śrāvaka* disciples, *pratyekabuddhas*, and all common people, all the roots of goodness garnered by all buddhas of the three periods of time in their past, present, and future realizations of *anuttarasamyaksaṃbodhi*, and all the roots of goodness garnered by all buddhas of the three periods of time in their speaking of the Dharma and their training of all beings, whether speaking in the past, speaking in the present, or speaking in the future, the bodhisattva-mahāsattva completely knows them all, believes in them deeply, joyfully accords with them, and happily aspires to cultivate them while never growing weary of doing so. This is the fifth of his types of oceanic wisdom;

In each successive mind-moment, the bodhisattva-mahāsattva enters all the ineffably many kalpas of the past in which, within a single kalpa, there may have been a hundred *koṭīs* of buddhas

正體字

或百億佛出世。或千億佛出世。或百千億佛出世。或無數或無量。或無邊或無等。或不可數。或不可稱。或不可思。或不可量。或不可說。或不可說不可說。超過算數。諸佛世尊。出興[1]于世。及彼諸佛。道場眾會。聲聞菩薩。說法調伏。一切眾生壽命延促。法住久近。如是一切。悉皆明見。如一劫。一切諸劫。皆亦如是。其無佛劫。所有眾生。有於阿耨多羅三藐三菩提。種諸善根亦悉了知。若有眾生。善根熟已。於未來世。當得見佛。亦悉了知。如是觀察過去世不可說不可說劫。心無厭足。是為第六如海智。菩薩摩訶薩。入未來世。觀察分別一切諸劫無量無邊。知何劫有佛。何劫無佛。何劫有幾如來出世。一一如來。名號何等。住何世界。世界名何。度幾眾生。壽命幾時。如是觀察。盡未來際。皆悉了知。不可窮盡。而無厭足。是為第七如海智。菩薩摩訶薩。入現在世。觀察思惟。於念念中。普見十方無邊品類不可說世界。

简体字

或百亿佛出世，或千亿佛出世，或百千亿佛出世，或无数、或无量、或无边、或无等、或不可数、或不可称、或不可思、或不可量、或不可说、或不可说不可说，超过算数诸佛世尊出兴于世，及彼诸佛道场众会声闻、菩萨说法调伏，一切众生寿命延促，法住久近，如是一切悉皆明见；如一劫，一切诸劫皆亦如是。其无佛劫所有众生，有于阿耨多罗三藐三菩提种诸善根，亦悉了知；若有众生善根熟已，于未来世当得见佛，亦悉了知。如是观察过去世不可说不可说劫，心无厌足，是为第六如海智。菩萨摩诃萨入未来世，观察分别一切诸劫无量无边，知何劫有佛，何劫无佛，何劫有几如来出世，一一如来名号何等，住何世界，世界名何，度几众生，寿命几时。如是观察，尽未来际皆悉了知，不可穷尽而无厌足，是为第七如海智。菩萨摩诃萨入现在世观察思惟，于念念中普见十方无边品类不可说世界，

who came forth into the world, or a thousand *koṭīs* of buddhas who came forth into the world, or a hundred thousand *koṭīs* of buddhas who came forth into the world, or a numberless number, or a measureless number, or a boundless number, or an incomparable number, or an innumerable number, or an inexpressible number, or an inconceivable number, or an incalculable number, or an ineffable number, or an ineffable-ineffable number, or a number of buddhas, *bhagavats*, who came forth into the world exceeding the capacity of calculation or enumeration during which kalpas he is able to completely and clearly see all buddhas such as these, their sites of enlightenment, congregations, *śrāvaka* disciples, and bodhisattvas, as well as the Dharma that they taught, their training of beings, the relative length or brevity of the life spans of those beings, the length of their Dharma's duration, and all other matters such as these.

And just as this is the case for a single kalpa, so too is it also the case that he completely knows this of all kalpas even as he also completely knows of those kalpas that have no buddhas all the roots of goodness planted by all their beings in relation to *anuttarasamyaksaṃbodhi*. In cases where there are beings within them whose roots of goodness have already become ripened to the point that they are thereby bound to succeed in seeing a buddha at some point in the future, he also completely knows all of those matters as well. It is in this way that he contemplates an ineffable-ineffable number of kalpas of the past, doing so without his mind ever growing weary of this. This is the sixth of his types of oceanic wisdom;

The bodhisattva-mahāsattva enters the future, contemplates and distinguishes all of its countlessly and boundlessly many kalpas, and knows which of those kalpas will have a buddha, which of those kalpas will have no buddha, which kalpas will have how many *tathāgatas* who will come forth into the world, and knows of each and every one of those *tathāgatas* what their names will be, which worlds they will abide in, what the names of those worlds will be, how many beings they will liberate, and how long their life spans will be. He endlessly and tirelessly engages in contemplations such as these which exhaust the bounds of the future. Thus he completely knows it all. This is the seventh of his types of oceanic wisdom;

The bodhisattva-mahāsattva enters the present, contemplating and reflecting upon it in such a way that, in each successive mind-moment, he everywhere sees the boundlessly many classes of beings throughout the ten directions in an ineffable number

正體字

290b10	皆有諸佛於無上菩提。已成今成當成。往詣
290b11	道場。菩提樹下。坐吉祥草。降伏魔軍。成阿耨
290b12	多羅三藐三菩提。從此起已。入於城邑。昇天
290b13	宮殿。說微妙法。轉大法輪。示現神通。調伏眾
290b14	生。乃至付囑阿耨多羅三藐三菩提法。捨於
290b15	壽命。入般涅槃。入涅槃已。結集法藏。令久住
290b16	世。莊嚴佛塔。種種供養。亦見彼世界所有眾
290b17	生。值佛聞法。受持諷誦。憶念思惟。增長慧
290b18	解。如是觀察。普遍十方。而於佛法。無有錯
290b19	謬。何以故。菩薩摩訶薩。了知諸佛。皆悉如
290b20	夢。而能往詣一切佛所。恭敬供養。菩薩爾時。
290b21	不著自身。不著諸佛。不著世界。不著眾會。不
290b22	著說法。不著劫數。然見佛聞法。觀察世界。入
290b23	[2]諸劫數。無有厭足。是為第八如海智。菩薩
290b24	摩訶薩。於不可說不可說劫一一劫中。供養
290b25	恭敬不可說不可說無量諸佛。示現自身。歿
290b26	此生彼。以出過三界一切供具。而為供養。并
290b27	及供養菩薩聲聞。一切大眾。

简体字

皆有诸佛于无上菩提已成、今成、当成，往诣道场菩提树下，坐吉祥草，降伏魔军，成阿耨多罗三藐三菩提；从此起已，入于城邑，升天宫殿，说微妙法，转大法轮，示现神通，调伏众生，乃至付嘱阿耨多罗三藐三菩提法，舍于寿命，入般涅槃；入涅槃已，结集法藏令久住世，庄严佛塔种种供养。亦见彼世界所有众生，值佛闻法，受持讽诵，忆念思惟，增长慧解。如是观察普遍十方，而于佛法无有错谬。何以故？菩萨摩诃萨了知诸佛皆悉如梦，而能往诣一切佛所恭敬供养。菩萨尔时，不著自身、不著诸佛、不著世界、不著众会、不著说法、不著劫数，然见佛闻法，观察世界，入诸劫数，无有厌足，是为第八如海智。菩萨摩诃萨于不可说不可说劫一一劫中，供养恭敬不可说不可说无量诸佛，示现自身殁此生彼，以出过三界一切供具而为供养，并及供养菩萨、声闻、一切大众；

of worlds in all of which there are buddhas who have already realized, now realize, or shall realize the unexcelled bodhi, observing with regard to them all their going forth to their sites of enlightenment, their sitting on the auspicious grass seat beneath the bodhi tree, their conquering of the armies of Māra, their realization of *anuttarasamyaksaṃbodhi*, their entering the cities and villages after rising from where they sat, their ascendance to the celestial palaces, their proclamation of the sublime Dharma, their turning of the great wheel of the Dharma, their manifestation of spiritual superknowledges, their training of beings, and so forth on through to their passing on the dharma of *anuttarasamyaksaṃbodhi*, their relinquishing of this life span, their entry into *parinirvāṇa*, the gathering together of their Dharma treasury after they have entered nirvāṇa whereby it is enabled to remain in the world for a long time, the raising of adorned commemorative buddha stupas, and the offerings to them of the many different kinds of offerings.

They also see all the beings in those worlds encountering the Buddha, hearing the Dharma, accepting it, retaining it, reciting it, bearing it in mind, meditating on it, and thereby increasing their wise understanding of it. He extends meditations such as these to include all places everywhere throughout the ten directions and still never becomes mistaken in his understanding of the Dharma of the Buddha. And why is this? This is because the bodhisattva-mahāsattva completely understands all buddhas as like a dream and yet he is still able to travel to the abodes of all buddhas, revering them and making offerings to them. At this time, the bodhisattva is not attached to his own body, is not attached to the buddhas, is not attached to worlds, is not attached to those congregations, is not attached to the teaching of the Dharma, and is not attached to any of those types of kalpas. So it is that he sees the Buddha, hears the Dharma, contemplates the worlds, and enters all the different types of kalpas without ever growing weary of doing so. This is the eighth of his types of oceanic wisdom;

Throughout every kalpa among an ineffable-ineffable number of kalpas, the bodhisattva-mahāsattva makes offerings and pays reverence to an ineffable-ineffable number of measurelessly many buddhas as he manifests his own bodies there, dying in this place and then taking rebirth in that place, making offerings to them exceeding the sum total of all gifts throughout the three realms of existence even as he also makes offerings to bodhisattvas, to *śrāvaka* disciples, and to all beings. When each

正體字

一一如來。般涅槃後。皆以無上供具。供養舍利。及廣行惠施。滿足眾生。佛子。菩薩摩訶薩。以不可思議心。不求報心。究竟心。饒益心。於不可說不可說劫。為阿耨多羅三藐三菩提故。供養諸佛。饒益眾生。護持正法。開示演說。是為第九如海智。菩薩摩訶薩。於一切佛所。一切菩薩所。一切法師所。一向專求菩薩所說法。菩薩所學法。菩薩所教法。菩薩修行法。菩薩清淨法。菩薩成熟法。菩薩調伏法。菩薩平等法。菩薩出離法。菩薩總持法。得此法已。受持讀誦。分別解說。無有厭足。令無量眾生。於佛法中。發一切智相應心。入真實相。於阿耨多羅三藐三菩提。得不退轉。菩薩如是。於不可說不可說劫。無有厭足。是為第十如海智。佛子。是為菩薩摩訶薩。十種入阿耨多羅三藐三菩提如海智。若諸菩薩。安住此法。則得一切諸佛無上大智慧海。佛子。菩薩摩訶薩。於阿耨多羅三藐三菩提。有十種如寶住。何等為十。佛子。菩薩摩訶薩。悉能往詣無數世界。諸如來所。瞻觀頂禮。承事供養。是為第一如寶住。

简体字

一一如来般涅槃后，皆以无上供具供养舍利，及广行惠施满足众生。佛子，菩萨摩诃萨以不可思议心、不求报心、究竟心、饶益心，于不可说不可说劫，为阿耨多罗三藐三菩提故，供养诸佛，饶益众生，护持正法，开示演说，是为第九如海智。菩萨摩诃萨于一切佛所、一切菩萨所、一切法师所，一向专求菩萨所说法、菩萨所学法、菩萨所教法、菩萨修行法、菩萨清净法、菩萨成熟法、菩萨调伏法、菩萨平等法、菩萨出离法、菩萨总持法；得此法已，受持读诵，分别解说，无有厌足；令无量众生，于佛法中，发一切智相应心，入真实相，于阿耨多罗三藐三菩提得不退转。菩萨如是于不可说不可说劫无有厌足，是为第十如海智。佛子，是为菩萨摩诃萨十种入阿耨多罗三藐三菩提如海智。若诸菩萨安住此法，则得一切诸佛无上大智慧海。

"佛子，菩萨摩诃萨于阿耨多罗三藐三菩提，有十种如宝住。何等为十？佛子，菩萨摩诃萨悉能往诣无数世界诸如来所，瞻觐顶礼，承事供养，是为第一如宝住。

Chapter 38 — *Transcending the World* 2827

of those *tathāgatas* enters *parinirvāṇa*, he presents unexcelled gifts as offerings to their *śarīra* while also engaging in extensive kindly giving sufficient to satisfy those beings.

Sons of the Buddha, the bodhisattva-mahāsattva uses an inconceivable mind, a mind that does not seek any reward, an ultimate mind, and a beneficial mind to make offerings to all buddhas, to benefit beings, to protect and preserve right Dharma, and to explain it and expound upon it, doing so for an ineffable-ineffable number of kalpas for the sake of *anuttarasamyaksaṃbodhi*. This is the ninth of his types of oceanic wisdom; and

In the presence of all buddhas, all bodhisattvas, and all masters of the Dharma, the bodhisattva-mahāsattva continuously and single-mindedly seeks the Dharma proclaimed by the bodhisattva, the Dharma studied by the bodhisattva, the Dharma taught by the bodhisattva, the Dharma cultivated by the bodhisattva, the Dharma by which the bodhisattva becomes purified, the Dharma by which the bodhisattva becomes ripened, the Dharma in which the bodhisattva trains, the bodhisattva's dharmas of equanimity, the bodhisattva's dharmas of emancipation, and the bodhisattva's *dhāraṇī* dharmas for complete-retention [of the Dharma]. Having acquired dharmas such as these, he absorbs them, retains them, studies them, recites them, and analyzes and explains them, never tiring of this, thereby enabling countless beings to resolve to attain all-knowledge in reliance on Dharma of the Buddha, to penetrate the character of reality, and to become irreversible in progressing toward the realization of *anuttarasamyaksaṃbodhi*. The bodhisattva tirelessly continues on in this way for an ineffable-ineffable number of kalpas. This is the tenth of his types of oceanic wisdom.

Sons of the Buddha, these are the bodhisattva-mahāsattva's ten kinds of oceanic wisdom with which he enters *anuttarasamyaksaṃbodhi*. If bodhisattvas abide in these dharmas, then they acquire all buddhas' ocean of unexcelled great wisdom.

Sons of the Buddha, the bodhisattva-mahāsattva has ten kinds of jewel-like abiding with regard to [accomplishing the realization of][107] *anuttarasamyaksaṃbodhi*. What are those ten? They are as follows:

Sons of the Buddha, the bodhisattva-mahāsattva is able to go to visit all the countless worlds, paying his respects to the *tathāgatas*, gazing up at them in admiration, bowing down to them in reverence, serving them, and making offerings to them. This is the first of his types of jewel-like abiding;

正體字	於不思議諸如來所。聽聞正法。受持憶念。不令忘失。分別思惟。覺慧增長。如是所作。充滿十方。是為第二如寶住。於此刹歿。餘處現生。而於佛法。無所迷惑。是為第三如寶住。知從一法。出一切法。而能各各分別演說。以一切法種種義。究竟皆是一義故。是為第四如寶住。知厭離煩惱。知止息煩惱。知防護煩惱。知除斷煩惱。修菩薩行。不證實際。究竟到於實際彼岸。方便善巧。善學所學。令往昔願行。皆得成滿。身不疲倦。是為第五如寶住。知一切眾生。心所分別。皆無處所。而亦說有種種方處。雖無分別。無所造作。為欲調伏一切眾生。而有修行。而有所作。是為第六如寶住。知一切法。皆同一性。所謂無性。無種種性。無無量性。無可算數性。無可稱量性。無色無相。若一若多。皆不可得。而決定了知。此是諸佛法。此是菩薩法。此是獨覺法。此是聲聞法。
简体字	于不思议诸如来所，听闻正法，受持忆念，不令忘失，分别思惟，觉慧增长，如是所作充满十方，是为第二如宝住。于此刹殁，余处现生，而于佛法无所迷惑，是为第三如宝住。知从一法出一切法，而能各各分别演说，以一切法种种义究竟皆是一义故，是为第四如宝住。知厌离烦恼，知止息烦恼，知防护烦恼，知除断烦恼，修菩萨行不证实际，究竟到于实际彼岸，方便善巧，善学所学，令往昔愿行皆得成满，身不疲倦，是为第五如宝住。知一切众生心所分别皆无处所，而亦说有种种方处；虽无分别、无所造作，为欲调伏一切众生而有修行、而有所作，是为第六如宝住。知一切法皆同一性，所谓：无性，无种种性，无无量性，无可算数性，无可称量性，无色无相，若一若多皆不可得，而决定了知此是诸佛法、此是菩萨法、此是独觉法、此是声闻法、

He listens to right Dharma from an inconceivable number of *tathāgatas*, absorbs it, retains it, bears it in mind, does not allow it to be forgotten, analyzes it, reflects upon it, and thus increases his awakened wisdom. The activities of this sort that he engages in fill the ten directions. This the second of his types of jewel-like abiding;

When he dies in this *kṣetra* and then manifests rebirth in some other place, he still remains free of any delusion regarding the Buddha's Dharma. This is the third of his types of jewel-like abiding;

He realizes that all dharmas come forth from a single dharma and thus he is able to analyze and expound upon every one of them because all the many different meanings of all dharmas ultimately constitute but a single meaning. This is the fourth of his types of jewel-like abiding;

He knows the renunciation of the afflictions, knows the stopping and extinguishing of the afflictions, knows the guarding against the arising of afflictions, and knows the severance of the afflictions. In his cultivation of the bodhisattva practices, he refrains from realizing the apex of reality even as he achieves ultimate perfection in fathoming the apex of reality. With clever skillful means, he studies well what is to be studied and thus enables his past vows and conduct to all become completely fulfilled, doing so without ever becoming physically wearied by this. This is the fifth of his types of jewel-like abiding;

He knows that all things distinguished by the minds of all beings have no place where they abide even as he still speaks of the existence of many different kinds of places. Although he is free of discriminations and has nothing that he creates, because he wishes to train all beings, he still has that which he cultivates and that which he accomplishes. This is the sixth of his types of jewel-like abiding;

He realizes that all dharmas have the same single nature, namely the absence of any nature at all. They are devoid of any of the many different kinds of natures, are devoid of any measureless nature, are devoid of any calculable nature, are devoid of any measurable nature, and are formless and signless. Whether one or many, they are all inapprehensible. And yet he still definitely and completely knows:

"This one is a dharma of all buddhas."

"This one is a dharma of the bodhisattva."

"This one is a dharma of the *pratyekabuddha*."

"This one is a dharma of the *śrāvaka* disciple."

正體字

此是凡夫法。此是善法。此是不善法。此是世間法。此是出世間法。此是過失法。此是無過失法。此是有漏法。此是無漏法。乃至此是有為法。此是無為法。是為第七如寶住。菩薩摩訶薩。求佛不可得。求菩薩不可得。求法不可得。求眾生不可得。而亦不捨調伏眾生。令於諸法。成正覺願。何以故。菩薩摩訶薩。善巧觀察。知一切眾生分別。知一切眾生境界。方便化導。令得涅槃。為欲滿足化眾生願。熾然修行菩薩行故。是為第八如寶住。菩薩摩訶薩。知善巧說法。示現涅槃。為度眾生。所有方便。一切皆是心想建立。非是顛倒。亦非虛誑。何以故。菩薩了知一切諸法三世平等。如如不動。實際無住。不見有一眾生。已受化今受化當受化。亦自了知。無所修行。無有少法。若生若滅。而可得者。而依於一切法。

简体字

此是凡夫法、此是善法、此是不善法、此是世间法、此是出世间法、此是过失法、此是无过失法、此是有漏法、此是无漏法，乃至此是有为法、此是无为法，是为第七如宝住。菩萨摩诃萨求佛不可得、求菩萨不可得、求法不可得、求众生不可得，而亦不舍调伏众生令于诸法成正觉愿。何以故？菩萨摩诃萨善巧观察，知一切众生分别，知一切众生境界，方便化导令得涅槃；为欲满足化众生愿，炽然修行菩萨行故。是为第八如宝住。菩萨摩诃萨知善巧说法、示现涅槃，为度众生所有方便，一切皆是心想建立，非是颠倒，亦非虚诳。何以故？菩萨了知一切诸法三世平等、如如不动、实际无住，不见有一众生已受化、今受化、当受化，亦自了知无所修行，无有少法若生若灭而可得者，而依于一切法，

Chapter 38 — *Transcending the World*

"This one is a dharma of the common person."

"This one is a good dharma whereas this other one is a bad dharma."

"This one is a worldly dharma whereas this other one is a world-transcending dharma."

"This one is a faulty dharma whereas this other one is a dharma free of faults."

"This is a contaminated dharma whereas this other one is a dharma free of all contaminants," and so forth, up to and including:

"This one is a conditioned dharma, whereas this other one is an unconditioned dharma."

This is the seventh of his types of jewel-like abiding;

In seeking to find any buddha, the bodhisattva-mahāsattva finds that no such thing can be found at all. In seeking to find any bodhisattva, he finds that no such thing can be found at all. In seeking to find any dharma, he finds that no such thing can be found at all. And in seeking to find any being, he finds that no such thing can be found at all. Even so, he never relinquishes his vow to train beings and enable them to attain right enlightenment with respect to all dharmas. And why is this? This is because the bodhisattva-mahāsattva skillfully contemplates and thereby knows the discriminations of all beings, knows all beings' spheres of cognition, and then uses skillful means to teach and guide them and enable them to reach *nirvāṇa*, doing so in order to completely fulfill his vow to teach beings and engage in brilliantly blazing cultivation of the bodhisattva practices. This is the eighth of his types of jewel-like abiding.

The bodhisattva-mahāsattva knows that using skillful means to teach the Dharma, manifesting entry into nirvāṇa, and all the skillful means used to liberate beings are all established on the basis of the mind and perceptions. They are not a function of inverted views and are not either false or deceptive. And how is this so? The bodhisattva fully realizes that all dharmas are the same throughout the three periods of time, are true suchness, are unmoving, are the apex of reality, and are non-abiding. He does not perceive the existence of even a single being who has ever undergone teaching, is now undergoing teaching, or ever will undergo teaching. He also fully realizes for himself that there is nothing that is cultivated, that there is not even the slightest dharma that is ever produced, that is ever destroyed, or that is at all apprehensible. Even so, relying on all dharmas,

正體字

令所願不空。是為第九如
寶住。菩薩摩訶薩。於不思議無量諸佛。一一
佛所。聞不可說不可說授記法名號各異。劫
數不同。從於一劫。乃至不可說不可說劫。常
如是聞。聞已修行。不驚不怖。不迷不惑。知如
來智不思議故。如來授記。言無二故。自身行
願。殊勝力故。隨應受化。令成阿耨多羅三藐
三菩提。滿等法界一切願故。是為第十如寶
住。佛子。是為菩薩摩訶薩。於阿耨多羅三藐
三菩提。十種如寶住。若諸菩薩。安住此法。則
得諸佛無上大智慧寶。佛子。菩薩摩訶薩。發
十種如金剛大乘誓願心。何等為十。佛子。菩
薩摩訶薩。作如是念。一切諸法。無有邊際。不
可窮盡。我當以盡三世智。普皆覺了。無有遺
餘。是為第一如金剛大乘誓願心。菩薩摩訶
薩。又作是念。於一毛端處。有無量無邊眾生。
何況一切法界。我當皆以無上涅槃。而滅度
之。是為第二如金剛大乘誓願心。菩薩摩訶
薩。又作是念。十方世界無量無邊。無有齊限。
不可窮盡

简体字

令所愿不空。是为第九如宝住。菩萨摩诃萨于不思议无量诸佛一一佛所，闻不可说不可说授记法，名号各异，劫数不同；从于一劫乃至不可说不可说劫常如是闻，闻已修行，不惊不怖，不迷不惑，知如来智不思议故，如来授记言无二故，自身行愿殊胜力故，随应受化令成阿耨多罗三藐三菩提满等法界一切愿故，是为第十如宝住。佛子，是为菩萨摩诃萨于阿耨多罗三藐三菩提十种如宝住。若诸菩萨安住此法，则得诸佛无上大智慧宝。

"佛子，菩萨摩诃萨发十种如金刚大乘誓愿心。何等为十？佛子，菩萨摩诃萨作如是念：'一切诸法，无有边际，不可穷尽。我当以尽三世智，普皆觉了，无有遗余。'是为第一如金刚大乘誓愿心。菩萨摩诃萨又作是念：'于一毛端处有无量无边众生，何况一切法界！我当皆以无上涅槃而灭度之。'是为第二如金刚大乘誓愿心。菩萨摩诃萨又作是念：'十方世界，无量无边，无有齐限，不可穷尽。

he enables whatever he has vowed to not have been in vain. This is the ninth of his types of jewel-like abiding.

In the abodes of every one of the buddhas among an inconceivable and measureless number of buddhas, the bodhisattva-mahāsattva hears an ineffable-ineffable number of instances of the dharma of bestowing predictions [of future buddhahood] in which the names [of the future buddhas] are each different and the number of kalpas [before attaining buddhahood] are not the same, varying from but a single kalpa all the way up to an ineffable-ineffable number of kalpas. He always hears them in this way and then, having heard them, he cultivates accordingly, is not frightened, is not fearful, is not confused, and is not deluded because he realizes that the wisdom of the Tathāgata is inconceivable, because he knows the words of the Tathāgata's bestowals of predictions are unequivocal, because of the especially superior power of his own practice and vows, and because, in accordance with those who should receive teaching, he enables their realization of *anuttarasamyaksaṃbodhi* and fulfills all his vows equal in their expansiveness to the Dharma realm. This is the tenth of his types of jewel-like abiding.

Sons of the Buddha, these are the bodhisattva-mahāsattva's ten kinds of jewel-like abiding in accomplishing the realization of *anuttarasamyaksaṃbodhi*. If bodhisattvas abide in these dharmas, then they acquire the jewel of all buddhas' unexcelled great wisdom.

Sons of the Buddha, the bodhisattva-mahāsattva arouses ten kinds of vajra-like Great Vehicle resolve. What are these ten? Sons of the Buddha:

The bodhisattva-mahāsattva has this thought: "All dharmas are so boundless as to be inexhaustible. I should use wisdom capable of exhaustively knowing the three periods of time to become completely awakened to all of them without exception." This is the first of his types of vajra-like Great Vehicle resolve;

The bodhisattva-mahāsattva also has this thought: "Even on the tip of but a single hair, there are incalculably and boundlessly many beings. How much the more is this so of the entire Dharma realm. I should enable them all to reach the liberation of cessation by resort to the unexcelled nirvāṇa." This is the second of his types of vajra-like Great Vehicle resolve;

The bodhisattva-mahāsattva also has this thought: "The worlds of the ten directions are so measureless, boundless, and unlimited as to be endless. I should use the most supreme adornments in

| 正體字 | 。我當以諸佛國土最上莊嚴。莊嚴
291b13 如是一切世界。所有莊嚴。皆悉真實。是為第
291b14 三如金剛大乘誓願心。菩薩摩訶薩。又作是
291b15 念。一切眾生。無量無邊。無有齊限。不可窮
291b16 盡。我當以一切善根。迴向於彼無上智光。照
291b17 [1]曜於彼。是為第四如金剛大乘誓願心。菩薩
291b18 摩訶薩。又作是念。一切諸佛無量無邊。無有
291b19 齊限。不可窮盡。我當以所種善根。迴向供養。
291b20 悉令周遍。無所闕少。然後我當成阿耨多羅
291b21 三藐三菩提。是為第五如金剛大乘誓願心。
291b22 佛子。菩薩摩訶薩。見一切佛。聞所說法。生大
291b23 歡喜。不著自身。不著佛身。解如來身。非實非
291b24 虛。非有非無。非性非無性。非色非無色。非相
291b25 非無相。非生非滅。實無所有。亦不壞有。何以
291b26 故。不可以一切性相。而取著故。是為第六如
291b27 金剛大乘誓願心。佛子。菩薩摩訶薩。或[2]有
291b28 眾生。訶罵毀呰。搥打楚撻。或截手足。或割耳
291b29 鼻。或挑其目。或級其頭。如是一切皆能忍受。
291c01 終不因此生患害心。於不可說不可說無央
291c02 數劫。修菩薩行。攝受眾生。恒無廢捨。何以
291c03 故。菩薩摩訶薩。已善觀察一切諸法。無有二
291c04 相。心不動亂。能捨自身。忍其苦故。是為第七
291c05 如金剛大乘誓願心。佛子。菩薩摩訶薩。又作
291c06 是念。未來世劫 |

| 简体字 | 我当以诸佛国土最上庄严,庄严如是一切世界,所有庄严皆悉真实。'是为第三如金刚大乘誓愿心。菩萨摩诃萨又作是念:'一切众生,无量无边,无有齐限,不可穷尽。我当以一切善根,回向于彼无上智光,照耀于彼。'是为第四如金刚大乘誓愿心。菩萨摩诃萨又作是念:'一切诸佛,无量无边,无有齐限,不可穷尽。我当以所种善根回向供养,悉令周遍,无所缺少,然后我当成阿耨多罗三藐三菩提。'是为第五如金刚大乘誓愿心。佛子,菩萨摩诃萨见一切佛,闻所说法生大欢喜,不著自身,不著佛身,解如来身非实非虚、非有非无、非性非无性、非色非无色、非相非无相、非生非灭,实无所有,亦不坏有。何以故?不可以一切性相而取著故。是为第六如金刚大乘誓愿心。佛子,菩萨摩诃萨,或被众生诃骂毁呰、挞打楚挞,或截手足,或割耳鼻,或挑其目,或级其头;如是一切皆能忍受,终不因此生患害心。于不可说不可说无央数劫修菩萨行,摄受众生恒无废舍。何以故?菩萨摩诃萨已善观察一切诸法无有二相,心不动乱,能舍自身忍其苦故。是为第七如金刚大乘誓愿心。佛子,菩萨摩诃萨又作是念:'未来世劫, |

Chapter 38 — Transcending the World

the lands of all buddhas to adorn all worlds such as these so that all their adornments are genuine. This is the third of his types of vajra-like Great Vehicle resolve;

The bodhisattva-mahāsattva also has this thought: "All beings are so measureless, boundless, and unlimited as to be endless. I should dedicate all roots of goodness to them and use the light of unexcelled wisdom to illuminate them with brilliant light." This is the fourth of his types of vajra-like Great Vehicle resolve;

The bodhisattva-mahāsattva also has this thought: "All buddhas are so measureless, boundless, and unlimited as to be endless. I should dedicate all the roots of goodness I have planted to making offerings to them so that [those offerings] are present everywhere and there is no shortage of anything. Afterward, I should accomplish the realization of *anuttarasamyaksaṃbodhi*." This is the fifth of his types of vajra-like Great Vehicle resolve;

Sons of the Buddha, when the bodhisattva-mahāsattva sees all buddhas and hears the Dharma that they proclaim, he is filled with great joy. He is not attached to his own body, is not attached to the Buddha's body, and understands the Tathāgata's body is neither real nor false, is neither existent nor nonexistent, is neither possessed of any nature nor devoid of a nature, is neither possessed of form nor formless, is neither possessed of signs nor signless, is neither produced nor destroyed, and, in truth, is devoid of anything that exists even as this does not undermine its existence. And why is this? This is because he cannot take any nature or sign as the basis for forming attachments. This the sixth of his types of vajra-like Great Vehicle resolve;

Sons of the Buddha, if the bodhisattva-mahāsattva encounters any being who scolds or disparages him, who beats or flogs him, who cuts off his hands and feet, who cuts off his ears and nose, who plucks out his eyes, or who even decapitates him, he is able to patiently endure all of this and never reacts to this by becoming angry or wanting to harm his attacker. Throughout an ineffable-ineffable and endless number of kalpas, he cultivates the bodhisattva practices, attracts beings [into the Dharma], and never abandons them. And why is this? This is because, having already skillfully contemplated all dharmas and realized they are devoid of any such dual opposition, his mind is never shaken or thrown into confusion. Hence he is able to relinquish even his own body and endure its sufferings. This is the seventh of his types of vajra-like Great Vehicle resolve;

Sons of the Buddha, the bodhisattva-mahāsattva also has this thought: "The kalpas of the future are so measureless,

正體字

無量無邊。無有齊限。不可窮
盡。我當盡彼劫。於一世界。行菩薩道。教化眾
生。如一世界。盡法界虛空界一切世界。悉亦
如是。而心不驚。不怖不畏。何以故。為菩薩道。
法應如是。為一切眾生。而修行故。是為第八
如金剛大乘誓願心。佛子。菩薩摩訶薩。又作
是念。阿耨多羅三藐三菩提。以心為本。心若
清淨。則能圓滿一切善根。於佛菩提。必得自
在。欲成阿耨多羅三藐三菩提。隨意即成。若
欲除斷一切取緣。住一向道。我亦能得。而我
不斷。為欲究竟佛菩提故。亦不即證無上菩
提。何以故。為滿本願盡一切世界。行菩薩行。
化眾生故。是為第九如金剛大乘誓願心。佛
子。菩薩摩訶薩。知佛不可得。菩提不可得。菩
薩不可得。一切法不可得。眾生不可得。心不
可得。行不可得。過去不可得。未來不可得。現
在不可得。一切世間不可得。有為無為不可
得。菩薩如是。寂靜住。甚深住。寂滅住。無諍
住。無言住。無二住。無等住。自性住。如理住。
解脫住。涅槃住。實際住。而亦不捨一切大願。
不捨薩婆若心。

简体字

无量无边，无有齐限，不可穷尽。我当尽彼劫，于一世界，行菩萨道教化众生；如一世界，尽法界、虚空界、一切世界悉亦如是，而心不惊、不怖、不畏。何以故？为菩萨道法应如是，为一切众生而修行故。'是为第八如金刚大乘誓愿心。佛子，菩萨摩诃萨又作是念：'阿耨多罗三藐三菩提以心为本，心若清净，则能圆满一切善根，于佛菩提必得自在，欲成阿耨多罗三藐三菩提随意即成。若欲除断一切取缘，住一向道，我亦能得，而我不断，为欲究竟佛菩提故，亦不即证无上菩提。何以故？为满本愿，尽一切世界行菩萨行化众生故。'是为第九如金刚大乘誓愿心。佛子，菩萨摩诃萨知佛不可得、菩提不可得、菩萨不可得、一切法不可得、众生不可得、心不可得、行不可得、过去不可得、未来不可得、现在不可得、一切世间不可得、有为无为不可得。菩萨如是寂静住、甚深住、寂灭住、无诤住、无言住、无二住、无等住、自性住、如理住、解脱住、涅槃住、实际住，而亦不舍一切大愿，不舍萨婆若心，

Chapter 38 — *Transcending the World* 2837

boundless, and unlimited as to be endless. I should exhaust all of those kalpas in practicing the bodhisattva path and teaching all the beings in one of those worlds and, just as I should do this in this one world, so too should I also do so in all worlds throughout the entire Dharma realm and the realms of empty space." In so doing, his mind is not terrified, frightened, or fearful. And why is this? In practicing for the sake of the bodhisattva path, this is the way the Dharma should be, for it is to benefit all beings that one cultivates in this way. This is the eighth of his types of vajra-like Great Vehicle resolve;

Sons of the Buddha, the bodhisattva-mahāsattva also has this thought: "It is the mind itself that constitutes the very root of *anuttarasamyaksaṃbodhi*. If one's mind is pure, then one is able to completely develop all roots of goodness. Then one is certainly bound to attain such sovereign mastery with respect to the Buddha's bodhi that one only needs to wish to realize *anuttarasamyaksaṃbodhi*, whereupon, whenever one decides to do so, one will immediately gain that very realization. If I but wished to cut off all grasping at conditions and abide in the direct path, then I too could succeed in doing so. However, I do not cut it all off because I wish to reach all the way to the complete realization of the bodhi of the Buddha. Thus I do not elect to immediately realize the unexcelled bodhi. Why is this? This is to fulfill my original vow to practice the bodhisattva practices throughout all worlds in order to teach the beings within them." This is the ninth of his types of vajra-like Great Vehicle resolve;

Sons of the Buddha, the bodhisattva-mahāsattva realizes that the buddha is inapprehensible,[108] that bodhi is inapprehensible, that bodhisattvas are inapprehensible, that all dharmas are inapprehensible, that beings are inapprehensible, that the mind is inapprehensible, that the practices are inapprehensible, that the past is inapprehensible, that the future is inapprehensible, that the present is inapprehensible, that the entire world is inapprehensible, and that both the conditioned and the unconditioned are inapprehensible. In this way, the bodhisattva abides in stillness, abides in the extremely profound, abides in quiescence, abides in noncontentiousness, abides in wordlessness, abides in non-duality, abides in peerlessness, abides in the essential nature, abides in accordance with principle, abides in liberation, abides in nirvāṇa, and abides in the apex of reality, and yet he still never relinquishes any of his great vows, never relinquishes the resolve to attain all-knowledge, never

正體字

不捨菩薩行。不捨教化眾生。不捨諸波羅蜜。不捨調伏眾生。不捨承事諸佛。不捨演說諸法。不捨莊嚴世界。何以故。菩薩摩訶薩。發大願故。雖復了達一切法相。大慈悲心。轉更增長。無量功德。皆具修行。於諸眾生。心不捨離。何以故。一切諸法。皆無所有。凡夫愚迷。不知不覺。我當令彼悉得開悟。於諸法性。分明照了。何以故。一切諸佛。安住寂滅。而以大悲心。於諸世間。說法教化。曾無休息。我今云何。而捨大悲。又我先發廣大誓願心。發決定利益一切眾生心。發積集一切善根心。發安住善巧迴向心。發出生甚深智慧心。發含受一切眾生心。發於一切眾生平等心。作真實語。不虛誑語。願與一切眾生。無上大法。願不斷一切諸佛種性。[1]令一切眾生。未得解脫。未成正覺。未具佛法。大願未滿。云何而欲捨離大悲。是為第十如金剛大乘誓願心。佛子。是為菩薩摩訶薩發十種如金剛大乘誓願心。若諸菩薩。安住此法。則得如來金剛性無上大神通智。佛子。菩薩摩訶薩。有十種大發起。何等為十。佛子。菩薩摩訶薩。作如是念。我當供養恭敬一切諸佛。是為第一大發起。

简体字

不舍菩萨行，不舍教化众生，不舍诸波罗蜜，不舍调伏众生，不舍承事诸佛，不舍演说诸法，不舍庄严世界。何以故？菩萨摩诃萨发大愿故，虽复了达一切法相，大慈悲心转更增长，无量功德皆具修行，于诸众生心不舍离。何以故？'一切诸法皆无所有，凡夫愚迷不知不觉，我当令彼悉得开悟，于诸法性分明照了。'何以故？'一切诸佛安住寂灭，而以大悲心，于诸世间说法教化曾无休息。我今云何而舍大悲？又我先发广大誓愿心，发决定利益一切众生心，发积集一切善根心，发安住善巧回向心，发出生甚深智慧心，发含受一切众生心，发于一切众生平等心；作真实语、不虚诳语，愿与一切众生无上大法，愿不断一切诸佛种性。今一切众生未得解脱、未成正觉、未具佛法，大愿未满，云何而欲舍离大悲？'是为第十如金刚大乘誓愿心。佛子，是为菩萨摩诃萨发十种如金刚大乘誓愿心。若诸菩萨安住此法，则得如来金刚性无上大神通智

"佛子，菩萨摩诃萨有十种大发起。何等为十？佛子，菩萨摩诃萨作如是念：'我当供养恭敬一切诸佛。'是为第一大发起。

Chapter 38 — *Transcending the World*

relinquishes the bodhisattva practices, never relinquishes the teaching of beings, never relinquishes any of the *pāramitās*, never relinquishes the training of beings, never relinquishes his serving of all buddhas, never relinquishes his expounding on all dharmas, and never relinquishes his adornment of worlds. And why is this so? This is because the bodhisattva-mahāsattva has made the great vow.

Although he completely comprehends the signs of all dharmas, his mind of great kindness and compassion grows ever stronger and he perfects the cultivation of all the countless meritorious qualities to the point that his mind is unwilling to ever abandon any being. And why is this? Although all dharmas are nonexistent, common people, being deluded and confused, do not know this and remain unaware of this. [Hence he thinks], "I should enable them all to awaken to the nature of all dharmas so that it becomes clearly and completely illuminated for them. Why? All buddhas abide in quiescence, and yet, relying on the mind of great compassion, they still proclaim the Dharma and teach it in all worlds, never desisting from this. How then could I now relinquish the great compassion?

Moreover, in the past, I produced the resolve of the vast vow by which I resolved to definitely benefit all beings, resolved to accumulate all roots of goodness, resolved to abide in skillful dedications [of merit], resolved to develop extremely deep wisdom, resolved to include all beings, and resolved to remain impartial toward all beings. I am one who speaks what is true and does not speak what is false or deceptive. I vowed to bestow the unexcelled great Dharma on all beings. I vowed to ensure that the lineage of all buddhas is never cut off. Now, it is still the case that all beings have not yet gained liberation, have not yet attained right enlightenment, and do not yet possess the Dharma of the Buddha. With my great vows not yet fulfilled, how could I wish to abandon the great compassion? This is the tenth of his types of vajra-like Great Vehicle resolve.

Sons of the Buddha, these are the ten kinds of vajra-like Great Vehicle resolve produced by the bodhisattva-mahāsattva. If bodhisattvas abide in these dharmas, then they acquire the Tathāgata's vajra-natured unexcelled great spiritual superknowledges and wisdom.

Sons of the Buddha, the bodhisattva-mahāsattva has ten kinds of great undertakings. What are those ten? They are as follows:

The bodhisattva-mahāsattva thinks: "I should make offerings to and revere all buddhas." This is the first of his great undertakings;

正體字

又作是念。我當長養一切菩薩所有善根。是為第二大發起。又作是念。我當於一切如來般涅槃後。莊嚴佛塔。以一切華。一切鬘。一切香。一切塗香。一切末香。一切衣一切蓋。一切幢一切幡。而供養之。受持守護彼佛正法。是為第三大發起。又作是念。我當教化調伏一切眾生。令得阿耨多羅三藐三菩提。是為第四大發起。又作是念。我當以諸佛國土無上莊嚴。而以莊嚴一切世界。是為第五大發起。又作是念。我當發大悲心。為一眾生。於一切世界。一一各盡未來際劫。行菩薩行。如為一眾生。為一切眾生。悉亦如是。皆令得佛無上菩提。乃至不生一念疲懈。是為第六大發起。又作是念。彼諸如來。無量無邊。我當於一如來所。經不思議劫。恭敬供養。如於一如來。於一切如來。悉亦如是。是為第七大發起。菩薩摩訶薩。又作是念。彼諸如來。滅度之後。我當為一一如來。所有舍利。各起寶塔。其量高廣。與不可說。諸世界等。造佛形像。亦復如是。於不可思議劫。以一切寶幢幡蓋。香華衣服。而為供養。不生一念。厭倦之心。為成就佛法故。為供養諸佛故。為教化眾生故。

简体字

又作是念：'我当长养一切菩萨所有善根。'是为第二大发起。又作是念：'我当于一切如来般涅槃后，庄严佛塔，以一切华、一切鬘、一切香、一切涂香、一切末香、一切衣、一切盖、一切幢、一切幡而供养之，受持守护彼佛正法。'是为第三大发起。又作是念：'我当教化调伏一切众生，令得阿耨多罗三藐三菩提。'是为第四大发起。又作是念：'我当以诸佛国土无上庄严，而以庄严一切世界。'是为第五大发起。又作是念：'我当发大悲心，为一众生，于一切世界，一一各尽未来际劫行菩萨行；如为一众生，为一切众生悉亦如是，皆令得佛无上菩提，乃至不生一念疲懈。'是为第六大发起。又作是念：'彼诸如来无量无边，我当于一如来所，经不思议劫恭敬供养；如于一如来，于一切如来悉亦如是。'是为第七大发起。菩萨摩诃萨又作是念：'彼诸如来灭度之后，我当为一一如来所有舍利各起宝塔，其量高广与不可说诸世界等；造佛形像亦复如是，于不可思议劫以一切宝幢、幡盖、香华、衣服而为供养，不生一念厌倦之心。为成就佛法故，为供养诸佛故，为教化众生故，

Chapter 38 — Transcending the World

He also thinks: "I should foster the growth of all bodhisattvas' roots of goodness." This is the second of his great undertakings;

He also thinks: "After the *parinirvāṇa* of all *tathāgatas*, I should adorn buddha stupas for them and make offerings to them of all kinds of flowers, all kinds of garlands, all kinds of incenses, all kinds of perfumes, all kinds of powdered incenses, all kinds of robes, all kinds of canopies, all kinds of banners, and all kinds of pennants while also absorbing, retaining, preserving, and protecting the right Dharma of those buddhas." This is the third of his great undertakings;

He also thinks: "I should teach and train all beings and enable them to attain *anuttarasamyaksaṃbodhi*." This is the fourth of his great undertakings;

He also thinks: "I should adorn all worlds with the unexcelled adornments of all buddha lands." This is the fifth of his great undertakings;

He also thinks: "Bringing forth the mind of great compassion, for the sake of a single being, I should practice the bodhisattva practices in all worlds, doing so in each and every one of them to the end of all future kalpas. And just as I should do this for a single being, so too should I also do so for all beings so that I can thereby enable them all to succeed in acquiring the Buddha's unexcelled bodhi while never in all this time ever generating even a single thought of weariness." This is the sixth of his great undertakings;

He also thinks: "All those *tathāgatas* are countlessly and boundlessly many. In the presence of one of those *tathāgatas*, I should revere him and make offerings to him for an inconceivably great number of kalpas. And just as I do so for that one *tathāgata*, so also should I do so for all *tathāgatas* in this very same manner." This is the seventh of his great undertakings;

The bodhisattva-mahāsattva also thinks: "After those *tathāgatas* pass into nirvāṇa, for the *śarīra* of every one of those *tathāgatas*, I should raise bejeweled stupas of such lofty and vast dimensions that they are equal in scale to an ineffable number of worlds. I should also create images of those buddhas in just this same way, making offerings to them of all kinds of bejeweled banners, pennants, canopies, incense, flowers, and robes, doing so for an inconceivably great number of kalpas during which I never have even a single mind-moment's thought of weariness in this, doing so to enable the complete success of the Buddha's Dharma, doing so to make offerings to all buddhas, doing so to teach beings, and doing so to protect and preserve

正體字

為護持正法。開示演說故。是為第八大發起。菩薩摩訶薩。又作是念。我當以此善根。成無上菩提。得入一切諸如來地。與一切如來體性平等。是為第九大發起。菩薩摩訶薩。復作是念。我當成正覺已。於一切世界不可說劫。演說正法示現不可思議自在神通。身語及意。不生疲倦。不離正法。以佛力所持故。為一切眾生。勤行大願故。大慈為首故。大悲究竟故。達無相法故。住真實語故。證一切法皆寂滅故。知一切眾生。悉不可得。而亦不違諸業所作故。與三世佛。同一體故。周遍法界。虛空界故。通達諸法無相故。成就不生不滅故。具足一切佛法故。以大願力。調伏眾生。作大佛事。無有休息。是為第十大發起。佛子。是為菩薩摩訶薩十種大發起。若諸菩薩。安住此法。則不斷菩薩行。具足如來無上大智。佛子。菩薩摩訶薩。有十種究竟大事。何等為十。所謂恭敬供養一切如來究竟大事。隨所念眾生。悉能救護究竟大事。專求一切佛法究竟大事。

简体字

为护持正法开示演说故。'是为第八大发起。菩萨摩诃萨又作是念：'我当以此善根成无上菩提，得入一切诸如来地，与一切如来体性平等。'是为第九大发起。菩萨摩诃萨复作是念：'我当成正觉已，于一切世界不可说劫，演说正法，示现不可思议自在神通，身、语及意不生疲倦，不离正法。以佛力所持故，为一切众生勤行大愿故，大慈为首故，大悲究竟故，达无相法故，住真实语故，证一切法皆寂灭故；知一切众生悉不可得而亦不违诸业所作故，与三世佛同一体故，周遍法界、虚空界故，通达诸法无相故，成就不生不灭故，具足一切佛法故，以大愿力调伏众生，作大佛事无有休息。'是为第十大发起。佛子，是为菩萨摩诃萨十种大发起。若诸菩萨安住此法，则不断菩萨行，具足如来无上大智。

"佛子，菩萨摩诃萨有十种究竟大事。何等为十？所谓：恭敬供养一切如来究竟大事；随所念众生悉能救护究竟大事；专求一切佛法究竟大事；

right Dharma by revealing it and expounding on it." This is the eighth of his great undertakings;

The bodhisattva-mahāsattva also thinks: "I should use these roots of goodness to gain unexcelled bodhi, to succeed in entering the ground of all *tathāgatas*, and to become of the same essential nature as all *tathāgatas*." This is the ninth of his great undertakings; and

The bodhisattva-mahāsattva also thinks: "After gaining right enlightenment, I should expound on right Dharma in all worlds for an ineffable number of kalpas, manifesting inconceivable sovereign mastery of the spiritual superknowledges, never becoming weary of this in body, speech, or mind, and never separating from right Dharma due to being sustained by the Buddha's powers, due to diligently implementing the great vows for the sake of all beings, due to taking the great kindness as foremost, due to taking the great compassion as what is most ultimate, due to comprehending the dharma of signlessness, due to abiding in truthful speech, due to gaining the realization that all dharmas are quiescent, due to realizing all beings are inapprehensible while still realizing this does not contradict the effects of karmic deeds, due to being of the same single essential nature as all buddhas of the three periods of time, due to pervading the Dharma realm and the realms of empty space, due to gaining a penetrating comprehension of the signlessness of all dharmas, due to completely realizing they are neither produced nor destroyed, due to completely fulfilling all dharmas of the Buddha, and due to relying on the power of great vows in incessantly training beings and accomplishing great buddha works." This is the tenth of his great undertakings.

Sons of the Buddha, these are the bodhisattva-mahāsattva's ten kinds of great undertakings. If bodhisattvas abide in these dharmas, then they incessantly continue in the bodhisattva practices and completely fulfill the Tathāgata's unexcelled great wisdom.

Sons of the Buddha, the bodhisattva-mahāsattva has ten kinds of ultimate and great endeavors. What are those ten? They are as follows:

The ultimate and great endeavor of revering and making offerings to all *tathāgatas*;

The ultimate and great endeavor of being able to rescue and protect whichever beings he brings to mind;

The ultimate and great endeavor of single-mindedly seeking all dharmas of the Buddha;

正體字

積集一
292c02 ‖ 切善根究竟大事。思惟一切佛法究竟大事。
292c03 ‖ 滿足一切誓願究竟大事。成就一切菩薩行
292c04 ‖ 究竟大事。奉事一切善知識究竟大事。往詣
292c05 ‖ 一切世界。諸如來所究竟大事。聞持一切諸
292c06 ‖ 佛正法究竟大事。是為十。若諸菩薩。安住此
292c07 ‖ 法。則得阿耨多羅三藐三菩提大智慧究竟
292c08 ‖ 事。佛子。菩薩摩訶薩。有十種不壞信。何等為
292c09 ‖ 十。所謂於一切佛不壞信。於一切佛法不壞
292c10 ‖ 信。於一切聖僧不壞信。於一切菩薩不壞信。
292c11 ‖ 於一切善知識不壞信。於一切眾生不壞信。
292c12 ‖ 於一切菩薩大願不壞信。於一切菩薩行不壞
292c13 ‖ 信。於恭敬供養一切諸佛不壞信。於菩薩巧密
292c14 ‖ 方便。教化調伏一切眾生不壞信。是為十。若
292c15 ‖ 諸菩薩。安住此法。則得諸佛無上大智慧不
292c16 ‖ 壞信。佛子。菩薩摩訶薩。有十種得授記。何等
292c17 ‖ 為十。所謂內有甚深解得授記。能[2]隨順起菩
292c18 ‖ 薩諸善根得授記。修廣大行得授記。

简体字

积集一切善根究竟大事；思惟一切佛法究竟大事；满足一切誓愿究竟大事；成就一切菩萨行究竟大事；奉事一切善知识究竟大事；往诣一切世界诸如来所究竟大事；闻持一切诸佛正法究竟大事。是为十。若诸菩萨安住此法，则得阿耨多罗三藐三菩提大智慧究竟事。

"佛子，菩萨摩诃萨有十种不坏信。何等为十？所谓：于一切佛不坏信；于一切佛法不坏信；于一切圣僧不坏信；于一切菩萨不坏信；于一切善知识不坏信；于一切众生不坏信；于一切菩萨大愿不坏信；于一切菩萨行不坏信；于恭敬供养一切诸佛不坏信；于菩萨巧密方便教化调伏一切众生不坏信。是为十。若诸菩萨安住此法，则得诸佛无上大智慧不坏信。

"佛子，菩萨摩诃萨有十种得授记。何等为十？所谓：内有甚深解得授记；能随顺起菩萨诸善根得授记；修广大行得授记；

Chapter 38 — *Transcending the World*

The ultimate and great endeavor of accumulating all roots of goodness;

The ultimate and great endeavor of the meditative contemplation of all dharmas of the Buddha;

The ultimate and great endeavor of completely fulfilling all vows;

The ultimate and great endeavor of accomplishing all the bodhisattva practices;

The ultimate and great endeavor of serving all good spiritual guides;

The ultimate and great endeavor of traveling to all worlds to pay respects to all *tathāgatas*; and

The ultimate and great endeavor of listening to and retaining the right Dharma of all buddhas.

These are the ten. If all bodhisattvas abide in these dharmas, then they accomplish the ultimate and great endeavor of acquiring the great wisdom of *anuttarasamyaksaṃbodhi*.

Sons of the Buddha, the bodhisattva-mahāsattva has ten kinds of indestructible faith. What are those ten? They are as follows:

Indestructible faith in all buddhas;

Indestructible faith in the Dharma of all buddhas;

Indestructible faith in all those in the *ārya* Sangha;

Indestructible faith in all bodhisattvas;

Indestructible faith in all good spiritual guides;

Indestructible faith in all beings;

Indestructible faith in all the great vows of the bodhisattvas;

Indestructible faith in all the practices of the bodhisattvas;

Indestructible faith in revering and making offerings to all buddhas; and

Indestructible faith in bodhisattvas' skillful and esoteric expedient means for teaching and training all beings.

These are the ten. If bodhisattvas abide in these dharmas, then they acquire indestructible faith in the unexcelled great wisdom of all buddhas.

Sons of the Buddha, the bodhisattva-mahāsattva has ten ways of receiving the prediction [of future buddhahood]. What are those ten? They are as follows:

Receiving the prediction through extremely profound inward understanding;

Receiving the prediction through the ability to accord with and produce the bodhisattva's roots of goodness;

Receiving the prediction through cultivating vast practices;

現前得授記。不現前得授記。因自心證菩提得授記。成就忍得授記。教化調伏眾生得授記。究竟一切劫數得授記。一切菩薩行自在得授記。是為十。若諸菩薩。安住此法。則於一切諸佛所。而得授記。佛子。菩薩摩訶薩。有十種善根迴向。菩薩由此。能以一切善根。悉皆迴向。何等為十。所謂以我善根。同善知識願。如是成就。莫別成就。以我善根。同善知識心。如是成就。莫別成就。以我善根。同善知識行。如是成就。莫別成就。以我善根。同善知識善根。如是成就。莫別成就。以我善根。同善知識平等。如是成就。莫別成就。以我善根。同善知識念。如是成就。莫別成就。以我善根。同善知識清淨。如是成就。莫別成就。以我善根。同善知識所住。如是成就。莫別成就。以我善根。同善知識成滿。如是成就。莫別成就。

现前得授记；不现前得授记；因自心证菩提得授记；成就忍得授记；教化调伏众生得授记；究竟一切劫数得授记；一切菩萨行自在得授记。是为十。若诸菩萨安住此法，则于一切诸佛所而得授记。

"佛子，菩萨摩诃萨有十种善根回向，菩萨由此能以一切善根悉皆回向。何等为十？所谓：以我善根同善知识愿，如是成就，莫别成就；以我善根同善知识心，如是成就，莫别成就；以我善根同善知识行，如是成就，莫别成就；以我善根同善知识善根，如是成就，莫别成就；以我善根同善知识平等，如是成就，莫别成就；以我善根同善知识念，如是成就，莫别成就；以我善根同善知识清净，如是成就，莫别成就；以我善根同善知识所住，如是成就，莫别成就；以我善根同善知识成满，如是成就，莫别成就；

Receiving the prediction directly;

Receiving the prediction indirectly;

Receiving the prediction due to his own mind's realization of bodhi;

Receiving the prediction through the complete realization of patience;[109]

Receiving the prediction through teaching and training beings;

Receiving the prediction through continuing on even to the very end of all kalpas; and

Receiving the prediction through sovereign mastery of all of the bodhisattva practices.

These are the ten. If bodhisattvas abide in these dharmas, then they receive the prediction [of future buddhahood] from all buddhas.

Sons of the Buddha, the bodhisattva-mahāsattva has ten ways of dedicating roots of goodness. Because of these, the bodhisattva is able to dedicate all his roots of goodness. What are those ten? They are as follows:

May my roots of goodness be perfected in the same way and no differently from my good spiritual guide as regards our vows;

May my roots of goodness be perfected in the same way and no differently from my good spiritual guide as regards our minds;

May my roots of goodness be perfected in the same way and no differently from my good spiritual guide as regards our practices;

May my roots of goodness be perfected in the same way and no differently from my good spiritual guide as regards our roots of goodness;

May my roots of goodness be perfected in the same way and no differently from my good spiritual guide as regards our equanimity;

May my roots of goodness be perfected in the same way and no differently from my good spiritual guide as regards our mindfulness;

May my roots of goodness be perfected in the same way and no differently from my good spiritual guide as regards our purity;

May my roots of goodness be perfected in the same way and no differently from my good spiritual guide as regards where we dwell;

May my roots of goodness be perfected in the same way and no differently from my good spiritual guide as regards our fulfillment; and

正體字

以我善根。同善知識
不壞。如是成就。莫別成就。是為十。若諸菩
薩。安住此法。則得無上善根迴向。佛子。菩薩
摩訶薩。有十種得智慧。何等為十。所謂於施
自在得智慧。深解一切佛法得智慧。入如來
無邊智得智慧。於一切問答中。能斷疑得智
慧。入於智者義得智慧。深解一切如來。於一
切佛法中。言音善巧得智慧。深解於諸佛所。
種少善根。必能滿足一切白淨法。獲如來無
量智得智慧。成就菩薩。不思議住得智慧。於
一念中。悉能往詣不可說佛剎得智慧。覺一
切佛菩提。入一切法界。聞持一切佛所說法。
深入一切如來種種莊嚴言音得智慧。是為
十。若諸菩薩。安住此法。則得一切諸佛無上
現證智。佛子。菩薩摩訶薩。有十種發無量無
邊廣大心。何等為十。所謂於一切諸佛所。發
無量無邊廣大心。觀一切眾生界。發無量無
邊廣大心。

简体字

以我善根同善知识不坏，如是成就，莫别成就。是为十。若诸菩萨安住此法，则得无上善根回向。

"佛子，菩萨摩诃萨有十种得智慧。何等为十？所谓：于施自在得智慧；深解一切佛法得智慧；入如来无边智得智慧；于一切问答中能断疑得智慧；入于智者义得智慧；深解一切如来于一切佛法中言音善巧得智慧；深解于诸佛所种少善根必能满足一切白净法获如来无量智得智慧；成就菩萨不思议住得智慧；于一念中悉能往诣不可说佛刹得智慧；觉一切佛菩提、入一切法界闻持一切佛所说法、深入一切如来种种庄严言音得智慧。是为十。若诸菩萨安住此法，则得一切诸佛无上现证智。

"佛子，菩萨摩诃萨有十种发无量无边广大心。何等为十？所谓：于一切诸佛所，发无量无边广大心；观一切众生界，发无量无边广大心；

Chapter 38 — *Transcending the World*

May my roots of goodness be perfected in the same way and no differently from my good spiritual guide as regards our indestructibility.

These are the ten. If bodhisattvas abide in these dharmas, then they acquire the unexcelled practice of dedicating roots of goodness.

Sons of the Buddha, the bodhisattva-mahāsattvas has ten ways of attaining wisdom. What are those ten? They are as follows:

Attaining wisdom through sovereign mastery in giving;

Attaining wisdom through deep understanding of all dharmas of the Buddha;

Attaining wisdom through entering the Tathāgata's boundless knowledge;

Attaining wisdom through the ability to sever doubts in all responses to queries;

Attaining wisdom through penetration of the meanings of the wise;

Attaining wisdom through the deep understanding of all *tathāgatas'* skillfulness in discourse on all dharmas of the Buddha;

Attaining wisdom through the deep understanding that even the most minor roots of goodness planted in the presence of buddhas results in the certain ability to completely fulfill all dharmas of purity and acquire the Tathāgata's measureless wisdom;

Attaining wisdom through complete development of the bodhisattva's inconceivable abodes;

Attaining wisdom through the ability to travel to and visit an ineffable number of buddha *kṣetras* in but a single mind-moment; and

Attaining wisdom through awakening to the bodhi of all buddhas, entering the entire Dharma realm, hearing and retaining the Dharma proclaimed by all buddhas, and deeply penetrating the many different adorned statements of all *tathāgatas*.

These are the ten. If bodhisattvas abide in these Dharmas, then they attain the unexcelled directly realized wisdom of all buddhas.

Sons of the Buddha, the bodhisattva-mahāsattva has ten ways of generating measurelessly and boundlessly vast resolve. What are those ten? They are as follows:

The arousal of measurelessly and boundlessly vast resolve in the presence of all buddhas;

The arousal of measurelessly and boundlessly vast resolve through contemplating all realms of beings;

正體字

觀一切刹一切世一切法界。發無量無邊廣大心。觀察一切法。皆如虛空。發無量無邊廣大心。觀察一切菩薩廣大行。發無量無邊廣大心。正念三世一切諸佛。發無量無邊廣大心。觀不思議諸業果報。發無量無邊廣大心。嚴淨一切佛刹。發無量無邊廣大心。遍入一切諸佛大會。發無量無邊廣大心。觀察一切如來妙音。發無量無邊廣大心。是為十。若諸菩薩。安住此心。則得一切佛法。無量無邊廣大智慧海。佛子。菩薩摩訶薩。有十種伏藏。何等為十。所謂知一切法。是起功德行藏。知一切法。是正思惟藏。知一切法。是陀羅尼照明藏。知一切法。是辯才開演藏。知一切法。是不可說善覺真實藏。知一切佛自在神通。是觀察示現藏。知一切法。是善巧出生平等藏。知一切法。是常見一切諸佛藏。

简体字

观一切刹、一切世、一切法界，发无量无边广大心；观察一切法皆如虚空，发无量无边广大心；观察一切菩萨广大行，发无量无边广大心；正念三世一切诸佛，发无量无边广大心；观不思议诸业果报，发无量无边广大心；严净一切佛刹，发无量无边广大心；遍入一切诸佛大会，发无量无边广大心；观察一切如来妙音，发无量无边广大心。是为十。若诸菩萨安住此心，则得一切佛法无量无边广大智慧海。

"佛子，菩萨摩诃萨有十种伏藏。何等为十？所谓：知一切法是起功德行藏；知一切法是正思惟藏；知一切法是陀罗尼照明藏；知一切法是辩才开演藏；知一切法是不可说善觉真实藏；知一切佛自在神通是观察示现藏；知一切法是善巧出生平等藏；知一切法是常见一切诸佛藏；

Chapter 38 — *Transcending the World*

The arousal of measurelessly and boundlessly vast resolve throughout contemplating all *kṣetras*, all periods of time, and the entire Dharma realm;

The arousal of measurelessly and boundlessly vast resolve through contemplating all dharmas as like empty space;

The arousal of measurelessly and boundlessly vast resolve through contemplating the vast practices of all bodhisattvas;

The arousal of measurelessly and boundlessly vast resolve through right mindfulness of all buddhas of the three periods of time;

The arousal of measurelessly and boundlessly vast resolve through contemplating the inconceivable rewards and consequences of all karmic deeds;

The arousal of measurelessly and boundlessly vast resolve through the purification of all buddha *kṣetras*;

The arousal of measurelessly and boundlessly vast resolve through everywhere entering the congregations of all buddhas; and

The arousal of measurelessly and boundlessly vast resolve through contemplating the sublime voice of all *tathāgatas*.

These are the ten. If bodhisattvas abide in these types of resolve, then they acquire the measurelessly and boundlessly vast ocean of wisdom of the Dharma of all buddhas.

Sons of the Buddha, the bodhisattva-mahāsattva has ten kinds of hidden treasures. What are those ten? They are as follows:

His knowing of all dharmas constitutes the treasure of generating the practice of meritorious qualities;

His knowing of all dharmas constitutes the treasure of right thought;

His knowing of all dharmas constitutes the treasure of illuminating radiance produced by *dhāraṇīs*;

His knowing of all dharmas constitutes the treasure of eloquent expository discourse;

His knowing of all dharmas constitutes the treasure of an ineffable number of thorough awakenings to reality;

His knowing of all buddhas' sovereign mastery of spiritual superknowledges constitutes the treasure of contemplations of their manifestations;

His knowing of all dharmas constitutes the treasure of the skillful generation of equanimity;

His knowing of all dharmas constitutes the treasure of always seeing all buddhas;

正體字

知一切不思議劫。是善了皆如幻住藏。知一切諸佛菩薩。是發生歡喜淨信藏。是為十。若諸菩薩。安住此法。則得一切諸佛無上智慧法藏。悉能調伏一切眾生。佛子。菩薩摩訶薩。有十種律儀。何等為十。所謂於一切佛法。不生誹謗律儀。於一切佛所。信樂心不可壞律儀。於一切菩薩所。起尊重恭敬律儀。於一切善知識所。終不捨愛樂心律儀。於一切聲聞獨覺。不生憶念心律儀。遠離一切退菩薩道律儀。不起一切損害眾生心律儀。修一切善根。皆令究竟律儀。於一切魔。悉能降伏律儀。於一切波羅蜜。皆令滿足律儀。是為十。若諸菩薩。安住此法。則得無上大智律儀。佛子。菩薩摩訶薩。有十種自在。何等為十。所謂命自在。於不可說劫。住壽命故。心自在。智慧能入阿僧祇諸三昧故。資具自在。能以無量莊嚴。莊嚴一切世界故。業自在。隨時受報故。

简体字

知一切不思议劫是善了皆如幻住藏；知一切诸佛菩萨是发生欢喜净信藏。是为十。若诸菩萨安住此法，则得一切诸佛无上智慧法藏，悉能调伏一切众生。

"佛子，菩萨摩诃萨有十种律仪。何等为十？所谓：于一切佛法不生诽谤律仪；于一切佛所信乐心不可坏律仪；于一切菩萨所起尊重恭敬律仪；于一切善知识所终不舍爱乐心律仪；于一切声闻、独觉不生忆念心律仪；远离一切退菩萨道律仪；不起一切损害众生心律仪；修一切善根皆令究竟律仪；于一切魔悉能降伏律仪；于一切波罗蜜皆令满足律仪。是为十。若诸菩萨安住此法，则得无上大智律仪。

"佛子，菩萨摩诃萨有十种自在。何等为十？所谓：命自在，于不可说劫住寿命故；心自在，智慧能入阿僧祇诸三昧故；资具自在，能以无量庄严庄严一切世界故；业自在，随时受报故；

Chapter 38 — *Transcending the World*

His knowing of all the inconceivably many kalpas constitutes the treasure of skillfully understanding all of them as abiding like mere conjurations; and

His knowing of all buddhas and bodhisattvas constitutes the treasure of the arousal of joyous delight and pure faith.

These are the ten. If bodhisattvas abide in these dharmas, then they acquire the Dharma treasure of all buddha's unexcelled wisdom with which they are able to train all beings.

Sons of the Buddha, the bodhisattva-mahāsattva has ten kinds of moral standards. What are those ten? They are as follows:

The moral standard of never slandering any of the Buddha's dharmas;

The moral standard of maintaining an indestructible mind of resolute faith in all buddhas;

The moral standard of arousing reverential respect for all bodhisattvas;

The moral standard of never abandoning their mind of fond devotion for all good spiritual guides;

The moral standard of refraining from thoughts recalling [the paths of] *śrāvaka* disciples or *pratyekabuddhas*;

The moral standard of abandoning any inclination to retreat from the bodhisattva path;

The moral standard of never producing any malicious thoughts toward other beings;

The moral standard of cultivating all roots of goodness so that they all reach a state of ultimate development;

The moral standard of maintaining the ability to conquer all *māras*; and

The moral standard of enabling the complete fulfillment of all the *pāramitās*.

These are the ten. If bodhisattvas abide in these dharmas, then they acquire the moral standard of unexcelled great wisdom.

Sons of the Buddha, the bodhisattva-mahāsattva has ten kinds of sovereign mastery. What are those ten? They are as follows:

Sovereign mastery of life span based on the ability to abide for a life span of ineffably many kalpas;

Sovereign mastery of mind based on having wisdom capable of entering an *asaṃkhyeya* of samādhis;

Sovereign mastery of resources based on the ability to use countless adornments to adorn all worlds;

Sovereign mastery in karmic actions based on the ability to receive their associated karmic rewards whenever they choose;

正體字

受生自在。
於一切世界。示現受生故。解自在。於一切世
界。見佛充滿故。願自在。隨欲隨時。於諸剎
中。成正覺故。神力自在。示現一切大神變故。
法自在。示現無邊諸法門故。智自在。於念念
中。示現如來十力無畏。成正覺故。是為十。若
諸菩薩。安住此法。則得圓滿一切諸佛。諸波
羅蜜。智慧神力。菩提自在

大方廣佛華嚴經[*]卷第五十六

離世間品第三十八之四

佛子。菩薩摩訶薩。有十種無礙用。何等為十。
所謂眾生無礙用。國土無礙用。法無礙用。身
無礙用。願無礙用。境界無礙用。智無礙用。神
通無礙用。神力無礙用。力無礙用。佛子。云何
為菩薩摩訶薩。眾生等無礙用。佛子。菩薩摩
訶薩。有十種眾生無礙用。何者為十。所謂知
一切眾生。無眾生無礙用。知一切眾生。但
想所持無礙用。為一切眾生。說法未曾失時
無礙用。普化現一切眾生界無礙用。

简体字

受生自在，于一切世界示现受生故；解自在，于一切世界见佛充满故；愿自在，随欲随时于诸刹中成正觉故；神力自在，示现一切大神变故；法自在，示现无边诸法门故；智自在，于念念中示现如来十力、无畏、成正觉故。是为十。若诸菩萨安住此法，则得圆满一切诸佛诸波罗蜜智慧神力菩提自在。

大方广佛华严经卷第五十六

离世间品第三十八之四

"佛子，菩萨摩诃萨有十种无碍用。何等为十？所谓：众生无碍用；国土无碍用；法无碍用；身无碍用；愿无碍用；境界无碍用；智无碍用；神通无碍用；神力无碍用；力无碍用。

"佛子，云何为菩萨摩诃萨众生等无碍用？

"佛子，菩萨摩诃萨有十种众生无碍用。何者为十？所谓：知一切众生无众生无碍用；知一切众生但想所持无碍用；为一切众生说法未曾失时无碍用；普化现一切众生界无碍用；

Sovereign mastery in the taking on of births based on the ability to manifest birth in all worlds;

Sovereign mastery in understanding based on the ability to see buddhas filling all worlds;

Sovereign mastery in vows based on the ability to attain right enlightenment in all *kṣetras* however and whenever they wish;

Sovereign mastery in spiritual powers based on the ability to manifest every kind of great spiritual transformation;

Sovereign mastery in Dharma based on the ability to manifest all of the boundlessly many Dharma gateways; and

Sovereign mastery of cognition based on the ability to manifest in each successive mind-moment the Tathāgata's ten powers, fearlessnesses, and realization of right enlightenment.

These are the ten. If bodhisattvas abide in these dharmas, then they acquire the sovereign mastery of the complete fulfillment of all buddhas' *pāramitās*, wisdom, spiritual powers, and bodhi.

Sons of the Buddha, the bodhisattva-mahāsattva has ten kinds of unimpeded functions. What are those ten? They are as follows:

Unimpeded function in relation to beings;
Unimpeded function in relation to lands;
Unimpeded function in relation to dharmas;
Unimpeded function in relation to bodies;
Unimpeded function in relation to vows;
Unimpeded function in relation to realms;
Unimpeded function in relation to knowledge;
Unimpeded function in relation to spiritual superknowledges;
Unimpeded function in relation to spiritual powers; and
Unimpeded function in relation to the powers.

Sons of the Buddha, what then constitutes the bodhisattva-mahāsattva's unimpeded functions in relation to beings and so forth? Sons of the Buddha, the bodhisattva-mahāsattva has ten kinds of unimpeded functions in relation to beings. What are those ten? They are as follows:

The unimpeded function of knowing all beings as devoid of any beings;

The unimpeded function of knowing all beings are sustained solely through thought;

The unimpeded function of never missing the right time in speaking Dharma for beings;

The unimpeded function of everywhere manifesting all realms of beings;

正體字

置一切
眾生。於一毛孔中。而不迫隘無礙用。為一切
眾生。示現他方一切世界。令其悉見無礙用。
為一切眾生。示現釋梵護世諸天身無礙用。
為一切眾生。示現聲聞辟支佛。寂靜威儀無
礙用。為一切眾生。示現菩薩行無礙用。為一
切眾生。示現諸佛。色身相好。一切智力。成等
正覺無礙用。是為十。佛子。菩薩摩訶薩。有十
種國土無礙用。何等為十。所謂一切刹作一
刹無礙用。一切刹入一毛孔無礙用。知一切
刹無有盡無礙用。一身結[1]跏坐。充滿一切刹
無礙用。一身中現一切刹無礙用。震動一切
刹。不令眾生恐怖無礙用。以一切刹莊嚴具。
莊嚴一刹無礙用。以一刹莊嚴具。莊嚴一切
刹無礙用。以一如來一眾會。遍一切佛刹。示
現眾生無礙用。一切小刹中刹大刹。廣刹深
刹。仰刹覆刹。側刹正刹。遍諸方網。無量差
別。以此普示一切眾生無礙用。是為十。佛子。
菩薩摩訶薩。有十種法無礙用。何等為十。所
謂

简体字

置一切众生于一毛孔中而不迫隘无碍用；为一切众生示现他方一切世界令其悉见无碍用；为一切众生示现释、梵、护世诸天身无碍用；为一切众生示现声闻、辟支佛寂静威仪无碍用；为一切众生示现菩萨行无碍用；为一切众生示现诸佛色身相好、一切智力、成等正觉无碍用。是为十。

"佛子，菩萨摩诃萨有十种国土无碍用。何等为十？所谓：一切刹作一刹无碍用；一切刹入一毛孔无碍用；知一切刹无有尽无碍用；一身结跏趺坐充满一切刹无碍用；一身中现一切刹无碍用；震动一切刹不令众生恐怖无碍用；以一切刹庄严具庄严一刹无碍用；以一刹庄严具庄严一切刹无碍用；以一如来一众会遍一切佛刹示现众生无碍用；一切小刹、中刹、大刹、广刹、深刹、仰刹、覆刹、侧刹、正刹，遍诸方网，无量差别，以此普示一切众生无碍用。是为十。

"佛子，菩萨摩诃萨有十种法无碍用。何等为十？所谓：

Chapter 38 — *Transcending the World* 2857

The unimpeded function of placing all beings within but a single pore without their being crowded;

The unimpeded function of manifesting for all beings all the worlds of other regions, thereby enabling them all to see them;

The unimpeded function of manifesting for all beings the bodies of the devas Śakra, Brahma, and the World Protecting Kings;

The unimpeded function of manifesting for all beings the serene awesome deportment of *śrāvaka* disciples and *pratyekabuddhas*;

The unimpeded function of manifesting for all beings the bodhisattva practices; and

The unimpeded function of manifesting for all beings the major marks and secondary signs of the buddhas' bodies, their powers of all-knowledge, and their realization of the right and perfect enlightenment.

These are the ten.

The bodhisattva-mahāsattva has ten kinds of unimpeded functions in relation to lands. What are those ten? They are as follows:

The unimpeded function of making all *kṣetras* into a single *kṣetra*;

The unimpeded function of making all *kṣetras* enter a single pore;

The unimpeded function of knowing the endlessness of all *kṣetras*;

The unimpeded function of causing a single body sitting in the lotus posture to completely fill all *kṣetras*;

The unimpeded function of showing all *kṣetras* appearing within a single body;

The unimpeded function of causing all *kṣetras* to quake even while not causing the beings within them to become frightened;

The unimpeded function of adorning a single *kṣetra* with the adornments of all *kṣetras*;

The unimpeded function of adorning all *kṣetras* with the adornments of a single *kṣetra*;

The unimpeded function of revealing to beings a single *tathāgata* and his single congregation pervading all buddha *kṣetras*; and

The unimpeded function of everywhere showing all beings all the countless differences in *kṣetras* everywhere throughout their network which pervades all the directions, including the small *kṣetras*, mid-sized *kṣetras*, large *kṣetras*, vast *kṣetras*, deep *kṣetras*, upward-facing *kṣetras*, inverted *kṣetras*, laterally facing *kṣetras*, and upright *kṣetras*.

These are the ten.

Sons of the Buddha, the bodhisattva-mahāsattva has ten kinds of unimpeded functions in relation to dharmas. What are those ten? They are as follows:

正體字	知一切法入一法。一法入一切法。而亦不違眾生心解無礙用。從般若波羅蜜。出生一切法。為他解說。悉令開悟無礙用。知一切法離文字。而令眾生。皆得悟入無礙用。知一切法入一相。而能演說無量法相無礙用。知一切法離言說。能為他說無邊法門無礙用。於一切法。善轉普門字輪無礙用。以一切法。入一法門。而不相違。於不可說劫。說不窮盡無礙用。以一切法。悉入佛法。令諸眾生。皆得悟解無礙用。知一切法。無有邊際無礙用。知一切法。無障礙際。猶如幻網。無量差別。於無量劫。為眾生說。不可窮盡無礙用。是為十。佛子。菩薩摩訶薩。有十種身無礙用。何等為十。所謂以一切眾生身。入己身無礙用。以己身。入一切眾生身無礙用。一切佛身。入一佛身無礙用。
简体字	知一切法入一法、一法入一切法，而亦不违众生心解无碍用；从般若波罗蜜出生一切法，为他解说悉令开悟无碍用；知一切法离文字，而令众生皆得悟入无碍用；知一切法入一相，而能演说无量法相无碍用；知一切法离言说，能为他说无边法门无碍用；于一切法善转普门字轮无碍用；以一切法入一法门而不相违，于不可说劫说不穷尽无碍用；以一切法悉入佛法，令诸众生皆得悟解无碍用；知一切法无有边际无碍用；知一切法无障碍际，犹如幻网无量差别，于无量劫为众生说不可穷尽无碍用。是为十。 　　"佛子，菩萨摩诃萨有十种身无碍用。何等为十？所谓：以一切众生身入己身无碍用；以己身入一切众生身无碍用；一切佛身入一佛身无碍用；

Chapter 38 — *Transcending the World*

- The unimpeded function of knowing all dharmas enter a single dharma and a single dharma enters all dharmas, and yet [still being able to explain this in such a way that] it does not contravene beings' capacity to comprehend this;
- The unimpeded function of bringing forth all dharmas from within the *prajñāpāramitā* and explaining them for others, thereby enabling them all to awaken;
- The unimpeded function of knowing all dharmas transcend expression in words even as he still enables all beings to successfully awaken to and penetrate them;
- The unimpeded function of knowing all dharmas enter but a single sign while still being able to expound on countless signs of dharmas;
- The unimpeded function of knowing all dharmas transcend words and speech even as he is still able to explain boundlessly many Dharma gateways for others;
- The unimpeded function of skillfully turning the universal gateway's syllabary wheel in relation to all dharmas;
- The unimpeded function of enabling all dharmas to enter a single Dharma gateway without any mutual contradiction between them as he expounds on them for an ineffable number of kalpas without ever coming to the end of them;
- The unimpeded function of enabling all dharmas to enter the Dharma of the Buddha, thereby enabling all beings to succeed in awakening and understanding;
- The unimpeded function of knowing all dharmas have no boundaries; and
- The unimpeded function of knowing all dharmas as devoid of obstructive boundaries and as like an illusory network possessed of countless differences which he explains for beings for countless kalpas without ever being able to come to the end of them all.

These are the ten.

Sons of the Buddha, the bodhisattva-mahāsattva has ten kinds of unimpeded functions in relation to bodies. What are these ten? They are as follows:

- The unimpeded function of causing the bodies of all beings to enter his own body;
- The unimpeded function of causing his own body to enter all beings' bodies;
- The unimpeded function of causing all buddhas' bodies to enter a single buddha's body;

正體字

一佛身。入一切佛身無礙用。一切剎
入己身無礙用。以一身。充遍一切三世法。示
現眾生無礙用。於一身。示現無邊身。入三昧
無礙用。於一身。示現眾生數等身。成正覺無
礙用。於一切眾生身。現一眾生身。於一眾生
身。現一切眾生身無礙用。於一切眾生身。示
現法身。於法身。示現一切眾生身無礙用。是
為十。佛子。菩薩摩訶薩。有十種願無礙用。何
等為十。所謂以一切菩薩願。作自願無礙用。
以一切佛成菩提願力。示現自成正覺無礙
用。隨所化眾生。自成阿耨多羅三藐三菩提
無礙用。於一切無邊際劫。大願不斷無礙用。
遠離識身。不著智身。以自在願現一切身。無
礙用。捨棄自身。成滿他願無礙用。普教化一
切眾生。而不捨大願無礙用。於一切劫。行菩
薩行。而大願不斷無礙用。於一毛孔。現成正
覺。以願力故。充遍一切諸佛國土。於不可說
不可說世界。為一一眾生。如是示現無礙用。

简体字

一佛身入一切佛身无碍用；一切剎入己身无碍用；以一身充遍一切三世法示现众生无碍用；于一身示现无边身入三昧无碍用；于一身示现众生数等身成正觉无碍用；于一切众生身现一众生身、于一众生身现一切众生身无碍用；于一切众生身示现法身、于法身示现一切众生身无碍用。是为十。

"佛子，菩萨摩诃萨有十种愿无碍用。何等为十？所谓：以一切菩萨愿作自愿无碍用；以一切佛成菩提愿力示现自成正觉无碍用；随所化众生自成阿耨多罗三藐三菩提无碍用；于一切无边际劫大愿不断无碍用；远离识身，不著智身，以自在愿现一切身无碍用；舍弃自身成满他愿无碍用；普教化一切众生而不舍大愿无碍用；于一切劫行菩萨行而大愿不断无碍用；于一毛孔现成正觉，以愿力故，充遍一切诸佛国土，于不可说不可说世界，为一一众生如是示现无碍用；

Chapter 38 — *Transcending the World*

The unimpeded function of causing a single buddha's body to enter all buddhas' bodies;

The unimpeded function of causing all *kṣetras* to enter his own body;

The unimpeded function of showing beings a single body completely pervading all dharmas of the three periods of time;

The unimpeded function of showing boundlessly many bodies entering samādhi in a single body;

The unimpeded function of showing bodies as numerous as beings realizing right enlightenment within a single body;

The unimpeded function of revealing a single being's body in all beings' bodies and revealing all beings' bodies in a single being's body; and

The unimpeded function of revealing the Dharma body in all beings' bodies and revealing all beings' bodies in the Dharma body.

These are the ten.

Sons of the Buddha, the bodhisattva-mahāsattva has ten kinds of unimpeded functions in relation to vows. What are those ten? They are as follows:

The unimpeded function of making the vows of all bodhisattvas his own vows;

The unimpeded function of using the vow power by which all buddhas realized bodhi to manifest his own realization of right enlightenment;

The unimpeded function of realizing *anuttarasamyaksaṃbodhi* in a manner adapted to the beings he teaches;

The unimpeded function of having great vows that remain interminable even throughout the course of all boundless kalpas;

The unimpeded function of leaving the conscious body far behind and not attaching to the wisdom body while using masterful vows to manifest all kinds of bodies;

The unimpeded function of sacrificing his own body to bring about the complete fulfillment of others' vows;

The unimpeded function of everywhere teaching all beings while still never abandoning his great vows;

The unimpeded function of practicing the bodhisattva practices in all kalpas while still never cutting short his great vows;

The unimpeded function of manifesting the realization of the right enlightenment in a single pore while, through the power of vows, everywhere filling all buddha lands, manifesting in this way for the sake of every one of those beings residing in an ineffable-ineffable number of worlds; and

正體字

說一句法。遍一切法界。興大正法雲。[1]耀解脫電光。震實法雷音。雨甘露味雨。以大願力。充洽一切諸眾生界無礙用。是為十。佛[2]子。菩薩摩訶薩。有十種境界無礙用。何等為十。所謂在法界境界。而不捨眾生境界無礙用。在佛境界。而不捨魔境界無礙用。在涅槃境界。而不捨生死境界無礙用。入一切智境界。而不斷菩薩種性境界無礙用。住寂靜境界。而不捨散亂境界無礙用。住無去無來。無戲論無相狀。無體性無言說。如虛空境界。而不捨一切眾生戲論境界無礙用。住諸力解脫境界。而不捨一切諸方所境界無礙用。入無眾生際境界。而不捨教化一切眾生無礙用。住禪定解脫。神通明智。寂靜境界。而於一切世界。示現受生無礙用。住如來一切行。莊嚴成正覺境界。而現一切聲聞辟支佛。寂靜威儀無礙用。

简体字

说一句法遍一切法界，兴大正法云，耀解脱电光，震实法雷音，雨甘露味雨，以大愿力充洽一切诸众生界无碍用。是为十。

"佛子，菩萨摩诃萨有十种境界无碍用。何等为十？所谓：在法界境界而不舍众生境界无碍用；在佛境界而不舍魔境界无碍用；在涅槃境界而不舍生死境界无碍用；入一切智境界而不断菩萨种性境界无碍用；住寂静境界而不舍散乱境界无碍用；住无去、无来、无戏论、无相状、无体性、无言说、如虚空境界而不舍一切众生戏论境界无碍用；住诸力解脱境界而不舍一切诸方所境界无碍用；入无众生际境界而不舍教化一切众生无碍用；住禅定解脱、神通明智、寂静境界而于一切世界示现受生无碍用；住如来一切行庄严成正觉境界而现一切声闻、辟支佛寂静威仪无碍用。

The unimpeded function of uttering a single sentence of Dharma that pervades the entire Dharma realm, brings forth a cloud of great right Dharma, sets loose the dazzling light of the lightning of liberation, creates the quaking thunder of the true Dharma, rains down the rain with the flavor of the elixir of immortality, and uses the power of great vows to drench all realms of beings.

These are the ten.

Sons of the Buddha, the bodhisattva-mahāsattva has ten kinds of unimpeded functions in relation to realms. What are those ten? They are as follows:

The unimpeded function of abiding in the realm of the Dharma realm even while still not abandoning the realms of beings;

The unimpeded function of abiding in the realm of the Buddha even while still not abandoning the realm of the *māras*;

The unimpeded function of abiding in the realm of nirvāṇa even while still not abandoning the realm of *saṃsāra*;

The unimpeded function of entering the realm of all-knowledge even while still never severing the realm of the bodhisattva's lineage;

The unimpeded function of abiding in the realm of quiescence even while never relinquishing the realms that conduce to distraction;

The unimpeded function of abiding in the realm that has no going and no coming, no conceptual proliferation, no appearances, no essential nature, no words and speech, and that is like empty space even while still not abandoning the realm of all beings' conceptual proliferation;

The unimpeded function of abiding in the realm of the powers and the liberations even while still not abandoning the realm that extends throughout all directions and places;

The unimpeded function of entering the realms without any beings even while still not abandoning the teaching of all beings;

The unimpeded function of abiding in the quiescent realms of the *dhyāna* absorptions, liberations, spiritual superknowledges, and clear knowledges even while still manifesting the taking on of birth in all worlds; and

The unimpeded function of abiding in the realm of all the Tathāgata's practices and adornments and his realization of right enlightenment even while still manifesting all the quiescence and awesome deportment of *śrāvaka* disciples and *pratyekabuddhas*.

正體字

是為十。佛子。菩薩摩訶薩。有十種智無礙用。何等為十。所謂無盡辯才無礙用。一切總持。無有忘失無礙用。能決定知決定說。一切眾生諸根無礙用。於一念中。以無礙智。知一切眾生心之所行無礙用。知一切眾生。欲樂隨眠。習氣煩惱病。隨應授藥無礙用。一念能入如來十力無礙用。以無礙智。知三世一切劫。及其中眾生無礙用。於念念中。現成正覺。示現眾生。無有斷絕無礙用。於一眾生想。知一切眾生業無礙用。於一眾生音。解一切眾生語無礙用。是為十。佛子。菩薩摩訶薩。有十種神通無礙用。何等為十。所謂於一身。示現一切世界身無礙用。於一佛眾會。聽受一切佛眾會中。所說法無礙用。於一眾生心念中。成就不可說無上菩提。開悟一切眾生心無礙用。

简体字

是为十。

"佛子,菩萨摩诃萨有十种智无碍用。何等为十?所谓:无尽辩才无碍用;一切总持无有忘失无碍用;能决定知、决定说一切众生诸根无碍用;于一念中以无碍智知一切众生心之所行无碍用;知一切众生欲乐、随眠、习气、烦恼病,随应授药无碍用;一念能入如来十力无碍用;以无碍智知三世一切劫及其中众生无碍用;于念念中现成正觉示现众生无有断绝无碍用;于一众生想知一切众生业无碍用;于一众生音解一切众生语无碍用。是为十。

"佛子,菩萨摩诃萨有十种神通无碍用。何等为十?所谓:于一身示现一切世界身无碍用;于一佛众会听受一切佛众会中所说法无碍用;于一众生心念中成就不可说无上菩提开悟一切众生心无碍用;

Chapter 38 — *Transcending the World*

These are the ten.

Sons of the Buddha, the bodhisattva-mahāsattva has ten kinds of unimpeded functions in relation to knowledge. What are those ten? They are as follows:

The unimpeded function of inexhaustible eloquence;

The unimpeded function of all the complete-retention *dhāraṇī* formulae by which he never forgets anything;

The unimpeded function of being able to definitely know and definitely explain all beings' faculties;

The unimpeded function of using unimpeded knowledge in knowing in but a single mind-moment the mental actions of all beings;

The unimpeded function of knowing the illnesses associated with all beings' dispositions, latent tendencies, habitual karmic propensities, and afflictions and then bestowing the appropriate medicine in accordance with what is fitting;

The unimpeded function of being able in but a single mind-moment to enter the Tathāgata's ten powers;

The unimpeded function of using unimpeded knowledge in knowing all kalpas of the three periods of time as well as the beings within them;

The unimpeded function of, in each successive mind-moment, endlessly revealing for beings the realization of right enlightenment;

The unimpeded function of knowing through the thoughts of but a single being the karmic actions of all beings; and

The unimpeded function of understanding through the voice of a single being the speech of all beings.

These are the ten.

Sons of the Buddha, the bodhisattva-mahāsattva has ten kinds of unimpeded functions in relation to the spiritual superknowledges. What are those ten? They are as follows:

The unimpeded function of revealing the bodies of all worlds in but a single body;

The unimpeded function of hearing in the congregation of a single buddha the Dharma spoken in the congregations of all buddhas;

The unimpeded function of using the thoughts in the mind of a single being to accomplish an ineffable number of realizations of unexcelled bodhi through which he awakens to the minds of all beings;

正體字

以一音。現一切世界差別言音。
294c16‖ 令[3]諸眾生。各得解了無礙用。一念中。現盡前
294c17‖ 際一切劫。所有業果。種種差別。令諸眾生。悉
294c18‖ 得知見無礙[4]用。令一切世界。具足莊嚴無礙
294c19‖ 用。普入一切三世無礙用。放大法光明。現一
294c20‖ 切諸佛菩提。眾生行願無礙用。善守護一切
294c21‖ 天龍夜叉乾闥婆阿脩羅迦樓羅緊那羅摩睺
294c22‖ 羅伽釋梵護世。聲聞獨覺。菩薩所有。如來十
294c23‖ 力。菩薩善根。無礙用是為十。若諸菩薩。得此
294c24‖ 無礙用。則能普入一切佛法。佛子。菩薩摩訶
294c25‖ 薩。有十種神力無礙用。何等為十。所謂以不
294c26‖ 可說世界。置一塵中無礙用。於一塵中。現等
294c27‖ 法界一切佛剎無礙用。以一切大海水。置一
294c28‖ 毛孔。周旋往返十方世界。而於眾生。無所觸
294c29‖ 嬈無礙用。以不可說世界內自身中。示現一切
295a01‖ 神通所作無礙用。以一毛。繫不可數金剛圍
295a02‖ 山。

简体字

以一音现一切世界差别言音，令诸众生各得解了无碍用；一念中现尽前际一切劫所有业果种种差别，令诸众生悉得知见无碍用；一微尘出现广大佛刹无量庄严无碍用；令一切世界具足庄严无碍用；普入一切三世无碍用；放大法光明现一切诸佛菩提、众生行愿无碍用；善守护一切天、龙、夜叉、乾闼婆、阿修罗、迦楼罗、紧那罗、摩睺罗伽、释、梵、护世、声闻、独觉、菩萨、所有如来十力、菩萨善根无碍用。是为十。若诸菩萨得此无碍用，则能普入一切佛法。

"佛子，菩萨摩诃萨有十种神力无碍用。何等为十？所谓：以不可说世界置一尘中无碍用；于一尘中现等法界一切佛刹无碍用；以一切大海水置一毛孔，周旋往返十方世界，而于众生无所触娆无碍用；以不可说世界内自身中，示现一切神通所作无碍用；以一毛系不可数金刚围山，

Chapter 38 — *Transcending the World*

The unimpeded function of using but a single voice to manifest all the different voices in all worlds, thereby enabling all beings to completely understand him;

The unimpeded function of revealing in but a single mind-moment all the many different karmic effects as they unfolded in all kalpas of the past, thereby enabling all beings to know and see them;

The unimpeded function of manifesting within a single atom the measureless adornments of a vast buddha *kṣetra*;[110]

The unimpeded function of causing all worlds to become completely adorned;

The unimpeded function of everywhere entering all three periods of time;

The unimpeded function of emanating great Dharma light which reveals the bodhi of all buddhas as well as the conduct and vows of all beings; and

The unimpeded function of skillfully protecting all devas, dragons, *yakṣas*, *gandharvas*, *asuras*, *garuḍas*, *kiṃnaras*, *mahoragas*, Śakra, Brahma, the World Protecting Heavenly Kings, *śrāvaka* disciples, *pratyekabuddhas*, bodhisattvas, the ten powers of all *tathāgatas*, and the bodhisattvas' roots of goodness.

These are the ten. If bodhisattvas acquire these unimpeded functions, then they are able to everywhere penetrate all dharmas of the Buddha.

Sons of the Buddha, the bodhisattva-mahāsattva has ten kinds of unimpeded functions in relation to the spiritual powers. What are those ten? They are as follows:

The unimpeded function of placing an ineffable number of worlds into but a single atom;

The unimpeded function of revealing in but a single atom all buddha *kṣetras* equal in number to all those contained in the entire Dharma realm;

The unimpeded function of placing the waters of all the great oceans into but a single pore and then traveling everywhere, going forth and returning from all worlds of the ten directions, yet doing so in a manner that involves no contact with or disturbance of any of those beings within them;

The unimpeded function of placing an ineffable number of worlds into his own body while revealing all the deeds accomplished with the spiritual superknowledges;

The unimpeded function of using a single strand of hair to string together an innumerable number of vajra ring mountains and

正體字

持以遊行一切世界。不令眾生。生恐怖心
無礙用。以不可說劫。作一劫。一劫。作不可說
劫。於中示現成壞差別。不令眾生。心有恐怖
無礙用。於一切世界。現水火風災。種種變壞。
而不惱眾生無礙用。一切世界。三災壞時。悉
能護持一切眾生資生之具。不令損缺無礙
用。以一手。持不思議世界。擲不可說世界之
外。不令眾生。有驚怖想無礙用。說一切剎。同
於虛空。令諸眾生。悉得悟解無礙用。是為十。
佛子。菩薩摩訶薩。有十種力無礙用。何等為
十。所謂眾生力無礙用。教化調伏。不捨離故。
剎力無礙用。示現不可說莊嚴。而莊嚴故。法
力無礙用。令一切身。入無身故。劫力無礙用。
修行不斷故。佛力無礙用。覺悟睡眠故。行力
無礙用。攝取一切菩薩行故。如來力無礙用。
度脫一切眾生故。

简体字

持以游行一切世界,不令众生生恐怖心无碍用;以不可说劫作一劫,一劫作不可说劫,于中示现成坏差别,不令众生心有恐怖无碍用;于一切世界现水、火、风灾种种变坏而不恼众生无碍用;一切世界三灾坏时,悉能护持一切众生资生之具不令损缺无碍用;以一手持不思议世界,掷不可说世界之外,不令众生有惊怖想无碍用;说一切刹同于虚空,令诸众生悉得悟解无碍用。是为十。

"佛子,菩萨摩诃萨有十种力无碍用。何等为十?所谓:众生力无碍用,教化调伏不舍离故;刹力无碍用,示现不可说庄严而庄严故;法力无碍用,令一切身入无身故;劫力无碍用,修行不断故;佛力无碍用,觉悟睡眠故;行力无碍用,摄取一切菩萨行故;如来力无碍用,度脱一切众生故;

Chapter 38 — *Transcending the World*

then carry them along as he roams to all worlds, doing so without ever causing any of the beings there to have any fearful thoughts;

The unimpeded function of making a single kalpa from an ineffable number of kalpas and making an ineffable number of kalpas from a single kalpa even while revealing the different phases of creation and destruction within them without ever frightening any beings;

The unimpeded function of revealing in all worlds the many different kinds of destructive changes produced by water, fire, and wind disasters while still not troubling any of their beings;

The unimpeded function of being able to protect all the life-sustaining possessions of all beings when the three kinds of disasters cause destruction in all worlds, thereby preventing them from becoming damaged or diminished;

The unimpeded function of being able to pick up in one hand an ineffable number of worlds and then pitch them beyond an ineffable number of worlds, all while not causing any of their beings to become terrified by this; and

The unimpeded function of enabling all beings to attain awakened understanding by speaking of all *kṣetras* as identical to empty space.

These are the ten.

Sons of the Buddha, the bodhisattva-mahāsattva has ten kinds of unimpeded functions in relation to the powers. What are those ten? They are as follows:

The unimpeded function of powers in relation to beings with which he teaches and trains them and never abandons them;

The unimpeded function of powers in relation to *kṣetras* with which he manifests an ineffable number of adornments and then adorns them;

The unimpeded function of powers in relation to the Dharma with which he causes all bodies to enter what is not a body at all;

The unimpeded function of powers in relation to kalpas with which he cultivates incessantly;

The unimpeded function of powers in relation to buddhahood with which he awakens beings from their slumber;

The unimpeded function of powers in relation to the practices with which he consolidates all the bodhisattva practices;

The unimpeded function of powers in relation to the Tathāgata with which he liberates all beings;

正體字

無師力無礙用。自覺一切諸
法故。一切智力無礙用。以一切智。成正覺故。
大悲力無礙用。不捨一切眾生故。是為十。佛
子。如是名為菩薩摩訶薩。十種無礙用。若有
得此十無礙用者。於阿耨多羅三藐三菩提。
欲成不成。隨意無違。雖成正覺。而亦不斷行
菩薩行。何以故。菩薩摩訶薩。發大誓願。入無
邊無礙用門。善巧示現故。佛子。菩薩摩訶薩。
有十種遊戲。何等為十。所謂以眾生身。作剎
身。而亦不壞眾生身。是菩薩遊戲。以剎身。作
眾生身。而亦不壞於剎身。是菩薩遊戲。於佛
身。示現聲聞獨覺身。而不損減如來身。是菩
薩遊戲。於聲聞獨覺身。示現如來身。而不增
長聲聞獨覺身。是菩薩遊戲。於菩薩行身。示
現成正覺身。而亦不斷菩薩行身。是菩薩遊
戲。

简体字

无师力无碍用，自觉一切诸法故；一切智力无碍用，以一切智成正觉故；大悲力无碍用，不舍一切众生故。是为十。

"佛子，如是名为菩萨摩诃萨十种无碍用。若有得此十无碍用者，于阿耨多罗三藐三菩提欲成、不成，随意无违，虽成正觉而亦不断行菩萨行。何以故？菩萨摩诃萨发大誓愿，入无边无碍用门，善巧示现故。

"佛子，菩萨摩诃萨有十种游戏，何等为十？所谓：以众生身作刹身，而亦不坏众生身，是菩萨游戏；以刹身作众生身，而亦不坏于刹身，是菩萨游戏；于佛身示现声闻、独觉身，而不损减如来身，是菩萨游戏；于声闻、独觉身示现如来身，而不增长声闻、独觉身，是菩萨游戏；于菩萨行身示现成正觉身，而亦不断菩萨行身，是菩萨游戏；

Chapter 38 — *Transcending the World*

    The unimpeded function of powers in relation to the absence of a teacher with which he becomes independently awakened to all dharmas;

    The unimpeded function of powers in relation to all-knowledge with which he attains right enlightenment through all-knowledge; and

    The unimpeded function of powers in relation to the great compassion with which he never abandons any being.

These are the ten.

Sons of the Buddha, factors such as these constitute what is meant by the bodhisattva-mahāsattva's ten kinds of unimpeded functions. Wherever there is anyone who acquires these ten kinds of unimpeded functions, he becomes one who, whether or not he wishes to gain *anuttarasamyaksaṃbodhi*, is but a matter of his own inclinations in which he would meet no opposition in either case. Although he could gain right enlightenment, he would still never cut off his practice of the bodhisattva practices. And why is this? This is because the bodhisattva-mahāsattva makes the great vow to enter boundlessly many gateways of unimpeded functions and uses skillful means to manifest them.

Sons of the Buddha, the bodhisattva-mahāsattva has ten kinds of easeful mastery. What are those ten? They are as follows:

    Using the body of a being, he creates the body of a *kṣetra* and yet still does not damage the body of that being. This is an instance of the bodhisattva's easeful mastery;

    Using the body of a *kṣetra*, he creates the body of a being and yet still does not damage the body of that *kṣetra*. This is an instance of the bodhisattva's easeful mastery;

    He manifests the bodies of *śrāvaka* disciples and *pratyekabuddhas* in the body of a buddha and yet still does not thereby diminish the body of that *tathāgata*. This is an instance of the bodhisattva's easeful mastery;

    He manifests the body of a *tathāgata* in the bodies of *śrāvaka* disciples and *pratyekabuddhas* and yet still does not thereby bring about any increase in the bodies of those *śrāvaka* disciples and *pratyekabuddhas*. This is an instance of the bodhisattva's easeful mastery;

    He manifests a body gaining right enlightenment in a body which practices the bodhisattva practices and yet still does not thereby cut short the actions of that body practicing the bodhisattva practices. This is an instance of the bodhisattva's easeful mastery;

正體字

於成正覺身。示現修菩薩行身。而亦不減
295b04 ∥ 成菩提身。是菩薩遊戲。於涅槃界。示現生死
295b05 ∥ 身。而不著生死。是菩薩遊戲。於生死界。示現
295b06 ∥ 涅槃。亦不究竟。入於涅槃。是菩薩遊戲。入於
295b07 ∥ 三昧。而示現行住坐臥一切業。亦不捨三昧
295b08 ∥ 正受。是菩薩遊戲。在一佛所。聞法受持。其身
295b09 ∥ 不動。而以三昧力。於不可說諸佛會中。各各
295b10 ∥ 現身。亦不分身。亦不起定。而聞法受持。相續
295b11 ∥ 不斷。如是念念。於一一三昧身。各出生不可
295b12 ∥ 說不可說三昧身。如是次第一切諸劫。猶可
295b13 ∥ 窮盡。而菩薩三昧身。不可窮盡。是菩薩遊戲。
295b14 ∥ 是為十。若諸菩薩安住此法。則得如來無上
295b15 ∥ 大智遊戲。佛子。菩薩摩訶薩。有十種境界。何
295b16 ∥ 等為十。所謂示現無邊法界門。令眾生得入。
295b17 ∥ 是菩薩境界。示現一切世界無量妙莊嚴。令
295b18 ∥ 眾生得入。是菩薩境界。化往一切眾生界。悉
295b19 ∥ 方便開悟。是菩薩境界。

简体字

于成正觉身示现修菩萨行身，而亦不减成菩提身，是菩萨游戏；于涅槃界示现生死身，而不著生死，是菩萨游戏；于生死界示现涅槃，亦不究竟入于涅槃，是菩萨游戏；入于三昧而示现行、住、坐、卧一切业，亦不舍三昧正受，是菩萨游戏；在一佛所闻法受持，其身不动，而以三昧力，于不可说诸佛会中各各现身，亦不分身，亦不起定，而闻法受持相续不断，如是念念于一一三昧身各出生不可说不可说三昧身，如是次第一切诸劫犹可穷尽，而菩萨三昧身不可穷尽，是菩萨游戏。是为十。若诸菩萨安住此法，则得如来无上大智游戏。

"佛子，菩萨摩诃萨有十种境界。何等为十？所谓：示现无边法界门，令众生得入，是菩萨境界；示现一切世界无量妙庄严，令众生得入，是菩萨境界；化往一切众生界，悉方便开悟，是菩萨境界；

Chapter 38 — *Transcending the World*

- He manifests a body cultivating the bodhisattva practices in the body that realizes the right enlightenment and yet still does not thereby diminish that body that realizes bodhi. This is an instance of the bodhisattva's easeful mastery;
- He manifests a *saṃsāra* body in the realm of nirvāṇa and yet does not become attached to *saṃsāra*. This is an instance of the bodhisattva's easeful mastery;
- He manifests nirvāṇa in the realm of *saṃsāra* and yet still does not then achieve the ultimate entry into nirvāṇa. This is an instance of the bodhisattva's easeful mastery;
- He enters samādhi and then manifests all of the actions of walking, standing, sitting, and lying down, and yet he still does not relinquish the right meditative absorption of samādhi. This is an instance of the bodhisattva's easeful mastery; and
- He resides with an unmoving body in the presence of a single buddha, listening to the Dharma, absorbing it, and retaining it even as, through the power of samādhi, he manifests bodies in the congregations of every one of an ineffable number of buddhas. Yet he still does not create any division bodies and still does not arise from meditative concentration as he continuously and ceaselessly listens to those expositions of Dharma, absorbing and retaining them. In this manner, in each successive mind-moment, he sends forth from each and every one of those samādhi-dwelling bodies an ineffable-ineffable number of additional samādhi-dwelling bodies. Though all the kalpas through which he sequentially passes in this way might still come to an end, those bodhisattva samādhi-dwelling bodies still could never come to an end. This is an instance of the bodhisattva's easeful mastery.

These are the ten. If bodhisattvas abide in these dharmas, then they acquire the easeful mastery of the Tathāgata's unexcelled great wisdom.

Sons of the Buddha, the bodhisattva-mahāsattva has ten kinds of spheres of action. What are those ten? They are as follows:

- Revealing boundlessly many gateways to the Dharma realm and enabling beings to enter them is a sphere of action of the bodhisattva;
- Revealing the countless marvelous adornments of all worlds and enabling beings to enter them is a sphere of action of the bodhisattva;
- Creating transformations that travel to the realms of all beings and use skillful means to awaken them all is a sphere of action of the bodhisattva;

正體字

於如來身。出菩薩身。
於菩薩身。出如來身。是菩薩境界。於虛空界。
現世界。於世界。現虛空界。是菩薩境界。於生
死界。現涅槃界。於涅槃界。現生死界。是菩薩
境界。於一眾生語言中。出生一切佛法語言。
是菩薩境界。以無邊身。現作一身。一身。作一
切差別身。是菩薩境界。以一身。充滿一切法
界。是菩薩境界。於一念中。令一切眾生。發菩
提心。各現無量身。成等正覺。是菩薩境界。是
為十。若諸菩薩。安住此法。則得如來無上大
智慧境界。佛子。菩薩摩訶薩。有十種力。何等
為十。所謂深心力。不雜一切世情故。增上深
心力。不捨一切佛法故。方便力。諸有所作究
竟故。智力。了知一切心行故。願力。一切所求
令滿故。行力。盡未來際不斷故。乘力。能出生
一切乘。而不捨大乘故。

简体字

于如来身出菩萨身，于菩萨身出如来身，是菩萨境界；于虚空界现世界，于世界现虚空界，是菩萨境界；于生死界现涅槃界，于涅槃界现生死界，是菩萨境界；于一众生语言中，出生一切佛法语言，是菩萨境界；以无边身现作一身，一身作一切差别身，是菩萨境界；以一身充满一切法界，是菩萨境界；于一念中，令一切众生发菩提心，各现无量身成等正觉，是菩萨境界。是为十。若诸菩萨安住此法，则得如来无上大智慧境界。

"佛子，菩萨摩诃萨有十种力。何等为十？所谓：深心力，不杂一切世情故；增上深心力，不舍一切佛法故；方便力，诸有所作究竟故；智力，了知一切心行故；愿力，一切所求令满故；行力，尽未来际不断故；乘力，能出生一切乘，而不舍大乘故；

Chapter 38 — *Transcending the World*

- To emanate bodhisattva bodies from a *tathāgata*'s body and emanate *tathāgata* bodies from a bodhisattva body is a sphere of action of the bodhisattva;
- To manifest worlds in the realm of empty space and manifest realms of empty space among worlds is a sphere of action of the bodhisattva;
- To manifest the realm of nirvāṇa in the realm of *saṃsāra* and manifest the realm of *saṃsāra* in the realm of *nirvāṇa* is a sphere of action of the bodhisattva;
- To produce the language of the Dharma of all buddhas from the language of a single being is a sphere of action of the bodhisattva;
- To use boundlessly many bodies to manifest the creation of a single body and to manifest the creation of all different kinds of bodies from a single body is a sphere of action of the bodhisattva;
- To use a single body to completely fill the entire Dharma realm is a sphere of action of the bodhisattva; and
- To enable all beings in but a single mind-moment to resolve to attain bodhi whereupon each of them manifests countless bodies realizing the right and perfect enlightenment is a sphere of action of the bodhisattva.

These are the ten. If bodhisattvas abide in these dharmas, then they gain the sphere of action of the Tathāgata's unexcelled great wisdom.

Sons of the Buddha, the bodhisattva-mahāsattva has ten [other] kinds of powers. What are those ten? They are as follows:

- The power of the deep mind by which he does not mix in any worldly sentiments;
- The power of the predominant deep mind by which he never abandons any of the dharmas of the Buddha;
- The power of skillful means by which whatever he does is ultimate;
- The power of knowledge by which he completely knows all mental actions;
- The power of vows by which he enables the fulfillment of whatever he strives to accomplish;
- The power of the practices by which he continues on to the very end of future time;
- The power of the vehicles by which he is able to manifest all the vehicles while still never abandoning the Great Vehicle;

正體字

神變力。於一一毛孔中。各各示現一切清淨世界。一切如來。出興世故。菩提力。令一切眾生。發心成佛。無斷絕故。轉法輪力。說一句法。悉稱一切眾生諸根性欲故。是為十。若諸菩薩。安住此法。則得諸佛無上一切智十力

佛子。菩薩摩訶薩。有十種無畏。何等為十。佛子。菩薩摩訶薩。悉能聞持一切言說。作如是念。設有眾生無量無邊。從十方來。以百千大法。而問於我。我於彼問。不見微少。難可答相。以不見故。心得無畏。究竟到彼大無畏岸。隨其所問。悉能[1]酬對。斷其疑惑。無有怯弱。是為菩薩第一無畏。佛子。菩薩摩訶薩。得如來灌頂。無礙辯才。到於一切文字言音。開示祕密究竟彼岸。作如是念。設有眾生無量無邊。從十方來。以無量法。而問於我。我於彼問。不見微少。難可答相。以不見故。心得無畏。究竟到彼大無畏岸。隨其所問。悉能[*]酬對。斷其疑惑。無有恐懼。是為菩薩第二無畏。佛子。菩薩摩訶薩。知一切法空。離我離我所。無作無作者。無知者。無命者。無養育者。

简体字

神变力，于一一毛孔中，各各示现一切清净世界一切如来出兴世故；菩提力，令一切众生发心成佛无断绝故；转法轮力，说一句法悉称一切众生诸根性欲故。是为十。若诸菩萨安住此法，则得诸佛无上一切智十力。

"佛子，菩萨摩诃萨有十种无畏。何等为十？佛子，菩萨摩诃萨悉能闻持一切言说，作如是念：'设有众生无量无边从十方来，以百千大法而问于我。我于彼问不见微少难可答相；以不见故，心得无畏，究竟到彼大无畏岸，随其所问悉能酬对，断其疑惑无有怯弱。'是为菩萨第一无畏。佛子，菩萨摩诃萨得如来灌顶无碍辩才，到于一切文字言音开示秘密究竟彼岸，作如是念：'设有众生无量无边从十方来，以无量法而问于我。我于彼问不见微少难可答相；以不见故，心得无畏，究竟到彼大无畏岸，随其所问悉能酬对，断其疑惑无有恐惧。'是为菩萨第二无畏。佛子，菩萨摩诃萨知一切法空，离我、离我所，无作、无作者，无知者，无命者，无养育者，

The power of spiritual transformations by which, in every pore, he reveals all the pure worlds and all the *tathāgatas* appearing in the world;

The power of bodhi by which he incessantly enables all beings to resolve to become buddhas; and

The power of turning the Dharma wheel by which, in explaining but a single sentence of Dharma, he matches the faculties, natures, and aspirations of all beings.

These are the ten. If bodhisattvas abide in these dharmas, then they acquire all buddhas' unexcelled all-knowledge and ten powers.

Sons of the Buddha, the bodhisattva-mahāsattva has ten kinds of fearlessness. What are those ten? They are as follows:

Sons of the Buddha, the bodhisattva-mahāsattva is so well able to hear and retain all speech that he hears that he reflects in this way: "Even if countlessly and boundlessly many beings were to come here from all the ten directions and then use a hundred thousand great dharmas to pose questions to me, I would not see in any of their questions even the slightest aspect worthy of considering their questions difficult to answer." Due to seeing no difficulty in this, his mind becomes fearless and he reaches the ultimate perfection of great fearlessness. No matter what they might ask, he is able to reply in a manner that severs the questioner's doubts without feeling any sort of timidity. This is the first of the bodhisattva's kinds of fearlessness;

Sons of the Buddha, the bodhisattva-mahāsattva acquires the Tathāgata's crown-anointing consecration and the unimpeded eloquence with which he achieves ultimate perfection in explaining the esoteric meaning of all writing and speech. He reflects in this way: "Even if countlessly and boundlessly many beings were to come here from all the ten directions and then used countless dharmas to question me, I would not see in any of their questions even the slightest aspect worthy of considering their questions difficult to answer." Due to seeing no difficulty in this, his mind becomes fearless and he reaches the ultimate perfection of great fearlessness. No matter what they might ask, he is able to reply in a manner that severs the questioner's doubts without feeling any sort of fearful trepidation. This is the second of the bodhisattva's kinds of fearlessness;

Sons of the Buddha, the bodhisattva-mahāsattva realizes that all dharmas are empty, are devoid of a self, are devoid of anything belonging to a self, are devoid of anything done, are devoid of any agent of actions, are devoid of any knower, are devoid of any entity possessed of a life span, are devoid of any soul,[111]

正體字

無補伽羅。離蘊界處。永出諸見。心如虛空。作如是念。不見眾生。有微少相。能損惱我。身語意業。何以故。菩薩遠離我我所故。不見諸法。有少性相。以不見故。心得無畏。究竟到彼大無畏岸。堅固勇猛。不可沮壞。是為菩薩第三無畏。佛子。菩薩摩訶薩。佛力所護。佛力所持。住佛威儀。所行真實。無有變易。作如是念。我不見有少分威儀。令諸眾生。生訶責相。以不見故。心得無畏。於大眾中。安隱說法。是為菩薩第四無畏。佛子。菩薩摩訶薩。身語意業。皆悉清淨。鮮白柔和。遠離眾惡。作如是念。我不自見身語意業。而有少分。可訶責相。以不見故。心得無畏。能令眾生。住於佛法。是為菩薩第五無畏。佛子。菩薩摩訶薩。金剛力士。天龍夜叉乾闥婆阿修羅。帝釋梵王。四天王等。常隨侍衛。一切如來。護念不捨。菩薩摩訶薩。作如是念。我不見有眾魔外道。有見眾生。能來障我。行菩薩道少分之相。以不見故。心得無畏。究竟到彼大無畏岸。

简体字

无补伽罗，离蕴、界、处，永出诸见，心如虚空，作如是念：'不见众生有微少相能损恼我身、语、意业。'何以故？菩萨远离我、我所故，不见诸法有少性相。以不见故，心得无畏，究竟到彼大无畏岸，坚固勇猛，不可沮坏，是为菩萨第三无畏。佛子，菩萨摩诃萨佛力所护、佛力所持，住佛威仪，所行真实，无有变易，作如是念：'我不见有少分威仪，令诸众生生诃责相。'以不见故，心得无畏，于大众中安隐说法，是为菩萨第四无畏。佛子，菩萨摩诃萨身、语、意业皆悉清净，鲜白柔和，远离众恶，作如是念：'我不自见身、语、意业而有少分可诃责相。'以不见故，心得无畏，能令众生住于佛法，是为菩萨第五无畏。佛子，菩萨摩诃萨，金刚力士、天、龙、夜叉、乾闼婆、阿修罗、帝释、梵王、四天王等常随侍卫，一切如来护念不舍。菩萨摩诃萨作如是念：'我不见有众魔外道有见众生能来障我行菩萨道少分之相。'以不见故，心得无畏，究竟到彼大无畏岸，

are devoid of any *pudgala*, and are apart from any of the aggregates, sense realms, or sense bases. He has forever transcended all views and his mind is like empty space. He reflects in this way: "I do not see even the slightest sign that there might be any being able to injure or trouble me through any physical, verbal, or mental action." And why is this so? This is because the bodhisattva has abandoned the self and all possessions of a self. He does not perceive the existence of any dharma at all that is possessed of even the slightest nature or characteristic. Because he sees no such thing, his mind becomes fearless and he reaches the ultimate perfection of great fearlessness. He is so steadfast and courageous that he cannot be obstructed. This is the third of the bodhisattva's kinds of fearlessness;

Sons of the Buddha, the bodhisattva-mahāsattva is protected by the Buddha's power, is sustained by the Buddha's power, and abides in the Buddha's awesome deportment. Whatever he practices is genuine and unchanging. He reflects in this way: "I do not perceive even the slightest aspect of this awesome deportment that might give any being cause to criticize it." On account of seeing no such thing, his mind gains that fearlessness by which, in the midst of the Great Assembly, he remains peaceful and secure in his expositions of the Dharma. This is the fourth of the bodhisattva's kinds of fearlessness;

Sons of the Buddha, the bodhisattva-mahāsattva's physical, verbal, and mental karmic actions are all pure, immaculate, gentle, and free of the many kinds of evil. He reflects in this way: "I do not perceive in any of my physical, verbal, or mental actions even the slightest aspect worthy of criticism." Due to seeing no such thing, his mind achieves that fearlessness by which he is able to cause beings to dwell in the Buddha's Dharma. This is the fifth of the bodhisattva's kinds of fearlessness;

Sons of the Buddha, the bodhisattva-mahāsattva is always followed and protected by vajra stalwarts, devas, dragons, *yakṣas*, *gandharvas*, *asuras*, Śakra, the Brahma Heaven King, the Four Heavenly Kings, and others. He is held in protective mindfulness by all *tathāgatas* and is never abandoned by them. The bodhisattva-mahāsattva reflects in this way: "I do not see even the slightest sign that any among the many *māras*, the adherents of the non-Buddhist traditions, or beings holding the view that existence is real might be able to come and obstruct my practice of the Bodhisattva path." Due to seeing no such thing, his mind becomes fearless and he reaches the ultimate perfection of great fearlessness. He brings forth a mind of joyous delight in

正體字

發歡喜心。行菩薩行。是為菩薩第六無畏。佛子。菩薩摩訶薩。已得成就第一念根。心無忘失。佛所悅可。作如是念。如來所說。成菩提道。文字句法。我不於中。見有少分忘失之相。以不見故。心得無畏。受持一切如來正法。行菩薩行。是為菩薩第七無畏。佛子。菩薩摩訶薩。智慧方便。悉已通達。菩薩諸力。皆得究竟。常勤教化一切眾生。恒以願心。繫佛菩提。而為悲愍眾生故。成就眾生故。於煩惱濁世。示現受生。種族尊貴。眷屬圓滿。所欲從心。歡娛快樂。而作是念。我雖與此眷屬聚會。不見少相而可貪著。廢我修行。禪定解脫。及諸三昧。總持辯才。菩薩道法。何以故。菩薩摩訶薩。於一切法。已得自在。到於彼岸。修菩薩行。誓不斷絕。不見世間。有一境界。而能惑亂菩薩道者。以不見故。心得無畏。究竟到彼大無畏岸。以大願力。於一切世界。示現受生。是為菩薩第八無畏。

简体字

发欢喜心行菩萨行,是为菩萨第六无畏。佛子,菩萨摩诃萨已得成就第一念根,心无忘失佛所悦可,作如是念:'如来所说成菩提道文字句法,我不于中见有少分忘失之相。'以不见故,心得无畏,受持一切如来正法行菩萨行,是为菩萨第七无畏。佛子,菩萨摩诃萨智慧方便悉已通达,菩萨诸力皆得究竟,常勤教化一切众生,恒以愿心系佛菩提,而为悲愍众生故,成就众生故,于烦恼浊世示现受生、种族尊贵、眷属圆满、所欲从心、欢娱快乐,而作是念:'我虽与此眷属聚会,不见少相而可贪著,废我修行禅定、解脱,及诸三昧、总持、辩才、菩萨道法。'何以故?菩萨摩诃萨于一切法已得自在到于彼岸,修菩萨行誓不断绝,不见世间有一境界而能惑乱菩萨道者。以不见故,心得无畏,究竟到彼大无畏岸,以大愿力于一切世界示现受生,是为菩萨第八无畏。

Chapter 38 — *Transcending the World*

his practice of the bodhisattva practices. This is the sixth of the bodhisattva's kinds of fearlessness;

Sons of the Buddha, the bodhisattva-mahāsattva has already perfected the foremost faculty of mindfulness. His mind has become free of forgetfulness and is approved of by the Buddha. He reflects in this way: "In the Dharma of the scriptures and statements of the path to bodhi as proclaimed by the Tathāgata, I do not see even the slightest sign that I might have forgotten any of it." Due to seeing no such sign, his mind becomes fearless in absorbing and sustaining the right Dharma of all Tathāgatas and in practicing the bodhisattva practices. This is the seventh of the bodhisattva's kinds of fearlessness;

Sons of the Buddha, the bodhisattva-mahāsattva has already gained a penetrating comprehension of wisdom and skillful means and he has already reached the ultimate development of all the powers of the bodhisattva. He always diligently teaches all beings and he constantly relies on the resolve of his vows to keep him connected to the bodhi of the Buddha. Even so, because of his compassionate pity for beings and because he is devoted to ripening beings, he manifests the appearance of taking birth in worlds beset by the turbidity of the afflictions, being born into a venerable and noble clan with a full retinue in circumstances where whatever he desires appears at will and he is able to delight in the pleasures and dwell in happiness. Still, he reflects in this way: "Although I have gathered together here with this retinue, I do not see even the slightest sign of anything worthy of any desire-based attachment which would lead to the deterioration of my cultivation of the dharmas of the bodhisattva path, including the *dhyāna* absorptions, the liberations, the samādhis, the complete-retention *dhāraṇīs*, and eloquence."

And why is this so? This is because the bodhisattva-mahāsattva has already achieved perfection in the sovereign mastery of all dharmas. He has vowed to never discontinue his cultivation of the bodhisattva practices and he does not see anywhere in the world even a single sphere of experience which could delude or confuse one who is on the bodhisattva path. Due to seeing no such thing, his mind becomes fearless and he reaches the ultimate perfection of great fearlessness. Hence, relying on the power of his great vows, he manifests the taking on of births in all worlds. This is the eighth of the bodhisattva's kinds of fearlessness;

正體字

佛子。菩薩摩
訶薩。恒不忘失薩婆若心。乘於大乘。行菩薩
行。以一切智。大心勢力。示現一切聲聞獨覺。
寂靜威儀。[1]作是念言。我不自見。當於二乘。
而取出離。少分之相。以不見故。心得無畏。到
彼無上大無畏岸。普能示現一切乘道。究竟
滿足平等大乘。是為菩薩第九無畏。佛子。菩
薩摩訶薩。成就一切諸白淨法。具足善根。圓
滿神通。究竟住於諸佛菩提。滿足一切諸菩
薩行。於諸佛所。受一切智灌頂之記。而常化
眾生。行菩薩道。作如是念。我不自見有一眾
生。應可成熟。而不能現諸佛自在。而成熟相。
以不見故。心得無畏。究竟到彼大無畏岸。不
斷菩薩行。不捨菩薩願。隨所應化一切眾生。
現佛境界。而化度之。是為菩薩第十無畏。佛
子。是為菩薩摩訶薩。十種無畏。若諸菩薩。安
住此法。則得諸佛無上大無畏。而亦不捨菩
薩無畏。佛子。菩薩摩訶薩。有十種不共法。何
等為十。佛子。菩薩摩訶薩。不由他教。自然修
行六波羅蜜。常樂大施。不生慳吝。恒持淨戒。
無所毀犯。具足忍辱。心不動搖。

简体字

佛子，菩萨摩诃萨恒不忘失萨婆若心，乘于大乘行菩萨行，以一切智大心势力，示现一切声闻、独觉寂静威仪，作如是念："我不自见当于二乘而取出离少分之相。"以不见故，心得无畏，到彼无上大无畏岸，普能示现一切乘道，究竟满足平等大乘，是为菩萨第九无畏。佛子，菩萨摩诃萨成就一切诸白净法，具足善根，圆满神通，究竟住于诸佛菩提，满足一切诸菩萨行，于诸佛所受一切智灌顶之记，而常化众生行菩萨道，作如是念："我不自见有一众生应可成熟而不能现诸佛自在而成熟相。"以不见故，心得无畏，究竟到彼大无畏岸，不断菩萨行，不舍菩萨愿，随所应化一切众生现佛境界而化度之，是为菩萨第十无畏。佛子，是为菩萨摩诃萨十种无畏。若诸菩萨安住此法，则得诸佛无上大无畏，而亦不舍菩萨无畏。

"佛子，菩萨摩诃萨有十种不共法。何等为十？佛子，菩萨摩诃萨不由他教，自然修行六波罗蜜——常乐大施，不生悭吝；恒持净戒，无所毁犯；具足忍辱，心不动摇；

Sons of the Buddha, the bodhisattva-mahāsattva never forgets his resolve to gain all-knowledge. Riding in the Great Vehicle, he practices the bodhisattva practices. Using the strength of his great resolve to gain all-knowledge, he manifests the serene awesome deportment of the *śrāvaka* disciple and *pratyekabuddha* practitioners. He reflects in this way: "I do not perceive in myself even the slightest sign of any inclination to seize on emancipation in reliance on the two vehicles." Due to seeing no such thing, his mind becomes fearless and he reaches the perfection of unexcelled great fearlessness. He is everywhere able to manifest the paths of all vehicles even as he achieves the ultimate fulfillment of the impartial Great Vehicle. This is the ninth of the bodhisattva's kinds of fearlessness; and

Sons of the Buddha, the bodhisattva-mahāsattva perfects all the dharmas of purity, completely fulfills the roots of goodness, perfectly fulfills the spiritual superknowledges, and ultimately comes to abide in the Buddha's bodhi. He completely fulfills all the bodhisattva practices and receives from all buddhas the crown-anointing prediction of all-knowledge even as he always continues to teach beings and practice the bodhisattva path. He reflects in this way: "I do not perceive any sign of even a single being appropriate for ripening for whom I would not be able to manifest all buddhas' sovereign mastery in bringing about their ripening." Due to seeing no such thing, his mind becomes fearless and he reaches the ultimate perfection of great fearlessness. He never ceases the bodhisattva practices, never abandons the bodhisattva vows, and reveals the realms of the Buddha for whichever beings should be taught and thereby teaches and liberates them. This is the tenth of the bodhisattva's kinds of fearlessness.

Sons of the Buddha, these are the bodhisattva-mahāsattva's ten kinds of fearlessness. If bodhisattvas abide in these dharmas, then they acquire the unexcelled fearlessness of the Buddha and yet still do not relinquish the fearlessness of the bodhisattva.

Sons of the Buddha, the bodhisattva-mahāsattva has ten kinds of exclusive dharmas. What are those ten? They are as follows:

Sons of the Buddha, even without depending on teachings provided by others, the bodhisattva-mahāsattva naturally cultivates the six *pāramitās*. Thus he always delights in great giving and does not become miserly. He constantly upholds the pure moral precepts and remains free of transgressions against them. He completely fulfills the practice of patience by which his mind is never shaken. He possesses great vigor by which

正體字

有大精進。未
296b24 ｜ 曾退轉。善入諸禪。永無散亂。巧修智慧。悉除
296b25 ｜ 惡見。是為第一不由他教隨順波羅蜜道修
296b26 ｜ 六度不共法。佛子。菩薩摩訶薩。普能攝受一
296b27 ｜ 切眾生。所謂以財[2]及法。而行惠施。正念現
296b28 ｜ 前。和顏愛語。其心歡喜。示如實義。令得悟解
296b29 ｜ 諸佛菩提。無有憎嫌。平等利益。是為第二不
296c01 ｜ 由他教順四攝道勤攝眾生不共法。佛子。菩
296c02 ｜ 薩摩訶薩。善巧迴向。所謂不求果報迴向。順
296c03 ｜ 佛菩提迴向。不著一切世間禪定三昧迴向。
296c04 ｜ 為利益一切眾生迴向。為不斷如來智慧迴
296c05 ｜ 向。是為第三不由他教為諸眾生發起善根
296c06 ｜ 求佛智慧不共法。佛子。菩薩摩訶薩。到善
296c07 ｜ 巧方便。究竟彼岸。心恒顧復一切眾生。不
296c08 ｜ 厭世俗凡愚境界。不樂二乘出離之道。不
296c09 ｜ 著己樂。唯勤化度。善能入出禪定解脫。於
296c10 ｜ 諸三昧。悉得自在。往來生死。如遊園觀。未
296c11 ｜ 曾暫起疲厭之心。或住魔宮。或為釋天。梵王
296c12 ｜ 世主。一切生處。靡不於中。而現其身。

简体字

有大精进，未曾退转；善入诸禅，永无散乱；巧修智慧，悉除恶见。是为第一不由他教随顺波罗蜜道修六度不共法。佛子，菩萨摩诃萨普能摄受一切众生。所谓：以财及法而行惠施，正念现前，和颜爱语，其心欢喜，示如实义，令得悟解诸佛菩提，无有憎嫌，平等利益。是为第二不由他教顺四摄道勤摄众生不共法。佛子，菩萨摩诃萨善巧回向，所谓：不求果报回向、顺佛菩提回向、不著一切世间禅定三昧回向、为利益一切众生回向、为不断如来智慧回向。是为第三不由他教为诸众生发起善根求佛智慧不共法。佛子，菩萨摩诃萨到善巧方便究竟彼岸，心恒顾复一切众生，不厌世俗凡愚境界，不乐二乘出离之道，不著己乐，唯勤化度，善能入出禅定解脱，于诸三昧悉得自在，往来生死如游园观，未曾暂起疲厌之心；或住魔宫，或为释天、梵王、世主，一切生处靡不于中而现其身；

he never retreats. He skillfully enters the *dhyānas* and never becomes scattered. And he skillfully cultivates wisdom and rids himself of all wrong views. This is the first of his exclusive dharmas, that by which, without depending on teachings provided by others, he follows the path of the *pāramitās* and thus cultivates the six perfections;

Sons of the Buddha, the bodhisattva-mahāsattva is everywhere able to attract and gather in all beings, in particular doing so: by practicing kindly giving of material wealth or the Dharma; by manifesting right mindfulness and a harmonious countenance as he uses pleasing words in such a way that others are delighted; by revealing to them meanings in accordance with reality, thereby causing them to awaken to and understand the bodhi of all buddhas; and by remaining free of dislike or disapproval as he benefits others equally. This is the second of his exclusive dharmas, that by which, without depending on teachings provided by others, he accords with the path of the four means of attraction as he diligently attracts and gathers in beings;

Sons of the Buddha, the bodhisattva-mahāsattva is skillful in making dedications, namely: dedications in which he does not seek any resulting rewards; dedications which accord with the Buddha's bodhi; dedications in which he is not attached to any worldly *dhyāna* absorptions or samādhis; dedications for the benefit of beings; and dedications to prevent the severance of the wisdom of the Tathāgata. This is the third of his exclusive dharmas, that by which, without depending on teachings provided by others, for the benefit of others, he produces roots of goodness and seeks the wisdom of the Buddha;

Sons of the Buddha, the bodhisattva-mahāsattva achieves ultimate perfection in skillful means. His mind is constantly concerned with caring for all beings. Thus he does not detest the mind states of the world's foolish common people, does not delight in the path of emancipation of adherents of the two vehicles, and does not become attached to his own pleasures. Rather he only devotes himself to diligently teaching and liberating them.

He is well able to enter and emerge from the *dhyāna* samādhis and liberations. He gains sovereign mastery of all the samādhis and goes forth and returns in *saṃsāra* as if wandering about in gardens and terraces, never even briefly wearying of this. He sometimes dwells in the palace of the *māras*, sometimes becomes Śakra Deva, sometimes becomes the Brahma Heaven King, and sometimes becomes a ruler in the world. Of all the places of rebirth, there are none in which he does not manifest his bodies.

正體字

	或於外
296c13	道眾中出家。而恒遠離一切邪見。一切世間。
296c14	文詞呪術。字印算數。乃至遊戲歌舞之法。悉
296c15	皆示現。無不精巧。或時示作端正婦人。智
296c16	慧才能。世中第一。於諸世間出世間法。能
296c17	[3]問能說。問答斷疑。皆得究竟。一切世間出
296c18	世間事。亦悉通達。到於彼岸。一切眾生。恒
296c19	來瞻仰。雖現聲聞辟支佛威儀。而不失大乘
296c20	心。雖念念中。示成正覺而不斷菩薩行。是為
296c21	第四不由他教方便善巧究竟彼岸不共法。
296c22	佛子。菩薩摩訶薩。善知權實雙行道。智慧自
296c23	在。到於究竟。所謂住於涅槃。而示現生死。知
296c24	無眾生。而勤行教化。究竟寂滅。而現起煩惱。
296c25	住一堅密智慧法身。而普現無量諸眾生身。
296c26	常入深禪定。而示受欲樂。常遠離三界。而不
296c27	捨眾生。常樂法樂。而現有[4]采女。歌詠嬉戲。

简体字

或于外道众中出家，而恒远离一切邪见；一切世间文词、咒术、字印、算数，乃至游戏、歌舞之法，悉皆示现，无不精巧；或时示作端正妇人，智慧才能世中第一；于诸世间、出世间法能问能说，问答断疑皆得究竟；一切世间、出世间事亦悉通达到于彼岸，一切众生恒来瞻仰；虽现声闻、辟支佛威仪，而不失大乘心；虽念念中示成正觉，而不断菩萨行。是为第四不由他教方便善巧究竟彼岸不共法。佛子，菩萨摩诃萨善知权实双行道，智慧自在，到于究竟。所谓：住于涅槃而示现生死，知无众生而勤行教化，究竟寂灭而现起烦恼，住一坚密智慧法身而普现无量诸众生身，常入深禅定而示受欲乐，常远离三界而不舍众生，常乐法乐而现有婇女歌咏嬉戏，

Chapter 38 — *Transcending the World*

He may become a monastic within the communities of non-Buddhist traditions, but always stays far away from all their erroneous views. He may manifest the skills associated with all of the world's literary abilities, mantra formulae, calligraphy, seal carving, mathematics, and so forth, including even the methods of entertainments, singing, and dancing, having none of these in which his skills are not especially refined.

He may manifest in the form of a beautiful woman possessed of such wisdom and talent that it is foremost in the entire world, as one who has acquired the most ultimate ability to pose questions on, discuss, answer questions, and sever doubts about both worldly and world-transcending dharmas, as one who has achieved perfection in the penetrating comprehension of all worldly and world transcending matters, as one whom all beings constantly come to and look up to with admiration.

Although he manifests the awesome deportment of *śrāvaka* disciples and *pratyekabuddhas*, he still never loses his resolve to abide in the Great Vehicle. Although he manifests the realization of right enlightenment in each successive mind-moment, he still never quits practicing the bodhisattva practices. This is the fourth of his exclusive dharmas, that by which, without depending on teachings provided by others, he reaches the ultimate perfection of skillful means;

Sons of the Buddha, the bodhisattva-mahāsattva knows well the path of joint practice of both the provisional and the true and has reached the ultimate degree of the sovereign mastery of wisdom. That is to say:

He abides in nirvāṇa and yet manifests in *saṃsāra*;

He realizes that no beings exist and yet he diligently practices teaching them;

He has reached ultimate quiescence and yet may manifest the arising of afflictions;

He abides in the one Dharma body of solid wisdom and yet may everywhere manifest countless bodies of beings;

He is always immersed in deep *dhyāna* absorptions and yet may manifest as one who enjoys the pleasures of the desires;

He has forever left the three realms of existence and yet never abandons beings;

He always delights in Dharma bliss and yet may appear as attended by talented ladies who sing and provide joyous entertainments;

正體字

296c28 ｜ 雖以眾相好。莊嚴其身。而示受醜陋貧賤之
296c29 ｜ 形。常積集眾善。無諸過惡。而現生地獄畜生
296c30 ｜ 餓鬼。雖已到於佛智彼岸。而亦不捨菩薩智
297a01 ｜ 身。菩薩摩訶薩。成就如是無量智慧。聲聞獨
297a02 ｜ 覺。尚不能知。何況一切童蒙眾生。是為第五
297a03 ｜ 不由他教權實雙行不共法。佛子。菩薩摩訶
297a04 ｜ 薩。身口意業。隨智慧行。皆悉清淨。所謂具足
297a05 ｜ 大慈。永離殺心。乃至具足正解。無有邪見。是
297a06 ｜ 為第六不由他教身口意業隨智慧行不共
297a07 ｜ 法。佛子。菩薩摩訶薩。具足大悲。不捨眾生。
297a08 ｜ 代一切眾生。而受諸苦。所謂地獄苦。畜生苦。
297a09 ｜ 餓鬼苦。為利益故。不生勞倦。唯專度脫一切
297a10 ｜ 眾生。未曾[1]耽染五欲境界。常為精勤。滅除
297a11 ｜ 眾苦。是為第七不由他教常起大悲不共法。
297a12 ｜ 佛子。菩薩摩訶薩。常為眾生之所樂見。梵王
297a13 ｜ 帝釋。四天王等。一切眾生。見無厭足。何以故。

简体字

虽以众相好庄严其身而示受丑陋贫贱之形，常积集众善无诸过恶而现生地狱、畜生、饿鬼，虽已到于佛智彼岸而亦不舍菩萨智身。菩萨摩诃萨成就如是无量智慧，声闻、独觉尚不能知，何况一切童蒙众生？是为第五不由他教权实双行不共法。佛子，菩萨摩诃萨身、口、意业，随智慧行皆悉清净。所谓：具足大慈永离杀心，乃至具足正解无有邪见。是为第六不由他教身、口、意业随智慧行不共法。佛子，菩萨摩诃萨具足大悲，不舍众生，代一切众生而受诸苦，所谓：地狱苦、畜生苦、饿鬼苦。为利益故，不生劳倦，唯专度脱一切众生，未曾耽染五欲境界，常为精勤灭除众苦。是为第七不由他教常起大悲不共法。佛子，菩萨摩诃萨常为众生之所乐见，梵王、帝释、四天王等一切众生见无厌足。何以故？

Although his body is adorned with the many major marks and secondary signs, he may still manifest in the form of one who is ugly, poor, or of low social class;

He always accumulates the many types of goodness, remains free of all faults, and yet may manifest as one born into the hell realms, the animal realms, or the hungry ghost realms; and

Although he has already reached perfection in the buddha's wisdom, he still never relinquishes the bodhisattva's wisdom body.

The bodhisattva-mahāsattva perfects such measureless wisdom as this which cannot even be known of by *śrāvaka* disciples or *pratyekabuddhas*, how much the less by any of the ignorant common beings. This is the fifth of his exclusive dharmas, that by which, without depending on teachings provided by others, he implements the joint practice of both the provisional and the true;

Sons of the Buddha, the physical, verbal, and mental actions of the bodhisattva-mahāsattva are enacted in accordance with the wisdom and are all pure. That is to say, he is fully possessed of great kindness, forever abandons the motivation to kill, is fully possessed of right understanding, and is free of wrong views. This is the sixth of his exclusive dharmas, that by which, without depending on teachings provided by others, his physical, verbal, and mental actions are enacted in accordance with wisdom;

Sons of the Buddha, the bodhisattva-mahāsattva is fully possessed of the great compassion, never abandons beings, and substitutes for all beings in undergoing sufferings, in particular, the sufferings of the hells, the sufferings of the animals, and the sufferings of the hungry ghosts, doing so in order to benefit beings and never growing weary of this. He wishes only to liberate all beings and never indulges in any of the defiled spheres of experience related to the five types of desire. He is always intensely diligent in extinguishing the many kinds of sufferings. This is the seventh of his exclusive dharmas, that by which, without depending on teachings provided by others, he always arouses the great compassion;

Sons of the Buddha, the bodhisattva-mahāsattva is one whom beings always delight in seeing. The Brahma Heaven King, Śakra, the Four Heavenly Kings, and the other devas as well as all beings never weary of seeing him. And why is this? From the long distant past on forward to the present, the

正體字

297a14 菩薩摩訶薩。久遠世來。行業清淨。無有過失。
297a15 是故眾生。見者無厭。是為第八不由他教一
297a16 切眾生皆悉樂見不共法。佛子。菩薩摩訶薩。
297a17 於薩婆若。大誓莊嚴。志樂堅固。雖處凡夫聲
297a18 聞獨覺。險難之處。終不退失一切智心明淨
297a19 妙寶。佛子。如有寶珠。名淨莊嚴。置泥[2]潦中。
297a20 光色不改。能令濁水。悉皆澄淨。菩薩摩訶薩。
297a21 亦復如是。雖在凡愚雜濁等處。終不失壞求
297a22 一切智清淨寶心。而能令彼諸惡眾生。遠離
297a23 妄見。煩惱穢濁。得求一切智清淨心寶。是為
297a24 第九不由他教在眾難處不失一切智心寶不
297a25 共法。佛子。菩薩摩訶薩。成就自覺境界智。無
297a26 師自悟。究竟自在。到於彼岸。離垢法繒。以冠
297a27 其首。而於善友。不捨親近。於諸如來。常樂尊
297a28 重。是為第十不由他教得最上法不離善知
297a29 識不捨尊重佛不共法。佛子。是為菩薩摩訶
297b01 薩。十種不共法。若諸菩薩。安住其中。則得如
297b02 來無上廣大不共法。佛子。菩薩摩訶薩。有十
297b03 種業。何等為十。所謂

简体字

菩萨摩诃萨久远世来,行业清净无有过失,是故众生见者无厌。是为第八不由他教一切众生皆悉乐见不共法。佛子,菩萨摩诃萨于萨婆若大誓庄严志乐坚固,虽处凡夫、声闻、独觉险难之处,终不退失一切智心明净妙宝。佛子,如有宝珠,名净庄严,置泥潦中光色不改,能令浊水悉皆澄净。菩萨摩诃萨亦复如是,虽在凡愚杂浊等处,终不失坏求一切智清净宝心,而能令彼诸恶众生远离妄见、烦恼、秽浊,得求一切智清净心宝。是为第九不由他教在众难处不失一切智心宝不共法。佛子,菩萨摩诃萨成就自觉境界智,无师自悟,究竟自在到于彼岸,离垢法缯以冠其首,而于善友不舍亲近,于诸如来常乐尊重,是为第十不由他教得最上法不离善知识、不舍尊重佛不共法。佛子,是为菩萨摩诃萨十种不共法。若诸菩萨安住其中,则得如来无上广大不共法。

"佛子,菩萨摩诃萨有十种业。何等为十?所谓:

bodhisattva-mahāsattva has practiced deeds which are pure and free of all faults. It is for this reason that beings who see him never grow weary of this. This is the eighth of his exclusive dharmas, that by which, without depending on teachings provided by others, he becomes one whom all beings delight in seeing;

Sons of the Buddha, the bodhisattva-mahāsattva's [quest to attain] all-knowledge is adorned with the great vow and characterized by solidly enduring zeal. Although he resides in the dangerous and difficult abodes of common people, *śrāvaka* disciples, and *pratyekabuddhas*, he never retreats from or loses the bright, pure, and marvelous jewel of his resolve to attain all-knowledge;

Sons of the Buddha, just as there is a precious jewel known as "pure adornment" which, when placed in muddy water, its radiance and color remain unchanged and it retains the capacity to clarify and purify those turbid waters, so too it is with the bodhisattva-mahāsattva. Although he resides in the foolish common person's places so characterized by the various kinds of turbidity and such, he still never loses his resolve to seek the pure jewel of all-knowledge, and yet he is still able to cause those beings ensconced in all kinds of evil to depart far from the filth and turbidity of their wrong views and afflictions and then become able themselves to seek the pure mind jewel of all-knowledge. This is the ninth of his exclusive dharmas, that by which, without depending on teachings provided by others and even when residing in the many kinds of difficult circumstances, he never loses the jewel of his resolve to attain all-knowledge; and

Sons of the Buddha, the bodhisattva-mahāsattva completely develops the knowledge of his self-enlightened sphere of cognition and reaches perfection in gaining ultimate sovereign mastery in his self-awakening attained without a teacher. He uses the headband of immaculately pure Dharma to crown his head, never abandons his close relationship with his good spiritual guide, and always delights in revering all the *tathāgatas*. This is the tenth of his exclusive dharmas, that by which, without depending on teachings provided by others, he acquires the most supreme Dharma, never parts from his good spiritual guide, and never abandons his veneration of the Buddha.

Sons of the Buddha, these are the bodhisattva-mahāsattva's ten kinds of exclusive dharmas. If bodhisattvas abide in these, then they acquire the Tathāgata's unexcelled and vast exclusive dharmas.

Sons of the Buddha, the bodhisattva-mahāsattva has ten kinds of works. What are those ten? They are as follows:

正體字

一切世界業。悉能嚴淨故。一切諸佛業。悉能供養故。一切菩薩業。同種善根故。一切眾生業。悉能教化故。一切未來業。盡未來際攝取故。一切神力業。不離一世界遍至一切世界故。一切光明業。放無邊色光明。一一光中。有蓮華座。各有菩薩。結[3]跏趺坐。而顯現故。一切三寶種不斷業。諸佛滅後。守護住持諸佛法故。一切變化業。於一切世界。說法教化諸眾生故。一切加持業。於一念中。隨諸眾生心之所欲。皆為示現。令一切願。悉成滿故。是為十。若諸菩薩。安住此法。則得如來無上廣大業。佛子。菩薩摩訶薩。有十種身。何等為十。所謂不來身。於一切世間。不受生故。不去身。於一切世間。求不得故。不實身。一切世間。如實得故。不虛身。以如實理。示世間故。不盡身。盡未來際。無斷絕故。堅固身。一切眾魔。不能壞故。不動身。眾魔外道。不能動故。

简体字

一切世界业，悉能严净故；一切诸佛业，悉能供养故；一切菩萨业，同种善根故；一切众生业，悉能教化故；一切未来业，尽未来际摄取故；一切神力业，不离一世界遍至一切世界故；一切光明业，放无边色光明，一一光中有莲华座，各有菩萨结跏趺坐而显现故；一切三宝种不断业，诸佛灭后，守护住持诸佛法故；一切变化业，于一切世界说法教化诸众生故；一切加持业，于一念中随诸众生心之所欲皆为示现，令一切愿悉成满故。是为十。若诸菩萨安住此法，则得如来无上广大业。

"佛子，菩萨摩诃萨有十种身。何等为十？所谓：不来身，于一切世间不受生故；不去身，于一切世间求不得故；不实身，一切世间如实得故；不虚身，以如实理示世间故；不尽身，尽未来际无断绝故；坚固身，一切众魔不能坏故；不动身，众魔外道不能动故；

Chapter 38 — *Transcending the World*

Works related to all worlds, based on his ability to purify them all;

Works related to all buddhas, based on his ability to make offerings to them all;

Works related to all bodhisattvas, based on his ability to plant roots of goodness the same as theirs;

Works related to all beings, based on his ability to teach them all;

Works related to all of future time, based on his continuing to attract and gather them in until the very end of future time;

Works related to all the spiritual powers, based on his never leaving one world even as he travels everywhere to all worlds;

Works related to all light, based on his emanation of rays of light of boundlessly many colors, every ray of which has a lotus flower throne on each of which he manifests a bodhisattva sitting there in the lotus posture;

Works related to preventing the lineages of all Three Jewels from ever being cut off, based on his continuing to preserve, protect, and sustain the Dharma of all buddhas after the buddhas have passed into *parinirvāṇa*;

Works related to all spiritual transformations, based on his proclaiming the Dharma and teaching beings in all worlds; and

Works related to all his empowerments, based on his adaptation in but a single mind-moment to whatever beings' minds wish for by manifesting for them all and enabling all their wishes to be completely fulfilled.

These are the ten. If bodhisattvas abide in these dharmas, then they acquire the Tathāgata's unexcelled vast works.

Sons of the Buddha, the bodhisattva-mahāsattva has ten kinds of bodies. What are those ten? They are as follows:

The body that does not come forth, so called because it does not take on births in any world;

The body that does not go forth, so called because it is inapprehensible in any world;

The unreal body, so called because, in all worlds, it is [only] as if truly acquired;[112]

The non-false body, so called because, it is by resort to reality-accordant noumenal principle[113] that it appears in the world;

The unending body, so called because it continues on to the very end of the future without being cut off;

The solid body, so called because none of all the many kinds of *māras* are able to destroy it;

The unmoving body, so called because it cannot be moved by any of the many kinds of *māras* or adherents of non-Buddhist paths;

正體字

具相身。示現清淨百福相
297b21 故。無相身。法相究竟。悉無相故。普至身。與
297b22 三世佛。同一身故。是為十。若諸菩薩。安住此
297b23 法。則得如來無上無盡之身
297b24 佛子。菩薩摩訶薩。有十種身業。何等為十。所
297b25 謂一身充滿一切世界身業。於一切眾生前。
297b26 悉能示現身業。於一切趣。悉能受生身業。遊
297b27 行一切世界身業。往詣一切諸佛。眾會身業。
297b28 能以一手。普覆一切世界身業。能以一手。磨
297b29 一切世界金剛圍山。碎如微塵身業。於自身
297c01 中。現一切佛剎成壞。示於眾生身業。以一身。
297c02 容受一切眾生界身業。於自身中。普現一切
297c03 清淨佛剎。一切眾生。於中成道身業。是為十。
297c04 若諸菩薩。安住此法。則得如來無上佛業。悉
297c05 能覺悟一切眾生。佛子。菩薩摩訶薩。復有十
297c06 種身。何等為十。所謂諸波羅蜜身。悉正修行
297c07 故。四攝身。不捨一切眾生故。

简体字

具相身，示现清净百福相故；无相身，法相究竟悉无相故；普至身，与三世佛同一身故。是为十。若诸菩萨安住此法，则得如来无上无尽之身。

"佛子，菩萨摩诃萨有十种身业。何等为十？所谓：一身充满一切世界身业；于一切众生前悉能示现身业；于一切趣悉能受生身业；游行一切世界身业；往诣一切诸佛众会身业；能以一手普覆一切世界身业；能以一手磨一切世界金刚围山碎如微尘身业；于自身中现一切佛刹成坏示于众生身业；以一身容受一切众生界身业；于自身中普现一切清净佛刹，一切众生于中成道身业。是为十。若诸菩萨安住此法，则得如来无上佛业，悉能觉悟一切众生。

"佛子，菩萨摩诃萨复有十种身。何等为十？所谓：诸波罗蜜身，悉正修行故；四摄身，不舍一切众生故；

Chapter 38 — *Transcending the World*

> The body possessed of the signs, so called because it manifests the pure signs arising from the hundredfold merits;
> The signless body, so called because the marks of dharmas are all devoid of any signs at all; and
> The body that reaches everywhere, so called because all buddhas of the three periods of time share this same single body.

These are the ten. If bodhisattvas abide in these dharmas, then they acquire the Tathāgata's unexcelled and endless body.

Sons of the Buddha, the bodhisattva-mahāsattva has ten kinds of physical actions. What are those ten? They are as follows:

> The physical actions by which a single body completely fills all worlds;
> The physical actions by which he is able to manifest directly before all beings;
> The physical actions by which he is able to take on births in all the destinies of rebirth;
> The physical actions by which he travels throughout all worlds;
> The physical actions by which he visits all buddhas and their congregations;
> The physical actions by which he is able to cover all worlds with one hand;
> The physical actions by which he is able with one hand to rub all worlds' vajra ring mountains and thus reduce them to atom-like particles;
> The physical actions by which he reveals within his own body the creation and destruction of all buddha *kṣetras* and shows this to beings;
> The physical actions by which he includes all realms of beings within a single body; and
> The physical actions by which he reveals within his own body all the pure buddha *kṣetras* in which all beings are attaining complete enlightenment.[114]

These are the ten. If bodhisattvas abide in these dharmas, then they acquire the Tathāgata's unexcelled actions of buddhas by which they are all able to awaken all beings.

Sons of the Buddha, the bodhisattva-mahāsattva has ten [other] kinds of bodies.[115] What are those ten? They are as follows:

> The body of the *pāramitās*, so called because of his correct cultivation of them all;
> The body of the four means of attraction, so called because he never abandons any being;

正體字

大悲身。代一切
眾生。受無量苦。無疲厭故。大慈身。救護一切
眾生故。福德身。饒益一切眾生故。智慧身。與
一切佛身。同一性故。法身。永離諸趣受生故。
方便身。於一切處現前故。神力身。示現一切
神變故。菩提身。隨樂隨時。成正覺故。是為十。
若諸菩薩。安住此法。則得如來無上大智慧
身。佛子。菩薩摩訶薩。有十種語。何等為十。
所謂柔軟語。使一切眾生。皆安隱故。甘露語。
令一切眾生。悉清涼故。不誑語。所有言說。皆
如實故。真實語。乃至夢中。無妄語故。廣大語。
一切釋梵。四天王等。皆尊敬故。甚深語。顯示
法性故。堅固語。說法無盡故。正直語。發言易
了故。種種語。隨時示現故。開悟一切眾生語。
隨其欲樂。令解了故。是為十。若諸菩薩。安住
此法。則得如來無上微妙語。佛子。菩薩摩訶
薩。有十種淨修語業。何等為十。所謂

简体字

大悲身，代一切众生受无量苦无疲厌故；大慈身，救护一切众生故；福德身，饶益一切众生故；智慧身，与一切佛身同一性故；法身，永离诸趣受生故；方便身，于一切处现前故；神力身，示现一切神变故；菩提身，随乐、随时成正觉故。是为十。若诸菩萨安住此法，则得如来无上大智慧身。

"佛子，菩萨摩诃萨有十种语。何等为十？所谓：柔软语，使一切众生皆安隐故；甘露语，令一切众生悉清凉故；不诳语，所有言说皆如实故；真实语，乃至梦中无妄语故；广大语，一切释、梵、四天王等皆尊敬故；甚深语，显示法性故；坚固语，说法无尽故；正直语，发言易了故；种种语，随时示现故；开悟一切众生语，随其欲乐令解了故。是为十。若诸菩萨安住此法，则得如来无上微妙语。

"佛子，菩萨摩诃萨有十种净修语业。何等为十？所谓：

The body of great compassion, so called because he tirelessly substitutes for all beings in enduring measureless suffering;

The body of great kindness, so called because he rescues all beings;

The body of merit, so called because he benefits all beings;

The body of wisdom, so called because it is of the same single nature as the bodies of all buddhas;

The body of the Dharma, so called because he forever transcends taking rebirth in any of the rebirth destinies;

The body of skillful means, so called because he appears in all places;

The body of spiritual powers, so called because he manifests all the spiritual transformations; and

The body of bodhi, so called because he gains right enlightenment however he pleases and whenever he chooses.

These are the ten. If bodhisattvas abide in these dharmas, then they acquire the Tathāgata's unexcelled great wisdom body.

Sons of the Buddha, the bodhisattva-mahāsattva has ten kinds of speech. What are those ten? They are as follows:

Gentle speech, so called because it enables all beings to feel safe;

Speech like the elixir of immortality, so called because it enables all beings to feel clear and cool;

Nondeceptive speech, so called because everything he says accords with reality;

Truthful speech, so called because, even in dreams, he is free of false speech;

Vast speech, so called because it is universally respected even by all devas such as Śakra, Brahma, the Four Heavenly Kings, and others;

Extremely profound speech, so called because it reveals the nature of dharmas;

Solid speech, so called because it endlessly speaks about the Dharma;

Direct speech, so called because it is easy to understand whatever he says;

Multifarious speech, so called because it manifests in accordance with the particular time; and

Speech that awakens all beings, so called because it accords with their inclinations and thereby enables them to fully understand.

These are the ten. If bodhisattvas abide in these dharmas, then they acquire the Tathāgata's unexcelled sublime speech.

Sons of the Buddha, the bodhisattva-mahāsattva has ten ways of purifying speech. What are those ten? They are as follows:

正體字

樂聽聞
如來音聲。淨修語業。樂聞說菩薩功德。淨修語業。不說一切眾生不樂聞語。淨修語業。真實遠離語四過失。淨修語業。歡喜踊躍讚歎如來。淨修語業。如來塔所高聲讚佛。如實功德淨修語業。以深淨心。施眾生法。淨修語業。音樂歌頌。讚歎如來。淨修語業。於諸佛所。聽聞正法。不惜身命。淨修語業。捨身承事一切菩薩。及諸法師。而受妙法。淨修語業。是為十。[1]佛子。若菩薩摩訶薩。以此十事淨修語業。則得十種守護。何等為十。所謂天王為首。一切天眾。而為守護。龍王為首。一切龍眾。而為守護。夜叉王為首。乾闥婆王為首。阿修羅王為首。迦樓羅王為首。緊那羅王為首。摩睺羅伽王為首。梵王為首。一一皆與自己[2]徒眾而為守護。如來法王為首。一切法師。皆悉守護。是為十。佛子。菩薩摩訶薩。得此守護已。則能成[3]辦十種大事。何等為十。所謂一切眾生皆令歡喜。

简体字

乐听闻如来音声净修语业；乐闻说菩萨功德净修语业；不说一切众生不乐闻语净修语业；真实远离语四过失净修语业；欢喜踊跃赞叹如来净修语业；如来塔所高声赞佛如实功德净修语业；以深净心施众生法净修语业；音乐歌颂赞叹如来净修语业；于诸佛所听闻正法不惜身命净修语业；舍身承事一切菩萨及诸法师而受妙法净修语业。是为十。

"若菩萨摩诃萨以此十事净修语业，则得十种守护。何等为十？所谓：天王为首，一切天众而为守护；龙王为首，一切龙众而为守护；夜叉王为首，乾闼婆王为首，阿修罗王为首，迦楼罗王为首，紧那罗王为首，摩睺罗伽王为首，梵王为首，一一皆与自己徒众而为守护；如来法王为首，一切法师皆悉守护。是为十。

"佛子，菩萨摩诃萨得此守护已，则能成办十种大事。何等为十？所谓：一切众生皆令欢喜，

Chapter 38 — *Transcending the World*

> Purifying speech by delighting in listening to the voice of the Tathāgata;
> Purifying speech by delighting in listening to discussions of the bodhisattva's meritorious qualities;
> Purifying speech by not saying what beings do not wish to hear;
> Purifying speech by truly abandoning the four speech faults;[116]
> Purifying speech by feeling exultant joy in praising all *tathāgatas*;
> Purifying speech by loudly praising the Buddha's true meritorious qualities at stupas commemorating the Tathāgata;
> Purifying speech by using a deeply pure mind in bestowing Dharma on beings;
> Purifying speech by praising the Tathāgata with music and songs;
> Purifying speech by not even sparing his own body or life for the sake of hearing right Dharma taught by the buddhas; and
> Purifying speech by being willing to sacrificing his own life to receive the sublime Dharma through serving all bodhisattvas and teachers of the Dharma.

These are the ten.

Sons of the Buddha, if bodhisattva-mahāsattvas use these ten means to purify their speech, they acquire ten kinds of protection. What are those ten? They are as follows:

> Protection provided by all the congregations of devas headed by the Heavenly Kings;
> Protection provided by all the congregations of dragons headed by the dragon kings themselves;
> Protection provided by the *yakṣa* kings and their followers;
> Protection provided by the *gandharva* kings and their followers;
> Protection provided by the *asura* kings and their followers;
> Protection provided by the *garuḍa* kings and their followers;
> Protection provided by the *kiṃnara* kings and their followers;
> Protection provided by the *mahoraga* kings and their followers;
> Protection provided by the Brahma Heaven Kings and their followers so that in every case, he is protected by these kings and their followers; and
> Protection provided by all the masters of the Dharma headed by the *tathāgatas*, the Dharma kings.

These are the ten.

Sons of the Buddha, having acquired protection such as this, the bodhisattva-mahāsattva is then able to accomplish ten kinds of great endeavors. What are those ten? They are as follows:

> They enable all beings to be happy;

正體字

一切世界悉能往詣。一切諸根
皆能了知。一切勝解悉令清淨。一切煩惱皆
令除斷。一切習氣皆令捨離。一切欲樂皆令
明潔。一切深心悉使增長。一切法界悉令周
遍。一切涅槃普令明見。是為十。佛子。菩薩摩
訶薩。有十種心。何等為十。所謂如大地心。能
持能長一切眾生諸善根故。如大海心。一切
諸佛。無量無邊。大智法水。悉流入故。如須彌
山王心。置一切眾生於出世間最上善根處
故。如摩尼寶王心。樂欲清淨無雜染故。如金
剛心。決定深入一切法故。如金剛圍山心。諸
魔外道。不能動故。如蓮華心。一切世法。不能
染故。如優曇鉢華心。一切劫中。難值遇故。如
淨日心。破闇障故。如虛空心。不可量故。是為
十。若諸菩薩。安住其中。則得如來無上大清
淨心。佛子。菩薩摩訶薩。有十種發心。何等為
十。所謂發我當度脫一切眾生心。

简体字

一切世界悉能往诣，一切诸根皆能了知，一切胜解悉令清净，一切烦恼皆令除断，一切习气皆令舍离，一切欲乐皆令明洁，一切深心悉使增长，一切法界悉令周遍，一切涅槃普令明见。是为十。

"佛子，菩萨摩诃萨有十种心。何等为十？所谓：如大地心，能持、能长一切众生诸善根故；如大海心，一切诸佛无量无边大智法水悉流入故；如须弥山王心，置一切众生于出世间最上善根处故；如摩尼宝王心，乐欲清净无杂染故；如金刚心，决定深入一切法故；如金刚围山心，诸魔外道不能动故；如莲华心，一切世法不能染故；如优昙钵华心，一切劫中难值遇故；如净日心，破暗障故；如虚空心，不可量故。是为十。若诸菩萨安住其中，则得如来无上大清净心。

"佛子，菩萨摩诃萨有十种发心。何等为十？所谓：发我当度脱一切众生心；

Chapter 38 — *Transcending the World*

They are able to travel and visit all worlds;
They are able to completely know all the faculties of others;
They purify all their resolute beliefs;
They eliminate all afflictions;
They relinquish all habitual karmic propensities;
They cause all their mental dispositions to be bright and immaculately pure;
They increase all kinds of profound mind;
They become pervasively present throughout the entire Dharma realm; and
They enable all instances of entering nirvāṇa to be clearly seen.

These are the ten.

Sons of the Buddha, the bodhisattva-mahāsattva has ten kinds of mind. What are those ten? They are as follows:

The mind that is like the great earth in its ability to support and promote the growth of all beings' roots of goodness;

The mind that is like the great ocean because all the Dharma waters of all buddhas' measureless and boundless great wisdom flow into it;

The mind that is like Sumeru, the king of mountains, in its ability to place all beings in the very highest place [for the growth] of the most superior roots of world-transcending goodness;

The mind that is like a sovereign *maṇi* jewel in the purity of its aspirations and in its absence of defilements;

The mind that is like vajra by virtue of its decisive and deep penetration of all dharmas;

The mind that is like the vajra ring mountains in its ability to remain unshaken by any of the *māras* or the followers of non-Buddhist traditions;

The mind that is like a lotus flower because it cannot be defiled by any of the worldly dharmas;

The mind that is like the *udumbara* flower because it is only rarely encountered in any kalpa;

The mind that is like the clearly shining sun because it dispels the obstacle of darkness; and

The mind that is like empty space because it is immeasurable.

These are the ten. If bodhisattvas abide in these, then they acquire the Tathāgata's unexcelled great and pure mind.

Sons of the Buddha, the bodhisattva-mahāsattva makes ten kinds of resolutions. What are those ten? They are as follows:

They resolve: "I shall liberate all beings";

正體字

發我當令
一切眾生除斷煩惱心。發我當令一切眾生
消滅習氣心。發我當斷除一切疑惑心。發我
當除滅一切眾生苦惱心。發我當除滅一切
惡道。諸難心。發我當敬順一切如來心。發我
當善學一切菩薩所學心。發我當於一切世
間一一毛端處。現一切佛成正覺心。發我當
於一切世界。[4]擊無上法鼓。令諸眾生。隨其
根欲。悉得悟解心。是為十。若諸菩薩。安住其
中。則得如來無上大發起能事心。佛子。菩薩
摩訶薩。有十種周遍心。何等為十。所謂周遍
一切虛空心。發意廣大故。周遍一切法界心。
深入無邊故。周遍一切三世心。一念悉知故。
周遍一切佛出現心。於入胎誕生。出家成道。
轉法輪。般涅槃。悉明了故。周遍一切眾生心。
悉知根欲習氣故。周遍一切智慧心。隨順了
知法界故。周遍一切無邊心。知諸幻網差別
故。周遍一切無生心。不得諸法自性故。

简体字

发我当令一切众生除断烦恼心；发我当令一切众生消灭习气心；发我当断除一切疑惑心；发我当除灭一切众生苦恼心；发我当除灭一切恶道诸难心；发我当敬顺一切如来心；发我当善学一切菩萨所学心；发我当于一切世间一一毛端处现一切佛成正觉心；发我当于一切世界击无上法鼓，令诸众生随其根欲悉得悟解心。是为十。若诸菩萨安住其中，则得如来无上大发起能事心。

"佛子，菩萨摩诃萨有十种周遍心。何等为十？所谓：周遍一切虚空心，发意广大故；周遍一切法界心，深入无边故；周遍一切三世心，一念悉知故；周遍一切佛出现心，于入胎、诞生、出家、成道、转法轮、般涅槃悉明了故；周遍一切众生心，悉知根、欲、习气故；周遍一切智慧心，随顺了知法界故；周遍一切无边心，知诸幻网差别故；周遍一切无生心，不得诸法自性故；

They resolve: "I shall enable all beings to cut off their afflictions";
They resolve: "I shall enable all beings to melt away their habitual karmic propensities";
They resolve: "I shall cut off all doubts";
They resolve: "I shall extinguish all beings' anguishing afflictions";
They resolve: "I shall do away with the wretched destinies and the difficulties";[117]
They resolve: "I shall respectfully follow all *tathāgatas*";
They resolve: "I shall thoroughly train in whatever all bodhisattvas train in";
They resolve: "I shall reveal all buddhas' realization of right enlightenment on the tip of every hair in all worlds"; and
They resolve: "I shall beat the drum of the unexcelled Dharma in all worlds and enable all beings to gain awakened understanding in a manner adapted to their faculties and inclinations."

These are the ten. If bodhisattvas abide in these, then they acquire the Tathāgata's unexcelled and great resolve to do what they are able to do.

Sons of the Buddha, the bodhisattva has ten kinds of all-pervasive mind. What are those ten? They are as follows:

The mind that pervades all of empty space due to the vastness of its resolve;
The mind that pervades the entire Dharma realm due to its infinitely deep penetration;
The mind that pervades all three periods of time due to knowing them all in but a single mind-moment;
The mind that is pervasively present wherever all buddhas appear due to its complete knowledge of whenever they enter the womb, take birth, leave the home life, attain complete enlightenment, turn the Dharma wheel, and enter *parinirvāṇa*;
The mind that pervades all [realms of] beings due to its knowing all their faculties, inclinations, and habitual karmic propensities;
The mind that is pervasively [cognizant] of all types of wisdom due to its accordance with and complete knowing of the Dharma realm;
The mind that pervades all that is boundless due to its knowing all the different aspects of the web of illusory phenomena;
The mind that pervades the unproduced due to not apprehending any inherently existent nature in any dharma;

正體字

周遍

298b17 一切無礙心。不住自心他心故。周遍一切自
298b18 在心。一念普現成佛故。是為十。若諸菩薩。安
298b19 住其中。則得無量無上佛法周遍莊嚴。佛子。
298b20 菩薩摩訶薩。有十種根。何等為十。所謂歡喜
298b21 根。見一切佛。信不壞故。希望根。所聞佛法。
298b22 皆悟解故。不退根。一切作事。皆究竟故。安住
298b23 根。不斷一切菩薩行故。微細根。入般若波羅
298b24 蜜。微妙理故。不休息根。究竟一切眾生事故。
298b25 如金剛根。證知一切諸法性故。金剛光焰根。
298b26 普照一切佛境界故。無差別根。一切如來。同
298b27 一身故。無礙際根。深入如來十種力故。是為
298b28 十。若諸菩薩。安住其中。則得如來無上大智
298b29 圓滿根。佛子。菩薩摩訶薩。有十種深心。何等
298c01 為十。所謂不染一切世間法深心。不雜一切
298c02 [5]二乘道深心。了達一切佛菩提深心。隨順一
298c03 切智智道深心。

简体字

周遍一切无碍心，不住自心、他心故；周遍一切自在心，一念普现成佛故。是为十。若诸菩萨安住其中，则得无量无上佛法周遍庄严。

"佛子，菩萨摩诃萨有十种根。何等为十？所谓：欢喜根，见一切佛信不坏故；希望根，所闻佛法皆悟解故；不退根，一切作事皆究竟故；安住根，不断一切菩萨行故；微细根，入般若波罗蜜微妙理故；不休息根，究竟一切众生事故；如金刚根，证知一切诸法性故；金刚光焰根，普照一切佛境界故；无差别根，一切如来同一身故；无碍际根，深入如来十种力故。是为十。若诸菩萨安住其中，则得如来无上大智圆满根。

"佛子，菩萨摩诃萨有十种深心。何等为十？所谓：不染一切世间法深心；不杂一切二乘道深心；了达一切佛菩提深心；随顺一切智智道深心；

Chapter 38 — *Transcending the World*

The mind that is unimpeded in pervading all things due to not dwelling in either his own mind or the minds of others; and

The mind that has sovereign mastery in pervading everything due to manifesting the realization of buddhahood everywhere in but a single mind-moment.

These are the ten. If bodhisattvas abide in these, then they acquire the pervasive adornment of the countless unexcelled dharmas of the Buddha.

Sons of the Buddha, the bodhisattva-mahāsattva has ten kinds of faculties. What are those ten? They are as follows:

The faculty of joyfulness by which he sees all buddhas and has indestructible faith;

The faculty of zeal by which he awakens to and understands all the Dharma of the Buddha that he hears;

The faculty of irreversibility by which he completes everything he does;

The faculty of secure abiding by which he never ceases practicing any of the bodhisattva practices;

The faculty of subtlety by which he penetrates the sublime principles of the *prajñāpāramitā*;

The faculty of never resting by which he completes all endeavors he does for the benefit of beings;

The faculty of being like vajra by which he realizes the nature of all dharmas;

The faculty of flaming vajra radiance by which he everywhere illuminates the sphere of action of all buddhas;

The faculty of nondifferentiation by which [he realizes] all *tathāgatas* share the same single body; and

The faculty of unimpeded boundlessness by which he deeply penetrates the Tathāgata's ten kinds of powers.

These are the ten. If bodhisattvas abide in these, then they acquire the faculty of the Tathāgata's unexcelled and perfectly fulfilled great wisdom.

Sons of the Buddha, the bodhisattva-mahāsattva has ten kinds of deep mind. What are those ten? They are as follows:

The deep mind that remains undefiled by any worldly dharma;

The deep mind that does not mix in any of the paths of the two vehicles;

The deep mind that completely comprehends the bodhi of all buddhas;

The deep mind that accords with the path to the wisdom of all-knowledge;

正體字

不為一切眾魔外道所動深
心。淨修一切如來圓滿智深心。受持一切所
聞法深心。不著一切受生處深心。具足一切
微細智深心。修一切諸佛法深心。是為十。若
諸菩薩。安住其中。則得一切智無上清淨深
心。佛子。菩薩摩訶薩。有十種增上深心。何等
為十。所謂不退轉增上深心。積集一切善根
故。離疑惑增上深心。解一切如來密語故。正
持增上深心。大願大行所流故。最勝增上深
心。深入一切佛法故。為主增上深心。一切佛
法自在故。廣大增上深心。普入種種法門故。
上首增上深心。一切所作成辦故。自在增上
深心。一切三昧。神通變化。莊嚴故。安住增
上深心。攝受本願故。無休息增上深心。成熟
一切眾生故。是為十。若諸菩薩。安住此法。則
得一切諸佛無上清淨增上深心。

简体字

不为一切众魔外道所动深心；净修一切如来圆满智深心；受持一切所闻法深心；不著一切受生处深心；具足一切微细智深心；修一切诸佛法深心。是为十。若诸菩萨安住其中，则得一切智无上清净深心。

"佛子，菩萨摩诃萨有十种增上深心。何等为十？所谓：不退转增上深心，积集一切善根故；离疑惑增上深心，解一切如来密语故；正持增上深心，大愿大行所流故；最胜增上深心，深入一切佛法故；为主增上深心，一切佛法自在故；广大增上深心，普入种种法门故；上首增上深心，一切所作成办故；自在增上深心，一切三昧神通变化庄严故；安住增上深心，摄受本愿故；无休息增上深心，成熟一切众生故。是为十。若诸菩萨安住此法，则得一切诸佛无上清净增上深心。

Chapter 38 — *Transcending the World*

The deep mind that remains unmoved by any of the many *māras* or followers of non-Buddhist paths;

The deep mind that purely cultivates the perfectly fulfilled wisdom of all *tathāgatas*;

The deep mind that absorbs and retains all Dharma that is heard;

The deep mind that remains unattached to any of the stations of rebirth;

The deep mind that is equipped with all forms of subtle wisdom; and

The deep mind that cultivates all dharmas of all buddhas.

These are the ten. If bodhisattvas abide in these, then they acquire the deep mind possessed of the unexcelled purity of the All-Knowing One.

Sons of the Buddha, the bodhisattva-mahāsattva has ten kinds of especially superior deep mind. What are those ten? They are as follows:

The especially superior deep mind of irreversibility, so called because he accumulates all roots of goodness;

The especially superior deep mind free of all doubts, so called because he understands the esoteric speech of all *tathāgatas*;

The especially superior deep mind of rightly maintaining [his cultivation], so called because of what flows from his great vows and great practices;

The especially superior deep mind of supremacy, so called because he deeply penetrates all dharmas of the Buddha;

The especially superior deep mind of mastery, so called because he has attained sovereign mastery in all dharmas of the Buddha;

The especially superior deep mind of vast penetration, so called because he everywhere penetrates the many different kinds of gateways into the Dharma;

The especially superior deep mind of supreme leadership, so-called because he completely accomplishes everything he does;

The especially superior deep mind of sovereign mastery, so called because he is adorned with all the samādhis, spiritual super-knowledges, and transformations;

The especially superior deep mind of secure abiding, so called because he embraces his original vows; and

The especially superior deep mind of incessant effort, so called because he fully ripens all beings.

These are the ten. If bodhisattvas abide in these dharmas, then they acquire all buddhas' especially superior mind of unexcelled purity.

正體字

佛子。菩薩摩訶薩。有十種勤修。何等為十。所謂布施勤修。悉捨一切。不求報故。持戒勤修。頭陀苦行。少欲知足。無所欺故。忍辱勤修。離自他想。忍一切惡。畢竟不生。患害心故。精進勤修。身語意業。未曾散亂。一切所作。皆不退轉。至究竟故。禪定勤修。解脫三昧。出現神通。離一切欲煩惱鬪諍。諸眷屬故。智慧勤修。修習積聚一切功德。無厭倦故。大慈勤修。知諸眾生。無自性故。大悲勤修。知諸法空。普代一切眾生受苦。無疲厭故。覺悟如來十力勤修。了達無礙。示眾生故。不退法輪勤修。轉至一切眾生心故。是為十。若諸菩薩。安住此法。則得如來無上大智慧勤修。佛子。菩薩摩訶薩。有十種決定解。何等為十。所謂最上決定解。種植尊重善根故。莊嚴決定解。出生種種莊嚴故。廣大決定解。其心未曾狹劣故。

简体字

"佛子，菩萨摩诃萨有十种勤修。何等为十？所谓：布施勤修，悉舍一切，不求报故；持戒勤修，头陀苦行，少欲知足，无所欺故；忍辱勤修，离自他想，忍一切恶，毕竟不生患害心故；精进勤修，身、语、意业未曾散乱，一切所作皆不退转，至究竟故；禅定勤修，解脱三昧，出现神通，离一切欲烦恼斗诤诸眷属故；智慧勤修，修习积聚一切功德无厌倦故；大慈勤修，知诸众生无自性故；大悲勤修，知诸法空，普代一切众生受苦无疲厌故；觉悟如来十力勤修，了达无碍示众生故；不退法轮勤修，转至一切众生心故。是为十。若诸菩萨安住此法，则得如来无上大智慧勤修。

"佛子，菩萨摩诃萨有十种决定解。何等为十？所谓：最上决定解，种植尊重善根故；庄严决定解，出生种种庄严故；广大决定解，其心未曾狭劣故；

Chapter 38 — *Transcending the World*

Sons of the Buddha, the bodhisattva-mahāsattva has ten kinds of diligent cultivation. What are those ten? They are as follows:

The diligent cultivation of giving in which he gives away everything and seeks no reward;

The diligent cultivation of upholding the moral precepts in which he is free of any deception in practicing the *dhūta* austerities and in being easily satisfied with but few wishes;

The diligent cultivation of patience in which he abandons concepts of "self" and "other," endures all kinds of evil treatment, and never arouses any thoughts of anger or malice;

The diligent cultivation of vigor in which he never becomes distracted in actions of body, speech, or mind, never retreats from any endeavors, and completes them all;

The diligent cultivation of *dhyāna* absorption in which he cultivates the liberations and samādhis and manifests the spiritual superknowledges while abandoning all desires, afflictions, contentiousness, and their associated manifestations;

The diligent cultivation of wisdom in which he tirelessly cultivates the accumulation of all the meritorious qualities;

The diligent cultivation of great kindness in which he realizes that all beings have no inherently existent nature;

The diligent cultivation of great compassion in which he realizes the emptiness of all dharmas and everywhere substitutes for all beings in tirelessly taking on their sufferings;

The diligent cultivation of awakening to the Tathāgata's ten powers in which he gains an unimpeded and complete comprehension of them and reveals them to beings; and

The diligent cultivation of turning the irreversible wheel of the Dharma so that it reaches the minds of all beings.

These are the ten. If bodhisattvas abide in these dharmas, then they acquire the diligent cultivation of the Tathāgata's unexcelled great wisdom.

Sons of the Buddha, the bodhisattva-mahāsattva has ten kinds of definite understanding. What are those ten? They are as follows:

The definite understanding of supremacy, so called because he plants roots of goodness of veneration;

The definite understanding of adornment, so called because he produces many different kinds of adornments;

The definite understanding of vastness, so called because his mind has never been inclined toward narrowness or inferiority;

正體字

寂滅
決定解。能入甚深法性故。普遍決定解。發心無所不及故。堪任決定解。能受佛力加持故。堅固決定解。摧破一切魔業故。明斷決定解。了知一切業報故。現前決定解。隨意能現神通故。紹隆決定解。一切佛所得記故。自在決定解。隨意隨時成佛故。是為十。若諸菩薩。安住此法。則得如來無上決定解。佛子。菩薩摩訶薩。有十種決定解知諸世界。何等為十。所謂知一切世界入一世界。知一世界入一切世界。知一切世界。一如來身。一蓮華座。皆悉周遍。知一切世界皆如虛空。知一切世界具佛莊嚴。知一切世界菩薩充滿。知一切世界入一毛孔。知一切世界入一眾生身。知一切世界一佛菩提樹。一佛道場。皆悉周遍。知一切世界。一音普遍。令諸眾生。各別了知。心生歡喜。是為十。若諸菩薩。安住此法。則得如來無上佛剎廣大決定解。

简体字

寂灭决定解，能入甚深法性故；普遍决定解，发心无所不及故；堪任决定解，能受佛力加持故；坚固决定解，摧破一切魔业故；明断决定解，了知一切业报故；现前决定解，随意能现神通故；绍隆决定解，一切佛所得记故；自在决定解，随意、随时成佛故。是为十。若诸菩萨安住此法，则得如来无上决定解。

"佛子，菩萨摩诃萨有十种决定解知诸世界。何等为十？所谓：知一切世界入一世界；知一世界入一切世界；知一切世界，一如来身、一莲华座皆悉周遍；知一切世界皆如虚空；知一切世界具佛庄严；知一切世界菩萨充满；知一切世界入一毛孔；知一切世界入一众生身；知一切世界，一佛菩提树、一佛道场皆悉周遍；知一切世界一音普遍，令诸众生各别了知，心生欢喜。是为十。若诸菩萨安住此法，则得如来无上佛刹广大决定解。

The definite understanding of quiescence, so called because he is able to penetrate the extremely deep nature of dharmas;

The definite understanding of universal pervasiveness, so called because his generation of the resolve has no place it does not reach;

The definite understanding of capacities, so called because he is able to receive the support of the Buddha's powers;

The definite understanding of solidity, so called because he demolishes all the works of the *māras*;

The definite understanding of clear judgment, so called because he completely knows the karmic results of all actions;

The definite understanding of direct manifestation, so called because he is able to manifest the spiritual superknowledges at will;

The definite understanding of continuing the legacy of the lineage, so called because he acquires predictions from all buddhas; and

The definite understanding of the sovereign masteries, so called because he can reach buddhahood whenever he pleases.

These are the ten. If bodhisattvas abide in these dharmas, then they acquire the Tathāgata's unexcelled definite understanding.

Sons of the Buddha, the bodhisattva-mahāsattva has ten kinds of definite understanding in knowing all worlds. What are those ten? They are as follows:

He knows all worlds enter a single world;

He knows all worlds enter all worlds;

He knows all worlds are everywhere pervaded by a single body of the Tathāgata and his single lotus flower throne;

He knows all worlds are like empty space;

He knows all worlds possess the adornment of the Buddha;

He knows all worlds as filled with bodhisattvas;

He knows all worlds enter a single pore;

He knows all worlds enter a single being's body;

He knows all worlds are everywhere pervaded by a single buddha's bodhi tree and a single buddha's site of enlightenment; and

He knows all worlds are everywhere pervaded by a single voice that enables all beings to each understand differently and thus be delighted.

These are the ten. If bodhisattvas abide in these dharmas, then they acquire the Tathāgata's unexcelled vast and definite understanding of the buddha *kṣetras*.

正體字

佛子。菩薩摩訶薩。有十種決定解知眾生界。何等為十。所謂知一切眾生界。本性無實。知一切眾生界。悉入一眾生身。知一切眾生界。悉入菩薩身。知一切眾生界。悉入如來藏。知一眾生身。普入一切眾生界。知一切眾生界。悉堪為諸佛法器。知一切眾生界。隨其所欲。為現釋梵護世身。知一切眾生界。隨其所欲。為現聲聞獨覺寂靜威儀。知一切眾生界。為現菩薩功德莊嚴身。知一切眾生界。為現如來相好。寂靜威儀。開悟眾生。是為十。若諸菩薩。安住此法。則得如來無上大威力決定解

大方廣佛華嚴經[*]卷第五十七

離世間品第三十八之五

佛子。菩薩摩訶薩。有十種習氣。何等為十。所謂菩提心習氣。善根習氣。教化眾生習氣。見佛習氣。於清淨世界受生習氣。行習氣。願習氣。波羅蜜習氣。思惟平等法習氣。

简体字

"佛子,菩萨摩诃萨有十种决定解知众生界。何等为十?所谓:知一切众生界本性无实;知一切众生界悉入一众生身;知一切众生界悉入菩萨身;知一切众生界悉入如来藏;知一众生身普入一切众生界;知一切众生界悉堪为诸佛法器;知一切众生界,随其所欲,为现释、梵、护世身;知一切众生界,随其所欲,为现声闻、独觉寂静威仪;知一切众生界,为现菩萨功德庄严身;知一切众生界,为现如来相好寂静威仪,开悟众生。是为十。若诸菩萨安住此法,则得如来无上大威力决定解。

大方广佛华严经卷第五十七

离世间品第三十八之五

"佛子,菩萨摩诃萨有十种习气。何等为十?所谓:菩提心习气;善根习气;教化众生习气;见佛习气;于清净世界受生习气;行习气;愿习气;波罗蜜习气;思惟平等法习气;

Chapter 38 — *Transcending the World* 2913

Sons of the Buddha, the bodhisattva-mahāsattva has ten kinds of definite understanding in knowing the realms of beings. What are those ten? They are as follows:

He knows all realms of beings have a fundamental nature of unreality;

He knows all realms of beings enter a single being's body;

He knows all realms of beings enter the bodhisattva's body;

He knows all realms of beings enter the matrix of the Tathāgata;[118]

He knows a single being's body everywhere enters all realms of beings;

He knows those in all realms of beings are capable of becoming vessels containing the Dharma of all buddhas;

He knows all realms of beings and accords with whatever they wish for by manifesting for them in the body of Śakra, Brahma, or a world-protecting heavenly king;

He knows all realms of beings and accords with whatever they wish for by manifesting for them the serene awesome deportment of a *śrāvaka* disciple or a *pratyekabuddha*;

He knows all realms of beings and manifests for them in the body of a bodhisattva adorned with the meritorious qualities; and

He knows all realms of beings and, to awaken beings, manifests for them a *tathāgata*'s major marks, secondary signs, and serene awesome deportment.

These are the ten. If bodhisattvas abide in these dharmas, then they acquire the definite understanding of the Tathāgata's unexcelled great awesome powers.

Sons of the Buddha, the bodhisattva-mahāsattva has ten kinds of habitual karmic propensities. What are those ten? They are as follows:

Habitual karmic propensities related to the resolve to attain bodhi;

Habitual karmic propensities related to roots of goodness;

Habitual karmic propensities related to teaching beings;

Habitual karmic propensities related to seeing buddhas;

Habitual karmic propensities related to being born in pure worlds;

Habitual karmic propensities related to practices;

Habitual karmic propensities related to vows;

Habitual karmic propensities related to the *pāramitās*;

Habitual karmic propensities related to contemplative meditation on the dharma of impartiality; and

正體字

種種境界

差別習氣。是為十。若諸菩薩。安住此法。則永
離一切煩惱習氣。得如來大智習氣。非習氣
智。佛子。菩薩摩訶薩。有十種取。以此不斷諸
菩薩行。何等為十。所謂取一切眾生界。究竟
教化故。取一切世界。究竟嚴淨故。取如來。修
菩薩行為供養故。取善根。積集諸佛相好功
德故。取大悲。滅一切眾生苦故。取大慈。與一
切眾生一切智樂故。取波羅蜜。積集菩薩諸
莊嚴故。取善巧方便。於一切處。皆示現故。取
菩提。得無礙智故。略說菩薩。取一切法。於一
切處。悉以明智。而現了故。是為十。若諸菩薩。
安住此取。則能不斷諸菩薩行。得一切如來
無上無所取法。佛子。菩薩摩訶薩。有十種修。
何等為十。所謂修諸波羅蜜。修學。修慧。修
義。修法。修出離。修示現。修勤行匪懈。

简体字

种种境界差别习气。是为十。若诸菩萨安住此法,则永离一切烦恼习气,得如来大智习气非习气智。

"佛子,菩萨摩诃萨有十种取,以此不断诸菩萨行。何等为十?所谓:取一切众生界,究竟教化故;取一切世界,究竟严净故;取如来,修菩萨行为供养故;取善根,积集诸佛相好功德故;取大悲,灭一切众生苦故;取大慈,与一切众生一切智乐故;取波罗蜜,积集菩萨诸庄严故;取善巧方便,于一切处皆示现故;取菩提,得无碍智故;略说菩萨取一切法,于一切处悉以明智而现了故。是为十。若诸菩萨安住此取,则能不断诸菩萨行,得一切如来无上无所取法。

"佛子,菩萨摩诃萨有十种修。何等为十?所谓:修诸波罗蜜;修学;修慧;修义;修法;修出离;修示现;修勤行匪懈;

Chapter 38 — *Transcending the World*

Habitual karmic propensities related to the many different kinds of spheres of experience.

These are the ten. If bodhisattvas abide in these dharmas, then they forever leave behind all habitual karmic propensities related to the afflictions and acquire habitual karmic propensities related to the Tathāgata's great wisdom, that wisdom which is not itself a function of habitual karmic propensities.

Sons of the Buddha, the bodhisattva-mahāsattva has ten kinds of grasping. It is because of these that he never discontinues any of the bodhisattva practices. What are those ten? They are as follows:

He grasps all realms of beings to ultimately teach them all;

He grasps all worlds to ultimately purify them all;

He grasps the *tathāgatas* to cultivate the bodhisattva practices as an offering to them;

He grasps roots of goodness to accumulate the meritorious qualities that produce all buddhas' major marks and secondary signs;

He grasps great compassion to extinguish the sufferings of all beings;

He grasps great kindness to bestow the happiness of all-knowledge on all beings;

He grasps the *pāramitās* to accumulate the bodhisattva's adornments;

He grasps the skillful means to appear in all places;

He grasps bodhi to acquire unimpeded wisdom; and

To state it briefly, he grasps all dharmas in all places to use radiant wisdom to completely reveal them all.

These are the ten. If bodhisattvas abide in these types of grasping, then they become able to never discontinue the bodhisattva practices and able to acquire all *tathāgatas'* unexcelled dharma of having nothing at all that they grasp.

Sons of the Buddha, the bodhisattva-mahāsattva has ten kinds of cultivation. What are those ten? They are as follows:

Cultivation of all of the *pāramitās*;

Cultivation of the trainings;

Cultivation of wisdom;

Cultivation of meaning;

Cultivation of Dharma;

Cultivation of emancipation;

Cultivation of manifestations;

Cultivation of incessantly diligent practice;

正體字	修成 等正覺。修轉正法輪。是為十。若諸菩薩。安住其中。則得無上修。修一切法。佛子。菩薩摩訶薩。有十種成就佛法。何等為十。所謂不離善知識。成就佛法。深信佛語。成就佛法。不謗正法。成就佛法。以無量無盡善根迴向。成就佛法。信解如來境界無邊際。成就佛法。知一切世界境界。成就佛法。不捨法界境界。成就佛法。遠離諸魔境界。成就佛法。正念一切諸佛境界。成就佛法。樂求如來十力境界。成就佛法。是為十。若諸菩薩。安住此法。則得成就如來無上大智慧。佛子。菩薩摩訶薩。有十種退失佛法。應當遠離。何等為十。所謂輕慢善知識。退失佛法。畏生死苦。退失佛法。厭修菩薩行。退失佛法。不樂住世間。退失佛法。
简体字	修成等正觉；修转正法轮。是为十。若诸菩萨安住其中，则得无上修修一切法。 　　"佛子，菩萨摩诃萨有十种成就佛法。何等为十？所谓：不离善知识成就佛法；深信佛语成就佛法；不谤正法成就佛法；以无量无尽善根回向成就佛法；信解如来境界无边际成就佛法；知一切世界境界成就佛法；不舍法界境界成就佛法；远离诸魔境界成就佛法；正念一切诸佛境界成就佛法；乐求如来十力境界成就佛法。是为十。若诸菩萨安住此法，则得成就如来无上大智慧。 　　"佛子，菩萨摩诃萨有十种退失佛法，应当远离。何等为十？所谓：轻慢善知识退失佛法；畏生死苦退失佛法；厌修菩萨行退失佛法；不乐住世间退失佛法；

Chapter 38 — *Transcending the World*

Cultivation of the realization of the right and perfect enlightenment; and

Cultivation of turning the wheel of right Dharma.

These are the ten. If bodhisattvas abide in these, then they attain unexcelled cultivation in their cultivation of all dharmas.

Sons of the Buddha, the bodhisattva has ten ways of fulfilling the dharmas of the Buddha. What are those ten? They are as follows:

Fulfillment of the Buddha's dharma of never abandoning the good spiritual guide;

Fulfillment of the Buddha's dharma of deep faith in the Buddha's words;

Fulfillment of the Buddha's dharma of never speaking ill of right Dharma;

Fulfillment of the Buddha's dharma of dedicating measureless and endless roots of goodness;

Fulfillment of the Buddha's dharma of resolute faith in the boundlessness of the Tathāgata's sphere of action;

Fulfillment of the Buddha's dharma of knowing all worlds' spheres of experience;

Fulfillment of the Buddha's dharma of never abandoning the Dharma realm as one's sphere of experience;

Fulfillment of the Buddha's dharma of abandoning the realms of the *māras*;

Fulfillment of the Buddha's dharma of right mindfulness of the sphere of action of all buddhas; and

Fulfillment of the Buddha's dharma of delighting in seeking to acquire the sphere of action of the Tathāgata's ten powers.

These are the ten. If bodhisattvas abide in these dharmas, then they succeed in fully developing the Tathāgata's unexcelled great wisdom.

Sons of the Buddha, the bodhisattva-mahāsattva has ten ways of retreating from the Buddha's Dharma that he should abandon. What are those ten? They are as follows:

Retreating from the Buddha's Dharma through slighting good spiritual guides;

Retreating from the Buddha's Dharma through becoming fearful of the sufferings of *saṃsāra*;

Retreating from the Buddha's Dharma through growing weary of cultivating the bodhisattva practices;

Retreating from the Buddha's Dharma through unhappiness in abiding in the world;

正體字

耽著
三昧。退失佛法。執取善根。退失佛法。誹謗正
法。退失佛法。斷菩薩行。退失佛法。樂二乘
道。退失佛法。嫌恨諸菩薩。退失佛法。是為
十。若諸菩薩。遠離此法。則入菩薩離生道。佛
子。菩薩摩訶薩。有十種離生道。何等為十。所
謂出生般若波羅蜜。而恒觀察一切眾生是
為一。遠離諸見。而度脫一切見縛眾生是為
二。不念一切相。而不捨一切著相眾生是為
三。超過三界。而常在一切世界是為四。永
離煩惱。而與一切眾生共居是為五。得離欲
法。而常以大悲。哀愍一切著欲眾生是為六。
常樂寂靜。而恒示現一切眷屬是為七。離世
間生。而死此生彼。起菩薩行是為八。不染一
切世間法。而不斷一切世間所作是為九。諸
佛菩提。已現其前。而不捨菩薩。一切願行是
為十。

简体字

耽著三昧退失佛法；执取善根退失佛法；诽谤正法退失佛法；断菩萨行退失佛法；乐二乘道退失佛法；嫌恨诸菩萨退失佛法。是为十。若诸菩萨远离此法，则入菩萨离生道。

"佛子，菩萨摩诃萨有十种离生道。何等为十？所谓：出生般若波罗蜜而恒观察一切众生，是为一；远离诸见而度脱一切见缚众生，是为二；不念一切相而不舍一切著相众生，是为三；超过三界而常在一切世界，是为四；永离烦恼而与一切众生共居，是为五；得离欲法而常以大悲哀愍一切著欲众生，是为六；常乐寂静而恒示现一切眷属，是为七；离世间生而死此生彼起菩萨行，是为八；不染一切世间法而不断一切世间所作，是为九；诸佛菩提已现其前而不舍菩萨一切愿行，是为十。

Chapter 38 — *Transcending the World*

Retreating from the Buddha's Dharma through indulgent attachment to samādhis;

Retreating from the Buddha's Dharma through becoming attached to roots of goodness;

Retreating from the Buddha's Dharma through disparaging right Dharma;

Retreating from the Buddha's Dharma through ceasing to practice the bodhisattva practices;

Retreating from the Buddha's Dharma through delighting in the paths of the two vehicles; and

Retreating from the Buddha's Dharma through hating bodhisattvas.

These are the ten. If bodhisattvas abandon these dharmas, then they enter the paths by which the bodhisattva gains emancipation from rebirths.

Sons of the Buddha, the bodhisattva-mahāsattva has ten kinds of paths for transcendence of rebirths. What are those ten? They are as follows:

He develops the *prajñāpāramitā*, and yet constantly contemplates all beings. This is the first;

He avoids all views, and yet liberates all view-bound beings. This is the second;

He does not bear any signs in mind, and yet he never abandons any of the beings who are so attached to signs. This is the third;

He steps beyond the three realms of existence, and yet he always resides in all worlds. This is the fourth;

He forever abandons the afflictions, and yet he resides together in the company of all beings. This is the fifth;

He acquires the dharmas used to abandon the desires, and yet, because of the great compassion, he feels deep sympathy for all beings who are so attached to the desires. This is the sixth;

He always delights in quiescence, and yet he constantly manifests with all kinds of retinues. This is the seventh;

He transcends birth in the world, and yet, having died here, he is reborn there and then takes up the bodhisattva practices. This is the eighth;

He remains unstained by any worldly dharmas, and yet he never ceases his endeavors in all worlds. This is the ninth; and

The bodhi of all buddhas has already manifested directly before him, and yet he still never abandons any of the bodhisattva's practices or vows. This is the tenth.

正體字

佛子。是為菩薩摩訶薩。十種離生道。出
離世間。不[1]與世共。而亦不雜二乘之行。若
諸菩薩。安住此法。則得菩薩決定法。佛子。菩
薩摩訶薩。有十種決定法。何等為十。所謂決
定於如來種族中生。決定於諸佛境界中住。
決定了知菩薩所作事。決定安住諸波羅蜜。
決定得預如來眾會。決定能顯如來種性。決
定安住如來力。決定深入佛菩提。決定與一
切如來。同一身。決定與一切如來。所住無有
二。是為十。佛子。菩薩摩訶薩。有十種出生佛
法道。何等為十。所謂隨順善友。是出生佛法
道。同種善根故。深心信解。是出生佛法道。知
佛自在故。發大誓願。是出生佛法道。其心寬
廣故。忍自善根。是出生佛法道。知業不失故。
一切劫修行無厭足。是出生佛法道。盡未來
際故。阿僧祇[出>世]界皆示現。是出生佛法道。成
熟眾生故。

简体字

佛子,是为菩萨摩诃萨十种离生道,出离世间,不与世共,而亦不杂二乘之行。若诸菩萨安住此法,则得菩萨决定法。

"佛子,菩萨摩诃萨有十种决定法。何等为十?所谓:决定于如来种族中生;决定于诸佛境界中住;决定了知菩萨所作事;决定安住诸波罗蜜;决定得预如来众会;决定能显如来种性;决定安住如来力;决定深入佛菩提;决定与一切如来同一身;决定与一切如来所住无有二。是为十。

"佛子,菩萨摩诃萨有十种出生佛法道。何等为十?所谓:随顺善友是出生佛法道,同种善根故;深心信解是出生佛法道,知佛自在故;发大誓愿是出生佛法道,其心宽广故;忍自善根是出生佛法道,知业不失故;一切劫修行无厌足是出生佛法道,尽未来际故;阿僧祇世界皆示现是出生佛法道,成熟众生故;

Sons of the Buddha, these are the bodhisattva-mahāsattva's ten paths by which he transcends rebirths and gains emancipation from the world. These are not held in common with those who abide in the world and they are they admixed with the practices of the two vehicles, either. If bodhisattvas abide in these dharmas, then they acquire the bodhisattva's definite dharmas.

Sons of the Buddha, the bodhisattva-mahāsattva has ten kinds of definite dharmas. What are those ten? They are as follows:

He definitely takes birth within the clan of the *tathāgatas*;
He definitely dwells in the realms of the buddhas;
He definitely completely knows the works done by the bodhisattva;
He definitely abides in the *pāramitās*;
He definitely joins the Tathāgata's congregations;
He is definitely able to manifest in the lineage of the Tathāgata;
He definitely abides in the Tathāgata's powers;
He definitely deeply enters the bodhi of the Buddha;
He definitely shares the same single body as all *tathāgatas*; and
The place in which he abides is definitely not other than where all *tathāgatas* abide.

These are the ten.

Sons of the Buddha, the bodhisattva-mahāsattva has ten kinds of paths by which he develops the dharmas of the Buddha. What are those ten? They are as follows:

Following along in accordance with the good spiritual guide is a path by which he develops the dharmas of the Buddha because he thereby plants the same roots of goodness;
Deep-minded resolute faith is a path by which he develops the dharmas of the Buddha because he thereby comes to know the sovereign masteries of the Buddha;
Making the great vows is a path by which he develops the dharmas of the Buddha because his mind thereby becomes vast;
Having patience in his own development of roots of goodness is a path by which he develops the dharmas of the Buddha because he thereby realizes that karmic actions are never lost;
Insatiable cultivation throughout all kalpas is a path by which he develops the dharmas of the Buddha because he thereby continues on to the very end of future time;
Manifesting in all the *asaṃkhyeyas* of worlds is a path by which he develops the dharmas of the Buddha because he thereby brings about the ripening of beings;

正體字

不斷菩薩行。是出生佛法道。增長
大悲故。無量心。是出生佛法道。一念遍一切
虛空界故。殊勝行。是出生佛法道。本所修行
無失壞故。如來種。是出生佛法道。令一切眾
生。樂發菩提心。以一切善法資持故。是為十。
若諸菩薩。安住此法。則得大丈夫名號。佛子。
菩薩摩訶薩。有十種大丈夫名號。何等為十。
所謂名為菩提薩埵。菩提智所生故。名為摩
訶薩埵。安住大乘故。名為第一薩埵。證第一
法故。名為勝薩埵。覺悟勝法故。名為最勝薩
埵。智慧最勝故。名為上薩埵。起上精進故。名
為無上薩埵。開示無上法故。名為力薩埵。廣
知十力故。名為無等薩埵。世間無比故。名為
不思議薩埵。一念成佛故。是為十。若諸菩薩。
得此名號。則成就菩薩道。佛子。菩薩摩訶薩。
有十種道。何等為十。所謂

简体字

不断菩萨行是出生佛法道,增长大悲故;无量心是出生佛法道,一念遍一切虚空界故;殊胜行是出生佛法道,本所修行无失坏故;如来种是出生佛法道,令一切众生乐发菩提心,以一切善法资持故。是为十。若诸菩萨安住此法,则得大丈夫名号。

"佛子,菩萨摩诃萨有十种大丈夫名号。何等为十?所谓:名为菩提萨埵,菩提智所生故;名为摩诃萨埵,安住大乘故;名为第一萨埵,证第一法故;名为胜萨埵,觉悟胜法故;名为最胜萨埵,智慧最胜故;名为上萨埵,起上精进故;名为无上萨埵,开示无上法故;名为力萨埵,广知十力故;名为无等萨埵,世间无比故;名为不思议萨埵,一念成佛故。是为十。若诸菩萨得此名号,则成就菩萨道。

"佛子,菩萨摩诃萨有十种道。何等为十?所谓:

Never ceasing the bodhisattva practices is a path by which he develops the dharmas of the Buddha because he thereby brings about the growth of the great compassion;

The immeasurable minds[119] constitute a path by which he develops the dharmas of the Buddha because, in but a single mind-moment, he pervades all realms of space;

Especially superior practice is a path by which he develops the dharmas of the Buddha because whatever he originally cultivated is never destroyed; and

The lineage of the Tathāgata is a path by which he develops the dharmas of the Buddha because it enables all beings to delight in making the bodhi resolve and because it is sustained by all good dharmas.

These are the ten. If bodhisattvas abide in these dharmas, then they acquire the names given to great men.

Sons of the Buddha, the bodhisattva-mahāsattva has ten names that are used for great men. What are those ten? They are as follows:

He is known as a "bodhisattva" because he is born from the wisdom of bodhi;

He is known as a "mahāsattva" because he abides in the Great Vehicle;

He is known as a "foremost *sattva*"[120] because he realizes the foremost Dharma;

He is known as a "supreme *sattva*" because he awakens to the supreme Dharma;

He is known as a "most supreme *sattva*" because his wisdom is the most supreme;

He is known as a "superior *sattva*" because he brings forth superior vigor;

He is known as an "unexcelled *sattva*" because he explains the unexcelled Dharma;

He is known as a "powerful *sattva*" because he possesses the vast knowledge of the ten powers;

He is known as a "peerless *sattva*" because he has no match anywhere in the entire world; and

He is known as an "inconceivable *sattva*" because he attains buddhahood in but a single mind-moment.

These are the ten. If the bodhisattva acquires these names, then he is one who completely fulfills the bodhisattva path.

Sons of the Buddha, the bodhisattva-mahāsattva has ten kinds of paths. What are those ten? They are as follows:

正體字

一道是菩薩道。不捨獨一菩提心故。二道是菩薩道。出生智慧及方便故。三道是菩薩道。行空無相無願。不著三界故。四行是菩薩道。懺除罪障。隨喜福德。恭敬尊重。勸請如來。善巧迴向。無休息故。五根是菩薩道。安住淨信。堅固不動。起大精進。所作究竟。一向正念。無異攀緣。巧知三昧入出方便。善能分別智慧境界故。六通是菩薩道。所謂天眼悉見一切世界所有眾色。知諸眾生死此生彼故。天耳悉聞諸佛說法。受持憶念。廣為眾生。隨根演暢故。他心智。能知他心。自在無礙故。宿命念。憶知過去一切劫數。增長善根故。神足通。隨所應化一切眾生。種種為現。令樂法故。漏盡智。現證實際。起菩薩行。不斷絕故。

简体字

一道是菩萨道，不舍独一菩提心故。二道是菩萨道，出生智慧及方便故。三道是菩萨道，行空、无相、无愿，不著三界故。四行是菩萨道，忏除罪障，随喜福德，恭敬尊重劝请如来，善巧回向无休息故。五根是菩萨道，安住净信坚固不动，起大精进所作究竟，一向正念无异攀缘，巧知三昧入出方便，善能分别智慧境界故。六通是菩萨道。所谓：天眼，悉见一切世界所有众色，知诸众生死此生彼故；天耳，悉闻诸佛说法，受持忆念，广为众生随根演畅故；他心智，能知他心，自在无碍故；宿命念，忆知过去一切劫数，增长善根故；神足通，随所应化一切众生，种种为现，令乐法故；漏尽智，现证实际，起菩萨行不断绝故。

A single path is the bodhisattva path because he never abandons the one bodhi resolve.

A twofold path is the bodhisattva path because it involves the development of wisdom and skillful means.

A threefold path serves as the bodhisattva path because, by practicing emptiness, signlessness, and wishlessness, he refrains from attachment to the three realms of existence.

A fourfold practice serves as the bodhisattva path based on incessantly eliminating karmic obstacles through repentance, rejoicing in others' meritorious deeds, respectfully venerating and entreating the Tathāgata [to teach the Dharma], and skillfully dedicating merit.

The five roots serve as the bodhisattva path based on:

Abiding in pure faith that is solid and unshakable;

Generating great vigor by which all that is done is completed;

Abiding in continuous right mindfulness by which one does not seize on extraneous objective conditions;

Skillfully knowing the means for entering and emerging from the samādhis; and

Being well able to distinguish wise spheres of experience.

The six spiritual superknowledges serve as the bodhisattva path based on the following:

With the heavenly eye, he sees the many forms in all worlds and knows of all beings that they died here and then were reborn there;

With the heavenly ear, he hears all the Dharma spoken by all buddhas, absorbs and upholds it, remembers it, and extensively expounds on it for beings in ways that are adapted to their faculties;

With the knowledge of others' thoughts, he possesses unimpeded sovereign mastery in knowing the thoughts of others;

Through the recall of previous lifetimes, he recalls and knows the growth of roots of goodness as it has occurred across the course of all past kalpas;

Through the superknowledge of psychic powers, he brings forth all kinds of different manifestations adapted to those beings he should teach, thereby causing them to delight in the Dharma; and

Through the knowledge of the complete cessation of all contaminants, he manifests the realization of the apex of reality, and ceaselessly develops the bodhisattva practices.

正體字

七念是菩薩道。所謂念

300b19 ｜ 佛。於一毛孔。見無量佛。開悟一切眾生心故。
300b20 ｜ 念法。不離一如來眾會。於一切如來眾會中。
300b21 ｜ 親承妙法。隨諸眾生。根性欲樂。而為演說。令
300b22 ｜ 悟入故。念僧。恒相續見。無有休息。於一切世
300b23 ｜ 間。見菩薩故。念捨。了知一切菩薩捨行。增長
300b24 ｜ 廣大布施心故。念戒。不捨菩提心。以一切善
300b25 ｜ 根。迴向眾生故。念天。常憶念兜率陀天宮一
300b26 ｜ 生補處菩薩故。念眾生。智慧方便。教化調伏。
300b27 ｜ 普及一切。無間斷故。隨順菩提。八聖道是菩
300b28 ｜ 薩道。所謂行正見道。遠離一切諸邪見故。起
300b29 ｜ 正思惟。捨妄分別。心常隨順一切智故。常行
300c01 ｜ 正語。離語四過。順聖言故。恒修正業。教化眾
300c02 ｜ 生。令調伏故。安住正命。頭陀知足。威儀審
300c03 ｜ 正。隨順菩提。行四聖種。一切過失。皆永離
300c04 ｜ 故。起正精進。勤修一切菩薩苦行。入佛十
300c05 ｜ 力無罣礙故。

简体字

七念是菩萨道。所谓：念佛，于一毛孔见无量佛，开悟一切众生心故；念法，不离一如来众会，于一切如来众会中亲承妙法，随诸众生根性欲乐而为演说，令悟入故；念僧，恒相续见无有休息，于一切世间见菩萨故；念舍，了知一切菩萨舍行，增长广大布施心故；念戒，不舍菩提心，以一切善根回向众生故；念天，常忆念兜率陀天宫一生补处菩萨故；念众生，智慧方便教化调伏，普及一切无间断故。随顺菩提八圣道是菩萨道。所谓：行正见道，远离一切诸邪见故；起正思惟，舍妄分别，心常随顺一切智故；常行正语，离语四过，顺圣言故；恒修正业，教化众生令调伏故；安住正命，头陀知足，威仪审正，随顺菩提行四圣种，一切过失皆永离故；起正精进，勤修一切菩萨苦行，入佛十力无挂碍故；

Chapter 38 — *Transcending the World*

The seven types of mindfulness serve as the bodhisattva path based on the following:

Mindfulness of the Buddha through seeing in but a single pore countless buddhas awakening the minds of all beings;

Mindfulness of the Dharma through never leaving the congregation of a single *tathāgata* even as he personally receives the sublime Dharma in the congregations of all *tathāgatas*, adapts to the nature of beings' faculties and inclinations, and then expounds on the Dharma for their sakes to enable them to awaken to it and enter it;

Mindfulness of the Sangha through constantly, continuously, and ceaselessly seeing bodhisattvas in all worlds;

Mindfulness of relinquishing through fully knowing all bodhisattvas' practice of relinquishing, thereby increasing the vastness of his mind of giving;

Mindfulness of the moral precepts through never abandoning the bodhi resolve while dedicating all roots of goodness to beings;

Mindfulness of the heavens through always bearing in mind the bodhisattva abiding in the Tuṣita Heaven palace who has but one more birth prior to buddhahood; and

Mindfulness of beings through the uninterrupted use of wisdom and skillful means in reaching all of them everywhere with his teaching and training.

The *āryas*' eightfold path to the realization of bodhi is the bodhisattva path based on the following:

Practicing the path of right views through abandoning all wrong views;

Bringing forth right thought through abandoning erroneous discriminations and causing the mind to always accord with [the path to] all-knowledge;

Always practicing right speech through abandoning the four speech faults and according with the words of the *āryas*;

Constantly cultivating right action through teaching beings and enabling them to take on the training;

Abiding in right livelihood through practicing the *dhūta* austerities, being easily satisfied, practicing the awesome deportment, reflecting critically on what is right, according with bodhi, practicing the four lineage bases of the *ārya*,[121] and forever abandoning all faults;

Arousing right vigor through diligently cultivating all the bodhisattva austerities and being unimpeded in entering the ten powers of the Buddha;

正體字

心常正念。悉能憶持一切言音。
除滅世間散動心故。心常正定。善入菩薩不
思議解脫門。於一三昧中。出生一切諸三昧
故。入九次第定。是菩薩道。所謂離欲患害。而
以一切語業。說法無礙。滅除覺觀。而以一切
智覺觀。教化眾生。捨離喜愛。而見一切佛。心
大歡喜。離世間樂。而隨順出世菩薩道樂。從
此不動。入無色定。而亦不捨欲色受生。雖住
滅一切想受定。而亦不息菩薩行故。學佛十
力。是菩薩道。所謂善知是處非處智。善知一
切眾生去來現在業報因果智。善知一切眾
生上中下根不同隨宜說法智。善知一切眾
生種種無量性智。善知一切眾生軟中上解
差別令入法方便智。遍一切世間一切剎一
切三世一切劫

简体字

心常正念，悉能忆持一切言音，除灭世间散动心故；心常正定，善入菩萨不思议解脱门，于一三昧中出生一切诸三昧故。入九次第定是菩萨道。所谓；离欲患害，而以一切语业说法无碍；灭除觉观，而以一切智觉观教化众生；舍离喜爱，而见一切佛，心大欢喜；离世间乐，而随顺出世菩萨道乐；从此不动，入无色定，而亦不舍欲、色受生；虽住灭一切想受定，而亦不息菩萨行故。学佛十力是菩萨道。所谓：善知是处、非处智；善知一切众生、去、来现在业报因果智；善知一切众生上、中、下根不同随宜说法智；善知一切众生种种无量性智；善知一切众生软、中、上解差别令入法方便智；遍一切世间、一切刹、一切三世、一切劫，

Chapter 38 — *Transcending the World*

- Always having the mind abide in right mindfulness through being able to remember all that is spoken while also extinguishing scattered worldly thoughts; and
- Always having the mind abide in right meditative concentration through skillfully entering the bodhisattva's inconceivable gates of liberation and through bringing forth all samādhis from within a single samādhi.

The nine sequential meditative absorptions[122] constitute the bodhisattva path based on the following:

- Abandoning the harm arising from desire and hatred even as he uses all forms of verbal actions in unimpeded discourse on the Dharma;
- Extinguishing both ideation and discursion even as he uses ideation and discursion arising from all-knowledge to teach beings;
- Relinquishing joy even as he feels great joy at the sight of all buddhas;
- Abandoning worldly bliss even as he accords with the world-transcending bliss of the bodhisattva path;
- Through remaining unshakable in this, he enters the formless meditative absorptions even as he does not abandon the taking on of births in both the desire realm and the formless realm; and
- Although he abides in the meditative absorption in which all perception and feeling are extinguished, he still never ceases the bodhisattva practices.

Training in the ten powers of the Buddha is the bodhisattva path, based on the following:

- The knowledge that well knows what can and cannot be;
- The knowledge that well knows all beings' karmic consequences, causes, and effects of the past, the future, and the present;
- The knowledge that well knows the differences in all beings superior, middling, and inferior faculties and accords with what is fitting in teaching them the Dharma;
- The knowledge that well knows the countless different natures of all beings;
- The knowledge that well knows the skillful means by which all beings of different weak, middling, or superior understanding may be enabled to enter the Dharma;
- The knowledge by which he pervades all worlds, all *kṣetras*, all three periods of time, and all kalpas, everywhere

正體字

普現如來形相威儀而亦不捨
300c20 ‖ 菩薩所行智。[2]善知一切諸禪解脫及諸三昧
300c21 ‖ 若垢若淨時與非時方便出生諸菩薩解脫門
300c22 ‖ 智。知一切眾生於諸趣中死此生彼差別智。
300c23 ‖ 於一念中悉知三世一切劫數智。善知一切
300c24 ‖ 眾生樂欲諸使惑習滅盡智。而不捨離諸菩
300c25 ‖ 薩行。是為十。若諸菩薩。安住此法。則得一切
300c26 ‖ 如來。無上巧方便道
300c27 ‖ 佛子。菩薩摩訶薩。有無量道。無量助道。無量
300c28 ‖ 修道。無量莊嚴道。佛子。菩薩摩訶薩。有十種
300c29 ‖ 無量道。何等為十。所謂虛空無量故。菩薩道
301a01 ‖ 亦無量。法界無邊故。菩薩道亦無量。眾生界
301a02 ‖ 無盡故。菩薩道亦無量。世界無際故。菩薩道
301a03 ‖ 亦無量。劫數不可盡故。菩薩道亦無量。一切
301a04 ‖ 眾生語言法無量故。菩薩道亦無量。如來身
301a05 ‖ 無量故。菩薩道亦無量。佛音聲無量故。菩薩
301a06 ‖ 道亦無量。如來力無量故。菩薩道亦無量。

简体字

普现如来形相威仪而亦不舍菩萨所行智；善知一切诸禅解脱及诸三昧若垢若净、时与非时，方便出生诸菩萨解脱门智；知一切众生于诸趣中死此生彼差别智；于一念中悉知三世一切劫数智；善知一切众生乐欲、诸使、惑习灭尽智，而不舍离诸菩萨行。是为十。若诸菩萨安住此法，则得一切如来无上巧方便道。

"佛子，菩萨摩诃萨有无量道、无量助道、无量修道、无量庄严道。

"佛子，菩萨摩诃萨有十种无量道。何等为十？所谓：虚空无量故，菩萨道亦无量；法界无边故，菩萨道亦无量；众生界无尽故，菩萨道亦无量；世界无际故，菩萨道亦无量；劫数不可尽故，菩萨道亦无量；一切众生语言法无量故，菩萨道亦无量；如来身无量故，菩萨道亦无量；佛音声无量故，菩萨道亦无量；如来力无量故，菩萨道亦无量；

Chapter 38 — *Transcending the World*

> manifesting the Tathāgata's form, signs, and awesome deportment even while still never abandoning the bodhisattva practices;
>
> The knowledge that well knows with regard to all the *dhyānas*, liberations, and samādhis what is defiled and what is pure as well as what is timely and what is untimely while using skillful means to bring forth the bodhisattvas' gates to liberation;[123]
>
> The knowledge that knows with regard to all beings in all the destinies of rebirth the differences in their dying in this place and being reborn in that place;
>
> The knowledge that knows in but a single mind-moment all kalpas of the three periods of time; and
>
> The knowledge that well knows the complete cessation of all the desires, latent tendencies, delusions, and habitual karmic propensities to which all beings are subject, yet never abandons any of the bodhisattva practices.

These are the ten. If beings abide in these dharmas, then they acquire all *tathāgatas'* unexcelled path of skillful means.

Sons of the Buddha, the bodhisattva-mahāsattva has measureless paths, measureless provisions for enlightenment, measureless ways of cultivating the path, and measureless adornments of the path.

Sons of the Buddha, the bodhisattva-mahāsattva has ten kinds of measureless path. What are those ten? They are as follows:

> Because empty space is measureless, so too is the bodhisattva's path also measureless;
>
> Because the Dharma realm is boundless, so too is the bodhisattva's path also measureless;
>
> Because the realms of beings are endless, so too is the bodhisattva's path also measureless;
>
> Because the worlds are boundless, so too is the bodhisattva's path also measureless;
>
> Because the number of kalpas is endless, so too is the bodhisattva's path also measureless;
>
> Because the dharmas associated with all beings' languages are measureless, so too is the bodhisattva's path also measureless;
>
> Because the Tathāgata's body is measureless, so too is the bodhisattva's path also measureless;
>
> Because the Buddha's voice is measureless, so too is the bodhisattva's path also measureless;
>
> Because the Tathāgata's powers are measureless, so too is the bodhisattva's path also measureless; and

正體字

```
301a07 | 切智智無量故。菩薩道亦無量。是為十。佛子。
301a08 | 菩薩摩訶薩。有十種無量助道。所謂如虛空
301a09 | 界無量。菩薩集助道亦無量。如法[1]界無邊。
301a10 | 菩薩集助道亦無邊。如眾生界無盡。菩薩集
301a11 | 助道亦無盡。如世界無際。菩薩集助道亦無
301a12 | 際。如劫數說不可盡。菩薩集助道亦一切世
301a13 | 間。說不能盡。如眾生語言法無量。菩薩集助
301a14 | 道。出生智慧。知語言法亦無量。如如來身無
301a15 | 量。菩薩集助道。遍一切眾生。一切剎。一切
301a16 | 世。一切劫亦無量。如佛音聲無量。菩薩出一
301a17 | 言音。周遍法界。一切眾生。無不聞知故。所集
301a18 | 助道亦無量。如佛力無量。菩薩承如來力。積
301a19 | 集助道亦無量。如一切智智無量。菩薩積集
301a20 | 助道亦如是無有量。是為十。若諸菩薩。安住
301a21 | 此法。則得如來無量智慧。
```

简体字

一切智智无量故,菩萨道亦无量。是为十。

"佛子,菩萨摩诃萨有十种无量助道。所谓:如虚空界无量,菩萨集助道亦无量;如法界无边,菩萨集助道亦无边;如众生界无尽,菩萨集助道亦无尽;如世界无际,菩萨集助道亦无际;如劫数说不可尽,菩萨集助道亦一切世间说不能尽;如众生语言法无量,菩萨集助道出生智慧知语言法亦无量;如如来身无量,菩萨集助道遍一切众生、一切刹、一切世、一切劫亦无量;如佛音声无量,菩萨出一言音周遍法界,一切众生无不闻知故,所集助道亦无量;如佛力无量,菩萨承如来力积集助道亦无量;如一切智智无量,菩萨积集助道亦如是无有量。是为十。若诸菩萨安住此法,则得如来无量智慧。

Chapter 38 — *Transcending the World*

Because the wisdom of all-knowledge is measureless, so too is the bodhisattva's path also measureless.

These are the ten.

Sons of the Buddha, the bodhisattva-mahāsattva has ten kinds of measurelessness of his provisions for enlightenment. They are as follows:

Just as the realms of empty space are measureless, so too are the provisions for enlightenment accumulated by the bodhisattva also measureless;

Just as the Dharma realm is boundless, so too are the provisions for enlightenment accumulated by the bodhisattva also boundless;

Just as the realms of beings are endless, so too are the provisions for enlightenment accumulated by the bodhisattva also endless;

Just as the worlds are boundless, so too are the provisions for enlightenment accumulated by the bodhisattva also boundless;

Just as the number of kalpas is inexhaustible through verbal description, so too are the provisions for enlightenment accumulated by the bodhisattva also inexhaustible through the verbal descriptions uttered by anyone in any world;

Just as the dharmas of all beings' languages are measureless, so too are the provisions for enlightenment measureless that are accumulated by the bodhisattva in producing the wisdom that knows all language dharmas;

Just as the Tathāgata's bodies are measureless, so too are the provisions for enlightenment measureless that are accumulated by the bodhisattva in pervading all [realms of] beings, all *kṣetras*, all worlds, and all kalpas;

Just as the Buddha's voices are measureless, so too are the provisions for enlightenment measureless that are accumulated by the bodhisattva in his utterance of but a single voice that reaches everywhere throughout the Dharma realm to all beings of whom none fail to hear and understand it;

Just as the Tathāgata's powers are measureless, so too are the provisions for enlightenment measureless that are accumulated by the bodhisattva through taking on the powers of the Tathāgata; and

Just as the wisdom of all-knowledge is measureless, so too are the provisions for enlightenment measureless that are accumulated by the bodhisattva.

These are the ten. If bodhisattvas abide in these dharmas, then they acquire the Tathāgata's measureless wisdom.

正體字

佛子。菩薩摩訶薩。
有十種無量修道。何等為十。所謂不來不去
修。身語意業。無動作故。不增不減修。如本性
故非有非無修。無自性故。如幻如夢。如影如
響。如鏡中像。如熱時焰。如水中月修。離一切
執著故。空無相無願無作修。明見三界。而集
福德。不休息故。不可說無言說離言說修。遠
離施設。安立法故。不壞法界修。智慧現知一
切法故。不壞真如實際修。普入真如實際虛
空際故。廣大智慧修。諸有所作力無盡故。住
如來十力四無所畏一切智智平等修。現見
一切法無疑惑故。是為十。若諸菩薩。安住此
法。則得如來一切智無上善巧修。佛子。菩薩
摩訶薩。有十種莊嚴道。何等為十。佛子。菩薩
摩訶薩。不離欲界。入色界無色界禪定解脫。
及諸三昧。亦不因此。而受彼生。是為第一莊
嚴道。

简体字

"佛子，菩萨摩诃萨有十种无量修道。何等为十？所谓：不来不去修，身、语、意业无动作故；不增不减修，如本性故；非有非无修，无自性故；如幻如梦、如影如响、如镜中像、如热时焰、如水中月修，离一切执著故；空、无相、无愿、无作修，明见三界而集福德不休息故；不可说、无言说、离言说修，远离施设安立法故；不坏法界修，智慧现知一切法故；不坏真如实际修，普入真如实际虚空际故；广大智慧修，诸有所作力无尽故；住如来十力、四无所畏、一切智智平等修，现见一切法无疑惑故。是为十。若诸菩萨安住此法，则得如来一切智无上善巧修。

"佛子，菩萨摩诃萨有十种庄严道。何等为十？佛子，菩萨摩诃萨不离欲界，入色界、无色界禅定解脱及诸三昧，亦不因此而受彼生，是为第一庄严道。

Chapter 38 — *Transcending the World*

Sons of the Buddha, the bodhisattva-mahāsattva has ten kinds of measureless cultivation of the path. What are those ten? They are as follows:

Cultivation in which he neither comes nor goes, this due to his remaining entirely motionlessness even in physical, verbal, and mental actions;

Cultivation in which there is neither any increase nor any decrease, this due to its accordance with the fundamental nature;

Cultivation that is neither existent nor nonexistent, this due to its absence of any inherently existent nature;

Cultivation that is like a conjuration, like a dream, like a shadow, like an echo, like an image reflected in a mirror, like the flames of a mirage in the hot-season, and like the moon reflected in the water, this due to having abandoned all attachments;

Cultivation characterized by emptiness, signlessness, wishlessness, and effortlessness, this due to his clear perception of the three realms of existence even as he ceaselessly accumulates merit;

Cultivation that is ineffable, wordless, and transcendent of words and speech, this due to having abandoned the creation or establishment of dharmas;

Cultivation that is not contradictory to the Dharma realm, this due to his wisdom's direct knowing of all dharmas;

Cultivation that does not contradict true suchness or the apex of reality, this due to his everywhere entering the realms of true suchness, the apex of reality, and empty space;

Cultivation imbued with vast wisdom, this due to his endless powers in whatever he does; and

Cultivation that equally abides in the Tathāgata's ten powers, four fearlessnesses, and wisdom of all-knowledge, this due to his freedom from doubt in the direct perception of all dharmas.

These are the ten. If bodhisattvas abide in these dharmas, then they acquire the Tathāgata's cultivation possessed of the unexcelled skillful means of all-knowledge.

Sons of the Buddha, the bodhisattva-mahāsattva has ten kinds of adornments of the path. What are those ten? They are as follows:

Sons of the Buddha, without leaving the desire realm, the bodhisattva-mahāsattva enters the *dhyāna* absorptions, liberations, and samādhis of the form and formless realms, and yet he still does not take rebirths there because of this. This is the first of his adornments of the path;

正體字

智慧現前。入聲聞道。不以此道。而取出
離。是為第二莊嚴道。智慧現前。入辟支佛道。
而起大悲。無有休息。是為第三莊嚴道。雖有
人天。眷屬圍遶。百千[2]采女。歌舞侍從。未曾
暫捨禪定解脫及諸三昧。是為第四莊嚴道。
與一切眾生。受諸欲樂。共相娛樂。乃至未曾
於一念間。捨離菩薩平等三昧。是為第五莊
嚴道。已到一切世間彼岸。於諸世法。悉無所
著。而亦不捨度眾生行。是為第六莊嚴道。安
住正道正智正見。而能示入一切邪道。不取
為實。不執為淨。令彼眾生。遠離邪法。是為第
七莊嚴道。常善護持如來淨戒。身語意業。無
諸過失。為欲教化犯戒眾生。示行一切凡愚
之行。雖已具足清淨福德。住菩薩趣。而示生
於一切地獄畜生餓鬼。及諸險難。貧窮等處。
令彼眾生。皆得解脫。而實菩薩。不生彼趣。是
為第八莊嚴道。不由他教。得無礙辯。智慧光
明。普能照了一切佛法。

简体字

智慧现前，入声闻道，不以此道而取出离，是为第二庄严道。智慧现前，入辟支佛道，而起大悲无有休息，是为第三庄严道。虽有人、天眷属围绕，百千婇女歌舞侍从，未曾暂舍禅定解脱及诸三昧，是为第四庄严道。与一切众生受诸欲乐共相娱乐，乃至未曾于一念间舍离菩萨平等三昧，是为第五庄严道。已到一切世间彼岸，于诸世法悉无所著，而亦不舍度众生行，是为第六庄严道。安住正道、正智、正见，而能示入一切邪道，不取为实，不执为净，令彼众生远离邪法，是为第七庄严道。常善护持如来净戒，身、语、意业无诸过失，为欲教化犯戒众生，示行一切凡愚之行，虽已具足清净福德住菩萨趣，而示生于一切地狱、畜生、饿鬼及诸险难、贫穷等处，令彼众生皆得解脱，而实菩萨不生彼趣，是为第八庄严道。不由他教，得无碍辩，智慧光明普能照了一切佛法，

Chapter 38 — *Transcending the World*

His wisdom directly manifests so that he could enter the path of the *śrāvaka* disciples, yet he still does not use this path to gain emancipation. This is the second of his adornments of the path;

His wisdom directly manifests so that he could enter the path of the *pratyekabuddhas*, yet he ceaselessly arouses the great compassion. This is the third of his adornments of the path;

Although he may be surrounded by a retinue of humans and devas and be attended by a hundred thousand female retainers who sing, dance, serve, and follow him, he still never for even a moment withdraws from his *dhyāna* absorptions, liberations, or samādhis. This is the fourth of his adornments of the path;

He may enjoy all kinds of pleasures and mutual amusements together with all other beings, yet he still never for even a single mind-moment withdraws from the bodhisattva's samādhi of equanimity. This is the fifth of his adornments of the path;

He has already achieved perfection in everything related to the world and is free of any attachments to worldly dharmas, yet he still never relinquishes his practice of liberating beings. This is the sixth of his adornments of the path;

He abides in right path, right knowledge, and right views, yet he is still able to manifest the appearance of entry into erroneous paths in which he does not seize on them as real and does not seize on them as pure, doing so to enable other beings to abandon erroneous dharmas. This is the seventh of his adornments of the path;

He always skillfully guards and upholds the Tathāgata's pure moral precepts so that he is free of all faults in his physical, verbal, and mental actions. Still, wishing to teach beings who transgress against the moral precepts, he may manifest the appearance of practicing all the actions of a foolish common person. Although he is fully equipped with pure merit and thus already dwells in the destinies of a bodhisattva, he still manifests the appearance of being reborn into the hell realms, the animal realms, and the hungry ghost realms as well as into all kinds of dangerous, difficult, and poverty-stricken circumstances, doing so in order to enable all the other beings there to gain liberation. Even so, in truth, the bodhisattva is never actually reborn in those rebirth destinies. This is the eighth of his adornments of the path;

Even without depending on instruction provided by others, he acquires unimpeded eloquence and the light of wisdom with which he is able to everywhere completely illuminate all dharmas of the Buddha. He is supported by the spiritual powers

正體字

為一切如來神力所
301b26 | 持。與一切諸佛。同一法身。成就一切堅固大
301b27 | 人明淨密法。安住一切平等諸乘。諸佛境界。
301b28 | 皆現其前。具足一切世智光明。照見一切諸
301b29 | 眾生界。能為眾生。作知法師。而示求正法。未
301c01 | 曾休息。雖實與眾生。作無上師。而示行尊敬
301c02 | 闍梨和[3]尚。何以故。菩薩摩訶薩。善巧方便。
301c03 | 住菩薩道。隨其所應。皆為示現。是為第九莊
301c04 | 嚴道。善根具足。諸行究竟。一切如來。所共灌
301c05 | 頂。到一切法自在彼岸。無礙法繒。以冠其首。
301c06 | 其身遍至一切世界。普現如來無礙之身。於
301c07 | 法自在。最上究竟。轉於無礙清淨法輪。一切
301c08 | 菩薩自在之法。皆已成就。而為眾生故。於一
301c09 | 切國土。示現受生。與三世諸佛。同一境界。而
301c10 | 不廢菩薩行。不捨菩薩法。不懈菩薩業。不離
301c11 | 菩薩道。不[4]弛菩薩儀。不斷菩薩取。不息菩
301c12 | 薩巧方便。不絕菩薩所作事。不厭菩薩生成
301c13 | 用。不止菩薩住持力。何以故。菩薩欲疾證阿
301c14 | 耨多羅三藐三菩提。觀一切智門。修菩薩行。
301c15 | 無休息故。是為第十莊嚴道。

简体字

为一切如来神力所持，与一切诸佛同一法身，成就一切坚固大人明净密法，安住一切平等诸乘，诸佛境界皆现其前，具足一切世智光明，照见一切诸众生界，能为众生作知法师，而示求正法未曾休息，虽实与众生作无上师，而示行尊敬闍梨和尚。何以故？菩萨摩诃萨善巧方便住菩萨道，随其所应皆为示现。是为第九庄严道。善根具足，诸行究竟，一切如来所共灌顶，到一切法自在彼岸，无碍法缯以冠其首；其身遍至一切世界，普现如来无碍之身，于法自在最上究竟，转于无碍清净法轮；一切菩萨自在之法皆已成就，而为众生故，于一切国土示现受生；与三世诸佛同一境界，而不废菩萨行，不舍菩萨法，不懈菩萨业，不离菩萨道，不弛菩萨仪，不断菩萨取，不息菩萨巧方便，不绝菩萨所作事，不厌菩萨生成用，不止菩萨住持力。何以故？菩萨欲疾证阿耨多罗三藐三菩提，观一切智门修菩萨行无休息故。是为第十庄严道。

Chapter 38 — *Transcending the World*

of all *tathāgatas*, shares the same single Dharma body as that of all buddhas, perfects the radiant and pure esoteric dharmas of all the steadfast great men, and securely dwells in all the uniformly equal vehicles. The spheres of action of all buddhas manifest directly before him. He becomes fully endowed with the light of all worldly knowledge, illuminates and sees all realms of beings, and is able to serve all beings as a knowledgeable master of the Dharma even as he manifests as never resting in his search for right Dharma. Although, in truth, he is one who serves beings as an unexcelled teacher, he still manifests the practice of venerating the *ācāryas* and *upādhyāyas*. And why is this so? This is because the bodhisattva-mahāsattva uses skillful means as he abides in the bodhisattva path, thereby manifesting for everyone in accordance with what is fitting. This is the ninth of his adornments of the path; and

Having become perfectly complete in his roots of goodness and having achieved the ultimate consummation of all of the practices, he becomes one who receives the simultaneous joint crown-anointing consecration from all *tathāgatas*. He reaches the far shore of perfection in the sovereign mastery of all dharmas and uses the headband of unimpeded Dharma to crown his head. His body everywhere reaches all worlds and everywhere manifests the Tathāgata's unimpeded body. He achieves the most supreme and ultimate sovereign mastery of the Dharma and turns the wheel of the unimpeded pure Dharma.

Having already achieved the complete development of all the bodhisattva's dharmas of sovereign mastery, for the sake of beings, he manifests as taking rebirths in all lands. He shares the same spheres of action as all buddhas of the three periods of time, yet still never neglects the bodhisattva practices, never relinquishes the bodhisattva's dharmas, never diminishes his accomplishment of the bodhisattva's works, never abandons the bodhisattva path, never relaxes his observance of the bodhisattva's demeanor, never ceases his grasp of whatever the bodhisattva grasps, never rests in implementing the bodhisattva's skillful means, never cuts off his accomplishment of the bodhisattva's endeavors, never wearies of the bodhisattva's initiation and achievement of whatever is useful, and never ceases providing the bodhisattva's supportive sustaining power. And why is this so? This is because, wishing to swiftly attain *anuttarasamyaksaṃbodhi*, the bodhisattva contemplates the gateway of all-knowledge and ceaselessly cultivates the bodhisattva practices. This is the tenth of his adornments of the path.

正體字

若諸菩薩。安住
此法。則得如來無上大莊嚴道。亦不捨菩薩
道。佛子。菩薩摩訶薩。有十種足。何等為十。
所謂持戒足。殊勝大願。悉成滿故。精進足。集
一切菩提分法。不退轉故。神通足。隨眾生欲。
令歡喜故。神力足。不離一佛剎。往一切佛剎
故。深心足。願求一切殊勝法故。堅誓足。一切
所作。咸究竟故。隨順足。不違一切尊者教故。
樂法足。聞持一切佛所說法。不疲懈故。法雨
足。為眾演說。無怯弱故。修行足。一切諸惡
悉遠離故。是為十。若諸菩薩。安住此法。則得
如來無上最勝足。若一舉步。悉能遍至一切
世界。佛子。菩薩摩訶薩。有十種手。何等為
十。所謂深信手。於佛所說。一向忍可。究竟受
持故。布施手。有來求者。隨其所欲。皆令充滿
故。先意問訊手。舒展右掌。相迎引故。供養諸
佛手。集眾福德。無疲厭故。多聞善巧手。悉斷
一切眾生疑故。

简体字

若诸菩萨安住此法，则得如来无上大庄严道，亦不舍菩萨道。

"佛子，菩萨摩诃萨有十种足。何等为十？所谓持戒足，殊胜大愿悉成满故；精进足，集一切菩提分法不退转故；神通足，随众生欲令欢喜故；神力足，不离一佛刹往一切佛刹故；深心足，愿求一切殊胜法故；坚誓足，一切所作咸究竟故；随顺足，不违一切尊者教故；乐法足，闻持一切佛所说法不疲懈故；法雨足，为众演说无怯弱故；修行足，一切诸恶悉远离故。是为十。若诸菩萨安住此法，则得如来无上最胜足，若一举步，悉能遍至一切世界。

"佛子，菩萨摩诃萨有十种手。何等为十？所谓：深信手，于佛所说，一向忍可，究竟受持故；布施手，有来求者，随其所欲皆令充满故；先意问讯手，舒展右掌相迎引故；供养诸佛手，集众福德无疲厌故；多闻善巧手，悉断一切众生疑故；

If bodhisattvas abide in these dharmas, then they acquire the Tathāgata's unexcelled and great adornments of the path even as they never abandon the bodhisattva path.

Sons of the Buddha, the bodhisattva-mahāsattva has ten kinds of feet. What are those ten? They are as follows:

- The feet of upholding the moral precepts with which he completely fulfills all of his extraordinarily superior great vows;
- The feet of vigor with which he irreversibly accumulates all the dharmas leading to bodhi;
- The feet of the spiritual superknowledges with which he gladdens beings by adapting to whatever they wish for;
- The feet of the spiritual powers with which he never leaves a single buddha *kṣetra* even as he goes to all buddha *kṣetras*;
- The feet of the deep resolve with which he vows to seek all the most especially superior dharmas;
- The feet of solid vows with which he completes everything he does;
- The feet of accordant compliance with which he never opposes the teachings of all the venerable ones;
- The feet of delight in the Dharma with which he never wearies of hearing and retaining all dharmas spoken by the Buddha;
- The feet of the Dharma rain with which he fearlessly expounds the Dharma for beings; and
- The feet of cultivation with which he abandons all forms of evil.

These are the ten. If bodhisattvas abide in these dharmas, then they acquire the Tathāgata's unexcelled and supreme feet with which, through the lifting of his foot to take but a single footstep, he is able to go everywhere throughout all worlds.

Sons of the Buddha, the bodhisattva-mahāsattva has ten kinds of hands. What are those ten? They are as follows:

- The hands of deep faith with which he continuously adopts and ultimately absorbs and upholds whatever the Buddha has taught;
- The hands of giving with which he completely fulfills the requests for whatever any supplicant desires;
- The hands that are the first to offer pressed-palms greetings followed by the extended right hand with which he welcomes and leads others;
- The hands that make offerings to all buddhas with which he tirelessly accumulates the many kinds of merit;
- The hands of skill in abundant learning with which he severs the doubts of all beings;

正體字

令超三界手。授與眾生。拔出
欲泥故。置於彼岸手。四暴流中。救溺眾生故。
不吝正法手。所有妙法。悉以開示故。善用眾
論手。以智慧[1]樂。滅身心病故。恒持智寶手。
開法光明。破煩惱闇故。是為十。若諸菩薩。安
住此法。則得如來無上手。普覆十方一切世
界。佛子。菩薩摩訶薩。有十種腹。何等為十。
所謂離諂曲腹。心清淨故。離幻偽腹。性質直
故。不虛假腹。無險詖故。無欺奪腹。於一切
物。無所貪故。斷煩惱腹。具智慧故。清淨心
腹。離諸惡故。觀察飲食腹。念如實法故。觀
察無作腹。覺悟緣起故。覺悟一切出離道腹。
善成熟深心故。遠離一切邊見垢腹。令一切
眾生。得入佛腹故。是為十。若諸菩薩。安住此
法。則得如來無上廣大腹。悉能容受一切眾
生。佛子。菩薩摩訶薩。有十種藏。何等為十。
所謂

简体字

令超三界手,授与众生拔出欲泥故;置于彼岸手,四暴流中救溺众生故;不吝正法手,所有妙法悉以开示故;善用众论手,以智慧药灭身心病故;恒持智宝手,开法光明破烦恼暗故。是为十。若诸菩萨安住此法,则得如来无上手,普覆十方一切世界。

"佛子,菩萨摩诃萨有十种腹。何等为十?所谓:离谄曲腹,心清净故;离幻伪腹,性质直故;不虚假腹,无险诐故;无欺夺腹,于一切物无所贪故;断烦恼腹,具智慧故;清净心腹,离诸恶故;观察饮食腹,念如实法故;观察无作腹,觉悟缘起故;觉悟一切出离道腹,善成熟深心故;远离一切边见垢腹,令一切众生得入佛腹故。是为十。若诸菩萨安住此法,则得如来无上广大腹,悉能容受一切众生。

"佛子,菩萨摩诃萨有十种藏。何等为十?所谓:

Chapter 38 — *Transcending the World*

> The hands that enable transcendence of the three realms of existence which he extends to beings to pull them out of the mire of desire;
>
> The hands that place beings on the far shore with which he rescues beings drowning in the four floods;[124]
>
> The hands that are never miserly with right Dharma with which he explains all the sublime Dharma that he possesses;
>
> The hands that skillfully use the many kinds of doctrines with which he uses the medicine of wisdom to extinguish all physical and mental disorders; and
>
> The hands that constantly hold the jewels of wisdom with which he shines the light of Dharma to dispel the darkness of afflictions.

These are the ten. If bodhisattvas abide in these dharmas, then they acquire the Tathāgata's unexcelled hands which cover all worlds of the ten directions.

Sons of the Buddha, the bodhisattva-mahāsattva has ten kinds of belly. What are those ten? They are as follows:

> The belly that abandons flattering deviousness, because his mind is pure;
>
> The belly that abandons deceptive artifice, because he has a straightforward character;
>
> The belly that is never false, because he is free of dishonesty;
>
> The belly that is free of any inclination to engage in bullying or forceful confiscation, because he has nothing that he covets;
>
> The belly that cuts off the afflictions, because he is wise;
>
> The belly with a pure mind, because he abandons all evils;
>
> The belly that subjects food and drink to analytic contemplation, because his mindfulness accords with the true Dharma;
>
> The belly that contemplates the uncreated, because he awakens to conditioned arising;
>
> The belly that awakens to all paths of emancipation, because he thoroughly ripens his deep resolve; and
>
> The belly that abandons the defilement of all extreme views, because he enables all beings to succeed in entering the belly of the Buddha.

These are the ten. If bodhisattvas abide in these dharmas, then they acquire the Tathāgata's unexcelled and vast belly that is able to take in and hold all beings.

Sons of the Buddha, the bodhisattva-mahāsattva has ten kinds of inner organs. What are those ten? They are as follows:

正體字

不斷佛種。是菩薩藏。開示佛法無量威
德故。增長法種。是菩薩藏。出生智慧廣大光
明故。住持僧種。是菩薩藏。令其得入不退法
輪故。覺悟正定眾生。是菩薩藏。善隨其時。不
逾一念故。究竟成熟不定眾生。是菩薩藏。令
因相續。無有間斷故。為邪定眾生。發起大悲。
是菩薩藏。令未來因。悉得成就故。滿佛十力
不可壞因。是菩薩藏。具降伏魔軍。無對善根
故。最勝無畏大師子吼。是菩薩藏。令一切眾
生。皆歡喜故。得佛十八不共法。是菩薩藏。智
慧普入一切處故。普了知一切眾生。一切剎。
一切法。一切佛。是菩薩藏。於一念中。悉明見
故。是為十。若諸菩薩。安住此法。則得如來無
上善根不可壞大智慧藏。佛子。菩薩摩訶薩。
有十種心。何等為十。所謂精勤心。一切所作。
悉究竟故。不懈心。積集相好。福德行故。大勇
健心。摧破一切諸魔軍故。

简体字

不断佛种是菩萨藏，开示佛法无量威德故；增长法种是菩萨藏，出生智慧广大光明故；住持僧种是菩萨藏，令其得入不退法轮故；觉悟正定众生是菩萨藏，善随其时不逾一念故；究竟成熟不定众生是菩萨藏，令因相续无有间断故；为邪定众生发起大悲是菩萨藏，令未来因悉得成就故；满佛十力不可坏因是菩萨藏，具降伏魔军无对善根故；最胜无畏大师子吼是菩萨藏，令一切众生皆欢喜故；得佛十八不共法是菩萨藏，智慧普入一切处故；普了知一切众生、一切刹、一切法、一切佛是菩萨藏，于一念中悉明见故。是为十。若诸菩萨安住此法，则得如来无上善根不可坏大智慧藏。

"佛子，菩萨摩诃萨有十种心。何等为十？所谓：精勤心，一切所作悉究竟故；不懈心，积集相好福德行故；大勇健心，摧破一切诸魔军故；

Never severing the lineage of the Buddha is a bodhisattva organ with which he explains the measureless awesome qualities of the Buddha's Dharma;

Extending the lineage of the Dharma is a bodhisattva organ with which he brings forth the vast light of wisdom;

Sustaining the lineage of the Sangha is a bodhisattva organ with which he enables others to succeed in gaining access to the irreversible wheel of the Dharma;

Awakening beings fixed in what is right[125] is a bodhisattva organ with which he skillfully accords with the right time for them, not missing it by even a single mind-moment;

Achieving the ultimate ripening of beings who are not fixed in [either what is right or what is wrong] is a bodhisattva organ with which he enables them to establish uninterrupted continuity of associated causes;

Bringing forth the great compassion for beings who are fixed in what is wrong is a bodhisattva organ with which he ensures that their future causes will all lead to their ripening;

Fulfillment of the indestructible causes for attaining the Buddha's ten powers is a bodhisattva organ with which he fully develops the roots of goodness by which he is unopposable in conquering the armies of Māra;

The lion's roar of supreme fearlessness is a bodhisattva organ with which he causes all beings to feel joyful;

Acquisition of the Buddha's eighteen dharmas exclusive to the buddhas is a bodhisattva organ with which his wisdom reaches everywhere; and

Universally and completely understanding all beings, all *kṣetras*, all dharmas, and all buddhas is a bodhisattva organ with which, in but a single mind-moment, he clearly sees them all.

These are the ten. If bodhisattvas abide in these dharmas, then they acquire the Tathāgata's unexcelled organ of roots of goodness and indestructible great wisdom.

Sons of the Buddha, the bodhisattva-mahāsattva has ten kinds of heart. What are those ten? They are as follows:

The heart that is energetically diligent by which he completes everything he does;

The heart that is never indolent by which he accumulates the merit-generating practices producing the major marks and secondary signs;

The heart that is immensely brave and strong by which he utterly vanquishes all the armies of Māra;

正體字

如理行心。除滅一
切諸煩惱故。不退轉心。乃至菩提。終不息故。
性清淨心。知心不動。無所著故。知眾生心。隨
其解欲。令出離故。令入佛法。大梵住心。知諸
眾生。種種解欲。不以別乘。而救護故。空無相
無願無作心。見三界相。不取著故。[2]卍字相
金剛堅固勝藏莊嚴心。一切眾生數等魔來。
乃至不能動一毛故。是為十。若諸菩薩。安住
此法。則得如來無上大智光明藏心。佛子。菩
薩摩訶薩。有十種被甲。何等為十。所謂被大
慈甲。救護一切眾生故。被大悲甲。堪忍一切
諸苦故。被大願甲。一切所作究竟故。被迴向
甲。建立一切佛莊嚴故。被福德甲。饒益一切
諸眾生故。被波羅蜜甲。度脫一切諸含識故。
被智慧甲。滅一切眾生。煩惱闇故。被善巧方
便甲。生普門善根故。被一切智心堅固不散
亂甲。不樂餘乘故。

简体字

如理行心，除灭一切诸烦恼故；不退转心，乃至菩提终不息故；性清净心，知心不动无所著故；知众生心，随其解欲令出离故；令入佛法大梵住心，知诸众生种种解欲，不以别乘而救护故；空、无相、无愿、无作心，见三界相不取著故；卍字相金刚坚固胜藏庄严心，一切众生数等魔来乃至不能动一毛故。是为十。若诸菩萨安住此法，则得如来无上大智光明藏心。

"佛子，菩萨摩诃萨有十种被甲。何等为十？所谓：被大慈甲，救护一切众生故；被大悲甲，堪忍一切诸苦故；被大愿甲，一切所作究竟故；被回向甲，建立一切佛庄严故；被福德甲，饶益一切诸众生故，被波罗蜜甲，度脱一切诸含识故，被智慧甲，灭一切众生烦恼暗故；被善巧方便甲，生普门善根故；被一切智心坚固不散乱甲，不乐余乘故；

Chapter 38 — *Transcending the World*

- The heart that accords with principle in its actions by which he gets rid of all afflictions;
- The heart that is irreversible by which he never rests until he achieves the realization of bodhi;
- The heart that is pure in nature by which his knowing mind is unshakable because it is free of attachments;
- The heart that knows beings by which he adapts to their understandings and desires and thereby enables them to gain emancipation;
- The heart of the great *brāhma-vihāras, [or four immeasurable minds]*,[126] which enable entry into the Dharma of the Buddha by which he knows all beings' various understandings and desires and rescues them without resorting to any other vehicle;
- The heart of emptiness, signlessness, wishlessness, and effortlessness by which he perceives the signs of the three realms of existence without ever seizing on any of them; and
- The heart that, adorned with the sign of the *svastika*, serves as a supreme treasury of vajra solidity by which, even if *māras* as numerous as all beings were to come and assail him, they would be unable to shake even a single hair on his body.

These are the ten. If bodhisattvas abide in these dharmas, then they acquire the Tathāgata's heart that is a treasury of the light of his unexcelled great wisdom.

Sons of the Buddha, the bodhisattva-mahāsattva has ten kinds of armor. What are those ten? They are as follows:

- He dons the armor of great kindness with which he rescues and protects all beings;
- He dons the armor of great compassion with which he is able to endure all sufferings;
- He dons the armor of great vows with which he completes everything he does;
- He dons the armor of dedications with which he establishes all the adornments of the buddhas;
- He dons the armor of merit with which he benefits all beings;
- He dons the armor of the *pāramitās* with which he liberates all sentient beings;
- He dons the armor of wisdom with which he dispels the darkness of all beings' afflictions;
- He dons the armor of skillful means with which he develops the roots of goodness of the universal gateways;
- He dons the armor of the solid and undistracted resolve to attain all-knowledge by which he does not delight in any of the other vehicles; and

正體字

被一心決定甲。於一切法。
離疑惑故。是為十。若諸菩薩。安住此法。則被如來無上甲冑。悉能摧伏一切魔軍。佛子。菩薩摩訶薩。有十種器仗。何等為十。所謂布施是菩薩器仗。摧破一切慳吝故。持戒是菩薩器仗。棄捨一切毀犯故。平等是菩薩器仗。斷除一切分別故。智慧是菩薩器仗。消滅一切煩惱故。正命是菩薩器仗。遠離一切邪命故。善巧方便是菩薩器仗。於一切處示現故。略說貪瞋癡等一切煩惱是菩薩器仗。以煩惱門。度眾生故。生死是菩薩器仗。不斷菩薩行。教化眾生故。說如實法。是菩薩器仗。能破一切執著故。一切智是菩薩器仗。不捨菩薩行門故。是為十。若諸菩薩。安住此法。則能除滅一切眾生。長夜所集。煩惱結使
佛子。菩薩摩訶薩。有十種首。何等為十。所謂涅槃首。無能見頂故。尊敬首。一切人天。所敬禮故。廣大勝解首。三千界中。最為勝故。第一善根首。三界眾生。咸供養故。荷戴眾生首。成就頂上肉髻相故。

简体字

被一心决定甲,于一切法离疑惑故。是为十。若诸菩萨安住此法,则被如来无上甲冑,悉能摧伏一切魔军。

"佛子,菩萨摩诃萨有十种器仗。何等为十?所谓:布施是菩萨器仗,摧破一切悭吝故;持戒是菩萨器仗,弃舍一切毁犯故;平等是菩萨器仗,断除一切分别故;智慧是菩萨器仗,消灭一切烦恼故;正命是菩萨器仗,远离一切邪命故;善巧方便是菩萨器仗,于一切处示现故;略说贪、瞋、痴等一切烦恼是菩萨器仗,以烦恼门度众生故;生死是菩萨器仗,不断菩萨行教化众生故;说如实法是菩萨器仗,能破一切执著故;一切智是菩萨器仗,不舍菩萨行门故。是为十。若诸菩萨安住此法,则能除灭一切众生长夜所集烦恼结使。

"佛子,菩萨摩诃萨有十种首。何等为十?所谓:涅槃首,无能见顶故;尊敬首,一切人、天所敬礼故;广大胜解首,三千界中最为胜故;第一善根首,三界众生咸供养故;荷戴众生首,成就顶上肉髻相故;

Chapter 38 — *Transcending the World*

He dons the armor of single-minded certainty with which he abandons doubts about any of the Dharma teachings.

These are the ten. If bodhisattvas abide in these dharmas, then they don the Tathāgata's unexcelled armor with which they are able to vanquish all the armies of Māra.

Sons of the Buddha, the bodhisattva-mahāsattva has ten kinds of weapons. What are those ten? They are as follows:

Giving is the bodhisattva's weapon with which he vanquishes all miserliness;

Upholding moral precepts is the bodhisattva's weapon with which he casts out all forms of transgressions;

Impartiality is the bodhisattva's weapon with which he cuts off all discriminations;

Wisdom is the bodhisattva's weapon with which he eliminates all afflictions;

Right livelihood is the bodhisattva's weapon with which he abandons all forms of wrong livelihood;

The use of skillful means is the bodhisattva's weapon with which he manifests in all places;

Briefly stated, greed, hatred, delusion, and all the other kinds of afflictions are the bodhisattva's weapons for it is through the gateway of the afflictions that he is able to liberate beings;

Saṃsāra is the bodhisattva's weapon by which he never ceases the bodhisattva practice of teaching beings;

The proclamation of Dharma in accordance with reality is the bodhisattva's weapon by which he is able to demolish all attachments; and

All-knowledge is the bodhisattva's weapon by which he never abandons the bodhisattva's gateways of practice.

These are the ten. If bodhisattvas abide in these dharmas, then they are able to rid all beings of the fetters and afflictions they have accumulated throughout the long night [of *saṃsāra*].

Sons of the Buddha, the bodhisattva-mahāsattva has ten kinds of head. What are those ten? They are as follows:

The head of nirvāṇa, the summit of which no one can see;

The venerated head, revered by all humans and devas;

The head of vast and supreme understanding, supreme of all in the trichiliocosm;

The head of foremost roots of goodness, to which beings of the three realms of existence all make offerings;

The head that supports beings, it has developed the fleshy prominence on the crown of the head;

正體字

不輕賤他首。於一切處。常
尊勝故。般若波羅蜜首。長養一切功德法故。
方便智相應首。普現一切同類身故。教化一
切眾生首。以一切眾生。為弟子故。守護諸佛
法眼首。能令三寶種。不斷絕故。是為十。若諸
菩薩。安住此法。則得如來無上大智慧首。佛
子。菩薩摩訶薩。有十種眼。所謂肉眼。見一切
色故。天眼。見一切眾生心故。慧眼。見一切眾
生。諸根境界故。法眼。見一切法。如實相故。
佛眼。見如來十力故。智眼。知見諸法故。光明
眼。見佛光明故。出生死眼。見涅槃故。無礙
眼。所見無障故。一切智眼。見普門法界故。是
為十。若諸菩薩。安住此法。則得如來無上大
智慧眼。佛子。菩薩摩訶薩。有十種耳。何等為
十。所謂聞讚歎聲。斷除貪愛。聞毀呰聲。斷除
瞋恚。聞說二乘。不著不求。聞菩薩道。歡喜踊
躍。

简体字

不轻贱他首,于一切处常尊胜故;般若波罗蜜首,长养一切功德法故;方便智相应首,普现一切同类身故;教化一切众生首,以一切众生为弟子故;守护诸佛法眼首,能令三宝种不断绝故。是为十。若诸菩萨安住此法,则得如来无上大智慧首。

"佛子,菩萨摩诃萨有十种眼。所谓:肉眼,见一切色故;天眼,见一切众生心故;慧眼,见一切众生诸根境界故;法眼,见一切法如实相故;佛眼,见如来十力故;智眼,知见诸法故;光明眼,见佛光明故;出生死眼,见涅槃故;无碍眼,所见无障故;一切智眼,见普门法界故。是为十。若诸菩萨安住此法,则得如来无上大智慧眼。

"佛子,菩萨摩诃萨有十种耳。何等为十?所谓:闻赞叹声,断除贪爱;闻毁呰声,断除瞋恚;闻说二乘,不著不求;闻菩萨道,欢喜踊跃;

Chapter 38 — *Transcending the World*

    The head that does not slight or look down on others, it is revered as supreme in all places;

    The *prajñāpāramitā* head, it promotes the growth of all dharmas of the meritorious qualities;

    The head that is compatible with the knowledge of skillful means, it everywhere manifests bodies the same as those of others;

    The head that teaches all beings, it takes all beings as disciples; and

    The head that preserves and protects the Dharma eye of all buddhas, it is able to prevent the lineage of the Three Jewels from being cut off.

These are the ten. If bodhisattvas abide in these dharmas, then they acquire the Tathāgata's head possessed of unexcelled great wisdom.

    Sons of the Buddha, the bodhisattva-mahāsattva has ten kinds of eyes, namely:

    The fleshly eye, so called because it sees all forms;

    The heavenly eye, so called because it sees all beings' minds;

    The wisdom eye, so called because it sees all beings' faculties and spheres of cognition;

    The Dharma eye, so called because it sees all dharmas in a manner consistent with their true character;

    The Buddha eye, so called because it sees the Tathāgata's ten powers;

    The eye of knowledge, so called because it knows and sees all dharmas;

    The light eye, so called because it sees the Buddha's light;

    The eye that transcends *saṃsāra*, so called because it sees nirvāṇa;

    The unimpeded eye, so called because it has unimpeded vision of everything it sees; and

    The eye of all-knowledge, so called because it sees the Dharma realm of the universal gateway.

These are the ten. If bodhisattvas abide in these dharmas, then they acquire the Tathāgata's eye of unexcelled great wisdom.

    Sons of the Buddha, the bodhisattva-mahāsattva has ten kinds of ears. What are those ten? They are as follows:

    The ear that, hearing the sounds of praise, severs all covetousness;

    The ear that, hearing the sounds of disparagement, severs all hatred;

    The ear that, on hearing of the two vehicles, is not attached to them and does not seek them;

    The ear that, hearing of the bodhisattva path, is filled with joyous exultation;

正體字

聞地獄等諸苦難處。起大悲心。發弘誓願。
聞說人天勝妙之事。知彼皆是無常之法。聞
有讚歎諸佛功德。勤加精進。令速圓滿。聞說
六度四攝等法。發心修行。願到彼岸。聞十方
世界一切音聲。悉知如響。入不可說甚深妙
義。菩薩摩訶薩。從初發心。乃至道場。常聞正
法。未曾暫息。而恒不捨化眾生事。是為十。若
諸菩薩。成就此法。則得如來無上大智慧耳。
佛子。菩薩摩訶薩。有十種鼻。何等為十。所謂
聞諸臭物。不以為臭。聞諸香氣。不以為香。香
臭俱聞。其心平等。非香非臭。安住於捨。若聞
眾生。衣服臥具。及其[1]肢體。所有香臭。則能
知彼貪恚愚癡。等分之行。若聞諸伏藏。草木
等香。皆如對目前。分明[2]辨了。

简体字

闻地狱等诸苦难处,起大悲心,发弘誓愿;闻说人、天胜妙之事,知彼皆是无常之法;闻有赞叹诸佛功德,勤加精进,令速圆满;闻说六度、四摄等法,发心修行,愿到彼岸;闻十方世界一切音声,悉知如响,入不可说甚深妙义;菩萨摩诃萨从初发心乃至道场,常闻正法未曾暂息,而恒不舍化众生事。是为十。若诸菩萨成就此法,则得如来无上大智慧耳。

"佛子,菩萨摩诃萨有十种鼻。何等为十?所谓:闻诸臭物不以为臭;闻诸香气不以为香;香臭俱闻,其心平等;非香非臭,安住于舍;若闻众生衣服、卧具及其肢体所有香臭,则能知彼贪、恚、愚痴等分之行;若闻诸伏藏草木等香,皆如对目前,分明辨了;

Chapter 38 — *Transcending the World*

- The ear that, on hearing of the hells and the other places beset by every sort of suffering and difficulty, arouses the mind of great compassion and makes the vast vow;
- The ear that, hearing of the supremely marvelous phenomena within the realms of humans and devas, realizes they are all impermanent dharmas;
- The ear that, hearing the praises of all buddhas' meritorious qualities, becomes diligently vigorous in causing them all to become quickly and completely fulfilled;
- The ear that, hearing of the dharmas of the six perfections, the four means of attraction, and other such dharmas, resolves to cultivate them and vows to perfect them;
- The ear that, hearing all the sounds of the worlds of the ten directions, knows them all as like mere echoes and then penetrates their ineffable and extremely profound and sublime meanings; and
- The ear that, from the time the bodhisattva-mahāsattva makes the initial resolve until he reaches the site of enlightenment, always listens to right Dharma, never ceasing for even a moment, and yet never relinquishes the work of teaching beings.

These are the ten. If bodhisattvas perfect these dharmas, then they acquire the Tathāgata's unexcelled ear of great wisdom.

Sons of the Buddha, the bodhisattva-mahāsattva has ten kinds of nose. What are those ten? They are as follows:

- The nose that, on smelling all kinds of things that are foul smelling, does not take them to be foul smelling;
- The nose that, on smelling all kinds of things that are pleasantly fragrant, does not take them to be pleasantly fragrant;
- The nose that, on smelling things that are both pleasantly fragrant and foul smelling remains even-minded;
- The nose that, on smelling that which is neither pleasantly fragrant nor foul smelling, abides in equanimity;
- The nose that, whenever it smells all the smells of the fragrances and foul smells of beings' clothes, bedding, or bodies is thereby able to know the character of their practice as associated with either greed, hatred, or delusion, or a relatively equal portion of all of these;
- The nose that, whenever it smells the fragrances of grasses, trees, and other such things at the site of hidden treasures is able to clearly distinguish them as if they were directly present before his very eyes;

正體字

若聞下至阿
鼻地獄。上至有頂眾生之香。皆知彼過去所
行之行。若聞諸聲聞。布施持戒。多聞慧香。住
一切智心。不令散動。若聞一切菩薩行香以
平等慧。入如來地。聞一切佛智境界香。亦不
廢捨諸菩薩行。是為十。若諸菩薩。成就此法。
則得如來無量無邊清淨鼻。佛子。菩薩摩訶
薩。有十種舌。何等為十。所謂開示演說無盡
眾生行舌。開示演說無盡法門舌。讚歎諸佛
無盡功德舌。演暢辭辯無盡舌。開闡大乘助
道舌。遍覆十方虛空舌。普照一切佛剎舌。普
使眾生悟解舌。悉令諸佛[3]歡喜舌。降伏一切
諸魔外道。除滅一切生死煩惱。令至涅槃舌。
是為十。若諸菩薩。成就此法。則得如來遍覆
一切諸佛國土無上舌。佛子。菩薩摩訶薩。有
十種身。何等為十。所謂

简体字

若闻下至阿鼻地狱、上至有顶众生之香，皆知彼过去所行之行；若闻诸声闻布施、持戒、多闻慧香，住一切智心，不令散动；若闻一切菩萨行香，以平等慧入如来地；闻一切佛智境界香，亦不废舍诸菩萨行。是为十。若诸菩萨成就此法，则得如来无量无边清净鼻。

"佛子，菩萨摩诃萨有十种舌。何等为十？所谓：开示演说无尽众生行舌；开示演说无尽法门舌；赞叹诸佛无尽功德舌；演畅词辩无尽舌；开阐大乘助道舌；遍覆十方虚空舌；普照一切佛刹舌；普使众生悟解舌；悉令诸佛欢喜舌；降伏一切诸魔外道，除灭一切生死烦恼，令至涅槃舌。是为十。若诸菩萨成就此法，则得如来遍覆一切诸佛国土无上舌。

"佛子，菩萨摩诃萨有十种身。何等为十？所谓：

Chapter 38 — Transcending the World

The nose that, whenever it smells any smell from anywhere at all, whether it be from as far down as the Avīci Hells or from as high as the peak of existence, he then knows the actions those beings practiced in the past;

The nose that, whenever it smells the fragrance of *śrāvaka* disciples' giving, moral-precept observance, or wisdom based on abundant learning, he still continues to abide in the resolve to gain all-knowledge and is not caused to become distracted by it;

The nose that, on smelling the fragrance associated with all the bodhisattva practices, uses equanimous wisdom to enter the ground of the Tathāgata; and

The nose that, even on smelling the fragrance of all buddhas' spheres of cognition, still refrains from abandoning the bodhisattva practices.

These are the ten. If bodhisattvas perfect these dharmas, then they acquire the Tathāgata's nose possessed of measureless and boundless purity.

Sons of the Buddha, the bodhisattva-mahāsattva has ten kinds of tongue. What are those ten? They are as follows:

The tongue that reveals and expounds upon the actions of infinitely many beings;

The tongue that reveals and expounds upon infinitely many Dharma gateways;

The tongue that praises all buddhas' endless meritorious qualities;

The tongue that preaches with endless eloquence;

The tongue that explains the Great Vehicle's provisions for enlightenment;

The tongue that everywhere covers the ten directions of space;

The tongue that everywhere illuminates all buddha *kṣetras*;

The tongue that everywhere enables beings to awaken and understand;

The tongue that elicits the praise and happiness of all buddhas; and

The tongue that conquers all *māras* and followers of non-Buddhist paths, extinguishes all of *saṃsāra*'s afflictions, and enables beings to reach nirvāṇa.

These are the ten. If bodhisattvas perfect these dharmas, then they acquire the Tathāgata's unexcelled tongue that everywhere covers all buddha lands.

Sons of the Buddha, the bodhisattva-mahāsattva has ten kinds of bodies. What are those ten? They are as follows:

正體字

人身。為教化一切諸
人故。非人身。為教化地獄畜生餓鬼故。天身。
為教化欲界色界無色界眾生故。學身。示現
學地故。無學身。示現阿羅漢地故。獨覺身。教
化令入辟支佛地故。菩薩身。令成就大乘故。
如來身。智水灌頂故。意生身。善巧出生故。無
漏法身。以無功用示現一切眾生身故。是為
十。若諸菩薩。成就此法。則得如來無上之身。
佛子。菩薩摩訶薩。有十種意。何等為十。所謂
上首意。發起一切善根故。安住意。深信堅固
不動故。深入意。隨順佛法而解故。內了意。知
諸眾生心樂故。無亂意。一切煩惱不雜故。明
淨意。客塵不能染著故。善觀眾生意。無有一
念失時故。善擇所作意。未曾一處生過故。密
護諸根意。調伏不令馳散故。

简体字

人身，为教化一切诸人故；非人身，为教化地狱、畜生、饿鬼故；天身，为教化欲界、色界、无色界众生故；学身，示现学地故；无学身，示现阿罗汉地故；独觉身，教化令入辟支佛地故；菩萨身，令成就大乘故；如来身，智水灌顶故；意生身，善巧出生故；无漏法身，以无功用示现一切众生身故。是为十。若诸菩萨成就此法，则得如来无上之身。

"佛子，菩萨摩诃萨有十种意。何等为十？所谓上首意，发起一切善根故；安住意，深信坚固不动故；深入意，随顺佛法而解故；内了意，知诸众生心乐故；无乱意，一切烦恼不杂故；明净意，客尘不能染著故；善观众生意，无有一念失时故；善择所作意，未曾一处生过故；密护诸根意，调伏不令驰散故；

Chapter 38 — *Transcending the World*

The human body, in order to teach all people;

The nonhuman body, in order to teach the hell-dwellers, the animals, and the hungry ghosts;

The deva body, in order to teach those beings in the desire realm, form realm, and formless realm;

The body of those still in training, in order to reveal the grounds of training;

The body of those beyond training, in order to reveal the grounds of the arhats;

The body of the *pratyekabuddha*, in order to teach beings and enable them to enter the grounds of the *pratyekabuddha*;

The body of the bodhisattva, in order to enable beings to achieve success in the Great Vehicle;

The body of a *tathāgata*, in order to enable crown-anointing consecrations with the waters of wisdom;

The mind-generated body, in order to use skillful means to manifest birth; and

The Dharma body free of contaminants, in order to effortlessly appear in the bodies of every kind of being.

These are the ten. If bodhisattvas perfect these dharmas, then they acquire the Tathāgata's unexcelled body.

Sons of the Buddha, the bodhisattva-mahāsattva has ten kinds of mind. What are those ten? They are as follows:

The supreme leader mind with which he produces all kinds of roots of goodness;

The securely abiding mind with which he maintains deep and unshakably solid faith;

The deeply penetrating mind with which he accords with the Buddha's Dharma and thus understands it;

The inwardly understanding mind with which he understands the mental dispositions of beings;

The undisturbed mind with which he is not contaminated by any of the afflictions;

The clear and pure mind with which he is invulnerable to being stained by the adventitious defilements;

The mind that skillfully contemplates beings with which he never misses the right time by even a single mind-moment;

The mind that skillfully chooses what is to be done with which he never has even a single circumstance in which he commits a transgression;

The mind that skillfully guards all the sense faculties with which he trains them and does not allow them to become scattered; and

正體字

善入三昧意。深入佛三昧無我我所故。是為十。若諸菩薩。安住此法。則得一切佛無上意。佛子。菩薩摩訶薩。有十種行。何等[有>為]十。所謂聞法行。愛樂於法故。說法行。利益眾生故。離貪恚癡怖畏行。調伏自心故。欲界行。教化欲界眾生故。色無色界三昧行。令速轉還故。趣向法義行。速得智慧故。一切生處行。自在教化眾生故。一切佛剎行。禮拜供養諸佛故。涅槃行。不斷生死相續故。成滿一切佛法行。不捨菩薩法行故。是為十。若諸菩薩。安住此法。則得如來無來無去行。佛子。菩薩摩訶薩。有十種住。何等為十。所謂菩提心住。曾不忘失故。波羅蜜住。不厭助道故。說法住。增長智慧故。阿蘭若住。證大禪定故。隨順一切智頭陀知足四聖種住。少欲少事故。深信住。荷負正法故。

简体字

善入三昧意，深入佛三昧无我、我所故。是为十。若诸菩萨安住此法，则得一切佛无上意。

"佛子，菩萨摩诃萨有十种行。何等为十？所谓：闻法行，爱乐于法故；说法行，利益众生故；离贪、恚，痴怖畏行，调伏自心故；欲界行，教化欲界众生故；色、无色界三昧行，令速转还故；趣向法义行，速得智慧故；一切生处行，自在教化众生故；一切佛刹行，礼拜供养诸佛故；涅槃行，不断生死相续故；成满一切佛法行，不舍菩萨法行故。是为十。若诸菩萨安住此法，则得如来无来无去行。

"佛子，菩萨摩诃萨有十种住。何等为十？所谓：菩提心住，曾不忘失故；波罗蜜住，不厌助道故；说法住，增长智慧故；阿兰若住，证大禅定故；随顺一切智头陀知足四圣种住，少欲少事故；深信住，荷负正法故；

The mind that skillfully enters samādhi with which he deeply enters the Buddha's samādhi free of a self or any possessions of a self.

These are the ten. If bodhisattvas abide in these dharmas, then they acquire the unexcelled mind of all buddhas.

Sons of the Buddha, the bodhisattva-mahāsattva has ten kinds of practices. What are those ten? They are as follows:

The practice of listening to the Dharma by which he enjoys the Dharma;

The practice of speaking the Dharma by which he benefits beings;

The practice of abandoning desire, hatred, delusion, and fear by which he trains his own mind;

Desire realm practice by which he teaches desire-realm beings;

Form and formless realm samādhi practice by which he causes those beings to quickly return;

Practice that pursues the meaning of Dharma by which he swiftly acquires wisdom;

Practice in all the stations of rebirth by which he exercises sovereign mastery in teaching beings;

Practice in all buddha *kṣetras* by which he reveres and makes offerings to all buddhas;

Nirvāṇa practice by which he never ceases his continuous presence in *saṃsāra*; and

Practice that achieves complete fulfillment of all the dharmas of the Buddha by which he never abandons his practice of the dharmas of the bodhisattva.

These are the ten. If bodhisattvas abide in these dharmas, then they acquire the Tathāgata's practice which is free of either coming or going.

Sons of the Buddha, the bodhisattva-mahāsattva has ten kinds of abiding. What are those ten? They are as follows:

Abiding in the resolve to attain bodhi, never forgetting it;

Abiding in the *pāramitās*, never wearying of the provisions for enlightenment;

Abiding in speaking the Dharma, increasing his wisdom;

Abiding in an *araṇya*, [a forest dwelling], realizing the great *dhyāna* absorptions;

Abiding in compliance with all-knowledge, the *dhūta* austerities, being easily satisfied, and the four lineage-bases of the *āryas*, having but few desires and few concerns;

Abiding in deep faith, supporting right Dharma;

正體字

親近如來住。學佛威儀故。出生神通住。圓滿大智故。得忍住。滿足授記故。道場住。具足力無畏一切佛法故。是為十。若諸菩薩。安住此法。則得一切智無上住。佛子。菩薩摩訶薩。有十種坐。何等為十。所謂轉輪王坐。興十善道故。四天王坐。於一切世間。自在安立佛法故。帝釋坐。與一切眾生。為勝主故。梵天坐。於自他心。得自在故。師子坐。能說法故。正法坐。以總持辯才力。而開示故。堅固坐。誓願究竟故。大慈坐。令惡眾生。悉歡喜故。大悲坐。忍一切苦。不疲厭故。金剛坐。降伏眾魔及外道故。是為十。若諸菩薩。安住此法。則得如來無上正覺坐。佛子。菩薩摩訶薩。有十種臥。何等為十。所謂寂靜臥。身心憺怕故。禪定臥。如理修行故。

简体字

亲近如来住，学佛威仪故；出生神通住，圆满大智故；得忍住，满足授记故；道场住，具足力、无畏、一切佛法故。是为十。若诸菩萨安住此法，则得一切智无上住。

"佛子，菩萨摩诃萨有十种坐。何等为十？所谓：转轮王坐，兴十善道故；四天王坐，于一切世间自在安立佛法故；帝释坐，与一切众生为胜主故；梵天坐，于自他心得自在故；师子坐，能说法故；正法坐，以总持辩才力而开示故；坚固坐，誓愿究竟故；大慈坐，令恶众生悉欢喜故；大悲坐，忍一切苦不疲厌故；金刚坐，降伏众魔及外道故。是为十。若诸菩萨安住此法，则得如来无上正觉坐。

"佛子，菩萨摩诃萨有十种卧。何等为十？所谓：寂静卧，身心憺怕故；禅定卧，如理修行故；

Chapter 38 — Transcending the World

> Abiding in drawing near to the Tathāgata, training in the Buddha's awesome deportment;
> Abiding in developing the spiritual superknowledges, achieving the complete fulfillment of great wisdom;
> Abiding in the realization of patience,[127] achieving the complete fulfillment of his prediction [of future buddhahood]; and
> Abiding at the site of enlightenment, reaching the complete fulfillment of the powers, the fearlessnesses, and all the other dharmas of the Buddha.

These are the ten. If bodhisattvas abide in these Dharmas, then they acquire the unexcelled abiding in all-knowledge.

Sons of the Buddha, the bodhisattva-mahāsattva has ten kinds of sitting. What are those ten? They are as follows:

> Sitting on the seat of the wheel-turning king from which he promotes the ten courses of good karmic action;
> Sitting on the seat of the Four Heavenly Kings from which he freely establishes the Buddha's Dharma in all worlds;
> Sitting on the seat of Lord Śakra from which he serves as the supreme lord of all beings;
> Sitting on the seat of the Brahma Heaven King from which he gains sovereignty over his own mind and others' minds;
> Sitting on the lion's seat from which he is able to teach the Dharma;
> Sitting on the seat of right Dharma from which he uses the power of complete-retention *dhāraṇīs* and eloquence to reveal and explain it;
> Sitting on the seat of solidity from which his vows are completely fulfilled;
> Sitting on the seat of the great kindness from which he gladdens even evil beings;
> Sitting on the seat of the great compassion from which he tirelessly endures all kinds of sufferings; and
> Sitting on the vajra seat from which he subdues the many *māras* and followers of non-Buddhist paths.

These are the ten. If bodhisattvas abide in these dharmas, then they are able to sit on the Tathāgata's unexcelled throne of right enlightenment.

Sons of the Buddha, the bodhisattva-mahāsattva has ten kinds of recumbence. What are those ten? They are as follows:

> Quiescent recumbence, with peacefulness in both body and mind;
> Recumbence in *dhyāna* absorption, cultivating in accordance with principle;

正體字

三昧

303c13　臥。身心柔軟故。梵天臥。不惱自他故。善業
303c14　臥。於後不悔故。正信臥。不可傾動故。正道
303c15　臥。善友開覺故。妙願臥。善巧迴向故。一切事
303c16　畢臥。所作成[4]辨故。捨諸功用臥。一切慣習
303c17　故。是為十。若諸菩薩。安住此法。則得如來無
303c18　上大法臥。悉能開悟一切眾生。佛子。菩薩摩
303c19　訶薩。有十種所住處。何等為十。所謂以大慈
303c20　為所住處。於一切眾生。心平等故。以大悲為
303c21　所住處。不輕未學故。以大喜為所住處。離一
303c22　切憂惱故。以大捨為所住處。於有為無為平
303c23　等故。以一切波羅蜜。為所住處。菩提心為首
303c24　故。以一切空。為所住處。善巧觀察故。以無相
303c25　為所住處。不出正位故。以無願為所住處。觀
303c26　察受生故。以念慧為所住處。忍法成滿故。以
303c27　一切法平等。為所住處。得授記[5]別故。是為
303c28　十。若諸菩薩。安住此法。則得如來無上無礙
303c29　所住處。佛子。菩薩摩訶薩。有十種所行處。何
304a01　等為十。所謂

简体字

三昧卧,身心柔软故;梵天卧,不恼自他故;善业卧,于后不悔故;正信卧,不可倾动故;正道卧,善友开觉故;妙愿卧,善巧回向故;一切事毕卧,所作成办故;舍诸功用卧,一切惯习故。是为十。若诸菩萨安住此法,则得如来无上大法卧,悉能开悟一切众生。

"佛子,菩萨摩诃萨有十种所住处。何等为十?所谓;以大慈为所住处,于一切众生心平等故;以大悲为所住处,不轻未学故;以大喜为所住处,离一切忧恼故;以大舍为所住处,于有为、无为平等故;以一切波罗蜜为所住处,菩提心为首故;以一切空为所住处,善巧观察故;以无相为所住处,不出正位故;以无愿为所住处,观察受生故;以念慧为所住处,忍法成满故;以一切法平等为所住处,得授记莂故。是为十。若诸菩萨安住此法,则得如来无上无碍所住处。

"佛子,菩萨摩诃萨有十种所行处。何等为十?所谓:

Chapter 38 — *Transcending the World*

Recumbence in samādhi, with pliancy in both body and mind;
Brahma Heaven recumbence, refraining from any disturbance of either self or others;
Recumbence in the good karmic deeds, not having regrets later on;
Recumbence in right faith, which cannot be shaken even slightly;
Recumbence in the right path, as awakened by the good spiritual guide;
Recumbence in marvelous vows, with skillful dedications;
Recumbence in the completion of all his endeavors, having done what is to be done; and
Recumbence in effortlessness, everything having become a matter of course.

These are the ten. If bodhisattvas abide in these dharmas, then they acquire the Tathāgata's recumbence in the unexcelled great Dharma in which they are all able to awaken all beings.

Sons of the Buddha, the bodhisattva-mahāsattva has ten kinds of places in which he abides. What are those ten? They are as follows:

He takes the great kindness as his abode, for his mind regards all beings equally;
He takes the great compassion as his abode, for he never slights those who have not yet received the training;
He takes the great sympathetic joy as his abode, for he has abandoned all worry and affliction;
He takes the great equanimity as his abode, for he regards the conditioned and the unconditioned equally;
He takes all the *pāramitās* as his abode, for he takes the resolve to attain bodhi as foremost;
He takes the emptiness of everything as his abode, for he is skillful in his contemplations;
He takes signlessness as his abode, for he never abandons the right and fixed position;[128]
He takes wishlessness as his abode, for he contemplates rebirth;
He takes mindfulness and wisdom as his abode, for his patience with dharmas has become completely fulfilled; and
He takes the uniform equality of all dharmas as his abode, for he has received his prediction [of future buddhahood].

These are the ten. If bodhisattvas abide in these dharmas, then they acquire the Tathāgata's unexcelled and unimpeded abode.

Sons of the Buddha, the bodhisattva-mahāsattva has ten kinds of bases of practice. What are those ten? They are as follows:

正體字

以正念為所行處。滿足念處故。以諸趣為所行處。正覺法趣故。以智慧為所行處。得佛歡喜故。以波羅蜜。為所行處。滿足一切智智故。以四攝為所行處。教化眾生故。以生死為所行處。積集善根故。以與一切眾生雜談戲。為所行處。隨應教化。令永離故。以神通為所行處。知一切眾生。諸根境界故。以善巧方便。為所行處。般若波羅蜜相應故。以道場為所行處。成一切智。而不斷菩薩行故。是為十。若諸菩薩。安住此法。則得如來無上大智慧所行處。佛子。菩薩摩訶薩。有十種觀察。何等為十。所謂知諸業觀察。微細悉見故。知諸趣觀察。不取眾生故。知諸根觀察。了達無根故。知諸法觀察。不壞法界故。見佛法觀察。勤修佛眼故。得智慧觀察。如理說法故。無生忍觀察。決了佛法故。

简体字

以正念为所行处,满足念处故;以诸趣为所行处,正觉法趣故;以智慧为所行处,得佛欢喜故;以波罗蜜为所行处,满足一切智智故;以四摄为所行处,教化众生故;以生死为所行处,积集善根故;以与一切众生杂谈戏为所行处,随应教化令永离故;以神通为所行处,知一切众生诸根境界故;以善巧方便为所行处,般若波罗蜜相应故;以道场为所行处,成一切智而不断菩萨行故。是为十。若诸菩萨安住此法,则得如来无上大智慧所行处。

"佛子,菩萨摩诃萨有十种观察。何等为十?所谓:知诸业观察,微细悉见故;知诸趣观察,不取众生故;知诸根观察,了达无根故;知诸法观察,不坏法界故;见佛法观察,勤修佛眼故;得智慧观察,如理说法故;无生忍观察,决了佛法故;

Chapter 38 — *Transcending the World*

He takes right mindfulness as his place of practice to completely fulfill [the practice of] the stations of mindfulness;

He takes all of the rebirth destinies as his place of practice for he is rightly enlightened to the aims of the Dharma;

He takes wisdom as his place of practice to be able to please the Buddha;

He takes the *pāramitās* as his place of practice to completely fulfill the wisdom of all-knowledge;

He takes the four means of attraction as his place of practice to teach beings;

He takes *saṃsāra* as his place of practice to accumulate roots of goodness;

He takes various sorts of talking and light-hearted interaction with beings as his place of practice to adapt to what is fitting in teaching them and enabling them to gain eternal emancipation;

He takes the spiritual superknowledges as his place of practice to know all beings' faculties and spheres of experience;

He takes skillful means as his place of practice in order to accord with the *prajñāpāramitā*; and

He takes the site of enlightenment as his place of practice to succeed in attaining all-knowledge while still never ceasing the bodhisattva practices.

These are the ten. If bodhisattvas abide in these dharmas, then they acquire the Tathāgata's unexcelled place of practicing great wisdom.

Sons of the buddha, the bodhisattva-mahāsattva has ten [other][129] kinds of contemplations. What are those ten? They are as follows:

The contemplation that knows all actions through perceiving all their subtleties;

The contemplation that knows all the rebirth destinies through not seizing on [the existence of] beings;

The contemplation that knows all faculties through completely comprehending the nonexistence of faculties;

The contemplation that knows all dharmas as not incompatible with the Dharma realm;

The contemplation that sees the Buddha's Dharma through diligently cultivating the Buddha eye;

The contemplation leading to the attainment of wisdom through explaining the Dharma in accordance with its principles;

The contemplation leading to the unproduced-dharmas patience through a definite and complete comprehension of the Buddha's Dharma;

正體字

不退地觀察。滅一切
煩惱。超出三界二乘地故。灌頂地觀察。於一
切佛法。自在不動故。善覺智三昧觀察。於一
切十方。施作佛事故。是為十。若諸菩薩。安住
此法。則得如來無上大觀察智。佛子。菩薩摩
訶薩。有十種普觀察。何等為十。所謂。普觀一
切諸來求者。以無違心。滿其意故。普觀一切
犯戒眾生。安置如來淨戒中故。普觀一切害
心眾生。安置如來忍力中故。普觀一切懈怠
眾生。勸令精勤。不捨荷負大乘擔故。普觀一
切亂心眾生。令住如來一切智地。無散動故。
普觀一切惡慧眾生。令除疑惑。破有見故。普
觀一切平等善友。順其教命。住佛法故。普觀
一切所聞之法。疾得證見最上義故。普觀一
切無邊眾生。常不捨離大悲力故。普觀一切
諸佛之法。速得成就一切智故。

简体字

不退地观察，灭一切烦恼，超出三界、二乘地故；灌顶地观察，于一切佛法自在不动故；善觉智三昧观察，于一切十方施作佛事故。是为十。若诸菩萨安住此法，则得如来无上大观察智。

"佛子，菩萨摩诃萨有十种普观察。何等为十？所谓：普观一切诸来求者，以无违心满其意故；普观一切犯戒众生，安置如来净戒中故；普观一切害心众生，安置如来忍力中故；普观一切懈怠众生，劝令精勤不舍荷负大乘担故；普观一切乱心众生，令住如来一切智地无散动故；普观一切恶慧众生，令除疑惑破有见故；普观一切平等善友，顺其教命住佛法故；普观一切所闻之法，疾得证见最上义故；普观一切无边众生，常不舍离大悲力故；普观一切诸佛之法，速得成就一切智故。

Chapter 38 — Transcending the World

- The contemplation leading to the ground of irreversibility through extinguishing all afflictions and stepping beyond the three realms of existence and the grounds of the two vehicles;
- The contemplation leading to the ground of the crown-anointing consecration through gaining unshakable sovereign mastery of all dharmas of the Buddha; and
- The contemplation leading to the samādhi of well awakened wisdom through doing the Buddha's works throughout the ten directions.

These are the ten. If bodhisattvas abide in these dharmas, then they acquire the Tathāgata's unexcelled great contemplative wisdom.

Sons of the Buddha, the bodhisattva-mahāsattva has ten kinds of universal contemplation. What are those ten? They are as follows:

- Universal contemplation of all who come as supplicants with which, free of any thoughts of opposition, he fulfills their wishes;
- Universal contemplation of all beings who transgress against the moral precepts with which he establishes them in the Tathāgata's pure moral precepts;
- Universal contemplation of all beings with harmful intentions with which he establishes them in the Tathāgata's power of patience;
- Universal contemplation of all indolent beings with which he encourages them and enables them to become energetically diligent in never give up bearing the Great Vehicle's burden;
- Universal contemplation of all beings with muddled minds with which he enables them to abide free of distraction on the Tathāgata's ground of all-knowledge;
- Universal contemplation of all evil-minded beings with which he enables them to become rid of doubts and dispels their existence-reifying views;
- Universal contemplation of all impartial good spiritual guides with which he complies with their instructions and abides in the Buddha's Dharma;
- Universal contemplation of all Dharma teachings he has heard with which he swiftly acquires realized perception of the ultimate meaning;
- Universal contemplation of all of the boundlessly many beings with which he never abandons the power of great compassion; and
- Universal contemplation of the Dharma of all buddhas with which he swiftly succeeds in fully realizing all-knowledge.

正體字

是為十。若諸菩薩。安住此法。則得如來無上大智慧普觀察。佛子。菩薩摩訶薩。有十種奮迅。何等為十。所謂牛王奮迅。映蔽一切天龍夜叉乾闥婆等。諸大眾故。象王奮迅。心善調柔。荷負一切諸眾生故。龍王奮迅。興大法密雲。[1]耀解脫電光。震如實義雷。降諸根力覺分禪定解脫三昧甘露雨故。大金翅鳥王奮迅。竭貪愛水。破愚癡[2][穀-禾+卵]。搏撮煩惱諸惡毒龍。令出生死大苦海故。大師子王奮迅。安住無畏平等大智。以為器仗。摧伏眾魔及外道故。勇健奮迅。能於生死大戰陣中。摧滅一切煩惱[3]怨故。大智奮迅。知蘊界處。及諸緣起。自在開示一切法故。陀羅尼奮迅。以念慧力。持法不忘。隨眾生根。為宣說故。辯才奮迅。無礙迅疾。分別一切咸令受益。心歡喜故。如來奮迅。一切智智助道之法。皆悉成滿。

简体字

是为十。若诸菩萨安住此法,则得如来无上大智慧普观察。

"佛子,菩萨摩诃萨有十种奋迅。何等为十?所谓:牛王奋迅,映蔽一切天、龙、夜叉、乾闼婆等诸大众故;象王奋迅,心善调柔,荷负一切诸众生故;龙王奋迅,兴大法密云,耀解脱电光,震如实义雷,降诸根、力、觉分、禅定、解脱、三昧甘露雨故;大金翅鸟王奋迅,竭贪爱水,破愚痴[穀-禾+卵],搏撮烦恼诸恶毒龙,令出生死大苦海故;大师子王奋迅,安住无畏平等大智以为器仗,摧伏众魔及外道故;勇健奋迅,能于生死大战阵中摧灭一切烦恼冤故;大智奋迅,知蕴、界、处及诸缘起,自在开示一切法故;陀罗尼奋迅,以念慧力持法不忘,随众生根为宣说故;辩才奋迅,无碍迅疾分别一切,咸令受益心欢喜故;如来奋迅,一切智智助道之法皆悉成满,

Chapter 38 — *Transcending the World*

These are the ten. If bodhisattvas abide in these dharmas, then they acquire the Tathāgata's unexcelled universal contemplation with great wisdom.

Sons of the Buddha, the bodhisattva-mahāsattva has ten kinds of swiftness. What are those ten? They are as follows:

The swiftness like that of the king of bulls with which he outshines that of everyone in all the great congregations of devas, dragons, *yakṣas*, *gandharvas*, and others;

The swiftness like that of the king of elephants with which his mind is well-regulated and pliant as it bears the burden of all beings;

The swiftness like that of the king of dragons with which he spreads forth the dense clouds of the great Dharma, shines the dazzling light of liberation's lightning flashes, causes the quaking thunder of reality-accordant meaning, and pours down the elixir of immortality of all the roots, powers, enlightenment factors, *dhyāna* absorptions, liberations, and samādhis;

The swiftness like that of the king of the great golden-winged *garuḍa* birds with which he is able to dry up the waters of desire, break the shell of delusion, pounce on and seize the poisonous dragons of afflictions' evils, and enables liberation from *saṃsāra*'s great ocean of suffering;

The swiftness like that of the great king of lions with which he abides in fearlessness, impartiality, and great wisdom and, using them as his weapons, he vanquishes the many *māras* and the followers of non-Buddhist paths;

The swiftness like that of the valiant stalwarts with which he is able to vanquish all the adversarial afflictions on the great battlefield of *saṃsāra*;

The swiftness like that of the great wisdom with which he knows the aggregates, the sense realms, the sense bases, and all aspects of conditioned arising and thus explains all dharmas with sovereign mastery;

The swiftness like that of the *dhāraṇīs* with which, using the power of mindfulness and wisdom, he retains dharmas, never forgets them, and, adapting to beings' faculties, expounds on them for their benefit;

The swiftness of eloquence with which, with unimpeded speed, he swiftly analyzes everything and then benefits and gladdens everyone; and

The swiftness like that of the Tathāgata with which he fulfills the wisdom of all-knowledge and all the dharmas of the provisions

正體字

以一念相應慧。所應得者。一切皆得。所應悟者。一切皆悟。坐師子座。降魔[*]怨敵。成阿耨多羅三藐三菩提故。是為十。若諸菩薩。安住此法。則得諸佛於一切法無上自在奮迅。佛子。菩薩摩訶薩。有十種[佛>師]子吼。何等為十。所謂唱言我當必定成正等覺。是菩提心大師子吼。我當令一切眾生。未度者度。未脫者脫。未安者安。未涅槃者。令得涅槃。是大悲大師子吼。我當令佛法僧種。無有斷絕。是報如來恩大師子吼。我當嚴淨一切佛剎。是究竟堅誓大師子吼。我當除滅一切惡道。及諸難處。是自持淨戒大師子吼。我當滿足一切諸佛身語及意。相好莊嚴。是求福無厭大師子吼。我當成滿一切諸佛。所有智慧。是求智無厭大師子吼。我當除滅一切眾魔。及諸魔業。是修正行斷諸煩惱大師子吼。我當了知一切諸法。無我無眾生。無壽命。無補伽羅。空無相無願。淨如虛空。是無生法忍大師子吼。最後生菩薩。震動一切諸佛國土。悉令嚴淨。是時一切釋梵四王。咸來讚請。

简体字

以一念相应慧，所应得者一切皆得，所应悟者一切皆悟，坐师子座降魔冤敌，成阿耨多罗三藐三菩提故。是为十。若诸菩萨安住此法，则得诸佛于一切法无上自在奋迅。

"佛子，菩萨摩诃萨有十种师子吼。何等为十？所谓：唱言：'我当必定成正等觉。'是菩提心大师子吼。'我当令一切众生，未度者度，未脱者脱，未安者安，未涅槃者令得涅槃。'是大悲大师子吼。'我当令佛、法、僧种无有断绝。'是报如来恩大师子吼。'我当严净一切佛刹。'是究竟坚誓大师子吼。'我当除灭一切恶道及诸难处。'是自持净戒大师子吼。'我当满足一切诸佛身、语及意相好庄严。'是求福无厌大师子吼。'我当成满一切诸佛所有智慧。'是求智无厌大师子吼。'我当除灭一切众魔及诸魔业。'是修正行断诸烦恼大师子吼。'我当了知一切诸法无我，无众生、无寿命、无补伽罗，空、无相、无愿，净如虚空。'是无生法忍大师子吼。最后生菩萨震动一切诸佛国土悉令严净，是时，一切释、梵、四王咸来赞请：

Chapter 38 — *Transcending the World*

for enlightenment and, using the wisdom which is responsive in but a single mind-moment, he sees to it that whatever should be realized is all realized, that whatever should be awakened to is all awakened to, and then, sitting on the lion throne, he conquers the *māra* adversaries and gains *anuttarasamyaksaṃbodhi*.

These are the ten. If bodhisattvas abide in these dharmas, then they acquire all buddhas' unexcelled and masterful swiftness in all dharmas.

Sons of the Buddha, the bodhisattva-mahāsattva has ten kinds of lion's roar. What are those ten? As follows, they are those in which he proclaims:

"I will certainly attain the right and perfect enlightenment." This is the great lion's roar of the bodhi resolve;

"I shall liberate all unliberated beings, emancipate all unemancipated beings, bring peace to all unpeaceful beings, and lead to nirvāṇa all beings who have not yet reached nirvāṇa." This is the great lion's roar of the great compassion;

"I shall prevent the lineage of the Buddha, Dharma, and Sangha from ever being cut off." This is the great lion's roar of repaying the Tathāgata's kindness;

"I shall purify all buddha *kṣetras*." This is the great lion's roar of ultimately solid of vows;

"I shall extinguish all the wretched destinies and the difficulties.[130]" This is the great lion's roar of personally upholding the pure moral precepts;

"I shall completely fulfill all the Buddha's physical, verbal, and mental adornments of the major marks and secondary signs." This is the great lion's roar of the tireless pursuit of merit;

"I shall completely fulfill the wisdom of all buddhas." This is the great lion's roar of the tireless pursuit of wisdom;

"I shall destroy all the many *māras* as well as all the works of the *māras*." This is the great lion's roar of the cultivation of right practice in severing all afflictions;

"I shall completely realize all dharmas as devoid of self, as devoid of any being, as devoid of any life span, as devoid of any *pudgala*, as empty, signless, and wishless, and as pure as space." This is the great lion's roar of the unproduced-dharmas patience; and

The bodhisattva who has reached his last birth causes quaking in all buddha *kṣetras* and purifies them all. At this time, Śakra, Brahma, and all the Four Heavenly Kings come to him, utter praises, and make the request: "We only pray that the Bodhisattva, by resort to the dharma of the birthless, will

正體字

唯願菩薩。以無生法。而現受生。菩薩
則以無礙慧眼。普觀世間一切眾生。無如我
者。即於王宮。示現誕生。自行七步大師子吼。
我於世間。最勝第一。我當永盡生死邊際。是
如說而作大師子吼。是為十。若諸菩薩。安住
此法。則得如來無上大師子吼

大方廣佛華嚴經[＊]卷第五十八

　　離世間品第三十八之六

佛子。菩薩摩訶薩。有十種清淨施。何等為十。
所謂平等施。不[4]揀眾生故。隨意施。滿其所
願故。不亂施。令得利益故。隨宜施。知上中下
故。不住施。不求果報故。開捨施。心不戀著
故。一切施。究竟清淨故。迴向菩提施。遠離有
為無為故。教化眾生施。乃至道場不捨故。三
輪清淨施。於施者受者。及以施物。正念觀察。
如虛空故。是為十。若諸菩薩。安住此法。則得
如來無上清淨廣大施。佛子。菩薩摩訶薩。有
十種清淨戒。何等為十。所謂身清淨戒。護身
三惡故。語清淨戒。離語四過故。心清淨戒。永
離貪瞋邪見故。

简体字

'唯愿菩萨以无生法而现受生！'菩萨则以无碍慧眼普观世间：'一切众生无如我者。'即于王宫示现诞生，自行七步大师子吼：'我于世间最胜第一，我当永尽生死边际。'是如说而作大师子吼。是为十。若诸菩萨安住此法，则得如来无上大师子吼。

大方广佛华严经卷第五十八

离世间品第三十八之六

　　"佛子，菩萨摩诃萨有十种清净施。何等为十？所谓：平等施，不拣众生故；随意施，满其所愿故；不乱施，令得利益故；随宜施，知上、中、下故；不住施，不求果报故；开舍施，心不恋著故；一切施，究竟清净故；回向菩提施，远离有为、无为故；教化众生施，乃至道场不舍故；三轮清净施，于施者、受者及以施物正念观察如虚空故。是为十。若诸菩萨安住此法，则得如来无上清净广大施。

　　"佛子，菩萨摩诃萨有十种清净戒。何等为十？所谓：身清净戒，护身三恶故；语清净戒，离语四过故；心清净戒，永离贪、瞋、邪见故；

manifest the taking on of birth." Then, using the eye of unimpeded wisdom, the Bodhisattva everywhere contemplates all beings in the world, realizes, "There are none among them like me," and then straightaway manifests birth into the palace of the King. Of his own accord, he strides seven steps and roars the great lion's roar, declaring: "I am the most supreme of all who abide in the world. I shall forever put an end to the boundaries imposed by *saṃsāra*." This is the great lion's roar of doing just as one has said.

These are the ten. If bodhisattvas abide in these dharmas, then they acquire the Tathāgata's unexcelled lion's roar.

Sons of the Buddha, the bodhisattva-mahāsattva has ten kinds of pure giving. What are those ten? They are as follows:

Equal giving, by which he does not discriminate among beings;

Giving that accords with others' wishes, by which he provides whatever they wish;

Undistracted giving, by which he causes others to benefit from it;

Giving which accords with whatever is fitting, by which he recognizes what is superior, middling, or inferior;

Non-abiding giving, by which he does not seek any reward;

Freely relinquishing giving, by which his mind does not retain any fond attachment;

The giving of everything, by which he attains ultimate purity;

Giving dedicated to the realization of bodhi, by which he abandons both the conditioned and the unconditioned;

Giving in the course of teaching beings, which he never relinquishes even on reaching the site of enlightenment; and

Giving in which the three spheres [involved in giving] have all been purified, by which, with right mindfulness, he contemplates the benefactor, the recipient, and the gift as like empty space.

These are the ten. If bodhisattvas abide in these, then they acquire the Tathāgata's unexcelled, pure, and vast giving.

Sons of the Buddha, the bodhisattva-mahāsattva has ten kinds of pure moral precepts. What are those ten? They are as follows:

The pure moral precepts of the body, by which he guards against the three evils of the body;[131]

The pure moral precepts of speech, by which he abandons the four transgressions in speech;[132]

The pure moral precepts of the mind, by which he forever abandons covetousness, ill will, and wrong views;[133]

正體字

不破一切學處清淨戒。於一切人天中。作尊主故。守護菩提心清淨戒。不樂小乘故。守護如來所制清淨戒。乃至微細罪。生大怖畏故。隱密護持清淨戒。[1]善拔犯戒眾生故。不作一切惡清淨戒。誓修一切善法故。遠離一切有見清淨戒。於戒無著故。守護一切眾生清淨戒。發起大悲故。是為十。若諸菩薩。安住此法。則得如來無上無過失清淨戒。佛子。菩薩摩訶薩。有十種清淨忍。何等為十。所謂安受詈辱清淨忍。護諸眾生故。安受刀杖清淨忍。善護自他故。不生患害清淨忍。其心不動故。不責卑賤清淨忍。為上能寬故。有歸咸救清淨忍。捨自身命故。遠離我慢清淨忍。不輕未學故。殘毀不瞋清淨忍。觀察如幻故。有犯無報清淨忍。不見自他故。

简体字

不破一切学处清净戒，于一切人、天中作尊主故；守护菩提心清净戒，不乐小乘故；守护如来所制清净戒，乃至微细罪生大怖畏故；隐密护持清净戒，善拔犯戒众生故；不作一切恶清净戒，誓修一切善法故；远离一切有见清净戒，于戒无著故；守护一切众生清净戒，发起大悲故。是为十。若诸菩萨安住此法，则得如来无上无过失清净戒。

"佛子，菩萨摩诃萨有十种清净忍。何等为十？所谓：安受詈辱清净忍，护诸众生故；安受刀杖清净忍，善护自他故；不生患害清净忍，其心不动故；不责卑贱清净忍，为上能宽故；有归咸救清净忍，舍自身命故；远离我慢清净忍，不轻未学故；残毁不瞋清净忍，观察如幻故；有犯无报清净忍，不见自他故；

The pure moral precept of refraining from transgressing against any of the aspects of the training, by which he becomes a venerated leader of all humans and devas;

The pure moral precept of preserving and protecting the resolve to attain bodhi, by which he does not delight in the small vehicle;

The pure moral precept of preserving and protecting whatever has been decreed by the Tathāgata, by which he remains immensely fearful of ever committing even the most subtle transgression;

The pure moral precept of guarding and upholding them even in secret, by which he skillfully rescues beings who transgress against the precepts;

The pure moral precept of not committing any kind of evil deed, by which he vows to cultivate all good dharmas;

The pure moral precept of abandoning all existence-reifying views, by which he remains free of attachment to the precepts themselves;[134] and

The pure moral precept of protecting all beings, by which he arouses the great compassion.

These are the ten. If bodhisattvas abide in these dharmas, then they acquire the Tathāgata's unexcelled flawless pure moral precepts.

Sons of the Buddha, the bodhisattva-mahāsattva has ten kinds of pure patience. What are those ten? They are as follows:

The pure patience that peacefully endures disparaging insults, by which he protects beings;

The pure patience that peacefully endures even attacks with knives and staves, by which he well protects both himself and others;

The pure patience that does not become angry or malicious, by which he maintains an unshakable mind;

The pure patience that refrains from censuring inferiors, by which he is able to be tolerant when serving as a superior;

The pure patience that rescues all who take refuge in him, by which he is willing to sacrifice even his own body and life;

The pure patience that abandons pride in self, by which he never slights those who are not yet well trained;

The pure patience that does not become angry even when subjected to cruelty or slander, by which he contemplates this as like a mere illusion;

The pure patience that does not seek to pay back offenses committed by others, by which he does not perceive the existence of either self or others;

正體字	不隨 305a19 ｜ 煩惱清淨忍。離諸境界故。隨順菩薩真實智 305a20 ｜ 知一切法無生清淨忍。不由他教。入一切智 305a21 ｜ 境界故。是為十。若諸菩薩。安住其中。則得一 305a22 ｜ 切諸佛。不由他悟無上法忍。佛子。菩薩摩訶 305a23 ｜ 薩。有十種清淨精進。何等為十。所謂身清淨 305a24 ｜ 精進。承事供養諸佛菩薩。及諸[2]師長。尊重 305a25 ｜ 福田。不退轉故。語清淨精進。隨所聞法。廣為 305a26 ｜ 他說。讚佛功德。無疲倦故。意清淨精進。善能 305a27 ｜ 入出慈悲喜捨禪定解脫及諸三昧。無休息 305a28 ｜ 故。正直[3]心清淨精進。無誑無諂。無曲無偽。 305a29 ｜ 一切勤修。無退轉故。增勝心清淨精進。志常 305b01 ｜ 趣求上上智慧。願具一切白淨法故。不唐捐 305b02 ｜ 清淨精進。攝取布施戒忍多聞。及不放逸。乃 305b03 ｜ 至菩提。無中息故。摧伏一切魔清淨精進。悉 305b04 ｜ 能除滅貪欲瞋恚愚癡邪見。一切煩惱。諸纏 305b05 ｜ 蓋故。成滿智慧光清淨精進。有所施為。悉善 305b06 ｜ 觀察。咸使究竟。不令後悔。得一切佛不共法 305b07 ｜ 故。無來無去清淨精進。得如實智。入法界門。 305b08 ｜ 身語及心。皆悉平等。了相非相。無所著故。
简体字	不随烦恼清净忍，离诸境界故；随顺菩萨真实智知一切法无生清净忍，不由他教，入一切智境界故。是为十。若诸菩萨安住其中，则得一切诸佛不由他悟无上法忍。 　　"佛子，菩萨摩诃萨有十种清净精进。何等为十？所谓：身清净精进，承事供养诸佛菩萨及诸师长，尊重福田不退转故；语清净精进，随所闻法广为他说，赞佛功德无疲倦故；意清净精进，善能入出慈、悲、喜、舍、禅定、解脱及诸三昧无休息故；正直心清净精进，无诳无谄，无曲无伪，一切勤修无退转故；增胜心清净精进，志常趣求上上智慧，愿具一切白净法故；不唐捐清净精进，摄取布施、戒、忍、多闻及不放逸乃至菩提无中息故；摧伏一切魔清净精进，悉能除灭贪欲、瞋恚、愚痴、邪见、一切烦恼、诸缠盖故；成满智慧光清净精进，有所施为悉善观察，咸使究竟，不令后悔，得一切佛不共法故；无来无去清净精进，得如实智，入法界门，身、语及心皆悉平等，了相非相，无所著故；

Chapter 38 — *Transcending the World*

- The pure patience that does not follow the afflictions, by which he transcends all spheres of experience; and
- The pure patience that accords with the bodhisattva's genuine wisdom and knows all dharmas as unarisen, by which he enters the sphere of cognition of all-knowledge even without depending on instruction from others.

These are the ten. If bodhisattvas abide in these, then they acquire all buddhas' unexcelled dharma patience to which they awaken without the assistance of others.

Sons of the Buddha, the bodhisattva-mahāsattva has ten kinds of pure vigor. What are those ten? They are as follows:

- The pure vigor of the body, with which he is irreversibly persistent in serving and making offerings to the buddhas and bodhisattvas as well as his teachers, elders, and other fields of merit;
- The pure vigor in speech, with which he extensively teaches others whatever Dharma he has heard while also tirelessly praising the meritorious qualities of the Buddha;
- The pure vigor of mind, with which he is well able to ceaselessly enter and emerge from meditations on kindness, compassion, sympathetic joy, and equanimity, the *dhyāna* absorptions, the liberations, and the samādhis;
- The pure vigor of the correct and straight mind, with which he remains free of deception, flattery, deviousness, and falseness as he irreversibly persists in all his diligent cultivation;
- The pure vigor of the increasingly superior resolve, with which he resolutely and constantly pursues the most supreme wisdom while vowing to possess all the dharmas of purity;
- The pure vigor not pursued in vain, with which, until he attains bodhi, he never rests in the midst of his accumulation of proficiency in giving, moral virtue, patience, and extensive learning;
- The pure vigor in vanquishing all *māras*, with which he is able to utterly extinguish all desire, hatred, delusion, and wrong views as well as all afflictions and all the entangling hindrances;
- The pure vigor in fully developing the light of wisdom, with which, in everything he does, he skillfully contemplates and ensures they are all completed so as to have no regrets and so as to acquire all buddhas' exclusive dharmas;
- The pure vigor without coming or going, with which he acquires reality-accordant wisdom, enters the gateway to the Dharma realm, realizes the equality of body, speech, and mind, understands signs as non-signs, and becomes free of attachments; and

正體字

成就法光清淨精進。超過諸地。得佛灌頂。以無漏身。而示歿生。出家成道。說法滅度。具足如是普賢事故。是為十。若諸菩薩。安住此法。則得如來無上大清淨精進。佛子。菩薩摩訶薩。有十種清淨禪。何等為十。所謂常樂出家清淨禪。捨一切所有故。得真善友清淨禪。示教正道故。住阿蘭若忍風雨等清淨禪。離我我所故。離憒鬧眾生清淨禪。常樂寂靜故。心業調柔清淨禪。守護諸根故。心智寂滅清淨[4]禪。一切音聲。諸禪定刺。不能亂故。覺道方便清淨禪。觀察一切皆現證故。離於味著清淨禪。不捨欲界故。發起通明清淨禪。知一切眾生根性故。自在遊戲清淨禪。入佛三昧。知無我故。是為十。若諸菩薩。安住其中。則得如來無上大清淨禪。佛子。菩薩摩訶薩。有十種清淨慧。何等為十。所謂知一切因清淨慧。不壞果報故。

简体字

成就法光清净精进，超过诸地，得佛灌顶，以无漏身而示殁生、出家、成道、说法、灭度，具足如是普贤事故。是为十。若诸菩萨安住此法，则得如来无上大清净精进。

"佛子，菩萨摩诃萨有十种清净禅。何等为十？所谓：常乐出家清净禅，舍一切所有故；得真善友清净禅，示教正道故；住阿兰若忍风雨等清净禅，离我、我所故；离愦闹众生清净禅，常乐寂静故；心业调柔清净禅，守护诸根故；心智寂灭清净禅，一切音声、诸禅定刺不能乱故；觉道方便清净禅，观察一切皆现证故；离于味著清净禅，不舍欲界故；发起通明清净禅，知一切众生根性故；自在游戏清净禅，入佛三昧，知无我故。是为十。若诸菩萨安住其中，则得如来无上大清净禅。

"佛子，菩萨摩诃萨有十种清净慧。何等为十？所谓：知一切因清净慧，不坏果报故；

The pure vigor that perfects the light of Dharma, with which he steps beyond all the grounds, acquires the Buddha's crown-anointing consecration, and uses the body free of contaminants to manifest dying and being born, leaving the home life, becoming enlightened, proclaiming the Dharma, and crossing into nirvāṇa, thus completely fulfilling the works of Samantabhadra such as these.

These are the ten. If bodhisattvas abide in these dharmas, then they acquire the Tathāgata's unexcelled great pure vigor.

Sons of the Buddha, the bodhisattva-mahāsattva has ten kinds of pure *dhyāna*. What are those ten? They are as follows:

The pure *dhyāna* in which he always delights in leaving the home life, by which he relinquishes all that he possesses;

The pure *dhyāna* in which he finds the true good spiritual guide, by which he is shown and taught the right path;

The pure *dhyāna* in which he dwells in the *araṇya*, the forest dwelling, enduring wind, rain, and other such things, by which he abandons self and possessions of a self;

The pure *dhyāna* in which he abandons the troublesome disturbances of beings, by which he always delights in quiescence;

The pure *dhyāna* in which his mental actions are pliant, by which he guards all his faculties;

The pure *dhyāna* in which the mind and its cognition are quiescent, by which no sounds or other thorns of *dhyāna* absorption can disturb him;

The pure *dhyāna* of the skillful means for awakening to the path, by which, in contemplating all things, they all lead to direct realization;

The pure *dhyāna* in which he abandons all attachment to delectable experiences, by which he still does not abandon the desire realm;

The pure *dhyāna* in which he brings forth the superknowledges, by which he knows the faculties and natures of all beings; and

The pure *dhyāna* of sovereign and easeful mastery, by which he enters the Buddha's samādhi and realizes the nonexistence of self.

These are the ten. If bodhisattvas abide in these, then they acquire the Tathāgata's unexcelled great pure *dhyānas*.

Sons of the Buddha, the bodhisattva-mahāsattva has ten kinds of pure wisdom. What are those ten? They are as follows:

The pure wisdom that knows all causes, by which he does not negate their effects;

正體字

知一切緣清淨慧。不違和合故。知不斷
不常清淨慧。了達緣起。皆如實故。拔一切見
清淨慧。於眾生相。無取捨故。觀一切眾生心
行清淨慧。了知如幻故。廣大辯才清淨慧。分
別諸法。問答無礙故。一切諸魔外道聲聞獨
覺所不能知清淨慧。深入一切如來智故。見
一切佛微妙法身見一切眾生本性清淨見一
切[5]法皆悉寂滅見一切剎同於虛空清淨慧。
知一切相。皆無礙故。一切總持辯才方便波
羅蜜清淨慧。令得一切最勝智故。一念相應
金剛智了一切法平等清淨慧。得一切法。最
尊智故。是為十。若諸菩薩。安住其中。則得如
來無障礙大智慧。佛子。菩薩摩訶薩。有十種
清淨慈。何等為十。所謂等心清淨慈。普攝眾
生。無所[6]揀擇故。饒益清淨慈。隨有所作。皆
令歡喜故。攝物同己清淨慈。究竟皆令出生
死故。不捨世間清淨慈。心常緣念集善根故。

简体字

知一切缘清净慧，不违和合故；知不断不常清净慧，了达缘起皆如实故；拔一切见清净慧，于众生相无取舍故；观一切众生心行清净慧，了知如幻故；广大辩才清净慧，分别诸法、问答无碍故；一切诸魔、外道、声闻、独觉所不能知清净慧，深入一切如来智故；见一切佛微妙法身、见一切众生本性清净、见一切法皆悉寂灭、见一切刹同于虚空清净慧，知一切相皆无碍故；一切总持、辩才、方便波罗蜜清净慧，令得一切最胜智故；一念相应金刚智了一切法平等清净慧，得一切法最尊智故。是为十。若诸菩萨安住其中，则得如来无障碍大智慧。

"佛子，菩萨摩诃萨有十种清净慈。何等为十？所谓：等心清净慈，普摄众生无所拣择故；饶益清净慈，随有所作皆令欢喜故；摄物同己清净慈，究竟皆令出生死故；不舍世间清净慈，心常缘念集善根故；

Chapter 38 — *Transcending the World*

The pure wisdom that knows all conditions, by which he does not oppose how they come together;

The pure wisdom that knows both annihilationism and eternalism are untrue, by which he always comprehends conditioned arising in accordance with reality;

The pure wisdom that removes all views, by which he neither seizes upon nor rejects any of the characteristics of beings;

The pure wisdom that contemplates the mental actions of all beings, by which he fully realizes they are like mere conjurations;

The pure wisdom that is possessed of vast eloquence, by which he has unimpeded skill in questions and responses revealing the distinctions in all dharmas;

The pure wisdom that no *māra*, no follower of non-Buddhist paths, no *śrāvaka* disciple, and no *pratyekabuddha* could ever know, by which he deeply penetrates the wisdom of all *tathāgatas*;

The pure wisdom that perceives the sublime Dharma body of all buddhas, that perceives the fundamentally pure nature of all beings, that perceives the complete quiescence of all dharmas, and that perceives all *kṣetras*' identity with empty space, by which he has an unimpeded knowledge of all signs;

The pure wisdom that knows all the complete-retention *dhāraṇīs*, all the kinds of eloquence, all the skillful means, and all the *pāramitās*, by which he is enabled to acquire all the most supreme forms of wisdom; and

The pure wisdom in which, in but a single mind-moment of vajra wisdom, he knows the equality of all dharmas, by which he acquires the most supreme knowledge of all dharmas.

These are the ten. If bodhisattvas abide in these, then they acquire the Tathāgata's unimpeded great wisdom.

Sons of the Buddha, the bodhisattva-mahāsattva has ten kinds of pure kindness. What are those ten? They are as follows:

The pure kindness of the impartial mind, by which he everywhere attracts all beings without any selective discriminations;

The pure kindness that benefits others, by which he causes them all to be delighted with whatever he does;

The pure kindness that, in attracting beings, takes them to be the same as himself, by which he ultimately enables them all to escape from *saṃsāra*;

The pure kindness that never abandons those in the world, by which he always bears them in mind as he accumulates roots of goodness;

正體字

能至解脫清淨慈。普使眾生。除滅一切諸煩惱故。出生菩提清淨慈。普使眾生。發求一切智心故。世間無礙清淨慈。放大光明。平等普照故。充滿虛空清淨慈。救護眾生。無處不至故。法緣清淨慈。證於如如真實法故。無緣清淨慈。入於菩薩離生性故。是為十。若諸菩薩。安住此法。則得如來無上廣大清淨慈。佛子。菩薩摩訶薩。有十種清淨悲。何等為十。所謂無儔伴清淨悲。獨發其心故。無疲厭清淨悲。代一切眾生受苦。不以為勞故。難處受生清淨悲。為度眾生故。善趣受生清淨悲。示現無常故。為邪定眾生清淨悲。歷劫不捨弘誓故。不著己樂清淨悲。普與眾生快樂故。不求恩報清淨悲。修潔其心故。能除顛倒清淨悲。說如實法故。菩薩摩訶薩。知一切法本性清淨。無染著。無熱惱。以客塵煩惱故。而受眾苦。

简体字

能至解脱清净慈，普使众生除灭一切诸烦恼故；出生菩提清净慈，普使众生发求一切智心故；世间无碍清净慈，放大光明平等普照故；充满虚空清净慈，救护众生无处不至故；法缘清净慈，证于如如真实法故；无缘清净慈，入于菩萨离生性故。是为十。若诸菩萨安住此法，则得如来无上广大清净慈。

"佛子，菩萨摩诃萨有十种清净悲。何等为十？所谓：无俦伴清净悲，独发其心故。无疲厌清净悲，代一切众生受苦，不以为劳故。难处受生清净悲，为度众生故。善趣受生清净悲，示现无常故。为邪定众生清净悲，历劫不舍弘誓故。不著己乐清净悲，普与众生快乐故。不求恩报清净悲，修洁其心故。能除颠倒清净悲，说如实法故。菩萨摩诃萨知一切法本性清净、无染著、无热恼，以客尘烦恼故而受众苦；

Chapter 38 — *Transcending the World*

The pure kindness that is able to reach liberation, by which he everywhere enables beings to extinguish all their afflictions;

The pure kindness that brings forth bodhi, by which he everywhere enables beings to generate the resolve to seek all-knowledge;

The pure kindness that is unimpeded in the world, by which he emanates great light that illuminates everyone equally;

The pure kindness that completely fills all of empty space, by which there is no place it does not reach as he strives to rescue beings;

The pure kindness that focuses on dharmas, by which he realizes the genuine dharma of true suchness; and

The pure kindness that is free of conditions, by which he enters the bodhisattva's rebirth-transcending nature.

These are the ten. If bodhisattvas abide in these dharmas, then they acquire the Tathāgata's unexcelled and vast pure kindness.

Sons of the Buddha, the bodhisattva-mahāsattva has ten kinds of pure compassion. What are those ten? They are as follows:

The pure compassion even in the absence of companions, with which it is he alone who arouses his resolve;

The pure compassion that remains free of weariness, with which he does not even find it toilsome to substitute for all beings in taking on their sufferings;

The pure compassion that takes on births even among the difficulties,[135] doing so in order to liberate beings;

The pure compassion that takes on births in the good rebirth destinies, with which he reveals impermanence;

The pure compassion manifested for the sake of beings fixed in what is wrong, with which he will even pass through kalpas without ever abandoning his vast vows;

The pure compassion in which one is not attached to his own bliss, with which he everywhere bestows happiness on other beings;

The pure compassion in which one does not seek any reward for one's kindness, with which he cultivates the purification of his own mind;

The pure compassion that is able to do away with the inverted views, with which he teaches Dharma in accordance with reality;

The bodhisattva-mahāsattva knows that the fundamental nature of all dharmas is pure, free of defiling attachments, and free of feverish afflictions while knowing too that it is because of adventitious afflictions that one experiences the many kinds

正體字

	如
305c29	是知已。於諸眾生。而起大悲。名本性清淨。為
306a01	說無垢清淨光明法故。菩薩摩訶薩。知一切
306a02	法。如空中鳥迹。眾生癡翳。不能照了。觀察
306a03	於彼。起大悲心。名真實智。為其開示涅槃法
306a04	故。是為十。若諸菩薩。安住此法。則得如來無
306a05	上廣大清淨悲。佛子。菩薩摩訶薩。有十種清
306a06	淨喜。何等為十。所謂發菩提心清淨喜。悉捨
306a07	所有清淨喜。不嫌棄破戒眾生而教化成就
306a08	清淨喜。能忍受造惡眾生誓願救度清淨喜。
306a09	捨身求法不生悔心清淨喜。自捨欲樂常樂
306a10	法樂清淨喜。令一切眾生捨資生樂常樂法
306a11	樂清淨喜。見一切佛恭敬供養無有厭足法
306a12	界平等清淨喜。令一切眾生愛樂禪定解脫
306a13	三昧遊戲入出清淨喜。心樂具行順菩薩道
306a14	一切苦行證得牟尼寂靜不動無上定慧清淨
306a15	喜。

简体字

如是知已，于诸众生而起大悲，名本性清净，为说无垢清净光明法故。菩萨摩诃萨知一切法如空中鸟迹，众生痴翳不能照了；观察于彼，起大悲心，名真实智，为其开示涅槃法故。是为十。若诸菩萨安住此法，则得如来无上广大清净悲。

"佛子，菩萨摩诃萨有十种清净喜。何等为十？所谓：发菩提心清净喜；悉舍所有清净喜；不嫌弃破戒众生而教化成就清净喜；能忍受造恶众生，誓愿救度清净喜；舍身求法不生悔心清净喜；自舍欲乐，常乐法乐清净喜；令一切众生舍资生乐，常乐法乐清净喜；见一切佛恭敬供养无有厌足，法界平等清净喜；令一切众生爱乐禅定、解脱、三昧游戏入出清净喜；心乐具行顺菩萨道一切苦行，证得牟尼寂静不动无上定慧清净喜。

Chapter 38 — Transcending the World

of suffering. Having come to know such things, he arouses a great compassion for all beings known as "[the compassion of] the pure fundamental nature," with which he teaches the undefiled, pure, and radiant Dharma for their benefit; and

The bodhisattva-mahāsattva knows that all dharmas are like the tracks of birds flying across the sky and knows that beings, having their vision obscured by the cataracts of their delusions, are unable to completely illuminate them. Contemplating beings, he arouses the mind of great compassion known as "[the compassion of] genuine wisdom" with which he reveals the dharma of nirvāṇa for their sakes.

These are the ten. If bodhisattvas abide in these dharmas, then they acquire the Tathāgata's unexcelled and vast pure compassion.

Sons of the Buddha, the bodhisattva-mahāsattva has ten kinds of pure sympathetic joy. What are those ten? They are as follows:

The pure sympathetic joy with which he resolves to attain bodhi;

The pure sympathetic joy with which he relinquishes everything he possesses;

The pure sympathetic joy with which he does not blame and reject beings who have broken the moral precepts, but rather teaches and ripens them;

The pure sympathetic joy with which he is able to tolerate beings who do evil deeds and vows to rescue and liberate them;

The pure sympathetic joy with which he is even willing to sacrifice his own body in seeking the Dharma and still not raise any thoughts of regret;

The pure sympathetic joy with which he relinquishes his own sensual bliss and always delights in Dharma bliss;

The pure sympathetic joy with which he enables all beings to relinquish the bliss arising from material possessions and then always delight in Dharma bliss;

The pure sympathetic joy of impartiality throughout the Dharma realm with which he is insatiable in going to see all buddhas to revere and make offerings to them;

The pure sympathetic joy with which he enables all beings to cherish and delight in easeful mastery in entering and arising from the *dhyāna* absorptions, liberations, and samādhis; and

The pure sympathetic joy with which he delights in according with the bodhisattva path while completely practicing all the austere practices and realizing the Muni's unshakably quiescent and unexcelled meditative absorptions and wisdom.

正體字

是為十。若諸菩薩。安住此法。則得如來無上廣大清淨喜。佛子。菩薩摩訶薩。有十種清淨捨。何等為十。所謂一切眾生恭敬供養不生愛著清淨捨。一切眾生輕慢毀辱不生瞋恚清淨捨。常行世間不為世間八法所染清淨捨。於法器眾生待時而化於無法器亦不生嫌清淨捨。不求二乘學無學法清淨捨。心常遠離一切欲樂順煩惱法清淨捨。不歎二乘厭離生死清淨捨。遠離一切世間語非涅槃語非離欲語不順理語惱亂他語聲聞獨覺語略說乃至一切障菩薩道語皆悉遠離清淨捨。或有眾生根已成熟發生念慧而未能知最上之法待時方化清淨捨。或有眾生菩薩往昔已曾教化至於佛地方可調伏彼亦待時清淨捨。菩薩摩訶薩於彼二人無高無下無取無捨

简体字

是为十。若诸菩萨安住此法，则得如来无上广大清净喜。

"佛子，菩萨摩诃萨有十种清净舍。何等为十？所谓：一切众生恭敬供养，不生爱著清净舍；一切众生轻慢毁辱，不生瞋恚清净舍；常行世间，不为世间八法所染清净舍；于法器众生待时而化，于无法器亦不生嫌清净舍；不求二乘学、无学法清净舍；心常远离一切欲乐、顺烦恼法清净舍；不叹二乘，厌离生死清净舍；远离一切世间语，非涅槃语、非离欲语、不顺理语、恼乱他语、声闻独觉语，略说乃至一切障菩萨道语皆悉远离清净舍；或有众生，根已成熟发生念慧而未能知最上之法，待时方化清净舍；或有众生，菩萨往昔已曾教化至于佛地方可调伏，彼亦待时清净舍；菩萨摩诃萨于彼二人，无高无下，无取无舍，

Chapter 38 — *Transcending the World*

These are the ten. If bodhisattvas abide in these dharmas, then they acquire the Tathāgata's unexcelled and vast pure sympathetic joy.

Sons of the Buddha, the bodhisattva-mahāsattva has ten kinds of pure equanimity. What are those ten? They are as follows:

- The pure equanimity with which he refrains from becoming fondly attached when all beings revere and make offerings to him and the pure equanimity with which he refrains from becoming angry when all beings slight and disparage him;[136]
- The pure equanimity with which he always remains in the world and yet is never defiled by the eight worldly dharmas;[137]
- The pure equanimity with which he awaits the right time to teach beings who are vessels of the Dharma and does not dislike those who are not vessels of the Dharma;
- The pure equanimity with which he does not seek the dharmas of the practitioners of the two vehicles who are either still in training or beyond training;
- The pure equanimity with which his mind always abandons all dharmas related to the desire-based pleasures which lead to the afflictions;
- The pure equanimity with which he refrains from praising the renunciation of *saṃsāra* as practiced by the practitioners of the two vehicles;
- The pure equanimity with which he abandons all worldly discourse, all discourse not associated with nirvāṇa, all discourse not abandoning the desires, all discourse that does not accord with principle, all discourse that torments or disturbs others, all discourse of *śrāvaka* disciples or *pratyekabuddhas*, and, in general, all other such discourse up to and including that which obstructs the bodhisattva path, all of which he leaves far behind;
- The pure equanimity with which, when there is some being whose faculties have already ripened to the point where they have developed mindfulness and wisdom but they have still not yet become able to know the most supreme Dharma, he awaits the right time and only then instructs them in it;
- The pure equanimity with which, when some being taught by the bodhisattva in the past must await his reaching the ground of buddhahood before he can successfully train him, he even then awaits the appropriate time; and
- The pure equanimity with which the bodhisattva-mahāsattva remains free of any conception of any of those two persons as either superior or inferior or as worthy of selection or rejection.

正體字

遠離一切種種分別恒住正定入如實
法心得堪忍清淨捨。是為十。若諸菩薩。安住
其中。則得如來無上廣大清淨捨
佛子。菩薩摩訶薩。有十種義。何等為十。所謂
多聞義。堅固修行故。法義。善巧思擇故。空
義。第一義空故。寂靜義。離諸眾生諠憒故。不
可說義。不著一切語言故。如實義。了達三世
平等故。法界義。一切諸法一味故。真如義。一
切如來順入故。實際義。了知究竟如實故。大
般涅槃義。滅一切苦。而修菩薩諸行故。是為
十。若諸菩薩。安住此法。則得一切智無上義。
佛子。菩薩摩訶薩。有十種法。何等為十。所謂
真實法。如說修行故。離取法。能取所取悉離
故。無諍法。無有一切惑諍故。寂滅法。滅除一
切熱惱故。離欲法。一切貪欲皆斷故。

简体字

远离一切种种分别,恒住正定,入如实法,心得堪忍清净舍。是为十。若诸菩萨安住其中,则得如来无上广大清净舍。

"佛子,菩萨摩诃萨有十种义。何等为十?所谓:多闻义,坚固修行故;法义,善巧思择故;空义,第一义空故;寂静义,离诸众生喧愦故;不可说义,不著一切语言故;如实义,了达三世平等故;法界义,一切诸法一味故;真如义,一切如来顺入故;实际义,了知究竟如实故;大般涅槃义,灭一切苦而修菩萨诸行故。是为十。若诸菩萨安住此法,则得一切智无上义。

"佛子,菩萨摩诃萨有十种法。何等为十?所谓:真实法,如说修行故;离取法,能取、所取悉离故;无诤法,无有一切惑诤故;寂灭法,灭除一切热恼故;离欲法,一切贪欲皆断故;

Chapter 38 — *Transcending the World*   2989

> In this, he abandons all the many different kinds of discrimination, constantly abides in right meditative absorption, and then penetrates reality-accordant Dharma, whereupon his mind achieves the realization of patience.[138]

These are the ten. If bodhisattvas abide in these, then they acquire the Tathāgata's unexcelled and vast pure equanimity.

Sons of the Buddha, the bodhisattva-mahāsattva has ten kinds of meaning. What are those ten? They are as follows:

> The meaning in extensive learning, by which he is steadfast in cultivation;
>
> The meaning in Dharma, by which he uses skillful means in contemplating and discerning [how to proceed];
>
> The meaning in emptiness, by which [he realizes] the supreme meaning;
>
> The meaning in quiescence, by which he separates from the noise and confusion of beings;
>
> The meaning in ineffability, by which he does not become attached to any speech or words;
>
> The meaning in according with reality, by which he fully comprehends the identity of the three periods of time;
>
> The meaning in the Dharma realm, by which [he realizes] all dharmas are of a single flavor;
>
> The meaning in true suchness, by which all *tathāgatas* accord with and enter it;
>
> The meaning in the apex of reality, by which he completely realizes the ultimate in accordance with reality; and
>
> The meaning in the great *parinirvāṇa*, by which he extinguishes all suffering and yet still cultivates all bodhisattva practices.

These are the ten. If bodhisattvas abide in these dharmas, then they acquire the unexcelled meaning of all-knowledge.

Sons of the Buddha, the bodhisattva-mahāsattva has ten kinds of dharmas. What are those ten? They are as follows:

> The dharma of reality, by which he cultivates in accordance with what has been taught;
>
> The dharma of abandoning grasping, by which he transcends both the agent of grasping and the object of grasping;
>
> The dharma of noncontentiousness, by which he is free of all deluded contentiousness;
>
> The dharma of quiescence, by which he extinguishes all the feverish afflictions;
>
> The dharma of dispassion, by which he cuts off all desire;

無分別

306b16	法。攀緣分別永息故。無生法。猶如虛空不動
306b17	故。無為法。離生住滅諸相故。本性法。自性無
306b18	染清淨故。捨一切烏波提涅槃法。能生一切
306b19	菩薩行。修習不斷故。是為十。若諸菩薩。安住
306b20	其中。則得如來無上廣大法。佛子。菩薩摩訶
306b21	薩。有十種福德助道具。何等為十。所謂勸眾
306b22	生起菩提心。是菩薩福德助道具。不斷三寶
306b23	種故。隨順十種迴向。是菩薩福德助道具。斷
306b24	一切不善法。集一切善法故。智慧誘誨。是菩
306b25	薩福德助道具。超過三界福德故。心無疲倦。
306b26	是菩薩福德助道具。究竟度脫一切眾生故。
306b27	悉捨內外一切所有。是菩薩福德助道具。於
306b28	一切物。無所著故。為滿足相好。精進不退。是
306b29	菩薩福德助道具。開門大施。無所限故。上中
306c01	下三品善根。悉以迴向無上菩提心無所輕。
306c02	是菩薩福德助道具。善巧方便相應故。

正體字

无分别法，攀缘分别永息故；无生法，犹如虚空不动故；无为法，离生、住、灭诸相故；本性法，自性无染清净故；舍一切乌波提涅槃法，能生一切菩萨行，修习不断故。是为十。若诸菩萨安住其中，则得如来无上广大法。

"佛子，菩萨摩诃萨有十种福德助道具。何等为十？所谓：劝众生起菩提心，是菩萨福德助道具；不断三宝种故。随顺十种回向，是菩萨福德助道具；断一切不善法，集一切善法故。智慧诱诲，是菩萨福德助道具；超过三界福德故。心无疲倦，是菩萨福德助道具；究竟度脱一切众生故。悉舍内外一切所有，是菩萨福德助道具；于一切物无所著故。为满足相好精进不退，是菩萨福德助道具；开门大施无所限故。上、中、下三品善根，悉以回向无上菩提，心无所轻，是菩萨福德助道具；善巧方便相应故。

简体字

Chapter 38 — Transcending the World

> The dharma of nondiscrimination, by which he forever puts to rest all discriminations involved in manipulating objective conditions;
>
> The dharma of the unproduced, by which he is as immovable as empty space;
>
> The dharma of the unconditioned, by which he transcends all the signs of arising, abiding, and destruction;
>
> The dharma of the original nature, by which the inherent nature is undefiled purity; and
>
> The dharma of abandoning all forms of mere *upādhi*, [or semblance] nirvāṇa dharmas,[139] by which he is able to bring forth all the bodhisattva practices and cultivate them incessantly.

These are the ten. If bodhisattvas abide in these, then they acquire the Tathāgata's unexcelled vast Dharma.

Sons of the Buddha, the bodhisattva-mahāsattva has ten kinds of merit-based provisions for enlightenment.[140] What are those ten? They are as follows:

> Encouraging beings to arouse the resolve to attain bodhi is a bodhisattva's merit-based provision for enlightenment, this because he thereby ensures that the lineage of the Three Jewels will never be cut off;
>
> Following along in accordance with the ten kinds of dedication is a bodhisattva's merit-based provision for enlightenment, this because he thereby cuts off all bad dharmas and accumulates all good dharmas;
>
> Using wisdom to guide and instruct is a bodhisattva's merit-based provision for enlightenment, this because he thereby steps entirely beyond all merit within the three realms of existence;
>
> Tireless resolve is a bodhisattva's merit-based provision for enlightenment, this because he thereby ultimately liberates all beings;
>
> Relinquishing all of one's inward and outward possessions is a bodhisattva's merit-based provision for enlightenment, this because he is thereby free of attachment to anything at all;
>
> Irreversible vigor for the sake of the complete fulfillment of the major marks and secondary signs is a bodhisattva's merit-based provision for enlightenment, this because he thereby opens the gateway to limitless great giving;
>
> Dedicating all three categories of superior, middling, and lesser roots of goodness to the realization of unexcelled bodhi, having none that one's mind looks on but lightly—this is a bodhisattva's merit-based provision for enlightenment, this because he thereby accords with skillful means;

正體字

於邪
定下劣。不善眾生。皆生大悲。不懷輕賤。是菩
薩福德助道具。常起大人。弘誓心故。恭敬供
養一切如來。於一切菩薩。起如來想。令一切
眾生。皆生歡喜。是菩薩福德助道具。守本志
願。極堅牢故。菩薩摩訶薩。於阿僧祇劫。積集
善根。自欲取證無上菩提。如在掌中。然悉捨
與一切眾生。心無憂惱。亦無悔恨。其心廣大。
等虛空界。此是菩薩福德助道具。起大智慧。
證大法故。是為十。若諸菩薩。安住其中。則具
足如來無上廣大福德聚。佛子。菩薩摩訶薩。
有十種智慧助道具。何等為十。所謂親近多
聞。真善知識。恭敬供養。尊重禮拜。種種隨
順。不違其教。是為一。一切正直。無虛矯故。
永離憍慢。常行謙敬。身語意業。無有麁[1]獷。
柔和善順。不偽不曲。是為二。其身堪作佛法
器故。念慧隨覺。未曾散亂。

简体字

于邪定、下劣、不善众生，皆生大悲，不怀轻贱，是菩萨福德助道具；常起大人弘誓心故。恭敬供养一切如来，于一切菩萨起如来想，令一切众生皆生欢喜，是菩萨福德助道具；守本志愿极坚牢故。菩萨摩诃萨于阿僧祇劫积集善根，自欲取证无上菩提如在掌中，然悉舍与一切众生，心无忧恼亦无悔恨，其心广大等虚空界，此是菩萨福德助道具；起大智慧证大法故。是为十。若诸菩萨安住其中，则具足如来无上广大福德聚。

"佛子，菩萨摩诃萨有十种智慧助道具。何等为十？所谓：亲近多闻真善知识，恭敬供养，尊重礼拜，种种随顺，不违其教，是为一；一切正直无虚矫故。永离憍慢，常行谦敬，身、语、意业无有粗犷，柔和善顺，不伪不曲，是为二；其身堪作佛法器故。念慧随觉未曾散乱，

Chapter 38 — *Transcending the World*

Arousing the great compassion even for all beings who are fixed in what is wrong, inferior, or unwholesome while not cherishing any slighting or disdainful attitude toward them—this is a bodhisattva's merit-based provision for enlightenment, this because he thereby always arouses the great man's mind of vast vows;

Reverently making offerings to all *tathāgatas*, conceiving of all bodhisattvas as *tathāgatas*, and gladdening all beings—this is a bodhisattva's merit-based provision for enlightenment, this because he thereby preserves his original vows with ultimate solidity and durability; and

For *asaṃkhyeyas* of kalpas, the bodhisattva-mahāsattva accumulates roots of goodness wishing himself to take up the realization of unexcelled bodhi, thus bringing it to the point that it is as if resting in the palm of his hand, yet he relinquishes it all and bestows it on all beings with a mind entirely free of distress or affliction and also free of regrets, doing so with his mind as vast as the realm of empty space—this is a bodhisattva's merit-based provision for enlightenment, this because he thereby brings forth great wisdom and realizes the great Dharma.

These are the ten. If bodhisattvas abide in these, then they completely fulfill the Tathāgata's unexcelled and vast accumulation of merit.

Sons of the Buddha, the bodhisattva-mahāsattva has ten kinds of wisdom-based provisions for enlightenment. What are those ten? They are as follows:

He draws near to a genuine good spiritual guide possessed of abundant learning, respectfully makes offerings to him, deeply esteems him, bows down in reverence to him, and follows along in accordance with him in many different ways while never opposing his teachings. This is what constitutes the first of them. It is based on being correct and straightforward in all things and on remaining free of any deception;

He forever abandons arrogance and pride, always practices humility and respectfulness, maintains physical, verbal, and mental deeds entirely free of coarse and uncivilized actions, remains gentle, harmonious, and accordant with goodness, refrains from deceptiveness, and abstains from deviousness. This is what constitutes the second of them. It is based on his being personally capable of becoming a vessel for the Buddha's Dharma;

He possesses mindfulness and wisdom that accord with awakening, never becomes scattered and confused, and maintains

正體字	慚愧柔和。心安不動。常憶六念。常行六敬。常隨順住六堅固法。是為三。與十種智。為方便故。樂法樂義。以法為樂。常樂聽聞。無有厭足。捨離世論及世言說。專心聽受。出世間語。遠離小乘。入大乘慧。是為四。一心憶念。無散動故。六波羅蜜。心專荷負。四種梵住。行已成熟。隨順明法。悉善修行。聰敏智人。皆勤請問。遠離惡趣。歸向善道。心常愛樂。正念觀察。調伏己情。守護他意。是為五。堅固修行真實行故。常樂出離。不著三有。恒覺自心。曾無惡念。三覺已絕。三業皆善。決定了知心之自性。是為六。能令自他心清淨故。觀察五蘊皆如幻事。界如毒蛇。處如空聚。一切諸法。如幻如焰。如水中月。如夢如影。如響如像。如空中畫。
简体字	慚愧柔和，心安不动，常忆六念，常行六敬，常随顺住六坚固法，是为三；与十种智为方便故。乐法、乐义，以法为乐，常乐听闻无有厌足，舍离世论及世言说，专心听受出世间语，远离小乘，入大乘慧，是为四；一心忆念无散动故。六波罗蜜心专荷负，四种梵住行已成熟，随顺明法悉善修行，聪敏智人皆勤请问，远离恶趣，归向善道，心常爱乐，正念观察，调伏己情，守护他意，是为五；坚固修行真实行故。常乐出离，不著三有，恒觉自心，曾无恶念，三觉已绝，三业皆善，决定了知心之自性，是为六；能令自他心清净故。观察五蕴皆如幻事，界如毒蛇，处如空聚，一切诸法如幻、如焰、如水中月、如梦、如影、如响、如像、如空中画、

(306c19–307a03)

Chapter 38 — *Transcending the World*

a sense of shame, dread of blame, and gentle harmoniousness in which his mind is peaceful and imperturbable, in which he always bears in mind the six kinds of mindfulness,[141] in which he always practices the six kinds of [harmony and] respect,[142] and in which he always follows along in accordance with and abides in the six dharmas of solidity.[143] This is what constitutes the third of them. It is based on its serving as a skillful means for development of the ten kinds of knowledge;[144]

- He delights in the Dharma, delights in meaning, and takes the Dharma as what is blissful. He always delights in listening to it and, in this, he is insatiable. He abandons worldly treatises and worldly discourse and especially focuses his mind on listening to world-transcending discourse while leaving the small vehicle far behind and entering the wisdom of the Great Vehicle. This is what constitutes the fourth of them. It is based on his being single-minded in his recollection and free of any scattered movement;
- His mind is focused on taking up the burden of the six *pāramitās*. His practice of the four abodes of Brahma[145] has already become completely ripened. He accords with the dharmas of the clarities and skillfully cultivates them all.[146] He is diligent in posing questions to persons who are intelligent, quick-witted, and wise, abandons the wretched destinies, and takes refuge in the courses of good karmic action. His mind always cherishes and delights in right mindfulness and contemplation, he subdues his own emotions, and he guards the minds of others. This is what constitutes the fifth of them. It is based on solidly enduring cultivation of the genuine practices;
- He always delights in emancipation from the three realms of existence and is not attached to them. He maintains constant awakened awareness of his own mind, is ever free of evil thoughts, and has already cut off the three types of ideation.[147] His three kinds of actions[148] are all good and he possesses a decisively resolute and complete knowledge of the mind's inherent nature. This is what constitutes the sixth of them. It is based on the ability to enable purity to arise in the minds of both himself and others;
- He contemplates the five aggregates as in every case like illusory phenomena, the sense realms as comparable to poisonous snakes, the sense fields as like an empty village, and all dharmas as like conjurations, like mirages, like the moon reflected in water, like dreams, like shadows, like echoes, like reflected images, like images drawn in space, like the wheel shape

正體字

如旋火輪。如虹霓色。如日月光。無相無形。非常非斷。不來不去。亦無所住。如是觀察。知一切法。無生無滅。是為七。知一切法性空寂故。菩薩摩訶薩。聞一切法無我無眾生。無壽者無補伽羅。無心無境。無貪瞋癡。無身無物。無主無待。無著無行。如是一切。皆無所有。悉歸寂滅。聞已深信。不疑不謗。是為八。以能成就圓滿解故。菩薩摩訶薩。善調諸根。如理修行。恒住止觀。心意寂靜。一切動念。皆悉不生。無我無人。無作無行。無計我想。無計我業。無有瘡疣。無有瘢痕。亦無於此所得之忍。身語意業。無來無去。無有精進。亦無勇猛。觀一切眾生。一切諸法。心皆平等。而無所住。非此岸非彼岸。此彼性離。無所從來。無所至去。常以智慧。如是思惟。是為九。到分別相。彼岸處故。菩薩摩訶薩。見緣起法故。見法清淨。見法清淨故。見國土清淨。見國土清淨故。見虛空清淨。

简体字

如旋火轮、如虹霓色、如日月光，无相无形，非常非断，不来不去，亦无所住，如是观察，知一切法无生无灭，是为七；知一切法性空寂故。菩萨摩诃萨闻一切法无我、无众生、无寿者、无补伽罗、无心、无境、无贪瞋痴、无身、无物、无主、无待、无著、无行，如是一切皆无所有、悉归寂灭，闻已深信，不疑不谤，是为八；以能成就圆满解故。菩萨摩诃萨善调诸根，如理修行，恒住止观，心意寂静，一切动念皆悉不生，无我、无人、无作、无行、无计我想、无计我业、无有疮疣、无有瘢痕，亦无于此所得之忍，身、语、意业无来无去，无有精进亦无勇猛，观一切众生、一切诸法，心皆平等而无所住，非此岸、非彼岸，此彼性离，无所从来，无所至去，常以智慧如是思惟，是为九；到分别相彼岸处故。菩萨摩诃萨见缘起法故见法清净，见法清净故见国土清净，见国土清净故见虚空清净，

created by a whirling firebrand, like the hues of rainbow, like the light of the sun or moon, as signless, as formless, as neither permanent nor annihilated, as neither coming nor going, and as having no place in which they abide. Contemplating them in this way, he knows that all dharmas are neither produced nor destroyed. This is what constitutes the seventh of them. It is based on realization that the nature of all dharmas is empty and quiescent;

When the bodhisattva-mahāsattva hears that all dharmas are devoid of self, devoid of any being, devoid of any life span, devoid of any *pudgala*, devoid of any mind, devoid of any objective realm, devoid of greed, hatred, or delusion, devoid of any body, devoid of any thing, devoid of any primary entity, devoid of any secondary entity, devoid of any attachment, devoid of any action, that all of these are in every case entirely nonexistent, and that they all trace back to quiescence—having heard this, he deeply believes it, does not doubt it, and does not repudiate it. This is what constitutes the eighth of them. It is based on the ability to develop perfectly fulfilled understanding;

The bodhisattva-mahāsattva skillfully trains all his faculties, cultivates in accordance with principle, and constantly dwells in the practice of calming and insight contemplation in which his mind is quiescent. None of the movements of thought arise at all. Thus there is no self, no other, no endeavors, no actions, no thought conceiving of a self, and no actions based on conceiving of a self. Thus he has no wounds, has no scars, and also does not even retain any of the patience he has acquired here.[149] In his actions of body, speech, and mind, he has neither any coming nor any going, has no vigor, and does not retain any valiant bravery, either.[150] In his contemplation of all beings and all dharmas, he observes them all impartially even as he has no place in which he abides, abiding thus neither on this shore nor on the far shore, for he has transcended any nature of either "this" or "that." He has no place from which he comes and no place to which he goes. He always uses wisdom in carrying out contemplations such as these. This is what constitutes the ninth of them. It is based on having reached the "far shore" of perfection in distinguishing signs; and

Because the bodhisattva-mahāsattva perceives the dharma of conditioned origination, he perceives dharmas as pure. Because he perceives dharmas as pure, he perceives lands as pure. Because he sees lands as pure, he perceives empty space as pure. Because he perceives empty space as pure, he perceives

正體字

見虛空
清淨故。見法界清淨。見法界清淨故。見智慧
清淨。是為十。修行積集一切智故。佛子。是為
菩薩摩訶薩十種智慧助道具。若諸菩薩。安
住此法。則得如來一切法。無障礙清淨。微妙
智慧聚。佛子。菩薩摩訶薩。有十種明足。何等
為十。所謂善分別諸法明足。不取著諸法明
足。離顛倒見明足。智慧光照諸根明足。巧發
起正精進明足。能深入真諦智明足。滅煩惱
業。成就盡智無生智明足。[2]大眼智普。觀察
明足。宿住念知前際清淨明足。漏盡神通智
斷眾生諸漏明足。是為十。若諸菩薩。安住此
法。則得如來於一切佛法無上大光明。佛子。
菩薩摩訶薩。有十種求法。何等為十。所謂直
心求法。無有諂誑故。

简体字

见虚空清净故见法界清净，见法界清净故见智慧清净，是为十；修行积集一切智故。佛子，是为菩萨摩诃萨十种智慧助道具。若诸菩萨安住此法，则得如来一切法无障碍清净微妙智慧聚。

"佛子，菩萨摩诃萨有十种明足。何等为十？所谓：善分别诸法明足；不取著诸法明足；离颠倒见明足；智慧光照诸根明足；巧发起正精进明足；能深入真谛智明足；灭烦恼业成就尽智无生智明足；天眼智普观察明足；宿住念知前际清净明足；漏尽神通智断众生诸漏明足。是为十。若诸菩萨安住此法，则得如来于一切佛法无上大光明。

"佛子，菩萨摩诃萨有十种求法。何等为十？所谓：直心求法，无有谄诳故；

Chapter 38 — *Transcending the World* 2999

the Dharma realm as pure. Because he perceives the Dharma realm as pure, he sees wisdom as pure. This is what constitutes the tenth of them. It is based on the cultivation and accumulation of all-knowledge.

Sons of the Buddha, these are what constitute the bodhisattva-mahāsattva's ten kinds of wisdom-based provisions for enlightenment. If bodhisattvas abide in these dharmas, then they acquire the Tathāgata's accumulation of unimpeded and pure sublime wisdom with respect to all dharmas.

Sons of the Buddha, the bodhisattva-mahāsattva has ten kinds of completely developed clarities. What are those ten? They are as follows:

The completely developed clarity of skill in distinguishing all dharmas;

The completely developed clarity of not seizing on or attaching to any dharma;

The completely developed clarity of abandoning the inverted views;

The completely developed clarity of illuminating all faculties with the light of wisdom;

The completely developed clarity of skillfully arousing right vigor;

The completely developed clarity of the ability to deeply penetrate the knowledge of the truths;[151]

The completely developed clarity of extinguishing affliction-based karma and completely developing the knowledge of cessation and the knowledge of the unproduced;

The completely developed clarity of universal contemplation with the cognition of the heavenly eye;

The pure and completely developed clarity of recollective awareness of previous-life existences throughout the past; and

The completely developed clarity of the spiritual superknowledge of the cessation of the contaminants with which he cuts off the contaminants of beings.

These are the ten. If bodhisattvas abide in these dharmas, then they acquire the Tathāgata's unexcelled great illumination of all dharmas of the Buddha.

Sons of the Buddha, the bodhisattva-mahāsattva has ten ways of seeking the Dharma. What are those ten? They are as follows:

He seeks the Dharma with a straightforward mind, this because he is free of any flattery or deviousness;

正體字

精進求法。遠離懈慢故。
307b06 ｜ 一向求法。不惜身命故。為斷一切眾生煩惱
307b07 ｜ 求法。不為名利恭敬故。為饒益自他一切眾
307b08 ｜ 生求法。不但自利故。為入智慧求法不樂文
307b09 ｜ 字故。為出生死求法。不貪世樂故。為度眾生
307b10 ｜ 求法。發菩提心故。為斷一切眾生疑求法。令
307b11 ｜ 無猶豫故。為滿足佛法求法。不樂餘乘故。是
307b12 ｜ 為十。若諸菩薩。安住此法。則得不由他教一
307b13 ｜ 切佛法大智慧。佛子。菩薩摩訶薩。有十種明
307b14 ｜ 了法。何等為十。所謂隨順世俗生長善根是
307b15 ｜ 童蒙凡夫明了法。得無礙不壞信覺法自性
307b16 ｜ 是隨信行人明了法。勤修習法隨順法住是
307b17 ｜ 隨法行人明了法。遠離八邪向八正道是
307b18 ｜ 第八人明了法。除滅眾結斷生死漏見真實
307b19 ｜ 諦

简体字

精进求法，远离懈慢故；一向求法，不惜身命故；为除一切众生烦恼求法，不为名利恭敬故；为饶益自他一切众生求法，不但自利故；为入智慧求法，不乐文字故；为出生死求法，不贪世乐故；为度众生求法，发菩提心故；为断一切众生疑求法，令无犹豫故；为满足佛法求法，不乐余乘故。是为十。若诸菩萨安住此法，则得不由他教一切佛法大智慧。

"佛子，菩萨摩诃萨有十种明了法。何等为十？所谓：随顺世俗生长善根，是童蒙凡夫明了法；得无碍不坏信，觉法自性，是随信行人明了法；勤修习法，随顺法住，是随法行人明了法；远离八邪，向八正道，是第八人明了法；除灭众结，断生死漏，见真实谛，

Chapter 38 — Transcending the World

- He seeks the Dharma with vigor, this because he has abandoned indolence;
- He seeks the Dharma wholeheartedly, this because he does not even begrudge his body or life to acquire it;
- He seeks the Dharma to sever the afflictions of all beings, this because he is not motivated by the desire for fame, personal benefit, or reverence;
- He seeks the Dharma to benefit self, others, and all beings, this because he does not seek to benefit only himself;
- He seeks the Dharma to penetrate its wisdom, this because he does not merely delight in its language;
- He seeks the Dharma to escape *saṃsāra*, this because he does not covet worldly happiness;
- He seeks the Dharma to liberate beings, this because he has brought forth the resolve to attain bodhi;
- He seeks the Dharma to sever the doubts of all beings, this because he wishes to enable them to be free of any hesitation; and
- He seeks the Dharma for the sake of completely fulfilling the dharma of buddhahood, this because he does not delight in any of the other vehicles.

These are the ten. If bodhisattvas abide in these dharmas, then they acquire the great wisdom of the Dharma of all buddhas that does not rely on instruction from others.

Sons of the Buddha, the bodhisattva-mahāsattva has ten kinds of dharmas for attaining complete understanding. What are those ten? They are as follows:

- According with mundane worldly conventions in producing and developing roots of goodness is a dharma for attaining complete understanding for common persons at beginning levels of practice;
- Acquiring unimpeded and indestructible faith and awakening to the inherent nature of dharmas is a dharma for attaining complete understanding for those whose practice accords with faith;
- Diligently cultivating and practicing the Dharma and dwelling in accordance with the Dharma is a dharma for attaining complete understanding for those whose practice accords with the Dharma;
- Abandoning the eightfold wrong path and following the eightfold right path is a dharma for attaining complete understanding for those at the level of the eighth person;[152]
- Extinguishing the many fetters, severing the contaminants associated with *saṃsāra*, and seeing the truths is a dharma for

正體字

是須陀洹人明了法。觀味是患知無往來
是斯陀含人明了法。不樂三界求盡有漏於
受生法乃至一念不生愛著是阿那含人明了
法。獲六神通得八解脫九定四辯悉皆成就
是阿羅漢人明了法。性樂觀察一味緣起心
常寂靜知足少事解因自得悟不由他成就種
種神通智慧是辟支佛人明了法。智慧廣大
諸根明利常樂度脫一切眾生勤修福智助道
之法如來所有十力無畏一切功德具足圓滿
是菩薩人明了法。是為十。若諸菩薩。安住此
法。則得如來無上大智明了法。佛子。菩薩摩
訶薩。有十種修行法。何等為十。所謂恭敬尊
重諸善知識修行法。常為諸天之所覺悟修
行法。於諸佛所常懷慚愧修行法。哀愍眾生
不捨生死修行法。事必究竟心無變動修行
法。

简体字

是须陀洹人明了法；观味是患，知无往来，是斯陀含人明了法；不乐三界，求尽有漏，于受生法乃至一念不生爱著，是阿那含人明了法；获六神通，得八解脱，九定、四辩悉皆成就，是阿罗汉人明了法；性乐观察一味缘起，心常寂静，知足少事，解因自得，悟不由他，成就种种神通智慧，是辟支佛人明了法；智慧广大，诸根明利，常乐度脱一切众生，勤修福智助道之法，如来所有十力、无畏、一切功德具足圆满，是菩萨人明了法。是为十。若诸菩萨安住此法，则得如来无上大智明了法。

"佛子，菩萨摩诃萨有十种修行法。何等为十？所谓：恭敬尊重诸善知识修行法；常为诸天之所觉悟修行法；于诸佛所常怀惭愧修行法；哀愍众生不舍生死修行法；事必究竟心无变动修行法；

Chapter 38 — Transcending the World

attaining complete understanding for who have reached the stage of a *srota-āpanna*;[153]

Regarding delectable meditation states as disastrous[154] and realizing there is neither any going nor any coming is a dharma for attaining complete understanding for a *sakṛd-āgāmin*;[155]

Not delighting in the three realms of existence, seeking to put an end to the contaminants, and not arousing so much as a single mind-moment of cherishing attachment for the dharmas of rebirth is a dharma for attaining complete understanding for an *anāgāmin*;[156]

Gaining the six spiritual superknowledges and acquiring the eight liberations, the nine meditative absorptions, and the four types of eloquence, completely developing them all—this is a dharma for attaining complete understanding for an arhat;

By nature delighting in contemplating single-flavored conditioned origination, having a mind that is always quiescent, being satisfied with but few things, reaching the understanding of causality himself, gaining awakening not reliant on others, and perfecting the many different kinds of spiritual superknowledges and wisdom—this is a dharma for attaining complete understanding for a *pratyekabuddha*; and

Acquiring vast wisdom and brilliantly sharp faculties, always delighting in liberating all beings, diligently cultivating the merit-based and wisdom-based dharmas of the provisions for enlightenment, and achieving the perfectly complete fulfillment of all of the Tathāgata's ten powers, fearlessnesses, and meritorious qualities is a dharma for attaining complete understanding for a bodhisattva.

These are the ten. If bodhisattvas abide in these dharmas, then they acquire the Tathāgata's dharma of complete understanding consisting of unexcelled great wisdom.

Sons of the Buddha, the bodhisattva-mahāsattva has ten kinds of cultivation dharmas. What are those ten? They are as follows:

The cultivation dharma of revering and honoring all good spiritual guides;

The cultivation dharma of always being awakened by the devas;

The cultivation dharma of always embracing a sense of shame and a dread of blame before the buddhas;

The cultivation dharma of deeply pitying beings and thus never leaving *saṃsāra*;

The cultivation dharma of certainly completely finishing all endeavors while maintaining an unchanging and unshakable resolve;

正體字

專念隨逐發大乘心諸菩薩眾精勤修學
修行法。遠離邪見勤求正道修行法。摧破眾
魔及煩惱業修行法。知諸眾生根性勝劣。而
為說法令住佛地修行法。安住無邊廣大法
界除滅煩惱令身清淨修行法。是為十。若諸
菩薩。安住其中。則得如來無上修行法。佛子。
菩薩摩訶薩。有十種魔。何等為十。所謂蘊魔。
生諸取故。煩惱魔。恒雜染故。業魔。能障礙
故。心魔。起高慢故。死魔。捨生處故。天魔。自
憍縱故。善根魔。恒執取故。三昧魔。久耽味
故。善知識魔。起著心故。菩提法智魔。不願捨
離故。是為十。菩薩摩訶薩。應作方便。速求遠
離。佛子。菩薩摩訶薩。有十種魔業。何等為
十。所謂

简体字

专念随逐发大乘心诸菩萨众精勤修学修行法；远离邪见勤求正道修行法；摧破众魔及烦恼业修行法；知诸众生根性胜劣而为说法令住佛地修行法；安住无边广大法界除灭烦恼令身清净修行法。是为十。若诸菩萨安住其中，则得如来无上修行法。

"佛子，菩萨摩诃萨有十种魔。何等为十？所谓：蕴魔，生诸取故；烦恼魔，恒杂染故；业魔，能障碍故；心魔，起高慢故；死魔，舍生处故；天魔，自憍纵故；善根魔，恒执取故；三昧魔，久耽味故；善知识魔，起著心故；菩提法智魔，不愿舍离故。是为十。菩萨摩诃萨应作方便，速求远离。

"佛子，菩萨摩诃萨有十种魔业。何等为十？所谓：

The cultivation dharma of single-minded energetic diligence in cultivating and training after the manner of the congregation of bodhisattvas who have aroused their resolve in the Great Vehicle;

The cultivation dharma of abandoning wrong views and diligently pursuing the path of what is right;

The cultivation dharma of vanquishing the many *māra*s as well as all affliction-based actions;

The cultivation dharma of knowing the relative superiority or inferiority of all beings' faculties and natures and then explaining the Dharma for them so as to enable them to dwell on the ground of buddhahood; and

The cultivation dharma of abiding in the boundlessly vast Dharma realm, extinguishing afflictions, and enabling the purification of the person.

These are the ten. If bodhisattvas abide in these, then they acquire the Tathāgata's unexcelled cultivation dharmas.

Sons of the Buddha, the bodhisattva-mahāsattva has ten kinds of *māra*s. What are those ten? They are as follows:

The *māra*s of the aggregates, so called because they induce grasping;

The *māra*s of the afflictions, so called because they constantly produce defilement;

The *māra*s of karma, so called because they are able to create obstacles;

The *māra*s of the mind, so called because they arouse arrogance;

The *māra*s of death, so called because they cause him to leave the place in which he lives;

Heavenly *māra*s, so called because they instigate arrogance and recklessness;

The *māra*s of roots of goodness, so called because they cause constant attachment;

The *māra*s of samādhi, so called because they cause him to develop an enduring obsession with delectable meditation states;

The *māra*s of good spiritual guides, so called because they cause him to arouse thoughts of attachment; and

The *māra*s of knowledge related to the dharma of bodhi, so called because they cause him to become unwilling to relinquish it.

These are the ten. Bodhisattva-mahāsattvas should create skillful means by which they swiftly seek to abandon them.

Sons of the Buddha, the bodhisattva-mahāsattva has ten kinds of *māra*-related actions. What are those ten? They are as follows:

正體字

忘失菩提心。修諸善根是為魔業。惡
心布施。瞋心持戒。捨惡性人。遠懈怠者。輕
慢亂意。譏嫌惡慧。是為魔業。於甚深法。心生
慳[3]吝。有堪化者。而不為說。若得財利。恭敬
供養。雖非法器。而強為說。是為魔業。不樂聽
聞諸波羅蜜。假使聞說。而不修行。雖亦修行。
多生懈怠。以懈怠故。志意狹劣。不求無上大
菩提法。是為魔業。遠善知識。近惡知識。樂求
二乘。不樂受生。志尚涅槃離欲寂靜。是為魔
業。於菩薩所。起瞋恚心。惡眼視之。求其罪
釁。說其過惡。斷彼所有。財利供養。是為魔
業。誹謗正法。不樂聽聞。假[4]使得聞。便生毀
呰。見人說法。不生尊重。言自說是。餘說悉
非。是為魔業。樂學世論。巧[1]術文詞。開闡二
乘。隱覆深法。或以妙義。授非其人。遠離菩
提。住於邪道。是為魔業。已得解脫。已安隱
者。常樂親近。而供養之。

简体字

忘失菩提心修诸善根，是为魔业；恶心布施，瞋心持戒，舍恶性人，远懈怠者，轻慢乱意，讥嫌恶慧，是为魔业；于甚深法心生悭吝，有堪化者而不为说，若得财利恭敬供养，虽非法器而强为说，是为魔业；不乐听闻诸波罗蜜，假使闻说而不修行，虽亦修行多生懈怠，以懈怠故，志意狭劣，不求无上大菩提法，是为魔业；远善知识，近恶知识，乐求二乘，不乐受生，志尚涅槃离欲寂静，是为魔业；于菩萨所起瞋恚心，恶眼视之，求其罪衅，说其过恶，断彼所有财利供养，是为魔业；诽谤正法不乐听闻，假使得闻便生毁呰，见人说法不生尊重，言自说是，余说悉非，是为魔业；乐学世论巧述文词，开阐二乘，隐覆深法，或以妙义授非其人，远离菩提住于邪道，是为魔业；已得解脱、已安隐者常乐亲近而供养之，

Forgetting the bodhi resolve as he cultivates roots of goodness is a work of the *māras*;

Giving with an evil mind, upholding the moral precepts with a mind of hatred, abandoning evil-natured people, distancing himself from those who are indolent, slighting those with slow and confused minds, and maintaining ridiculing disdain for those who are evil-minded—these are works of the *māras*;

Becoming miserly with extremely profound Dharma so that, even when there are those capable of being taught, he does not explain it for them, and, although someone else is not Dharma vessel, if he has the prospect of receiving material benefits, reverence, or offerings for doing so, he insists on teaching it to him—these are works of the *māras*;

If he does not delight in hearing teachings on the *pāramitās*, if he hears them explained but does not cultivate them, if he does cultivate them but for the most part becomes indolent, or if, because of such indolence, his resolve becomes so feeble and inferior that he does not seek the Dharma of the unexcelled great bodhi—these are works of the *māras*;

If he distances himself from good spiritual guides, if he draws near to bad spiritual guides, or if he delights in pursuing the two vehicles in which one does not delight in taking on births and resolves to pursue nirvāṇa, transcendence of desires, and quiescence—these are works of the *māras*;

If he arouses thoughts of anger toward bodhisattvas, glowers at them with a loathing gaze, seeks out their transgressions and errors, or discusses their transgressions and faults so as to cut off all their material benefits and offerings—these are works of the *māras*;

If he slanders right Dharma, if he does not delight in hearing it, if he succeeds in hearing it but then disparages it, if he sees someone speak Dharma but does not revere it, or if he claims that when he speaks it, it is right, but when others speak it, it is wrong—these are works of the *māras*;

If he delights in studying worldly treatises, arts, or literary writings, if he presents explanations of the two vehicles while concealing the profound Dharma, if perhaps he does teach the marvelous meaning, but does so to those unfit to receive it, or if he abandons bodhi and then dwells in erroneous paths—these are works of the *māras*;

If he always delights in drawing near to and making offerings to those who have already gained liberation and who have already attained peace and security but cannot bring himself to draw near to or teach those who have not yet gained liberation and

正體字

未得解脫。未安隱
者。不肯親近。亦不教化。是為魔業。增長我
慢。無有恭敬。於諸眾生。多行惱害。不求正
法真實智慧。其心弊惡。難可開悟。是為魔業。
是為十。菩薩摩訶薩。應速遠離。勤求佛業。佛
子。菩薩摩訶薩。有十種捨離魔業。何等為十。
所謂近善知識。恭敬供養。捨離魔業。不自尊
舉。不自讚歎。捨離魔業。於佛深法。信解不
謗。捨離魔業。未曾忘失一切智心。捨離魔業。
勤修妙行。恒不放逸。捨離魔業。常求一切菩
薩藏法。捨離魔業。恒演說法。心無疲倦。捨離
魔業。歸依十方一切諸佛。起救護想。捨離魔
業。信受憶念。一切諸佛。神力加持。捨離魔
業。與一切菩薩。同種善根。平等無二。捨離魔
業。是為十。若諸菩薩。安住此法。則能出離一
切魔道
佛子。菩薩摩訶薩。有十種見佛。何等為十。所
謂於安住世間成正覺佛無著見。

简体字

未得解脱、未安隐者不肯亲近亦不教化，是为魔业；增长我慢，无有恭敬，于诸众生多行恼害，不求正法真实智慧，其心弊恶难可开悟，是为魔业。是为十。菩萨摩诃萨应速远离，勤求佛业。

"佛子，菩萨摩诃萨有十种舍离魔业。何等为十？所谓：近善知识恭敬供养，舍离魔业；不自尊举，不自赞叹，舍离魔业；于佛深法信解不谤，舍离魔业；未曾忘失一切智心，舍离魔业；勤修妙行恒不放逸，舍离魔业；常求一切菩萨藏法，舍离魔业；恒演说法，心无疲倦，舍离魔业；归依十方一切诸佛，起救护想，舍离魔业；信受忆念一切诸佛，神力加持，舍离魔业；与一切菩萨同种善根，平等无二，舍离魔业。是为十。若诸菩萨安住此法，则能出离一切魔道。

"佛子，菩萨摩诃萨有十种见佛。何等为十？所谓：于安住世间成正觉佛无著见；

Chapter 38 — Transcending the World

who have not yet attained peace and security—these are works of the *māras*; and

If his pride in self increases, if he has no respect for others, if he often torments or injures beings, if he does not seek right Dharma and genuine wisdom, or if his mind becomes so inferior and evil that he is difficult to awaken—these are works of the *māras*.

These are the ten. the bodhisattva-mahāsattva should swiftly abandon them and diligently seek the works of the Buddha.

Sons of the Buddha, the bodhisattva-mahāsattva has ten ways of abandoning the works of the *māras*. What are those ten? They are as follows:

He abandons the works of the *māras* by drawing near to good spiritual guides, revering them, and making offerings to them;

He abandons the works of the *māras* by refraining from honoring and elevating himself and by refraining from praising himself;

He abandons the works of the *māras* by having resolute faith in and not disparaging the profound Dharma of the Buddha;

He abandons the works of the *māras* by never forgetting his resolve to attain all-knowledge;

He abandons the works of the *māras* by diligently cultivating the sublime practices and never becoming neglectful in this;

He abandons the works of the *māras* by always seeking the Dharma of the canon of all bodhisattvas;

He abandons the works of the *māras* by constantly and tirelessly expounding on the Dharma;

He abandons the works of the *māras* by taking refuge in all buddhas of the ten directions and bringing forth the motivation to rescue and protect others;

He abandons the works of the *māras* by faith, acceptance, and recollection of all buddhas' use of spiritual powers in providing supportive assistance; and

He abandons the works of the *māras* by joining with all bodhisattvas in planting roots of goodness that are the same and no different from theirs.

These are the ten. If bodhisattvas abide in these dharmas, then they are able to escape from all the paths of the *māras*.

Sons of the Buddha, the bodhisattva-mahāsattva has ten ways of seeing the Buddha. What are those ten? They are as follows:

Seeing the buddha abiding in the world, achieving the right enlightenment, due to nonattachment;

願佛出生

正體字

見。業報佛深信見。住持佛隨順見。涅槃佛深
入見。法界佛普至見。心佛安住見。三昧佛無
量無依見。本性佛明了見。隨樂佛普受見。是
為十。若諸菩薩。安住此法。則常得見無上如
來。佛子。菩薩摩訶薩。有十種佛業。何等為
十。所謂隨時開導是佛業。令正修行故。夢中
令見是佛業。覺昔善根故。為他演說所未聞
經是佛業。令生智斷疑故。為悔纏所纏者。說
出離法是佛業。令離疑心故。若有眾生。起慳
悋心。乃至惡慧心。二乘心。損害心。疑惑心。
散動心。憍慢心。為現如來眾相莊嚴身是佛
業。生長過去善根故。於正法難遇時。廣為說
法。令其聞已。得陀羅尼智。神通智。普能利益
無量眾生是佛業。勝解清淨故。若有魔事起。
能以方便。現虛空界等聲。

简体字

愿佛出生见；业报佛深信见；住持佛随顺见；涅槃佛深入见；法界佛普至见；心佛安住见；三昧佛无量无依见；本性佛明了见；随乐佛普受见。是为十。若诸菩萨安住此法，则常得见无上如来。

"佛子，菩萨摩诃萨有十种佛业。何等为十？所谓：随时开导，是佛业；令正修行故。梦中令见，是佛业；觉昔善根故。为他演说所未闻经，是佛业；令生智断疑故。为悔缠所缠者说出离法，是佛业；令离疑心故。若有众生起悭吝心，乃至恶慧心、二乘心、损害心、疑惑心、散动心、憍慢心，为现如来众相庄严身，是佛业；生长过去善根故。于正法难遇时，广为说法，令其闻已，得陀罗尼智、神通智，普能利益无量众生，是佛业；胜解清净故。若有魔事起，能以方便现虚空界等声，

Seeing the vow buddha, due to coming forth and taking birth;
Seeing the karmic rewards buddha, due to deep faith;
Seeing the abiding and sustaining buddha, due to adaptations;
Seeing the nirvāṇa buddha, due to deep penetration;
Seeing the Dharma realm buddha, due to universal reach;
Seeing the mind buddha, due to secure abiding;
Seeing the samādhi buddha, due to measureless independence;
Seeing the original nature buddha, due to clear comprehension; and
Seeing the buddha adapting to whatever delights others, due to universal acceptance.

These are the ten. If bodhisattvas abide in these dharmas, then they always succeed in seeing the unexcelled Tathāgata.

Sons of the Buddha, the bodhisattva-mahāsattva has ten kinds of buddha works. What are those ten? They are as follows:

Providing guidance in accordance with the right time is a buddha work done to enable right cultivation;

Causing beings to have visions in their dreams is a buddha work done to awaken them to roots of goodness from the past;

Expounding for beings sutras they have not yet heard is a buddha work done to enable them to develop wisdom and cut off doubts;

Teaching dharmas of emancipation for those bound up by the bonds of regretfulness is a buddha work done to enable separation from doubt-ridden thoughts;

Where there are beings who produce miserly thoughts and so forth, including evil-minded thoughts, thoughts of the two vehicles, thoughts of injuring others, doubt-ridden thoughts, scattered thoughts, or arrogant thoughts, manifesting for their sakes the Tathāgata's body adorned with the many signs is a buddha work done to enable the growth of past roots of goodness;

Extensively teaching the Dharma for others at a time when right Dharma has become difficult to encounter so that, having enabled them to hear it, they acquire the knowledge of the *dhāraṇīs* and the knowledge of the spiritual superknowledges— being able to everywhere benefit countless beings in this way is a buddha work done to enable them to acquire decisive understanding that is pure;

When works of *māras* are arising, being able to use skillful means to manifest a voice equal in its range to all of space that, in order to counter these endeavors, speaks Dharma encouraging

正體字	
	說不損惱他法。以
308b09	為對治。令其開悟。眾魔聞已。威光歇滅是佛
308b10	業。志樂殊勝。威德大故。其心無間。常自守
308b11	護。不令證入二乘正位。若有眾生。根性未熟。
308b12	終不為說解脫境界是佛業。本願所作故。生
308b13	死結漏。一切皆離。修菩薩行。相續不斷。以大
308b14	悲心。攝取眾生。令其起行。究竟解脫是佛業。
308b15	不斷修行菩薩行故。菩薩摩訶薩。了達自身
308b16	及以眾生。本來寂滅。不驚不怖。而勤修福智。
308b17	無有厭足。雖知一切法無有造作。而亦不捨
308b18	諸法自相。雖於諸境界。永離貪欲。而常樂瞻
308b19	奉諸佛色身。雖知不由他悟入於法。而種種
308b20	方便。求一切智。雖知諸國土皆如虛空。而常
308b21	樂莊嚴一切佛剎。雖恒觀察無人無我。而教
308b22	化眾生。無有疲厭。雖於法界本來不動。而以
308b23	神通智力。現眾變化。雖已成就一切智智。而
308b24	修菩薩行。無有休息。

简体字

说不损恼他法以为对治，令其开悟，众魔闻已威光歇灭，是佛业；志乐殊胜，威德大故。其心无间，常自守护，不令证入二乘正位，若有众生根性未熟，终不为说解脱境界，是佛业；本愿所作故。生死结漏一切皆离，修菩萨行相续不断，以大悲心摄取众生，令其起行究竟解脱，是佛业；不断修行菩萨行故。菩萨摩诃萨了达自身及以众生本来寂灭不惊不怖而勤修福智无有厌足，虽知一切法无有造作而亦不舍诸法自相，虽于诸境界永离贪欲而常乐瞻奉诸佛色身，虽知不由他悟入于法而种种方便求一切智，虽知诸国土皆如虚空而常乐庄严一切佛刹，虽恒观察无人无我而教化众生无有疲厌，虽于法界本来不动而以神通智力现众变化，虽已成就一切智智而修菩萨行无有休息，

Chapter 38 — *Transcending the World*

refraining from injurious torment of others, thus enabling their awakening so that, once the many *māra*s have heard this, their awesomely strong radiance recedes and disappears—this is a buddha work done to engender especially superior aspirations and vast awesome virtue;

To always guard his uninterrupted resolve by not allowing himself to gain realized entry into the right and fixed position of the two vehicles, and also, wherever there are beings whose faculties and natures are not yet ripened, to never teach them that sphere of liberation—this is a buddha work done to accord with his original vows;

To abandon all of *saṃsāra*'s fetters and contaminants, to continuously and uninterruptedly cultivate the bodhisattva practices, and to use the mind of great compassion to attract beings and enable them to begin the practices and ultimately reach liberation—this is a buddha work done to ceaselessly cultivate the bodhisattva practices; and

When the bodhisattva-mahāsattva fully comprehends that his own body as well as those of beings, from their very origin onward, are quiescent, he is neither startled or frightened, but rather proceeds then to insatiably pursue the diligent cultivation of merit and wisdom. In this:

Although he realizes all dharmas are uncreated, he still does not abandon dharmas' individual characteristics.

Although he has forever abandoned desire for any of the sense realms, he still always delights in looking up to and serving the buddhas manifesting in their form bodies.

Although he realizes that awakening and entering the Dharma does not depend on others, he still uses many different kinds of skillful means in his quest to reach all-knowledge.

Although he realizes all lands are like empty space, he still always delights in adorning all buddha *kṣetras*.

Although he constantly contemplates the nonexistence of others and the nonexistence of self, he still tirelessly teaches beings.

Although he is as originally unmoving as the Dharma realm itself, he still uses the power of his knowledge of the spiritual superknowledges to manifest a multitude of spiritual transformations.

Although he has already fully developed the wisdom of all-knowledge, he still incessantly cultivates the bodhisattva practices.

正體字

雖知諸法不可言說。而轉淨法輪。令眾心喜。雖能示現諸佛神力。而不厭捨菩薩之身。雖現入於大般涅槃。而一切處。示現受生。能作如是權實雙行法是佛業。是為十。若諸菩薩。安住其中。則得不由他教無上無師廣大業。佛子。菩薩摩訶薩。有十種慢業。何等為十。所謂於師僧父母。沙門婆羅門。住於正道。向正道者。尊重福田所。而不恭敬。是慢業。或有法師。獲最勝法。乘於大乘。知出要道。得陀羅尼。演說契經廣大之法。無有休息。而於其所。起高慢心。及於所說法。不生恭敬。是慢業。於眾會中。聞說妙法。不肯歎美。令人信受。是慢業。好起過慢。自高陵物。不見己失。不知自短。是慢業。好起過過慢。見有德人。應讚不讚。見他讚歎。不生歡喜。是慢業。見有法師為人說法。知是法是律。是真實是佛語。為嫌其人。亦嫌其法。自起誹謗。亦令他謗。是慢業。

简体字

虽知诸法不可言说而转净法轮令众心喜，虽能示现诸佛神力而不厌舍菩萨之身，虽现入于大般涅槃而一切处示现受生，能作如是权实双行法，是佛业。是为十。若诸菩萨安住其中，则得不由他教无上无师广大业。

"佛子，菩萨摩诃萨有十种慢业。何等为十？所谓：于师、僧、父母、沙门、婆罗门、住于正道向正道者，尊重福田所而不恭敬，是慢业；或有法师获最胜法，乘于大乘，知出要道，得陀罗尼，演说契经广大之法无有休息，而于其所起高慢心，及于所说法不生恭敬，是慢业；于众会中闻说妙法，不肯叹美令人信受，是慢业；好起过慢，自高陵物，不见己失，不知自短，是慢业；好起过过慢，见有德人应赞不赞，见他赞叹不生欢喜，是慢业；见有法师为人说法，知是法、是律、是真实、是佛语，为嫌其人亦嫌其法，自起诽谤亦令他谤，是慢业；

Chapter 38 — Transcending the World

- Although he realizes all dharmas are indescribable, he still turns the wheel of the pure Dharma, thereby enabling beings' minds to rejoice in it.
- Although he is able to manifest the spiritual powers of all buddhas, he still does not disdain or relinquish the body of a bodhisattva.
- Although he manifests the appearance of entering the great *parinirvāṇa*, he still manifests as taking rebirth everywhere.

The ability to carry out dharmas of simultaneous conventional and ultimate reality practice such as these is a buddha work.

These are the ten. If bodhisattvas abide in them, then they acquire the unexcelled and vast teacherless works not reliant on teaching provided by others.

Sons of the Buddha, the bodhisattva-mahāsattva has ten kinds of arrogant actions. What are those ten? They are as follows:

- If he fails to respect teachers, members of the Sangha, parents, *śramaṇas*, brahmans, those who abide in the right path, those on the threshold of the right path, or other venerable fields of merit, this is an arrogant action;
- If there is a master of the Dharma who has acquired the supreme Dharma, who has ascended to the Great Vehicle, who knows the path to emancipation, who has acquired the *dhāraṇīs*, and who ceaselessly expounds on the vast dharmas of the sutras, yet he generates thoughts of arrogance toward him or does not respect the Dharma that he teaches, this is an arrogant action;
- If he hears the proclamation of the sublime Dharma in the midst of a congregation but cannot bring himself to praise its excellence and thereby cause others to believe and accept it, this is an arrogant action;
- If he delights in thoughts of elevating arrogance[157] in which he elevates himself, assails others, fails to see his own faults, and fails to realize his own shortcomings, this is an arrogant action;
- If he delights in thoughts of over-reaching arrogance[158] by which, on seeing a virtuous person, he does not praise him even though he should praise him and is not pleased when he sees him being praised by others, this is an arrogant action;
- If he sees that there is a master of the Dharma teaching the Dharma for others and he realizes that this is indeed the Dharma, the moral code, the truth, and the words of the Buddha, yet, because he dislikes that person, he criticizes the Dharma as he teaches it and deliberately slanders him and causes others to slander him, this is an arrogant action;

正體字

自求高座。自稱法師。應受供給。不
應執事。見有耆舊久修行人。不起逢迎。不肯
承事。是慢業。見有德人。[2]顰蹙不喜。言辭麁
獷。伺其過失。是慢業。見有聰慧知法之人。不
肯親近恭敬供養。不肯諮問。何等為善。何等
不善。何等應作。何等不應作。作何等業。於長
夜中。而得種種利益安樂。愚癡頑很。我慢所
吞。終不能見出要之道。是慢業。復有眾生。慢
心所覆。諸佛出世不能親近恭敬供養。新善
不起。舊善消滅。不應說而說。不應諍而諍。未
來必墮險難深坑。於百千劫。尚不值佛。何況
聞法。但以曾發菩提心故。終自醒悟。是慢業。
是為十。若諸菩薩。離此慢業。則得十種智業。
何等為十。所謂信解業報。不壞因果。是智業。
不捨菩提心。常念諸佛。是智業。近善知識。恭
敬供養。其心尊重。終無厭怠。是智業。樂法樂
義。無有厭足。遠離邪念。勤修正念。是智業。

简体字

自求高座，自称法师，应受供给，不应执事，见有耆旧久修行人不起逢迎、不肯承事，是慢业；见有德人，颦蹙不喜，言辞粗犷，伺其过失，是慢业；见有聪慧知法之人，不肯亲近恭敬供养，不肯咨问：'何等为善？何等不善？何等应作？何等不应作？作何等业，于长夜中而得种种利益安乐？'愚痴顽很，我慢所吞，终不能见出要之道，是慢业；复有众生慢心所覆，诸佛出世不能亲近恭敬供养，新善不起，旧善消灭，不应说而说，不应诤而诤，未来必堕险难深坑，于百千劫尚不值佛，何况闻法！但以曾发菩提心故，终自醒悟，是慢业。是为十。

"若诸菩萨离此慢业，则得十种智业。何等为十？所谓：信解业报，不坏因果，是智业；不舍菩提心，常念诸佛，是智业；近善知识恭敬供养，其心尊重终无厌怠，是智业；乐法、乐义无有厌足，远离邪念，勤修正念，是智业；

Chapter 38 — *Transcending the World*

If he seeks the high seat, calls himself a master of the Dharma worthy of offerings and support, claims he therefore should not have to do his usual work, and fails to greet and welcome senior and long-tenured cultivators while also being unwilling to serve them, this is an arrogant action;

If he sees that there is a virtuous person, but he knits his brows, acts displeased, and narrates his faults in coarse and fiercely rude terms, this is an arrogant action;

If he sees that there is an intelligent and wise person who knows the Dharma, yet he cannot bring himself to draw near to that person to pay his respects and present offerings and cannot bring himself to inquire as to what is good, what is not good, what he should do, what he should not do, and what actions there are that, pursued throughout the long night [of *saṃsāra*], would bring about all kinds of benefit and happiness, being so beset by delusion and dullness that he is swallowed up by self-imputing arrogance[159] and can never see the path to emancipation, this is an arrogant action;

And further, if there is a being whose mind is so covered over by arrogance that, even when buddhas come forth into the world, he is unable to draw near to them, revere them, or make offerings to them—one in whom new acts of goodness do not arise and old acts of goodness have passed away, one who says what should not be said and disputes what should not be disputed—in the future, he will certainly fall into a deep pit of hazards and difficulties and, even in a hundred thousand kalpas, he will never encounter a buddha, how much the less hear the Dharma. It is only due to having once already resolved to attain bodhi that he might finally eventually awaken on his own. This is an arrogant action.

These are the ten. If bodhisattvas abandon these arrogant actions, then they acquire the ten kinds of wise actions. What are those ten? They are as follows:

Maintaining resolute faith in karmic consequences that does not contradict cause and effect is a wise action;

Never relinquishing the resolve to attain bodhi and always remaining mindful of all buddhas—these are wise actions;

Drawing near to a good spiritual guide, respectfully making offerings to him with a reverential mind, and never wearying of this—these are wise actions;

Insatiably delighting in the Dharma and delighting in meaning while abandoning wrong mindfulness and diligently cultivating right mindfulness—these are wise actions;

正體字

| 308c29 | 於一切眾生。離於我慢。於諸菩薩。起如來想。
| 309a01 | 愛重正法。如惜己身。尊奉如來。如護己命。於
| 309a02 | 修行者。生諸佛想。是智業。身語意業。無諸不
| 309a03 | 善。讚美賢聖。隨順菩提。是智業。不壞緣起。
| 309a04 | 離諸邪見。破闇得明。照一切法。是智業。十種
| 309a05 | 迴向。隨順修行。於諸波羅蜜。起慈母想。於善
| 309a06 | 巧方便。起慈父想。以深淨心。入菩提舍。是智
| 309a07 | 業。施戒多聞。止觀福慧。如是一切助道之法。
| 309a08 | 常勤積集。無有厭倦。是智業。若有一業。為佛
| 309a09 | 所讚。能破眾魔煩惱鬪諍。能離一切障蓋纏
| 309a10 | 縛。能教化調伏一切眾生。能隨順智慧。攝取
| 309a11 | 正法。能嚴淨佛剎。能發起通明。皆勤修習。無
| 309a12 | 有懈退。是智業。是為十。若諸菩薩。安住其
| 309a13 | 中。則得如來一切善巧方便無上大智業。佛
| 309a14 | 子。菩薩摩訶薩。有十種魔所攝持。何等為十。
| 309a15 | 所謂懈怠心。魔所攝持。志樂狹劣。魔所攝持。
| 309a16 | 於少行生足。魔所攝持。受一非餘。魔所攝持。

简体字

于一切众生离于我慢,于诸菩萨起如来想,爱重正法如惜己身,尊奉如来如护己命,于修行者生诸佛想,是智业;身、语、意业无诸不善,赞美贤圣,随顺菩提,是智业;不坏缘起,离诸邪见,破暗得明,照一切法,是智业;十种回向随顺修行,于诸波罗蜜起慈母想,于善巧方便起慈父想,以深净心入菩提舍,是智业;施、戒、多闻、止观、福慧,如是一切助道之法常勤积集无有厌倦,是智业;若有一业为佛所赞,能破众魔烦恼斗诤,能离一切障、盖、缠、缚,能教化调伏一切众生,能随顺智慧摄取正法,能严净佛剎,能发起通明,皆勤修习无有懈退,是智业。是为十。若诸菩萨安住其中,则得如来一切善巧方便无上大智业。

"佛子,菩萨摩诃萨有十种魔所摄持。何等为十?所谓:懈怠心,魔所摄持;志乐狭劣,魔所摄持;于少行生足,魔所摄持;受一非余,魔所摄持;

Chapter 38 — *Transcending the World*

- Abandoning self-imputing arrogance in relating to other beings, conceiving of all bodhisattvas as *tathāgatas*, cherishing and revering right Dharma as he would his own person, honoring and serving the Tathāgata just as he would protect his own life, and conceiving of all cultivators as buddhas—these are wise actions;
- Keeping his physical, verbal, and mental actions free of all that is not good, praising the worthies and the *āryas*, and compliantly pursuing bodhi—these are wise actions;
- Refraining from acting in contradiction to conditioned origination, abandoning all wrong views, dispelling darkness and acquiring brilliance, and illuminating all dharmas—these are wise actions;
- According with and cultivating the ten kinds of dedications, thinking of the *pāramitās* as he would a kindly mother, thinking of excellent skillful means as he would a kindly father, and using the deep and pure mind to enter the abode of bodhi—these are wise actions;
- Always diligently accumulating giving, moral precepts, abundant learning, calming and contemplation, merit, and wisdom, all such provisions for enlightenment as these, doing so insatiably and tirelessly—these are wise actions; and
- If there is one action that is praised by the Buddha, that is able to demolish the afflictions and disputation associated with the *māras*, that is able to cause one to abandon all obstructing hindrances and entangling bonds, that is able to bring about the teaching and training of all beings, that is able to accord with wisdom and accumulate right Dharma, that is able to purify the buddha *kṣetras*, and that is able to produce the superknowledges and clarities—where one always diligently cultivates it and never withdraws in retreat—this is a wise action.

These are the ten. If bodhisattvas abide in them, then they acquire all of the Tathāgata's skillful means and unexcelled wise actions.

Sons of the Buddha, the bodhisattva-mahāsattva has ten ways of being possessed by Māra. What are those ten? They are as follows:

- To have an indolent mind is to be possessed by Māra;
- To have narrow and inferior aspirations is to be possessed by Māra;
- To be satisfied with but a minor level of practice is to be possessed by Māra;
- Accepting but a single approach while regarding all others as wrong is to be possessed by Māra;

正體字

```
309a17  不發大願。魔所攝持。樂處寂滅。斷除煩惱。魔
309a18  所攝持。永斷生死。魔所攝持。捨菩薩行。魔所
309a19  攝持。不化眾生。魔所攝持。疑謗正法。魔所攝
309a20  持。是為十。若諸菩薩。能棄捨此魔所攝持。則
309a21  得十種佛所攝持。何等為十。所謂初始能發
309a22  菩提之心。佛所攝持。於生生中。持菩提心。不
309a23  令忘失。佛所攝持。覺諸魔事。悉能遠離。佛所
309a24  攝持。聞諸波羅蜜。如說修行。佛所攝持。知生
309a25  死苦。而不厭惡。佛所攝持。觀甚深法。得無量
309a26  果。佛所攝持。為諸眾生。說二乘法。而不證取
309a27  彼乘解脫。佛所攝持。樂觀無為法。而不住其
309a28  中。於有為無為。不生二想。佛所攝持。至無生
309a29  處。而現受生。佛所攝持。雖證得一切智。而起
309b01  菩薩行。不斷菩薩種。佛所攝持。是為十。若諸
309b02  菩薩。安住其中。則得諸佛無上攝持力。佛子。
309b03  菩薩摩訶薩。有十種法所攝持。何等為十。所
309b04  謂
```

简体字

不发大愿，魔所摄持；乐处寂灭，断除烦恼，魔所摄持；永断生死，魔所摄持；舍菩萨行，魔所摄持；不化众生，魔所摄持；疑谤正法，魔所摄持。是为十。

"若诸菩萨能弃舍此魔所摄持，则得十种佛所摄持。何等为十？所谓：初始能发菩提之心，佛所摄持；于生生中持菩提心不令忘失，佛所摄持；觉诸魔事，悉能远离，佛所摄持；闻诸波罗蜜，如说修行，佛所摄持；知生死苦而不厌恶，佛所摄持；观甚深法，得无量果，佛所摄持；为诸众生说二乘法，而不证取彼乘解脱，佛所摄持；乐观无为法而不住其中，于有为、无为不生二想，佛所摄持；至无生处而现受生，佛所摄持；虽证得一切智，而起菩萨行，不断菩萨种，佛所摄持。是为十。若诸菩萨安住其中，则得诸佛无上摄持力。

"佛子，菩萨摩诃萨有十种法所摄持。何等为十？所谓：

Chapter 38 — *Transcending the World*

To fail to make great vows is to be possessed by Māra;
To delight [only] in abiding in quiescence and cutting off afflictions is to be possessed by Māra;
To forever cut off *saṃsāra* is to be possessed by Māra;
To abandon the bodhisattva practices is to be possessed by Māra;
To refrain from teaching beings is to be possessed by Māra; and
To doubt and slander right Dharma is to be possessed by Māra.

These are the ten. If bodhisattvas are able to cast off these ways of being possessed by Māra, then they acquire ten ways of being possessed by the Buddha. What are those ten? They are as follows:

With the initial instance of being able to resolve to attain bodhi, they are possessed by the Buddha;
When in life after life they maintain the resolve to attain bodhi and are not allowed to forget it, they are possessed by the Buddha;
When they are aware of all the works of the *māras* and are able to avoid them all, they are possessed by the Buddha;
When they hear the teaching of the *pāramitās* and then cultivate them as they were taught, they are possessed by the Buddha;
When they know the sufferings of *saṃsāra*, yet do not detest and abhor it, they are possessed by the Buddha;
When they contemplate the extremely profound Dharma and attain its measureless fruits, they are possessed by the Buddha;
When they explain the dharmas of the two vehicles for beings, yet do not opt for the realization of those vehicles' liberations, they are possessed by the Buddha;
When they delight in contemplating unconditioned dharmas, yet do not abide in them and do not form a dualistic conception of the conditioned and the unconditioned, they are possessed by the Buddha;
When they reach the station of the unproduced[160] and yet still manifest the appearance of taking on births, they are possessed by the Buddha; and
When, although they have realized the attainment of all-knowledge, they still bring forth the bodhisattva practices and do not cut off the lineage of the bodhisattvas, they are possessed by the Buddha.

These are the ten. If bodhisattvas abide in them, then they acquire the unexcelled power of being possessed by all buddhas.

Sons of the Buddha, the bodhisattva-mahāsattva has ten ways in which he is possessed by the Dharma. What are those ten? They are as follows:

正體字

知一切行無常。法所攝持。知一切行苦。法
所攝持。知一切行無我。法所攝持。知一切法。
寂滅涅槃。法所攝持。知諸法從緣起。無緣則
不起。法所攝持。知不正思惟故。起於無明。無
明起故。乃至老死起。不正思惟滅故。無明滅。
無明滅故。乃至老死滅。法所攝持。知三解脫
門出生聲聞乘。證無諍法出生獨覺乘。法所
攝持。知六波羅蜜。四攝法。出生大乘。法所攝
持。知一切剎。一切法。一切眾生。一切世。是
佛智境界。法所攝持。知斷一切念。捨一切取。
離前後際。隨順涅槃。法所攝持。是為十。若諸
菩薩。安住其中。則得一切諸佛無上。法所攝
持

佛子。菩薩摩訶薩。住兜率天。有十種所作業。
何等為十。所謂為欲界諸天子。說厭離法言。
一切自在。皆是無常。一切快樂。悉當衰謝。

简体字

知一切行无常，法所摄持；知一切行苦，法所摄持；知一切行无我，法所摄持；知一切法寂灭涅槃，法所摄持；知诸法从缘起，无缘则不起，法所摄持；知不正思惟故起于无明，无明起故乃至老死起，不正思惟灭故无明灭，无明灭故乃至老死灭，法所摄持；知三解脱门出生声闻乘，证无诤法出生独觉乘，法所摄持；知六波罗蜜、四摄法出生大乘，法所摄持；知一切刹、一切法、一切众生、一切世是佛智境界，法所摄持；知断一切念，舍一切取，离前后际，随顺涅槃，法所摄持。是为十。若诸菩萨安住其中，则得一切诸佛无上法所摄持。

"佛子，菩萨摩诃萨住兜率天，有十种所作业。何等为十？所谓：为欲界诸天子说厌离法言：'一切自在皆是无常，一切快乐悉当衰谢。'

Chapter 38 — *Transcending the World*

> When he realizes that all karmic formative factors are characterized by impermanence, he is possessed by the Dharma;
> When he realizes that all karmic formative factors are characterized by suffering, he is possessed by the Dharma;
> When he realizes that all karmic formative factors are characterized by the absence of any "self," he is possessed by the Dharma;
> When he realizes that all dharmas are characterized by quiescence and nirvāṇa, he is possessed by the Dharma;
> When he realizes that dharmas arise from conditions and that, in the absence of conditions, they do not arise at all, he is possessed by the Dharma;
> When he realizes that: it is due to wrong thought that ignorance arises; that due to the arising of ignorance, the other links in the causal chain up to and including aging-and-death arise; that it is due to the extinguishing of wrong thought that ignorance is extinguished; and that due to the extinguishing of ignorance, the other links of the causal chain up to and including aging and death are extinguished, then he is possessed by the Dharma;
> When he realizes that the three gates to liberation[161] are the basis for the arising of the *śrāvaka*-disciple vehicle and that realization of the dharma of non-contentiousness is the basis for the arising of the *pratyekabuddha* vehicle, he is possessed by the Dharma;
> When he realizes that the six *pāramitās* and the dharmas constituting the four means of attraction are the bases for the arising of the Great Vehicle, he is possessed by the Dharma;
> When he realizes that all *kṣetras*, all dharmas, all beings, and all worlds are realms of the Buddha's knowledge, he is possessed by the Dharma; and
> When he realizes that cutting off all thought, relinquishing all grasping, and transcending the past and future are in accordance with nirvāṇa, he is possessed by the Dharma.

These are the ten. If bodhisattvas abide in them, then they acquire all buddhas' unexcelled possession by the Dharma.

Sons of the Buddha, the bodhisattva-mahāsattva who dwells in the Tuṣita Heaven has ten kinds of works he accomplishes. What are those ten? They are as follows:

> For the sake of the young devas of the desire realm, he teaches the dharma of renunciation and tells them that all their sovereign powers are impermanent and that all their types of happiness are bound to wither and fade. He then exhorts all those devas to

正體字

勸彼諸天。發菩提心。是為第一所作業。為色界諸天。說入出諸禪。解脫三昧。若於其中。而生愛著。因愛復起身見邪見無明等者。則為其說如實智慧。若於一切色非色法。起顛倒想。以為清淨。為說不淨皆是無常。勸其令發菩提之心。是為第二所作業。菩薩摩訶薩。住兜率天。入三昧。名光明莊嚴。身放光明。遍照三千大千世界。隨眾生心。以種種音。而為說法。眾生聞已。信心清淨。命終生於兜率天中。勸其令發菩提之心。是為第三所作業。菩薩摩訶薩。在兜率天。以無障礙眼。普見十方兜率天中。一切菩薩。彼諸菩薩。皆亦見此。互相見已。論說妙法。謂降神母胎。初生出家。往詣道場。具大莊嚴。而復示現往昔已來。所行之行。以彼行故。成此大智。所有功德。不離本處。而能示現如是等事。是為第四所作業。菩薩摩訶薩。住兜率天。十方一切兜率天宮。諸菩薩眾。皆悉來集。恭敬圍遶。爾時菩薩摩訶薩。欲令彼諸菩薩皆滿其願。生歡喜故。

简体字

劝彼诸天发菩提心。是为第一所作业。为色界诸天说入出诸禅解脱三昧，若于其中而生爱著，因爱复起身见、邪见、无明等者，则为其说如实智慧；若于一切色、非色法起颠倒想，以为清净，为说不净皆是无常，劝其令发菩提之心。是为第二所作业。菩萨摩诃萨住兜率天，入三昧，名光明庄严，身放光明，遍照三千大千世界，随众生心，以种种音而为说法；众生闻已，信心清净，命终生于兜率天中，劝其令发菩提之心。是为第三所作业。菩萨摩诃萨在兜率天，以无障碍眼普见十方兜率天中一切菩萨，彼诸菩萨皆亦见此；互相见已，论说妙法，谓：降神母胎、初生、出家、往诣道场、具大庄严；而复示现往昔已来所行之行，以彼行故成此大智；所有功德不离本处，而能示现如是等事。是为第四所作业。菩萨摩诃萨住兜率天，十方一切兜率天宫诸菩萨众，皆悉来集，恭敬围绕；尔时，菩萨摩诃萨欲令彼诸菩萨皆满其愿生欢喜故，

Chapter 38 — *Transcending the World*

resolve to attain bodhi. This is the first of the works he accomplishes;

For the sake of the devas of the form realm, he teaches entry into and emergence from all the *dhyāna* absorptions, liberations, and samādhis. For those who develop cravings-based attachments to them, or then, because of such craving, also develop the body-centered identity view, other wrong views, ignorance, and so forth, he then teaches them with reality-accordant wisdom. For those who develop inverted conceptions imputing purity to all form and formless dharmas, he teaches them that they are impure and that they are all impermanent, whereupon he exhorts them and causes them to resolve to attain bodhi. This is the second of the works he accomplishes;

When the bodhisattva-mahāsattva dwells in the Tuṣita Heaven, he enters a samādhi known as "radiant adornment" in which his body emanates light that everywhere illuminates the worlds of the great trichiliocosm. Adapting to beings' minds, he uses all different kinds of voices with which he teaches the Dharma for their sakes. After those beings hear this, their minds of faith are purified. When their lives come to an end, they are then reborn in the Tuṣita Heaven where he exhorts them in ways that enable them to resolve to attain bodhi. This is the third of the works he accomplishes;

When the bodhisattva-mahāsattva is in the Tuṣita Heaven, with his unimpeded eye, he everywhere sees all the bodhisattvas in the Tuṣita heavens throughout the ten directions. All those other bodhisattvas also see this place. After they have all seen each other, they then discuss the sublime Dharma and speak of spiritually descending into the womb of their mother, taking birth, leaving the home life, and going to the site of enlightenment possessed of magnificent adornments. They then also manifest the appearances of the practices they have pursued from the past on forward to the present by which, because of those practices, they have perfected this great wisdom and all their meritorious qualities. Even without ever leaving their original place, they are able to reveal phenomena such as these. This is the fourth of the works he accomplishes;

When the bodhisattva-mahāsattva is dwelling in the Tuṣita Heaven, all those in the congregations of bodhisattvas in all the Tuṣita heaven palaces throughout the ten directions then come and respectfully gather around him. At that time, wishing to enable all those other bodhisattvas to fulfill their vows and be filled with joyous delight, the bodhisattva-mahāsattva adapts

隨彼菩薩。所應住地。所行所斷。所修所證。演說法門。彼諸菩薩。聞說法已。皆大歡喜。得未曾有。各還本土所住宮殿。是為第五所作業。菩薩摩訶薩。住兜率天時。欲界主。天魔波旬。為欲壞亂菩薩業故。眷屬圍遶。詣菩薩所。爾時菩薩。為摧伏魔軍故。住金剛道所攝般若波羅蜜方便善巧智慧門。以柔軟麁獷二種語。而為說法。令[1]魔波旬。不得其便。魔見菩薩自在威力。皆發阿耨多羅三藐三菩提心。是為第六所作業。菩薩摩訶薩。住兜率天。知欲界諸天子。不樂聞法。爾時菩薩。出大音聲。遍告之言。今日菩薩。當於宮中。現希有事。若欲見者。宜速往詣。時諸天子。聞是語已。無量百千億那由[2]他。皆來集會。爾時菩薩。見諸天眾皆來集已。為現宮中諸希有事。彼諸天子。曾未見聞。既得見已。皆大歡喜。其心醉沒。又於樂中。出聲告言。諸仁者。一切諸行。皆悉無常。一切諸行。皆悉是苦。一切諸法。皆悉無我。涅槃寂滅。又復告言。汝等皆應修菩薩行。

随彼菩萨所应住地、所行所断、所修所证,演说法门;彼诸菩萨闻说法已,皆大欢喜,得未曾有,各还本土所住宫殿。是为第五所作业。菩萨摩诃萨住兜率天时,欲界主天魔波旬,为欲坏乱菩萨业故,眷属围绕诣菩萨所;尔时,菩萨为摧伏魔军故,住金刚道所摄般若波罗蜜方便善巧智慧门,以柔软、粗犷二种语而为说法,令魔波旬不得其便;魔见菩萨自在威力,皆发阿耨多罗三藐三菩提心。是为第六所作业。菩萨摩诃萨住兜率天,知欲界诸天子不乐闻法;尔时,菩萨出大音声,遍告之言:'今日菩萨当于宫中现希有事,若欲见者宜速往诣。'时,诸天子闻是语已,无量百千亿那由他皆来集会;尔时,菩萨见诸天众皆来集已,为现宫中诸希有事;彼诸天子曾未见闻,既得见已,皆大欢喜,其心醉没;又于乐中出声告言:'诸仁者,一切诸行皆悉无常,一切诸行皆悉是苦,一切诸法皆悉无我,涅槃寂灭。'又复告言:'汝等皆应修菩萨行,

Chapter 38 — Transcending the World

to whichever grounds those bodhisattvas should dwell on, to whatever they practice, to whatever they have already cut off, to whatever they have cultivated, and to whatever they have already realized and then expounds on Dharma gateways for their sakes. After those bodhisattvas have heard his teachings on the Dharma, they are all filled with great joyous delight and experience what they have never before experienced, whereupon they each return to the palaces where they dwell in the lands from which they came. This is the fifth of the works he accomplishes;

When the bodhisattva-mahāsattva dwells in the Tuṣita Heaven, wishing to damage and throw into disorder the bodhisattva's works, the lord of the desire realm, Pāpīyān, the *māra* of the heavens, surrounded by his retinue, goes to where the bodhisattva dwells. Then, to vanquish the armies of *māra*s, dwelling in the *prajñāpāramitā*'s gateway of the vajra path's skillful means and expedient wisdom, the bodhisattva uses both gentle and harsh statements as he speaks the Dharma for their sakes. So it is that he prevents that *māra*, Pāpīyān, from having his way. When those *māra*s see the awesome powers of the bodhisattva's sovereign masteries, they all resolve to attain *anuttarasamyaksaṃbodhi*. This is the sixth of the works he accomplishes;

When the bodhisattva-mahāsattva dwells in the Tuṣita Heaven, he realizes that the young devas of the desire realm do not delight in hearing the Dharma. At that time, the bodhisattva emanates a loud voice with which he everywhere announces to them: "Today, the bodhisattva shall manifest rare phenomena in his palace. If anyone wishes to see this, it would be fitting for them to quickly go there." Having heard these words, the young devas who number in measurelessly many hundreds of thousands of *koṭīs* of *nayuta*s all come and gather together there. At that time, having observed that the congregation of devas has all come and assembled there, the bodhisattva then manifests for them all kinds of rare phenomena within his palace. Then, having been able to see what they had never before seen or heard, those young devas are all so moved to feelings of great joy that their minds are as if inebriated.

He then also emanates from the midst of musical sounds a voice that tells them, "O Worthy Ones, you should realize that all karmic formative factors are impermanent, all karmic formative factors are suffering, and all dharmas are devoid of any self and are characterized by the quiescence of nirvāṇa." He also informs them, "All of you should cultivate the bodhisattva practices and

正體字

皆當圓滿一切智智。彼諸天子。聞此法音。憂歎諮嗟。而生厭離。靡不皆發菩提之心。是為第七所作業。菩薩摩訶薩。住兜率宮。不捨本處。悉能往詣十方無量一切佛所。見諸如來。親近禮拜。恭敬聽法。爾時諸佛。欲令菩薩。獲得最上灌頂法故。為說菩薩地。名一切神通。以一念相應慧。具足一切最勝功德。入一切智智位。是為第八所作業。菩薩摩訶薩。住兜率宮。為欲供養諸如來故。以大神力。興起種種諸供養具。名殊勝可樂。遍法界虛空界。一切世界。供養諸佛。彼世界中。無量眾生。見此供養。皆發阿耨多羅三藐三菩提心。是為第九所作業。菩薩摩訶薩。住兜率天。出無量無邊如幻如影法門。周遍十方一切世界。示現種種色。種種相。種種形體。種種威儀。種種事業。種種方便。種種譬諭。種種言說。隨眾生心。皆令歡喜。是為第十所作業。佛子。是為菩薩摩訶薩。住兜率天。十種所作業。若諸菩薩。成就此法。則能於後。下生人[1]間。

简体字

皆当圆满一切智智。'彼诸天子闻此法音,忧叹咨嗟而生厌离,靡不皆发菩提之心。是为第七所作业。菩萨摩诃萨住兜率宫,不舍本处,悉能往诣十方无量一切佛所,见诸如来亲近礼拜恭敬听法;尔时,诸佛欲令菩萨获得最上灌顶法故,为说菩萨地,名一切神通,以一念相应慧,具足一切最胜功德,入一切智智位。是为第八所作业。菩萨摩诃萨住兜率宫,为欲供养诸如来故,以大神力兴起种种诸供养具,名殊胜可乐,遍法界、虚空界、一切世界供养诸佛;彼世界中无量众生见此供养,皆发阿耨多罗三藐三菩提心。是为第九所作业。菩萨摩诃萨住兜率天,出无量无边如幻如影法门,周遍十方一切世界,示现种种色、种种相、种种形体、种种威仪、种种事业、种种方便、种种譬喻、种种言说,随众生心皆令欢喜。是为第十所作业。佛子,是为菩萨摩诃萨住兜率天十种所作业。若诸菩萨成就此法,则能于后下生人间。

gain the complete fulfillment of the wisdom of all-knowledge." On hearing these sounds of the Dharma, those young devas are all moved to worried sighing and mutual exclamations of lamentation, whereupon they develop thoughts of renunciation. Then there are none among them who fail to resolve to attain bodhi. This is the seventh of the works he accomplishes;

- Without ever leaving his original place, the bodhisattva-mahāsattva dwelling in the Tuṣita Heaven palace is able to go to the abodes of all the countless buddhas of the ten directions to see all *tathāgatas*, draw near to them, bow down in reverence to them, and respectfully listen to the Dharma. At that time, because the buddhas wish to enable the bodhisattva to acquire the dharma of the most supreme crown-anointing consecration, they speak for his sake on the bodhisattva ground known as "all superknowledges" through which, with but a single mind-moment of corresponding wisdom, he completely perfects all of the most supreme meritorious qualities and enters the station of the wisdom of all-knowledge. This is the eighth of the works he accomplishes;
- Wishing to make offerings to all *tathāgatas*, the bodhisattva-mahāsattva dwelling in the Tuṣita Heaven palace uses great spiritual powers to offer up many different kinds of offering gifts known as "especially superior and delightful" which, as offerings to all buddhas, pervade all the worlds of the Dharma realm and the realms of space. On seeing these offerings, the countless beings in those worlds all resolve to attain *anuttarasamyaksaṃbodhi*. This is the ninth of the works he accomplishes; and
- The bodhisattva-mahāsattva dwelling in the Tuṣita Heaven brings forth countlessly and boundlessly many Dharma gateways like illusions and like reflections which pervade all worlds of the ten directions, displaying all different kinds of colors, all different kinds of signs, all different kinds of bodies, all different kinds of awesome deportment, all different kinds of endeavors, all different kinds of skillful means, all different kinds of analogies, and all different kinds of expositions which, adapting to the minds of beings, cause them all to be filled with joyous delight. This is the tenth of the works he accomplishes.

Sons of the Buddha, these are the ten kinds of works accomplished by the bodhisattva-mahāsattva dwelling in the Tuṣita Heaven. If bodhisattvas perfect these dharmas, later on they are able to descend to take rebirth among humans.

正體字

佛子。菩薩摩訶薩。於兜率天。將下生時。現十種事。何等為十。佛子。菩薩摩訶薩。於兜率天。下生之時。從於足下。放大光明。名安樂莊嚴。普照三千大千世界一切惡趣。諸難眾生。觸斯光者。莫不皆得離苦安樂。得安樂已。悉知將有奇特大人。出興[2]于世。是為第一所示現事。佛子。菩薩摩訶薩。於兜率天。下生之時。從於眉間白毫相中。放大光明。名曰覺悟。普照三千大千世界。照彼宿世一切同行。諸菩薩身。彼諸菩薩。蒙光照已。咸知菩薩將欲下生。各各出興。無量供具。詣菩薩所。而為供養。是為第二所示現事。佛子。菩薩摩訶薩。於兜率天。將下生時。於右掌中。放大光明。名清淨境界。悉能嚴淨一切三千大千世界。其中若有已得無漏諸辟支佛。覺斯光者。即捨壽命。若不覺者。光明力故。[3]徙置他方。餘世界中。一切諸魔。及諸外道。有見眾生。皆亦徙置他方世界。唯除諸佛神力所持應化眾生。是為第三所示現事。佛子。菩薩摩訶薩。於兜率天。將下生時。

简体字

"佛子,菩萨摩诃萨于兜率天将下生时,现十种事。何等为十?佛子,菩萨摩诃萨于兜率天下生之时,从于足下放大光明,名安乐庄严,普照三千大千世界一切恶趣诸难众生;触斯光者,莫不皆得离苦安乐;得安乐已,悉知将有奇特大人出兴于世。是为第一所示现事。佛子,菩萨摩诃萨于兜率天下生之时,从于眉间白毫相中放大光明,名曰觉悟,普照三千大千世界,照彼宿世一切同行诸菩萨身;彼诸菩萨蒙光照已,咸知菩萨将欲下生,各各出兴无量供具,诣菩萨所而为供养。是为第二所示现事。佛子,菩萨摩诃萨于兜率天将下生时,于右掌中放大光明,名清净境界,悉能严净一切三千大千世界,其中若有已得无漏诸辟支佛觉斯光者,即舍寿命;若不觉者,光明力故,徙置他方;余世界中一切诸魔及诸外道、有见众生,皆亦徙置他方世界,唯除诸佛神力所持应化众生。是为第三所示现事。佛子,菩萨摩诃萨于兜率天将下生时,

Chapter 38 — *Transcending the World*

Sons of the Buddha, when the bodhisattva-mahāsattva dwelling in the Tuṣita Heaven is about to descend to take birth, he manifests ten kinds of phenomena. What are those ten? [They are as follows]:

Sons of the Buddha, when the bodhisattva-mahāsattva dwelling in the Tuṣita Heaven is about to descend to take birth, he emanates from beneath his feet a great light known as "adornment with happiness" that everywhere illuminates all the wretched destinies in the worlds of the great trichiliocosm. When the beings beset with difficulties there are touched by this light, there are none among them who are not then able to abandon their sufferings and become happy. Having attained happiness, they all then realize that there is about to be some especially great man who is about to appear in the world. This is the first of the phenomena that he manifests;

Sons of the Buddha, when the bodhisattva-mahāsattva dwelling in the Tuṣita Heaven is about to descend to take birth, from the white hair mark between his brows, he emanates a great light known as "awakening" that everywhere illuminates the worlds of the trichiliocosm and illuminates the bodies of all the bodhisattvas with whom he has practiced together in previous lifetimes. When those bodhisattvas are illuminated by this light, they all realize that the bodhisattva is about to descend to take birth, whereupon each one of them then brings forth countless offering gifts which they take to the bodhisattva to present to him as offerings. This is the second of the phenomena that he manifests;

Sons of the Buddha, when the bodhisattva-mahāsattva dwelling in the Tuṣita Heaven is about to descend to take birth, he emanates a great light from his right palm known as "pure realms" that is able to purify all the worlds of the great trichiliocosm. If there are any *pratyekabuddhas* within them who have already succeeded in becoming free of the contaminants, on becoming aware this light, they immediately relinquish this lifetime. If they do not become aware of it, due to the power of this light, they then move away to some other world in some other region. If any *māra*s, adherents of non-Buddhist paths, or beings clinging to existence-reifying views, they too then all also move off to some other world in some other region, leaving only those beings who should be taught who are supported by the spiritual powers of the buddhas. This is the third of the phenomena that he manifests;

Sons of the Buddha, when the bodhisattva-mahāsattva dwelling in the Tuṣita Heaven is about to descend to take birth, he

正體字

從其兩膝。放大光明。名清淨莊嚴。普照一
切諸天宮殿。下從護世。上至淨居。靡不周遍。
彼諸天等。咸知菩薩於兜率天。將欲下生。俱
懷戀慕。悲歎憂惱。各持種種華鬘衣服。塗香
末香。幡蓋[4]妓樂。詣菩薩所。恭敬供養。隨逐
下生。乃至涅槃。是為第四所示現事。佛子。菩
薩摩訶薩。在兜率天。將下生時。於[5]卍字金
剛莊嚴心藏中。放大光明。名無能勝幢。普照
十方一切世界金剛力士。時有百億金剛力
士。皆悉來集。隨逐侍衛。始於下生。乃至涅
槃。是為第五所示現事。佛子。菩薩摩訶薩。於
兜率天。將下生時。從其身上。一切毛孔。放大
光明。名分別眾生。普照一切大千世界。遍觸
一切諸菩薩身。復觸一切諸天世人。諸菩薩
等。咸作是念。我應住此。供養如來。教化眾
生。是為第六所示現事。佛子。菩薩摩訶薩。於
兜率天。將下生時。從大摩尼寶藏殿中。放大
光明。名善住觀察。照此菩薩當生之處。所託
王宮。其光照已。諸餘菩薩。皆共隨逐。下閻浮
提。

简体字

从其两膝放大光明,名清净庄严,普照一切诸天宫殿,下从护世,上至净居,靡不周遍;彼诸天等,咸知菩萨于兜率天将欲下生,俱怀恋慕,悲叹忧恼,各持种种华鬘、衣服、涂香、末香、幡盖、妓乐,诣菩萨所恭敬供养,随逐下生乃至涅槃。是为第四所示现事。佛子,菩萨摩诃萨在兜率天将下生时,于卍字金刚庄严心藏中放大光明,名无能胜幢,普照十方一切世界金刚力士;时,有百亿金刚力士皆悉来集,随逐侍卫,始于下生,乃至涅槃。是为第五所示现事。佛子,菩萨摩诃萨于兜率天将下生时,从其身上一切毛孔放大光明,名分别众生,普照一切大千世界,遍触一切诸菩萨身,复触一切诸天世人;诸菩萨等咸作是念:'我应住此,供养如来,教化众生。'是为第六所示现事。佛子,菩萨摩诃萨于兜率天将下生时,从大摩尼宝藏殿中放大光明,名善住观察,照此菩萨当生之处所托王宫;其光照已,诸余菩萨皆共随逐下阎浮提,

Chapter 38 — Transcending the World

emanates a great light from his two knees known as "pure adornment" that everywhere illuminates all heavenly palaces down to those of the World-Protecting devas and up to those of the Pure Dwelling devas, having none that it does not thoroughly pervade. All those devas, realizing that the bodhisattva is about to descend to take birth, are then filled with feelings of fond admiration, are moved to sighing with sadness and sorrow. They then each take up all different kinds of floral garlands, robes, perfumes, powdered incenses, banners, canopies, and music and then go to where the bodhisattva dwells where they respectfully present these gifts as offerings, and then follow him as he descends to take birth, continuing to accompany him all along until he enters nirvāṇa. This is the fourth of the phenomena that he manifests;

Sons of the Buddha, when the bodhisattva-mahāsattva dwelling in the Tuṣita Heaven is about to descend to take birth, from his heart adorned with the vajra *svastika* emblem he emanates a great light known as "invincible banner" that then everywhere illuminates the vajra stalwarts in all worlds of the ten directions at which time a hundred *koṭīs* of vajra stalwarts all come and assemble there, following and serving him then as guardians, doing so beginning with his descent to take birth and continuing on in this manner all the way until he reaches nirvāṇa. This is the fifth of the phenomena that he manifests;

Sons of the Buddha, when the bodhisattva-mahāsattva dwelling in the Tuṣita Heaven is about to descend to take birth, from all the pores of his body, he emanates a great light known as "distinguishing beings" that then everywhere illuminates all the worlds of the great chiliocosm and everywhere falls on the bodies of all bodhisattvas while also falling on all the devas and all the humans in the world. All the bodhisattvas and the others then think: "I should remain here, make offerings to the Tathāgata, and provide teachings to beings." This is the sixth of the phenomena that he manifests;

Sons of the Buddha, when the bodhisattva-mahāsattva dwelling in the Tuṣita Heaven is about to descend to take birth, from within the great Maṇi Jewel Treasury Palace, he emanates a great light known as "skillfully abiding contemplation" that illuminates the place where this bodhisattva is about to take birth and the royal palace wherein he is about to dwell. After his light illuminates them, all the other bodhisattvas then follow along together with him in descending to the continent of Jambudvīpa, taking rebirth there either within his clan, within

正體字

若於其家。若其聚落。若其城邑。而現受生。為欲教化諸眾生故。是為第七所示現事。佛子。菩薩摩訶薩。於兜率天。臨下生時。從天宮殿。及大樓閣諸莊嚴中。放大光明。名一切宮殿清淨莊嚴。照所生母腹。光明照已。令菩薩母。安隱快樂。具足成就一切功德。其母腹中。自然而有廣大樓閣。大摩尼寶。而為莊嚴。為欲安處菩薩身故。是為第八所示現事。佛子。菩薩摩訶薩。於兜率天。臨下生時。從兩足下。放大光明。名為善住。若諸天子。及諸梵天。其命將終。蒙光照觸。皆得住壽。供養菩薩。從初下生。乃至涅槃。是為第九所示現事。佛子。菩薩摩訶薩。於兜率天。臨下生時。從隨好中。放大光明。名[6]曰眼莊嚴。示現菩薩種種諸業。時諸人天。或見菩薩。住兜率天。或見入胎。或見初生。或見出家。或見成道。或見降魔。或見轉法輪。或見入涅槃。是為第十所示現事。佛子。菩薩摩訶薩。於身於座。於宮殿。於樓閣中。放如是等百萬阿僧祇光明。悉現種種諸菩薩業。現是業已。具足一切功德法故。從兜率天。下生人間

大方廣佛華嚴經[*]卷第五十九

離世間品第三十八之七

简体字

若于其家、若其聚落、若其城邑而现受生，为欲教化诸众生故。是为第七所示现事。佛子，菩萨摩诃萨于兜率天临下生时，从天宫殿及大楼阁诸庄严中放大光明，名一切宫殿清净庄严，照所生母腹；光明照已，令菩萨母安隐快乐，具足成就一切功德，其母腹中自然而有广大楼阁大摩尼宝而为庄严，为欲安处菩萨身故。是为第八所示现事。佛子，菩萨摩诃萨于兜率天临下生时，从两足下放大光明，名为善住；若诸天子及诸梵天其命将终，蒙光照触皆得住寿，供养菩萨从初下生乃至涅槃。是为第九所示现事。佛子，菩萨摩诃萨于兜率天临下生时，从随好中放大光明，名日月庄严，示现菩萨种种诸业；时，诸人、天或见菩萨住兜率天，或见入胎，或见初生，或见出家，或见成道，或见降魔，或见转法轮，或见入涅槃。是为第十所示现事。佛子，菩萨摩诃萨于身、于座、于宫殿、于楼阁中，放如是等百万阿僧祇光明，悉现种种诸菩萨业；现是业已，具足一切功德法故，从兜率天下生人间。

大方广佛华严经卷第五十九

离世间品第三十八之七

Chapter 38 — *Transcending the World*

his village, or within his city and its outlying precincts, doing so for the purpose of teaching all beings. This is the seventh of the phenomena that he manifests;

Sons of the Buddha, when the bodhisattva-mahāsattva dwelling in the Tuṣita Heaven is about to descend to take birth, from the adornments of his heavenly palace and its great towers, he emanates a great light known as "pure adornments of all palaces" that illuminates the belly of the mother to whom he is to be born. After this light has cast its illumination, it causes the bodhisattva's mother to feel safe, secure, and happy and fully possessed of all meritorious qualities. Then, within his mother's belly, there spontaneously manifests a vast tower adorned with immense *maṇi* jewels in order to provide a peaceful dwelling place for the bodhisattva's body. This is the eighth of the phenomena that he manifests;

Sons of the Buddha, when the bodhisattva-mahāsattva dwelling in the Tuṣita Heaven is about to descend to take birth, from beneath his two feet he emanates a great light known as "excellent dwelling." If any of the young devas or Brahma Heaven devas reaching the imminent end of their lives receive this light's illumination, they all succeed in continuing to abide in this lifetime to make offerings to the bodhisattva from the time when he takes birth all the way until he reaches his nirvāṇa. This is the ninth of the phenomena that he manifests;

Sons of the Buddha, when the bodhisattva-mahāsattva dwelling in the Tuṣita Heaven is about to descend to take birth, from his secondary signs he emanates a great light known as "adornment for the eyes" that manifests the appearances of all the many different kinds of deeds the bodhisattva has done. At that time, all the humans and devas may see the bodhisattva dwelling in the Tuṣita Heaven, or may see him entering the womb, or may see him when he is first born, or may see him when he leaves the home life, or may see him when he attains enlightenment, or may see him when he vanquishes the *māra*s, or may see him when he turns the wheel of the Dharma, or may see him when he enters nirvāṇa. This is the tenth of the phenomena that he manifests.

Sons of the Buddha, the bodhisattva-mahāsattva emanates hundreds of myriads of *asaṃkhyeyas* of light rays such as these from his body, from his throne, from his palace, and from his towers, all of which display the many different kinds of bodhisattva works. Having revealed these works, due to having completely fulfilled all dharmas of the meritorious qualities, he then descends from the Tuṣita heaven and takes birth among humans.

正體字

| 310c27 | 佛子。菩薩摩訶薩。示現處胎。有十種事。何等
| 310c28 | 為十。佛子。菩薩摩訶薩。為欲成就小心劣解
| 310c29 | 諸眾生故。不欲令彼起如是念。今此菩薩。自
| 311a01 | 然化生。智慧善根。不從修得。是故菩薩。示現
| 311a02 | 處胎。是為第一事。菩薩摩訶薩。為成熟父母。
| 311a03 | 及諸眷屬。宿世同行。眾生善根。示現處胎。何
| 311a04 | 以故。彼皆應以見於處胎。成熟所有諸善根
| 311a05 | 故。是為第二事。菩薩摩訶薩。入母胎時。正念
| 311a06 | 正知。無有迷惑。住母胎已。心恒正念。亦無錯
| 311a07 | 亂。是為第三事。菩薩摩訶薩。在母胎中。常演
| 311a08 | 說法。十方世界。諸大菩薩。釋梵四王。皆來集
| 311a09 | 會。悉令獲得無量神力。無邊智慧。菩薩處胎。
| 311a10 | 成就如是。辯才勝用。是為第四事。菩薩摩訶
| 311a11 | 薩。在母胎中。集大眾會。以本願力。教化一切
| 311a12 | 諸菩薩眾。是為第五事。菩薩摩訶薩。於人中
| 311a13 | 成佛。應具人間最勝受生。以此示現處於母
| 311a14 | 胎。是為第六事。菩薩摩訶薩。在母胎中。三千
| 311a15 | 大千世界眾生。悉見菩薩。

简体字

"佛子，菩萨摩诃萨示现处胎，有十种事。何等为十？佛子，菩萨摩诃萨为欲成就小心劣解诸众生故，不欲令彼起如是念：'今此菩萨自然化生，智慧善根不从修得。'是故菩萨示现处胎。是为第一事。菩萨摩诃萨为成熟父母及诸眷属、宿世同行众生善根，示现处胎。何以故？彼皆应以见于处胎成熟所有诸善根故。是为第二事。菩萨摩诃萨入母胎时，正念正知，无有迷惑；住母胎已，心恒正念，亦无错乱。是为第三事。菩萨摩诃萨在母胎中常演说法，十方世界诸大菩萨、释、梵、四王皆来集会，悉令获得无量神力、无边智慧，菩萨处胎成就如是辩才、胜用。是为第四事。菩萨摩诃萨在母胎中集大众会，以本愿力教化一切诸菩萨众。是为第五事。菩萨摩诃萨于人中成佛，应具人间最胜受生，以此示现处于母胎。是为第六事。菩萨摩诃萨在母胎中，三千大千世界众生悉见菩萨，

Chapter 38 — *Transcending the World*

Sons of the Buddha, there are ten phenomena associated with the bodhisattva-mahāsattva's manifesting as dwelling in the womb. What are those ten? They are as follows:

Sons of the Buddha, wishing to ripen beings with petty minds and inferior understanding, the bodhisattva-mahāsattva wishes to prevent them from generating such thoughts as this: "This bodhisattva has now been spontaneously transformationally born. Hence his wisdom and roots of goodness have not been acquired through cultivation." Therefore the bodhisattva manifests the appearance of abiding in the womb. This is the first of these phenomena;

In order to ripen the roots of goodness of his parents, family, and beings with whom he has practiced together in past lives, the bodhisattva-mahāsattva manifests as abiding in the womb. Why is this? They should all be able to ripen all their roots of goodness by seeing him dwelling in the womb. This is the second of these phenomena;

When the bodhisattva-mahāsattva enters his mother's womb, he maintains right mindfulness and right knowing free of confusion. Once he has come to abide in his mother's womb, his mind constantly remains in a state of right mindfulness in which he is free of either error or confusion. This is the third of these phenomena;

When the bodhisattva-mahāsattva is abiding in his mother's womb, he is always expounding on the Dharma. All the great bodhisattvas, Śakra, Brahma, and the four heavenly kings throughout the worlds of the ten directions all come and gather together there where he enables them all to acquire measureless spiritual powers and boundless wisdom. Even as the bodhisattva is abiding in the womb, he is implementing supreme functions of eloquence such as these. This is the fourth of these phenomena;

When the bodhisattva-mahāsattva is abiding in his mother's womb, he assembles a great congregation and, through the power of his original vows, teaches all the congregations of bodhisattvas. This is the fifth of these phenomena;

When the bodhisattva-mahāsattva appears among humans to realize buddhahood, it is only fitting that he have the best of human births. It is for this reason that he manifests as dwelling in his mother's womb. This is the sixth of these phenomena;

When the bodhisattva-mahāsattva abides in his mother's womb, the beings in the worlds of the great trichiliocosm all see the bodhisattva as clearly as if they were looking at their own

正體字

如明鏡中。見其面像。爾時大心。天龍夜叉乾闥婆阿脩羅迦樓羅緊那羅摩睺羅伽人非人等。皆詣菩薩。恭敬供養。是為第七事。菩薩摩訶薩。在母胎中。他方世界。一切最後生菩薩。在母胎者。皆來共會。說大集法門。名廣大智慧藏。是為第八事。菩薩摩訶薩。在母胎時。入離垢藏三昧。以三昧力。於母胎中。現大宮殿。種種嚴飾。悉皆妙好。兜率天宮。不可為比。而令母身。安隱無患。是為第九事。菩薩摩訶薩。住母胎時。以大威力。興供養具。名開大福德離垢藏。普遍十方一切世界。供養一切諸佛如來。彼諸如來。咸為演說無邊菩薩。住處法界藏。是為第十事。佛子。是為菩薩摩訶薩。示現處胎十種事。若諸菩薩了達此法則能示現甚微細趣。佛子。菩薩摩訶薩。有十種甚微細趣。何等為十。所謂在母胎中。示現初發菩提心。乃至灌頂地。在母胎中。示現住兜率天。在母胎中。示現初生。

简体字

如明镜中见其面像；尔时，大心天、龙、夜叉、乾闼婆、阿修罗、迦楼罗、紧那罗、摩睺罗伽、人非人等，皆诣菩萨，恭敬供养。是为第七事。菩萨摩诃萨在母胎中，他方世界一切最后生菩萨在母胎者，皆来共会，说大集法门，名广大智慧藏。是为第八事。菩萨摩诃萨在母胎时，入离垢藏三昧，以三昧力，于母胎中现大宫殿，种种严饰悉皆妙好，兜率天宫不可为比，而令母身安隐无患。是为第九事。菩萨摩诃萨住母胎时，以大威力兴供养具，名开大福德离垢藏，普遍十方一切世界，供养一切诸佛如来，彼诸如来咸为演说无边菩萨住处法界藏。是为第十事。佛子，是为菩萨摩诃萨示现处胎十种事。若诸菩萨了达此法，则能示现甚微细趣。

"佛子，菩萨摩诃萨有十种甚微细趣。何等为十？所谓：在母胎中，示现初发菩提心，乃至灌顶地；在母胎中，示现住兜率天；在母胎中，示现初生；

Chapter 38 — Transcending the World

faces in a brightly polished mirror. At that time, all of those possessed of great minds among the devas, dragons, *yakṣas*, *gandharvas*, *asuras*, *garuḍas*, *kiṃnaras*, *mahoragas*, humans, and nonhumans—they all come there to meet the bodhisattva and reverently present offerings. This is the seventh of these phenomena;

When the bodhisattva-mahāsattva is abiding in his mother's womb, all the bodhisattvas from the worlds of other regions who have reached their very last birth and are abiding in their mothers' wombs—they all come and gather together there whereupon he teaches a Dharma gateway of great accumulation known as "vast wisdom treasury." This is the eighth of these phenomena;

When the bodhisattva-mahāsattva is abiding in his mother's womb, he enters the immaculate treasury samādhi and, with the power of that samādhi, he manifests an immense palace in his mother's womb that has all kinds of different adornments, all of which are so wondrously fine that not even the Tuṣita Heaven Palace could compare with it. In doing so, he ensures that his mother's body is safe and free of any troubles. This is the ninth of these phenomena; and

When the bodhisattva-mahāsattva abides in his mother's womb, he uses his great awe-inspiring power to bring forth a collection of offering gifts known as "the opening of the immaculate treasury of great merit." He then makes offerings to all buddhas, the *tathāgatas*, everywhere throughout all worlds of the ten directions. All those *tathāgatas* then expound for him teachings on the boundless bodhisattva dwelling place, the treasury of the Dharma realm. This is the tenth of these phenomena.

Sons of the Buddha, these are the ten phenomena associated with the bodhisattva-mahāsattva's manifesting as dwelling in the womb. If bodhisattvas completely comprehend these dharmas, then they become able to manifest subtle endeavors.

Sons of the Buddha, the bodhisattva-mahāsattva has ten kinds of subtle endeavors. What are those ten? They are as follows:

While in his mother's womb, he manifests the initial resolve to attain bodhi and so forth up to and including the ground of the crown-anointing consecration;

While in his mother's womb, he manifests dwelling in the Tuṣita Heaven;

While in his mother's womb, he manifests first taking on birth;

正體字

在母胎中。示現童子地。在母胎中。示現
處王宮。在母胎中。示現出家。在母胎中。示現
苦行。往詣道場。成等正覺。在母胎中。示現轉
法輪。在母胎中。示現般涅槃。在母胎中。示現
大微細。謂一切菩薩行。一切如來。自在神力。
無量差別門。佛子。是為菩薩摩訶薩。在母胎
中。十種微細趣。若諸菩薩。安住此法。則得如
來無上大智慧微細趣。佛子。菩薩摩訶薩。有
十種生。何等為十。所謂遠離愚癡正念正知
生。放大光明網普照三千大千世界生。住最
後有更不受後身生。不生不起生。知三界如
幻生。於十方世界普現身生。證一切智智身
生。放一切佛光明普覺悟一切眾生身生。入
大智觀察三昧身生。佛子。菩薩生時。震動一
切佛剎。解脫一切眾生。

简体字

在母胎中，示现童子地；在母胎中，示现处王宫；在母胎中，示现出家；在母胎中，示现苦行，往诣道场，成等正觉；在母胎中，示现转法轮；在母胎中，示现般涅槃；在母胎中，示现大微细，谓：一切菩萨行一切如来自在神力无量差别门。佛子，是为菩萨摩诃萨在母胎中十种微细趣。若诸菩萨安住此法，则得如来无上大智慧微细趣。

"佛子，菩萨摩诃萨有十种生。何等为十？所谓：远离愚痴正念正知生；放大光明网普照三千大千世界生；住最后有更不受后身生；不生不起生；知三界如幻生；于十方世界普现身生；证一切智智身生；放一切佛光明普觉悟一切众生身生；入大智观察三昧身生；佛子，菩萨生时，震动一切佛刹，解脱一切众生，

Chapter 38 — *Transcending the World*

While in his mother's womb, he manifests abiding on the ground of the pure youth;

While in his mother's womb, he manifests dwelling in the royal palace;

While in his mother's womb, he manifests leaving the household life;

While in his mother's womb, he manifests engaging in the austerities, going to the site of enlightenment, and realizing the right and perfect enlightenment;

While in his mother's womb, he manifests turning the wheel of the Dharma;

While in his mother's womb, he manifests *parinirvāṇa*; and

While in his mother's womb, he manifests the appearance of great subtle endeavors, namely the countless different gateways of all bodhisattvas' practices and all *tathāgatas'* sovereign spiritual powers.

Sons of the Buddha, these are the bodhisattva-mahāsattva's ten subtle endeavors while abiding in his mother's womb. If bodhisattvas abide in these dharmas, then they acquire the subtle endeavor of the Tathāgata's unexcelled great wisdom.

Sons of the Buddha, the bodhisattva-mahāsattva has ten kinds of birth. What are those ten? They are as follows:

The birth of abandoning delusion while abiding in right mindfulness and right knowing;

The birth of emanating a great net of light rays which everywhere illuminate the worlds of the great trichiliocosm;

The birth of abiding in his last existence after which he never receives another body;

The birth with no production and no arising;

The birth in which he realizes that the three realms of existence are like an illusion;

The birth in which he manifests bodies everywhere throughout the worlds of the ten directions;

The birth of the body in which he realizes the wisdom of all-knowledge;

The birth of the body in which he emanates the light of all buddhas which everywhere awakens all beings;

The birth of the body in which he enters the great wisdom contemplation samādhi; and

Sons of the Buddha, when the bodhisattva takes birth, he causes the shaking of all buddha *kṣetras*, liberates all beings,

正體字

除滅一切惡道。映蔽一切諸魔。無量菩薩。皆來集會。佛子。是為菩薩摩訶薩十種生。為調伏眾生故。如是示現。

佛子。菩薩摩訶薩。以十事故。示現微笑心自誓。何等為十。所謂菩薩摩訶薩念言。一切世間。歿在欲泥。除我一人。無能[1]免濟。如是知已。熙怡微笑心自誓。復念言。一切世間。煩惱所盲。唯我今者。具足智慧。如是知已。熙怡微笑心自誓。又念言。我今因此假名身故。當得如來充滿三世無上法身。如是知已。熙怡微笑心自誓。菩薩爾時。以無障礙眼。遍觀十方所有梵天。乃至一切大自在天。作是念言。此等眾生。皆自謂為有大智力。如是知已。熙怡微笑心自誓。菩薩爾時。觀諸眾生。久種善根。今皆退沒。如是知已。熙怡微笑心自誓。菩薩觀見世間種子。所種雖少。獲果甚多。如是知已。熙怡微笑心自誓。菩薩觀見一切眾生。蒙佛所教。必得利益。如是知已。熙怡微笑心自誓。菩薩觀見過去世中。同行菩薩。

简体字

除灭一切恶道,映蔽一切诸魔,无量菩萨皆来集会。佛子,是为菩萨摩诃萨十种生,为调伏众生故,如是示现。

"佛子,菩萨摩诃萨以十事故,示现微笑心自誓。何等为十?所谓:菩萨摩诃萨念言:'一切世间没在欲泥,除我一人无能勉济。'如是知已,熙怡微笑心自誓。复念言:'一切世间烦恼所盲,唯我今者具足智慧。'如是知已,熙怡微笑心自誓。又念言:'我今因此假名身故,当得如来充满三世无上法身。'如是知已,熙怡微笑心自誓。菩萨尔时,以无障碍眼,遍观十方所有梵天,乃至一切大自在天,作是念言:'此等众生,皆自谓为有大智力。'如是知已,熙怡微笑心自誓。菩萨尔时观诸众生,久种善根,今皆退没;如是知已,熙怡微笑心自誓。菩萨观见世间种子,所种虽少,获果甚多;如是知已,熙怡微笑心自誓。菩萨观见一切众生,蒙佛所教,必得利益;如是知已,熙怡微笑心自誓。菩萨观见过去世中同行菩萨,

extinguishes all the wretched destinies, outshines all *māra*s, and causes countless bodhisattvas to all come and gather together.

Sons of the Buddha, these are the bodhisattva-mahāsattva's ten kinds of birth. They are manifested in these ways in order to train beings.

Sons of the Buddha, it is due to ten kinds of circumstances that the bodhisattva-mahāsattva manifests a subtle smile and spontaneously makes a vow. What are those ten? They are as follows:

The bodhisattva-mahāsattva thinks, "Everyone in the world has sunken into the mud of the desires. With the exception of myself, this one person, there is no one able to rescue them." Having realized this, he subtly smiles and makes a vow to himself;

He also thinks, "Everyone in the world is blinded by the afflictions. There is only myself who now has developed completely fulfilled wisdom." Having realized this, he subtly smiles and makes a vow to himself;

He additionally thinks, "Because of this conventionally designated body, I shall now succeed in acquiring the Tathāgata's unexcelled Dharma body that completely fills up all three periods of time. Having realized this, he subtly smiles and makes a vow to himself;

At this time, the bodhisattva uses his unimpeded eye to everywhere contemplate throughout the ten directions all the Brahma Heaven devas and so forth on up to all the devas of the Great Maheśvara Heaven and thinks, "All of these beings are of the opinion that they possess the power of great wisdom." Having realized this, he subtly smiles and makes a vow to himself;

At this time, the bodhisattva contemplates all beings and observes that, having planted roots of goodness in the past, they now all regress. Having realized this, he subtly smiles and makes a vow to himself;

The bodhisattva contemplates and observes that, although seeds planted in the world may be but few, the fruits that are thereby reaped may be extremely abundant. Having realized this, he subtly smiles and makes a vow to himself;

The bodhisattva contemplates and observes that, when beings receive the Buddha's teachings, they become certain to realize benefits from this. Having realized this, he subtly smiles and makes a vow to himself;

The bodhisattva contemplates and observes that bodhisattvas with whom he cultivated together in past lives have developed

正體字

染著餘事。
311c08 ｜ 不得佛法廣大功德。如是知已。熙怡微笑心
311c09 ｜ 自誓。菩薩觀見過去世中。[2]同共集會。諸天人
311c10 ｜ 等。至今猶在凡夫之地。不能捨離。亦不疲厭。
311c11 ｜ 如是知已。熙怡微笑心自誓。菩薩爾時。為一
311c12 ｜ 切如來光明所觸。倍加欣慰。熙怡微笑心自
311c13 ｜ 誓。是為十。佛子。菩薩為調伏眾生故。如是示
311c14 ｜ 現。佛子。菩薩摩訶薩。以十事故。示行七步。
311c15 ｜ 何等為十。所謂現菩薩力故。示行七步。現施
311c16 ｜ 七財故。示行七步。滿地神願故。示行七步。現
311c17 ｜ 超三界相故。示行七步。現菩薩最勝行。超過
311c18 ｜ 象王牛王。師子王行故。示行七步。現金剛地
311c19 ｜ 相故。示行七步。現欲與眾生勇猛力故。示行
311c20 ｜ 七步。現修行七覺寶故。示行七步。現所得法。
311c21 ｜ 不由他教故。示行七步。現於世間。最勝無比
311c22 ｜ 故。示行七步。是為十。佛子。菩薩為調伏眾生
311c23 ｜ 故。如是示現。

简体字

染著余事，不得佛法广大功德；如是知已，熙怡微笑心自誓。菩萨观见过去世中同共集会诸天人等，至今犹在凡夫之地，不能舍离，亦不疲厌；如是知已，熙怡微笑心自誓。菩萨尔时，为一切如来光明所触，倍加欣慰，熙怡微笑心自誓。是为十。佛子，菩萨为调伏众生故，如是示现。

"佛子，菩萨摩诃萨以十事故，示行七步。何等为十？所谓：现菩萨力故，示行七步；现施七财故，示行七步；满地神愿故，示行七步；现超三界相故，示行七步；现菩萨最胜行超过象王、牛王、师子王行故，示行七步；现金刚地相故，示行七步；现欲与众生勇猛力故，示行七步；现修行七觉宝故，示行七步；现所得法不由他教故，示行七步；现于世间最胜无比故，示行七步。是为十。佛子，菩萨为调伏众生故，如是示现。

defiling attachments to other things and thus have failed to acquire the vastly meritorious qualities associated with the Buddha's Dharma. Having realized this, he subtly smiles and makes a vow to himself;

The bodhisattva contemplates and observes that the devas, humans, and others with whom he gathered together in past lives—they even now still abide on the ground of the common person where they remain unable to abandon it and have not yet even grown weary of it. Having realized this, he subtly smiles and makes a vow to himself; and

At this time, the bodhisattva, touched by the light of all the *tathāgatas*, experiences doubly increased delight and happiness. He then subtly smiles and makes a vow to himself.

These are the ten. Sons of the Buddha, it is for the purpose of training beings that the bodhisattva appears in ways such as these.

Sons of the Buddha, it is for ten reasons that the bodhisattva-mahāsattva manifests the act of walking seven steps. What are those ten? They are as follows:

It is to reveal the power of the bodhisattva that he manifests the act of walking seven steps;

It is to reveal his bestowing of the seven kinds of wealth[162] that he manifests the act of walking seven steps;

It is to fulfill the wishes of the earth spirits that he manifests the act of walking seven steps;

It is to reveal the signs of stepping beyond the three realms that he manifests the act of walking seven steps;

It is to reveal the bodhisattva's supreme walk surpassing the walk of the king of elephants, the king of bulls, and the king of lions that he manifests the act of walking seven steps;

It is to reveal the signs of the vajra ground that he manifests the act of walking seven steps;

It is to reveal his wish to bestow on beings the power of courage that he manifests the act of walking seven steps;

It is to reveal the cultivation of the jewels of the seven enlightenment factors that he manifests the act of walking seven steps;

It is to reveal that the Dharma he has acquired did not arise from the teachings of others that he manifests the act of walking seven steps; and

It is to reveal that, of all who abide in the world, he is incomparably supreme that he manifests the act of walking seven steps.

These are the ten. Sons of the Buddha, it is for the purpose of training beings that the bodhisattva appears in ways such as these.

正體字

佛子。菩薩摩訶薩。以十事故。現處童子地。何等為十。所謂為現通達一切世間文字算計圖書印璽種種業故。處童子地。為現通達一切世間象馬車乘弧矢劍戟種種業故。處童子地。為現通達一切世間文筆談論博弈嬉戲種種事故。處童子地。為現遠離身語意業諸過失故。處童子地。為現入定住涅槃門周遍十方無量世界故。處童子地。為現其力超過一切天龍夜叉乾闥婆阿脩羅迦樓羅緊那羅摩睺羅伽釋梵護世人非人等故。處童子地。為現菩薩色相威光超過一切釋梵護世故。處童子地。為令耽著欲樂眾生歡喜樂法故。處童子地。為尊重正法勤供養佛周遍十方一切世界故。處童子地。為現得佛加被蒙法光明故。處童子地。是為十。佛子。菩薩摩訶薩。現童子地已。

简体字

"佛子,菩萨摩诃萨以十事故,现处童子地。何等为十?所谓:为现通达一切世间文字、算计、图书、印玺种种业故,处童子地;为现通达一切世间象马、车乘、弧矢、剑戟种种业故,处童子地;为现通达一切世间文笔、谈论、博弈、嬉戏种种事故,处童子地;为现远离身、语、意业诸过失故,处童子地;为现入定住涅槃门,周遍十方无量世界故,处童子地;为现其力超过一切天、龙、夜叉、乾闼婆、阿修罗、迦楼罗、紧那罗、摩睺罗伽、释、梵、护世、人非人等故,处童子地;为现菩萨色相威光超过一切释、梵、护世故,处童子地;为令耽著欲乐众生欢喜乐法故,处童子地;为尊重正法,勤供养佛,周遍十方一切世界故,处童子地;为现得佛加被蒙法光明故,处童子地。是为十。

"佛子,菩萨摩诃萨现童子地已,

Chapter 38 — *Transcending the World*

Sons of the Buddha, it is for ten reasons that the bodhisattva-mahāsattva manifests as abiding on the ground of the pure youth. What are those ten? They are as follows:

He manifests as abiding on the ground of the pure youth to demonstrate the complete comprehension of all the world's languages, mathematics, painting, calligraphy, seal-carving, and all the many other kinds of skills;

He manifests as abiding on the ground of the pure youth to demonstrate the complete comprehension of all the many different kinds of worldly skills such as riding elephants and horses, driving carriages and other vehicles, and wielding bows and arrows, swords, and halberds;

He manifests as abiding on the ground of the pure youth to demonstrate the complete comprehension of all the many different kinds of worldly arts such as literary composition, discussion, games, and entertainments;

He manifests as abiding on the ground of the pure youth to demonstrate the renunciation of all the faults in physical, verbal, and mental deeds;

He manifests as abiding on the ground of the pure youth for the sake of demonstrating entry into meditative absorption and abiding in the gateway of nirvāṇa throughout the countless worlds of the ten directions;

He manifests as abiding on the ground of the pure youth to demonstrate his powers surpassing those of all the devas, dragons, *yakṣas, gandharvas, asuras, garuḍas, kiṃnaras, mahoragas,* Śakra, Brahma, the world-protecting devas, humans, nonhumans, and others;

He manifests as abiding on the ground of the pure youth to reveal the bodhisattva's physical marks and awe-inspiring radiance surpassing those of all of the devas such as Śakra, Brahma, or the world-protecting devas;

He manifests as abiding on the ground of the pure youth to enable beings obsessively attached to the pleasures of the desires to find happiness and delight in the Dharma;

He manifests as abiding on the ground of the pure youth to revere right Dharma and diligently make offerings to the buddhas everywhere throughout all worlds of the ten directions; and

He manifests as abiding on the ground of the pure youth to show his empowerment by the Buddha and his illumination by the light of the Dharma.

These are the ten. Sons of the Buddha, after the bodhisattva-mahāsattva has manifested as abiding on the ground of the pure

正體字

以十事故。現處

王宮。何等為十。所謂為令宿世同行眾生。善
根成熟故。現處王宮。為顯示菩薩善根力故。
現處王宮。為諸人天耽著樂具。示現菩薩大
威德樂具故。現處王宮。順五濁世眾生心故。
現處王宮。為現菩薩大威德力。能於深宮入
三昧故。現處王宮。為令宿世同願眾生滿其
意故。現處王宮。欲令父母親戚眷屬滿所願
故。現處王宮。欲以[1]妓樂出妙法音供養一切
諸如來故。現處王宮。欲於宮內住微妙三昧
始從成佛乃至涅槃皆示現故。現處王宮。為
隨順守護諸佛法故。現處王宮。是為十。最後
身菩薩。如是示現處王宮已。然後出家。佛子。
菩薩摩訶薩。以十事故。示現出家。何等為十。
所謂為厭居家故。示現出家。為著家眾生令
捨離故。示現出家。為隨順信樂聖人道故。示
現出家。

简体字

以十事故现处王宫。何等为十？所谓：为令宿世同行众生善根成熟故,现处王宫；为显示菩萨善根力故,现处王宫；为诸人、天耽著乐具,示现菩萨大威德乐具故,现处王宫；顺五浊世众生心故,现处王宫；为现菩萨大威德力能于深宫入三昧故,现处王宫；为令宿世同愿众生满其意故,现处王宫；欲令父母、亲戚、眷属满所愿故,现处王宫；欲以妓乐出妙法音供养一切诸如来故,现处王宫；欲于宫内住微妙三昧,始从成佛乃至涅槃皆示现故,现处王宫；为随顺守护诸佛法故,现处王宫。是为十。最后身菩萨如是示现处王宫已,然后出家。

"佛子,菩萨摩诃萨以十事故,示现出家。何等为十？所谓：为厌居家故,示现出家；为著家众生令舍离故,示现出家；为随顺信乐圣人道故,示现出家；

Chapter 38 — *Transcending the World*

youth, he manifests as abiding in the royal palace for ten reasons. What are those ten? They are as follows:

> He manifests as abiding in the royal palace to ripen the roots of goodness of those beings with whom he practiced together in previous lives;
>
> He manifests as abiding in the royal palace to reveal the power of the bodhisattva's roots of goodness;
>
> He manifests as abiding in the royal palace to reveal to devas and humans obsessively attached to sources of bliss the bodhisattva's greatly awe-inspiring sources of bliss;
>
> He manifests as abiding in the royal palace to accord with the minds of beings abiding in the world of the five turbidities;[163]
>
> He manifests as abiding in the royal palace to reveal the bodhisattva's great awe-inspiring powers and his ability to enter samādhi even in the depths of the palace;
>
> He manifests as abiding in the royal palace to enable the fulfillment of the aspirations of those beings with whom he shared the same vows in previous lives;
>
> He manifests as abiding in the royal palace to enable his parents, relatives, and retinue to fulfill their vows;
>
> He manifests as abiding in the royal palace to use music to send forth the sounds of the sublime Dharma as offerings to all *tathāgatas*;
>
> He manifests as abiding in the royal palace wishing within the inner palace to abide in the sublime samādhi which reveals everything beginning from his realization of buddhahood to his entry into nirvāṇa; and
>
> He manifests as abiding in the royal palace to accord with and preserve the Dharma of all buddhas.

These are the ten. After the bodhisattva in his very last body manifests his abiding within the royal palace in these ways, he then leaves the householder's life.

Sons of the Buddha, it is for ten reasons that the bodhisattva-mahāsattva manifests as leaving the household life. What are those ten? They are as follows:

> He manifests as leaving the household life to renounce dwelling in the household;
>
> He manifests as leaving the household life to enable beings attached to the household to abandon it;
>
> He manifests as leaving the household life to accord with his resolute faith in in the path of the *āryas*;

正體字

為宣揚讚歎出家功德故。示現出家。
為顯永離二邊見故。示現出家。為令眾生。離
欲樂我樂故。示現出家。為先現出三界相故。
示現出家。為現自在不屬他故。示現出家。為
顯當得如來十力無畏法故。示現出家。最後
菩薩。法應爾故。示現出家。是為十。菩薩以此
調伏眾生。佛子。菩薩摩訶薩。為十種事故。示
行苦行。何等為十。所謂為成就劣解眾生故。
示行苦行。為拔邪見眾生故。示行苦行。為不
信業報眾生。令見業報故。示行苦行。為隨順
雜染世界法應爾故。示行苦行。示能忍劬勞。
勤修道故。示行苦行。為令眾生。樂求法故。示
行苦行。為著欲樂我樂眾生故。示行苦行。為
顯菩薩起行殊勝。乃至最後生。猶不捨勤精
進故。示行苦[2]行。為諸天世人。諸根未熟。待
時成熟故。示行苦行。是為十。菩薩以此方便。
調伏一切眾生。佛子。菩薩摩訶薩。往詣道場。
有十種事。何等為十。所謂

简体字

为宣扬赞叹出家功德故,示现出家;为显永离二边见故,示现出家;为令众生离欲乐、我乐故,示现出家;为先现出三界相故,示现出家;为现自在不属他故,示现出家;为显当得如来十力、无畏法故,示现出家;最后菩萨法应尔故,示现出家。是为十。菩萨以此调伏众生。

"佛子,菩萨摩诃萨为十种事故,示行苦行。何等为十?所谓:为成就劣解众生故,示行苦行;为拔邪见众生故,示行苦行;为不信业报众生令见业报故,示行苦行;为随顺杂染世界法应尔故,示行苦行;示能忍劬劳勤修道故,示行苦行;为令众生乐求法故,示行苦行;为著欲乐、我乐众生故,示行苦行;为显菩萨起行殊胜,乃至最后生犹不舍勤精进故,示行苦行;为令众生乐寂静法,增长善根故,示行苦行;为诸天、世人诸根未熟,待时成熟故,示行苦行。是为十。菩萨以此方便调伏一切众生。

"佛子,菩萨摩诃萨往诣道场有十种事。何等为十?所谓:

Chapter 38 — Transcending the World

He manifests as leaving the household life to proclaim and praise the meritorious qualities of leaving the householder's life;

He manifests as leaving the household life to demonstrate detaching forever from the two extreme views;[164]

He manifests as leaving the household life to enable beings to leave behind delight in the desires and delight in the self;

He manifests as leaving the household life to be the first to show the appearance of transcending the three realms of existence;

He manifests as leaving the household life to demonstrate sovereign mastery not dependent on anyone else;

He manifests as leaving the household life to show that he is bound to gain the dharmas of the Tathāgata's ten powers and fearlessnesses; and

He manifests as leaving the household life because the dharma of the bodhisattva in his very last body should be of this very sort.

These are the ten. The bodhisattva uses these to train beings.

Sons of the Buddha, it is for ten reasons that the bodhisattva-mahāsattva manifests as practicing the austerities. What are those ten? They are as follows:

He manifests as practicing the austerities to enable the development of beings with inferior levels of understanding;

He manifests as practicing the austerities to remove the wrong views of beings with wrong views;

He manifests as practicing the austerities to enable beings who do not believe in karmic consequences to perceive the consequences arising from karmic actions;

He manifests as practicing the austerities because it is only fitting to do so when adapting to the dharmas of a defiled world;

He manifests as practicing the austerities to demonstrate the ability to endure even such strenuous exertion in diligent cultivation of the path;

He manifests as practicing the austerities to enable beings to delight in seeking the Dharma;

He manifests as practicing the austerities for the sake of beings attached to delighting in the desires and delighting in the self;

He manifests as practicing the austerities to show that the bodhisattva begins with especially supreme practice and continues on with it to the very last birth, even then still never relinquishing his diligence and vigor;

He manifests as practicing the austerities to enable beings to delight in the dharma of quiescence and increase their roots of goodness;[165] and

正體字

詣道場時。照[3]耀
312b14 | 一切世界。詣道場時。震動一切世界。詣道場
312b15 | 時。於一切世界。普現其身。詣道場時。覺悟一
312b16 | 切菩薩。及一切宿世。同行眾生。詣道場時。示
312b17 | 現道場一切莊嚴。詣道場時。隨諸眾生心之
312b18 | 所欲。而為現身。種種威儀。及菩提樹一切莊
312b19 | 嚴。詣道場時。現見十方一切如來。詣道場時。
312b20 | 舉足下足。常入三昧。念念成佛。無有超隔。詣
312b21 | 道場時。一切天龍夜叉乾闥婆阿脩羅迦樓
312b22 | 羅緊那羅摩睺羅伽釋梵護世一切諸王各不
312b23 | 相知。而興種種。上妙供養。詣道場時以無礙
312b24 | 智。普觀一切諸佛如來。於一切世界修菩薩
312b25 | 行。而成正覺。是為十。菩薩以此。教化眾生。
312b26 | 佛子。菩薩摩訶薩。坐道場。[4]有十種事。何等
312b27 | 為十。所[5]謂

简体字

诣道场时，照耀一切世界；诣道场时，震动一切世界；诣道场时，于一切世界普现其身；诣道场时，觉悟一切菩萨及一切宿世同行众生；诣道场时，示现道场一切庄严；诣道场时，随诸众生心之所欲，而为现身种种威仪，及菩提树一切庄严；诣道场时，现见十方一切如来；诣道场时，举足、下足常入三昧，念念成佛无有超隔；诣道场时，一切天、龙、夜叉、乾闼婆、阿修罗、迦楼罗、紧那罗、摩睺罗伽、释、梵、护世一切诸王各不相知，而兴种种上妙供养；诣道场时，以无碍智，普观一切诸佛如来于一切世界修菩萨行而成正觉。是为十。菩萨以此教化众生。

"佛子，菩萨摩诃萨坐道场有十种事。何等为十？所谓：

Chapter 38 — *Transcending the World*

He manifests as practicing the austerities for the sake of devas and humans in the world whose faculties have not yet become ripened, thus awaiting the right time for their ripening.

These are the ten. The bodhisattva uses these skillful means to train all beings.

Sons of the Buddha, there are ten phenomena that occur when the bodhisattva-mahāsattva goes to the site of enlightenment. What are those ten? They are as follows.

When he goes to the site of enlightenment, he illuminates all worlds with shining light;

When he goes to the site of enlightenment, he causes shaking and movement in all worlds;

When he goes to the site of enlightenment, he manifests his body in all worlds;

When he goes to the site of enlightenment, he awakens all bodhisattvas as well as all those beings with whom he practiced together in previous lifetimes;

When he goes to the site of enlightenment, he reveals all the adornments of the site of enlightenment;

When he goes to the site of enlightenment, adapting to the aspirations in beings' minds, he manifests bodies for them which are possessed of all the many different types of awesome deportment and also manifests all the adornments of the bodhi tree;

When he goes to the site of enlightenment, he manifests the seeing of all *tathāgatas* of the ten directions;

When he goes to the site of enlightenment, even with every time he lifts his foot or sets down his foot, he is always immersed in samādhi and in each successive mind-moment, without interruption, he is realizing buddhahood;

When he goes to the site of enlightenment, all the devas, dragons, *yakṣas*, *gandharvas*, *asuras*, *garuḍas*, *kiṃnaras*, *mahoragas*, Śakra, Brahma, the world-protecting devas, and all kings, each unaware of the others, bring forth many different kinds of different supremely sublime offerings; and

When he goes to the site of enlightenment, using his unimpeded wisdom, he everywhere contemplates the cultivation of the bodhisattva practices and the realization of right enlightenment as carried out in all worlds by all buddhas, the *tathāgatas*.

These are the ten. The bodhisattva uses these to teach beings.

Sons of the Buddha, there are ten phenomena that occur when the bodhisattva-mahāsattva sits at the site of enlightenment. What are those ten? They are as follows:

正體字

坐道場時。種種[6]震動一切世界。
312b28 ‖ 坐道場時。平等照[*]耀一切世界。坐道場時。
312b29 ‖ 除滅一切諸惡趣苦。[7]坐道場時。令一切世界
312c01 ‖ 金剛所成。坐道場時。普[8]觀一切諸佛如來。
312c02 ‖ 師子之座。坐道場時。心如虛空。無所分別。坐
312c03 ‖ 道場時。隨其所應。現身威儀。坐道場時。隨順
312c04 ‖ 安住金剛三昧。坐道場時。受一切如來神力
312c05 ‖ 所持。清淨妙處。坐道場時。自善根力。悉能加
312c06 ‖ 被一切眾生。是為十。佛子。菩薩摩訶薩。坐道
312c07 ‖ 場時。有十種奇特未曾有事。何等為十。佛子。
312c08 ‖ 菩薩摩訶薩。坐道場時。十方世界。一切如來。
312c09 ‖ 皆現其前。咸舉右手。而稱讚言。善哉善哉。無
312c10 ‖ 上導師。是為第一未曾有事。菩薩摩訶薩。坐
312c11 ‖ 道場時。一切如來。皆悉護念。與其威力。是為
312c12 ‖ 第二未曾有事。菩薩摩訶薩。坐道場時。宿世
312c13 ‖ 同行。諸菩薩眾。悉來圍遶。以種種莊嚴具。恭
312c14 ‖ 敬供養。是為第三未曾有事。

简体字

坐道场时，种种震动一切世界；坐道场时，平等照耀一切世界；坐道场时，除灭一切诸恶趣苦；坐道场时，令一切世界金刚所成；坐道场时，普观一切诸佛如来师子之座；坐道场时，心如虚空，无所分别；坐道场时，随其所应，现身威仪；坐道场时，随顺安住金刚三昧；坐道场时，受一切如来神力所持清净妙处；坐道场时，自善根力悉能加被一切众生。是为十。

"佛子，菩萨摩诃萨坐道场时，有十种奇特未曾有事。何等为十？佛子，菩萨摩诃萨坐道场时，十方世界一切如来皆现其前，咸举右手而称赞言：'善哉！善哉！无上导师！'是为第一未曾有事。菩萨摩诃萨坐道场时，一切如来皆悉护念，与其威力，是为第二未曾有事。菩萨摩诃萨坐道场时，宿世同行诸菩萨众悉来围绕，以种种庄严具恭敬供养，是为第三未曾有事。

Chapter 38 — *Transcending the World*

- When he sits at the site of enlightenment, he creates the many different kinds of shaking and movement in all worlds;
- When he sits at the site of enlightenment, he equally illuminates all worlds;
- When he sits at the site of enlightenment, he extinguishes all the sufferings of the wretched destinies;
- When he sits at the site of enlightenment, he causes all worlds to be composed of vajra;
- When he sits at the site of enlightenment, he everywhere contemplates the lion thrones of all buddhas, the *tathāgatas*;
- When he sits at the site of enlightenment, his mind is like empty space, free of any discriminations;
- When he sits at the site of enlightenment, he manifests bodies and types of awesome deportment in accordance with whatever is appropriate;
- When he sits at the site of enlightenment, he accords with and securely abides in the vajra samādhi;
- When he sits at the site of enlightenment, he receives the pure and sublime place supported by the spiritual powers of all *tathāgatas*; and
- When he sits at the site of enlightenment, the power of his own roots of goodness is able to assist all beings.

These are the ten.

Sons of the Buddha, when the bodhisattva-mahāsattva sits at the site of enlightenment, ten kinds of extraordinary and unprecedented phenomena occur. What are those ten? They are as follows:

- Sons of the Buddha, when the bodhisattva-mahāsattva sits at the site of enlightenment, all *tathāgatas* throughout the worlds of the ten directions appear directly before him, raise their right hands, and praise him, saying, "This is good indeed, good indeed, O Unexcelled Guide." This is the first of these unprecedented phenomena;
- Sons of the Buddha, when the bodhisattva-mahāsattva sits at the site of enlightenment, all *tathāgatas* are protectively mindful of him and bestow on him their awesome powers. This is the second of these unprecedented phenomena;
- Sons of the Buddha, when the bodhisattva-mahāsattva sits at the site of enlightenment, the congregation of all bodhisattvas with whom he cultivated together in the past surrounds him and reverently makes offerings to him of all different kinds of adornments. This is the third of these unprecedented phenomena;

正體字

菩薩摩訶薩。坐道場時。一切世界。草木叢林。諸無情物。皆曲身低影。歸向道場。是為第四未曾有事。菩薩摩訶薩。坐道場時。入三昧。名觀察法界。此三昧力。能令菩薩一切諸行。悉得圓滿。是為第五未曾有事。菩薩摩訶薩。坐道場時。得陀羅尼。名最上離垢妙光海藏。能受一切諸佛如來大雲法雨。是為第六未曾有事。菩薩摩訶薩。坐道場時。以威德力。興上妙供具。遍一切世界。供養諸佛。是為第七未曾有事。菩薩摩訶薩。坐道場時。住最勝智。悉現了知一切眾生。諸根意行。是為第八未曾有事。菩薩摩訶薩。坐道場時。入三昧。名善覺。此三昧力。能令其身。充滿三世盡虛空界一切世界。是為第九未曾有事。菩薩摩訶薩。坐道場時。得離垢光明無礙大智。令其身業。普入三世。是為第十未曾有事。佛子。是為菩薩摩訶薩。坐道場時。

简体字

菩萨摩诃萨坐道场时，一切世界草木、丛林诸无情物，皆曲身低影，归向道场，是为第四未曾有事。菩萨摩诃萨坐道场时，入三昧，名观察法界，此三昧力能令菩萨一切诸行悉得圆满，是为第五未曾有事。菩萨摩诃萨坐道场时，得陀罗尼，名最上离垢妙光海藏，能受一切诸佛如来大云法雨，是为第六未曾有事。菩萨摩诃萨坐道场时，以威德力兴上妙供具，遍一切世界供养诸佛，是为第七未曾有事。菩萨摩诃萨坐道场时，住最胜智，悉现了知一切众生诸根意行，是为第八未曾有事。菩萨摩诃萨坐道场时，入三昧，名善觉，此三昧力能令其身充满三世尽虚空界一切世界，是为第九未曾有事。菩萨摩诃萨坐道场时，得离垢光明无碍大智，令其身业普入三世，是为第十未曾有事。佛子，是为菩萨摩诃萨坐道场时，十种奇特未曾有事。

"佛子，菩萨摩诃萨坐道场时，

Chapter 38 — *Transcending the World*

Sons of the Buddha, when the bodhisattva-mahāsattva sits at the site of enlightenment, the grasses, trees, forests, and insentient things all bow their bodies and bend down their shadows in the direction of the site of enlightenment. This is the fourth of these unprecedented phenomena;

Sons of the Buddha, when the bodhisattva-mahāsattva sits at the site of enlightenment, he enters a samādhi known as "contemplation of the Dharma realm." The power of this samādhi is able to cause all the bodhisattva's practices to become completely fulfilled. This is the fifth of these unprecedented phenomena;

Sons of the Buddha, when the bodhisattva-mahāsattva sits at the site of enlightenment, he acquires a *dhāraṇī* known as "oceanic treasury of the most supremely pure and sublime light" with which he is able to take in all the Dharma rain falling from the great Dharma clouds of all buddhas, the *tathāgatas*. This is the sixth of these unprecedented phenomena;

Sons of the Buddha, when the bodhisattva-mahāsattva sits at the site of enlightenment, by the power of his awesome virtue, he raises up supremely marvelous gifts which everywhere pervade all worlds as offerings to all buddhas. This is the seventh of these unprecedented phenomena;

Sons of the Buddha, when the bodhisattva-mahāsattva sits at the site of enlightenment, he abides in the most supreme wisdom through which he manifests the complete knowing of the faculties, minds, and actions of all beings. This is the eighth of these unprecedented phenomena;

Sons of the Buddha, when the bodhisattva-mahāsattva sits at the site of enlightenment, he enters a samādhi known as "well awakened." By the power of this samādhi, he is able to cause his body to completely fill all worlds in all of space throughout the three periods of time. This is the ninth of these unprecedented phenomena; and

Sons of the Buddha, when the bodhisattva-mahāsattva sits at the site of enlightenment, he acquires the unimpeded great wisdom of immaculate radiance by which his physical actions everywhere enter all three periods of time. This is the tenth of these unprecedented phenomena.

Sons of the Buddha, these are the ten kinds of extraordinary and unprecedented phenomena that occur when the bodhisattva-mahāsattva sits at the site of enlightenment.

Sons of the Buddha, when the bodhisattva-mahāsattva sits at the site of enlightenment, it is due to contemplating ten meaningful

正體字

十種奇特未曾有事。佛子。菩薩摩訶薩。坐道場時。觀十種義故。示現降魔。何等為十。所謂為濁世眾生。樂於鬪戰。欲顯菩薩威德力故。示現降魔。為諸天世人。有懷疑者。斷彼疑故。示現降魔。為教化調伏諸魔軍故。示現降魔。為欲令諸天世人。樂軍陣者。咸來聚觀。心調伏故。示現降魔。為顯示菩薩所有威力。世無能敵故。示現降魔。為欲發起一切眾生勇猛力故。示現降魔。為哀愍末世諸眾生故。示現降魔。為欲顯示乃至道場。猶有魔軍。而來觸惱。此後乃得超魔境界故。示現降魔。為顯煩惱業用羸劣。大慈善根勢力強盛故。示現降魔。為欲隨順濁惡世界所行法故。示現降魔。是為十。佛子。菩薩摩訶薩。有十種成如來力。何等為十。所謂超過一切眾魔煩惱[1]業故。成如來力。具足一切菩薩行。遊戲一切菩薩三昧門故。成如來力。具足一切菩薩廣大禪定故。成如來力。

简体字

观十种义故，示现降魔。何等为十？所谓：为浊世众生乐于斗战，欲显菩萨威德力故，示现降魔；为诸天、世人有怀疑者，断彼疑故，示现降魔；为教化调伏诸魔军故，示现降魔；为欲令诸天、世人乐军阵者，咸来聚观，心调伏故，示现降魔；为显示菩萨所有威力世无能敌故，示现降魔；为欲发起一切众生勇猛力故，示现降魔；为哀愍末世诸众生故，示现降魔；为欲显示乃至道场犹有魔军而来触恼，此后乃得超魔境界故，示现降魔；为显烦恼业用羸劣，大慈善根势力强盛故，示现降魔；为欲随顺浊恶世界所行法故，示现降魔。是为十。

"佛子，菩萨摩诃萨有十种成如来力。何等为十？所谓：超过一切众魔烦恼业故，成如来力；具足一切菩萨行，游戏一切菩萨三昧门故，成如来力；具足一切菩萨广大禅定故，成如来力；

considerations that he manifests the subduing of the *māras*. What are those ten? They are as follows:

> Wishing to demonstrate the power of the bodhisattva's awesome virtue for beings in the world of the turbidities who are fond of fighting, he therefore manifests the subduing of the *māras*;
>
> To cut off the doubts of devas and people of the world who cherish doubts, he therefore manifests the subduing of the *māras*;
>
> To teach and subdue the armies of Māra, he therefore manifests the subduing of the *māras*;
>
> Wishing to cause the subduing of the minds of devas and people of the world who so delight in the ranks of the army that they all come, congregate, and observe them, he therefore manifests the subduing of the *māras*;
>
> To reveal all the awesome powers of the bodhisattva which no one in the world can oppose, he therefore manifests the subduing of the *māras*;
>
> Wishing to bring forth the courageous power of all beings, he therefore manifests the subduing of the *māras*;
>
> Out of deep sympathetic pity for all beings of the Dharma-ending age, he therefore manifests the subduing of the *māras*;
>
> Wishing to reveal that, even when he reaches the site of enlightenment, Māra's armies still come to create disturbances and only after that does he go beyond the sphere of interference by the *māras*, he therefore manifests the subduing of the *māras*;
>
> To reveal that the karmic functions of the afflictions are but thin and weak whereas the power of the roots of goodness of great kindness are strong and flourishing, he therefore manifests the subduing of the *māras*; and
>
> Wishing to accord with the dharmas practiced in the evil world of the turbidities, he therefore manifests the subduing of the *māras*.

These are the ten.

Sons of the Buddha, the bodhisattva-mahāsattva has ten ways in which he perfects the Tathāgata's powers. What are those ten? They are as follows:

> He perfects the Tathāgata's powers by stepping beyond the affliction-based actions of all the many *māras*;
>
> He perfects the Tathāgata's powers by completely fulfilling all the bodhisattva practices and achieving easeful mastery in all the samādhi gateways of the bodhisattva;
>
> He perfects the Tathāgata's powers by perfecting all the vast *dhyāna* absorptions of the bodhisattva;

正體字

圓滿一切白淨助道法故。
成如來力。得一切法智慧光明。善思惟分別
故。成如來力。其身周遍一切世界故。成如來
力。所出言音。悉與一切眾生心等故。成如來
力。能以神力加持一切故。成如來力。與三世
諸佛身語意業。等無有異。於一念中。了三世
法故。成如來力。得善覺智三昧。具如來十力。
所謂是處非處智力。乃至漏盡智力故。成如
來力。是為十。若諸菩薩。具此十力。則名如來
應正等覺。佛子。如來應正等覺。轉大法輪。有
十種事。何等為十。一者具足清淨四無畏智。
二者出生四辯隨順音聲。三者善能開闡四
真諦相。四者隨順諸佛無礙解脫。五者能令
眾生心皆淨信。六者所有言說皆不唐捐。能
拔眾生諸苦毒箭。七者大悲願力之所加持。

简体字

圆满一切白净助道法故，成如来力；得一切法智慧光明，善思惟分别故，成如来力；其身周遍一切世界故，成如来力；所出言音悉与一切众生心等故，成如来力；能以神力加持一切故，成如来力；与三世诸佛身、语、意业等无有异，于一念中了三世法故，成如来力；得善觉智三昧，具如来十力，所谓：是处非处智力乃至漏尽智力故，成如来力。是为十。若诸菩萨具此十力，则名如来、应、正等觉。

"佛子，如来、应、正等觉转大法轮有十种事。何等为十？一者、具足清净四无畏智；二者、出生四辩随顺音声；三者、善能开阐四真谛相；四者、随顺诸佛无碍解脱；五者、能令众生心皆净信；六者、所有言说皆不唐捐，能拔众生诸苦毒箭；七者、大悲愿力之所加持；

Chapter 38 — *Transcending the World*

> He perfects the Tathāgata's powers by completely fulfilling all the pure dharmas among the provisions for enlightenment;
>
> He perfects the Tathāgata's powers by acquiring the light of wisdom with respect to all dharmas through skillful meditative analysis;
>
> He perfects the Tathāgata's powers through his body's[166] pervasive presence everywhere in all worlds;
>
> He perfects the Tathāgata's powers through making his voice match the minds of all beings;
>
> He perfects the Tathāgata's powers through his ability to use spiritual powers to assist and support everyone;
>
> He perfects the Tathāgata's powers through actions of body, speech, and mind that are equal to and no different from those of all buddhas of the three periods of time and through completely understanding the dharmas of the three periods of time in but a single mind-moment; and
>
> He perfects the Tathāgata's ten powers through acquiring the samādhi of well awakened knowledge. In particular, these refer to the wisdom power by which he knows what can be as what can be and what cannot be as what cannot be, and so forth, on through to the wisdom power that knows the complete cessation of all the contaminants.

These are the ten. If bodhisattvas perfect these ten powers, then they are known as "Tathāgata," "Arhat," and "The One of Right and Perfect Enlightenment."

Sons of the Buddha, when the Tathāgata, the Arhat, the One of Right and Universal Enlightenment turns the wheel of the great Dharma, this is attended by ten kinds of phenomena. What are those ten? They are as follows:

> First, he is perfectly fulfilled in the purification of the knowledge of the four types of fearlessness;
>
> Second, he produces statements corresponding to the four types of unimpeded knowledge;
>
> Third, he is well able to explain the aspects of the four truths;
>
> Fourth, he accords with the unimpeded liberation of all buddhas;
>
> Fifth, he is able to enable all beings' minds to acquire purified faith;
>
> Sixth, nothing that he utters is spoken in vain, for it is able to extricate from beings the arrows smeared with the poison of suffering;
>
> Seventh, he is aided in this by the power of greatly compassionate vows;

正體字

八者隨出音聲普遍。十方一切世界。九者於阿僧祇劫。說法不斷。十者隨所說法。皆能生起根力覺道禪定解脫三昧等法。佛子。諸佛如來。轉於法輪。有如是等無量種事。佛子。如來應正等覺。轉法輪時。以十事故。於眾生心中。種白淨法。無空過者。何等為十。所謂過去願力故。大悲所持故。不捨眾生故。智慧自在隨其所樂為說法故。必應其時未曾失故。隨其所宜無妄說故。知三世智善了知故。其身最勝無與等故。言辭自在無能測故。智慧自在隨所發言悉開悟故。是為十。佛子。如來應正等覺。作佛事已。觀十種義故。示般涅槃。何等為十。所謂示一切行實無常故。示一切有為非安隱故。示大涅槃是安隱處無怖畏故。

简体字

八者、随出音声普遍十方一切世界；九者、于阿僧祇劫说法不断；十者、随所说法皆能生起根、力、觉道、禅定、解脱、三昧等法。佛子，诸佛如来转于法轮，有如是等无量种事。

"佛子，如来、应、正等觉转法轮时，以十事故，于众生心中种白净法，无空过者。何等为十？所谓：过去愿力故；大悲所持故；不舍众生故；智慧自在，随其所乐为说法故；必应其时，未曾失故；随其所宜，无妄说故；知三世智，善了知故；其身最胜，无与等故；言辞自在，无能测故；智慧自在，随所发言悉开悟故。是为十。

"佛子，如来、应、正等觉作佛事已，观十种义故，示般涅槃。何等为十？所谓：示一切行实无常故；示一切有为非安隐故；示大涅槃是安隐处，无怖畏故；

Chapter 38 — Transcending the World

Eighth, whatever utterances he produces pervade all worlds throughout the ten directions;

Ninth, he ceaselessly proclaims the Dharma for *asaṃkhyeyas* of kalpas; and

Tenth, whatever dharmas he teaches are all able to produce the roots, the powers, the factors of enlightenment, the components of the path, the *dhyāna* concentrations, the liberations, the samādhis, and other such dharmas.

Sons of the Buddha, when the Buddha, the Tathāgata, turns the wheel of the Dharma, this is attended by countless other such phenomena as these.

Sons of the Buddha, when the Tathāgata, the Arhat, the One of Right and Perfect Enlightenment, turns the wheel of the Dharma, it is due to ten things that he plants the dharmas of purity in beings' minds and does not do so in vain. What are those ten? They are as follows:

It is due to the power of past vows;

It is due to being sustained by the great compassion;

It is due to never abandoning beings;

It is due to speaking Dharma for them with wisdom and sovereign mastery adapted to whatever they delight in;

It is due to definitely according with and never missing the right time;

It is due to adapting to what is fitting without speaking wrongly;

It is due to knowing the wisdom of the three periods of time, knowing it thoroughly and completely;

It is due to having a body which is most excellent and without peer;

It is due to his mastery of verbal expression which no one can completely fathom; and

It is due to his sovereign mastery of wisdom with which, whatever he says, it awakens everyone.

These are the ten.

Sons of the Buddha, after the Tathāgata, the Arhat, the One of Right and Perfect Enlightenment finishes accomplishing his buddha works, it is due to contemplating ten meaningful considerations that he then manifests entry into *parinirvāṇa*. What are those ten? They are as follows:

To demonstrate that all actions are truly impermanent;

To demonstrate that all conditioned phenomena are unstable;

To demonstrate that the great nirvāṇa is the station of peace and security free of anything to fear;

正體字	313b19 ∥ 以諸人天。樂著色身。為現色身。是無常法。令 313b20 ∥ 其願住淨法身故。示無常力不可轉故。示一 313b21 ∥ 切有為。不隨心住。不自在故。示一切三有。皆 313b22 ∥ 如幻化。不堅牢故。示涅槃性。究竟堅牢。不可 313b23 ∥ 壞故。示一切法。無生無起。而有聚集散壞相 313b24 ∥ 故。佛子。諸佛世尊。作佛事已。所願滿已。轉 313b25 ∥ 法輪已。應化度者。皆化度已。有諸菩薩。應受 313b26 ∥ 尊號。成記[2]別已。法應如是入於不變大般涅 313b27 ∥ 槃。佛子。是為如來應正等覺。觀十義故。示般 313b28 ∥ 涅槃 313b29 ∥ 佛子。此法門名菩薩廣大清淨行。無量諸佛。 313c01 ∥ 所共宣說。能令智者。了無量義。皆生歡喜。令 313c02 ∥ 一切菩薩。大願大行。皆得相續。佛子。若有眾 313c03 ∥ 生。得聞此法。聞已信解。解已修行。必得疾成 313c04 ∥ 阿耨多羅三藐三菩提。何以故。以如說修行 313c05 ∥ 故。佛子。若諸菩薩。不如說行。
简体字	以诸人、天乐著色身,为现色身是无常法,令其愿住净法身故;示无常力不可转故;示一切有为不随心住,不自在故;示一切三有皆如幻化,不坚牢故;示涅槃性究竟坚牢,不可坏故;示一切法无生无起而有聚集、散坏相故;佛子,诸佛世尊作佛事已,所愿满已,转法轮已,应化度者皆化度已,有诸菩萨应受尊号成记莂已,法应如是入于不变大般涅槃。佛子,是为如来、应、正等觉观十义故,示般涅槃。 　　"佛子,此法门名菩萨广大清净行。无量诸佛所共宣说,能令智者了无量义皆生欢喜,令一切菩萨大愿、大行皆得相续。佛子,若有众生得闻此法,闻已信解,解已修行,必得疾成阿耨多罗三藐三菩提。何以故?以如说修行故。佛子,若诸菩萨不如说行,

Chapter 38 — *Transcending the World*

Because all humans and devas take pleasure in and are attached to the physical body, he does this to demonstrate that the physical body is an impermanent dharma and to induce them to wish to abide in the pure Dharma body;

To demonstrate that the power of impermanence cannot be turned aside;

To demonstrate that all conditioned phenomena do not exist in accordance with one's intentions and have no inherent existence of their own;

To demonstrate that all things in the three realms of existence are like magical conjurations which are not durable;

To demonstrate that the nature of nirvāṇa is ultimately solid and indestructible;

To demonstrate that all dharmas are unproduced and non-arising and yet they present the appearance of coming together and being destroyed; and

Sons of the Buddha, once the buddhas, the *bhagavats*, have finished their buddha works, have fulfilled whatever they have vowed to do, have turned the wheel of the Dharma, have taught and liberated those whom they should rightly teach and liberate, and have bestowed predictions on those bodhisattvas deserving of receiving their venerable titles, as a matter of what the Dharma should rightly entail, they then enter the changeless great *parinirvāṇa*.

Sons of the Buddha, these are what constitute the ten meaningful considerations of the Tathāgata, the Arhat, the One of Right and Perfect Enlightenment on account of which he manifests entry into *parinirvāṇa*.

Sons of the Buddha, this gateway into the Dharma is known as "the bodhisattva's vast pure practice" which countless buddhas all join in proclaiming. It enables the wise to completely comprehend countless meanings and become filled with joyous delight. It enables the great vows and great practices of all bodhisattvas to be continuously sustained.

Sons of the Buddha, if there are any beings who are able to hear this Dharma and, having heard it, then believe and understand it, and having understood it, then cultivate it—they will definitely be able to swiftly realize *anuttarasamyaksaṃbodhi*. And why is this? This is due to their having cultivated it in accordance with what has been taught.

Sons of the Buddha, if bodhisattvas do not practice in accordance with what has been taught, one should realize these people

正體字

當知是人。於佛
313c06 菩提。則為永離。是故菩薩。應如說行。佛子。
313c07 此一切菩薩功德行處決定義華普入一切法。
313c08 普生一切智。超諸世間。離二乘道。不與一切
313c09 諸眾生共。悉能照了一切法門。增長眾生出
313c10 世善根。離世間法門品。應尊重。應聽受。應誦
313c11 持。應思惟。應願樂。應修行。若能如是。當知
313c12 是人。疾得阿耨多羅三藐三菩提。說此品時。
313c13 佛神力故。及此法門。法如是故。十方無量無
313c14 邊阿僧祇世界。皆大震動。大光普照。爾時十
313c15 方諸佛。皆現普賢菩薩前。讚言。善哉善哉。佛
313c16 子。乃能說此諸菩薩摩訶薩。功德行處決定
313c17 義華普入一切佛法出世間法門品。佛子。汝
313c18 已善學此法。善說此法。汝以威力。護持此法。
313c19 我等諸佛。悉皆隨喜。如我等諸佛隨喜於汝。
313c20 一切諸佛。悉亦如是。佛子。我等諸佛。悉共同
313c21 心。護持此經。令現在未來諸菩薩眾。未曾聞
313c22 者。皆當得聞。爾時普賢菩薩摩訶薩。承佛神
313c23 力。觀察十方一切大眾。[3]洎于法界。而說頌
313c24 言

简体字

当知是人于佛菩提则为永离，是故菩萨应如说行。佛子，此一切菩萨功德行处决定义华，普入一切法，普生一切智，超诸世间，离二乘道，不与一切诸众生共，悉能照了一切法门，增长众生出世善根，离世间法门品，应尊重，应听受，应诵持，应思惟，应愿乐，应修行；若能如是，当知是人疾得阿耨多罗三藐三菩提。"

说此品时，佛神力故，及此法门法如是故，十方无量无边阿僧祇世界皆大震动，大光普照。

尔时，十方诸佛皆现普贤菩萨前，赞言："善哉！善哉！佛子，乃能说此诸菩萨摩诃萨功德行处决定义华普入一切佛法出世间法门品。佛子，汝已善学此法，善说此法。汝以威力护持此法，我等诸佛悉皆随喜；如我等诸佛随喜于汝，一切诸佛悉亦如是。佛子，我等诸佛悉共同心护持此经，令现在、未来诸菩萨众未曾闻者皆当得闻。"

尔时，普贤菩萨摩诃萨承佛神力，观察十方一切大众洎于法界而说颂言：

Chapter 38 — *Transcending the World*

will forever remain apart from the bodhi of the Buddha. Therefore the bodhisattva should practice in accordance with what has been taught.

Sons of the Buddha, this "Transcending the World" chapter is the basis for the practice of all bodhisattvas' meritorious qualities and is the flower of the definitive meaning which everywhere enters all dharmas, which everywhere produces all-knowledge, which steps beyond all worlds, which abandons the paths of the two vehicles, which is not held in common with any other class of being, which is able to completely illuminate all Dharma gateways, and which increases beings' world-transcending roots of goodness. One should revere it, listen to it, recite it, remember it, reflect on it, admire and delight in it, and cultivate it. If one is able to proceed in this manner, one should realize that such a person will swiftly gain *anuttarasamyaksaṃbodhi*.

When the proclamation of this chapter concluded, due to the Buddha's spiritual powers and also because the Dharma of this Dharma gateway is of this very sort, the countlessly and boundlessly many *asaṃkhyeyas* of worlds throughout the ten directions all quaked and shook and bright light illuminated them all.

At that time, the buddhas of the ten directions all appeared directly before Samantabhadra Bodhisattva and praised him, saying:

It is good indeed, good indeed, O Son of the Buddha, that you have now been able to proclaim this "Transcending the World" chapter, the basis for the practice of the meritorious qualities of all bodhisattva-mahāsattvas and the flower of the definitive meaning which everywhere enters all dharmas of the Buddha.

O Son of the Buddha, you have already well trained in this Dharma and well proclaimed this Dharma. With your awesome powers, you guard and preserve this Dharma. We buddhas all rejoice in accord with this and, just as we buddhas all rejoice in accord with what you do, so too is this true of all other buddhas as well.

O Son of the Buddha, we buddhas are all of the same mind in protecting and preserving this sutra to enable it to be heard by all present and future bodhisattva congregations who have not yet heard it.

At that time, aided by the Buddha's spiritual powers, Samantabhadra Bodhisattva-mahāsattva surveyed all the great assemblies throughout the ten directions of the Dharma realm and then spoke these verses:

正體字	313c25　於無量劫修苦行　從無量佛正法生	
	313c26　令無量眾住菩提　彼無等行聽我說	
	313c27　供無量佛而捨著　廣度群生不作想	
	313c28　求佛功德心無依　彼勝妙行我今說	
	313c29　離三界魔煩惱業　具聖功德最勝行	
	314a01　滅諸癡惑心寂然　我今說彼所行道	
	314a02　永離世間諸誑幻　種種變化示眾生	
	314a03　心生住滅現眾事　說彼所能令眾喜	
	314a04　見諸眾生生老死　煩惱憂橫所纏迫	
	314a05　欲令解脫教發心　彼功德行應聽受	
	314a06　施戒忍進禪智慧　方便慈悲喜捨等	
	314a07　百千萬劫常修行　彼人功德仁應聽	
	314a08　千萬億劫求菩提　所有身命皆無[1]吝	
	314a09　願益群生不為己　彼慈愍行我今說	
	314a10　無量億劫演其德　如海一滴未為少	
	314a11　功德無比不可[2]諭　以佛威神今略說	
	314a12　其心[3]無高下　求道無厭倦	
	314a13　普使諸眾生　住善增淨法	
	314a14　智慧普饒益　如樹如河泉	
	314a15　亦如於大地　一切所依處	

简体字

"于无量劫修苦行，从无量佛正法生，
令无量众住菩提，彼无等行听我说。
供无量佛而舍著，广度群生不作想，
求佛功德心无依，彼胜妙行我今说。
离三界魔烦恼业，具圣功德最胜行，
灭诸痴惑心寂然，我今说彼所行道。
永离世间诸诳幻，种种变化示众生，
心生住灭现众事，说彼所能令众喜。
见诸众生生老死，烦恼忧横所缠迫，
欲令解脱教发心，彼功德行应听受。
施戒忍进禅智慧，方便慈悲喜舍等，
百千万劫常修行，彼人功德仁应听。
千万亿劫求菩提，所有身命皆无吝，
愿益群生不为己，彼慈愍行我今说。
无量亿劫演其德，如海一滴未为少，
功德无比不可喻，以佛威神今略说。
其心不高下，求道无厌倦，
普使诸众生，住善增净法。
智慧普饶益，如树如河泉，
亦如于大地，一切所依处。

Chapter 38 — *Transcending the World*

Having cultivated austere practices for countless kalpas,
he is born from the right Dharma of countless buddhas.
He enables countless beings to abide in bodhi.
Listen as I speak of his unexcelled practice.

His offerings to countless buddhas, his forsaking of attachments,
his extensive liberation of beings while not even conceiving of them,
his quest for a buddha's qualities with a mind depending on nothing,
and his supremely marvelous practices—I shall now speak of them.

He abandons the *māras* of the three realms and affliction-based karma,
perfects the *āryas*' meritorious qualities and most supreme practices,
and extinguishes all delusions with a quiescent mind.
I shall now describe the path that he travels.

He forever abandons all the world's deceptive illusions,
emanates many different transformations to teach beings.
The minds' arising, abiding, and ceasing—he manifests many things.
I shall describe his abilities to gladden the multitude.

His seeing of all beings' birth, aging, death, and
entanglement and oppression by afflictions' worries and calamities,
and his wish to liberate them and teach them to make the resolve—
You should listen as I describe his meritorious practices.

Giving, moral virtue, patience, vigor, dhyāna, wisdom, skillful means,
kindness, compassion, sympathetic joy, equanimity, and such—
always cultivating these for a hundred thousand myriads of kalpas—
You Worthy Ones should hear of that man's meritorious qualities.

Seeking bodhi for thousands of myriads of *koṭīs* of kalpas,
never being sparing of any of his bodies or lives,
wishing to benefit the many beings, not doing so for himself—
I shall now describe his kindly and sympathetic practices.

Even if one expounded on his qualities for countless *koṭīs* of kalpas,
it would be like but one drop in an ocean, not even a minor part of it.
His qualities are incomparable and indescribable even by analogy.
Aided by Buddha's awesome powers, I will now briefly tell of them.

His mind is free of any conception of anyone being either high or low
and, in seeking the path, he never grows weary.
He everywhere enables all beings
to abide in goodness and in the dharmas of increasing purity.

His wisdom everywhere benefits others
like a tree, like a river, like a spring,
and also like the great earth itself
which serves as the place upon which all things depend.

正體字	314a16 ‖	菩薩如蓮華	慈根安隱莖
	314a17 ‖	智慧為眾蘂	戒品為香潔
	314a18 ‖	佛放法光明	令彼得開敷
	314a19 ‖	不著有為水	見者皆欣樂
	314a20 ‖	菩薩妙法樹	生於直心地
	314a21 ‖	信種慈悲根	智慧以為身
	314a22 ‖	方便為枝幹	五度為繁密
	314a23 ‖	定葉神通華	一切智為果
	314a24 ‖	最上力為[4]鳥	垂陰覆三界
	314a25 ‖	菩薩師子王	白淨法為身
	314a26 ‖	四諦為其足	正念以為頸
	314a27 ‖	慈眼智慧首	頂繫解脫繒
	314a28 ‖	勝義空谷中	吼法怖眾魔
	314a29 ‖	菩薩為商主	普見諸群生
	314b01 ‖	在生死曠野	煩惱險惡處
	314b02 ‖	魔賊之所攝	癡盲失正道
	314b03 ‖	示其正直路	令入無畏城
	314b04 ‖	菩薩見眾生	三毒煩惱病
	314b05 ‖	種種諸苦惱	長夜所煎迫
	314b06 ‖	為發大悲心	廣說對治門
简体字	菩萨如莲华,慈根安隐茎, 智慧为众蕊,戒品为香洁。 佛放法光明,令彼得开敷, 不著有为水,见者皆欣乐。 菩萨妙法树,生于直心地, 信种慈悲根,智慧以为身, 方便为枝干,五度为繁密, 定叶神通华,一切智为果。 最上力为茑,垂阴覆三界。 菩萨师子王,白净法为身。 四谛为其足,正念以为颈, 慈眼智慧首,顶系解脱缯, 胜义空谷中,吼法怖众魔。 菩萨为商主,普见诸群生, 在生死旷野,烦恼险恶处, 魔贼之所摄,痴盲失正道, 示其正直路,令入无畏城。 菩萨见众生,三毒烦恼病, 种种诸苦恼,长夜所煎迫; 为发大悲心,广说对治门,		

Chapter 38 — *Transcending the World*

The bodhisattva is like a lotus flower
with roots of kindness, a stem of peace and security,
with wisdom forming its many stamens,
and moral virtue forming its fragrance and purity.

The Buddha emanates the light of the Dharma,
which enables him to bloom
and remain unattached to the waters of conditioned existence.
All who see him are delighted.

The bodhisattva's tree of the sublime Dharma
grows on the ground of the straight mind.
His faith forms its seed, kindness and compassion forms its roots,
and wisdom forms its trunk.

Skillful means form its boughs.
Five perfections form their dense growth.
Concentration forms its leaves, the superknowledges form its flowers,
and all-knowledge forms the fruit.
The most supreme powers are the birds.[167]
It lets fall its shade to shelter those in three realms of existence.

The bodhisattva lion king
takes the dharmas of pristine purity as his body,
the four truths as his feet,
and right mindfulness as his neck.

Kindness forms his eyes and wisdom his head.
The crown of his head is tied with the silk headband of the liberations.
In the valley of the emptiness of the supreme meaning,
he roars the Dharma and frightens the many *māra*s.

The bodhisattva acts as a caravan leader
who everywhere sees the many kinds of beings
residing in the wasteland wilderness of *saṃsāra*
in hazardous and evil places beset by the afflictions.

Having been lured there by Māra's bandits
and having been blinded by delusion, they have lost the right path.
He shows them the right and straight road
and enables them to enter the city of fearlessness.

The bodhisattva sees beings
sickened by the afflictions of the three poisons,
and tormented and persecuted through the long night [of *saṃsāra*]
by the many different kinds of misery and distress.

Having aroused the greatly compassionate mind for their sakes,
he extensively explains the means of counteractive treatment,

正體字	314b07 314b08 314b09 314b10 314b11 314b12 314b13 314b14 314b15 314b16 314b17 314b18 314b19 314b20 314b21 314b22 314b23 314b24 314b25 314b26	八萬四千種　　滅除眾苦患 菩薩為法王　　正道化眾生 令遠惡修善　　專求佛功德 一切諸佛所　　灌頂[5]授尊記 廣施眾聖財　　菩提分珍寶 菩薩轉法輪　　如佛之所轉 戒轂三昧輞　　智莊慧為劍 既破煩惱賊　　亦殄眾魔怨 一切諸外道　　見之無不散 菩薩智慧海　　深廣無涯際 正法味盈洽　　覺分寶充滿 大心無邊岸　　一切智為潮 眾生莫能測　　說之不可盡 菩薩須彌山　　超出於世間 神通三昧峯　　大心安不動 若有親近者　　同其智慧色 迥絕眾境界　　一切無不覩 菩薩如金剛　　志求一切智 信心及苦行　　堅固不可動 其心無所畏　　饒益諸群生
简体字		八万四千种，灭除众苦患。 菩萨为法王，正道化众生， 令远恶修善，专求佛功德； 一切诸佛所，灌顶受尊记， 广施众圣财，菩提分珍宝。 菩萨转法轮，如佛之所转， 戒轂三昧辋，智庄慧为剑， 既破烦恼贼，亦殄众魔怨， 一切诸外道，见之无不散。 菩萨智慧海，深广无涯际， 正法味盈洽，觉分宝充满， 大心无边岸，一切智为潮， 众生莫能测，说之不可尽。 菩萨须弥山，超出于世间， 神通三昧峰，大心安不动； 若有亲近者，同其智慧色， 迥绝众境界，一切无不睹。 菩萨如金刚，志求一切智， 信心及苦行，坚固不可动； 其心无所畏，饶益诸群生，

that, in their eighty-four thousand different varieties,
extinguish the illnesses of the many types of suffering.

The bodhisattva serves as a king of the Dharma
who uses the path of what is right to teach beings,
enabling them to distance themselves from evil, cultivate goodness,
and single-mindedly seek the Buddha's meritorious qualities.

In the abodes of all buddhas, he receives
the crown-anointing consecration and the *bhagavats'* predictions
and extensively gives to others the many kinds of wealth of the *aryas*
and the precious jewels of the enlightenment factors.

The bodhisattva turns the wheel of the Dharma
just like that which is turned by the Buddha.
Moral virtue forms its hubs and samādhi forms its rims.
Wisdom's strong intelligence serves as his sword.

Having destroyed the insurgents of the afflictions,
he then also puts an end to the many *māra* adversaries.
Of all those who follow non-Buddhist paths,
there are none who do not scatter when they see him.

The bodhisattva's ocean of wisdom
is deep, vast, and unbounded.
It is suffused with the flavor of right Dharma
and is filled with the jewels of the enlightenment factors.

His great mind has no bounding shore.
All-knowledge forms its tides.
Among beings, there are none able to fathom it.
Any attempt to describe it could never come to the end.

The bodhisattva's Sumeru Mountain
rises up beyond the world.
The spiritual superknowledges and samādhi are its peaks
and it is made stable and unshakable by his great resolve.

If anyone draws near to it,
they take on its same color of wisdom
which goes far beyond the many other spheres of cognition
and is such that no one does not see it.

The bodhisattva is like vajra
in his resolve to seek all-knowledge
His mind of faith and practice of the austerities
are steadfast and unshakable.

His mind has nothing that it fears
as he strives to benefit the many kinds of beings.

正體字	314b27　眾魔與煩惱　一切悉摧滅 314b28　菩薩大慈悲　譬如重密雲 314b29　三明發電光　神足震雷音 314c01　普以四辯才　雨八功德水 314c02　潤洽於一切　令除煩惱熱 314c03　菩薩正法城　般若以為牆 314c04　慚愧為深塹　智慧為却敵 314c05　廣開解脫門　正念恒防守 314c06　四諦坦[6]王道　六通集兵仗 314c07　復建大法幢　周迴遍其下 314c08　三有諸魔眾　一切無能入 314c09　菩薩迦樓羅　如意為堅足 314c10　方便勇猛翅　慈悲明淨眼 314c11　住一切智樹　觀三有大海 314c12　搏撮天人龍　安置涅槃岸 314c13　菩薩正法日　出現於世間 314c14　戒品圓滿輪　神足速疾行 314c15　照以智慧光　長諸根力藥 314c16　滅除煩惱闇　消竭愛欲海 314c17　菩薩智光月　法界以為輪
简体字	众魔与烦恼，一切悉摧灭。 菩萨大慈悲，譬如重密云， 三明发电光，神足震雷音， 普以四辩才，雨八功德水， 润洽于一切，令除烦恼热。 菩萨正法城，般若以为墙， 惭愧为深堑，智慧为却敌， 广开解脱门，正念恒防守， 四谛坦王道，六通集兵仗， 复建大法幢，周回遍其下； 三有诸魔众，一切无能入。 菩萨迦楼罗，如意为坚足， 方便勇猛翅，慈悲明净眼， 住一切智树，观三有大海， 搏撮天人龙，安置涅槃岸。 菩萨正法日，出现于世间， 戒品圆满轮，神足速疾行， 照以智慧光，长诸根力药， 灭除烦恼暗，消竭爱欲海。 菩萨智光月，法界以为轮，

Chapter 38 — Transcending the World

As for the many *māra*s as well as the afflictions,
he has completely vanquished them all.

The bodhisattva's great kindness and compassion
are like clouds that are layered and dense
from which the three clarities[168] send down their lightning flashes
and the quaking thunder of the spiritual powers resounds.

He everywhere uses the four types of eloquence[169]
to rain down the waters of the eight qualities
which moisten and soak everything
and cause the heat of the afflictions to be dispelled.

In the bodhisattva's city of right Dharma,
it is *prajñā* that forms its walls,
his sense of shame and dread of blame that form its deep moats,
and wisdom that forms its enemy-repelling battlements.

He opens wide the gates to liberation and
relies on right mindfulness for constant protection and preservation,
the four truths to level the King's path,
and the six superknowledges to assemble his troops and armaments.

In addition, he raises the great Dharma banners
that are arrayed all around below him
so that, of all the hordes of *māra*s of the three realms of existence,
there are none at all who are able to enter there.

For the bodhisattva, like a *garuḍa*,
it is his foundations of psychic power[170] that serve as his solid footing,
his skillful means that serve as the wings of his courage,
and kindness and compassion that serve him as bright and clear eyes.

Dwelling in the tree of all-knowledge
he surveys the great ocean of the three realms of existence,
pounces upon and clutches up the celestial and human dragons,
and sets them then on the shore of nirvāṇa.

The bodhisattva's sun of right Dharma
rises and appears in the world.
The moral precepts form its round and full orb
and the spiritual power of psychic travel propels its swift transit.

Its illumination with the light of wisdom
grows the medicinal herbs of the roots and the powers,
extinguishes the darkness of the afflictions,
and dries up the ocean of desire.

The bodhisattva's moon of wisdom light
takes the Dharma realm as its orbit

正體字	314c18　遊於畢竟空　世[7]間無不見 314c19　三界識心內　隨時有增減 314c20　二乘星宿中　一切無儔匹 314c21　菩薩大法王　功德莊嚴身 314c22　相好皆具足　人天悉瞻仰 314c23　方便清淨目　智慧金剛杵 314c24　於法得自在　以道化群生 314c25　菩薩大梵王　自在超三有 314c26　業惑悉皆斷　慈捨靡不具 314c27　處處示現身　開悟以法音 314c28　於彼三界中　拔諸邪見根 314c29　菩薩自在天　超過生死地 315a01　境界常清淨　智慧無退轉 315a02　絕彼下乘道　受諸灌頂法 315a03　功德智慧具　名稱靡不聞 315a04　菩薩智慧心　清淨如虛空 315a05　無性無依處　一切不可得 315a06　有大自在力　能成世間事 315a07　自具清淨行　令眾生亦然 315a08　菩薩方便地　饒益諸眾生	
简体字	游于毕竟空，世间无不见； 三界识心内，随时有增减； 二乘星宿中，一切无俦匹。 菩萨大法王，功德庄严身， 相好皆具足，人天悉瞻仰， 方便清净目，智慧金刚杵， 于法得自在，以道化群生。 菩萨大梵王，自在超三有， 业惑悉皆断，慈舍靡不具， 处处示现身，开悟以法音， 于彼三界中，拔诸邪见根。 菩萨自在天，超过生死地， 境界常清净，智慧无退转， 绝彼下乘道，受诸灌顶法， 功德智慧具，名称靡不闻。 菩萨智慧心，清净如虚空， 无性无依处，一切不可得， 有大自在力，能成世间事， 自具清净行，令众生亦然。 菩萨方便地，饶益诸众生；	

Chapter 38 — *Transcending the World*

as it travels through the emptiness of the ultimate truth.
Of those who abide in the world, there are none who do not see it.

In the minds of the conscious beings within the three realms
it waxes and wanes in accordance with the time.
Among all the stars and constellations of the two vehicles,
there are none who are capable of comparing to it.

The body adorned with the meritorious qualities
possessed by the bodhisattva, the great king of the Dharma,
is complete in all the major marks and secondary signs
to which all humans and devas gaze up in admiration.

With the pure eyes of skillful means
and the vajra scepter of wisdom,
he attains sovereign mastery in the Dharma
and uses the path to teach the many kinds of beings.

The bodhisattva, like a great Brahma Heaven king,
with sovereign mastery, steps beyond the three realms of existence,
cuts off all the karma and afflictions, and, of kindness,[171] [compassion, sympathetic joy], and equanimity, there are none he does not possess.

He manifests his body in every place
and, using the sound of the Dharma, instigates awakening,
and, in all those three realms of existence,
he extricates the very roots of all the wrong views.

The bodhisattva, like a *parinirmita-vaśavartin* deva,
steps beyond the grounds of *saṃsāra*,
has spheres of cognition that are always pure,
and possesses wisdom that has become irreversible.

He cuts off the paths of those lower vehicles,
receives the dharmas of the crown-anointing consecration,
becomes completely equipped with merit and wisdom,
and achieves such fame that no one does not hear of him.

The bodhisattva's mind of wisdom
is as pure as empty space.
It has no inherently existent nature, has nothing it depends upon,
and, for it, there is nothing at all that is apprehensible.

He is possessed of the power of the great sovereign masteries
by which he is able to accomplish works in the world.
Possessed of pure practice himself,
he enables beings to also do the same.

The bodhisattva's earth of skillful means
bestows benefit on all beings.

正體字	315a09 ‖	菩薩慈悲水	[1]澣滌諸煩惱
	315a10 ‖	菩薩智慧火	燒諸惑習薪
	315a11 ‖	菩薩無住風	遊行三有空
	315a12 ‖	菩薩如珍寶	能濟貧窮厄
	315a13 ‖	菩薩如金剛	能摧顛倒見
	315a14 ‖	菩薩如瓔珞	莊嚴三有身
	315a15 ‖	菩薩如摩尼	增長一切行
	315a16 ‖	菩薩德如華	常發菩提分
	315a17 ‖	菩薩願如鬘	恒繫眾生首
	315a18 ‖	菩薩淨戒香	堅持無缺犯
	315a19 ‖	菩薩智塗香	普熏於三界
	315a20 ‖	菩薩力如帳	能遮煩惱塵
	315a21 ‖	菩薩智如幢	能摧我慢敵
	315a22 ‖	妙行為繒綵	莊嚴於智慧
	315a23 ‖	慚愧作衣服	普覆諸群生
	315a24 ‖	菩薩無礙乘	巾之出三界
	315a25 ‖	菩薩大力象	其心善調伏
	315a26 ‖	菩薩神足馬	騰步超諸有
	315a27 ‖	菩薩說法龍	普雨眾生心
	315a28 ‖	菩薩優曇華	世間難值遇
简体字	菩萨慈悲水，浣涤诸烦恼；菩萨智慧火，烧诸惑习薪；菩萨无住风，游行三有空。菩萨如珍宝，能济贫穷厄；菩萨如金刚，能摧颠倒见；菩萨如璎珞，庄严三有身；菩萨如摩尼，增长一切行。菩萨德如华，常发菩提分；菩萨愿如鬘，恒系众生首。菩萨净戒香，坚持无缺犯；菩萨智涂香，普熏于三界。菩萨力如帐，能遮烦恼尘；菩萨智如幢，能摧我慢敌。妙行为缯彩，庄严于智慧，惭愧作衣服，普覆诸群生。菩萨无碍乘，巾之出三界；菩萨大力象，其心善调伏；菩萨神足马，腾步超诸有；菩萨说法龙，普雨众生心；菩萨优昙华，世间难值遇；		

Chapter 38 — *Transcending the World*

The bodhisattva's water of kindness and compassion
washes away all the afflictions.

The bodhisattva's fire of wisdom
burns up the tinder of all afflictions and habitual karmic propensities.
The bodhisattva's wind of non-abiding
roams through the emptiness of the three realms of existence.[172]

The bodhisattva is like a precious jewel
that is able to rescue beings from poverty and hardship.
The bodhisattva is like vajra
that is able to smash the inverted views.

The bodhisattva is like a pearl necklace
adorning the body of the three realms of existence.
The bodhisattva is like a [wish-fulfilling] *maṇi* jewel[173]
that is able to produce growth in all the practices.

The bodhisattva's qualities are like flowers
that always bloom with the enlightenment factors.[174]
The bodhisattva's vows are like garlands
that constantly tie [the topknots atop] the heads of beings.

The bodhisattva's fragrance of purity in the moral precepts
stems from solidly observing them without deficiency or infraction.
The bodhisattva's perfume of wisdom
everywhere imbues the three realms of existence with its scent.

The bodhisattva's powers are like screens
that are able to block the dust of the afflictions.
The bodhisattva's wisdom is like a banner
that is able to vanquish the enemy of pride.

His sublime practices are like silk pennants
serving as adornments for his wisdom.
A sense of shame and dread of blame serve as robes
everywhere covering the many kinds of beings.

The bodhisattva's unimpeded vehicle,
when mounted, allows him to escape from the three realms.
The bodhisattva's elephant of his great powers
is possessed of the mind that is well trained.

The bodhisattva's horse of travel by spiritual powers
leaps up and steps beyond all realms of existence.
The bodhisattvas Dharma-proclaiming dragon
everywhere rains Dharma into the minds of beings.

The bodhisattva, like the *udumbara* flower,
is only rarely ever encountered in the world.

正體字	315a29	菩薩大勇將	眾魔悉[2]降伏
	315b01	菩薩轉法輪	如佛之所轉
	315b02	菩薩燈破闇	眾生見正道
	315b03	菩薩功德河	恒順正道流
	315b04	菩薩精進橋	廣度諸群品
	315b05	大智與弘誓	共作堅牢船
	315b06	引接諸眾生	安置菩提岸
	315b07	菩薩遊戲園	真實樂眾生
	315b08	菩薩解脫華	莊嚴智宮殿
	315b09	菩薩如妙藥	滅除煩惱病
	315b10	菩薩如雪山	出生智慧藥
	315b11	菩薩等於佛	覺悟諸群生
	315b12	佛心豈有他	正覺覺世間
	315b13	如佛之所來	菩薩如是來
	315b14	亦如一切智	以智入普門
	315b15	菩薩善開導	一切諸群生
	315b16	菩薩自然覺	一切智境界
	315b17	菩薩無量力	世間莫能壞
	315b18	菩薩無畏智	知眾生及法
	315b19	一切諸世間	色相各差別
简体字	菩萨大勇将，众魔悉降伏； 菩萨转法轮，如佛之所转； 菩萨灯破暗，众生见正道； 菩萨功德河，恒顺正道流； 菩萨精进桥，广度诸群品。 大智与弘誓，共作坚牢船， 引接诸众生，安置菩提岸。 菩萨游戏园，真实乐众生； 菩萨解脱华，庄严智宫殿； 菩萨如妙药，灭除烦恼病； 菩萨如雪山，出生智慧药。 菩萨等于佛，觉悟诸群生， 佛心岂有他，正觉觉世间。 如佛之所来，菩萨如是来； 亦如一切智，以智入普门。 菩萨善开导，一切诸群生； 菩萨自然觉，一切智境界。 菩萨无量力，世间莫能坏； 菩萨无畏智，知众生及法。 一切诸世间，色相各差别，		

Chapter 38 — Transcending the World

The bodhisattva, like the greatly courageous general,
conquers all the many *māras*.

The bodhisattva's turning of the wheel of the Dharma
is like that turned by the Buddha.
The bodhisattva's lamp dispels the darkness
so that beings then see the right path.

The bodhisattva's river of meritorious qualities
constantly follows the flow of the right path.
The bodhisattva's bridge of vigor
extensively takes across to liberation all the many kinds of beings.

His great wisdom and vast vows
together create a solid and durable ship
into which he welcomes all beings
before he then places them securely on the shore of bodhi.

In the bodhisattva's gardens of easeful mastery,
he provides beings with genuine bliss.
The bodhisattva's flowers of liberation
adorn his temple of wisdom.

The bodhisattva is like a marvelous herbal medicine
that utterly extinguishes the illness of the afflictions.
The bodhisattva is like a snowy mountain
on which there grows the herbal medicine of wisdom.

The bodhisattva is the same as the Buddha
in his awakening of the many kinds of beings.
How could there be anything else in the mind of the Buddha
other than right enlightenment and the enlightenment of the world?

Just as the Buddha has come forth,
so too does the bodhisattva come forth.
So too, like the Omniscient One,
he uses wisdom to enter the universal gateway.

The bodhisattva skillfully guides
all the many kinds of beings.
The bodhisattva naturally awakens
to the sphere of cognition of all-knowledge.

The bodhisattva's measureless powers
are such that no one in the world can destroy them.
With his fearlessnesses and wisdom, the bodhisattva
knows beings as well as dharmas.

All of the worlds,
the differences in their forms and characteristics,

正體字	315b20	音聲及名字	悉能分別知
	315b21	雖離於名色	而現種種相
	315b22	一切諸眾生	莫能測其道
	315b23	如是等功德	菩薩悉成就
	315b24	了性皆無性	有無無所著
	315b25	如是一切智	無盡無所依
	315b26	我今當演說	令眾生歡喜
	315b27	雖知諸法相	如幻悉空寂
	315b28	而以悲願心	及佛威神力
	315b29	現神通變化	種種無量事
	315c01	如是諸功德	汝等應聽受
	315c02	一身能示現	無量差別身
	315c03	無心無境界	普應一切眾
	315c04	一音中具演	一切諸言音
	315c05	眾生語言法	隨類皆能作
	315c06	永離煩惱身	而現自在身
	315c07	知法不可說	而作種種說
	315c08	其心常寂滅	清淨如虛空
	315c09	而普莊嚴剎	示現一切眾
	315c10	於身無所著	而能示現身

简体字

音声及名字，悉能分别知。
虽离于名色，而现种种相；
一切诸众生，莫能测其道。
如是等功德，菩萨悉成就，
了性皆无性，有无无所著。
如是一切智，无尽无所依，
我今当演说，令众生欢喜。
虽知诸法相，如幻悉空寂，
而以悲愿心，及佛威神力，
现神通变化，种种无量事；
如是诸功德，汝等应听受。
一身能示现，无量差别身，
无心无境界，普应一切众。
一音中具演，一切诸言音；
众生语言法，随类皆能作。
永离烦恼身，而现自在身，
知法不可说，而作种种说。
其心常寂灭，清净如虚空，
而普庄严刹，示现一切众。
于身无所著，而能示现身；

Chapter 38 — *Transcending the World*

their languages, and also their names—
He is able to distinguish and know them all.

Although he has transcended both name and form,
he still manifests the many different kinds of appearances.
Of all the beings there are,
there are none who are able to fathom his path.

All such meritorious qualities as these—
the bodhisattva perfects them all.
He understands all natures as having no [inherently existent] nature
and has no attachment to either existence or nonexistence.

In this way, all-knowledge
is endless and free of anything on which it depends.
I shall now expound on this
to enable beings to rejoice.

Although he knows all the characteristic marks of dharmas
as like mere conjured illusions that are all empty and quiescent,
he still uses the resolve of his compassionate vows
as well as the Buddha's awesome spiritual powers,

manifesting transformations with his spiritual superknowledges
by which he brings forth countless phenomena of all different sorts.
You should all listen
as I speak of meritorious qualities such as these.

With a single body, he is able to manifest
countless different bodies as,
without mind or object,
he everywhere responds to all beings.

With but a single sound, he completely expounds
in all different kinds of voices
with the methods of beings' speech,
so that, as befits their type, he is able to interact with them all.

He forever transcends the body affected by the afflictions
and instead manifests bodies possessed of sovereign mastery.
Though he realizes that dharmas are beyond explanation,
he still engages in all kinds of different explanations.

His mind is always quiescent,
pure, and like empty space,
and yet he everywhere adorns *kṣetras*
and appears in all congregations.

He has no attachment to the body,
and yet he is able to manifest bodies.

正體字	315c11 ‖	一切世間中	隨應而受生
	315c12 ‖	雖生一切處	亦不住受生
	315c13 ‖	知身如虛空	種種隨心現
	315c14 ‖	菩薩身無邊	普現一切處
	315c15 ‖	常恭敬供養	最勝兩足尊
	315c16 ‖	香華眾[3]妓樂	幢幡及寶蓋
	315c17 ‖	恒以深淨心	供養於諸佛
	315c18 ‖	不離一佛會	普在諸佛所
	315c19 ‖	於彼大眾中	問難聽受法
	315c20 ‖	聞法入三昧	一一無量門
	315c21 ‖	起定亦復然	示現無窮盡
	315c22 ‖	智慧巧方便	了世皆如幻
	315c23 ‖	而能現世間	無邊諸幻法
	315c24 ‖	示現種種色	亦現心及語
	315c25 ‖	入諸想網中	而恒無所著
	315c26 ‖	或現初發心	利益於世間
	315c27 ‖	或現久修行	廣大無邊際
	315c28 ‖	施戒忍精進	禪定及智慧
	315c29 ‖	四梵四攝等	一切最勝法
	316a01 ‖	或現行成滿	得忍無分別
简体字	一切世间中，随应而受生。 虽生一切处，亦不住受生， 知身如虚空，种种随心现。 菩萨身无边，普现一切处， 常恭敬供养，最胜两足尊。 香华众妓乐，幢幡及宝盖， 恒以深净心，供养于诸佛。 不离一佛会，普在诸佛所， 于彼大众中，问难听受法。 闻法入三昧，一一无量门， 起定亦复然，示现无穷尽。 智慧巧方便，了世皆如幻， 而能现世间，无边诸幻法。 示现种种色，亦现心及语， 入诸想网中，而恒无所著。 或现初发心，利益于世间； 或现久修行，广大无边际， 施戒忍精进，禅定及智慧， 四梵四摄等，一切最胜法。 或现行成满，得忍无分别；		

Within all the worlds,
he takes on births according to whatever is fitting.

Although he takes birth in all places,
he still does not abide in taking on births,
for he realizes the body is like empty space
as, according with beings' minds, he appears in various ways.

The body of the bodhisattva is boundless
and everywhere appears in all places.
He always reveres and makes offerings
to the most revered ones of all who stand on two feet.[175]

Whether it be incense, flowers, the many kinds of music,
banners, pennants or bejeweled canopies,
he constantly uses a deep and pure mind
in presenting offerings to all buddhas.

He never leaves the assembly of any single buddha,
and yet he is everywhere in the presence of all buddhas
where, in the midst of their great assemblies,
he inquires on difficult points and listens to the Dharma.

He listens to the Dharma and enters samādhi
through every one of its countless gateways.
So too it is when he arises from these meditative absorptions,
manifesting endless appearances.

With his wisdom and skillful means,
he completely understands the world as like a mere illusion
and yet is still able to manifest in the world
boundlessly many illusory dharmas.

He manifests in many different forms
while also manifesting thoughts and words.
He enters into the web of conceptions,
and yet remains forever free of attachments.

Sometimes he manifests as one making the initial resolve
or as one who benefits those in the world.
Sometimes he manifests as one who has long cultivated
practices that are boundlessly vast

of giving, moral virtue, patience, vigor,
dhyāna concentration, wisdom,
the four *brāhma-vihāras*, the four means of attraction, and the others
among all those most supreme of dharmas.

Sometimes he manifests as one whose practice has become fulfilled
and has attained the patience free of discriminations.

正體字	316a02 ‖	或現一生繫	諸佛與灌頂
	316a03 ‖	或現聲聞相	或復現緣覺
	316a04 ‖	處處般涅槃	不捨菩提行
	316a05 ‖	或現為帝釋	或現為梵王
	316a06 ‖	或天女圍遶	或時獨宴默
	316a07 ‖	或現為比丘	寂靜調其心
	316a08 ‖	或現自在王	統理世間法
	316a09 ‖	或現巧術女	或現修[1]苦行
	316a10 ‖	或現受五欲	或現入諸禪
	316a11 ‖	或現初始生	或少或老死
	316a12 ‖	若有思議者	心疑發狂亂
	316a13 ‖	或現在天宮	或現始降神
	316a14 ‖	或入或住胎	或佛轉法輪
	316a15 ‖	或生或涅槃	或現入學堂
	316a16 ‖	或在[2]采女中	或離俗修禪
	316a17 ‖	或坐菩提樹	自然成正覺
	316a18 ‖	或現轉法輪	或現始求道
	316a19 ‖	或現為佛身	宴坐無量剎
	316a20 ‖	或修不退道	積集菩提具
	316a21 ‖	深入無數劫	皆悉到彼岸
简体字		或现一生系，诸佛与灌顶。 或现声闻相，或复现缘觉， 处处般涅槃，不舍菩提行。 或现为帝释，或现为梵王， 或天女围绕，或时独宴默。 或现为比丘，寂静调其心； 或现自在王，统理世间法。 或现巧术女，或现修苦行， 或现受五欲，或现入诸禅。 或现初始生，或少或老死。 若有思议者，心疑发狂乱。 或现在天宫，或现始降神， 或入或住胎，或佛转法轮。 或生或涅槃，或现入学堂， 或在婇女中，或离俗修禅。 或坐菩提树，自然成正觉； 或现转法轮，或现始求道。 或现为佛身，宴坐无量刹； 或修不退道，积集菩提具。 深入无数劫，皆悉到彼岸；		

Sometimes he manifests as one tied to but one more birth
upon whom all buddhas bestow the crown-anointing consecration.

Sometimes he manifests as bearing the marks of a *śrāvaka* disciple,
or instead manifests as a *pratyekabuddha*,
or as, in place after place, entering *parinirvāṇa*,
even as he still never relinquishes the bodhi practices.

Sometimes he manifests as Lord Śakra,
sometimes manifests as a Brahma Heaven king,
sometimes as surrounded by celestial maidens,
and sometimes as alone in silent meditation.

Sometimes he manifests as a *bhikṣu*,
abiding in quiescence, training his own mind.
Sometimes he manifests as a Paranirmita Vaśavartin Heaven king
who governs over the laws of the world.

Sometimes he manifests as a woman skilled in the arts,
sometimes manifests as one who cultivates austere practices,
sometimes manifests as indulging the five types of desire,
and sometimes manifests as entering the *dhyāna* absorptions.

Sometimes he manifests as one but newly born,
sometimes as a youth, or sometimes as one who is old or dying.
Were someone to try to contemplate and conceive of these matters,
his mind might become so plagued by doubts as to be driven mad.

Sometimes he manifests as abiding in a celestial palace,
sometimes manifests as having just spiritually descended from there,
sometimes as entering and sometimes as abiding in the womb, and
sometimes as attaining buddhahood and turning the Dharma wheel.

Sometimes it is as being born, sometimes as entering nirvāṇa,
and sometimes he manifests as entering the halls of study.
Sometimes it is as abiding in the midst of courtesans and
sometimes it is as leaving a common man's life to cultivate *dhyāna*.

Sometimes it is as sitting beneath the bodhi tree,
and then naturally gaining right enlightenment.
Sometimes he manifests as turning the wheel of the Dharma
and sometimes he manifests as having just begun to seek the path.

Sometimes he manifests in the body of a buddha,
calmly sitting in meditation in countless *kṣetras*.
Sometimes it is as cultivating irreversibility in the path,
accumulating the provisions essential to realizing bodhi,

or as deeply entering innumerable kalpas in which,
in every case, he reaches the far shore of perfection,

正體字	316a22 ‖	無量劫一念	一念無量劫
	316a23 ‖	一切劫非劫	為世示現劫
	316a24 ‖	無來無積集	成就諸劫事
	316a25 ‖	於一微塵中	普見一切佛
	316a26 ‖	十方一切處	無處而不有
	316a27 ‖	國土眾生法	次第悉皆見
	316a28 ‖	經無量劫數	究竟不可盡
	316a29 ‖	菩薩知眾生	廣大無有邊
	316b01 ‖	彼一眾生身	無量因緣起
	316b02 ‖	如知一無量	一切悉亦然
	316b03 ‖	隨其所通達	教諸未學者
	316b04 ‖	悉知眾生根	上中下不同
	316b05 ‖	亦知根轉移	應化不應化
	316b06 ‖	一根一切根	展轉因緣力
	316b07 ‖	微細各差別	次第無錯亂
	316b08 ‖	又知其欲解	一切煩惱習
	316b09 ‖	亦知去來今	所有諸心行
	316b10 ‖	了達一切行	無來亦無去
	316b11 ‖	既知其行已	為說無上法
	316b12 ‖	雜染清淨行	種種悉了知
简体字	无量劫一念，一念无量劫。 一切劫非劫，为世示现劫， 无来无积集，成就诸劫事。 于一微尘中，普见一切佛； 十方一切处，无处而不有。 国土众生法，次第悉皆见； 经无量劫数，究竟不可尽。 菩萨知众生，广大无有边； 彼一众生身，无量因缘起。 如知一无量，一切悉亦然； 随其所通达，教诸未学者。 悉知众生根，上中下不同； 亦知根转移，应化不应化； 一根一切根，展转因缘力， 微细各差别，次第无错乱。 又知其欲解，一切烦恼习； 亦知去来今，所有诸心行。 了达一切行，无来亦无去； 既知其行已，为说无上法。 杂染清净行，种种悉了知，		

making countless kalpas become but a single mind-moment,
and making a single mind-moment include countless kalpas,

realizing all kalpas as but non-kalpas even as,
for the sake of the world, he manifests kalpas, and even as,
though he has no coming forth and has no such accumulation,
he accomplishes all his works in all those kalpas.

In but a single atom,
he everywhere sees all buddhas
and sees that, throughout the ten directions, and in all places,
there is no place where they do not exist.

He perceives in a sequentially orderly fashion
all dharmas associated with the lands and their beings
and their passing through a measureless number of kalpas,
the bounds of which, one could ultimately never exhaust.

The bodhisattva's knowing of beings
is so vast as to be boundless.
Even but a single one of those beings' bodies
arises due to countless causes and conditions.

Just as he knows these countless factors for any single one of them,
so too is this true of all others as well.
As befits whatever his penetrating comprehension has understood,
he proceeds then to teach all those who have not yet been trained.

He knows the faculties of all beings,
the differences in those who are superior, middling, and inferior,
and also knows how such faculties transform and develop,
and whether they should or should not then be taught.

Whether it be but a single faculty or all faculties,
or how they evolve through the power of causes and conditions,
he distinguishes the different subtleties involved in these
in a sequentially precise way free of error or disorder.

He also knows their desires and understandings,
all their afflictions and habitual karmic propensities,
and also knows with respect to their past, future, and present,
the course of all their thoughts and actions.

He completely comprehends all their actions
and that they neither come nor go.
Having thus known their actions,
he then explains for them the unexcelled Dharma.
As for their defiled actions and their pure actions,
he completely knows them all in all their many different varieties.

正體字	316b13 ‖	一念得菩提	成就一切智
	316b14 ‖	住佛不思議	究竟智慧心
	316b15 ‖	一念悉能知	一切眾生行
	316b16 ‖	菩薩神通智	功力已自在
	316b17 ‖	能於一念中	往詣無邊剎
	316b18 ‖	如是速疾往	盡於無數劫
	316b19 ‖	無處而不周	莫動毫端分
	316b20 ‖	譬如工幻師	示現種種色
	316b21 ‖	於彼幻中求	無色無非色
	316b22 ‖	菩薩亦如是	以方便智幻
	316b23 ‖	種種皆示現	充滿於世間
	316b24 ‖	譬如淨日月	皎鏡在虛空
	316b25 ‖	影現於眾水	不為水所雜
	316b26 ‖	菩薩淨法輪	當知亦如是
	316b27 ‖	現世間心水	不為世所雜
	316b28 ‖	如人睡夢中	造作種種事
	316b29 ‖	雖經億千歲	一夜未終盡
	316c01 ‖	菩薩住法性	示現一切事
	316c02 ‖	無量劫可極	一念智無盡
	316c03 ‖	譬如山谷中	及以宮殿[3]間

简体字

一念得菩提，成就一切智。
住佛不思议，究竟智慧心，
一念悉能知，一切众生行。
菩萨神通智，功力已自在，
能于一念中，往诣无边刹。
如是速疾往，尽于无数劫，
无处而不周，莫动毫端分。
譬如工幻师，示现种种色，
于彼幻中求，无色无非色。
菩萨亦如是，以方便智幻，
种种皆示现，充满于世间。
譬如净日月，皎镜在虚空，
影现于众水，不为水所杂。
菩萨净法轮，当知亦如是，
现世间心水，不为世所杂。
如人睡梦中，造作种种事，
虽经亿千岁，一夜未终尽。
菩萨住法性，示现一切事，
无量劫可极，一念智无尽。
譬如山谷中，及以宫殿间，

Chapter 38 — *Transcending the World*

In but a single mind-moment, he attains bodhi
and achieves the perfection of all-knowledge.
He abides in the Buddha's inconceivable
mind of ultimate wisdom in which,
in but a single mind-moment, he is able to know
all the actions in which beings engage.

The bodhisattva's spiritual superknowledges, wisdom, and
power of skill in these has already attained such sovereign mastery
that he is able in but a single mind-moment
to travel and visit boundlessly many *kṣetras*.

He goes forth with such swiftness as this
throughout countless kalpas
in which there is no place he has not thus been everywhere present
even as, in all of this, he never moves even as far as the tip of a hair.

Just as in a case where a master conjurer
manifests all kinds of different forms,
if one searches in the midst of those illusions,
there would be nothing there that either has form or is formless,

so too it is with the bodhisattva when,
using the conjurations of skillful means and wisdom,
he produces all different kinds of manifestations
which completely fill the world.

Just as when the clearly shining sun and moon
beaming brightly in the midst of space
are reflected in the many bodies of water
and yet never become mixed with those waters,

one should realize that this is also just so
in the case of the bodhisattva's sphere of pure Dharma
when it appears in the waters of worldlings' minds
and yet never becomes mixed up with the world.

Just as, in a sleeping person's dream,
he may accomplish many different endeavors in which,
though he seems to have passed through thousands of *koṭīs* of years,
he has not yet even reached the end of that one single night,

so too, the bodhisattva, abiding in the nature of dharmas,
manifests all kinds of phenomena
that could stretch to the end of countless kalpas
even as his single mind-moment of wisdom is endless.

Just as in a mountain valley
or within a palace

正體字	316c04 ‖	種種皆響應	而實無分別
	316c05 ‖	菩薩住法性	能以自在智
	316c06 ‖	廣出隨類音	亦復無分別
	316c07 ‖	如有見陽焰	[4]想之以為水
	316c08 ‖	馳逐不得飲	展轉更增渴
	316c09 ‖	眾生煩惱心	應知亦如是
	316c10 ‖	菩薩起慈愍	救之令出離
	316c11 ‖	觀色如聚沫	受如水上泡
	316c12 ‖	想如熱時焰	諸行如芭蕉
	316c13 ‖	心識猶如幻	示現種種事
	316c14 ‖	如是知諸蘊	智者無所著
	316c15 ‖	諸處悉空寂	如機關動轉
	316c16 ‖	諸界性永離	妄現於世間
	316c17 ‖	菩薩住真實	寂滅第一義
	316c18 ‖	種種廣宣暢	而心無所依
	316c19 ‖	無來亦無去	亦復無有住
	316c20 ‖	煩惱業苦因	三種恒流轉
	316c21 ‖	緣起非有無	非實亦非虛
	316c22 ‖	如是入中道	說之無所[5]著
	316c23 ‖	能於一念中	普現三世心
简体字	种种皆响应，而实无分别。 菩萨住法性，能以自在智， 广出随类音，亦复无分别。 如有见阳焰，想之以为水， 驰逐不得饮，展转更增渴。 众生烦恼心，应知亦如是； 菩萨起慈愍，救之令出离。 观色如聚沫，受如水上泡， 想如热时焰，诸行如芭蕉。 心识犹如幻，示现种种事； 如是知诸蕴，智者无所著。 诸处悉空寂，如机关动转； 诸界性永离，妄现于世间。 菩萨住真实，寂灭第一义， 种种广宣畅，而心无所依。 无来亦无去，亦复无有住， 烦恼业苦因，三种恒流转。 缘起非有无，非实亦非虚， 如是入中道，说之无所著。 能于一念中，普现三世心，		

Chapter 38 — *Transcending the World*

many different sounds are all echoed
when, in truth, they do not distinguish among them,

so too, the bodhisattva abiding in the nature of dharmas
is able with masterful wisdom
to extensively emanate sounds according to each person's type
even as he is still free of any discriminations about them.

Just as, if one sees a mirage,
he may imagine it to be water
and race off after it, only to never find anything to drink,
so that, as a consequence, he becomes ever more thirsty,

so too it is with beings' affliction-ridden minds.
One should realize they are also just like this.
The bodhisattva arouses kindness and sympathy
to rescue them and enable them to make their escape.

He contemplates "form" as like a mass of sea foam,
"feelings" as like bubbles floating atop the water,
"perceptions" as like heat-wave mirages in the hot season,
"karmic formative factors" as like the stalk of the plantain,[176]

and the mind's "consciousnesses" as like conjured illusions
manifesting the many different kinds of phenomena.
Just so does he know the aggregates
for which the wise one has no attachment.

All the sense bases[177] are empty, quiescent, and
like a mechanism as they move and turn about.
All the sense realms[178] are forever free of any nature
even as they present a false appearance in the world.

The bodhisattva abides in the genuine
quiescence of the ultimate truth,
extensively and freely proclaiming it in many different ways,
and yet his mind remains free of anything upon which it depends.

He has neither any coming nor any going
and also has no abiding either.
The causes of suffering in the karma of the afflictions
constantly flow on and transform in three different ways.[179]

Conditioned origination is neither existent nor nonexistent,
and neither real nor insubstantial.
It is in this way that he enters the middle way.
In explaining it, he remains free of any attachment at all.

He is able in but a single mind-moment
to everywhere manifest the mind of the three periods of time

	316c24 ‖	欲色無色界　　一切種種事
	316c25 ‖	隨順三律儀　　演說三解脫
	316c26 ‖	建立三乘道　　成就一切智
	316c27 ‖	了達處非處　　諸業及諸根
	316c28 ‖	界解與禪定　　一切至處道
	316c29 ‖	宿命念天眼　　滅除一切惑
	317a01 ‖	知佛十種力　　而未能成就
	317a02 ‖	了達諸法空　　而常求妙法
正體字	317a03 ‖	不與煩惱合　　而亦不盡漏
	317a04 ‖	廣知出離道　　而以度眾生
	317a05 ‖	於此得無畏　　不捨修諸行
	317a06 ‖	無謬無違道　　亦不失正念
	317a07 ‖	精進欲三昧　　觀慧無損減
	317a08 ‖	三聚皆清淨　　三世悉明達
	317a09 ‖	大慈愍眾生　　一切無障礙
	317a10 ‖	由入此法門　　得成如是行
	317a11 ‖	我說[1]其少分　　　功德莊嚴義
	317a12 ‖	窮於無數劫　　說彼行無盡
	317a13 ‖	我今說少分　　如大地一塵
	317a14 ‖	依於佛智住　　起於奇特[2]想

简体字	欲色无色界，一切种种事。 随顺三律仪，演说三解脱， 建立三乘道，成就一切智。 了达处非处，诸业及诸根， 界解与禅定，一切至处道。 宿命念天眼，灭除一切惑， 知佛十种力，而未能成就。 了达诸法空，而常求妙法， 不与烦恼合，而亦不尽漏。 广知出离道，而以度众生， 于此得无畏，不舍修诸行。 无谬无违道，亦不失正念， 精进欲三昧，观慧无损减。 三聚皆清净，三世悉明达， 大慈愍众生，一切无障碍。 由入此法门，得成如是行， 我说其少分，功德庄严义。 穷于无数劫，说彼行无尽， 我今说少分，如大地一尘。 依于佛智住，起于奇特想，

Chapter 38 — *Transcending the World*

in all the many different kinds of phenomena
within the desire realm, the form realm, and the formless realm.

He accords with the three types of moral deportment,[180]
expounds on the three gates to liberation,[181]
establishes the paths of the Three Vehicles,[182]
and achieves the complete realization of all-knowledge.

He attains the complete comprehension of what is and is not possible,
of all karmic actions, of all faculties,
of the realms, understandings, and dhyāna concentrations,
of the points to which all paths lead,

of past life recall, of the heavenly eye,
and of the complete extinguishing of all delusions.
He knows the Buddha's ten powers,
but is not yet able to bring them to complete fulfillment.

He completely comprehends the emptiness of all dharmas,
and yet he always seeks the sublime Dharma.
He does not become involved with the afflictions,
and yet he still does not completely put an end to the contaminants.

He possesses a vast knowledge of the paths to emancipation,
and yet he uses them to liberate beings.
In this, he has attained the fearlessnesses
and still never relinquishes his cultivation of all the practices.

He remains free of error and free of any contradiction of the path,
and still never loses right mindfulness.
His vigor, zeal, and samādhi
as well as his wisdom arising from contemplation never diminish.[183]

He remains pure in all three accumulations of moral virtue,[184]
has a clear comprehension of all three periods of time,
treats beings with great kindness and sympathetic pity,
and, in all that he does, remains free of all obstacles.

It is due to having entered these gateways into the Dharma
that he has succeeded in perfecting practices such as these.
I describe here but a minor measure
of the meaning of his adornments with such meritorious qualities.

Even if one exhausted countless kalpas in trying to do so,
one could still never finish describing all his practices.
I now only describe but a small portion of them
comparable to a single mote of dust as contrasted with the great earth.

Abiding in reliance upon the Buddha's wisdom,
he brings forth extraordinary thought,

正體字	317a15 317a16 317a17 317a18 317a19 317a20 317a21 317a22 317a23 317a24 317a25 317a26 317a27 317a28 317a29 317b01 317b02 317b03 317b04 317b05	修行最勝行　　具足大慈悲 精勤自安[3]隱　教化諸含識 安住淨戒中　　具諸授記行 能入佛功德　　眾生行及剎 劫世悉亦知　　無有疲厭想 差別智總持　　通達真實義 思惟說無比　　寂靜等正覺 發於普賢心　　及修其行願 慈悲因緣力　　趣道意清淨 修行波羅蜜　　究竟隨覺智 證知力自在　　成無上菩提 成就平等智　　演說最勝法 能持具妙辯　　逮得法王處 遠離於諸著　　演說心平等 出生於智慧　　變化得菩提 住持一切劫　　智者大欣慰 深入及依止　　無畏無疑惑 了達不思議　　巧密善分別 善入諸三昧　　普見智境界 究竟諸解脫　　遊戲諸通明
简体字		修行最胜行，具足大慈悲。 精勤自安隐，教化诸含识， 安住净戒中，具诸授记行。 能入佛功德，众生行及刹， 劫世悉亦知，无有疲厌想。 差别智总持，通达真实义， 思惟说无比，寂静等正觉。 发于普贤心，及修其行愿， 慈悲因缘力，趣道意清净。 修行波罗蜜，究竟随觉智， 证知力自在，成无上菩提。 成就平等智，演说最胜法， 能持具妙辩，逮得法王处。 远离于诸著，演说心平等， 出生于智慧，变化得菩提。 住持一切劫，智者大欣慰， 深入及依止，无畏无疑惑。 了达不思议，巧密善分别， 善入诸三昧，普见智境界。 究竟诸解脱，游戏诸通明，

cultivates the most supreme practices,
and achieves complete fulfillment of great kindness and compassion.

Intensely diligent, yet personally abiding in tranquility,
he carries on the teaching of all sentient beings.
Having established himself in the pure precepts of moral virtue,
he fulfills all the practices leading to the bestowal of the prediction.[185]

He is able to penetrate the meritorious qualities of the Buddha,
the practices related to beings, and the *kṣetras*.
He also knows all the kalpas and periods of time,[186]
and yet never has any thoughts of weariness.

With differentiating wisdom and the complete-retention *dhāraṇīs*,
he reaches a penetrating comprehension of the true meaning.
He contemplates and expounds upon the incomparable,
and quiescently proceeds toward the right and perfect enlightenment.

He has brought forth the resolve of Samantabhadra
and also cultivates his conduct and vows.
By the power of kindness and compassion's causes and conditions,
he proceeds along the path with purity of mind.

He cultivates the *pāramitās*
and perfects the wisdom arising pursuant to awakening.
He achieves the realization of the powers and the sovereign masteries
and then attains the unexcelled bodhi.

He perfects the wisdom cognizing uniform equality
and expounds the most supreme Dharma.
He is able to preserve it and possesses sublime eloquence
and then arrives at the position of the king of the Dharma.

He abandons all attachments
and expounds on impartiality of mind.
Bringing forth his wisdom,
he transformationally manifests the realization of bodhi.

He preserves [the Dharma] in all kalpas
in ways that please and comfort the wise.
He deeply penetrates it, relies on it,
and becomes fearless and free of doubts.

He completely comprehends the inconceivable,
ably distinguishes the expedient and esoteric,
skillfully enters all the samādhis,
and everywhere perceives the spheres of wisdom.

He completely attains all the liberations,
achieves easeful mastery in the superknowledges,

正體字	317b06　　纏縛悉永離　　園林恣遊處 317b07　　白法為宮殿　　諸行可欣樂 317b08　　現無量莊嚴　　於世心無動 317b09　　深心善觀察　　妙辯能開演 317b10　　清淨菩提印　　智光照一切 317b11　　所住無等比　　其心不下劣 317b12　　立志如大山　　種德若深海 317b13　　如寶安住法　　被甲誓願心 317b14　　發起於大事　　究竟無能壞 317b15　　得授菩提記　　安住廣大心 317b16　　祕藏無窮盡　　覺悟一切法 317b17　　世智皆自在　　妙用無障礙 317b18　　眾生一切剎　　及以種種法 317b19　　身願與境界　　智慧神通等 317b20　　示現於世間　　無量百千億 317b21　　遊戲及境界　　自在無能制 317b22　　力無畏不共　　一切業莊嚴 317b23　　諸身及身業　　語及淨修語 317b24　　以得守護故　　成[4]辨十種事 317b25　　菩薩心[5]初發　　及以心周遍
简体字	缠缚悉永离，园林恣游处。 白法为宫殿，诸行可欣乐， 现无量庄严，于世心无动。 深心善观察，妙辩能开演， 清净菩提印，智光照一切。 所住无等比，其心不下劣， 立志如大山，种德若深海。 如宝安住法，被甲誓愿心， 发起于大事，究竟无能坏。 得授菩提记，安住广大心， 秘藏无穷尽，觉悟一切法。 世智皆自在，妙用无障碍， 众生一切刹，及以种种法。 身愿与境界，智慧神通等， 示现于世间，无量百千亿。 游戏及境界，自在无能制， 力无畏不共，一切业庄严。 诸身及身业，语及净修语， 以得守护故，成办十种事。 菩萨心发心，及以心周遍，

Chapter 38 — *Transcending the World*

forever abandons all of the entangling bonds,
and, in this, is as if roaming at will, abiding in parks and groves.

The dharmas of purity serve as his palace
and he finds all the practices to be delightful.
He manifests measureless adornments
and abides in the world with an unmoving mind.

With the deep mind, he skillfully contemplates,
and with marvelous eloquence, he is able to expound the Dharma.
He acquires the seal of pure bodhi
and illuminates everything with the light of wisdom.

The place where he dwells is one that no one can equal.
His mind does not involve itself with anything inferior.
He establishes resolve as [solid as] a great mountain
and the meritorious qualities he possesses are like a deep ocean.

He abides in the Dharma like a jewel,
dons the armor of the resolve of his vows,
and initiates all the great works
which can never be ruined by anyone.

He acquires the prediction of his realization of bodhi
and securely dwells in his vast resolve.
His treasury of esoteric knowledge is inexhaustible
and he becomes awakened in all the dharmas.

He attains sovereign mastery of all worldly knowledge
and is unimpeded in the sublime uses to which he applies it,
whether it be among beings, in all the *kṣetras*,
or in the sphere of the many different dharmas.

Through his bodies, vows, spheres of action,
wisdom, spiritual superknowledges, and such,
he brings forth manifestations within the world
numbering in countless hundreds of thousands of *koṭīs*.

Whether in his easeful mastery or in his spheres of action,
he possesses sovereign mastery which none can constrain.
All of his karmic actions are adorned
with the powers, the fearlessnesses, and the exclusive dharmas.[187]

In all his bodies and physical actions
and in his speaking as well as in his purified speech,
through having become one who is protected,
he succeeds in accomplishing ten kinds of things.[188]

In the bodhisattva's initial generation of the resolve
as well as in his mind's universally pervasive presence,

	317b26	諸根無散動	獲得最勝根
	317b27	深心增勝心	遠離於諂誑
	317b28	種種決定解	普入於世間
	317b29	捨彼煩惱習	取茲最勝道
	317c01	巧修使圓滿	逮成一切智
	317c02	離退入正位	決定證寂滅
	317c03	出生佛法道	成就功德號
	317c04	道及無量道	乃至莊嚴道
正體字	317c05	次第善安住	悉皆無所著
	317c06	手足及腹藏	金剛以為心
	317c07	被以慈哀[6]甲	具足眾器仗
	317c08	智首明達眼	菩提行為耳
	317c09	清淨戒為鼻	滅闇無障礙
	317c10	辯才以為舌	無處不至身
	317c11	最勝智為心	行住修諸業
	317c12	道場師子坐	梵臥空為住
	317c13	所行及觀察	普照如來境
	317c14	遍觀眾生行	奮迅及哮吼
	317c15	離[7]貪行淨施	捨慢持淨戒
	317c16	不瞋常忍辱	不懈恒精進

简体字	诸根无散动，获得最胜根。 深心增胜心，远离于谄诳； 种种决定解，普入于世间。 舍彼烦恼习，取兹最胜道， 巧修使圆满，逮成一切智。 离退入正位，决定证寂灭， 出生佛法道，成就功德号。 道及无量道，乃至庄严道， 次第善安住，悉皆无所著。 手足及腹藏，金刚以为心， 被以慈哀甲，具足众器仗。 智首明达眼，菩提行为耳， 清净戒为鼻，灭暗无障碍。 辩才以为舌，无处不至身； 最胜智为心，行住修诸业。 道场师子座，梵卧空为住， 所行及观察，普照如来境。 遍观众生行，奋迅及哮吼， 离贪行净施，舍慢持净戒， 不瞋常忍辱，不懈恒精进，

Chapter 38 — *Transcending the World*

all of his faculties become undistracted
and he thus acquires the most supreme faculties.

Abiding in the deep mind and the especially superior mind,
he abandons all flattery and deception
and, through all different kinds of decisive understanding,
he everywhere enters the worlds.

He relinquishes his afflictions and habitual karmic propensities,
takes up this most supreme of paths,
skillfully cultivates it and brings it to complete fulfillment,
and then arrives at the realization of all-knowledge.

He goes beyond reversibility, enters the right and fixed position,[189]
achieves the definite realization of quiescence,
brings forth the path of the Buddha's Dharma, and
perfects the bases for the names of those with meritorious qualities.[190]

The path, the path of the immeasurable,
and so forth, on through to the path of adornment—
He successively becomes well established in each of them,
yet remains free of attachment to any of them.

His hands, feet, belly, and organs,
his heart made of vajra—
He cloaks them in the armor of kindness and deep sympathy
and thus becomes completely protected with the many weapons.

Wisdom serves as his head, clear comprehension as his eyes,
the bodhi practices as his ears,
and purity in the moral precepts as his nose.
Thus he dispels the darkness and remains free of obstacles.

He takes the types of eloquence as his tongue,
his ability to have no place he does not go as his body,
and the most supreme wisdom as his mind.
Walking and standing, he cultivates his actions.
He sits on the lion throne at the site of enlightenment,
lies down as in the Brahma heavens, and stands in emptiness.

In whatever he practices and contemplates,
he everywhere illuminates the Tathāgata's sphere of action.
He everywhere contemplates the actions of beings,
enters the lion-stretch [samādhi], and roars the lion's roar.

He abandons covetousness, practices pure giving,
relinquishes arrogance, and upholds purity in the moral precepts.
He does not become angry, always abides in patience,
does not become indolent, and is constantly vigorous.

	317c17 ‖	禪定得自在	智慧無所行
	317c18 ‖	慈濟悲無倦	喜法捨煩惱
	317c19 ‖	於諸境界中	知義亦知法
	317c20 ‖	福德悉成滿	智慧如利劍
	317c21 ‖	普照樂多聞	明了趣向法
	317c22 ‖	知魔及魔道	誓願咸捨離
	317c23 ‖	見佛與佛業	發心皆攝取
	317c24 ‖	離慢修智慧	不為魔力持
正體字	317c25 ‖	為佛所攝持	亦為法所持
	317c26 ‖	現住兜率天	又現彼命終
	317c27 ‖	示現住母胎	亦現微細趣
	317c28 ‖	現生及微笑	亦現行七步
	317c29 ‖	示修眾技術	亦示處深宮
	318a01 ‖	出家修苦行	往詣於道場
	318a02 ‖	端坐放光明	覺悟諸群生
	318a03 ‖	降魔成正覺	轉無上法輪
	318a04 ‖	所現悉已終	入於大涅槃
	318a05 ‖	彼諸菩薩行	無量劫修習
	318a06 ‖	廣大無有邊	我今說少分
	318a07 ‖	雖令無量眾	安住佛功德

简体字

禅定得自在，智慧无所行，
慈济悲无倦，喜法舍烦恼；
于诸境界中，知义亦知法。
福德悉成满，智慧如利剑，
普照乐多闻，明了趣向法。
知魔及魔道，誓愿咸舍离；
见佛与佛业，发心皆摄取，
离慢修智慧，不为魔力持；
为佛所摄持，亦为法所持。
现住兜率天，又现彼命终；
示现住母胎，亦现微细趣。
现生及微笑，亦现行七步；
示修众技术，亦示处深宫。
出家修苦行，往诣于道场，
端坐放光明，觉悟诸群生，
降魔成正觉，转无上法轮，
所现悉已终，入于大涅槃。
彼诸菩萨行，无量劫修习，
广大无有边，我今说少分。
虽令无量众，安住佛功德；

Chapter 38 — *Transcending the World*

He attains sovereign mastery in the *dhyāna* absorptions,
and, in his exercise of wisdom, has nothing at all that he practices.
With kindness he rescues beings and in compassion he is tireless.
He rejoices in the Dharma and with equanimity abandons afflictions.

In all spheres of experience,
he knows the meaning and he knows the Dharma.
His stock of merit has been brought to complete fulfillment
and his wisdom has become like sharp sword.

He everywhere casts his illumination, delights in extensive learning,
and progresses in the Dharma with complete understanding.
He is aware of the *māra*s and the paths of the *māra*s
and vows to leave them all behind.

He observes the Buddha as well as the works of the Buddha
and resolves to accumulate them all.
He abandons pride, cultivates wisdom,
and does not become possessed by the power of Māra.

He is drawn forth and supported by the Buddha
and is also supported by the Dharma.
He manifests as dwelling in the Tuṣita Heaven,
and then also appears to reach the end of his life there.

He then manifests as dwelling in his mother's womb
even as he also manifests subtle endeavors.
He manifests taking birth as well as the subtle smile,
and also appears as walking seven steps.

He manifests the cultivation of the many skills and arts
and also manifests as dwelling deep within the palace,
leaving the home life, cultivating the austerities,
and then going to the site of enlightenment.

There he sits up straight, emanating light,
and awakens the many kinds of beings.
He subdues the *māra*s, gains right enlightenment,
turns the wheel of the unexcelled Dharma,
and then when his manifestations have come to an end,
he then enters the great nirvāṇa.

As for all of those bodhisattva practices
which he cultivates for countless kalpas,
they are so boundlessly expansive,
that I now describe only a small fraction of them.

Although he enables countless beings
to become established in the Buddha's meritorious qualities,

正體字

318a08	眾生及法中 畢竟無所取
318a09	具足如是行 遊戲諸神通
318a10	毛端置眾剎 經於億千劫
318a11	掌持無量剎 遍往身無倦
318a12	還來置本處 眾生不知覺
318a13	菩薩以一切 種種莊嚴剎
318a14	置於一毛孔 真實悉令見
318a15	復以一毛孔 普[1]納一切海
318a16	大海無增減 眾生不嬈害
318a17	無量鐵圍山 手執碎為塵
318a18	一塵下一剎 盡此諸塵數
318a19	以此諸塵剎 復更末為塵
318a20	如是塵可知 菩薩智難量
318a21	於一毛孔中 放無量光明
318a22	日月星宿光 摩尼珠火光
318a23	及以諸天光 一切皆映蔽
318a24	滅諸惡道苦 為說無上法
318a25	一切諸世間 種種差別音
318a26	[2]菩薩以一音 一切皆能演
318a27	決定分別說 一切諸佛法

简体字

众生及法中，毕竟无所取。
具足如是行，游戏诸神通；
毛端置众刹，经于亿千劫；
掌持无量刹，遍往身无倦，
还来置本处，众生不知觉。
菩萨以一切，种种庄严刹，
置于一毛孔，真实悉令见。
复以一毛孔，普纳一切海，
大海无增减，众生不娆害。
无量铁围山，手执碎为尘，
一尘下一刹，尽此诸尘数。
以此诸尘刹，复更末为尘；
如是尘可知，菩萨智难量。
于一毛孔中，放无量光明；
日月星宿光，摩尼珠火光，
及以诸天光，一切皆映蔽，
灭诸恶道苦，为说无上法。
一切诸世间，种种差别音；
菩萨以一音，一切皆能演。
决定分别说，一切诸佛法，

Chapter 38 — *Transcending the World*

of those beings and those dharmas,
there is ultimately nothing on which he seizes.

He completely fulfills practices such as these,
gains such easeful mastery of all the spiritual superknowledges
that he can place the many *kṣetras* on the tip of a single hair
and pass through thousands of *koṭīs* of kalpas.

Holding countless *kṣetras* in his palm,
he travels everywhere, never feeling any physical weariness,
and then returns to place them in their original location,
as the beings in them remain unaware.

The bodhisattva may take all
the many different kinds of adorned *kṣetras*
and place them in a single pore
so that everyone can see them as they truly are.

He may also take all the oceans
and place them in but a single pore
without those great oceans either increasing or diminishing
and without those beings being either disturbed or harmed.

Suppose he took countless iron ring mountains,
grasped them in his hand, ground them to particles,
then set down but one of those particles in each *kṣetra*,
doing so until all those particles were used up.

Suppose too that he took all those *kṣetras* as many as those particles
and again ground them all into particles.
Though one might calculate the number of all those particles,
he would still find it difficult to measure this bodhisattva's wisdom.

He may emanate so countlessly many light rays
from within but a single pore
that the light of the sun, moon, stars, and constellations,
the blazing light of the *maṇi* jewels,

and the light of all the devas
are all completely outshone by that light
which extinguishes all the sufferings in the wretched destinies
as he then proclaims for them the unexcelled Dharma.

The many different kinds of voices
within all worlds—
with but a single voice, the bodhisattva
is able to speak them all.

He decisively distinguishes and explains
all dharmas of all buddhas,

正體字	318a28 ‖	普使諸群生	聞之大歡喜
	318a29 ‖	過去一切劫	安置未來今
	318b01 ‖	未來現在劫	迴置過去世
	318b02 ‖	示現無量剎	燒然及成住
	318b03 ‖	一切諸世間	悉在一毛孔
	318b04 ‖	[3]未來及現在	一切十方佛
	318b05 ‖	靡不於身中	分明而顯現
	318b06 ‖	深知變化法	善應眾生心
	318b07 ‖	示現種種身	而皆無所著
	318b08 ‖	或現於六趣	一切眾生身
	318b09 ‖	[4]梵釋護世身	諸天人眾身
	318b10 ‖	聲聞緣覺身	諸佛如來身
	318b11 ‖	或現菩薩身	修行一切智
	318b12 ‖	善入軟中上	眾生諸想[綱>網]
	318b13 ‖	示現成菩提	及以諸佛剎
	318b14 ‖	了知諸想網	於想得自在
	318b15 ‖	示修菩薩行	一切方便事
	318b16 ‖	示現如是等	廣大諸神變
	318b17 ‖	如是諸境界	舉世莫能知
	318b18 ‖	雖現無所現	究竟轉增上
简体字		普使诸群生，闻之大欢喜。 过去一切劫，安置未来今； 未来现在劫，迴置过去世。 示现无量剎，烧燃及成住； 一切诸世间，悉在一毛孔。 未来及现在，一切十方佛， 靡不于身中，分明而显现。 深知变化法，善应众生心， 示现种种身，而皆无所著。 或现于六趣，一切众生身， 释梵护世身，诸天人众身， 声闻缘觉身，诸佛如来身； 或现菩萨身，修行一切智。 善入软中上，众生诸想网， 示现成菩提，及以诸佛剎。 了知诸想网，于想得自在， 示修菩萨行，一切方便事。 示现如是等，广大诸神变； 如是诸境界，举世莫能知。 虽现无所现，究竟转增上，		

Chapter 38 — *Transcending the World*

everywhere enabling the many kinds of beings
to feel immense joy upon hearing them explained.

He is able to take all kalpas of the past
and place them into the future and the present
and is able to take the kalpas of the future and present
and place them far back into the past.

He shows countless *kṣetras*
burning, forming, and abiding,
and shows all worlds
entirely contained in a single pore.

Of all the buddhas throughout the ten directions
of the future as well as of the present,
there are none of them that are not clearly revealed
within his very own body.

Deeply knowing the methods of transformation,
he skillfully responds to the minds of beings
by manifesting all kinds of different bodies,
and even so, he retains no attachment to any of them.

He may appear within the six destinies of rebirth
in the bodies of all kinds of beings,
appearing in the body of Brahma, Śakra, or a world-protecting deva,
in the body of a deva or human,

in the body of a *śrāvaka* disciple or *pratyekabuddha*,
in the body of buddhas, the *tathāgatas*,
or he may appear in the body of a bodhisattva
who is cultivating the path to all-knowledge.

He skillfully enters into the web of thought
of beings possessed of weak, middling, and superior capacities,
manifesting the realization of bodhi
as well as all the buddha *kṣetras*.

He completely knows the web of all thought,
attains sovereign mastery in such thought,
and then reveals the cultivation of the bodhisattva practices
and all the works in which he uses skillful means.

He manifests all such as these
of his vast spiritual transformations.
All his spheres of action such as these
are such that no one in the entire world could ever know.

Although he manifests them, he has no manifestations at all,
for ultimately they are transmutations of what is most supreme

正體字	318b19 ‖	隨順眾生心	令[5]行真實道
	318b20 ‖	身語及與心	平等如虛空
	318b21 ‖	淨戒為塗香	眾行為衣服
	318b22 ‖	法繒嚴淨髻	一切智摩尼
	318b23 ‖	功德靡不周	灌頂[6]昇王位
	318b24 ‖	波羅蜜為輪	諸通以為象
	318b25 ‖	神足以為馬	智慧為明珠
	318b26 ‖	妙行為[7]采女	四攝主藏[8]臣
	318b27 ‖	方便為主兵	菩薩轉輪王
	318b28 ‖	三昧為城廓	空寂為宮殿
	318b29 ‖	慈甲智慧劍	念弓明利箭
	318c01 ‖	高張神力蓋	迥建智慧幢
	318c02 ‖	忍力不動搖	直破魔王軍
	318c03 ‖	總持為平地	眾行為河水
	318c04 ‖	淨智為涌泉	妙慧作樹林
	318c05 ‖	空為澄淨池	覺分菡萏華
	318c06 ‖	神力自莊嚴	三昧常娛樂
	318c07 ‖	思惟為[*]采女	甘露為美食
	318c08 ‖	解脫味為漿	遊戲於三乘
	318c09 ‖	此諸菩薩行	微妙轉增上
简体字		随顺众生心,令行真实道。 身语及与心,平等如虚空, 净戒为涂香,众行为衣服, 法缯严净髻,一切智摩尼, 功德靡不周,灌顶升王位。 波罗蜜为轮,诸通以为象, 神足以为马,智慧为明珠。 妙行为婇女,四摄主藏神, 方便为主兵,菩萨转轮王。 三昧为城郭,空寂为宫殿, 慈甲智慧剑,念弓明利箭。 高张神力盖,迥建智慧幢, 忍力不动摇,直破魔王军。 总持为平地,众行为河水, 净智为涌泉,妙慧作树林。 空为澄净池,觉分菡萏华, 神力自庄严,三昧常娱乐。 思惟为婇女,甘露为美食, 解脱味为浆,游戏于三乘。 此诸菩萨行,微妙转增上,		

Chapter 38 — *Transcending the World*

which are thus adapted to the minds of beings
to enable them to practice the genuine path.
His body, speech, and mind
are all equally comparable to empty space.

His purity in the moral precepts is his perfume
and his many practices are his robes.
His silken headband of Dharma adorns his topknot of purity
which is crested by the *maṇi* jewel of all-knowledge.

Of all the meritorious qualities, there are none that are not complete.
By the crown-anointing consecration, he ascends to the royal throne.
Taking the *pāramitās* as his wheel,
all the spiritual superknowledges as his elephant,

the spiritual power of psychic travel as his horse,
wisdom as his shining jewel,
the sublime practices as his maiden retainers,
the four means of attraction as his minister overseeing the treasury,

and the skillful means as the lord's armies,
the bodhisattva thus appears like a wheel-turning king.
His samādhis serve as his city's surrounding walls,
and emptiness and quiescence serve as his palace and royal hall.[191]

Kindness is his armor and wisdom his sword,
whereas mindfulness is his bow and sharp faculties[192] are his arrows.
He raises high the canopy of his spiritual powers,
erects the banners of his wisdom,

remains unshaken due to the power of patience,
and straightaway demolishes the armies of the king of the *māras*.
His complete-retention *dhāraṇīs* serve him as level ground,
his manifold practices are his rivers and streams,

his pure wisdom serves as gushing springs,
and his sublime wisdom serves as his forest groves.
Emptiness serves as his limpid pristine ponds
and the enlightenment factors serve as his lotus flowers.

He adorns himself with the spiritual powers,
and always delights in samādhi.
He takes meditative contemplations as his maiden retainers,
takes the elixir of immortality as his delectable sustenance,
and takes the flavors of liberation as his broth
as he roams with easeful mastery in the Three Vehicles.

As for all of these bodhisattva practices,
their sublimity becomes ever more supreme.

正體字	318c10 ‖ 無量劫修行 其心不厭足	
	318c11 ‖ 供養一切佛 嚴淨一切刹	
	318c12 ‖ 普令一切眾 安住一切智	
	318c13 ‖ 一切刹微塵 悉可知其數	
	318c14 ‖ 一切虛空界 一沙可度量	
	318c15 ‖ 一切眾生心 念念可數知	
	318c16 ‖ 佛子諸功德 說之不可盡	
	318c17 ‖ 欲具此功德 及諸上妙法	
	318c18 ‖ 欲使諸眾生 離苦常安樂	
	318c19 ‖ 欲令身語意 悉與諸佛等	
	318c20 ‖ 應發金剛心 學此功德行	

简体字

无量劫修行，其心不厌足。
供养一切佛，严净一切刹，
普令一切众，安住一切智。
一切刹微尘，悉可知其数；
一切虚空界，一沙可度量；
一切众生心，念念可数知；
佛子诸功德，说之不可尽。
欲具此功德，及诸上妙法，
欲使诸众生，离苦常安乐，
欲令身语意，悉与诸佛等，
应发金刚心，学此功德行。"

He cultivates them for measurelessly many kalpas
during which his resolve remains ever tireless.

He makes offerings to all buddhas
and purifies all the *kṣetras*
as he everywhere enables all beings
to become securely established in all-knowledge.

Though one might be able to know the number
of all the atoms in all *kṣetras*,
though one might measure all the realms of empty space
using but a single sand grain [as his ruler],

and though one might be able to count all beings' thoughts
in every successive mind-moment—
one could still never reach the end of any description
of all the meritorious qualities possessed by this Buddha's son.

If one wishes to possess these meritorious qualities
as well as all of these superior and sublime dharmas—
If one wishes too to cause all beings
to abandon suffering and always abide in happiness—

And if one wishes to enable his own body, speech, and mind
to become the same as those of all the buddhas,
then one should arouse the vajra-like resolve
and train in these meritorious qualities and practices.

The End of Chapter Thirty-Eight

Volume Four Endnotes

1. As is clear from referencing the extant Sanskrit of Chapter 39, *zizai* (自在) is often used in SA's translation to translate not only the usual *vaśī* or *vaśitā*, "mastery" or "sovereign masteries" but also *adhipateya*, "dominance," or, as is likely in this case, *vikurvita*, "magic" or "feats of spiritual power." My support for this is the BB translation's rendering of this line as "the buddhas' sovereign mastery of the spiritual powers is inconceivable." (諸佛神力自在不可思議。/ T09n0278_p0590b18)
2. Both QL and HH interpret these "three kinds of sovereign mastery" (三種自在) as referring to sovereign mastery in the three types of karmic actions (physical, verbal, mental).
3. HH says this refers to "in a single mind-moment, manifesting the Dharma body of all buddhas of the past, the present, and the future." (在一念中，現出過去、現在、未來三世諸佛的法身。/ HYQS)
4. HH notes that "Dharma position" corresponds to realization of the unproduced-dharmas patience (*anutpattika-dharma-kṣānti*).
5. Number six in this list was left out in this SA translation. It is however included in the BB translation: "一切諸佛。常度一切眾生。" (BB = T09n0278_p0592b10). Hence its inclusion in brackets here as a suggested emendation.
6. What I translate here as "syllables" (味身), per BCSD, p. 250, is *vyañjana-kāya*. Perhaps this is referring to esoteric issues related to either mantras or *sandhi*.
7. "Right and fixed position" corresponds to the Sanskrit *samyktva-niyāma*. It is synonymous with irreversibility on the path.
8. Although with the first glance at the Chinese text it would be natural to suppose that the deeply abstruse concept of "non-duality" is somehow being referenced here, it is definitely not a topic anywhere in this entire passage. What I translate ten times in this paragraph as "it could definitely not be otherwise" is literally "definitely, without a second [outcome]" (決定無二). Per DDB, this *wu'er* (無二) can also mean: "The lack of a second (thing) (Skt. *advitīya*) [Charles Muller]."
9. "Three spheres of action" refers to a buddha's physical, verbal, and mental actions.
10. Again, "right and fixed position" corresponds to the Sanskrit *samyaktva-niyāma*. It is synonymous with irreversibility on the path.
11. Again, "three spheres of action" refers to a buddha's physical, verbal, and mental actions.
12. As should become evident soon to most readers, the descriptions of the physical adornments of the Tathāgatha described in this chapter and

13. QL interprets this as referring to the list also found in the *Yogācārabhūmi-śāstra* (T1579.30.565c16): the *pāramitās*; the practice of the enlightenment factors, the practice of the superknowledges; and the practice of maturing beings (當知略有四菩薩行。何等爲四。一者波羅蜜多行。二者菩提分法行。三者神通行。四者成熟有情行。). HH explains this as referring to the four bodhisattva vows or the four means of attraction.

14. According to Soothill (digital edition), this *ganpu* (紺蒲) is a transliteration of *"kamboja,"* "described as a round, reddish fruit, the Buddha having something resembling it on his neck, one of his characteristic marks." HH points out that this is referring to the three horizontal creases in the flesh of the Buddha's soft and smooth neck (HYQS). Translator's note: One also sees these three creases in the neck flesh on the majority of bodhisattva images as well. Further investigation suggests that this is referring to the deep creases in the outer shape of *Garcinia gummi-gutta* or one of its subspecies, these being according to Wikipedia (as of 12/15/2021) "tropical species of *Garcinia* native to South Asia and Southeast Asia. Common names include *Garcinia cambogia* (a former scientific name), as well as brindle berry, and Malabar tamarind. The fruit looks like a small pumpkin and is green to pale yellow in color." As referenced in the text, one could probably rightly visualize it as like a small yellow pumpkin with very deep creases in its outer flesh. As of this writing, images are available in abundance on the internet.

15. "Jewel King" (寶王 / *rāja-ratna*) is one of the titles of the Buddha. Although all three jewels of "the Three Jewels" are finally equally important, in this "Jewel King" or "King of Jewels" name, the inference appears to be that the buddhas are the most supreme of the Three Jewels (Buddha, Dharma, Sangha), for without them there would not be their teaching of the Dharma or their community of enlightened Sangha members.

16. As unequivocally specified in the BB translation (T09n0278_p0607a17: "生八難處障," or "The obstacle of being born in to the eight difficult circumstances."), "difficult circumstances" here refers to "birth into the eight difficult circumstances (*aṣṭa kṣaṇa*) consisting of inopportune rebirths: in the hells; among hungry ghosts; as an animal; in the long-life heavens; in a border region (where the Dharma does not exist); as deaf, blind, or mute; as one possessed of oratorical skill tethered to merely worldly knowledge; or at a time before or after a buddha appears in the world.

(following chapter would be those associated with the Buddha's reward body or *saṃbhogakāya* as seen in a pure land setting.)

Endnotes

17. What I translate here as "unintelligent" is more literally "stupid" (頑鈍). Typically this is referring to rebirth among animals, among the hungry ghosts, or in the hells where the beings lives are so dominated by the three poisons and basic instincts that they remain unable to understand karma, unable to reliably distinguish right from wrong, and unable to understand the path of liberation from karma-bound suffering in *saṃsāra*.

18. *Xinle* (信樂), which would seem to mean "having faith in and being pleased by" is actually a Chinese translation of the Sanskrit *adhimukti* which, at least in this context, simply means "resolute faith."

19. The BB translation makes it clear that this refers directly to a *kalyāṇamitra* (T09n0278_p0607a22: "不見善知識障") and not merely to the SA translation's slightly ambiguous "good friends" (善友), hence my more specific translation: "good spiritual guide," what in common parlance one might refer to as "the good guru."

20. "Restraining difficulties" (*liunan* / 留難) often implies interference wrought by demonic influences which lead to the slowing or halting of a cultivator's attempts to advance on the path.

21. HH: "Although reborn as a human—but one's six sense faculties are incomplete, one's five sense organs are not normal—this is also an obstacle." (雖生為人，但六根不全，五官不正，這也是障。)

    BB translated this as: "the obstacle of being born among evil people" (生惡人中障, T09n0278_p0607a23).

22. Comparison with the Sanskrit of the Ten Grounds Sutra shows that *shenxin* (深心) is one of Śikṣānanda's translations of *āśaya* ("resolution," "resolute intention," "intention," "inclination," etc.).

23. For the skill the absence of which is said to be an obstacle here "skill in dealing with various possible and impossible situations" (處非處善巧), BCSD (p. 1033), gives the Sanskrit as *sthāna-asthāna-kauśalya*. BHSD (p. 85, column 1) translates essentially the same phrase (*sthānāsthānakuśalāḥ*) as: *"clever in regard to various sound and unsound conclusions* (or, *possibilities and impossibilities*)."

    The BB translation is perhaps a little clearer: "The obstacle of not knowing the skillful means [appropriate for dealing with various] possible or impossible situations." (不知是處非處方便障。 / T09n0278_p0607b10–11.)

24. Regarding the "ten eyes," in Chapter 38, "Transcending the World," we have:

    > Sons of the Buddha, the bodhisattva-*mahāsattva* has ten kinds of eyes, namely:
    >
    > The fleshly eye, this associated with the seeing of all forms.

> The heavenly eye, this associated with the seeing of all beings' minds.
> The wisdom eye, this associated with the seeing of all beings' faculties and objective states.
> The Dharma eye, this associated with the seeing of all dharmas in a manner consistent with their real character.
> The Buddha eye, this associated with the perception of the Tathāgata's ten powers.
> The eye of knowledge, this associated with the knowing perception of all dharmas.
> The radiance eye, this associated with the seeing of the Buddha's light.
> The eye that transcends the realm of births and deaths, this associated with the perception of nirvāṇa.
> The unimpeded eye, this associated with its being unobstructed in all that it sees.
> The eye of all-knowledge, this associated with the seeing of the Dharma realm's universal gateways.
>
> These are the ten. If bodhisattvas abide in these dharmas, then they acquire the Tathāgata's eye of unexcelled great wisdom. (T10n0279_p302c17–25).

25. This is a reference to the three moral failings in physical conduct as listed in the ten courses of unwholesome karmic action, namely killing, stealing, and sexual misconduct.
26. This is a reference to the four moral failings in verbal conduct as listed in the ten courses of unwholesome karmic action, namely false speech, abusive speech, divisive speech, and frivolous or lewd speech.
27. This is a reference to the three moral failings in mental conduct as listed in the ten courses of unwholesome karmic action, namely covetousness, ill-will, and wrong views.
28. "Right and fixed position" corresponds here to the Sanskrit technical term, *samyaktva-niyāma*, which in the context of Two Vehicles practice refers to reaching a state of irreversibility on the path to arhatship. It is characterized as an obstacle here for anyone otherwise pursuing the bodhisattva path because to enter on such a state amounts to an immediate and permanent termination of the ability to ever complete the path to buddhahood. Nāgārjuna is emphatically clear in warning the aspiring bodhisattva against pursuing realization of this "right and fixed position."
29. Per BCSD, p. 1140, the Sanskrit antecedent for the Chinese (辭辯) which I translate as "unimpeded knowledge of eloquent phrasing" is *nirukti pratisaṃvid*, an unambiguous reference to the fourth of the Buddha's four unimpeded knowledges.

Endnotes 3117

30. An "ineffable" (*anabhilāpya*) is an inexpressibly large number, the 121st highest level of 123 levels of Sanskrit denominational numbers described in the Āsaṃkhyeya chapter of the Avataṃsaka Sutra. In this numbering schema, each level of denomination is the square of the immediately previous denominational number. (The first and lowest of those 123 levels is a *lakṣa* [100,000].)

31. Although *yihuo* (疑惑) here would appear to mean "doubts and delusions," it usually translates the Sanskrit *vicikitsā* which is simply "skeptical doubt" or "doubt," the fifth of the five hindrances.

32. Although the SA text is slightly ambiguous as to whether this *yiqie shi* (一切世) is meant to refer to "all worlds" or "all periods of time," because the BB translation instead refers to *san shi* (三世) which *always* refers to "periods of time," I translate this as referring to "time" in accordance with the BB translation's corroborating evidence.

33. *Pingdeng fa* (平等法), translated here and subsequently as "equally accessible Dharma," although slightly opaque at the first glance as simply "equal Dharma," generally refers directly and specifically to the fact that the Dharma of the Buddha and eventual highest enlightenment are equally accessible to all beings.

34. Through comparison with the BB translation, it appears that this list component is an accidentally included redundancy repeating the essential meaning of number six. It has no correlate at this point in the BB translation's tenfold list.

35. As the reader may readily observe, there are eleven items in this supposedly tenfold list. This appears to be the result of the accidental inclusion as item number ten of a repetition of the meaning found in item number six. I believe this "tenth" of eleven list items may be a textual corruption because it has no correlate at this point in the tenfold list preserved in the BB translation.

36. "Lion Among Men" is an often-encountered reference to a buddha. In his exegesis on the *Mahāprajñāpāramitā* Sūtra, Nāgārjuna says, "Just as the lion walks alone among the four-legged animals without fear because he is able to subdue them all, so too it is with the Buddha. Because he is fearless in subduing the proponents of all of the ninety-six types of spiritual paths, he is referred to as 'the Lion Among Men.'" (T25n1509_p0111b06–08)

37. "Lion of reasoned discourse" is an epithet that refers to the Buddha's and great bodhisattvas' fearlessness in debating any and all challengers.

38. This is a reference to the ten powers of a buddha.

39. "Length" here translates a standard idiomatic expression for this concept, *xiuduan* (修短), lit. "length and brevity."
40. "Worthy" here can refer either to: a) anyone on any of the preparatory levels on the bodhisattva path prior to becoming an *ārya*; or b) via a play on words, to Samantabhadra Bodhisattva whose name in Chinese is usually rendered as "Universally Worthy."
41. "Achieved complete perfection" here is literally "succeeded in reaching the far shore" (得至於彼岸). "To reach the far shore" is just a Chinese translation of the Sanskrit term for "perfection" (*pāramitā*).
42. Both BB translation and HH clarify that it is these bodhisattvas that are the ones who are able to know these matters.
43. This is probably a reference to the ten types of sovereign mastery (*vaśitā*) listed in the discussion of the eighth bodhisattva ground in the Ten Grounds chapter of the Avataṃsaka Sutra and also in the same section of the Ten Grounds Sutra itself: sovereign mastery of the life span (*āyur-vaśitā*); sovereign mastery of the mind (*cittavaśitā*); sovereign mastery of equipage (*pariṣkāra-vaśitā*); sovereign mastery of karmic actions (*karma-vaśitā*); sovereign mastery of rebirths (*upapatti-vaśitā*); sovereign mastery of vows (*praṇidhāna-vaśitā*), sovereign mastery of resolute faith (*adhimukti-vaśitā*); sovereign mastery of spiritual powers (*r̥ddhivaśitā*); sovereign mastery of the knowledges (*jñāna-vaśitā*); and sovereign mastery of Dharma (*dharma-vaśitā*).
44. Again, what would otherwise appear here to mean "[reaching] the far shore" (彼岸) is just a reference to the quaint etymology of the Sanskrit word for "perfection" (*pāramitā*).
45. A *kṣaṇa* is the shortest possible span of time. To say here that, "To never even perceive 'long' as opposed to 'short' is the ultimate *kṣaṇa* dharma" appears to mean that not making such discriminations is the ultimately correct relationship to the concept of time. In his oral commentary on this quatrain, HH mentioned the extreme relativity of time as it occurs when a meditator enters the *dhyānas* and then emerges in what seemed to him to be only a short while when in fact three weeks may have passed. He also mentioned the extreme relativity of the experience of time as demonstrated by fifty years among humans being equivalent to only a day and a night in the Heaven of the Four Heavenly Kings (HYQS).
46. Given that the "body" here is described as possessed of so many ultimately transcendent qualities, it would be reasonable to conclude that this verse is referring to the Dharma body.
47. Here, "Samantabhadra" is not just a reference to the name of that great bodhisattva, but also a play on words intended to refer to the qualities of these particular bodhisattvas, this because "Samantabhadra" means

"universally worthy" (or "universally good," "universally excellent," etc.).

48. QLSC cites scriptural bases for understanding these lotuses to be many, not just one as rendered by Cheng Chien Bhikshu and BTTS (in its preliminary digital manuscript as of 06/28/20): "Ānanda, why is this known as 'the Worthy (*bhadra*) Kalpa?' Ānanda, when this great trichiliocosm is about to be established, everything is a single body of water. The devas of the Pure Abode Heavens use their heavenly eyes to see that, on this world's singular body of water, *there are a thousand marvelous lotus flowers*, seeing too that every one of these lotus flowers has a thousand petals that are especially lovely. Due to seeing these flowers, the minds of those Pure Abode Heaven devas are filled with measureless delight and exultation whereupon they utter praises, saying, 'How very strange and rare! How very strange and rare it is that in a kalpa such as this there will be a thousand buddhas who appear in the world!' It is for this reason that this kalpa came to be named 'the Worthy Kalpa.' After my entry into nirvāṇa, there will be another nine hundred and ninety-six buddhas." (經云阿難何故名為賢劫阿難此三千大千世界劫欲成時盡為一水淨居天子以天眼觀見此世界唯一大水見有千枝諸妙蓮華一一蓮華各有千葉甚可愛樂彼淨居天子因見此華心生歡喜踴躍無量而皆讚言奇哉希有奇哉希有如此劫中當有千佛出興於世以是因緣遂名此劫號之為賢 / L130n1557_836b04-837a01)

Additionally, this passage in the BB translation reads, "Then, after Maheśvara and the other devas of the Pure Abode Heavens have seen these lotus flowers, they immediately know with certainty that, *in accordance with the number of lotus flowers, the buddhas will appear in the world.*" (時摩醯首羅淨居天等。見蓮華已。即決定知如蓮華數諸佛興世。 / T09n0278_p0613b21–23)

49. The earlier part of this chapter (at 263c10–11) and the BB translation both specify this ruler as "Maheśvara" (摩醯首羅).

50. The BB translation says, "Because the rains are able to give rise to the winds, the winds are able to give rise to the world" (因雨能起風, 風能起世界。 / T09n0278_p0615c22).

51. These are references to the five roots, the five powers, and the seven limbs of enlightenment, a.k.a. "the seven enlightenment factors."

52. Of the two relatively standard Sanskrit antecedents for 邪定, lit. "erroneous fixation," namely *mithyātva-niyata* ("fixated on what is erroneous or wrong") and *mithyā-samādhi* ("wrong meditative absorption,"), a review of the uses of this binome in the SA translation makes it clear that "fixated on what is wrong" is intended here and generally throughout all of its other occurrences in this scripture. In fact,

the term is fairly nicely defined in fascicle thirty-eight as referring to beings who are fixated on wrong views, who are fixated on the five evil deeds leading to rebirth in the unremitting hells, who are fixated on the eight transgressions against the eightfold path of right practice, or who are deeply attached to wrong dharmas.

53. The BB translation refers here not to "capable of cultivating mindfulness and wisdom" (堪修念智) but rather to "complete perfection of the dharmas of the four stations of mindfulness." (具足成就四念處法. / T09_n278_616c28–29)
54. The BB translation refers only to "emanating eight kinds of sublime voices of the Tathāgata." (演出八種如來妙音. / T09_n278_617a04–05)
55. Here, "all actions" (一切諸行) clearly refers to "karmic formative factors" or "volitional factors" (saṃskāras), as a component of the five aggregates (skandhas) and the twelve links of conditioned co-production.
56. "Difficulties" here is a clear reference to the standard list of eight difficulties. Indeed, the BB translation refers at this point twice to "the eight difficulties." (T09_n278_619a15–16)
57. This is an allusion to various punishments found in the hot hells such as the one in which one is forced to swallow pellets so hot that they burn all the way through the body and then drop to the ground below.
58. This is listed as the first of the ten kinds of patience (十忍). See Foguang Dictionary, p. 438.
59. Per HH's HYQS (digital version), "Patience" here refers to the unproduced-dharmas patience (無生法忍, anutpattika-dharma-kṣānti).
60. "Bodhisattvas at the stages of the dwellings, the dedications, or the practices" (住向行菩薩) is a reference to the ten dwellings, the ten dedications, and the ten practices.
61. "All formations" here translates zhu heng (諸行) which in turn usually translates sarva-saṃskāra, otherwise rendered as "karmic formative factors," "fabrications," etc.
62. "Scattered goodness" (散善) usually refers to goodness done with a scattered mind as opposed to goodness done with a mind abiding in samādhi (定善).
63. Here the BB translation says, "From the edge of the sphere of water...." Just below SA himself refers to "the edge of the sphere of water" (水輪際). Based on this evidence, I interpolate here "sphere of" which SA leaves out at this point, probably due to a rather standard stylistic preference for four-character phrases.
64. Although both the BB and SA translations seem to literally refer to the Tathāgata's wisdom as "fully present in the bodies of beings" (具足在於

眾生身中), because this is only a manner of speaking, I have instead translated it as "fully present in beings," as "present in the persons of all beings," etc. because, in classical Chinese, *shen* (身) does not just refer to the physical body, but rather also to what we think of as the "person." (Of course "person" in this context is itself a mere conventional way of speaking and a merely imputed concept devoid of any inherent existence of its own, hence it is not an ultimately real entity.) What this passage is really referring to is the fact that all beings fully possess *the potential* to awaken to the wisdom of the Tathāgata. It is only because of their erroneous perceptions, etc. that they have as yet remained unable to do so.

65. "Three spheres" (三輪), usually from the Sanskrit *trimaṇḍala*, refers to the body, speech, and mind of a buddha.

66. This rather opaquely phrased list item is probably intending to refer to the well-known ability of the Buddha to speak with a single voice and have all beings hear him as if he was speaking directly to them, addressing their particular individual concerns. The BB translation isn't much clearer: "He knows and sees all voices as constituting a single voice. It is by means of this that the Tathāgata turns the wheel of Dharma, for there is no subjective agent." (知見一切音聲皆是一聲。如來以此而轉法輪。佛轉法輪無有主故。T09n0278_p627c12-14) Of course the most impenetrable phrase is SA's "for there is ultimately no subjective agent" rendered by BB as "for there is no subjective agent." This seems to be referring to there being no "self" involved and hence perhaps no single subjective point from which the Buddha's voice emanates.

67. The BB translation indicates that this refers to cultivating a state of uniformly equal purity that is like empty space.

68. HH explains "two kinds of actions" (二行) here as referring to "views-based actions" (見行) and "cravings-based actions" (愛行), whereas QL obliquely refers to another of the several standard lists for "two kinds of actions" consisting of actions reflective of the two kinds of obstacles consisting of "affliction-associated obstacles" (煩惱障) and the "cognition-associated obstacles" (所知障).

69. In explaining this, QL quotes Vasubandhu: "As for 'dwelling where the buddhas dwell,' it is the place where one does not dwell anywhere." (L130n1557_p0076a06 / 世親云謂住佛所住無所住處.)

70. QL says: "This refers to all buddhas having three matters in which they are no different, namely: 1) The knowledge on which they rely is the same; 2) Their aspiration to benefit beings is the same; and 3) The actions which their reward bodies and transformation bodies perform are the same." (謂諸佛有三事無差。一所依智同。二益生意樂同。三報化作業同。 / L130n1557_p0076a06)

71. Per QL, "The Dharma that cannot be overturned" refers to that with which one "vanquishes all non-Buddhists." (不可轉法即降伏一切外道 / L130n1557_p0076a06)
72. Per QL, "He was unimpeded in his actions" refers to "being born in the world, but not being impeded by worldly dharmas." (所行無礙即生在世間不為世法所礙。/ L130n1557_p0076a06)
73. Per QL: "'He had established what is inconceivable' is just the establishment of right Dharma." (立不思議即安立正法 / L130n1557_p0076a06)
74. HH: "As for his having completed all the practices, he had already reached the realm in which there is no [further] cultivation and no [further] realization." (了一切行: 已到無修無證的境界。/ HYQS
75. "Universal Worthy" is the sino-translation of the Sanskrit name for "Samantabhadra" which is otherwise used throughout this text. I go ahead and translate it into English here to show the parallelism in the naming of these ten bodhisattvas.
76. The slightly different corresponding discussion later in the text begins with "The bodhisattva-mahāsattva speaks of ten kinds of buddhas." (菩薩摩訶薩。說十種佛。)
77. The Sanskrit for the famous bodhisattva's name "Samantabhadra" translates as "Universally Worthy." Its adjectival connotations in this and many of the following passages are twofold: a) as indicating a direct connection with Samantabhadra Bodhisattva; and b) as having the character of being, in the spiritual cultivation sense, "universally worthy." The contexts in which the binome occurs lean somewhat in the direction of the latter, but also equally clearly reference the former, hence I have chosen to selectively include both of these meanings by including "Samantabhadra" in brackets to reflect the full range of implications intended by the text.
78. I enclose "wise" in brackets to accord with the ten kinds of "wise contemplation" (智慧觀察) listed later on in the chapter as the answer to this question. I also do this to distinguish this question from the otherwise identical question number one hundred and fifty-two (at 280a15).
79. I add "other kinds of" purity in brackets to help distinguish from the exact same question above as question number twenty-six (279c01). BB escapes this accidental duplication of questions by translating this not as "purity," but rather as "absence of defilement" (無垢).
80. What I translate here and later on as "easeful mastery" (遊戲) might ordinarily be more literally rendered as something like "roaming and sporting," however, scanning the extant Sanskrit texts for Chapter Thirty-Nine makes it clear that this is SA's translation of the Sanskrit *vikrīḍita* which, per BHSD (p. 482, Column 1), definition number two is

"oftener, fig., something like *easy mastery*..." This "easeful mastery" seems to be a much better fit in most instances in SA's translation of this text than definition number one's "sporting."

81. The BB translation renders these as "supreme practices" (勝行).
82. I add "other kinds of" in brackets to help distinguish from the exact same question above as question number thirty.
83. This is another tenfold list of bodies, in this case bodies associated with important bodhisattva path factors such as the *pāramitās*, the four means of attraction, great compassion, and so forth. I include "other" in brackets to distinguish this question from the identical question two questions earlier.
84. In the subsequent discussion later in the chapter this is instead referred to as "ten kinds of definite understanding in knowing all worlds." (十種決定解知諸世界。/ 299a13–21)
85. In the subsequent discussion later in the chapter this is instead referred to as "ten kinds of definite understanding in knowing the realms of beings." (十種決定解知眾生界。/ 299a23–b03)
86. In the subsequent discussion later in the chapter this is instead referred to as "ten ways of retreating from the Buddha's Dharma." (十種退失佛法。/ 299c12–c18)
87. Here and elsewhere in this chapter, this "provisions for enlightenment" (助道), literally "path-assisting [dharmas]" is most likely intended to be a reference not to "the thirty-seven aids to enlightenment" or "thirty-seven enlightenment factors" (*saptatriṃśat bodhipakṣika dharma*) which were often also translated into Chinese by this same term, but rather to "the provisions for enlightenment" (*bodhi-saṃbhāra*) consisting primarily of the merit-based and wisdom-based provisions for enlightenment which are each given their own separate questions and corresponding tenfold lists later on in this chapter.
88. This is later referred to instead as his "measureless cultivation of the path." (無量修道 / 301a22)
89. I insert the bracketed "other" both here and later in the chapter to distinguish this question and its later explanation from the otherwise identical question posed earlier as question number sixty-two.
90. The Ming edition (and now Cbeta as well) include this "Practices related to all the spiritual superknowledges, to facilitate sovereign mastery in spiritual transformations." (一切神通行。變化自在故。/ T10n0279_p0280b27) which I place here in brackets. It is missing in Taisho and in nearly all other received editions, hence there are otherwise only nine. HH follows QL in including this practice as a tenth

list item (unlike the Ming and Cbeta editions which place it as sixth in this list). It is not found at all in the BB translation.

91. As for the "inapprehensibility" (不可得 / *anupalabdha*) of all dharmas, this is just a reference to the absence of any inherent existence in any and all phenomena, this because they are mere names, mere false conceptions, and mere conjunctions of subsidiary conditions and sequences of conditional causality which are in every case entirely devoid of any ultimate reality of their own.

92. This is most likely intended to refer to what Vasubandhu referred to in his Abhidharma works as the five "pure" accumulations (skandha) of: precepts, samādhi, *prajñā*, liberation, and the knowledge and vision of liberation.

93. QL identifies this "knowledge" *pāramitā* with the "skillful means" *pāramitā* of the standard list of ten *pāramitās*.

94. QL identifies this "Dharma" *pāramitā* with the "knowledges" *pāramitā* of the standard list of ten *pāramitās*.

95. Per HH's HYQS, "latent tendencies" (使) here refers to the ten latent tendencies (十使, *daśa-anuśaya*). These are usually said to consist of five views affecting even those of sharp faculties (personality view, extreme view, wrong view, views attaching to views, and the view attaching to moral prohibitions as constituting the path) and another five especially affecting those of duller faculties (desire, hatred, delusion, pride or conceit, and skeptical doubt).

96. "Fear of the awesome virtue of great assemblies" (大眾威德畏) refers to being fearful of speaking before a large audience of advanced practitioners of the path.

97. The "four means of attraction" consist of: giving, pleasing words, beneficial actions, and joint endeavors.

98. "Kindly father" here is a reference to the Buddha.

99. The "four abodes of Brahma" or "four pure abodes" (四梵住 / *catvāro brahma-vihārāḥ*) are identical to the four immeasurable minds (四無量心 / *catvāri-apramāna-citta*): loving-kindness, compassion, sympathetic joy, and equanimity. The "*dhyāna* absorption" alluded to here correspond to the first *dhyāna* heavens of the form realm.

100. "Stations beset by the difficulties" is almost certainly a reference to the eight difficulties.

101. Here, "ultimate truth" (*paramārtha*) is literally "the primary meaning" (一義).

102. These three, together, are known as "the three sufferings." My rendering of the third of them (*saṃskāra-duḥkhatā*), "the suffering of the

saṃskāras' karmic formative factors" is simply a conjunction of the Sanskrit (*saṃskāra*) and the English for the fourth of the five aggregates that is here referenced as having inherent suffering as a cardinal quality.

103. "Zeal" here (欲), otherwise translatable as "desire," doubtless refers to *chanda*, the undefiled aspiration to achieve a wholesome objective which Nāgārjuna teaches is an indispensable component of vigor (*vīrya*), one of the six perfections.

104. By "types of kalpas," literally "kalpa numbers" or "kalpa denominations" (劫數) I am assuming the text is referring to the various designations based on kalpa size such as, "small kalpa," "large kalpa," "*asaṃkhyeya* kalpa," etc.

105. What I translate here as "flawless resolve" is literally "resolve that is free of inferior aspects" (無下劣心). The BB translation refers to these as "resolve free of indolence" (無懈怠心).

106. With regard to the rationale for these kinds of especially superior mind being referred to as "mountain-like," QL mentions that this has to do with: a) their being so lofty, one only gazes up to their heights with difficulty; and b) their being, (like a mountain), utterly unshakable in their progression toward bodhi. (L130n1557_0139b13)

107. Here I follow the sense of the BB translation to fill in (in brackets) what SA leaves out, namely the nature of the relationship between this jewel-like abiding and *anuttarasamyaksaṃbodhi*: "The bodhisattva-mahāsattva has ten kinds of jewel-like abiding in realizing *anuttarasamyaksaṃbodhi*." (菩薩摩訶薩。有十種寶住成阿耨多羅三藐三菩提。/ T09n0278_p0644b19–20)

108. "Inapprehensibility" (不可得 / *anupalabdha*) here and throughout this text is just a reference to the absence of any inherent existence in any and all phenomena, this because they are mere names, mere false conceptions, and mere conjunctions of subsidiary conditions which are devoid of any ultimate reality of their own.

109. BB makes it clear that this refers specifically to "the unproduced dharmas patience" (*anutpattika-dharma-kṣānti*). (得法忍菩薩授記。 – T09n0278_p0646c11).

110. In their extant editions, both BB and SA have only nine unimpeded functions related to the spiritual superknowledges. However, one alternative edition of SA (the Ming edition) contains this unimpeded function as the sixth of a complete list of ten. I insert it here to accord with Cbeta's judgment that it should be adopted into the definitive edition of the canon. (一微塵出現廣大佛剎無量莊嚴無礙用 - T10n0279_p0294c18).

111. The Sanskrit for what I translate here as "devoid of any soul" (無養育者), per BCSD, p. 786 is *niṣpoṣa* or "no *poṣa*" which, per BHSD, p. 355, Column 1 would mean "[no] person, [no] individuality, [no] soul, [no] spirit," this apparently due to *poṣa* somehow being derived from *puruṣa*, "person." (Conze's MDPPL, p. 235 also defines *niṣpoṣa* as "no individuality.") Although the very unintuitive Chinese looks like it should be "no one who is raised up (or nourished)," this almost always occurs in statements about the emptiness of inherent existence of any "self," and, in particular, in a string of similar "no-self" similes, nearly always right before, as in this case, "no *pudgala*," so, no matter how seemingly odd SA's choice for a Chinese translation, there really can be no mistaking its intended meaning as synonymous with "no self." Incidentally, BB's translation is just as unintuitive and along the very same lines (無長養者無福伽羅), meaning, again, "no one who is raised up (or "nourished"), no *pudgala*," etc. The unintuitive translations of *niṣpoṣa* in both BB and SA reveal this to be as a result of their mixing it up with a different definition of the same Sanskrit word which does indeed mean "not being nourished" but which is instead derived from the root *puṣ*- which in nearly all cases *does* refer to "nourishment," etc.

112. In his HYQS, HH points out here how, because the body is reducible to the four codepedent great elements (earth, water, fire, and wind), it is unreal and hence false.

113. In his HYQS, HH points out that this "[noumenal] principle" (理) is a reference to true suchness (真如 / *tathatā*). "Noumenal principle" (理), otherwise perhaps translatable as just "noumenon," is not and never was really a Buddhist term at all. Rather it was used by sino-hermeneutic traditions such as the Huayan School as a terminological stand-in for "emptiness" and "true suchness." It may have occurred here due to the influence of Fazang (法藏) who was both a member of SA's translation team and the third patriarch of the Huayan School whose own writings and the writings of his predecessors relied very heavily on the use of this very term in explaining this very sutra, especially as it occurs in its tenfold schema (理事無礙十門) which treats in ten ways the unimpeded interrelationship of "noumenon" (理) and "phenomena" (事), sino-Buddhist philosophical substitutes for "the unconditioned" versus "the conditioned" and "emptiness" versus "conventional existence," etc.

114. What I translate as "gaining complete enlightenment" would appear in the somewhat euphemistic semi-Taoist Chinese rendering to be "realizing the path" (成道). However, the Sanskrit for this translation into Chinese shows that it is instead referring rather precisely to the attainment of "complete enlightenment" (*abhisaṃbodhi*, BCSD, p. 0517).

115. Again, this is another tenfold list of bodies, in this case bodies associated with important bodhisattva path factors such as the *pāramitās*, the four means of attraction, great compassion, and so forth. I include "other" in brackets to distinguish this question from the identical question and its associated list two questions earlier.
116. Here, what is referred to as "the four speech faults" (語四過失) is explained by HH to be lying, frivolous or lewd speech, harsh speech, and divisive speech. These are the four verbal transgressions against the ten courses of good karmic action.
117. "Difficulties" (諸難) here is primarily a reference to the eight difficulties.
118. This is most likely referring to the *tathāgata-garbha*.
119. "Immeasurable minds" (無量心) is a reference to the four immeasurable minds (四無量心 / *apramāṇa-citta*), namely: loving kindness; compassion; sympathetic joy; and equanimity.
120. "*Sattva*," here and in the following names means "being."
121. The four lineage bases of the *ārya* (四聖種 / *catur-ārya-vaṃśa*) refers to being pleased with mere sufficiency in robes, food and drink, and bedding, while delighting in severance and cultivation.
122. This refers to the four *dhyānas*, the four formless absorptions, and the meditative concentration in which the functioning of both the feeling and the perception aggregates is extinguished.
123. "Gates to liberation" in this context usually refers to the three gates to liberation (三解脫門) consisting of emptiness (*śūnyatā*), signlessness (*animitta*), and wishlessness (*apraṇihita*).
124. The four floods (四暴流 / *catur-ogha*) refer to: desire, existence, ignorance, and [wrong] views.
125. This list item and next two list items together refer to what is known in slightly varying order in nearly all Buddhist traditions as the "three groups [of beings]" (三聚, *tri-skandha*): 1) those who are fixed in what is right; 2) those who are not fixed [in either what is right or what is wrong], i.e. those who are as yet "unfixed" with regard to their inclinations toward doing what is right or what is wrong; and 3) those who are fixed in what is wrong.
126. This "*brāhma-vihāra*," otherwise known as "the four abodes of Brahma," or "the four immeasurable minds" refers to loving-kindness, compassion, sympathetic joy, and equanimity (慈, 悲, 喜, 捨).
127. The BB translation specifies what the SA translation only implies: "Abiding in the unproduced-dharmas patience." (無生忍住.)

128. "Right and fixed position" (usually *samyaktva-niyāma* as defined in Conze's MDPPL, p. 415 as "certainty to have got safely out of this world.") is generally associated with realization of the unproduced-dharmas patience (*anutpattika-dharma-kṣānti*) and the achievement of irreversibility in one's chosen path of liberation.
129. Again, I include the bracketed "other" here and earlier in the list of corresponding questions to distinguish this question and discussion from the otherwise identical question number sixty-two and its corresponding discussion.
130. Again, "difficulties" here is a reference to the eight difficulties.
131. The "three evils of the body" (身三惡) are killing, stealing, and sexual misconduct. These are the three physical transgressions against the ten courses of good karmic action.
132. The "four transgressions in speech" (語四過) are lying, harsh speech, divisive speech, and frivolous or lewd speech. These are the four verbal transgressions against the ten courses of good karmic action.
133. Covetousness, ill will, and wrong views are the three mental transgressions against the ten courses of good karmic action.
134. Lest one misinterpret the intent of this line, it is not that one should not be attached to according with the moral precepts, for, indeed, adherence to the moral precepts absolutely *does* constitute an indispensable prerequisite to gaining liberation. Rather it is that one should not see adherence to the precepts alone as constituting, in and of itself, the entire path to liberation. That is a function of *all three* of the three trainings: a) moral virtue; b) samādhi; and c) wisdom.
135. "Difficulties" here is a reference to the eight difficulties involving rebirth in inauspicious circumstances.
136. I string together these first two kinds of pure equanimity because, otherwise, the SA translation creates eleven rather than ten kinds of pure equanimity by breaking into two kinds of pure equanimity what the BB translation preserves as the first of ten kinds of pure equanimity as follows: "The pure equanimity with which he refrains from becoming fondly attached when all beings revere and make offerings to him and with which he refrains from becoming angry when all beings slight and disparage him." (一切眾生恭敬供養不生愛著，一切眾生輕慢毀辱，不生瞋恚淨捨. T09n0278_p0661b10–12)
137. The eight worldly dharmas (*aṣṭa-loka-dharma*) are: gain and loss, fame and disrepute, praise and blame, pleasure and pain.
138. HH points out that "patience" here refers to the unproduced-dharmas patience (*anutpattika-dharma-kṣānti*). Also, QL notes here that the BB edition does indeed have but ten of these pure patiences, this through

its preserving as a single patience what has been broken into numbers one and two in the SA translation, thereby implying that the presence of eleven here in the SA edition is simply the result of a minor textual corruption.

139. Per MW (p. 213, Column 2), *upādhi* is "that which is put in the place of another thing, a substitute, substitution R.; anything which may be taken for or has the mere name or appearance of another thing, appearance, phantom, disguise…. " Hence the term "*upādhi* nirvāṇa" refers to all forms of mere semblance nirvāṇa clung to by non-Buddhist traditions that do not really constitute any form of genuine nirvāṇa as understood by Buddhists.

140. "Provisions for enlightenment" refers to the "provisions for the realization of bodhi" (*bodhi-saṃbhāra*) of which there are primarily two main categories: merit and wisdom. This list of ten represents the former. The ensuing list of ten constitutes the latter.

141. The six kinds of mindfulness are: mindfulness of the Buddha, mindfulness of the Dharma, mindfulness of the Sangha, mindfulness of the precepts, mindfulness of giving, and mindfulness of the heavens.

142. The six kinds of harmony and respect are six ways in which monastics live in harmony which refer to harmony in body, mouth, mind, precepts, views, and benefits.

143. The six dharmas of solidity (六堅固法) refer to solidity in faith, Dharma, cultivation, virtue, supremacy, and awakening.

144. There are many different lists of ten knowledges. In his HYQS, HH lists the ten kinds of knowledge (十種智) as: dharma knowledge, relative knowledge, knowledge of others' thoughts, worldly knowledge, knowledge of the truth of suffering, knowledge of the truth of origination, knowledge of the truth of cessation, knowledge of the truth of the path, knowledge of cessation, and knowledge of the unproduced.

145. The "four abodes of Brahma" or "four pure abodes" (四梵住 / *catvāro brahma-vihārāḥ*) are identical to the four immeasurable minds (四無量心 / *catvāri-apramāna-citta*): loving-kindness, compassion, sympathetic joy, and equanimity.

146. "Clarities" is a general reference to all of the spiritual powers, but more specifically to the "three clarities" (*tri-vidya*), namely: clarity with regard to past lives of self and others, clarity with regard to the power of the heavenly eye, and clarity with regard to the cessation of all the contaminants.

147. QL identifies the three types of ideation as desire, hatred, and maliciousness (欲恚害).

148. "Three kinds of actions" (三業) refers to physical, verbal, and mental actions.
149. QL indicates that conceptions of a "self" and "karmic actions" performed by some supposed "self" in effect "wound" the Dharma body and that karmic transgressions not yet extinguished constitute its "scars." (L130n1557_p0224a05)
    HH specifically points to delusive ignorance and afflictions as constituting "wounds" and karmic transgressions as constituting "scars." (HYQS, v. 18, p. 185)
150. Both QL and HH note that this entire passage down to the references to the absence of any conceptions of "vigor" or "valiant bravery" are related to the "calming" of "calming and contemplation" (śamatha-vipaśyanā), whereas the rest of the ensuing passage specifically correlates to the "contemplation" of "calming and contemplation." "Patience" here likely refers to his realization of "the unproduced-dharmas patience" (anutpattika-dharma-kṣānti).
151. The phrasing of the term for "truths" in the text (真諦) makes it clear that it is referring specifically and exclusively to the four truths of the āryas.
152. "Those at the level of the eighth person" refers specifically to those who are at the third of the ten stages common to śrāvaka disciples, pratyekabuddhas, and bodhisattvas who have reached the threshold stage immediately prior to realizing the "stream entry" of the srota-āpanna. This threshold stage is that of the srota-āpatti-pratipannaka.
153. A srota-āpanna or "stream enterer" has gained the first fruit on the path to arhatship.
154. Because delectable meditation states are more ecstatically pleasurable than any other experiences in the world, the meditator is prone to become attached to them and proceed no farther on the path. Worse yet, he may be then be led astray by māras so that he falls off the path completely.
155. A sakṛd-āgāmin or "once returner" has gained the second fruit on the path to arhatship.
156. An anāgāmin or "never returner" has gained the third fruit on the path to arhatship.
157. Per the fifth chapter ("Right Practice for Monastics") of Nāgārjuna's Ratnāvalī (in which he concisely and precisely defines the seven types of arrogance), "elevating arrogance" corresponds to the Sanskrit atimāna. Nāgārjuna says there that "It stems from elevating oneself to equality with superior persons." (See pages 159-61 of my Kalavinka

Endnotes 3131

Press translation: *A Strand of Dharma Jewels, A Bodhisattva's Profound Teachings on Happiness, Liberation, and the Path*.)

158. Again, per the *Ratnāvalī*, "over-reaching arrogance" corresponds to the Sanskrit *māna atimāna*. Nāgārjuna says there that "It is compared to developing a pustule on top of an abscess."

159. Again, per the *Ratnāvalī*, "Self-imputing arrogance" corresponds to the Sanskrit *asmi-māna*. Referring to the five aggregates, Nāgarjuna says there that "When, because of delusion, one imputes existence of a 'self' therein, this is known as 'self-imputing arrogance.'"

160. HH equates this "reaches the station of the unproduced" with the realization of the unproduced dharmas patience: "The bodhisattva gains the realization of the unproduced dharmas patience and thus puts an end to births and deaths." (菩薩證得無生法忍，而了生死…. / HYQS)

161. The three gates to liberation (三解脫門) consist of emptiness (*śūnyatā*), signlessness (*animitta*), and wishlessness (*apraṇihita*).

162. Lists of "the seven kinds of wealth" (七財) vary slightly, depending on the source. In his Treatise on the Ten Bodhisattva Grounds, Nāgārjuna lists: faith, moral virtue, a sense of shame, a dread of blame, relinquishing (i.e. "giving"), learning, and wisdom (信戒慚愧捨聞慧 / SZPPS_ T26n1521_p0091c01–02.)

163. The "five turbidities" (五濁) are five kinds of deterioration occurring as each kalpa progresses past the point when beings' life spans begin to decrease. This refers then to deterioration in the quality of the kalpa, views, afflictions, beings, and life spans.

164. The "two extreme views" (二邊見) refers to views such as eternalism versus annihilationism, existence versus nonexistence, etc.

165. Here I follow the Ming Edition and more recent editions of Cbeta in restoring this ninth list item missing in all other editions: "He manifests as practicing the austerities to enable beings to delight in the dharma of quiescence and increase their roots of goodness." (為令眾生樂寂靜法增長善根故。示行苦行。 / T10n0279_p0312b10)

166. HH explains that this refers to the pervasive presence of the Buddha's Dharma body throughout all worlds. (HYQS)

167. Although Cbeta now incorporates "mistletoe" (蔦) into the text instead of Taisho's "birds" (鳥), prior to Cbeta's emendation, "mistletoe" only ever appeared in the Ming edition of the sutra. HH explains it as "birds." QL also has "birds." (最上力為鳥。 / T36n1736_p0135a25) Moreover, all the editions of the BB translation have "birds" (鳥) and none of them have the mistletoe character. Since mistletoe is a

parasitic plant, it seems odd that Cbeta would think it wise to make this emendation.

168. The "three clarities" (三明) or *trividya* are the heavenly eye, cognition of past lives, and cessation of the contaminants.

169. "Four types of eloquence" (四辯) is actually a reference to the "four unimpeded knowledges" (四無礙智) with regard to dharmas, meanings, phrasing, and delight in speaking.

170. Although the SA translation is vague as to whether this refers to psychic powers in general or specifically to the four bases of psychic power. The BB translation makes it quite clear that it is the latter: "The four bases of psychic power are its feet." (四如意為足 / T09n0278_p0670c11). The four bases of psychic power (四如意足, *catvāra ṛddhi-pādāḥ*) consist of zeal (*chanda*), vigor (*vīrya*), concentration (*citta*), and investigation (*mīmāṃsa*).

171. By specifying all four members of the list, the BB translation makes it clear that it is all four of "the four immeasurable minds" of kindness, compassion, sympathetic joy, and equanimity that are being referred to in this verse, not merely the "kindness and equanimity" of the SA translation which was forced to leave out the middle two (compassion and sympathetic joy) only because of the constraints of the five-character line length. Hence I include in brackets here "compassion, sympathetic joy" to fill in the contraction which, for a Chinese Buddhist reader, would have been obviously implicitly included, whereas, for a reader of this English translation, this implicitly intended inclusion might not have been at all obvious.

    Also, since this list is otherwise known as "the four abodes of Brahma" (四梵住 / *catvāro brahma-vihārāḥ*), the fact that this quatrain compares the bodhisattva to "a Brahma Heaven King" should make all of this doubly obvious to an experienced reader.

172. The BB translation makes it very clear that this *huo* character (惑) in the second line of this verse, otherwise very commonly and rightly translatable as "delusions" (*moha*), is here translating the Sanskrit for afflictions (*kleśa*): "…burns up the afflictions and habitual karmic propensities." (燒盡煩惱習 / T09n0278_p0671a12)

173. I add "wish-fulfilling" in brackets both because it is implicit in the meaning of the verse and also because magical wish-fulfillment is a connotation built in to the Sanskrit word *maṇi*. In short, all by itself, the word "*maṇi*" can mean "wish-fulfilling jewel."

174. "Enlightenment factors" (菩提分) is more specifically translated as "the seven enlightenment factors" (七覺) in the BB translation's: "…enable the seven enlightenment factors to bloom." (七覺令開敷 / T09n0278_p0671a18)

175. "The most revered ones of all who stand on two feet" is a reference to the buddhas that is interpreted in either a literal or metaphoric manner. In the former case, they are the most supreme among humans and devas as two-legged beings. In the latter case, they are the most supreme in the complete development of the two foundations of buddhahood: merit and wisdom.

176. The comparison for this fourth of the five aggregates is aimed at demonstrating that karmic formative factors have no true substantiality, for they are just like the plantain stalk which consists solely of layers which, when peeled away, leave nothing whatsoever.

177. This is a reference to the twelve sense bases consisting of the six sense faculties and their six respective sense objects.

178. This is a reference to the eighteen sense realms consisting of the six sense faculties, the six corresponding sense objects, and the six associated sense consciousnesses.

179. HH interprets these as the three obstacles: karmic obstacles, retribution obstacles, and affliction obstacles, though one might just as easily interpret them in accordance with the BB edition's "three sufferings" (三苦), usually explained as: the suffering of physical and mental pain (*duḥkha-duḥkha*), the suffering inherent in change (*vipariṇāma-duḥkha*), and the suffering inherent in the karmic formative factors (*saṃskāra-duḥka*).

180. The three types of moral precepts (三律儀) per HH are the moral precepts of individual liberation (別解脫律儀), the moral precepts produced by *dhyāna* (靜慮律儀), and the moral precepts of the cessation of the contaminants (無漏律儀). (HYQS)

181. Again, the "three gates to liberation" (三解脫門) consist of emptiness (*śūnyatā*), signlessness (*animitta*), and wishlessness (*apraṇihita*).

182. "Three Vehicles" refers to the vehicles of the *śrāvaka* disciples, the *pratyekabuddhas*, and the bodhisattvas.

183. Although one might otherwise translate these last two lines of this verse as "He remains vigorous in his zeal to abide in samādhi / and his wisdom arising from contemplation never diminishes," the language used in both the SA and BB translations makes it clear that this verse is instead referring to "the eighteen dharmas exclusive to the buddhas" (十八不共法) of which "right mindfulness," "vigor," "zeal," "samādhi," and "wisdom" are here serving as emblematic elements implying the presence of all the others as well.

184. The three types of accumulation of moral virtue (三聚戒) refer to: 1) the aggregation of the particular categories of moral precept obligation such as the five precepts, the eight precepts, or the ten precepts;

2) the aggregation of all good dharmas; and 3) the drawing forth of all beings through benefiting them with Dharma.
185. "Bestowal of the prediction" refers to receiving the Buddha's prediction of one's future buddhahood.
186. Although the SA translation is ambiguous, the BB translation makes it clear that the *shi* character (世) here is referring to "periods of time" and not to "worlds" as one might otherwise expect.
187. This line is alluding specifically to the Buddha's ten powers, four fearlessnesses, and eighteen dharmas exclusive to the Buddha.
188. HH explains these "ten kinds of things" according to the ten courses of good karmic action. (HYQS)
189. "Right and fixed position" refers to *samyaktva-niyāma* which corresponds to the stage of irreversibility on one's chosen path.
190. HH interprets this line as referring to the ten names of the Buddha. (HYQS, V. 18, p. 308)
191. Dividing into "palace" and "hall" the compound which in Chinese ordinarily means "palace" (宮殿), HH explains "palace" (宮) as referring to the place where the ruler takes his rest and "royal hall" (殿) as referring to the place where he conducts the business of the king's court. (HYQS)
192. Although ambiguous in the SA translation, the BB translation makes it clear that *mingli* (明利), ordinarily "sharp," is referring to "sharp faculties" (明利根 / T09n0278_p0674c18).

www.ingramcontent.com/pod-product-compliance
Lightning Source LLC
Chambersburg PA
CBHW031128160426
43193CB00008B/65